Date: 2/2/18

THE DELUXE EDITION BOOK THREE

THE INVISIBLES

Grant Morrison
Writer

Phil Jimenez
John Stokes
Michael Lark
Chris Weston
Keith Aiken
Marc Hempel
Ray Kryssing
Artists

Daniel Vozzo
Kevin Somers
Rick Taylor
Colorists

Todd Klein
Letterer

Brian Bolland
Cover Art and
Original Series Covers

THE INVISIBLES created by Grant Morrison

THE INVISIBLES: THE DELUXE EDITION BOOK THREE
Published by DC Comics. Compilation Copyright © 2015 Grant Morrison. All Rights Reserved.
Originally published in single magazine form in THE INVISIBLES VOL. 2 1-13 Copyright © 1997,
1998 Grant Morrison. All Rights Reserved. All characters, their distinctive likenesses and related
elements featured in this publication are trademarks of Grant Morrison. VERTIGO is a trademark of
DC Comics. The stories, characters and incidents featured in this publication are entirely fictional.
DC Comics does not read or accept unsolicited submissions of ideas, stories or artwork.
DC Comics 1700 Broadway, New York, NY 10019. A Warner Bros. Entertainment Company.
Printed in Canada. First Printing. ISBN: 978-1-4012-4951-9

Library of Congress Cataloging-in-Publication Data

Morrison, Grant.
 The Invisibles : The Deluxe Edition, Book Three / Grant Morrison, writer ; Phil Jimenez, John Stokes,
artists.
   pages cm
 ISBN 978-1-4012-4951-9 (hardback)
 1. Graphic novels. I. Jimenez, Phil, illustrator. II. Stokes, John, illustrator. III. Title.
 PN6728.I58M678 2015
 741.5'973—dc23
                                2014039275

THE INVISIBLES

THE DELUXE EDITION

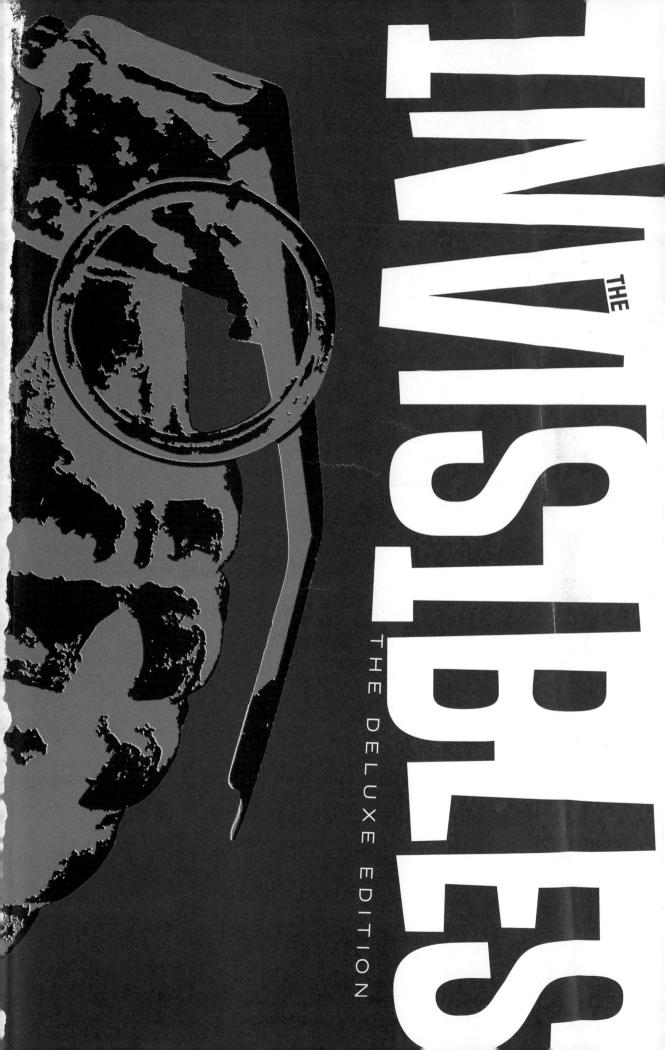

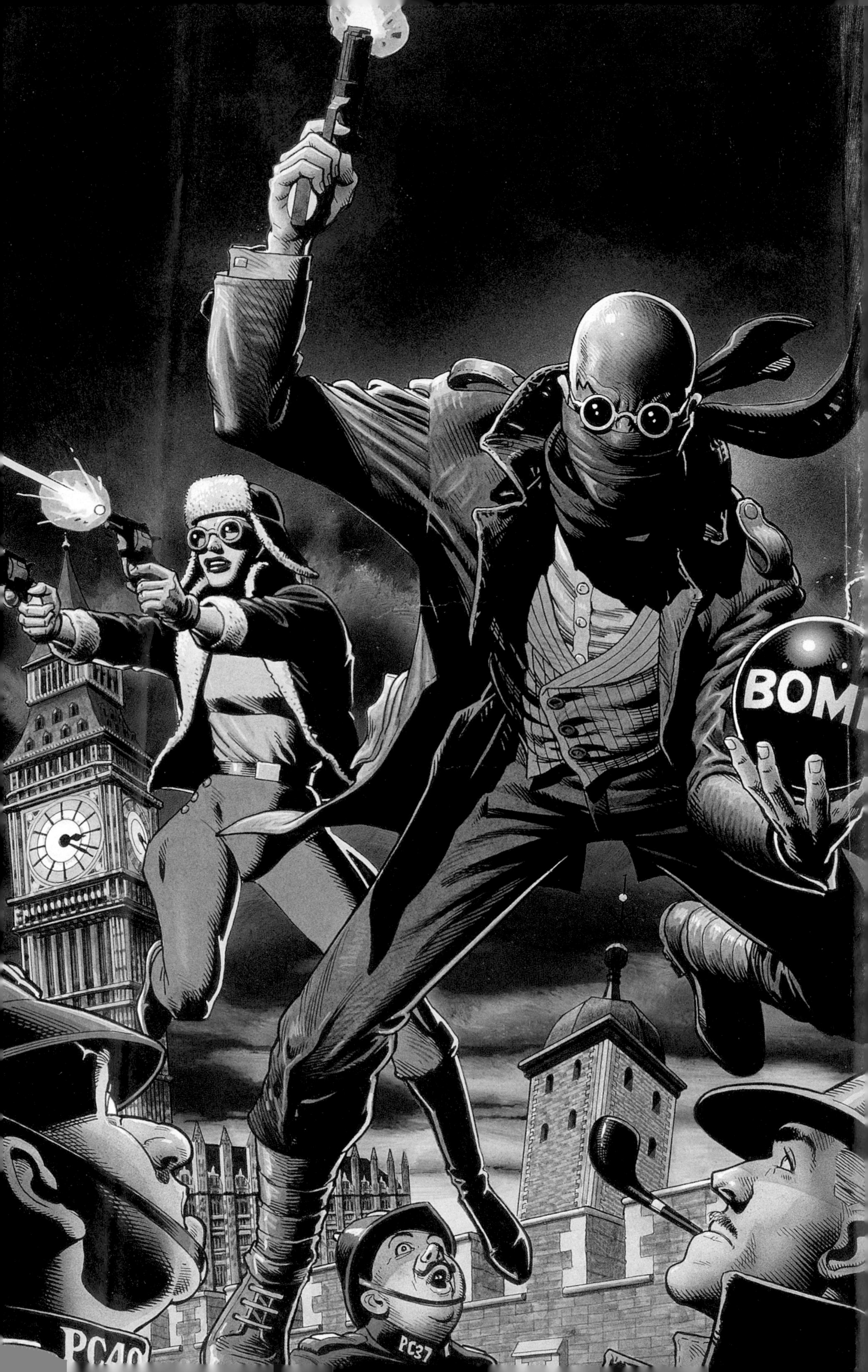
BOM
PC37

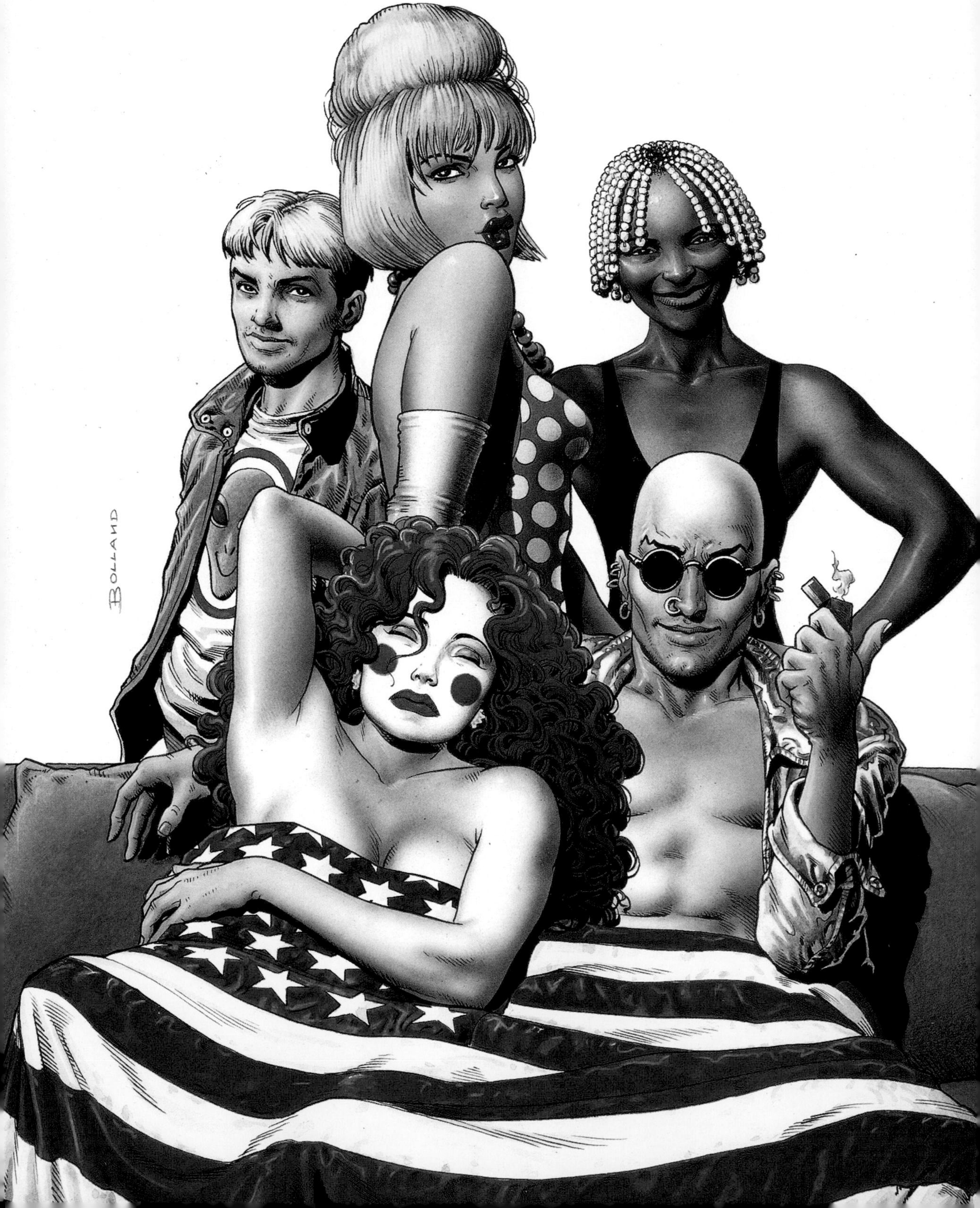
BOLLAND

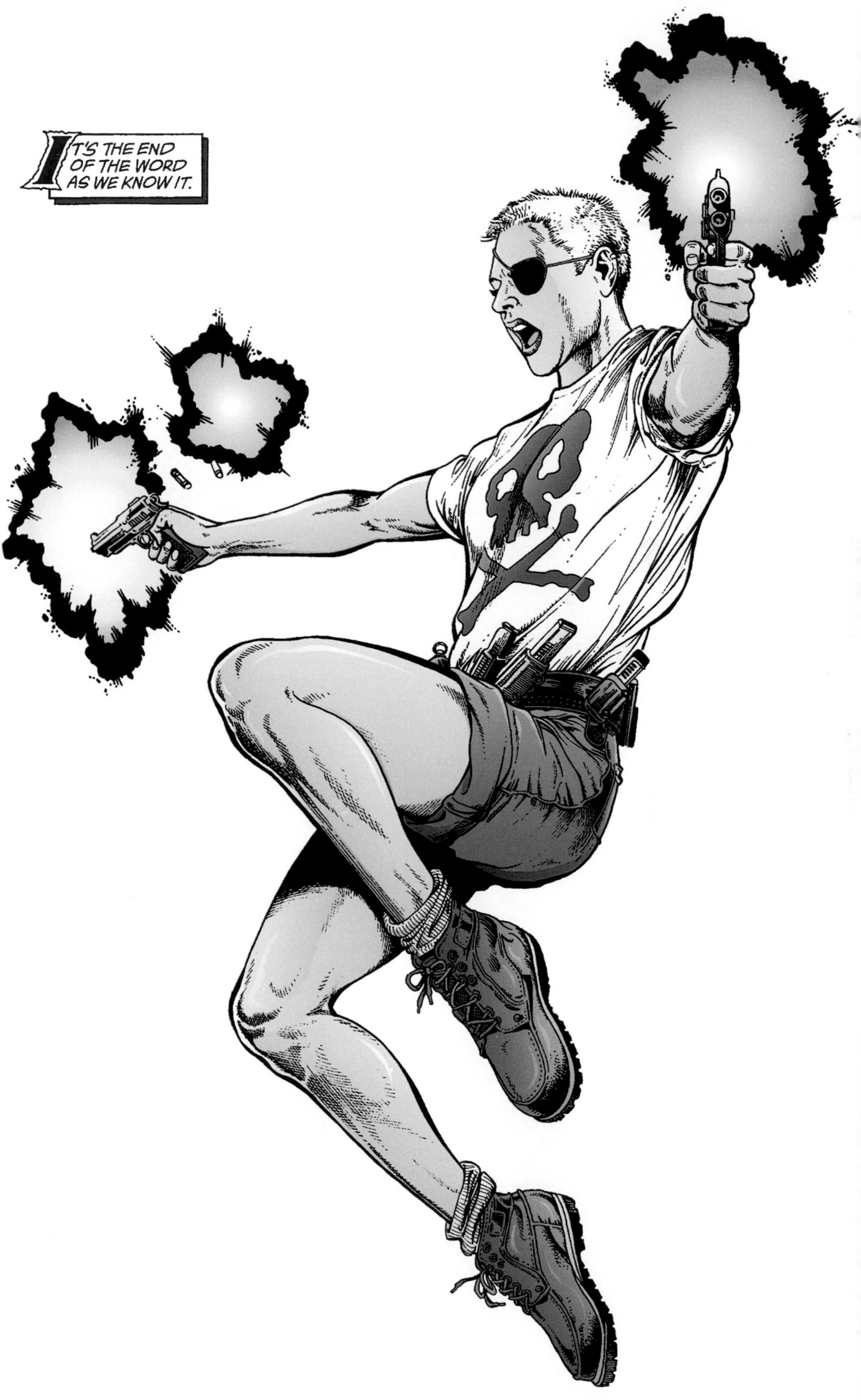
IT'S THE END OF THE WORD AS WE KNOW IT.

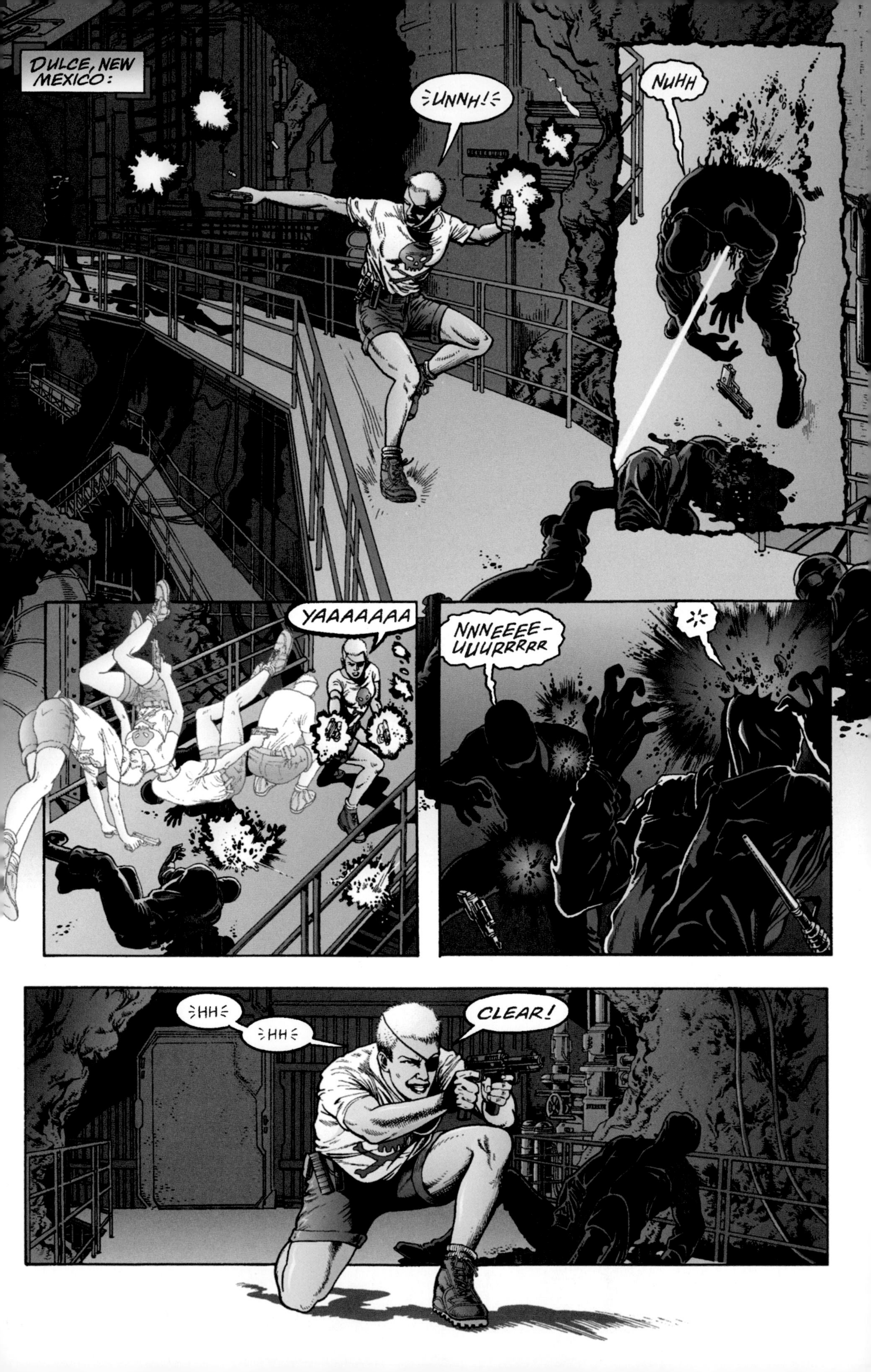
DULCE, NEW MEXICO:
UNNH!
NUHH
YAAAAAAA
NNNEEEE-UUURRRRR
HH
HH
CLEAR!

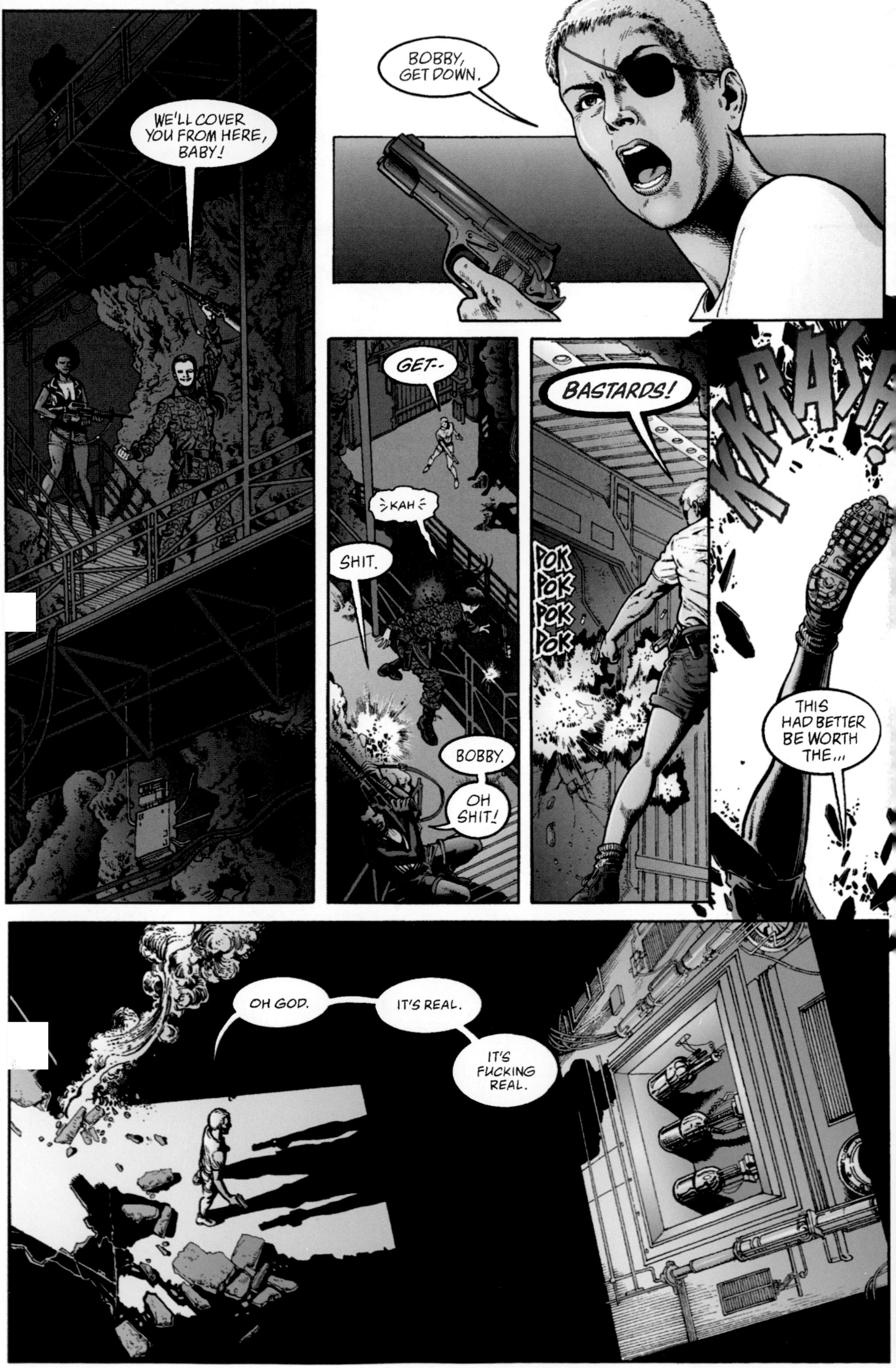
WE'LL COVER YOU FROM HERE, BABY!
BOBBY, GET DOWN.
GET--
KAH
SHIT.
BOBBY.
OH SHIT!
BASTARDS!
POK POK POK POK
KKRASH
THIS HAD BETTER BE WORTH THE...
OH GOD.
IT'S REAL.
IT'S FUCKING REAL.

BLACK SCIENCE

part one: BANGIN'

GRANT MORRISON: writer
PHIL JIMENEZ: penciller
JOHN STOKES: inker

DANIEL VOZZO: colors & separations
TODD KLEIN: letterer
SHELLY ROEBERG: editor

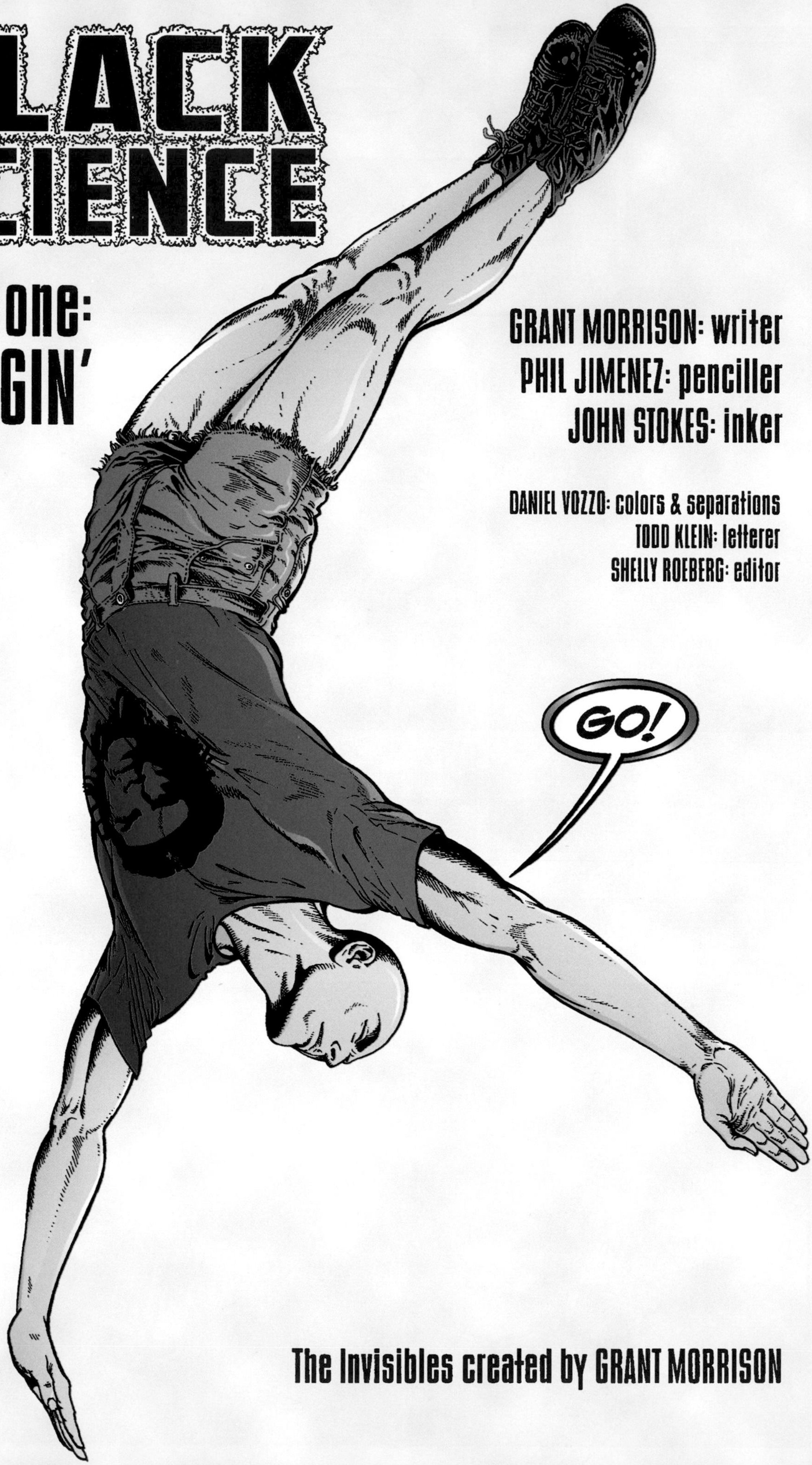
GO!

The Invisibles created by GRANT MORRISON

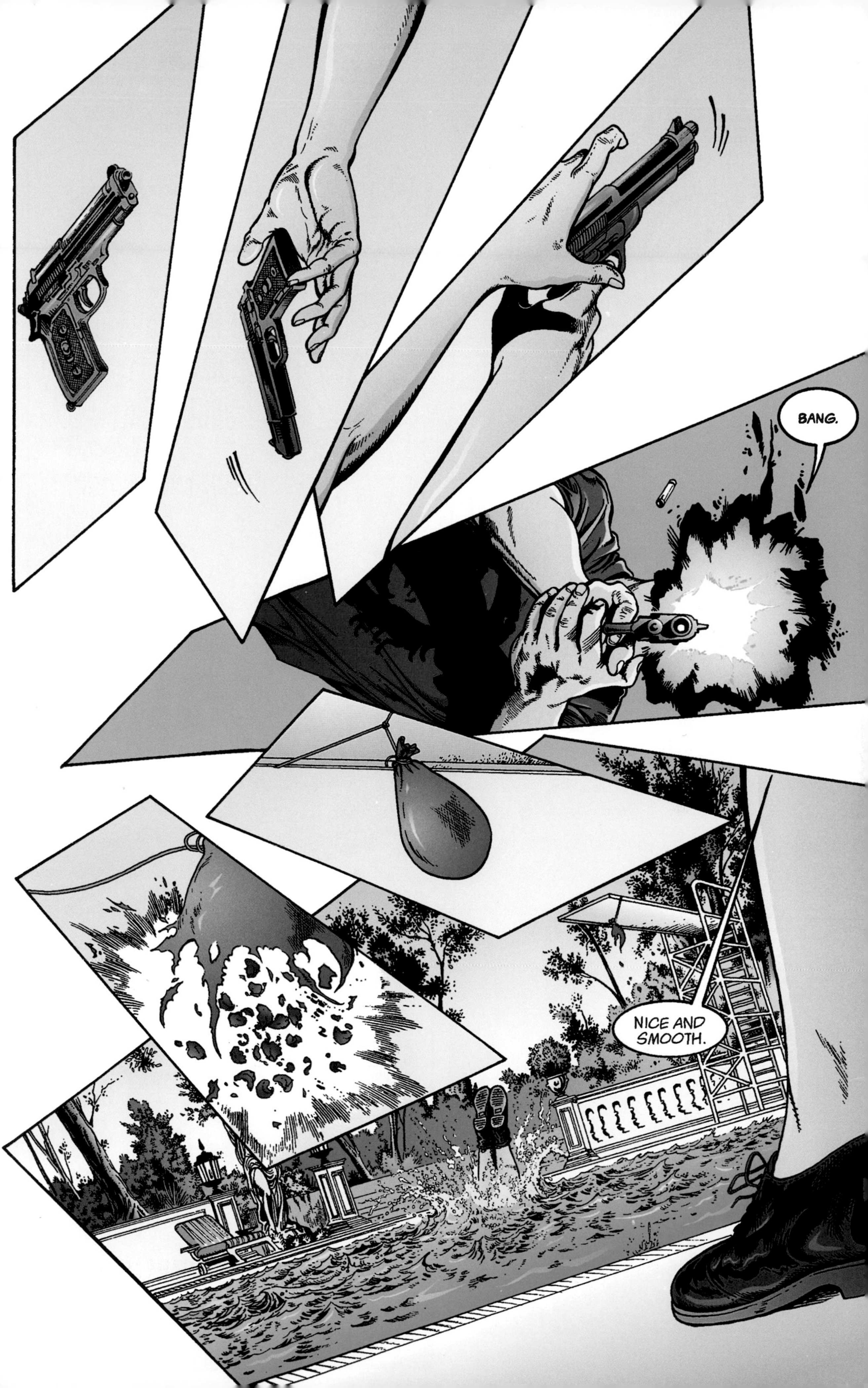
BANG.
NICE AND SMOOTH.

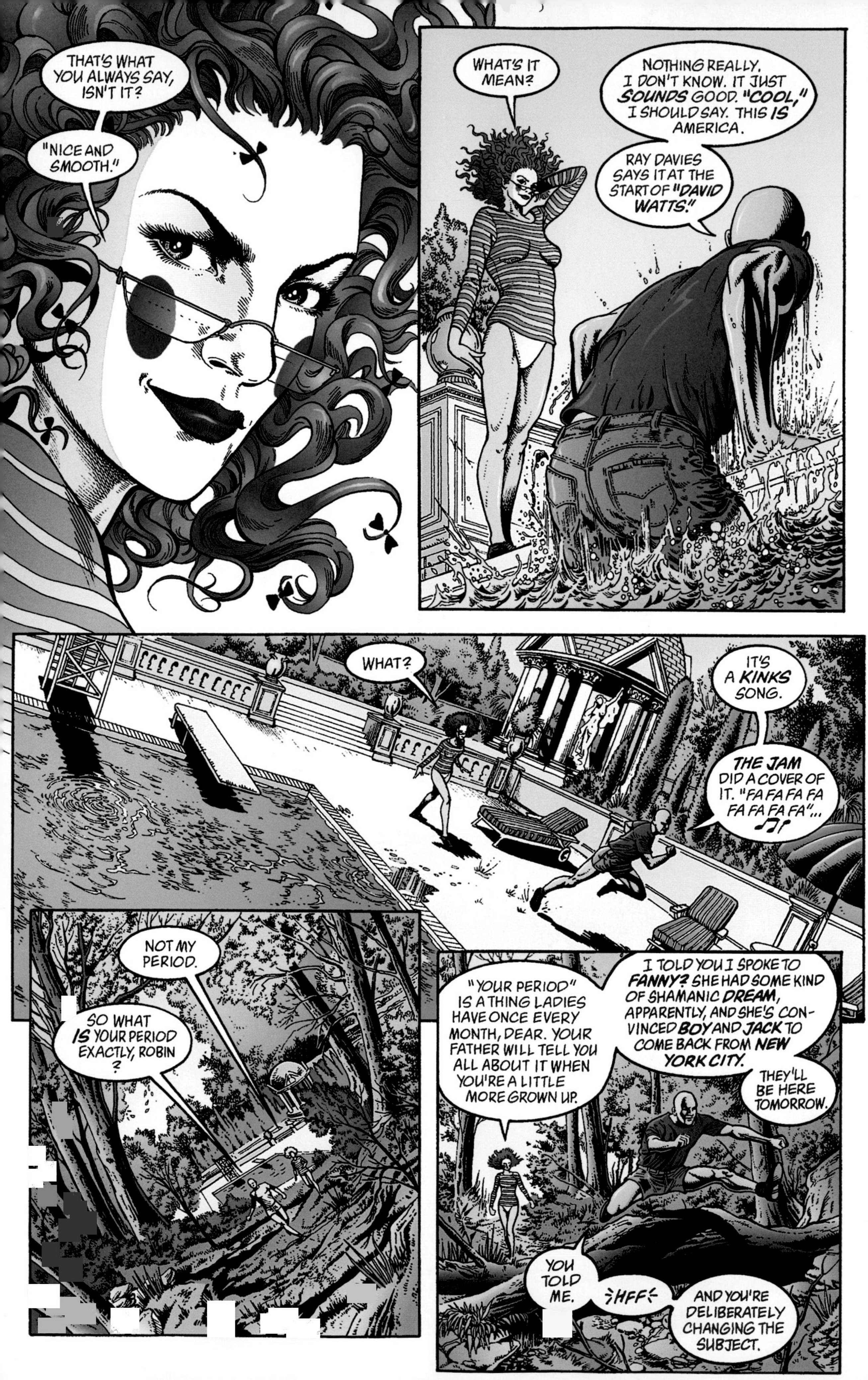

THAT'S WHAT YOU ALWAYS SAY, ISN'T IT?
"NICE AND SMOOTH."
WHAT'S IT MEAN?
NOTHING REALLY. I DON'T KNOW. IT JUST SOUNDS GOOD. "COOL," I SHOULD SAY. THIS IS AMERICA.
RAY DAVIES SAYS IT AT THE START OF "DAVID WATTS."
WHAT?
IT'S A KINKS SONG.
THE JAM DID A COVER OF IT. "FA FA FA FA FA FA FA FA"...
NOT MY PERIOD.
SO WHAT IS YOUR PERIOD EXACTLY, ROBIN?
"YOUR PERIOD" IS A THING LADIES HAVE ONCE EVERY MONTH, DEAR. YOUR FATHER WILL TELL YOU ALL ABOUT IT WHEN YOU'RE A LITTLE MORE GROWN UP.
I TOLD YOU I SPOKE TO FANNY? SHE HAD SOME KIND OF SHAMANIC DREAM, APPARENTLY, AND SHE'S CONVINCED BOY AND JACK TO COME BACK FROM NEW YORK CITY.
THEY'LL BE HERE TOMORROW.
YOU TOLD ME.
HFF
AND YOU'RE DELIBERATELY CHANGING THE SUBJECT.

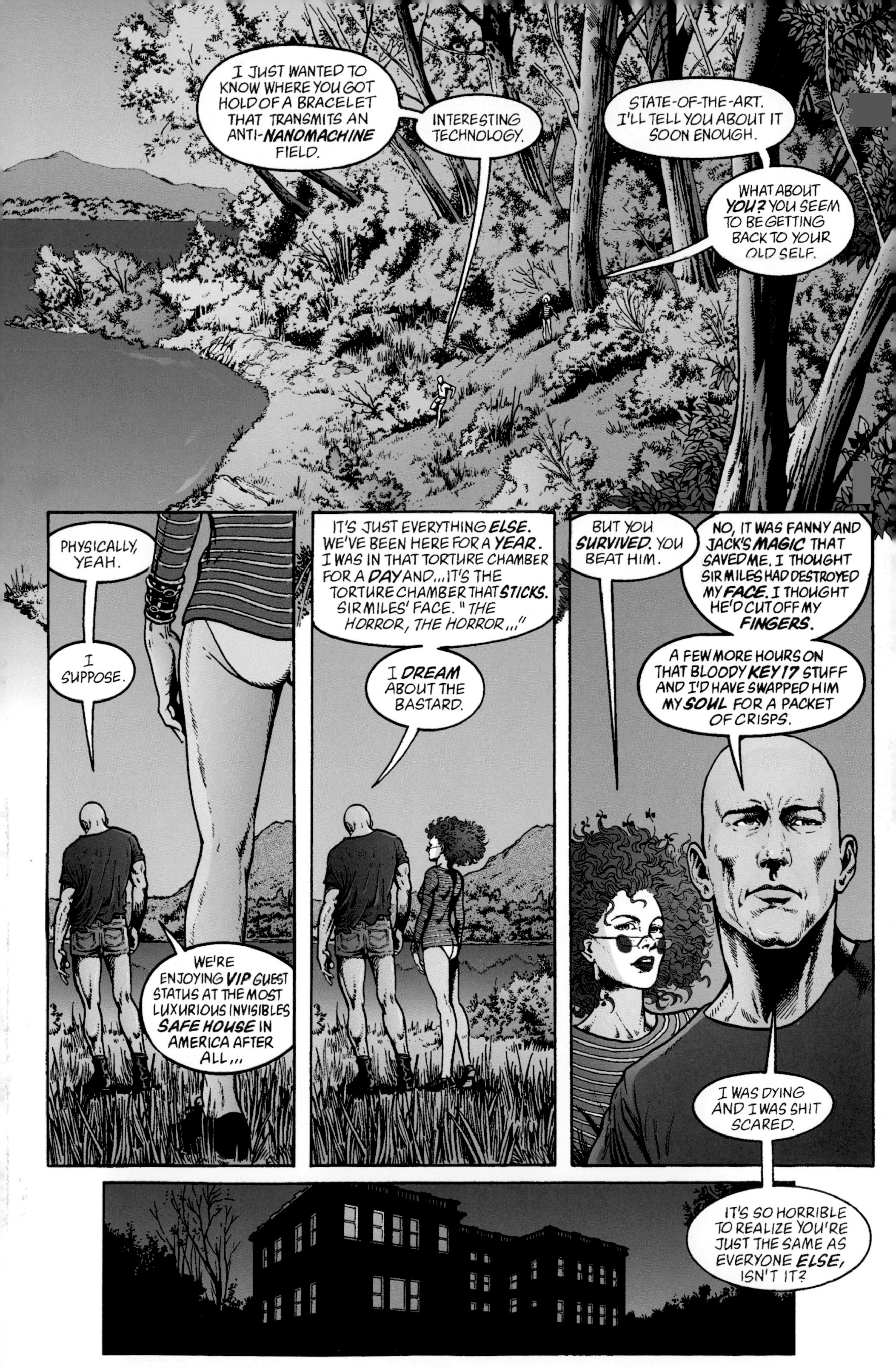
I JUST WANTED TO KNOW WHERE YOU GOT HOLD OF A BRACELET THAT TRANSMITS AN ANTI-NANOMACHINE FIELD.
INTERESTING TECHNOLOGY.
STATE-OF-THE-ART. I'LL TELL YOU ABOUT IT SOON ENOUGH.
WHAT ABOUT YOU? YOU SEEM TO BE GETTING BACK TO YOUR OLD SELF.
PHYSICALLY, YEAH.
I SUPPOSE.
WE'RE ENJOYING VIP GUEST STATUS AT THE MOST LUXURIOUS INVISIBLES SAFE HOUSE IN AMERICA AFTER ALL...
IT'S JUST EVERYTHING ELSE. WE'VE BEEN HERE FOR A YEAR. I WAS IN THAT TORTURE CHAMBER FOR A DAY AND...IT'S THE TORTURE CHAMBER THAT STICKS. SIR MILES' FACE. "THE HORROR, THE HORROR..."
I DREAM ABOUT THE BASTARD.
BUT YOU SURVIVED. YOU BEAT HIM.
NO, IT WAS FANNY AND JACK'S MAGIC THAT SAVED ME. I THOUGHT SIR MILES HAD DESTROYED MY FACE. I THOUGHT HE'D CUT OFF MY FINGERS.
A FEW MORE HOURS ON THAT BLOODY KEY 17 STUFF AND I'D HAVE SWAPPED HIM MY SOUL FOR A PACKET OF CRISPS.
I WAS DYING AND I WAS SHIT SCARED.
IT'S SO HORRIBLE TO REALIZE YOU'RE JUST THE SAME AS EVERYONE ELSE, ISN'T IT?

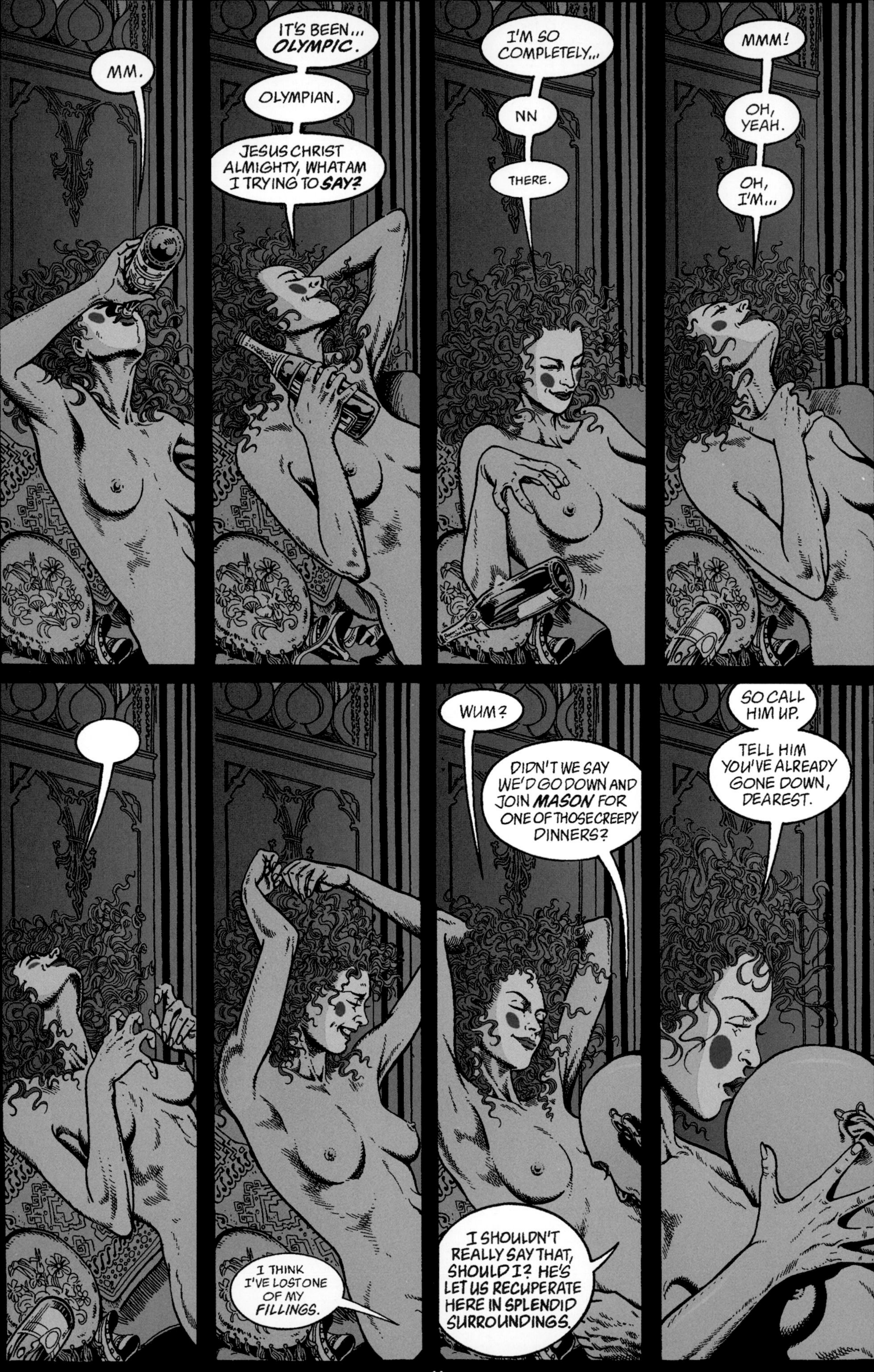
MM.
IT'S BEEN... OLYMPIC.
OLYMPIAN.
JESUS CHRIST ALMIGHTY, WHAT AM I TRYING TO SAY?
I'M SO COMPLETELY...
NN
THERE.
MMM!
OH, YEAH.
OH, I'M...
I THINK I'VE LOST ONE OF MY FILLINGS.
WUM?
DIDN'T WE SAY WE'D GO DOWN AND JOIN MASON FOR ONE OF THOSE CREEPY DINNERS?
I SHOULDN'T REALLY SAY THAT, SHOULD I? HE'S LET US RECUPERATE HERE IN SPLENDID SURROUNDINGS.
SO CALL HIM UP.
TELL HIM YOU'VE ALREADY GONE DOWN, DEAREST.

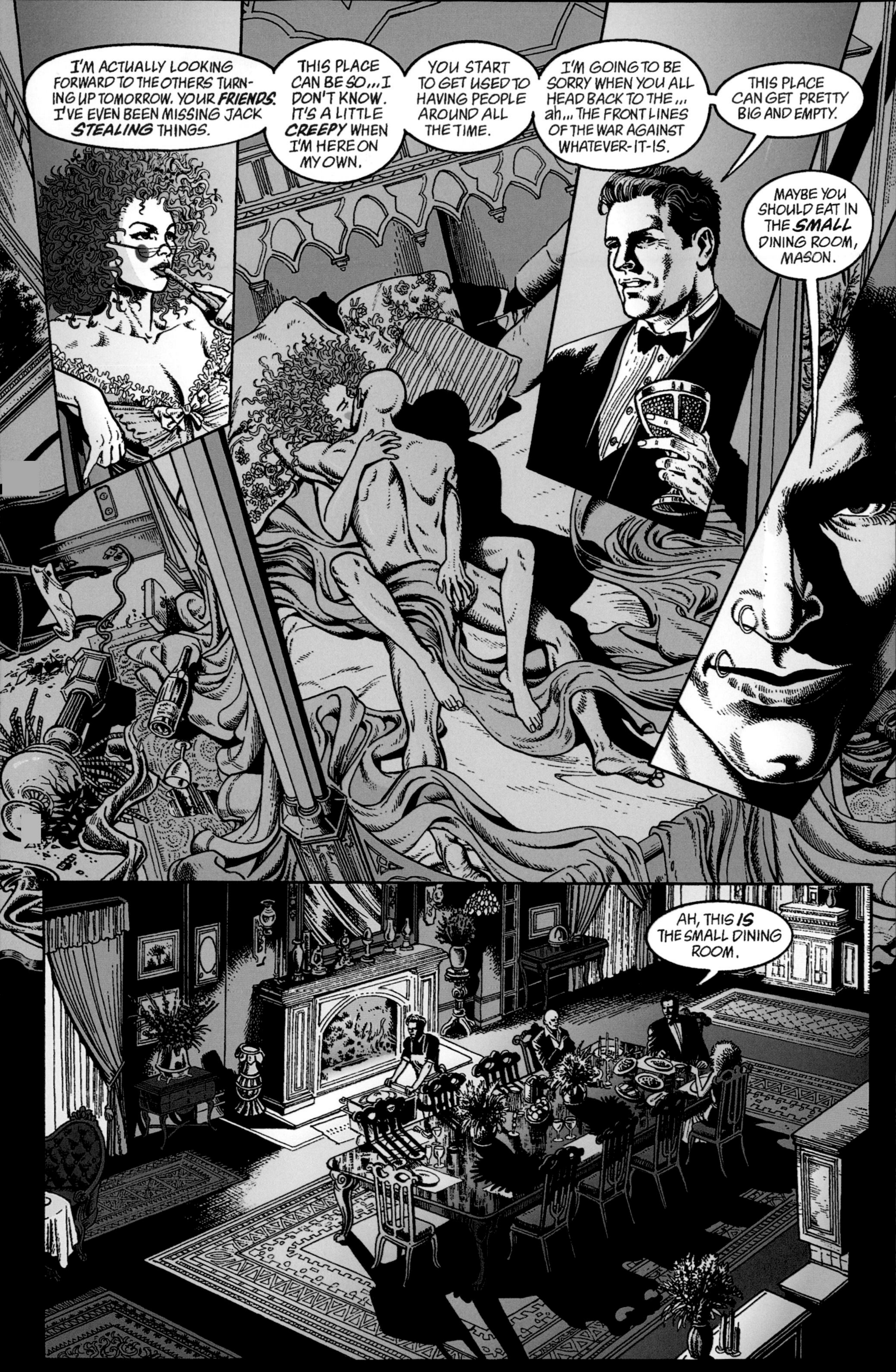
I'M ACTUALLY LOOKING FORWARD TO THE OTHERS TURNING UP TOMORROW. YOUR **FRIENDS**. I'VE EVEN BEEN MISSING JACK **STEALING** THINGS.
THIS PLACE CAN BE SO... I DON'T KNOW. IT'S A LITTLE **CREEPY** WHEN I'M HERE ON MY OWN.
YOU START TO GET USED TO HAVING PEOPLE AROUND ALL THE TIME.
I'M GOING TO BE SORRY WHEN YOU ALL HEAD BACK TO THE... ah... THE FRONT LINES OF THE WAR AGAINST WHATEVER-IT-IS.
THIS PLACE CAN GET PRETTY BIG AND EMPTY.
MAYBE YOU SHOULD EAT IN THE **SMALL** DINING ROOM, MASON.
AH, THIS **IS** THE SMALL DINING ROOM.

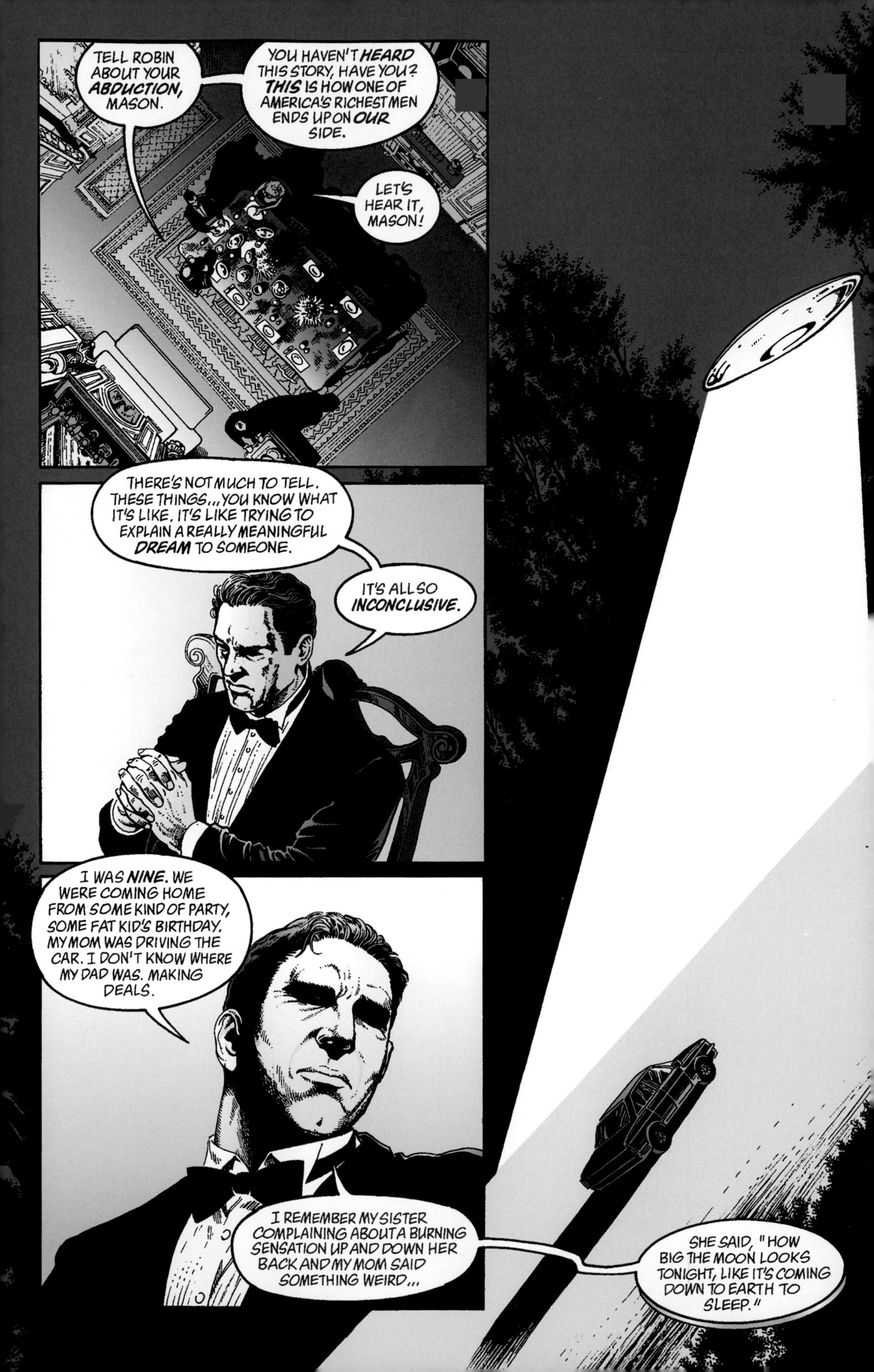
TELL ROBIN ABOUT YOUR ABDUCTION, MASON.
YOU HAVEN'T HEARD THIS STORY, HAVE YOU? THIS IS HOW ONE OF AMERICA'S RICHEST MEN ENDS UP ON OUR SIDE.
LET'S HEAR IT, MASON!
THERE'S NOT MUCH TO TELL. THESE THINGS... YOU KNOW WHAT IT'S LIKE. IT'S LIKE TRYING TO EXPLAIN A REALLY MEANINGFUL DREAM TO SOMEONE.
IT'S ALL SO INCONCLUSIVE.
I WAS NINE. WE WERE COMING HOME FROM SOME KIND OF PARTY, SOME FAT KID'S BIRTHDAY. MY MOM WAS DRIVING THE CAR. I DON'T KNOW WHERE MY DAD WAS. MAKING DEALS.
I REMEMBER MY SISTER COMPLAINING ABOUT A BURNING SENSATION UP AND DOWN HER BACK AND MY MOM SAID SOMETHING WEIRD...
SHE SAID, "HOW BIG THE MOON LOOKS TONIGHT, LIKE IT'S COMING DOWN TO EARTH TO SLEEP."

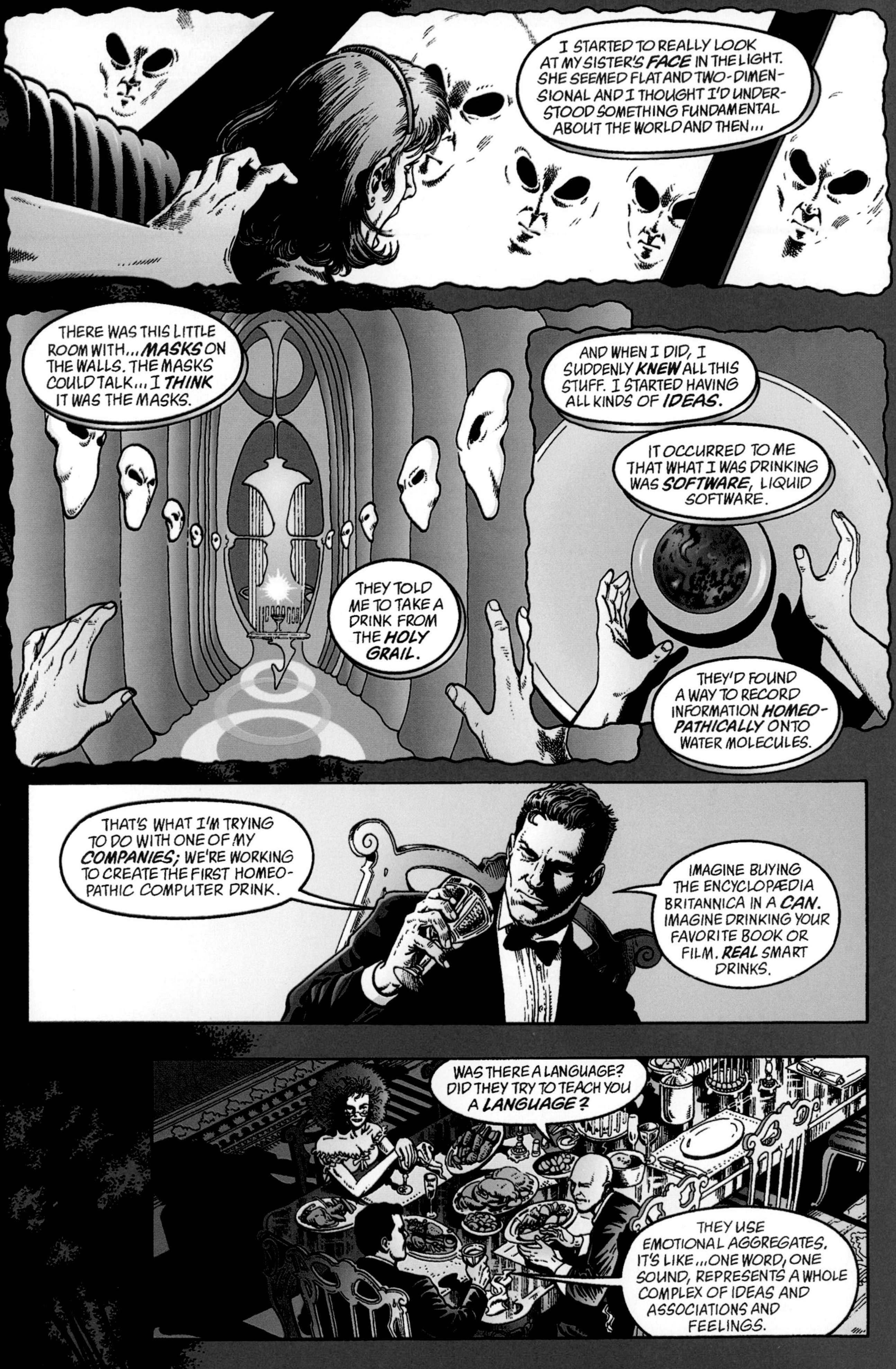
I STARTED TO REALLY LOOK AT MY SISTER'S FACE IN THE LIGHT. SHE SEEMED FLAT AND TWO-DIMENSIONAL AND I THOUGHT I'D UNDERSTOOD SOMETHING FUNDAMENTAL ABOUT THE WORLD AND THEN...
THERE WAS THIS LITTLE ROOM WITH... MASKS ON THE WALLS. THE MASKS COULD TALK... I THINK IT WAS THE MASKS.
THEY TOLD ME TO TAKE A DRINK FROM THE HOLY GRAIL.
AND WHEN I DID, I SUDDENLY KNEW ALL THIS STUFF. I STARTED HAVING ALL KINDS OF IDEAS.
IT OCCURRED TO ME THAT WHAT I WAS DRINKING WAS SOFTWARE, LIQUID SOFTWARE.
THEY'D FOUND A WAY TO RECORD INFORMATION HOMEOPATHICALLY ONTO WATER MOLECULES.
THAT'S WHAT I'M TRYING TO DO WITH ONE OF MY COMPANIES; WE'RE WORKING TO CREATE THE FIRST HOMEOPATHIC COMPUTER DRINK.
IMAGINE BUYING THE ENCYCLOPÆDIA BRITANNICA IN A CAN. IMAGINE DRINKING YOUR FAVORITE BOOK OR FILM. REAL SMART DRINKS.
WAS THERE A LANGUAGE? DID THEY TRY TO TEACH YOU A LANGUAGE?
THEY USE EMOTIONAL AGGREGATES. IT'S LIKE... ONE WORD, ONE SOUND, REPRESENTS A WHOLE COMPLEX OF IDEAS AND ASSOCIATIONS AND FEELINGS.

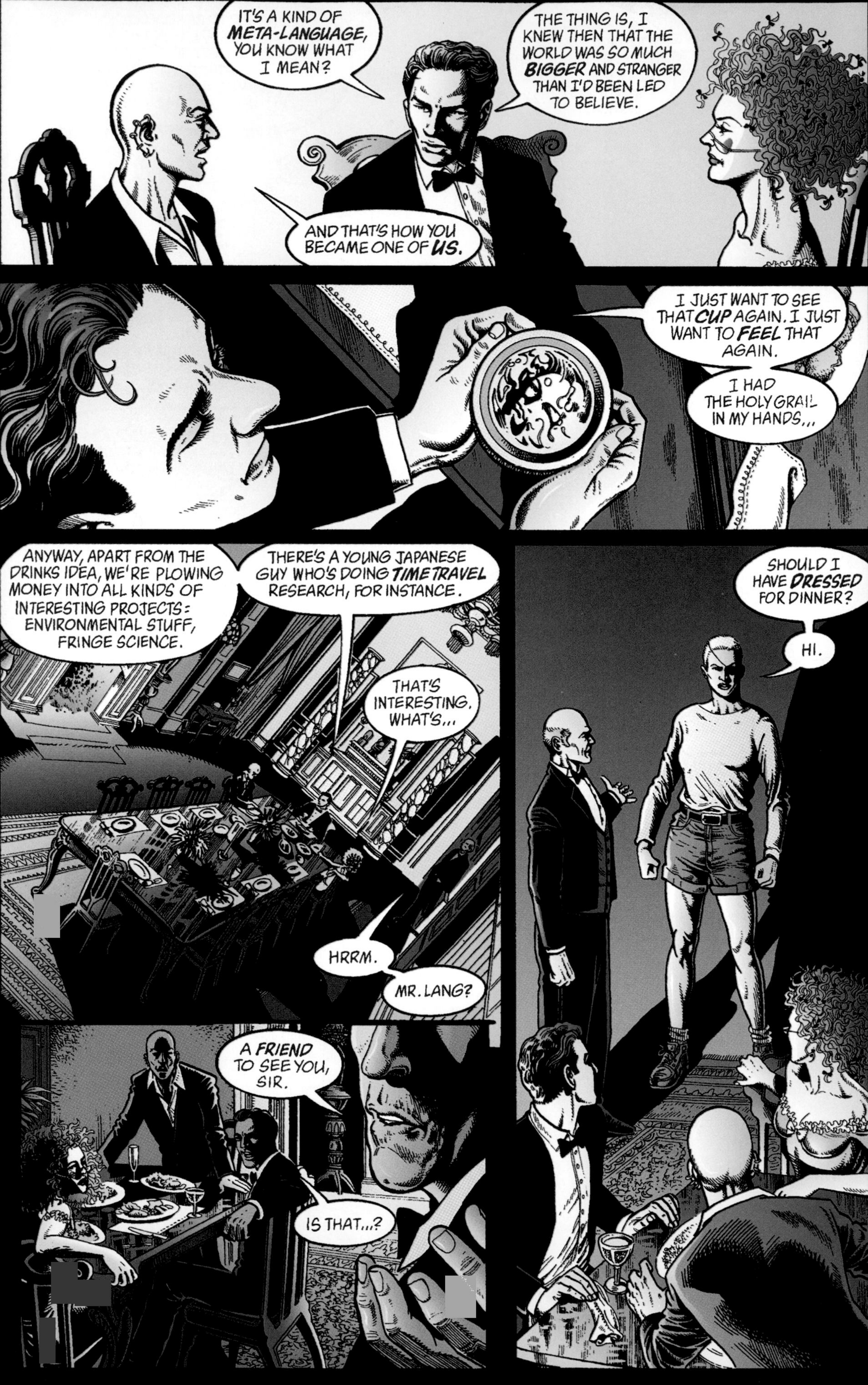
IT'S A KIND OF META-LANGUAGE, YOU KNOW WHAT I MEAN?
THE THING IS, I KNEW THEN THAT THE WORLD WAS SO MUCH BIGGER AND STRANGER THAN I'D BEEN LED TO BELIEVE.
AND THAT'S HOW YOU BECAME ONE OF US.
I JUST WANT TO SEE THAT CUP AGAIN. I JUST WANT TO FEEL THAT AGAIN.
I HAD THE HOLY GRAIL IN MY HANDS...
ANYWAY, APART FROM THE DRINKS IDEA, WE'RE PLOWING MONEY INTO ALL KINDS OF INTERESTING PROJECTS: ENVIRONMENTAL STUFF, FRINGE SCIENCE.
THERE'S A YOUNG JAPANESE GUY WHO'S DOING TIME TRAVEL RESEARCH, FOR INSTANCE.
THAT'S INTERESTING. WHAT'S...
HRRM.
MR. LANG?
A FRIEND TO SEE YOU, SIR.
IS THAT...?
SHOULD I HAVE DRESSED FOR DINNER?
HI.

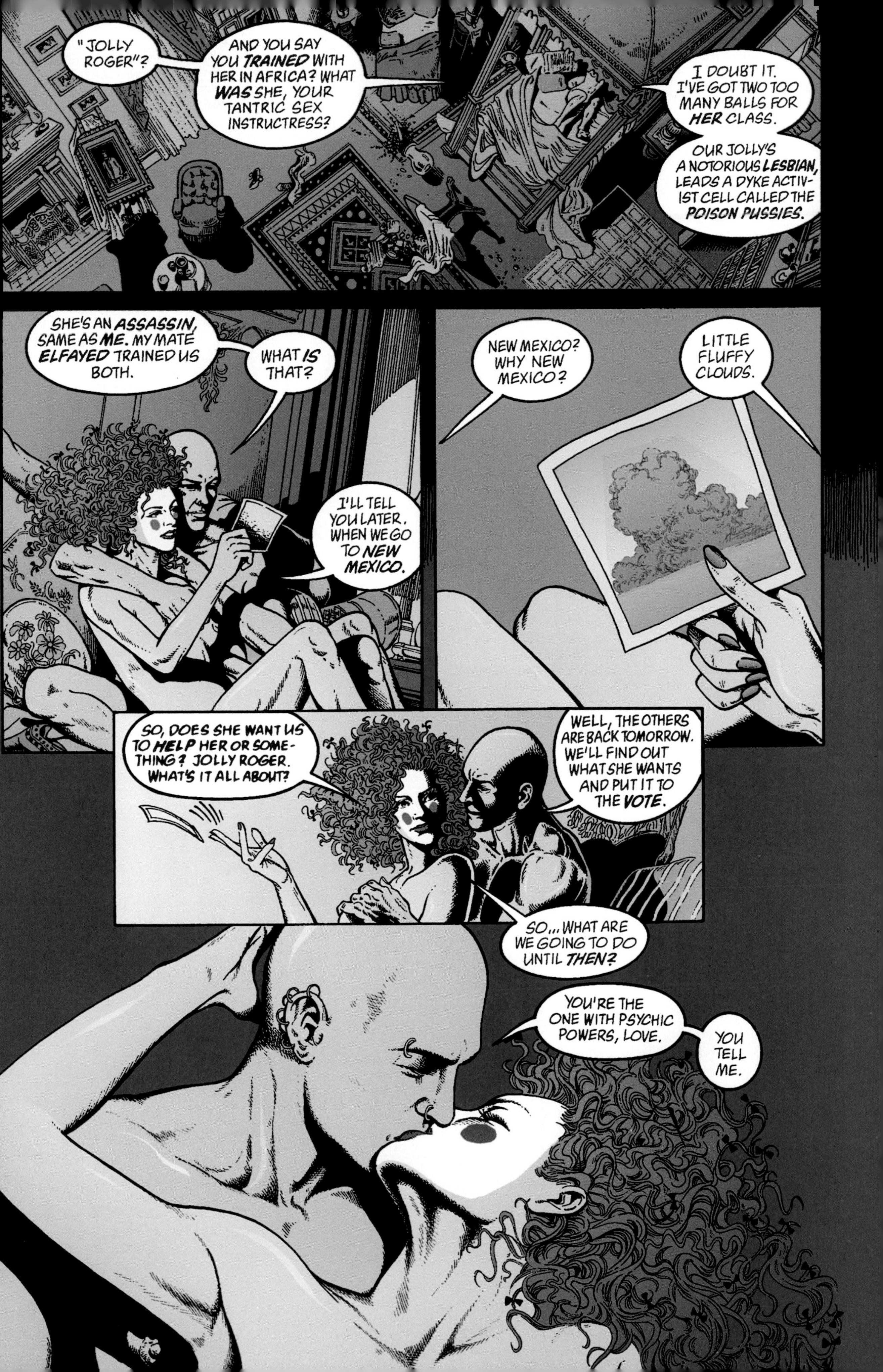
"JOLLY ROGER"?
AND YOU SAY YOU TRAINED WITH HER IN AFRICA? WHAT WAS SHE, YOUR TANTRIC SEX INSTRUCTRESS?
I DOUBT IT. I'VE GOT TWO TOO MANY BALLS FOR HER CLASS.
OUR JOLLY'S A NOTORIOUS LESBIAN, LEADS A DYKE ACTIVIST CELL CALLED THE POISON PUSSIES.
SHE'S AN ASSASSIN, SAME AS ME. MY MATE ELFAYED TRAINED US BOTH.
WHAT IS THAT?
I'LL TELL YOU LATER. WHEN WE GO TO NEW MEXICO.
NEW MEXICO? WHY NEW MEXICO?
LITTLE FLUFFY CLOUDS.
SO, DOES SHE WANT US TO HELP HER OR SOMETHING? JOLLY ROGER. WHAT'S IT ALL ABOUT?
WELL, THE OTHERS ARE BACK TOMORROW. WE'LL FIND OUT WHAT SHE WANTS AND PUT IT TO THE VOTE.
SO... WHAT ARE WE GOING TO DO UNTIL THEN?
YOU'RE THE ONE WITH PSYCHIC POWERS, LOVE.
YOU TELL ME.

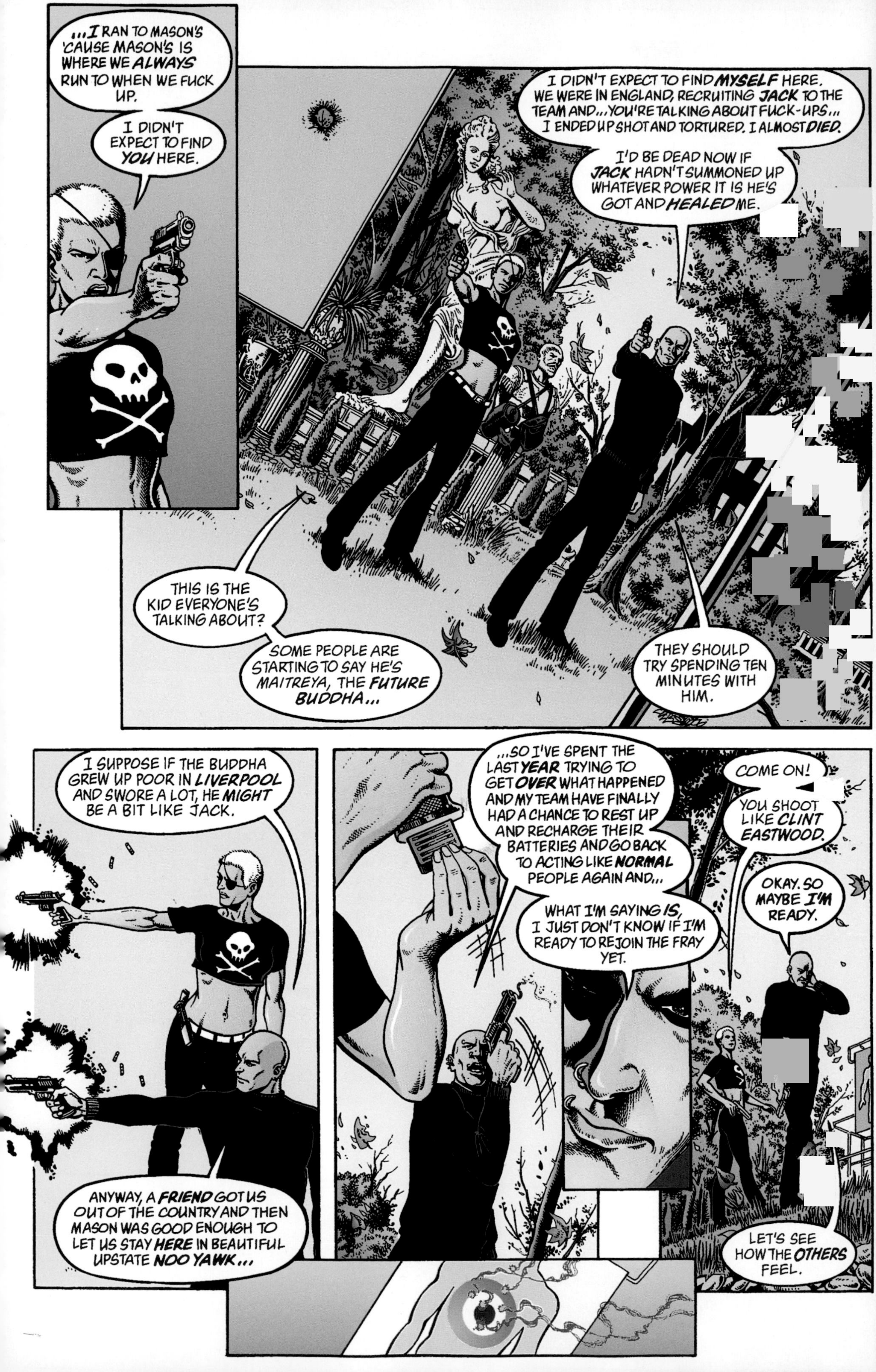
...I RAN TO MASON'S 'CAUSE MASON'S IS WHERE WE ALWAYS RUN TO WHEN WE FUCK UP.
I DIDN'T EXPECT TO FIND YOU HERE.
I DIDN'T EXPECT TO FIND MYSELF HERE. WE WERE IN ENGLAND, RECRUITING JACK TO THE TEAM AND... YOU'RE TALKING ABOUT FUCK-UPS... I ENDED UP SHOT AND TORTURED. I ALMOST DIED.
I'D BE DEAD NOW IF JACK HADN'T SUMMONED UP WHATEVER POWER IT IS HE'S GOT AND HEALED ME.
THIS IS THE KID EVERYONE'S TALKING ABOUT?
SOME PEOPLE ARE STARTING TO SAY HE'S MAITREYA, THE FUTURE BUDDHA...
THEY SHOULD TRY SPENDING TEN MINUTES WITH HIM.
I SUPPOSE IF THE BUDDHA GREW UP POOR IN LIVERPOOL AND SWORE A LOT, HE MIGHT BE A BIT LIKE JACK.
ANYWAY, A FRIEND GOT US OUT OF THE COUNTRY AND THEN MASON WAS GOOD ENOUGH TO LET US STAY HERE IN BEAUTIFUL UPSTATE NOO YAWK...
...SO I'VE SPENT THE LAST YEAR TRYING TO GET OVER WHAT HAPPENED AND MY TEAM HAVE FINALLY HAD A CHANCE TO REST UP AND RECHARGE THEIR BATTERIES AND GO BACK TO ACTING LIKE NORMAL PEOPLE AGAIN AND...
WHAT I'M SAYING IS, I JUST DON'T KNOW IF I'M READY TO REJOIN THE FRAY YET.
COME ON!
YOU SHOOT LIKE CLINT EASTWOOD.
OKAY. SO MAYBE I'M READY.
LET'S SEE HOW THE OTHERS FEEL.

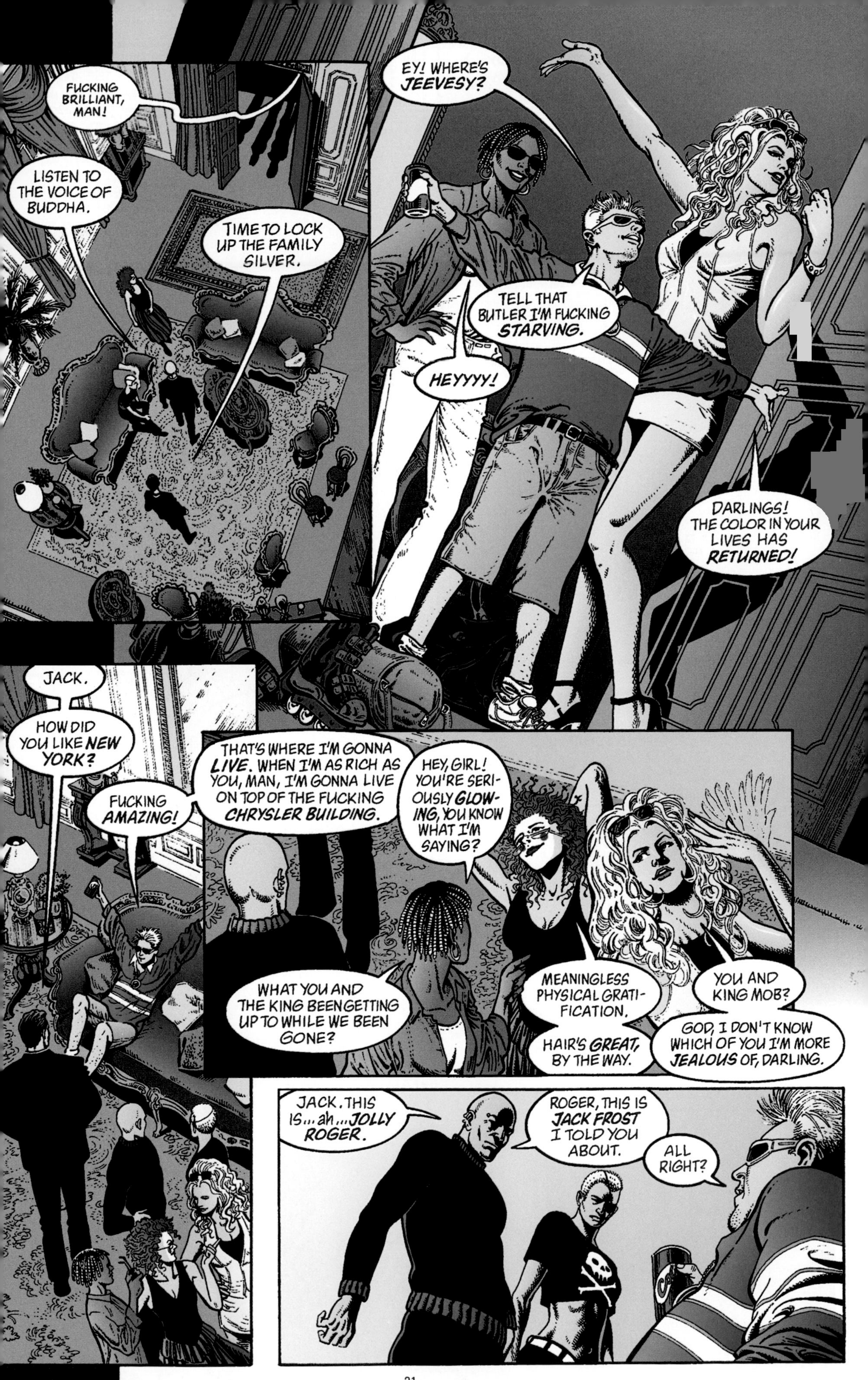
FUCKING BRILLIANT, MAN!
LISTEN TO THE VOICE OF BUDDHA.
TIME TO LOCK UP THE FAMILY SILVER.
EY! WHERE'S JEEVESY?
TELL THAT BUTLER I'M FUCKING STARVING.
HEYYYY!
DARLINGS! THE COLOR IN YOUR LIVES HAS RETURNED!
JACK.
HOW DID YOU LIKE NEW YORK?
FUCKING AMAZING!
THAT'S WHERE I'M GONNA LIVE. WHEN I'M AS RICH AS YOU, MAN, I'M GONNA LIVE ON TOP OF THE FUCKING CHRYSLER BUILDING.
HEY, GIRL! YOU'RE SERIOUSLY GLOWING, YOU KNOW WHAT I'M SAYING?
WHAT YOU AND THE KING BEEN GETTING UP TO WHILE WE BEEN GONE?
MEANINGLESS PHYSICAL GRATIFICATION.
HAIR'S GREAT, BY THE WAY.
YOU AND KING MOB?
GOD, I DON'T KNOW WHICH OF YOU I'M MORE JEALOUS OF, DARLING.
JACK. THIS IS... ah ...JOLLY ROGER.
ROGER, THIS IS JACK FROST I TOLD YOU ABOUT.
ALL RIGHT?

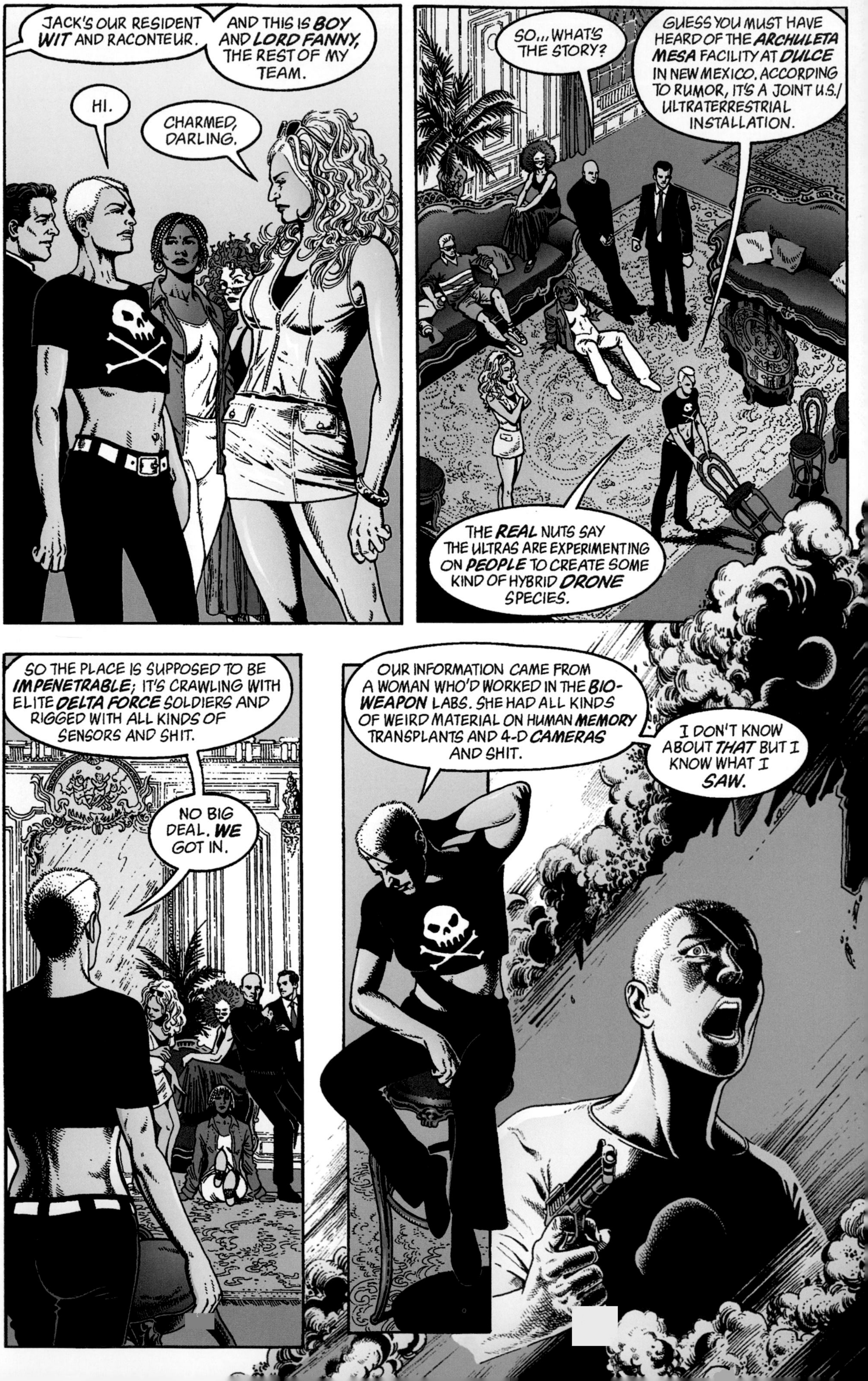
JACK'S OUR RESIDENT WIT AND RACONTEUR.
AND THIS IS BOY AND LORD FANNY, THE REST OF MY TEAM.
HI.
CHARMED, DARLING.
SO... WHAT'S THE STORY?
GUESS YOU MUST HAVE HEARD OF THE ARCHULETA MESA FACILITY AT DULCE IN NEW MEXICO. ACCORDING TO RUMOR, IT'S A JOINT U.S./ ULTRATERRESTRIAL INSTALLATION.
THE REAL NUTS SAY THE ULTRAS ARE EXPERIMENTING ON PEOPLE TO CREATE SOME KIND OF HYBRID DRONE SPECIES.
SO THE PLACE IS SUPPOSED TO BE IMPENETRABLE; IT'S CRAWLING WITH ELITE DELTA FORCE SOLDIERS AND RIGGED WITH ALL KINDS OF SENSORS AND SHIT.
NO BIG DEAL. WE GOT IN.
OUR INFORMATION CAME FROM A WOMAN WHO'D WORKED IN THE BIO-WEAPON LABS. SHE HAD ALL KINDS OF WEIRD MATERIAL ON HUMAN MEMORY TRANSPLANTS AND 4-D CAMERAS AND SHIT.
I DON'T KNOW ABOUT THAT BUT I KNOW WHAT I SAW.

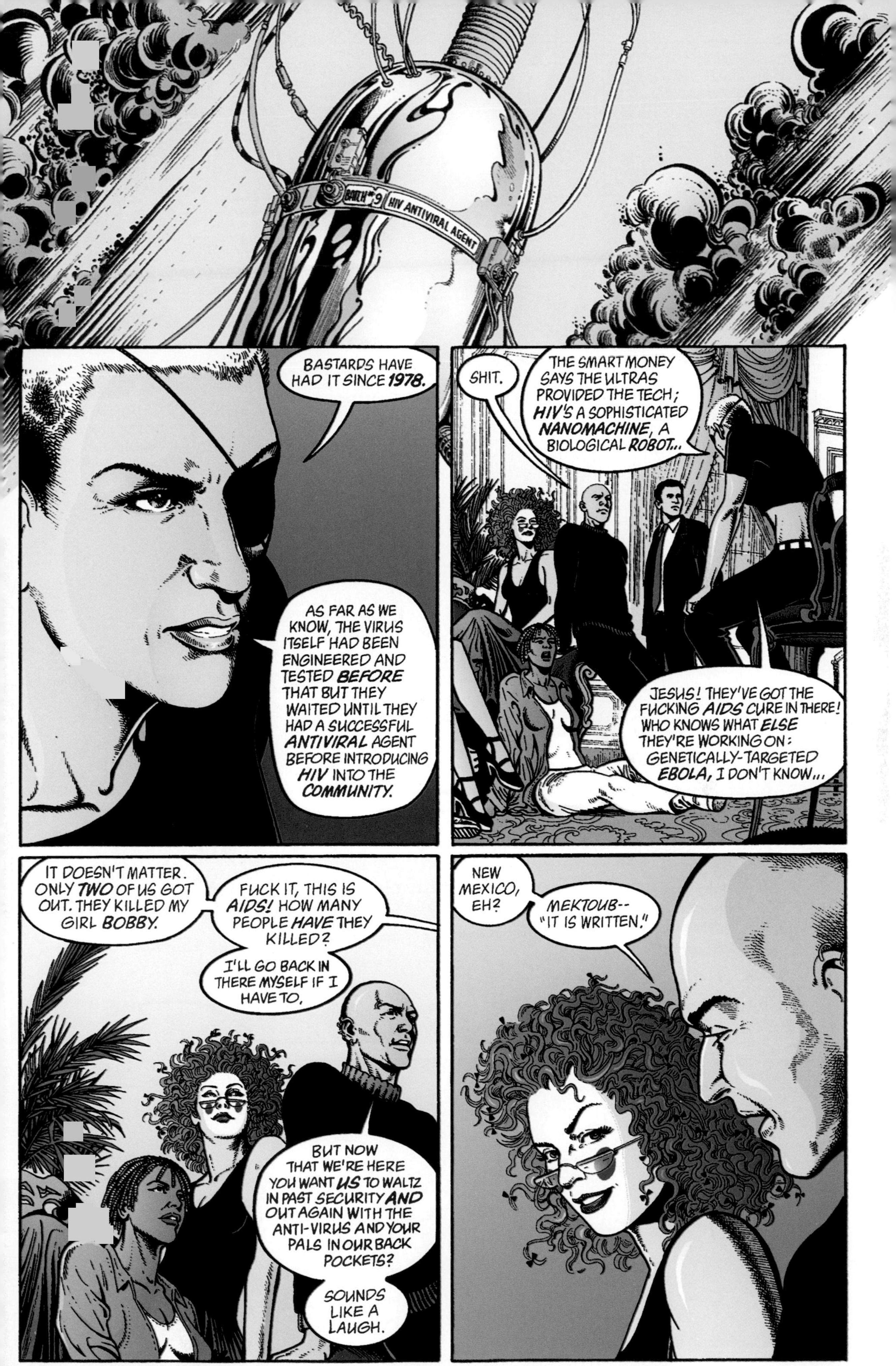
BATCH #9 HIV ANTIVIRAL AGENT
BASTARDS HAVE HAD IT SINCE 1978.
AS FAR AS WE KNOW, THE VIRUS ITSELF HAD BEEN ENGINEERED AND TESTED BEFORE THAT BUT THEY WAITED UNTIL THEY HAD A SUCCESSFUL ANTIVIRAL AGENT BEFORE INTRODUCING HIV INTO THE COMMUNITY.
SHIT.
THE SMART MONEY SAYS THE ULTRAS PROVIDED THE TECH; HIV'S A SOPHISTICATED NANOMACHINE, A BIOLOGICAL ROBOT...
JESUS! THEY'VE GOT THE FUCKING AIDS CURE IN THERE! WHO KNOWS WHAT ELSE THEY'RE WORKING ON: GENETICALLY-TARGETED EBOLA, I DON'T KNOW...
IT DOESN'T MATTER. ONLY TWO OF US GOT OUT. THEY KILLED MY GIRL BOBBY.
FUCK IT, THIS IS AIDS! HOW MANY PEOPLE HAVE THEY KILLED?
I'LL GO BACK IN THERE MYSELF IF I HAVE TO.
BUT NOW THAT WE'RE HERE YOU WANT US TO WALTZ IN PAST SECURITY AND OUT AGAIN WITH THE ANTI-VIRUS AND YOUR PALS IN OUR BACK POCKETS?
SOUNDS LIKE A LAUGH.
NEW MEXICO, EH?
MEKTOUB-- "IT IS WRITTEN."

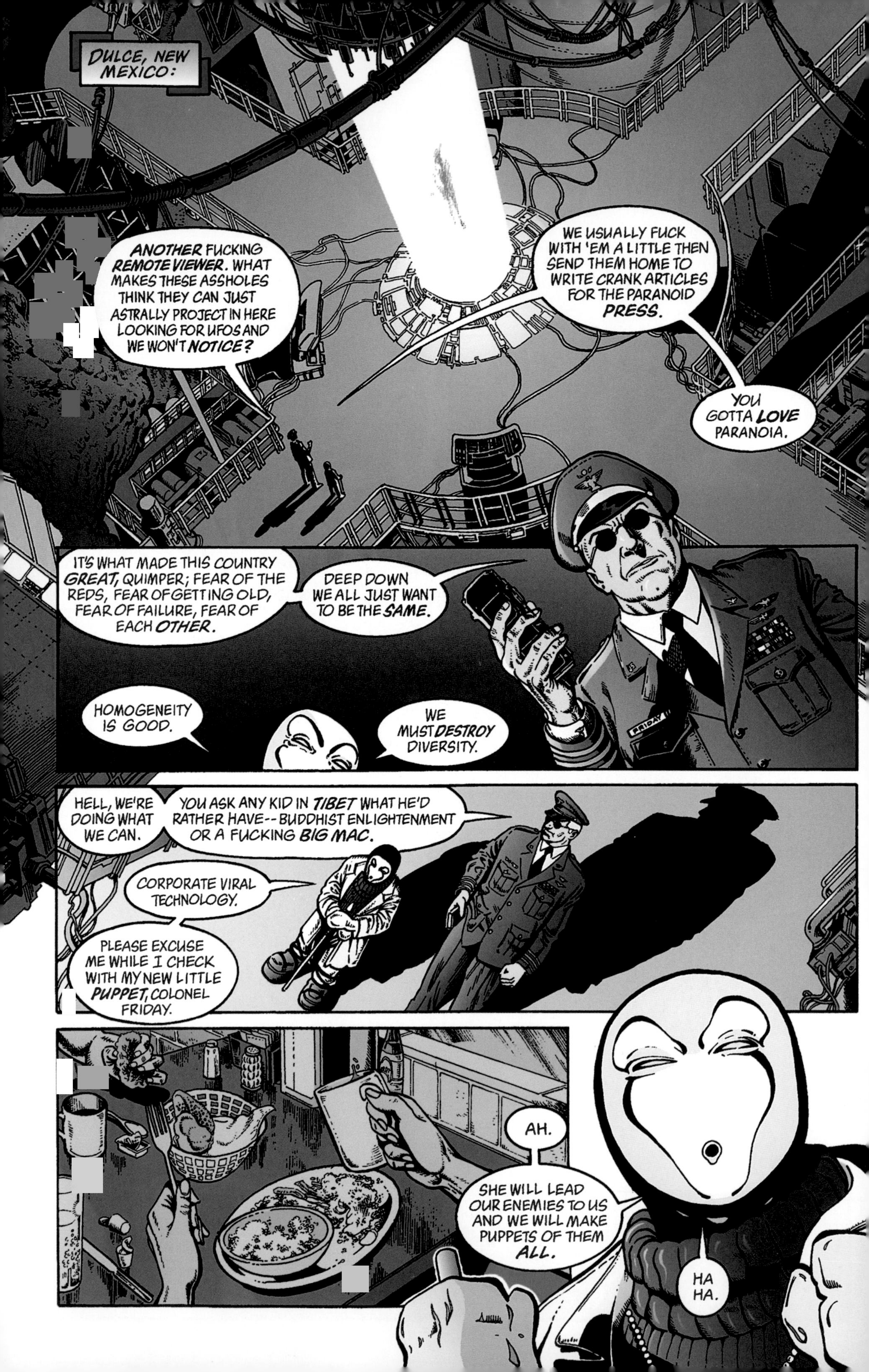
DULCE, NEW MEXICO:
ANOTHER FUCKING REMOTE VIEWER. WHAT MAKES THESE ASSHOLES THINK THEY CAN JUST ASTRALLY PROJECT IN HERE LOOKING FOR UFOS AND WE WON'T NOTICE?
WE USUALLY FUCK WITH 'EM A LITTLE THEN SEND THEM HOME TO WRITE CRANK ARTICLES FOR THE PARANOID PRESS.
YOU GOTTA LOVE PARANOIA.
IT'S WHAT MADE THIS COUNTRY GREAT, QUIMPER; FEAR OF THE REDS, FEAR OF GETTING OLD, FEAR OF FAILURE, FEAR OF EACH OTHER.
DEEP DOWN WE ALL JUST WANT TO BE THE SAME.
HOMOGENEITY IS GOOD.
WE MUST DESTROY DIVERSITY.
FRIDAY
HELL, WE'RE DOING WHAT WE CAN.
YOU ASK ANY KID IN TIBET WHAT HE'D RATHER HAVE-- BUDDHIST ENLIGHTENMENT OR A FUCKING BIG MAC.
CORPORATE VIRAL TECHNOLOGY.
PLEASE EXCUSE ME WHILE I CHECK WITH MY NEW LITTLE PUPPET, COLONEL FRIDAY.
AH.
SHE WILL LEAD OUR ENEMIES TO US AND WE WILL MAKE PUPPETS OF THEM ALL.
HA HA.

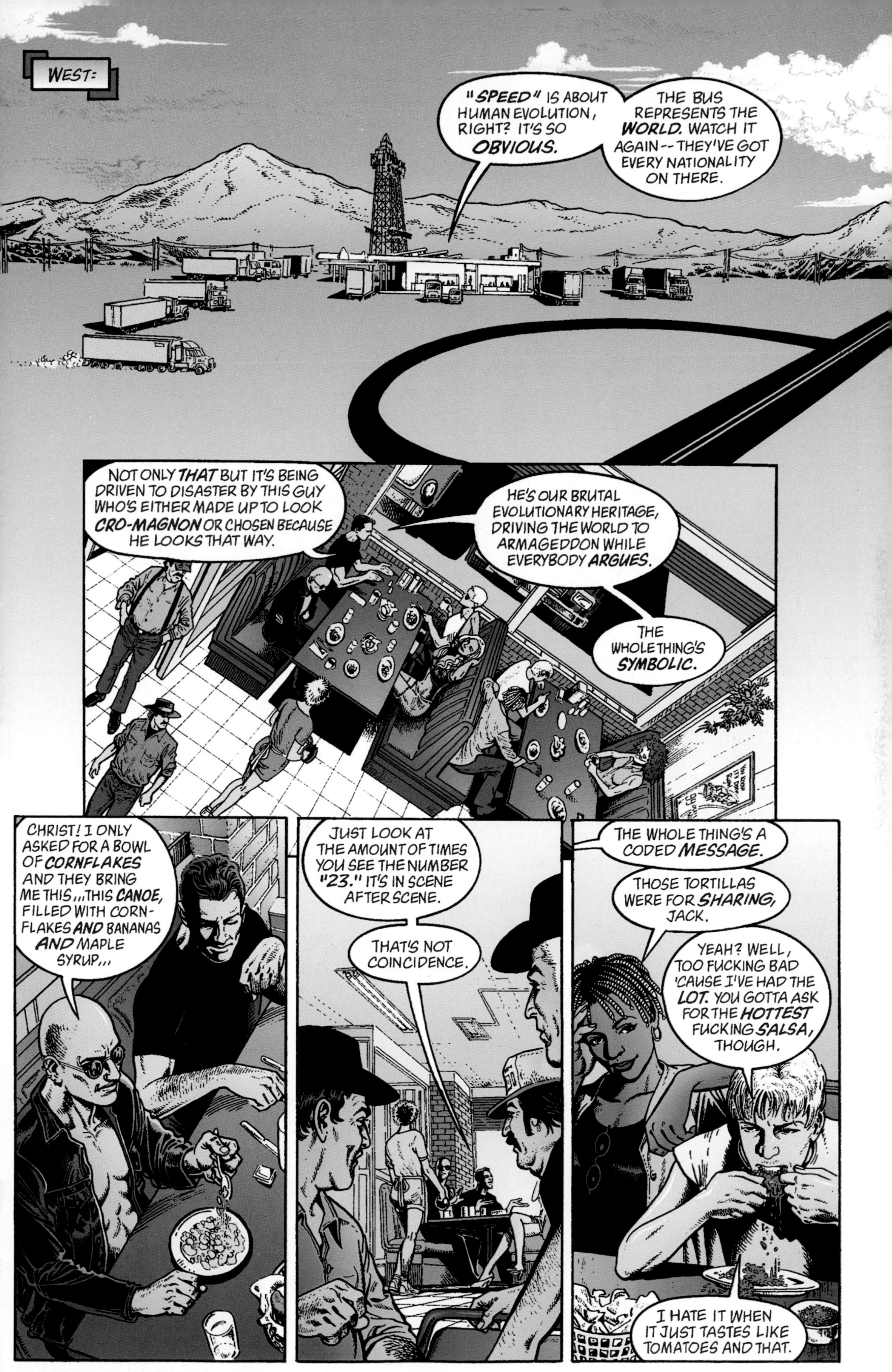
WEST:
"SPEED" IS ABOUT HUMAN EVOLUTION, RIGHT? IT'S SO OBVIOUS.
THE BUS REPRESENTS THE WORLD. WATCH IT AGAIN -- THEY'VE GOT EVERY NATIONALITY ON THERE.
NOT ONLY THAT BUT IT'S BEING DRIVEN TO DISASTER BY THIS GUY WHO'S EITHER MADE UP TO LOOK CRO-MAGNON OR CHOSEN BECAUSE HE LOOKS THAT WAY.
HE'S OUR BRUTAL EVOLUTIONARY HERITAGE, DRIVING THE WORLD TO ARMAGEDDON WHILE EVERYBODY ARGUES.
THE WHOLE THING'S SYMBOLIC.
CHRIST! I ONLY ASKED FOR A BOWL OF CORNFLAKES AND THEY BRING ME THIS,,,THIS CANOE, FILLED WITH CORN-FLAKES AND BANANAS AND MAPLE SYRUP,,,
JUST LOOK AT THE AMOUNT OF TIMES YOU SEE THE NUMBER "23." IT'S IN SCENE AFTER SCENE.
THAT'S NOT COINCIDENCE.
THE WHOLE THING'S A CODED MESSAGE.
THOSE TORTILLAS WERE FOR SHARING, JACK.
YEAH? WELL, TOO FUCKING BAD 'CAUSE I'VE HAD THE LOT. YOU GOTTA ASK FOR THE HOTTEST FUCKING SALSA, THOUGH.
I HATE IT WHEN IT JUST TASTES LIKE TOMATOES AND THAT.

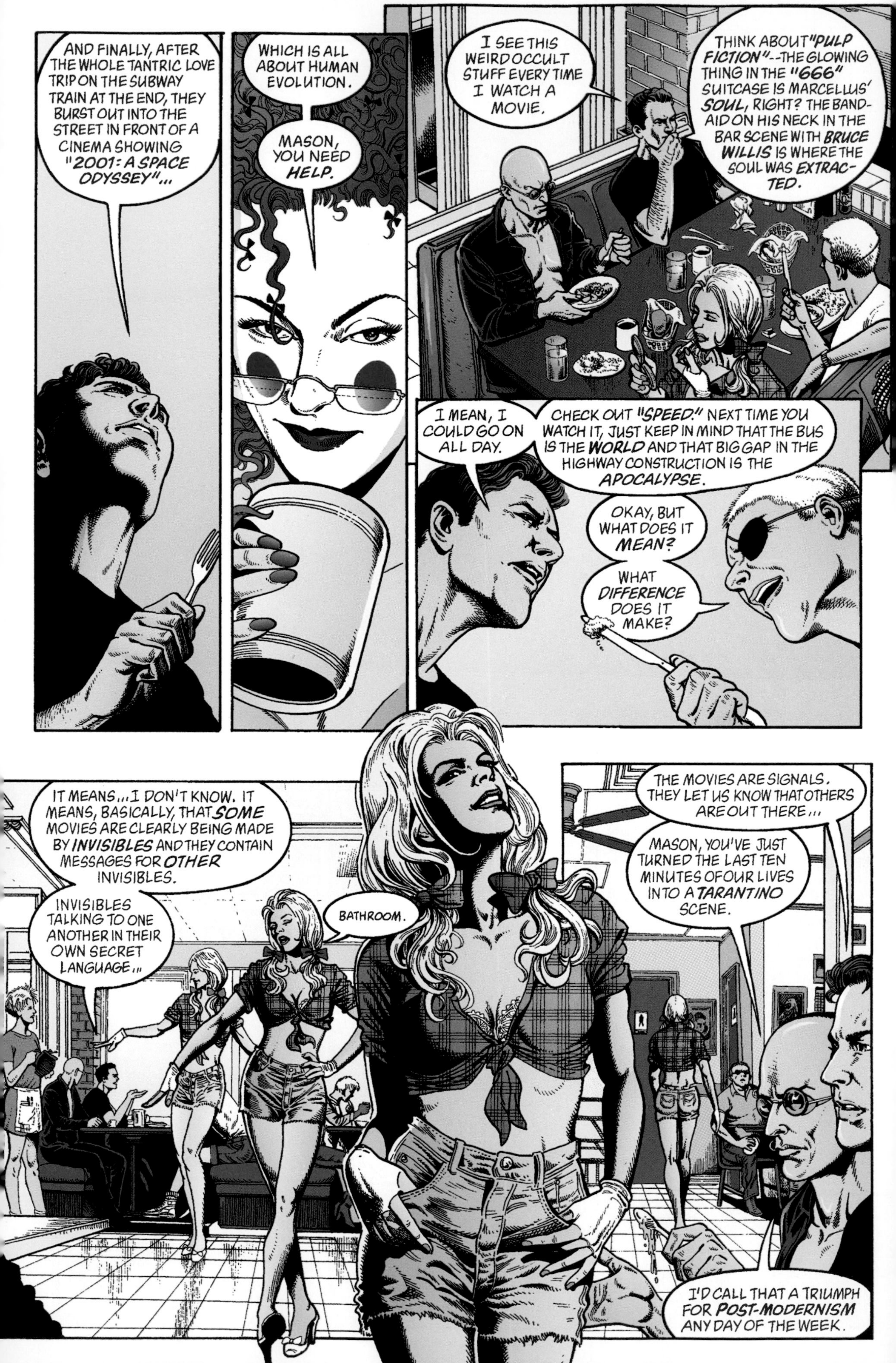
AND FINALLY, AFTER THE WHOLE TANTRIC LOVE TRIP ON THE SUBWAY TRAIN AT THE END, THEY BURST OUT INTO THE STREET IN FRONT OF A CINEMA SHOWING "2001: A SPACE ODYSSEY"...
WHICH IS ALL ABOUT HUMAN EVOLUTION.
MASON, YOU NEED HELP.
I SEE THIS WEIRD OCCULT STUFF EVERY TIME I WATCH A MOVIE.
THINK ABOUT "PULP FICTION"--THE GLOWING THING IN THE "666" SUITCASE IS MARCELLUS' SOUL, RIGHT? THE BAND-AID ON HIS NECK IN THE BAR SCENE WITH BRUCE WILLIS IS WHERE THE SOUL WAS EXTRACTED.
I MEAN, I COULD GO ON ALL DAY.
CHECK OUT "SPEED." NEXT TIME YOU WATCH IT, JUST KEEP IN MIND THAT THE BUS IS THE WORLD AND THAT BIG GAP IN THE HIGHWAY CONSTRUCTION IS THE APOCALYPSE.
OKAY, BUT WHAT DOES IT MEAN?
WHAT DIFFERENCE DOES IT MAKE?
IT MEANS...I DON'T KNOW. IT MEANS, BASICALLY, THAT SOME MOVIES ARE CLEARLY BEING MADE BY INVISIBLES AND THEY CONTAIN MESSAGES FOR OTHER INVISIBLES.
INVISIBLES TALKING TO ONE ANOTHER IN THEIR OWN SECRET LANGUAGE...
BATHROOM.
THE MOVIES ARE SIGNALS. THEY LET US KNOW THAT OTHERS ARE OUT THERE...
MASON, YOU'VE JUST TURNED THE LAST TEN MINUTES OF OUR LIVES INTO A TARANTINO SCENE.
I'D CALL THAT A TRIUMPH FOR POST-MODERNISM ANY DAY OF THE WEEK.

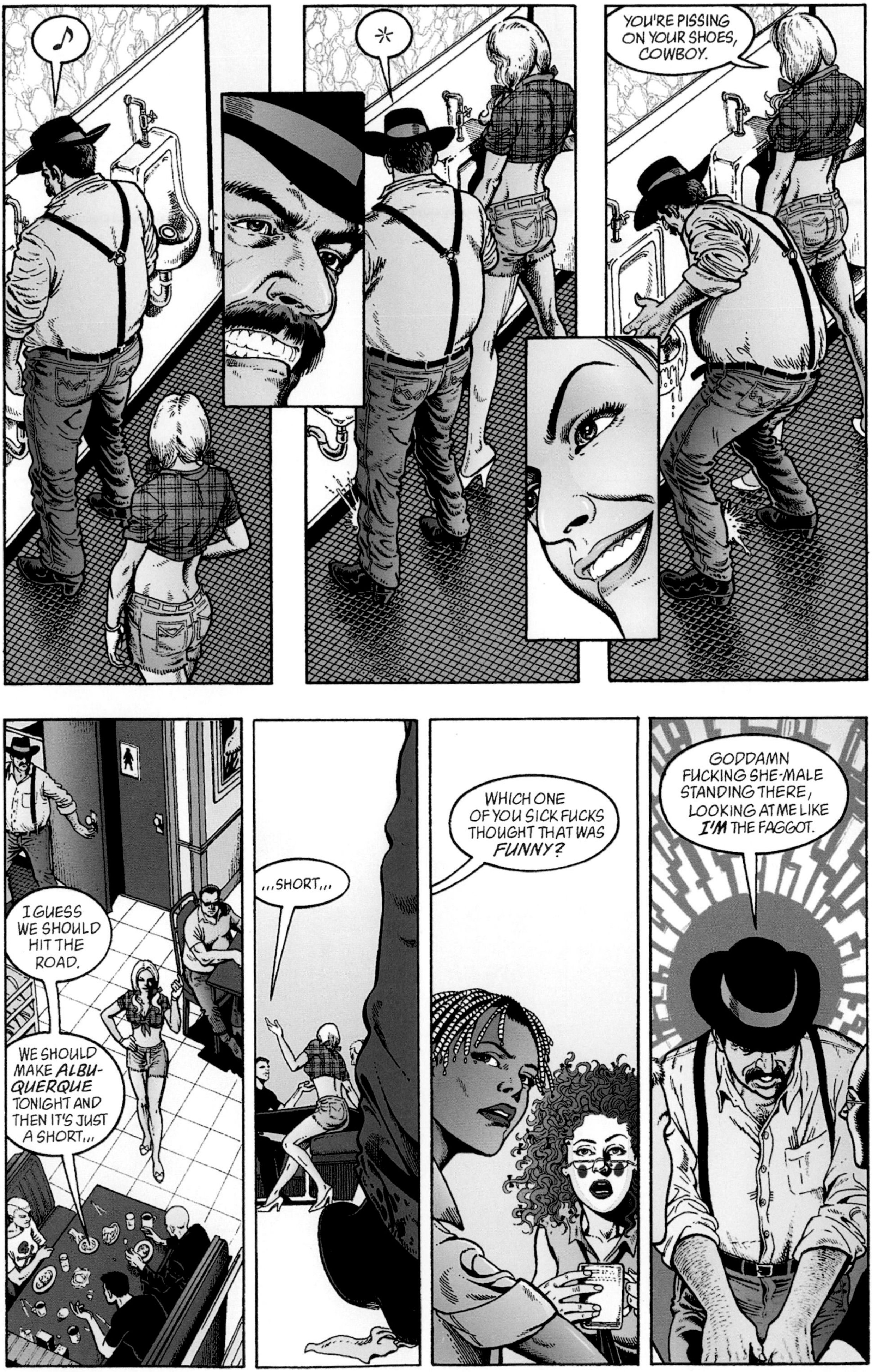
♪
*
YOU'RE PISSING ON YOUR SHOES, COWBOY.
I GUESS WE SHOULD HIT THE ROAD.
WE SHOULD MAKE ALBUQUERQUE TONIGHT AND THEN IT'S JUST A SHORT,,,
,,,SHORT,,,
WHICH ONE OF YOU SICK FUCKS THOUGHT THAT WAS FUNNY?
GODDAMN FUCKING SHE-MALE STANDING THERE, LOOKING AT ME LIKE I'M THE FAGGOT.

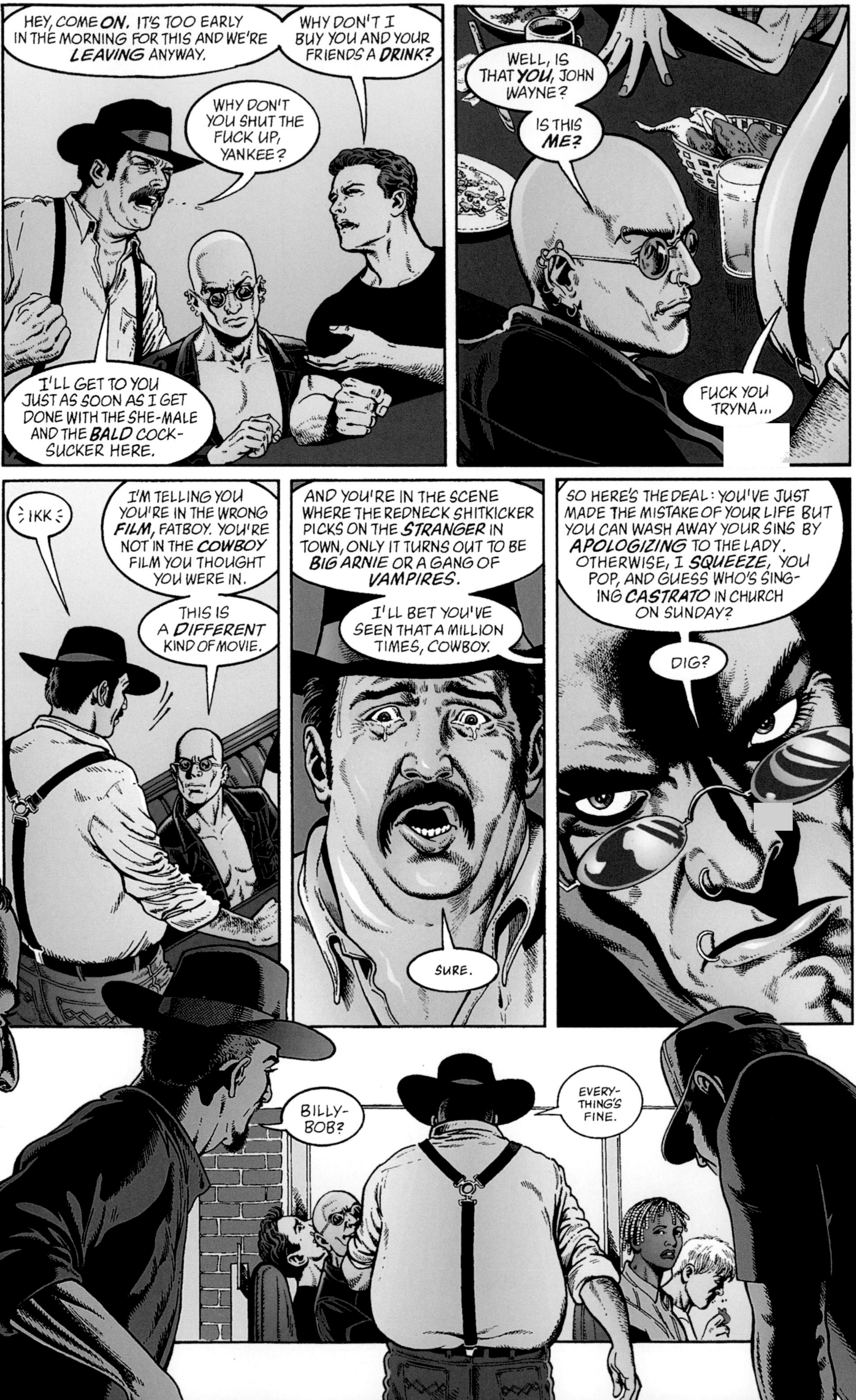
HEY, COME ON. IT'S TOO EARLY IN THE MORNING FOR THIS AND WE'RE LEAVING ANYWAY.
WHY DON'T I BUY YOU AND YOUR FRIENDS A DRINK?
WHY DON'T YOU SHUT THE FUCK UP, YANKEE?
I'LL GET TO YOU JUST AS SOON AS I GET DONE WITH THE SHE-MALE AND THE BALD COCK-SUCKER HERE.
WELL, IS THAT YOU, JOHN WAYNE?
IS THIS ME?
FUCK YOU TRYNA...
IKK
I'M TELLING YOU YOU'RE IN THE WRONG FILM, FATBOY. YOU'RE NOT IN THE COWBOY FILM YOU THOUGHT YOU WERE IN.
THIS IS A DIFFERENT KIND OF MOVIE.
AND YOU'RE IN THE SCENE WHERE THE REDNECK SHITKICKER PICKS ON THE STRANGER IN TOWN, ONLY IT TURNS OUT TO BE BIG ARNIE OR A GANG OF VAMPIRES.
I'LL BET YOU'VE SEEN THAT A MILLION TIMES, COWBOY.
SURE.
SO HERE'S THE DEAL: YOU'VE JUST MADE THE MISTAKE OF YOUR LIFE BUT YOU CAN WASH AWAY YOUR SINS BY APOLOGIZING TO THE LADY. OTHERWISE, I SQUEEZE, YOU POP, AND GUESS WHO'S SING-ING CASTRATO IN CHURCH ON SUNDAY?
DIG?
BILLY-BOB?
EVERY-THING'S FINE.

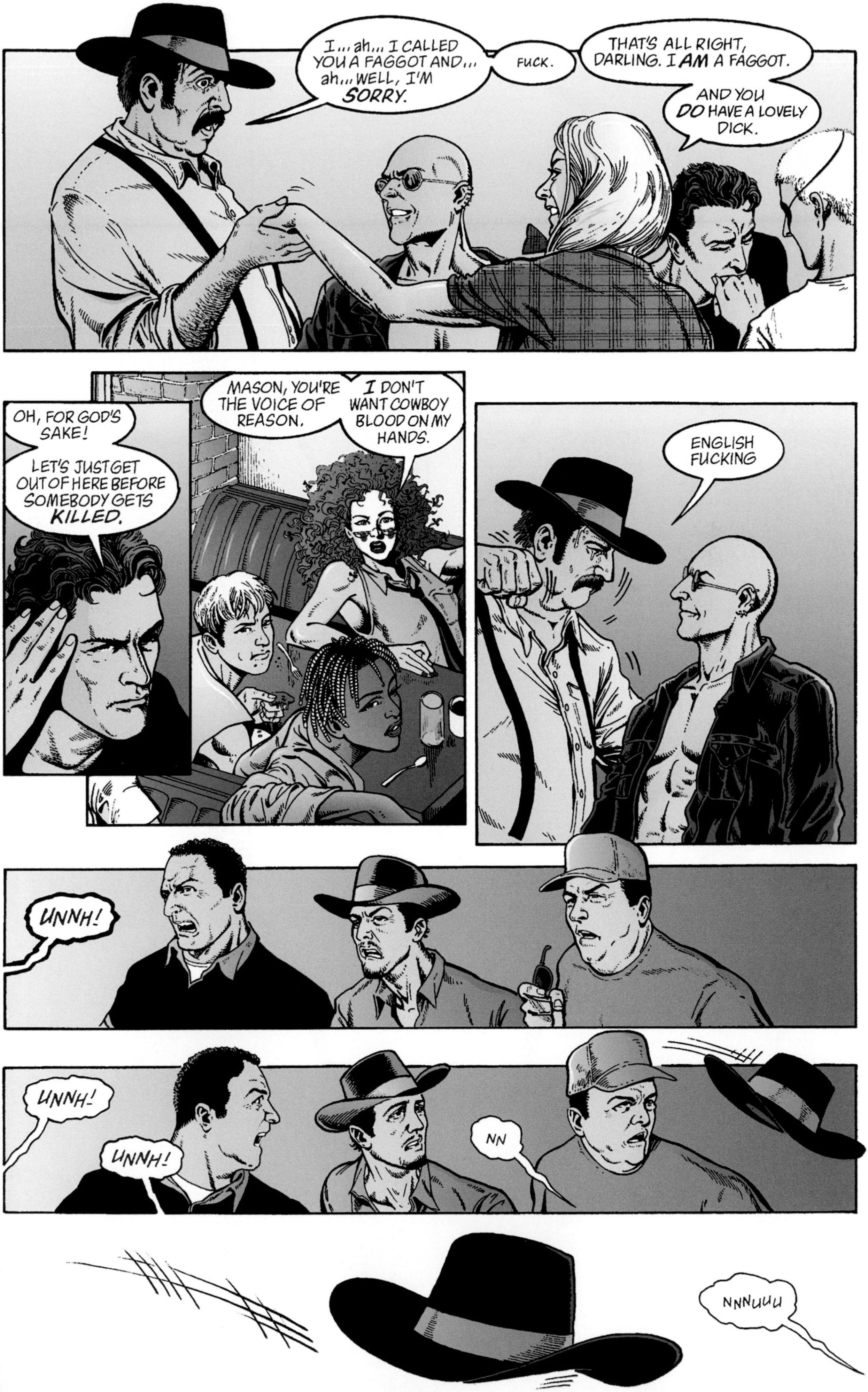
I... ah... I CALLED YOU A FAGGOT AND... ah... WELL, I'M SORRY.
FUCK.
THAT'S ALL RIGHT, DARLING. I AM A FAGGOT.
AND YOU DO HAVE A LOVELY DICK.
OH, FOR GOD'S SAKE!
LET'S JUST GET OUT OF HERE BEFORE SOMEBODY GETS KILLED.
MASON, YOU'RE THE VOICE OF REASON.
I DON'T WANT COWBOY BLOOD ON MY HANDS.
ENGLISH FUCKING
UNNH!
UNNH!
UNNH!
NN
NNNUUU

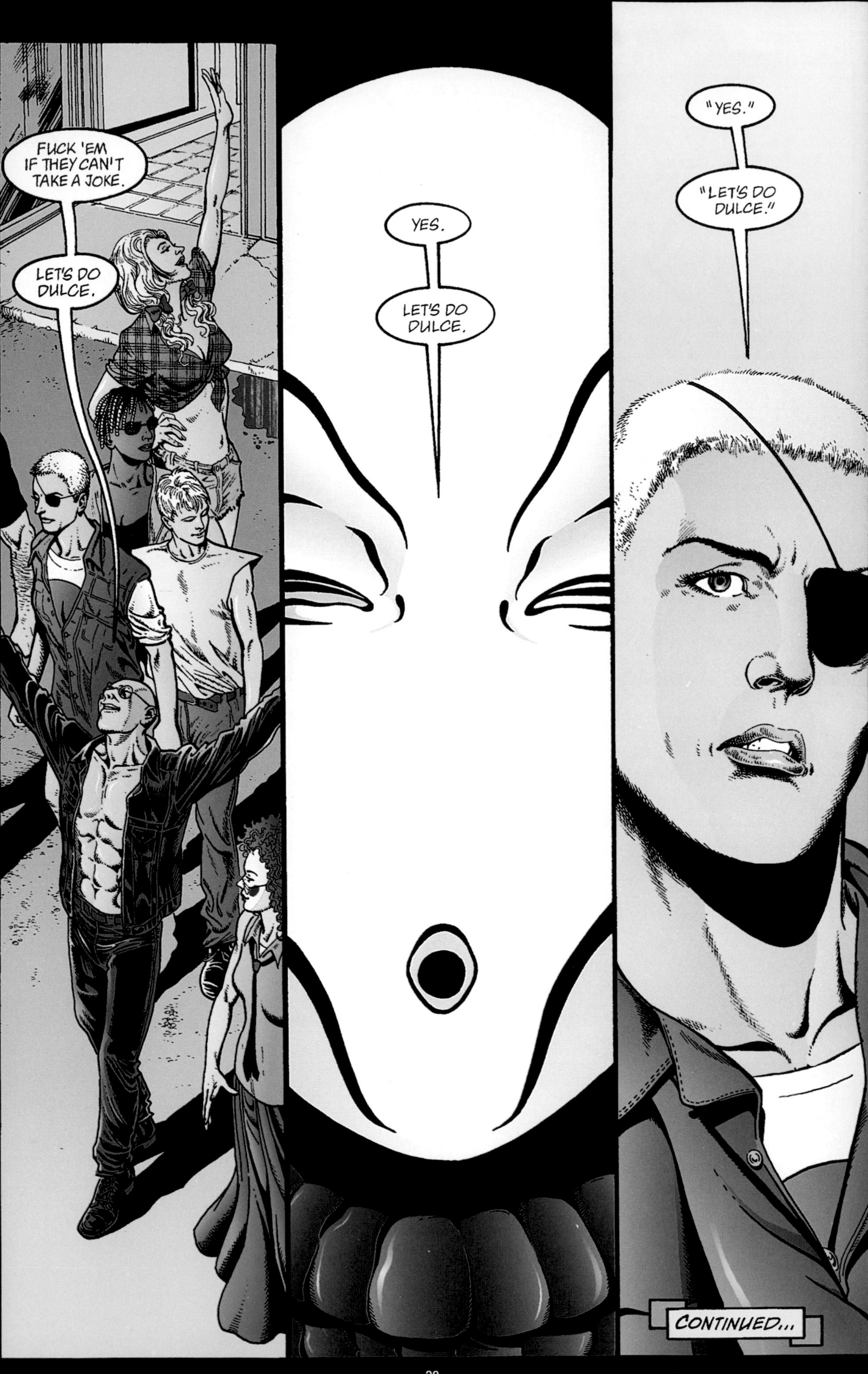
FUCK 'EM IF THEY CAN'T TAKE A JOKE.
LET'S DO DULCE.
YES.
LET'S DO DULCE.
"YES."
"LET'S DO DULCE."
CONTINUED...

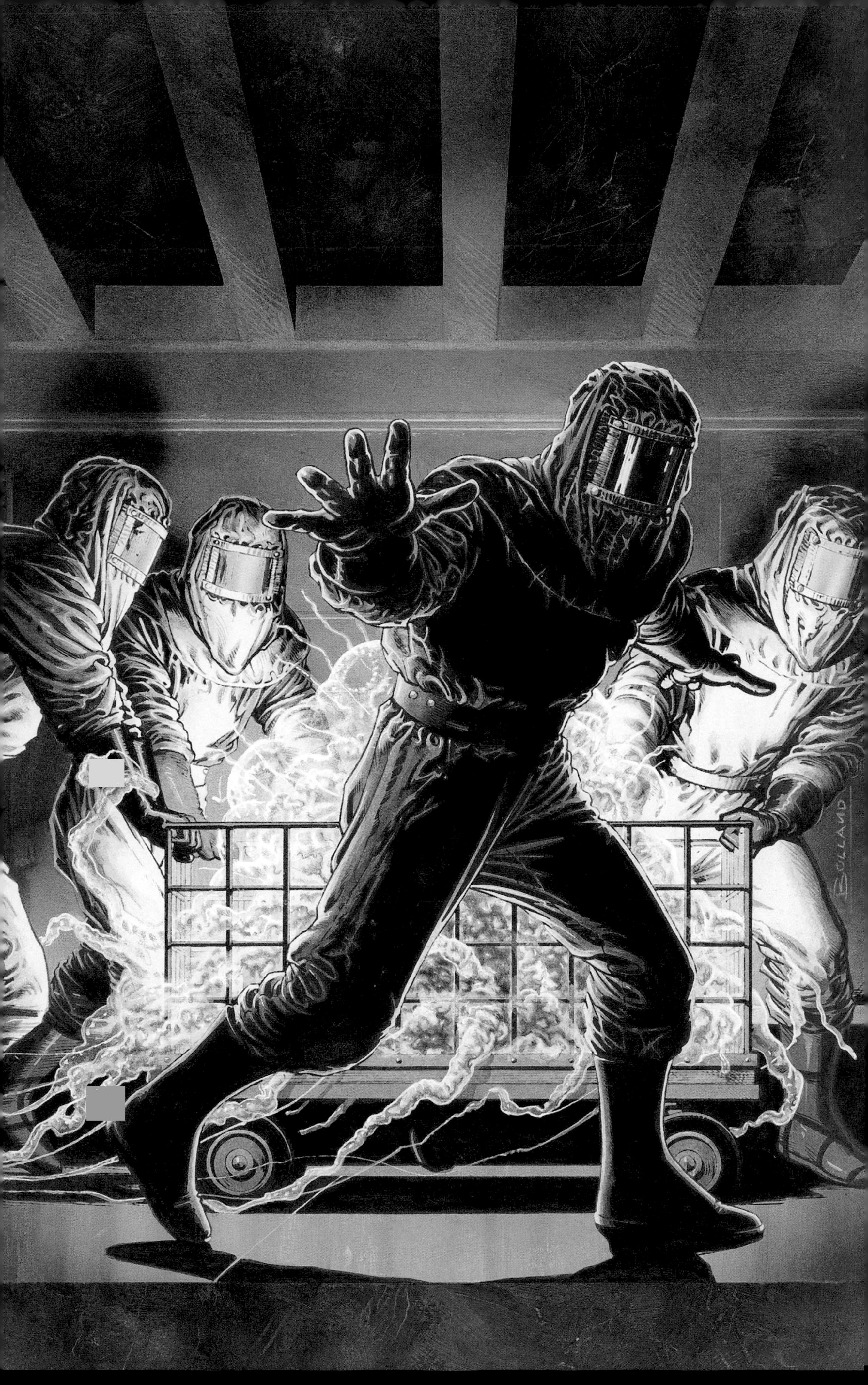
BOLLAND

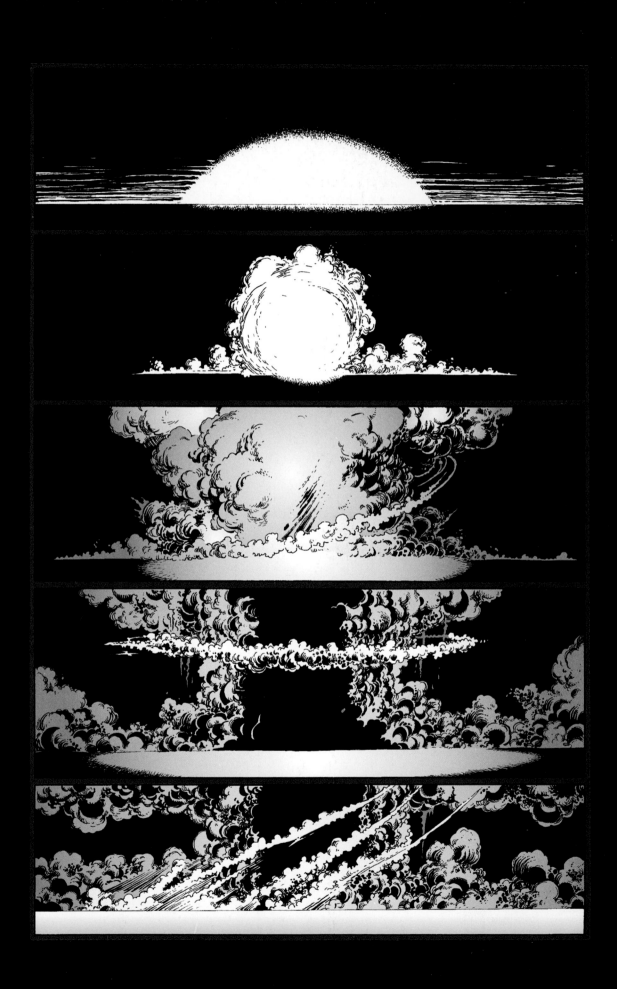

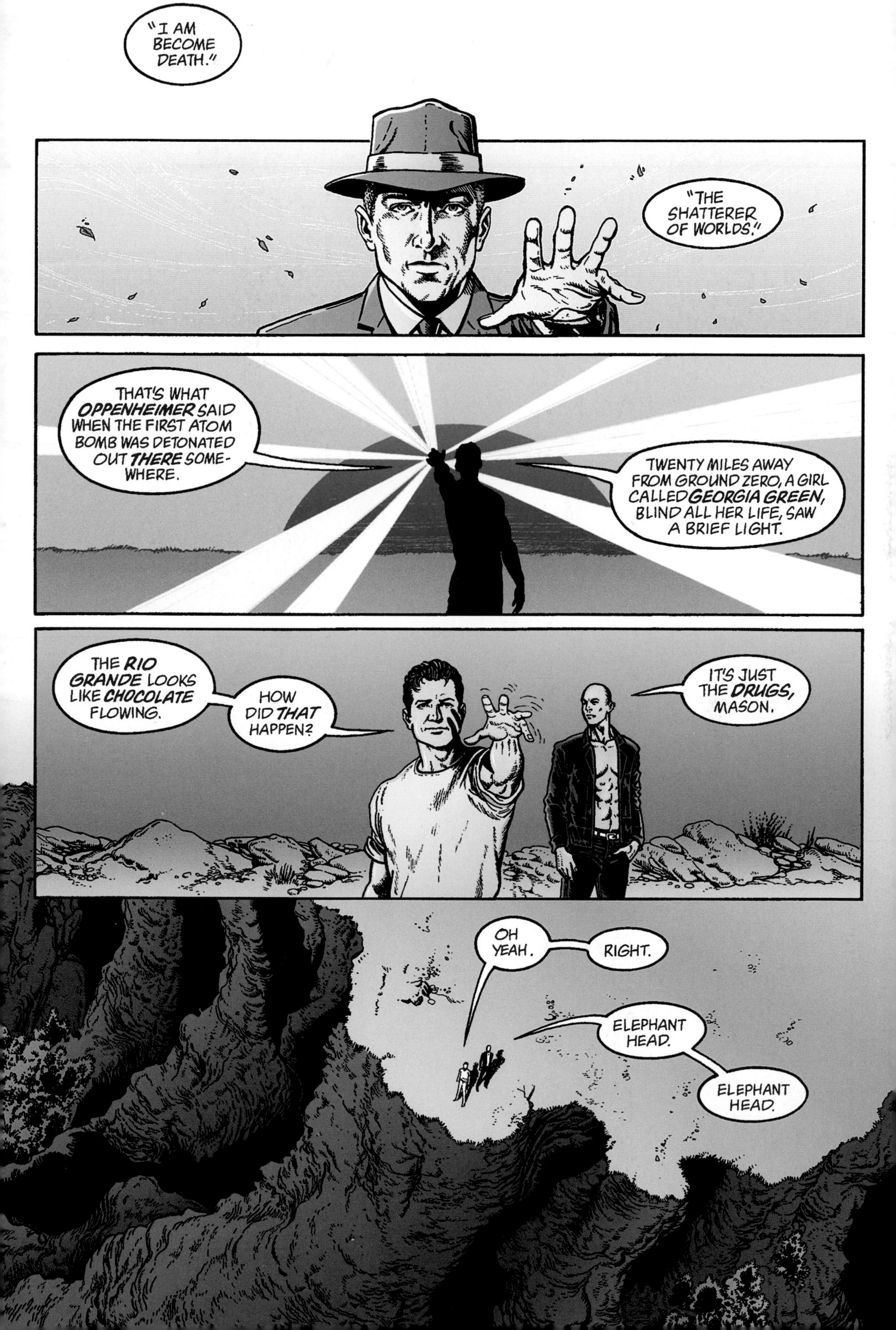
"I AM BECOME DEATH."
"THE SHATTERER OF WORLDS."
THAT'S WHAT OPPENHEIMER SAID WHEN THE FIRST ATOM BOMB WAS DETONATED OUT THERE SOME-WHERE.
TWENTY MILES AWAY FROM GROUND ZERO, A GIRL CALLED GEORGIA GREEN, BLIND ALL HER LIFE, SAW A BRIEF LIGHT.
THE RIO GRANDE LOOKS LIKE CHOCOLATE FLOWING.
HOW DID THAT HAPPEN?
IT'S JUST THE DRUGS, MASON.
OH YEAH.
RIGHT.
ELEPHANT HEAD.
ELEPHANT HEAD.

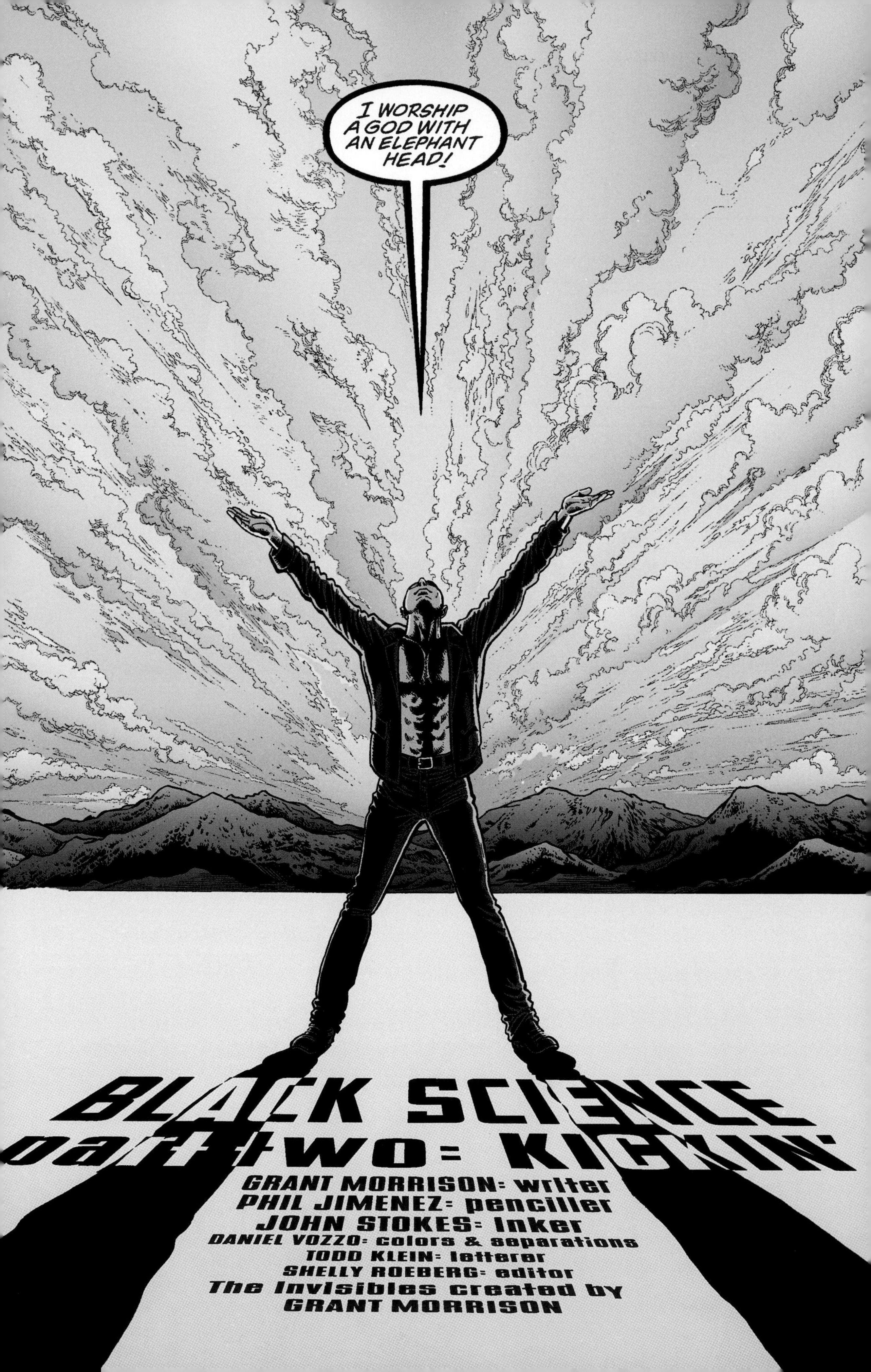
I WORSHIP A GOD WITH AN ELEPHANT HEAD!
BLACK SCIENCE
part two: KICKIN'
GRANT MORRISON: writer
PHIL JIMENEZ: penciller
JOHN STOKES: inker
DANIEL VOZZO: colors & separations
TODD KLEIN: letterer
SHELLY ROEBERG: editor
The Invisibles created by GRANT MORRISON

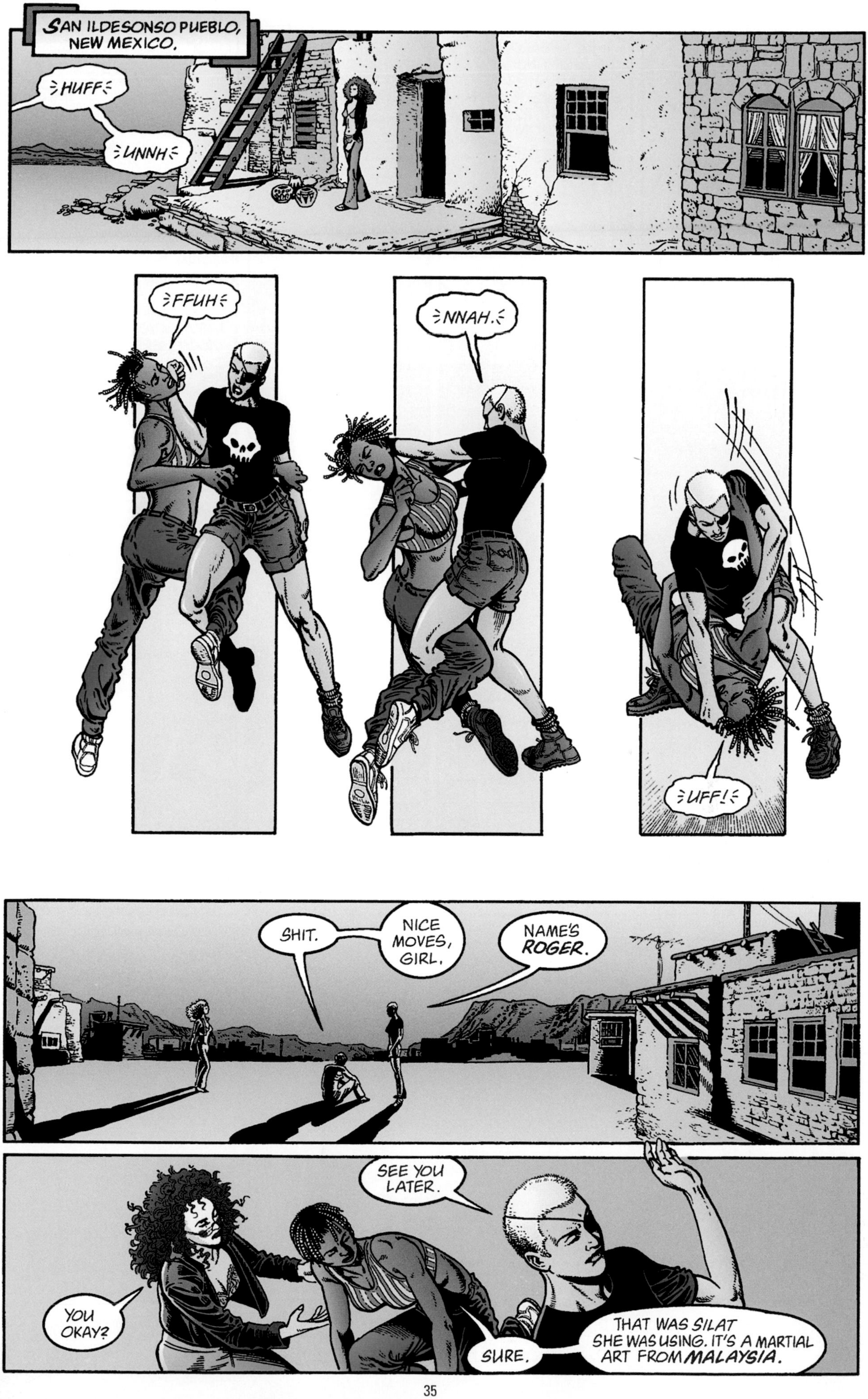
SAN ILDESONSO PUEBLO, NEW MEXICO.
HUFF
UNNH
FFUH
NNAH.
UFF!
SHIT.
NICE MOVES, GIRL.
NAME'S ROGER.
SEE YOU LATER.
YOU OKAY?
SURE.
THAT WAS SILAT SHE WAS USING. IT'S A MARTIAL ART FROM MALAYSIA.

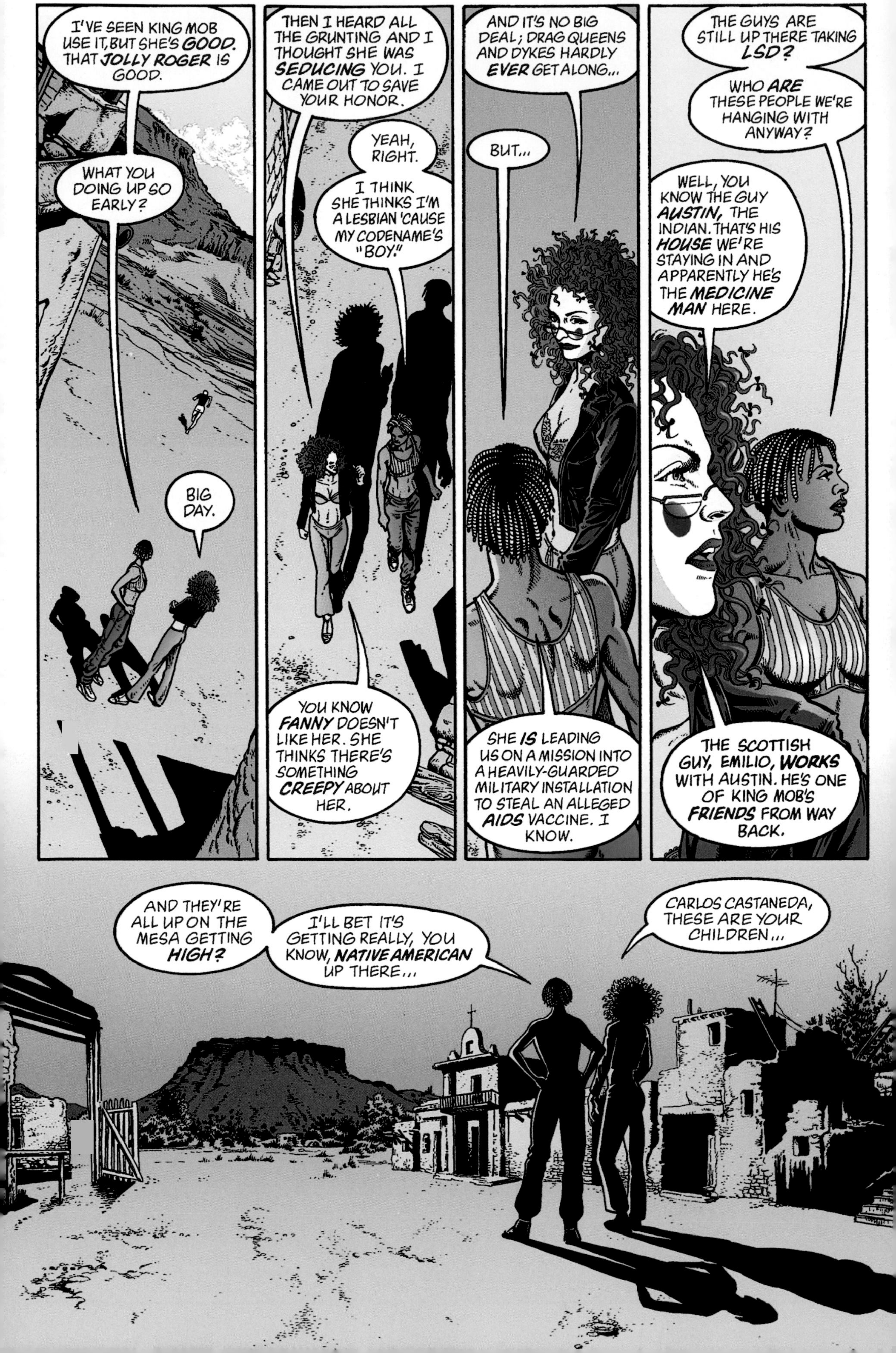
I'VE SEEN KING MOB USE IT, BUT SHE'S GOOD. THAT JOLLY ROGER IS GOOD.
WHAT YOU DOING UP SO EARLY?
BIG DAY.
THEN I HEARD ALL THE GRUNTING AND I THOUGHT SHE WAS SEDUCING YOU. I CAME OUT TO SAVE YOUR HONOR.
YEAH, RIGHT.
I THINK SHE THINKS I'M A LESBIAN 'CAUSE MY CODENAME'S "BOY."
YOU KNOW FANNY DOESN'T LIKE HER. SHE THINKS THERE'S SOMETHING CREEPY ABOUT HER.
AND IT'S NO BIG DEAL; DRAG QUEENS AND DYKES HARDLY EVER GET ALONG...
BUT...
SHE IS LEADING US ON A MISSION INTO A HEAVILY-GUARDED MILITARY INSTALLATION TO STEAL AN ALLEGED AIDS VACCINE. I KNOW.
THE GUYS ARE STILL UP THERE TAKING LSD?
WHO ARE THESE PEOPLE WE'RE HANGING WITH ANYWAY?
WELL, YOU KNOW THE GUY AUSTIN, THE INDIAN. THAT'S HIS HOUSE WE'RE STAYING IN AND APPARENTLY HE'S THE MEDICINE MAN HERE.
THE SCOTTISH GUY, EMILIO, WORKS WITH AUSTIN. HE'S ONE OF KING MOB'S FRIENDS FROM WAY BACK.
AND THEY'RE ALL UP ON THE MESA GETTING HIGH?
I'LL BET IT'S GETTING REALLY, YOU KNOW, NATIVE AMERICAN UP THERE...
CARLOS CASTANEDA, THESE ARE YOUR CHILDREN...

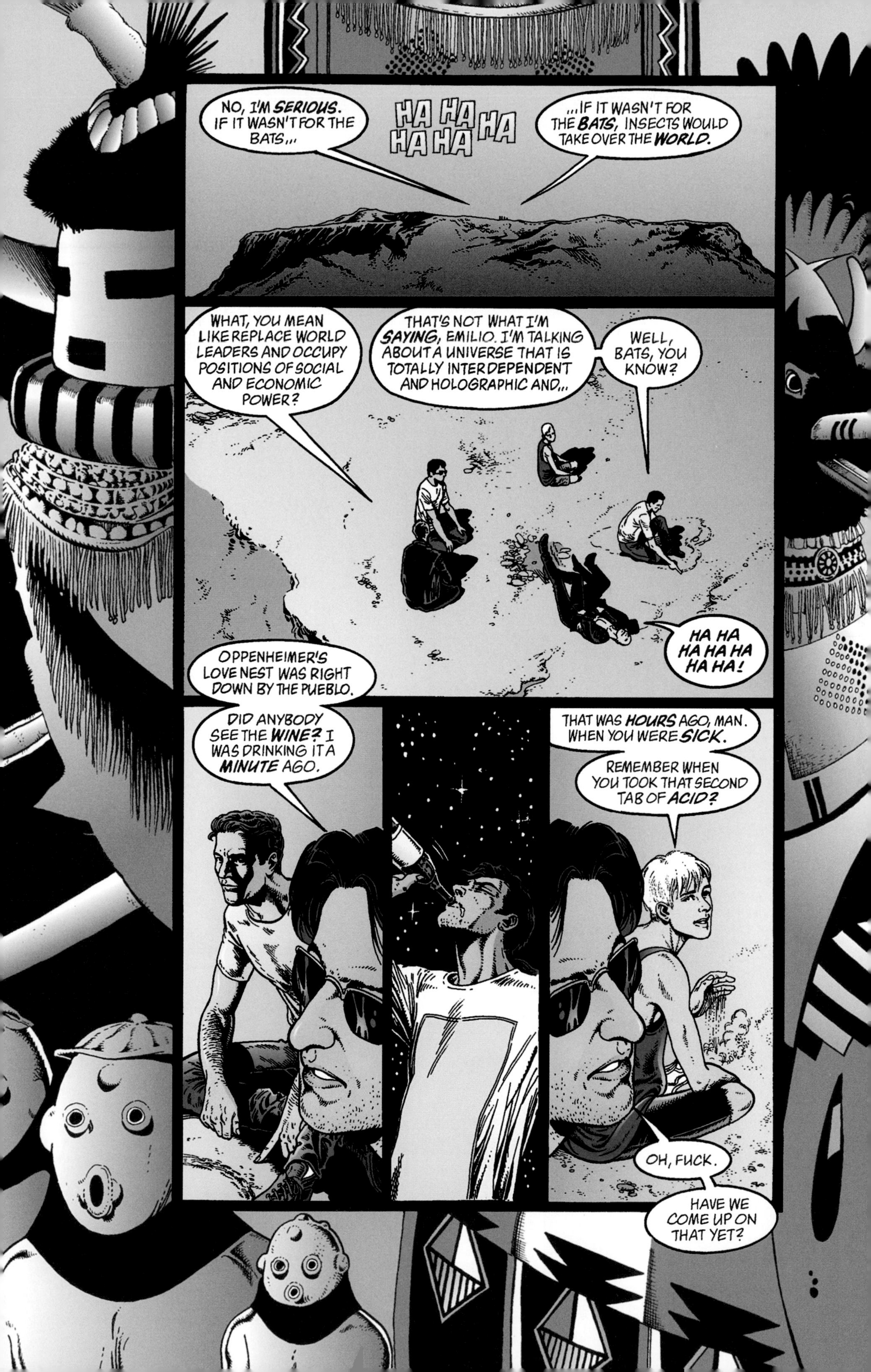
NO, I'M SERIOUS. IF IT WASN'T FOR THE BATS...
HA HA HA HA HA
...IF IT WASN'T FOR THE BATS, INSECTS WOULD TAKE OVER THE WORLD.
WHAT, YOU MEAN LIKE REPLACE WORLD LEADERS AND OCCUPY POSITIONS OF SOCIAL AND ECONOMIC POWER?
THAT'S NOT WHAT I'M SAYING, EMILIO. I'M TALKING ABOUT A UNIVERSE THAT IS TOTALLY INTERDEPENDENT AND HOLOGRAPHIC AND...
WELL, BATS, YOU KNOW?
HA HA HA HA HA HA HA!
OPPENHEIMER'S LOVE NEST WAS RIGHT DOWN BY THE PUEBLO.
DID ANYBODY SEE THE WINE? I WAS DRINKING IT A MINUTE AGO.
THAT WAS HOURS AGO, MAN. WHEN YOU WERE SICK.
REMEMBER WHEN YOU TOOK THAT SECOND TAB OF ACID?
OH, FUCK.
HAVE WE COME UP ON THAT YET?

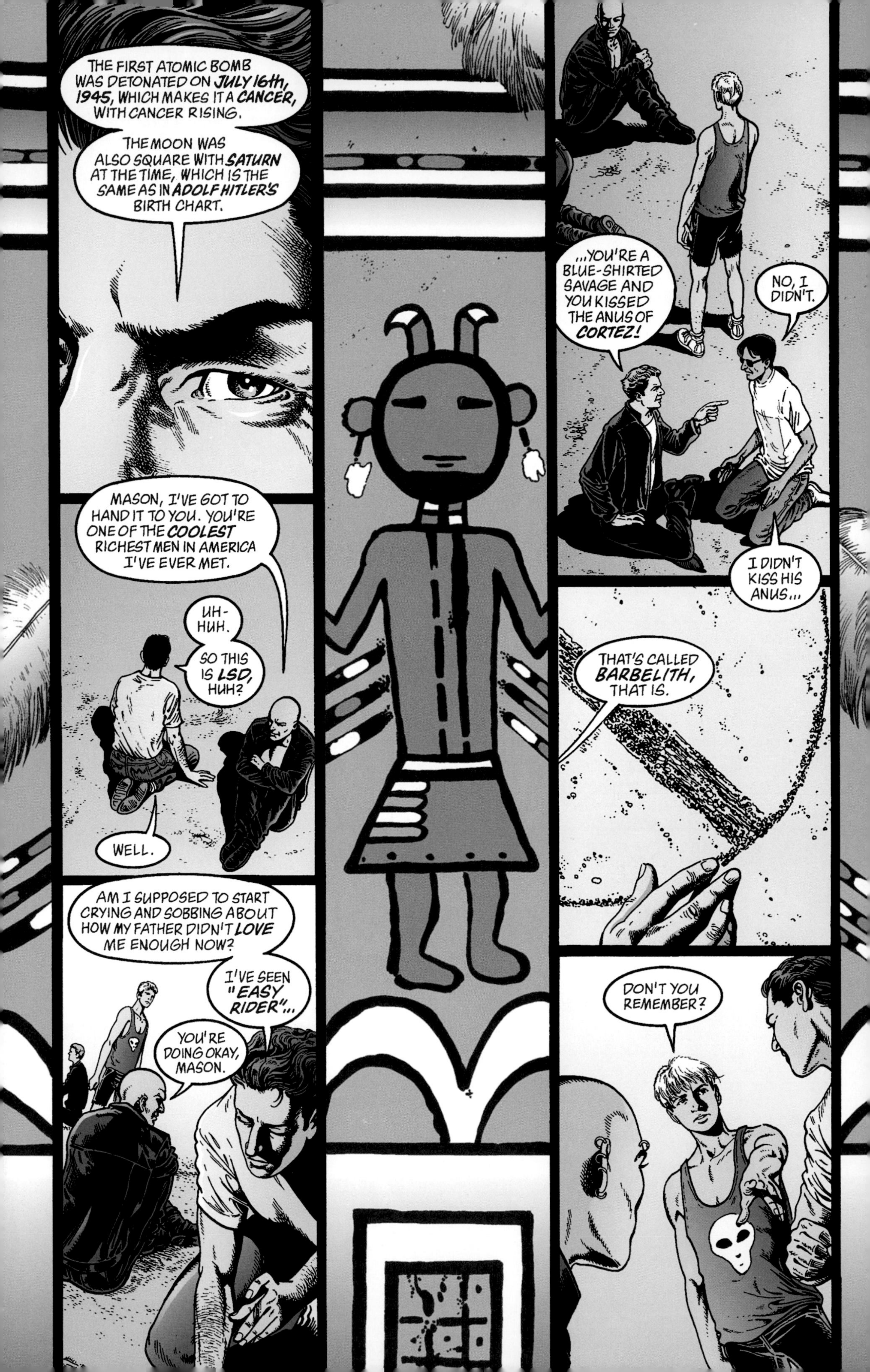
THE FIRST ATOMIC BOMB WAS DETONATED ON JULY 16th, 1945, WHICH MAKES IT A CANCER, WITH CANCER RISING.
THE MOON WAS ALSO SQUARE WITH SATURN AT THE TIME, WHICH IS THE SAME AS IN ADOLF HITLER'S BIRTH CHART.
MASON, I'VE GOT TO HAND IT TO YOU. YOU'RE ONE OF THE COOLEST RICHEST MEN IN AMERICA I'VE EVER MET.
UH-HUH.
SO THIS IS LSD, HUH?
WELL.
AM I SUPPOSED TO START CRYING AND SOBBING ABOUT HOW MY FATHER DIDN'T LOVE ME ENOUGH NOW?
I'VE SEEN "EASY RIDER"...
YOU'RE DOING OKAY, MASON.
...YOU'RE A BLUE-SHIRTED SAVAGE AND YOU KISSED THE ANUS OF CORTEZ!
NO, I DIDN'T.
I DIDN'T KISS HIS ANUS...
THAT'S CALLED BARBELITH, THAT IS.
DON'T YOU REMEMBER?

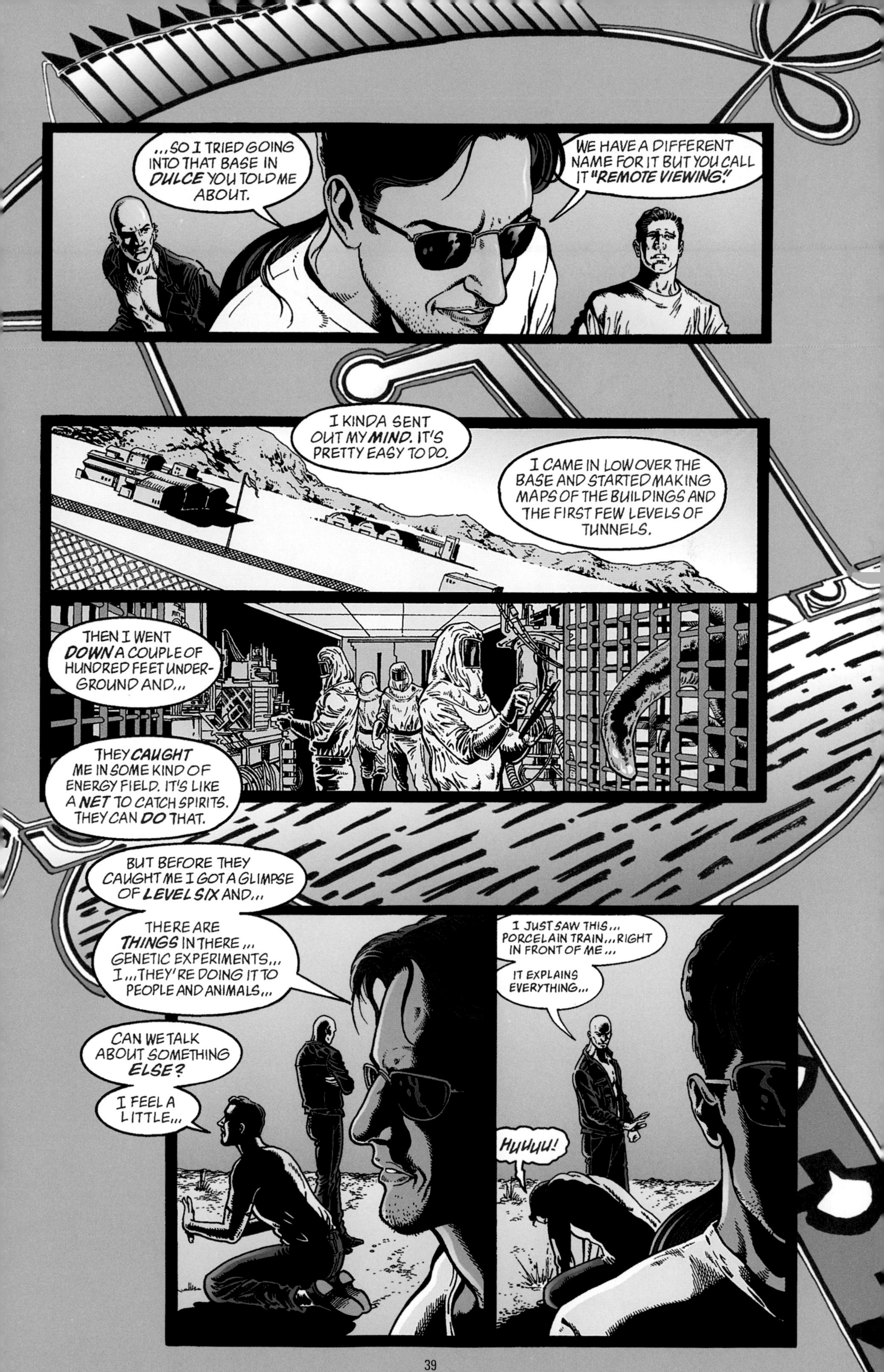
...SO I TRIED GOING INTO THAT BASE IN DULCE YOU TOLD ME ABOUT.
WE HAVE A DIFFERENT NAME FOR IT BUT YOU CALL IT "REMOTE VIEWING."
I KINDA SENT OUT MY MIND. IT'S PRETTY EASY TO DO.
I CAME IN LOW OVER THE BASE AND STARTED MAKING MAPS OF THE BUILDINGS AND THE FIRST FEW LEVELS OF TUNNELS.
THEN I WENT DOWN A COUPLE OF HUNDRED FEET UNDER-GROUND AND...
THEY CAUGHT ME IN SOME KIND OF ENERGY FIELD. IT'S LIKE A NET TO CATCH SPIRITS. THEY CAN DO THAT.
BUT BEFORE THEY CAUGHT ME I GOT A GLIMPSE OF LEVEL SIX AND...
THERE ARE THINGS IN THERE... GENETIC EXPERIMENTS... I... THEY'RE DOING IT TO PEOPLE AND ANIMALS...
CAN WE TALK ABOUT SOMETHING ELSE?
I FEEL A LITTLE...
I JUST SAW THIS... PORCELAIN TRAIN... RIGHT IN FRONT OF ME...
IT EXPLAINS EVERYTHING...
HUUUU!

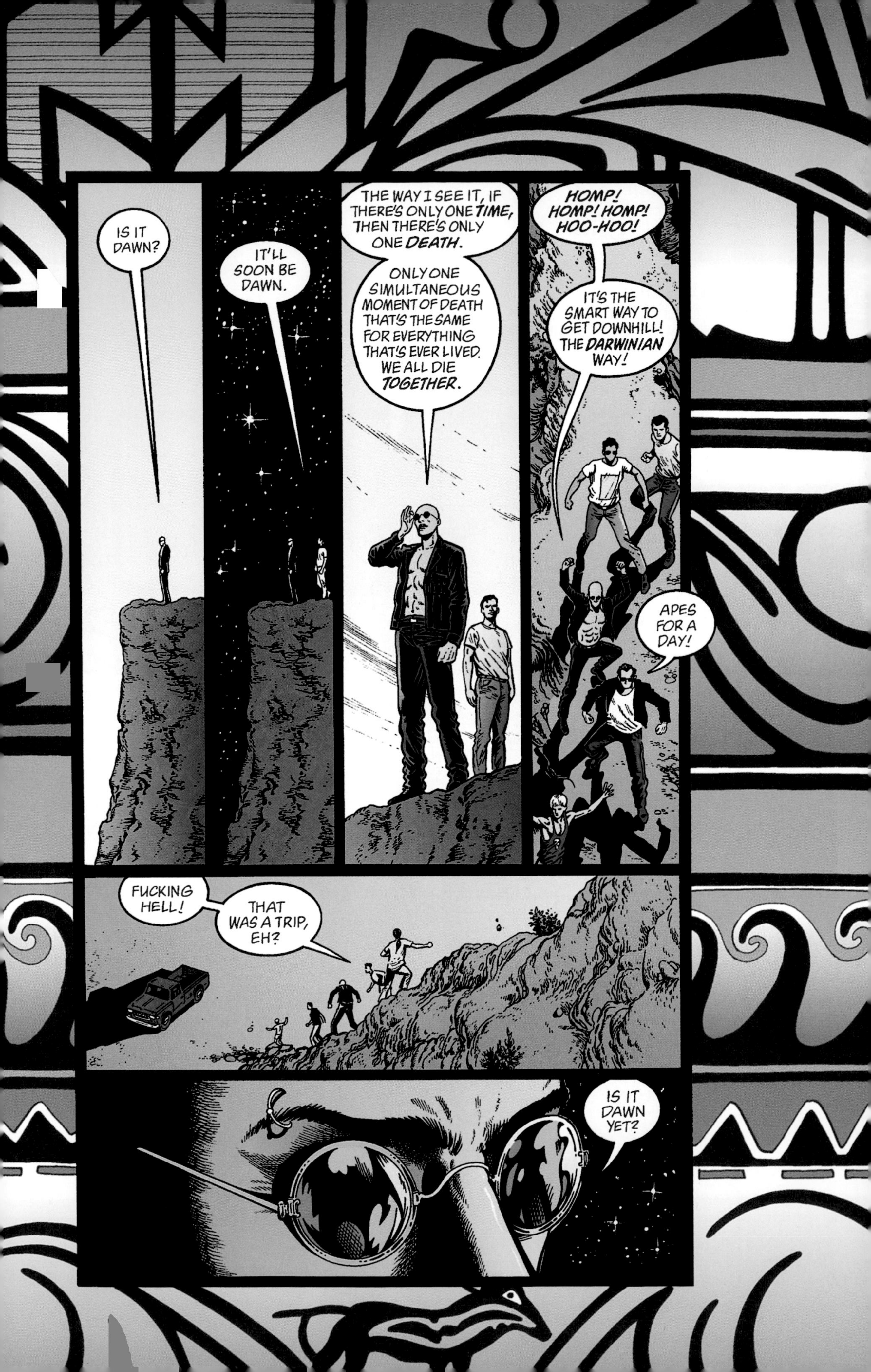
IS IT DAWN?
IT'LL SOON BE DAWN.
THE WAY I SEE IT, IF THERE'S ONLY ONE TIME, THEN THERE'S ONLY ONE DEATH.
ONLY ONE SIMULTANEOUS MOMENT OF DEATH THAT'S THE SAME FOR EVERYTHING THAT'S EVER LIVED. WE ALL DIE TOGETHER.
HOMP! HOMP! HOMP! HOO-HOO!
IT'S THE SMART WAY TO GET DOWNHILL! THE DARWINIAN WAY!
APES FOR A DAY!
FUCKING HELL!
THAT WAS A TRIP, EH?
IS IT DAWN YET?

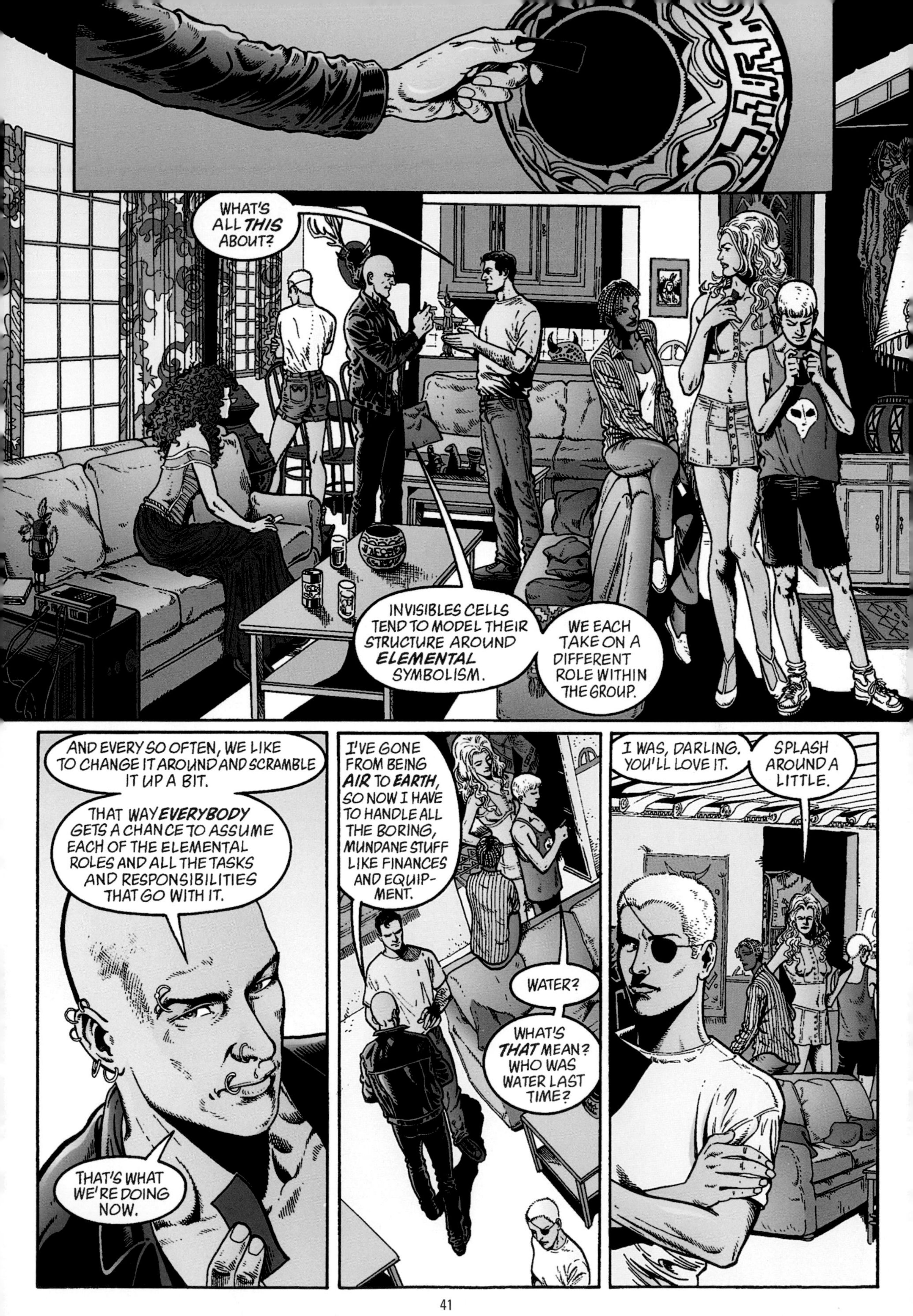
WHAT'S ALL THIS ABOUT?
INVISIBLES CELLS TEND TO MODEL THEIR STRUCTURE AROUND ELEMENTAL SYMBOLISM.
WE EACH TAKE ON A DIFFERENT ROLE WITHIN THE GROUP.
AND EVERY SO OFTEN, WE LIKE TO CHANGE IT AROUND AND SCRAMBLE IT UP A BIT.
THAT WAY EVERYBODY GETS A CHANCE TO ASSUME EACH OF THE ELEMENTAL ROLES AND ALL THE TASKS AND RESPONSIBILITIES THAT GO WITH IT.
THAT'S WHAT WE'RE DOING NOW.
I'VE GONE FROM BEING AIR TO EARTH, SO NOW I HAVE TO HANDLE ALL THE BORING, MUNDANE STUFF LIKE FINANCES AND EQUIPMENT.
WATER?
WHAT'S THAT MEAN? WHO WAS WATER LAST TIME?
I WAS, DARLING. YOU'LL LOVE IT.
SPLASH AROUND A LITTLE.

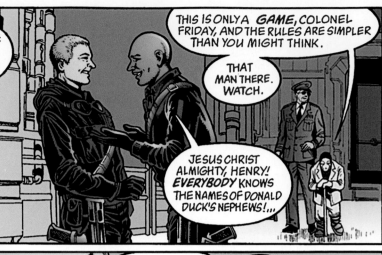

OUR ENEMIES WILL BE WITH US SHORTLY. I *PLAYED* WITH THE WOMAN LAST NIGHT.

SHE THOUGHT I WAS A BAD DREAM.

SO YOU'RE ABLE TO KEEP CONTROL OF MORE THAN ONE OF 'EM AT A TIME, *QUIMPER?*

THIS IS ONLY A *GAME,* COLONEL FRIDAY, AND THE RULES ARE SIMPLER THAN YOU MIGHT THINK.

THAT MAN THERE. WATCH.

JESUS CHRIST ALMIGHTY, HENRY! *EVERYBODY* KNOWS THE NAMES OF DONALD DUCK'S NEPHEWS!...

DOMINATION.

SUBMISSION.

OBEDIENCE.

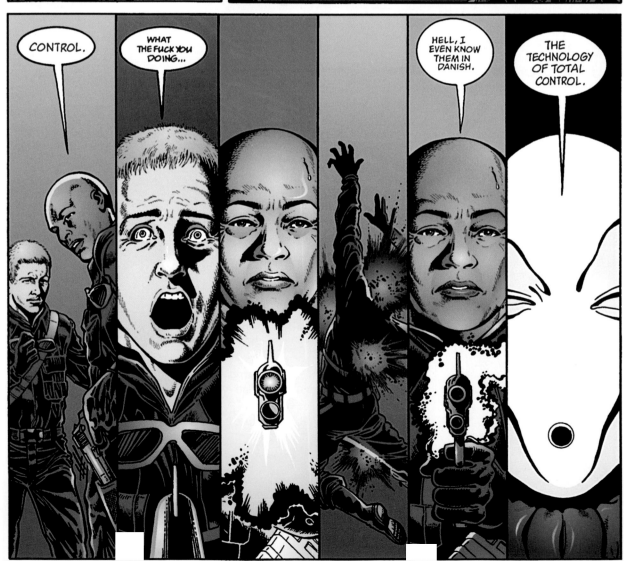

CONTROL.

WHAT THE FUCK YOU DOING...

HELL, I EVEN KNOW THEM IN DANISH.

THE TECHNOLOGY OF TOTAL CONTROL.

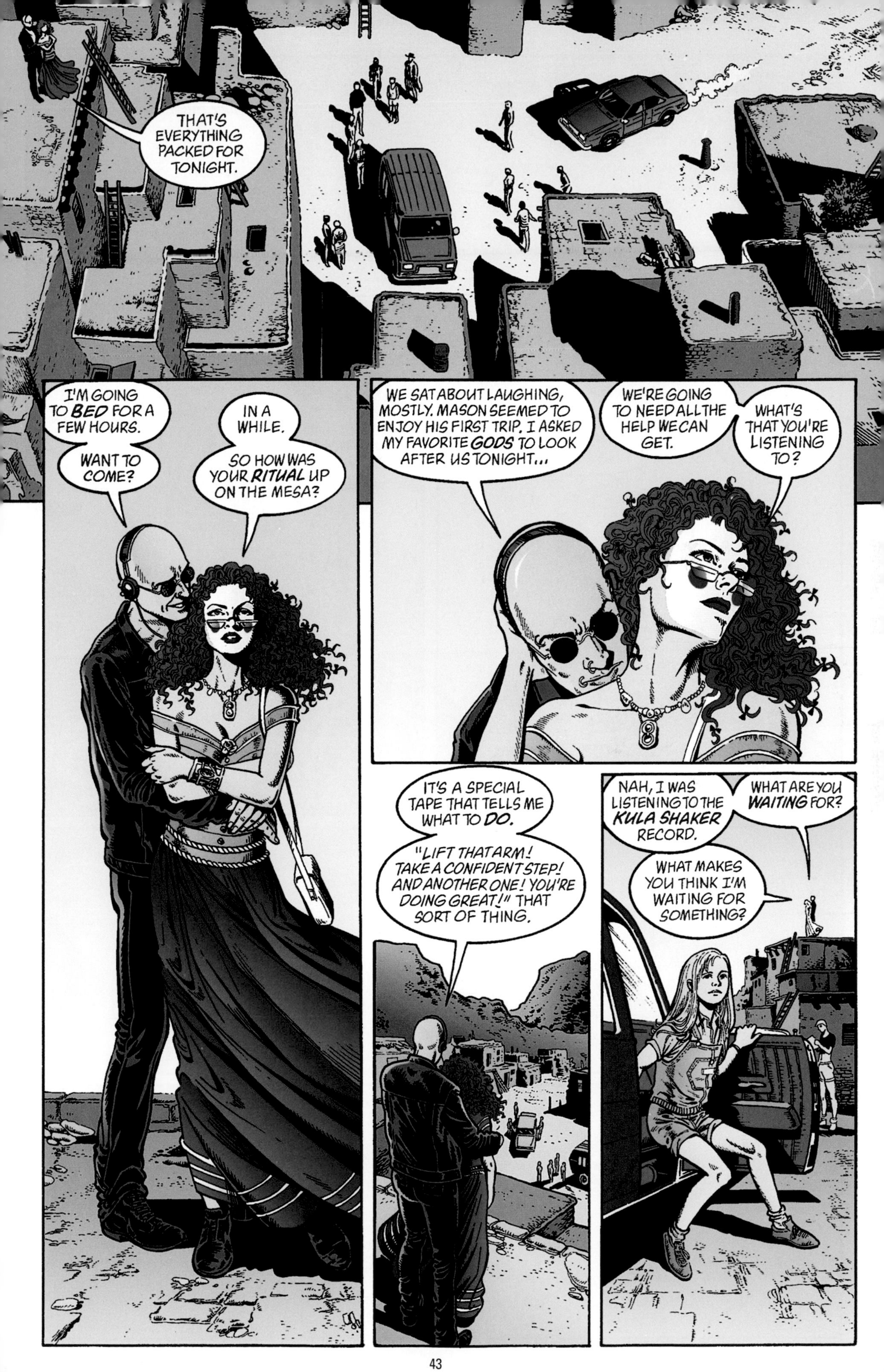
THAT'S EVERYTHING PACKED FOR TONIGHT.
I'M GOING TO BED FOR A FEW HOURS.
WANT TO COME?
IN A WHILE.
SO HOW WAS YOUR RITUAL UP ON THE MESA?
WE SAT ABOUT LAUGHING, MOSTLY. MASON SEEMED TO ENJOY HIS FIRST TRIP. I ASKED MY FAVORITE GODS TO LOOK AFTER US TONIGHT...
WE'RE GOING TO NEED ALL THE HELP WE CAN GET.
WHAT'S THAT YOU'RE LISTENING TO?
IT'S A SPECIAL TAPE THAT TELLS ME WHAT TO DO.
"LIFT THAT ARM! TAKE A CONFIDENT STEP! AND ANOTHER ONE! YOU'RE DOING GREAT!" THAT SORT OF THING.
NAH, I WAS LISTENING TO THE KULA SHAKER RECORD.
WHAT ARE YOU WAITING FOR?
WHAT MAKES YOU THINK I'M WAITING FOR SOMETHING?

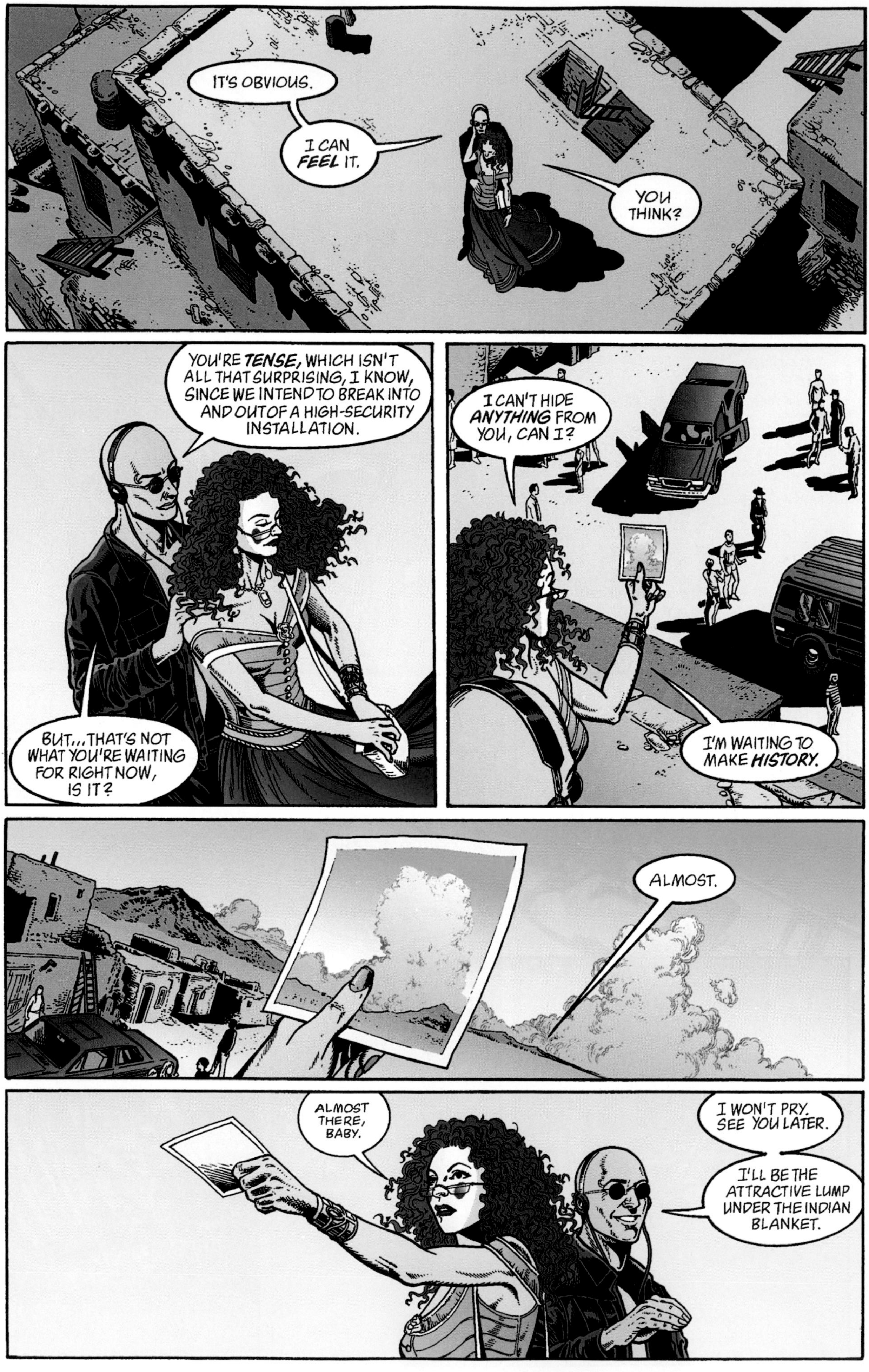
IT'S OBVIOUS.
I CAN FEEL IT.
YOU THINK?
YOU'RE TENSE, WHICH ISN'T ALL THAT SURPRISING, I KNOW, SINCE WE INTEND TO BREAK INTO AND OUT OF A HIGH-SECURITY INSTALLATION.
BUT... THAT'S NOT WHAT YOU'RE WAITING FOR RIGHT NOW, IS IT?
I CAN'T HIDE ANYTHING FROM YOU, CAN I?
I'M WAITING TO MAKE HISTORY.
ALMOST.
ALMOST THERE, BABY.
I WON'T PRY. SEE YOU LATER.
I'LL BE THE ATTRACTIVE LUMP UNDER THE INDIAN BLANKET.

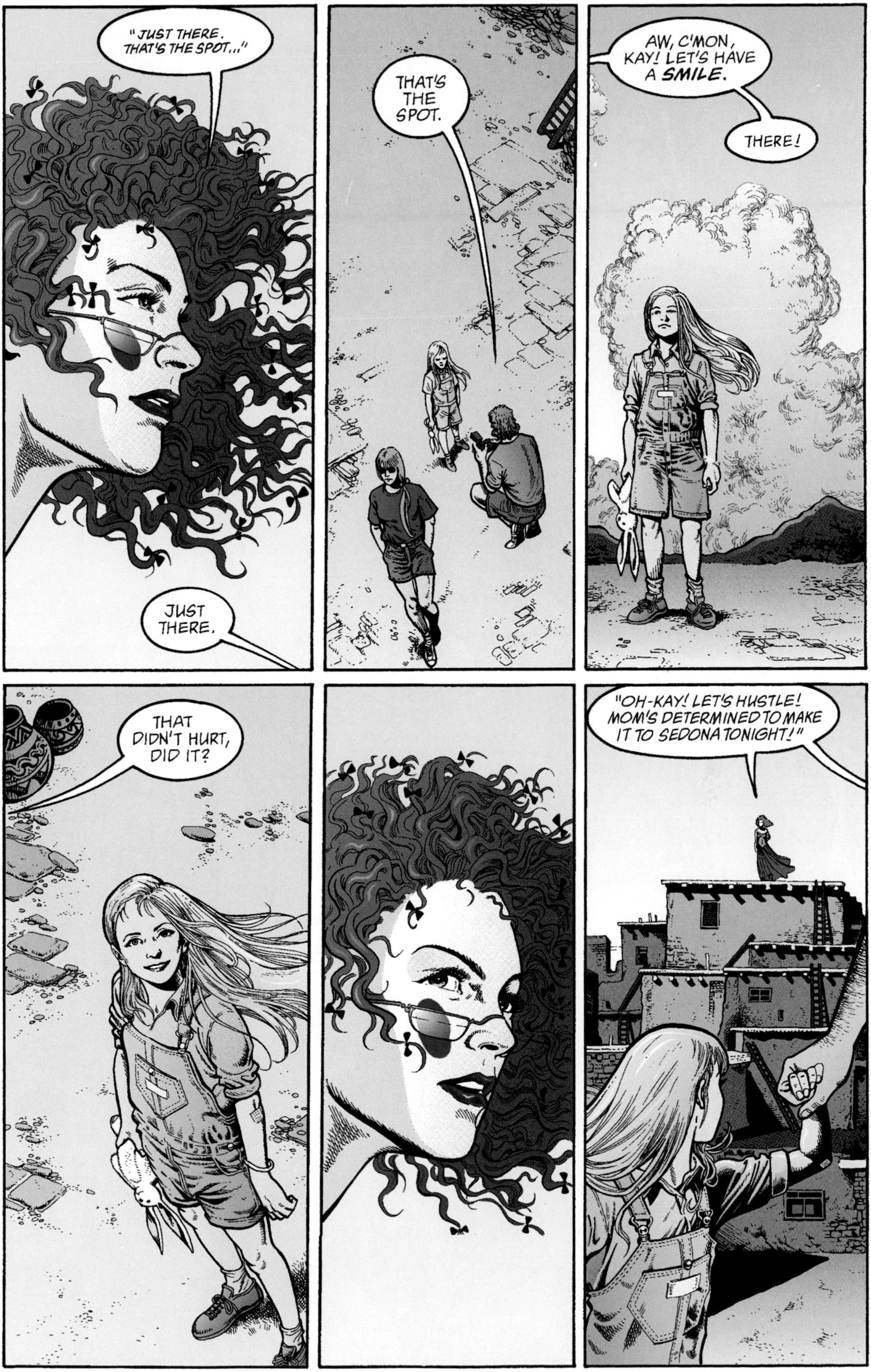
"JUST THERE. THAT'S THE SPOT..."
JUST THERE.
THAT'S THE SPOT.
AW, C'MON, KAY! LET'S HAVE A **SMILE**.
THERE!
THAT DIDN'T HURT, DID IT?
"OH-KAY! LET'S HUSTLE! MOM'S DETERMINED TO MAKE IT TO SEDONA TONIGHT!"

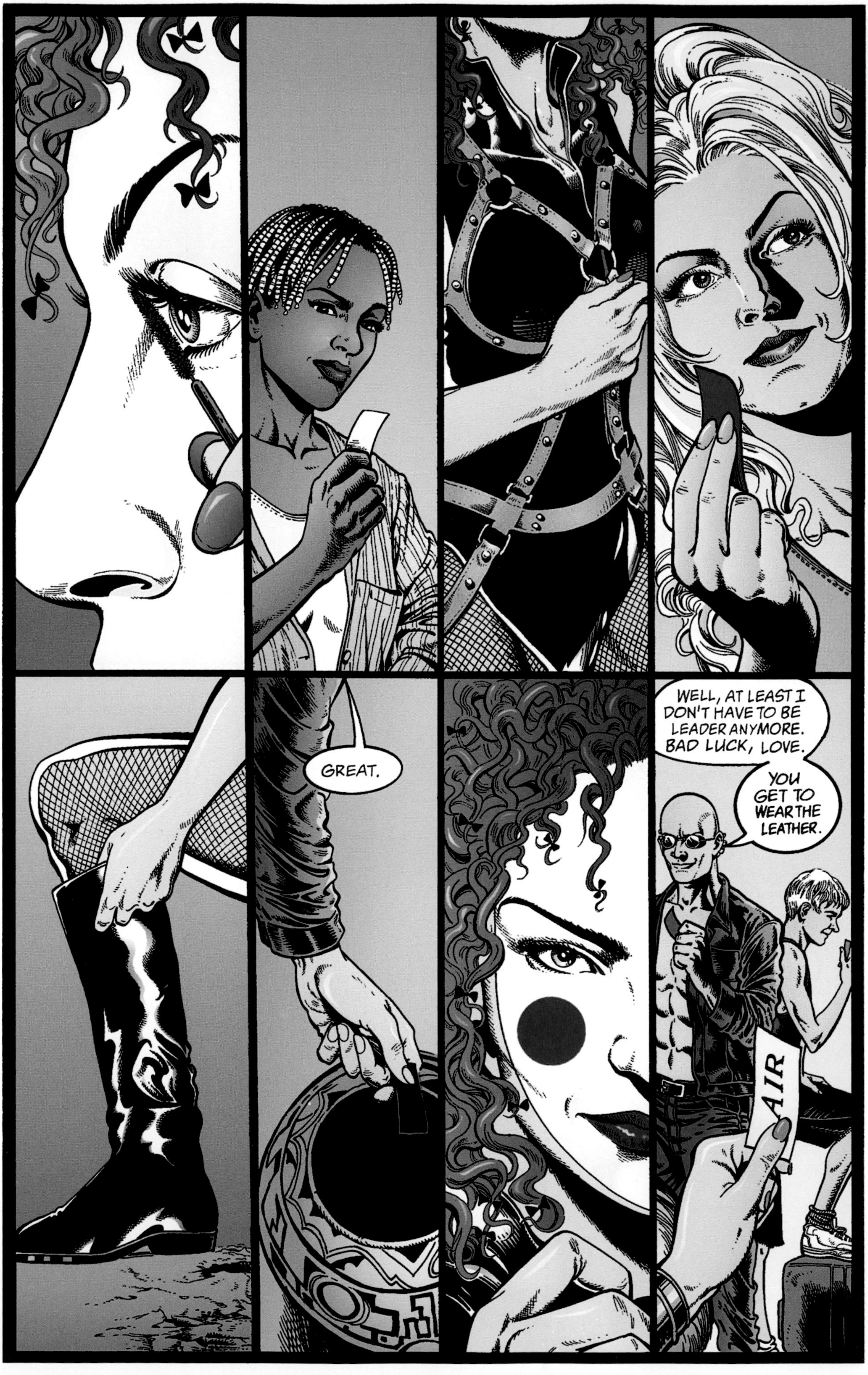
GREAT.
WELL, AT LEAST I DON'T HAVE TO BE LEADER ANYMORE. BAD LUCK, LOVE.
YOU GET TO WEAR THE LEATHER.
AIR

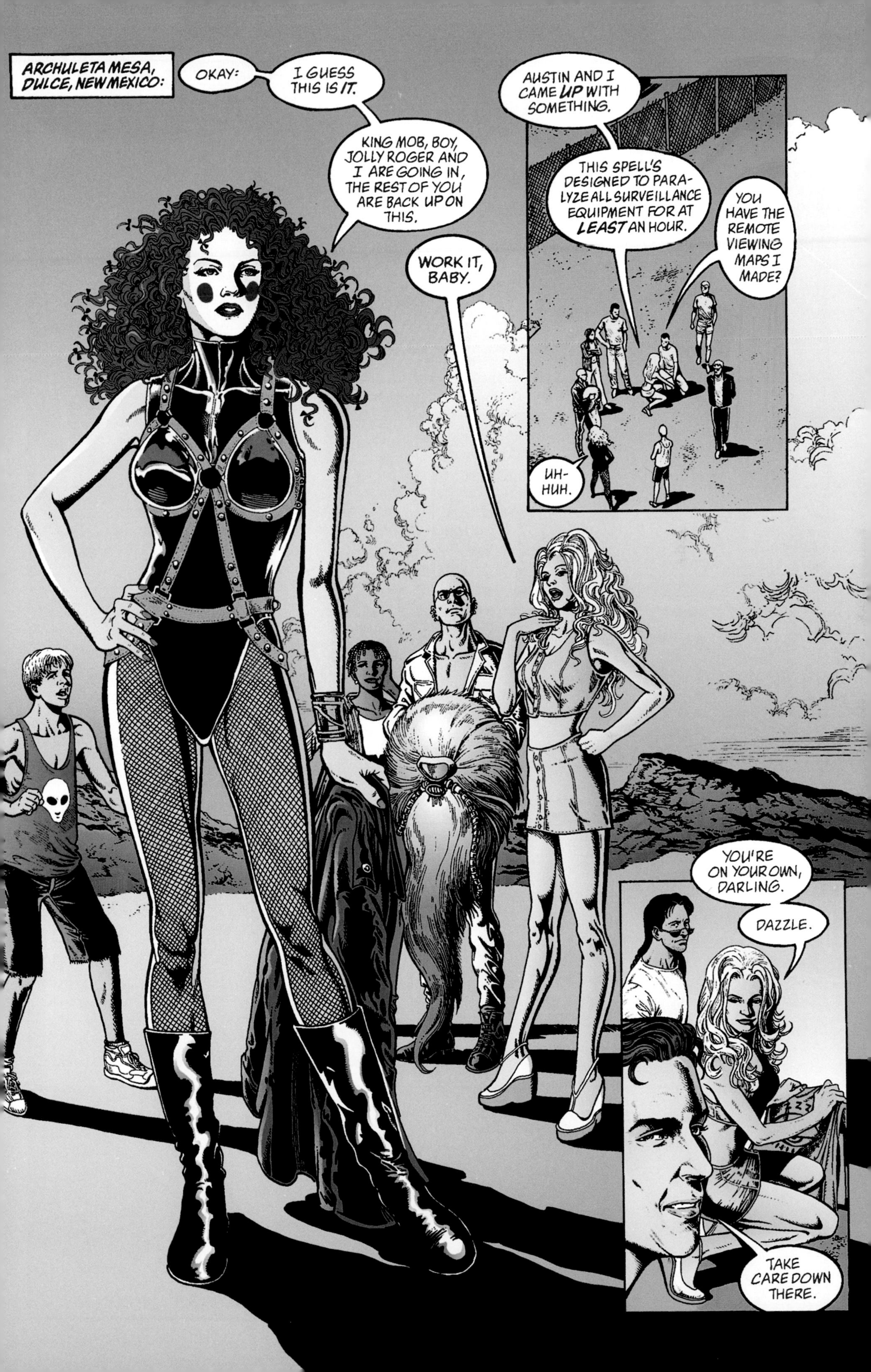
ARCHULETA MESA, DULCE, NEW MEXICO:
OKAY:
I GUESS THIS IS IT.
KING MOB, BOY, JOLLY ROGER AND I ARE GOING IN, THE REST OF YOU ARE BACK UP ON THIS.
WORK IT, BABY.
AUSTIN AND I CAME UP WITH SOMETHING.
THIS SPELL'S DESIGNED TO PARA-LYZE ALL SURVEILLANCE EQUIPMENT FOR AT LEAST AN HOUR.
YOU HAVE THE REMOTE VIEWING MAPS I MADE?
UH-HUH.
YOU'RE ON YOUR OWN, DARLING.
DAZZLE.
TAKE CARE DOWN THERE.

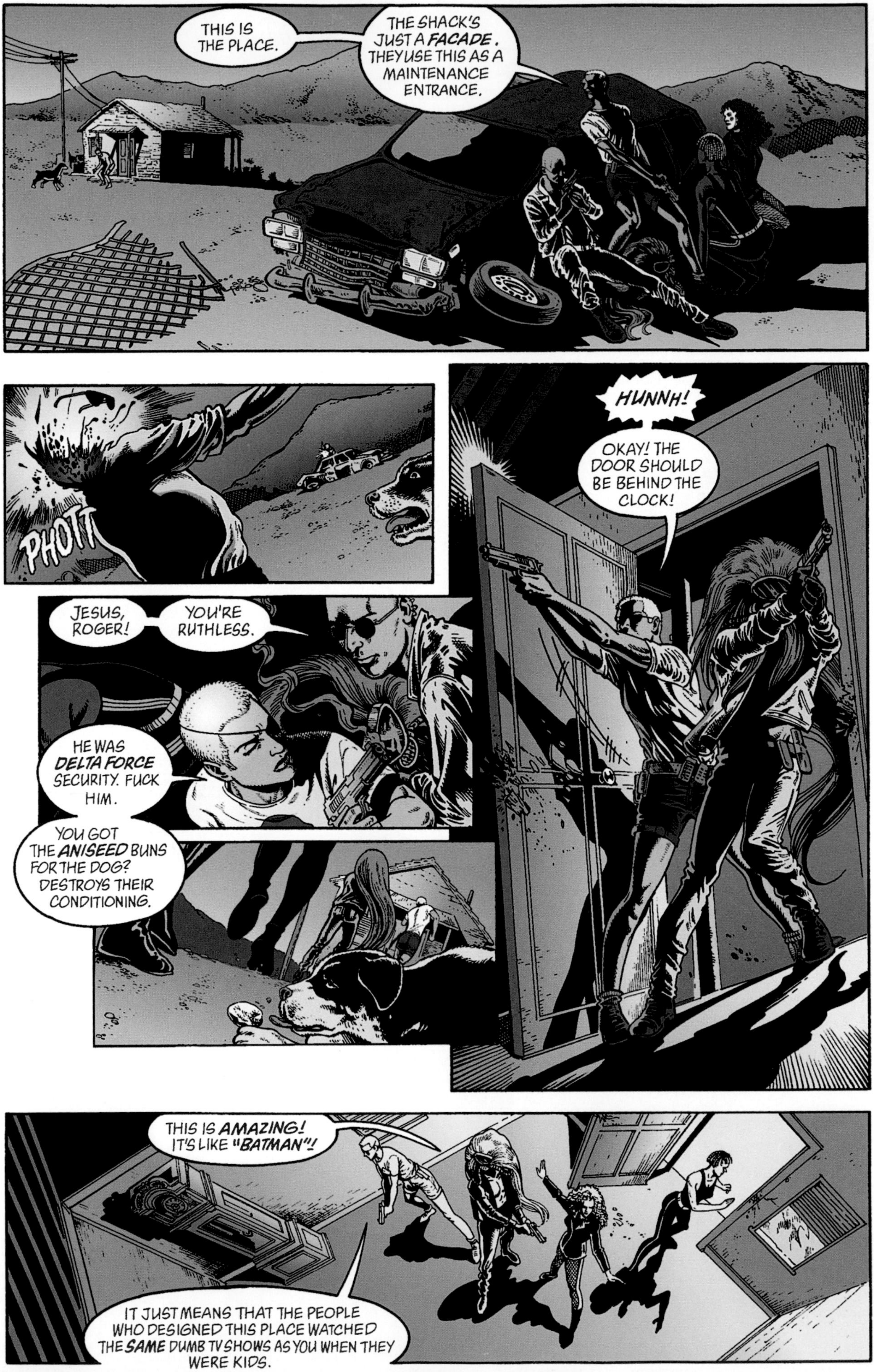
THIS IS THE PLACE.
THE SHACK'S JUST A FACADE. THEY USE THIS AS A MAINTENANCE ENTRANCE.
PHOTT
JESUS, ROGER!
YOU'RE RUTHLESS.
HE WAS DELTA FORCE SECURITY. FUCK HIM.
YOU GOT THE ANISEED BUNS FOR THE DOG? DESTROYS THEIR CONDITIONING.
HUNNH!
OKAY! THE DOOR SHOULD BE BEHIND THE CLOCK!
THIS IS AMAZING! IT'S LIKE "BATMAN"!
IT JUST MEANS THAT THE PEOPLE WHO DESIGNED THIS PLACE WATCHED THE SAME DUMB TV SHOWS AS YOU WHEN THEY WERE KIDS.

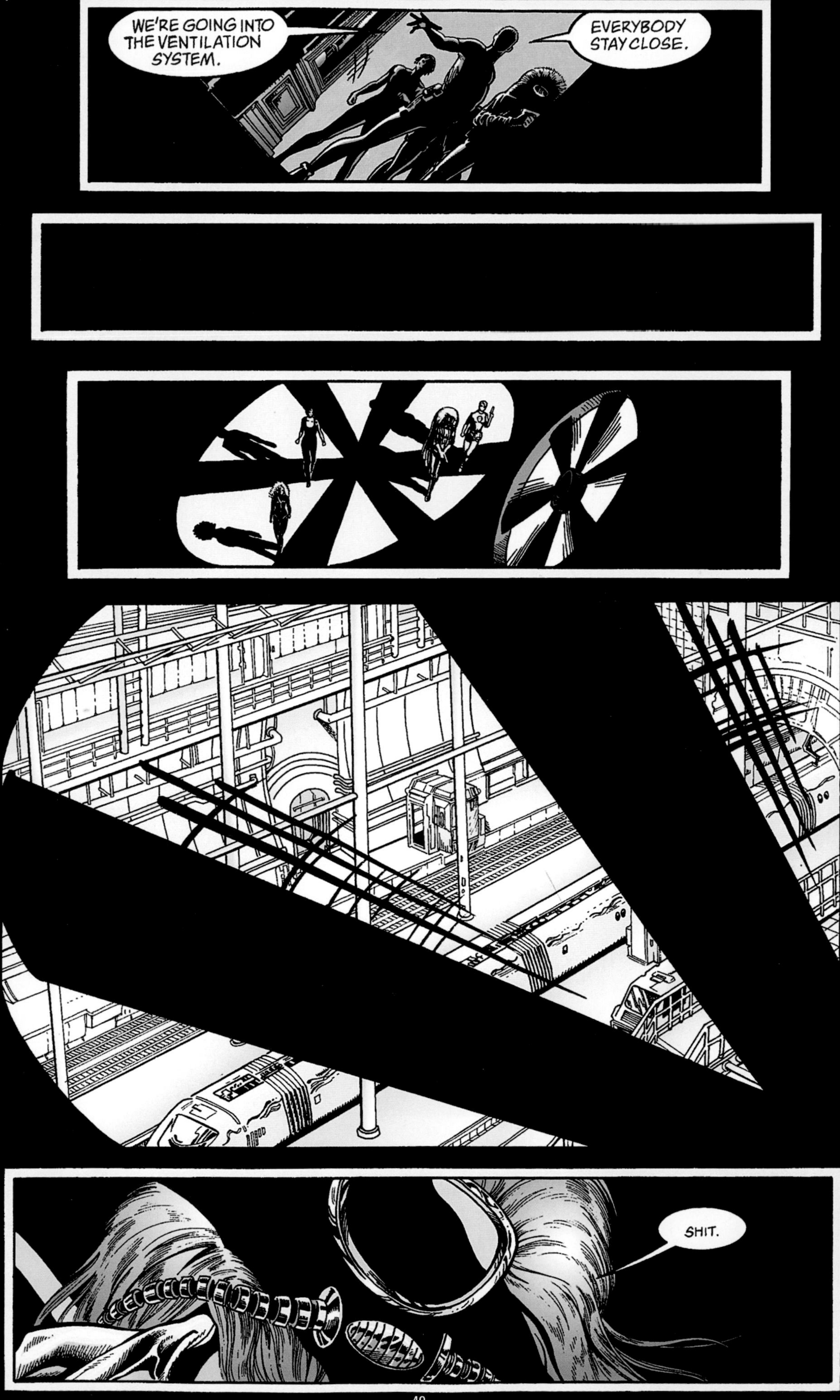
WE'RE GOING INTO THE VENTILATION SYSTEM.
EVERYBODY STAY CLOSE.
SHIT.

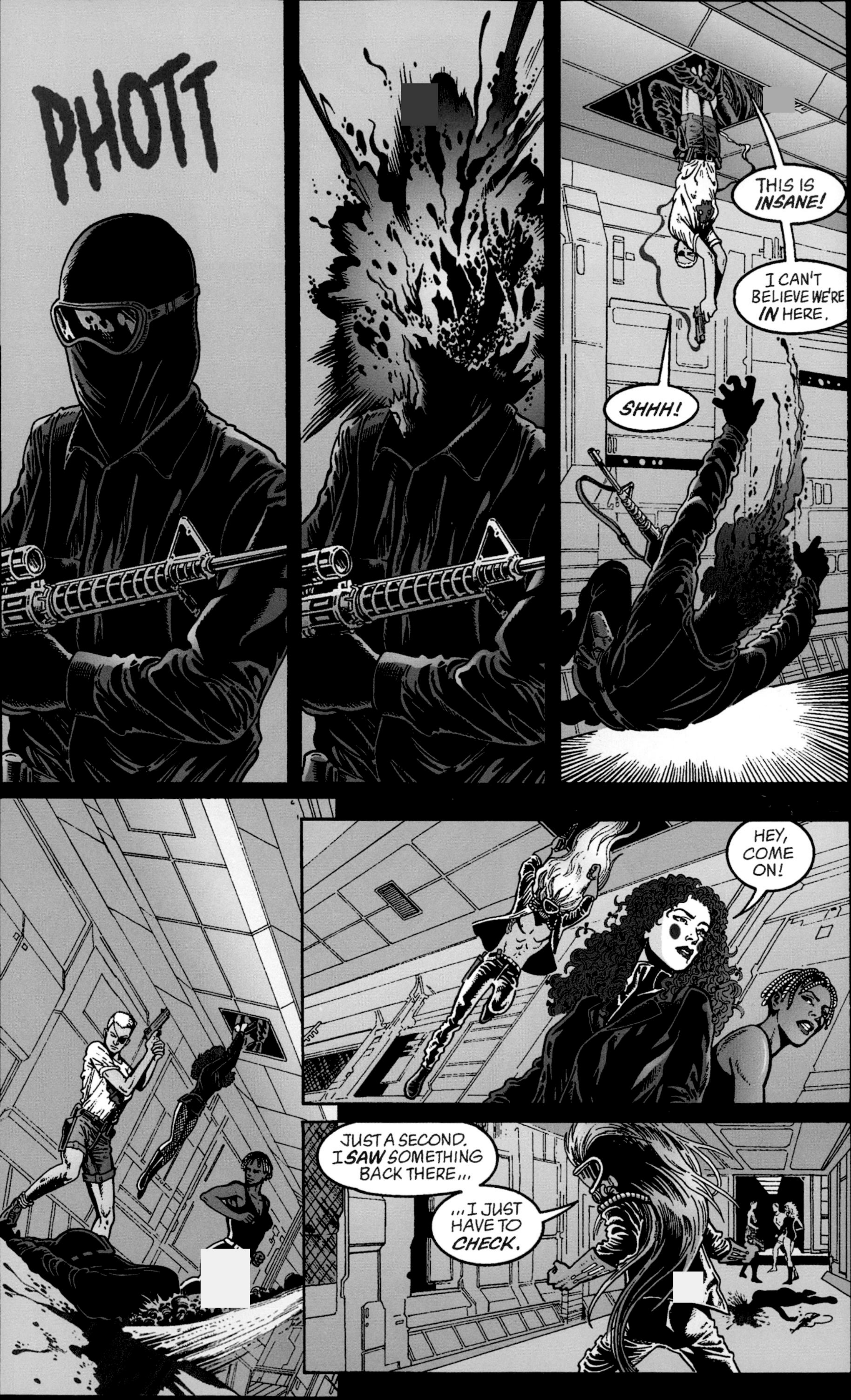
PHOTT
THIS IS INSANE!
I CAN'T BELIEVE WE'RE IN HERE.
SHHH!
HEY, COME ON!
JUST A SECOND. I SAW SOMETHING BACK THERE...
...I JUST HAVE TO CHECK.

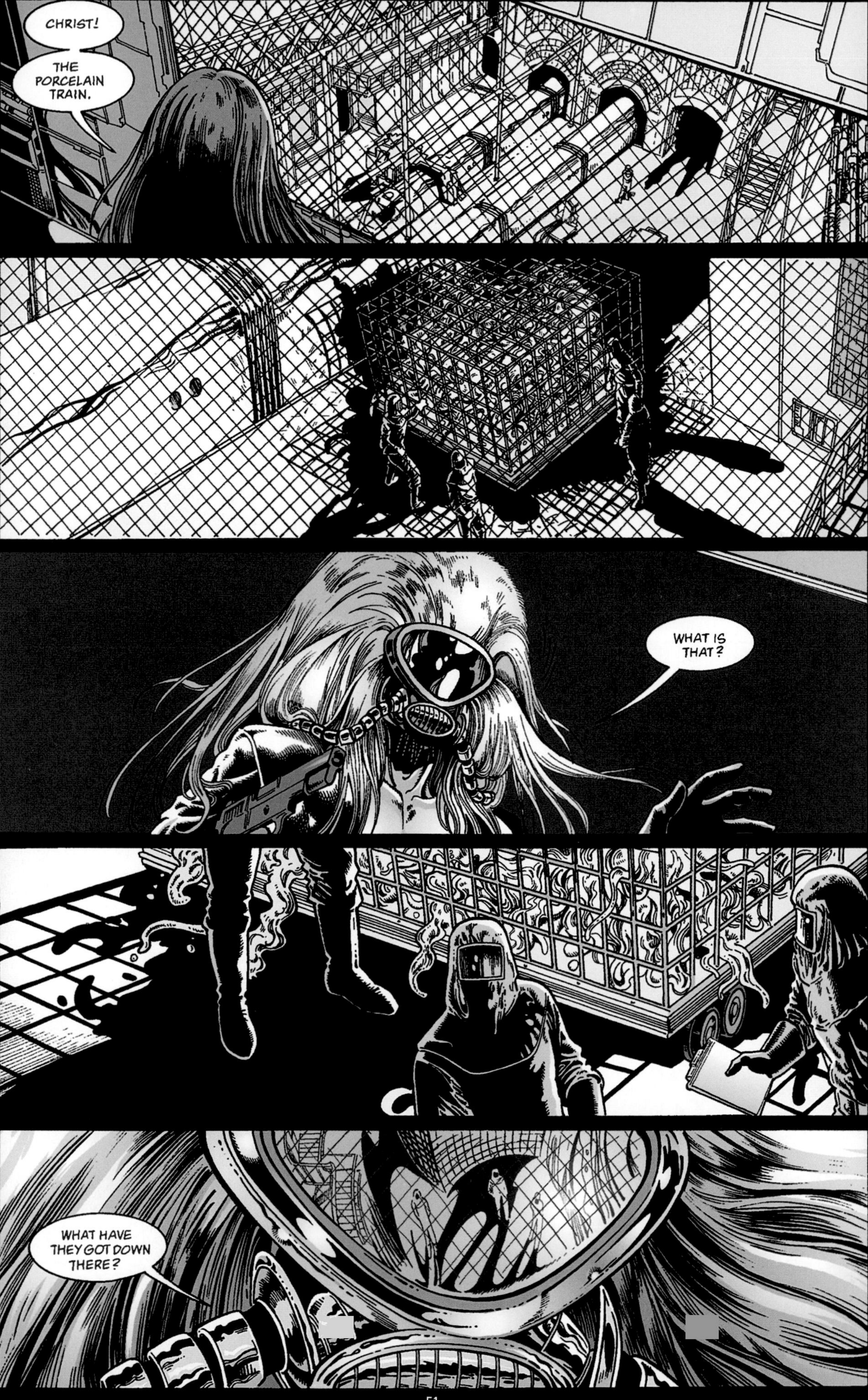
CHRIST!
THE PORCELAIN TRAIN.
WHAT IS THAT?
WHAT HAVE THEY GOT DOWN THERE?

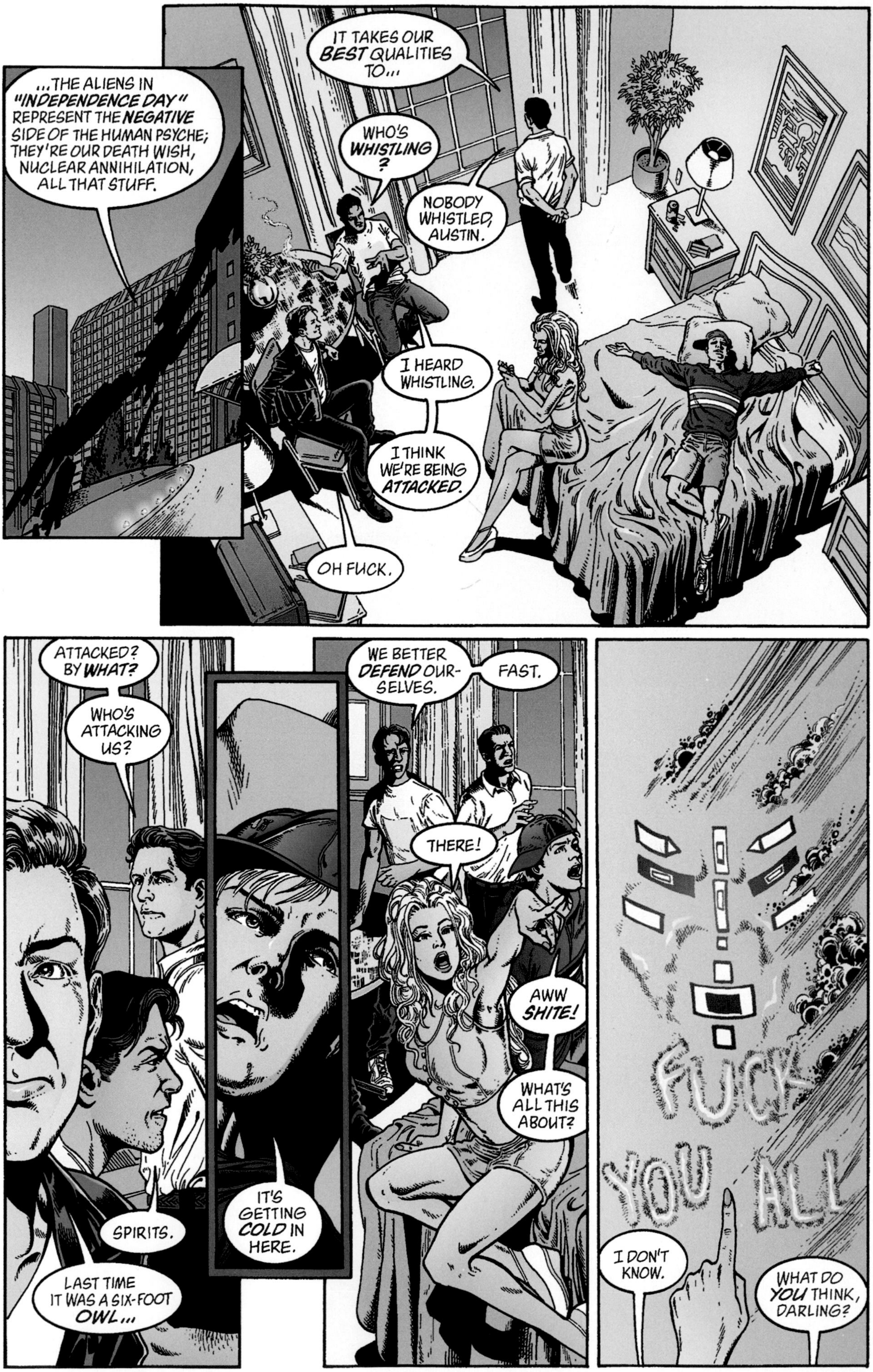
...THE ALIENS IN "INDEPENDENCE DAY" REPRESENT THE NEGATIVE SIDE OF THE HUMAN PSYCHE; THEY'RE OUR DEATH WISH, NUCLEAR ANNIHILATION, ALL THAT STUFF.
IT TAKES OUR BEST QUALITIES TO...
WHO'S WHISTLING?
NOBODY WHISTLED, AUSTIN.
I HEARD WHISTLING.
I THINK WE'RE BEING ATTACKED.
OH FUCK.
ATTACKED? BY WHAT?
WHO'S ATTACKING US?
SPIRITS.
LAST TIME IT WAS A SIX-FOOT OWL...
IT'S GETTING COLD IN HERE.
WE BETTER DEFEND OURSELVES.
FAST.
THERE!
AWW SHITE!
WHAT'S ALL THIS ABOUT?
FUCK YOU ALL
I DON'T KNOW.
WHAT DO YOU THINK, DARLING?

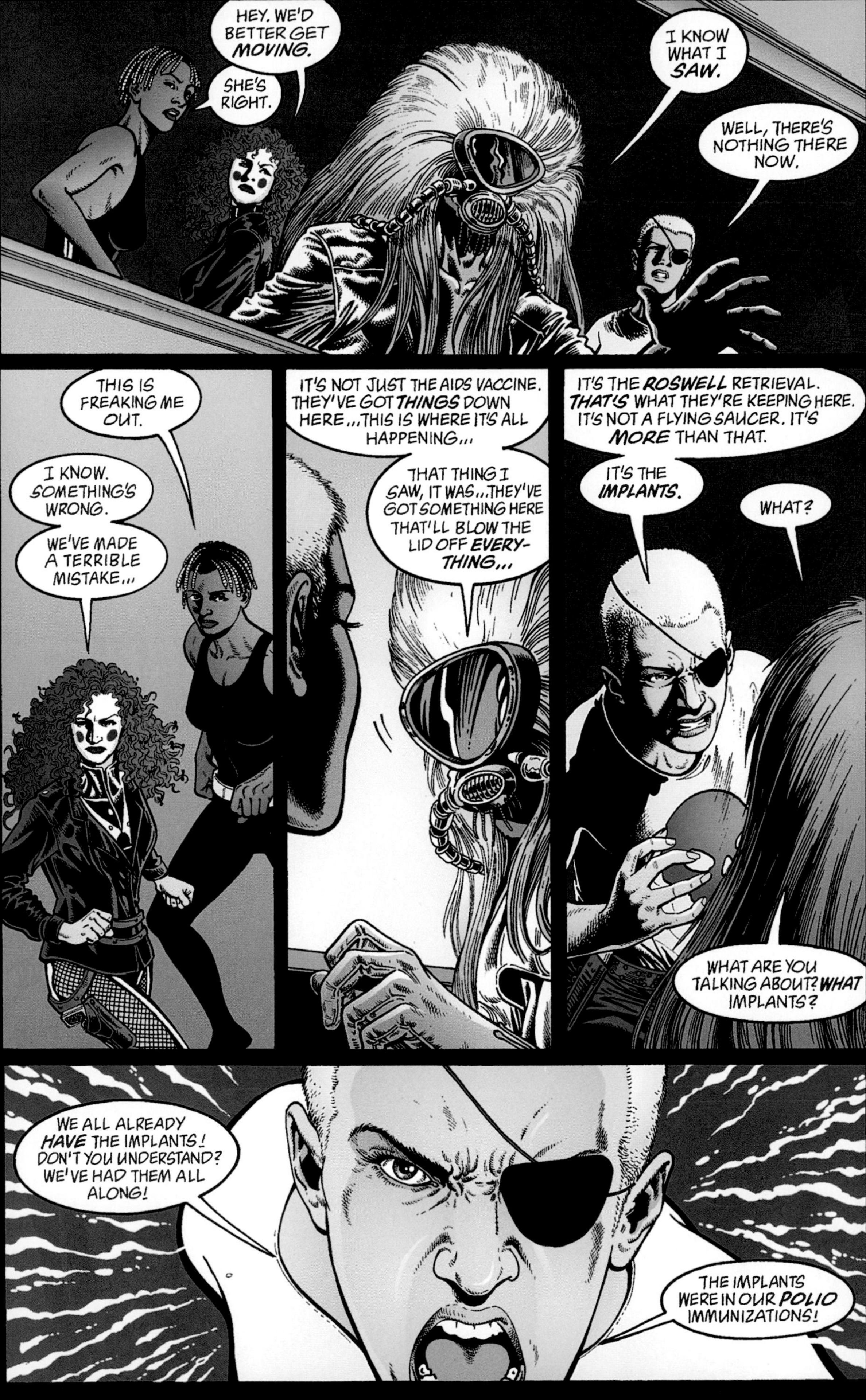

HEY. WE'D BETTER GET MOVING.
SHE'S RIGHT.
I KNOW WHAT I SAW.
WELL, THERE'S NOTHING THERE NOW.
THIS IS FREAKING ME OUT.
I KNOW. SOMETHING'S WRONG.
WE'VE MADE A TERRIBLE MISTAKE...
IT'S NOT JUST THE AIDS VACCINE. THEY'VE GOT THINGS DOWN HERE... THIS IS WHERE IT'S ALL HAPPENING...
THAT THING I SAW, IT WAS... THEY'VE GOT SOMETHING HERE THAT'LL BLOW THE LID OFF EVERY-THING...
IT'S THE ROSWELL RETRIEVAL. THAT'S WHAT THEY'RE KEEPING HERE. IT'S NOT A FLYING SAUCER. IT'S MORE THAN THAT.
IT'S THE IMPLANTS.
WHAT?
WHAT ARE YOU TALKING ABOUT? WHAT IMPLANTS?
WE ALL ALREADY HAVE THE IMPLANTS! DON'T YOU UNDERSTAND? WE'VE HAD THEM ALL ALONG!
THE IMPLANTS WERE IN OUR POLIO IMMUNIZATIONS!

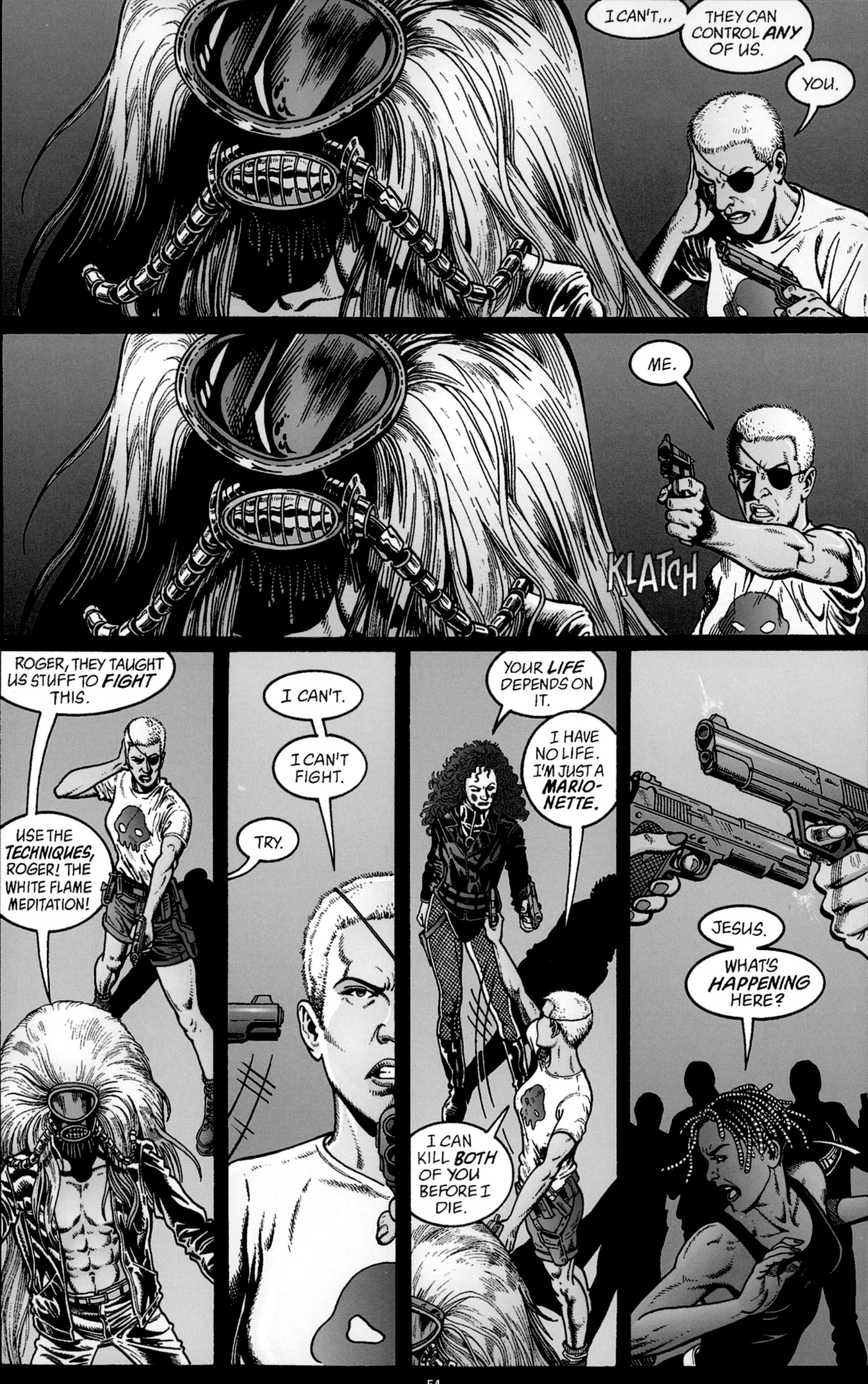
I CAN'T...
THEY CAN CONTROL ANY OF US.
YOU.
ME.
KLATCH
ROGER, THEY TAUGHT US STUFF TO FIGHT THIS.
USE THE TECHNIQUES, ROGER! THE WHITE FLAME MEDITATION!
I CAN'T.
I CAN'T FIGHT.
TRY.
YOUR LIFE DEPENDS ON IT.
I HAVE NO LIFE. I'M JUST A MARIO-NETTE.
I CAN KILL BOTH OF YOU BEFORE I DIE.
JESUS.
WHAT'S HAPPENING HERE?

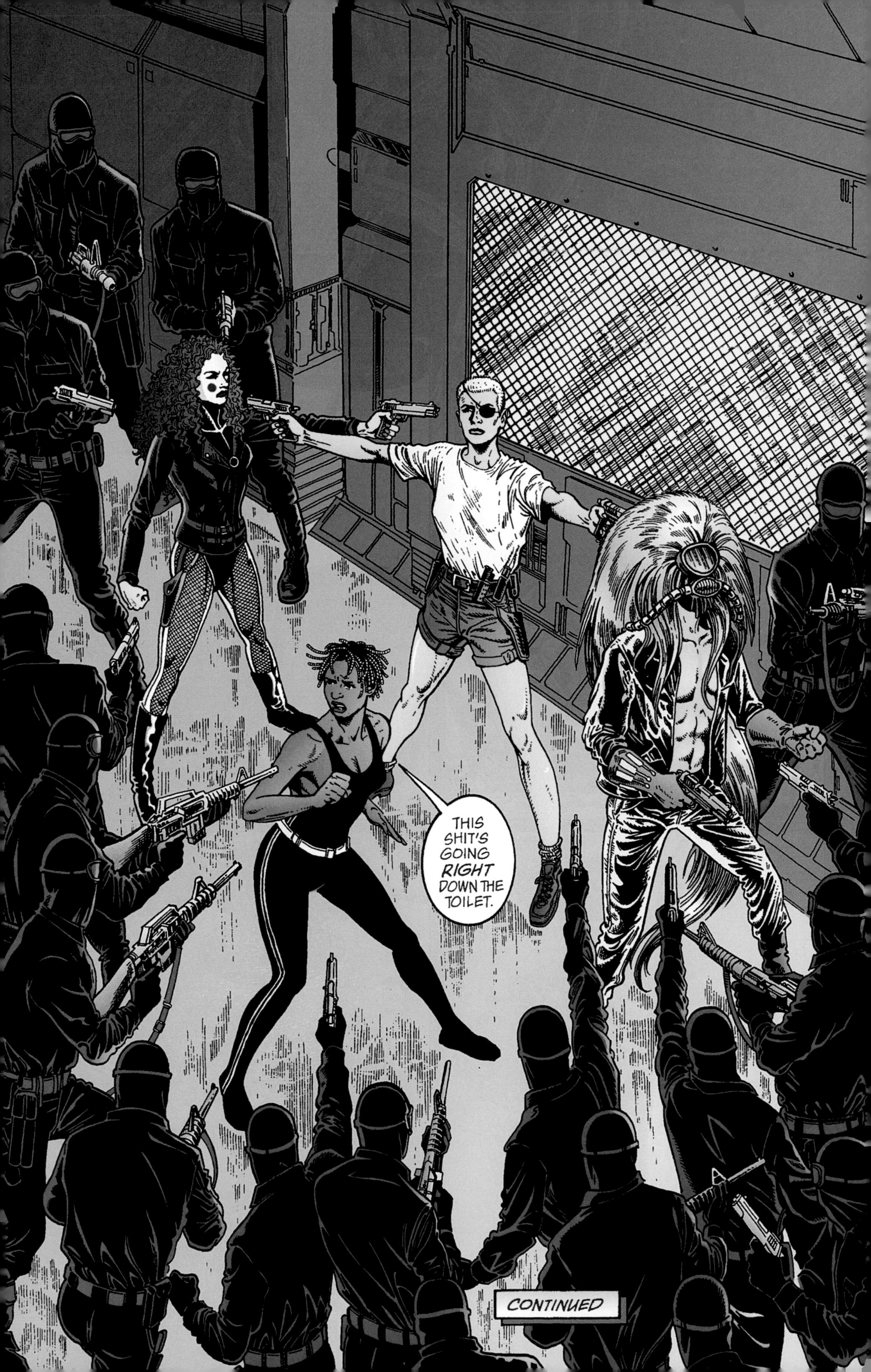
THIS SHIT'S GOING RIGHT DOWN THE TOILET.
CONTINUED

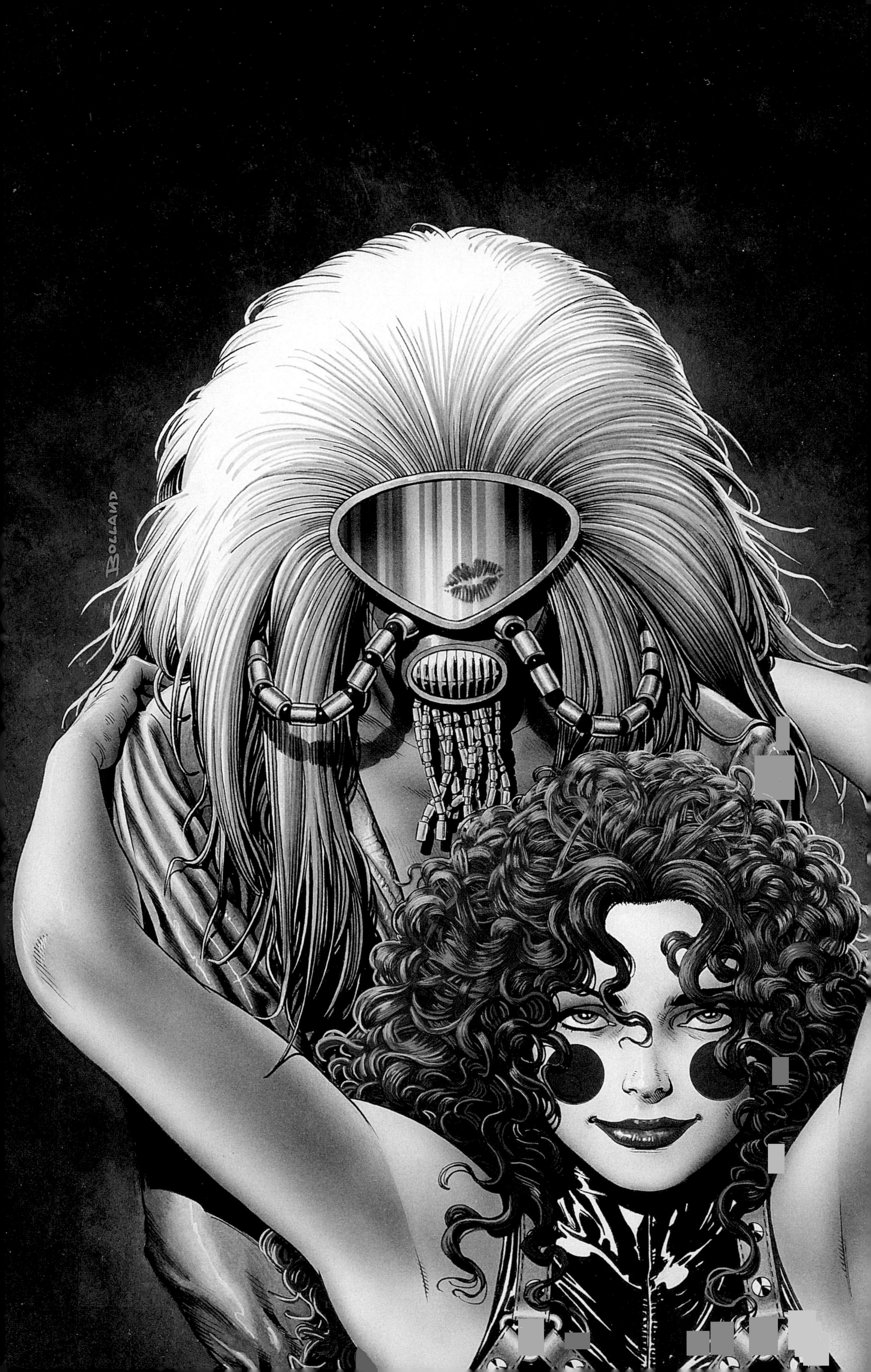
BOLLAND

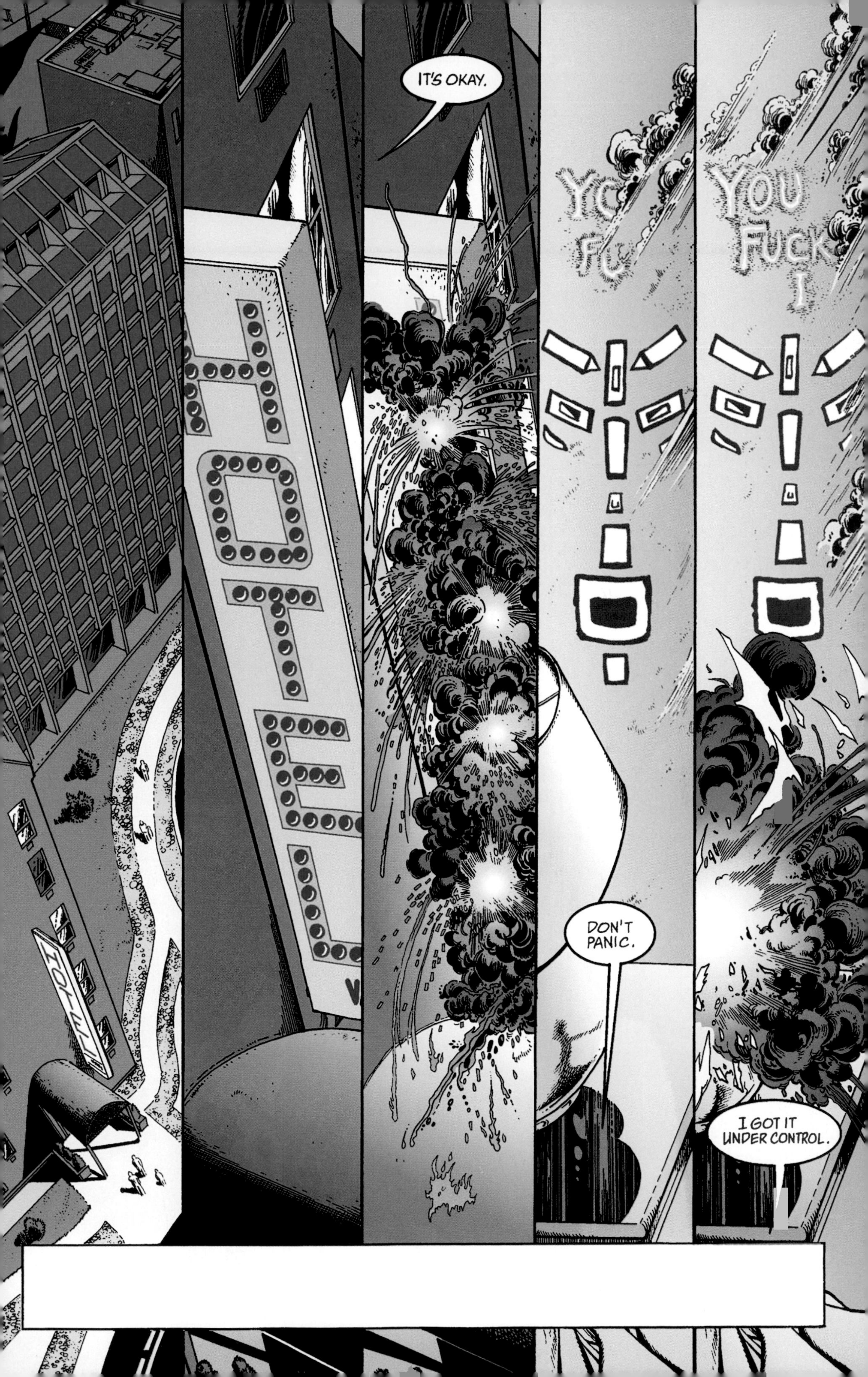

IT'S OKAY.
YO
FU
DON'T PANIC.
YOU
FUCK
I
I GOT IT UNDER CONTROL.

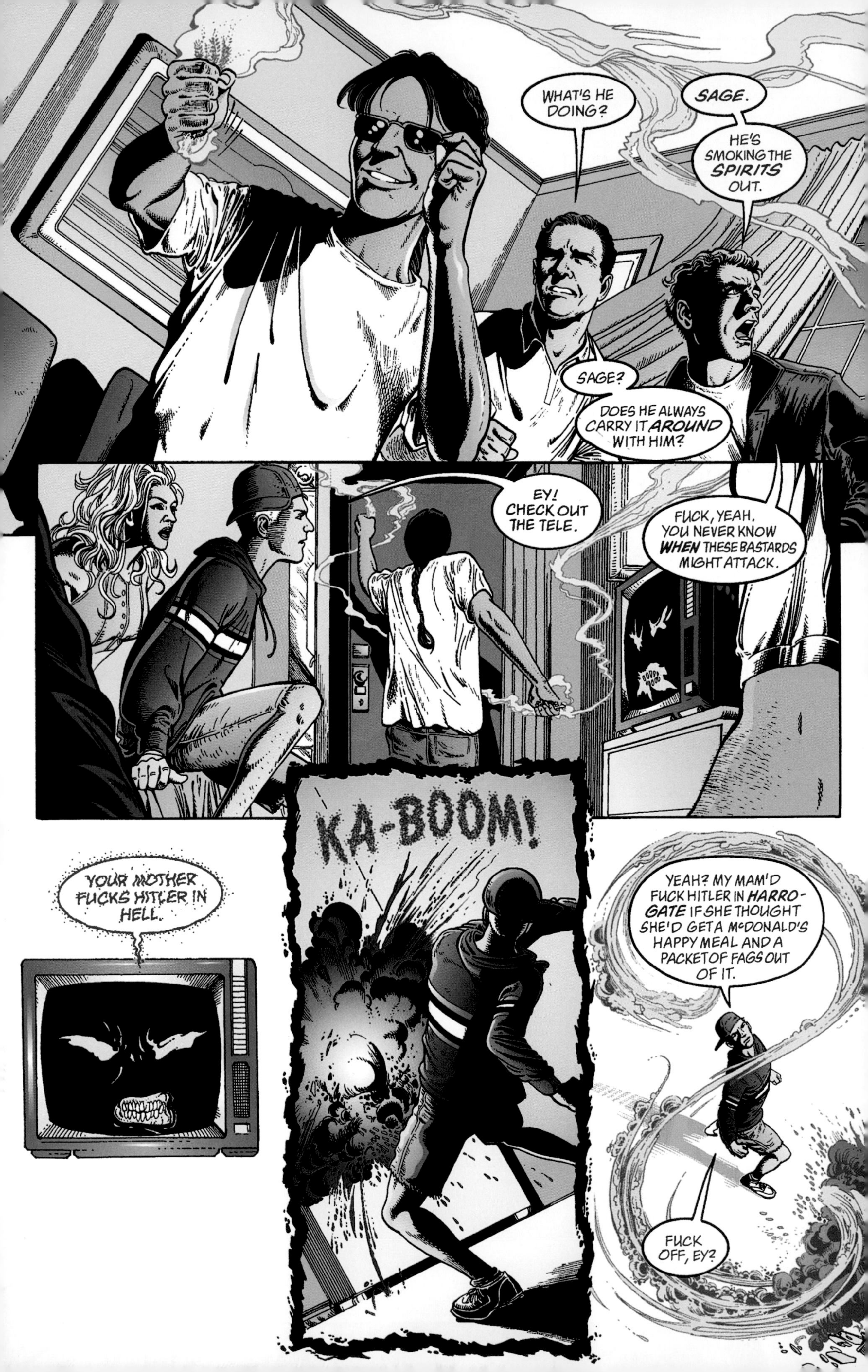
WHAT'S HE DOING?
SAGE.
HE'S SMOKING THE SPIRITS OUT.
SAGE?
DOES HE ALWAYS CARRY IT AROUND WITH HIM?
EY! CHECK OUT THE TELE.
FUCK, YEAH. YOU NEVER KNOW WHEN THESE BASTARDS MIGHT ATTACK.
YOUR MOTHER FUCKS HITLER IN HELL.
KA-BOOM!
YEAH? MY MAM'D FUCK HITLER IN HARRO-GATE IF SHE THOUGHT SHE'D GET A McDONALD'S HAPPY MEAL AND A PACKET OF FAGS OUT OF IT.
FUCK OFF, EY?

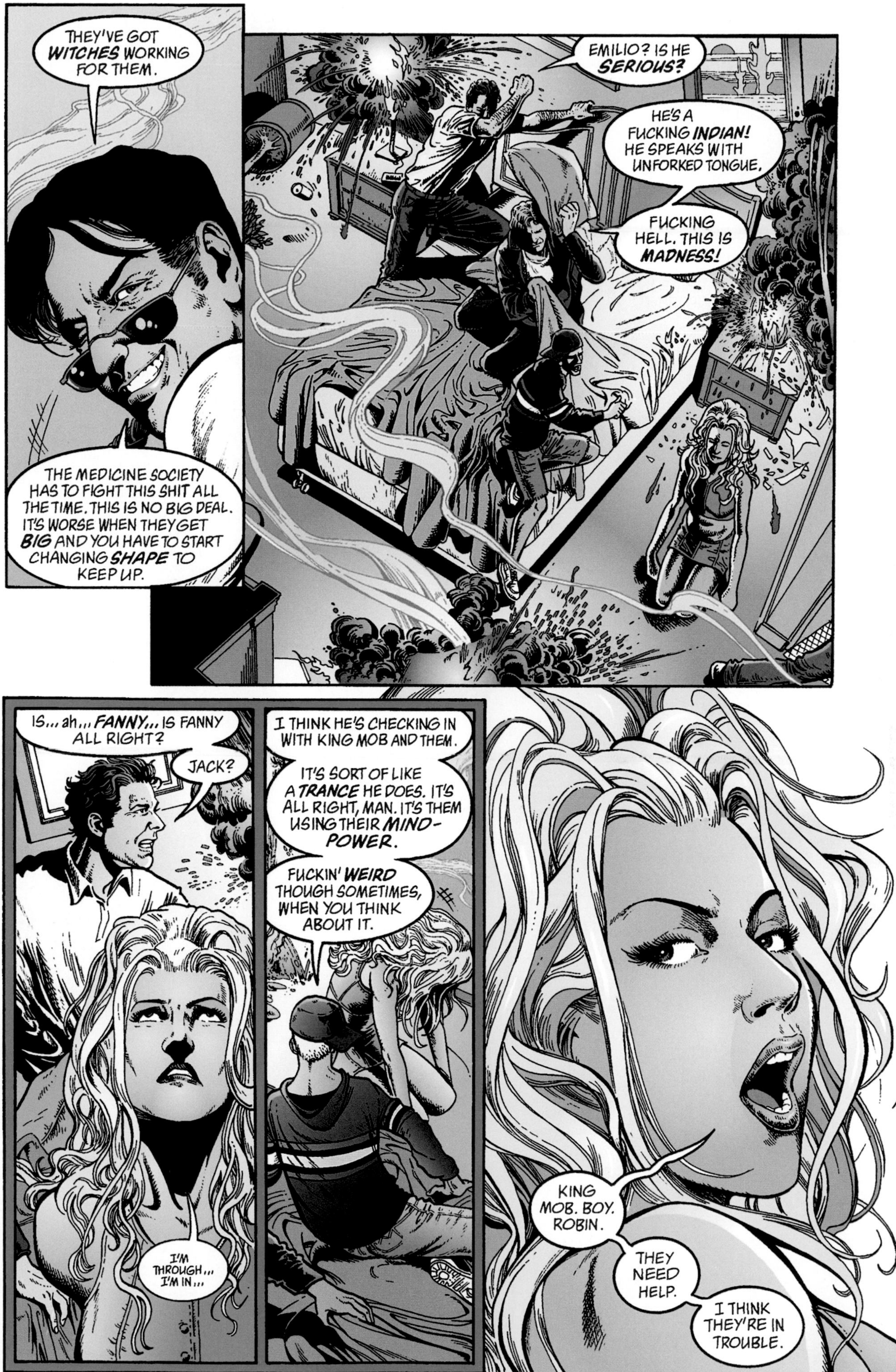
THEY'VE GOT WITCHES WORKING FOR THEM.
THE MEDICINE SOCIETY HAS TO FIGHT THIS SHIT ALL THE TIME. THIS IS NO BIG DEAL. IT'S WORSE WHEN THEY GET BIG AND YOU HAVE TO START CHANGING SHAPE TO KEEP UP.
EMILIO? IS HE SERIOUS?
HE'S A FUCKING INDIAN! HE SPEAKS WITH UNFORKED TONGUE.
FUCKING HELL. THIS IS MADNESS!
IS... ah... FANNY... IS FANNY ALL RIGHT?
JACK?
I'M THROUGH... I'M IN...
I THINK HE'S CHECKING IN WITH KING MOB AND THEM.
IT'S SORT OF LIKE A TRANCE HE DOES. IT'S ALL RIGHT, MAN. IT'S THEM USING THEIR MIND-POWER.
FUCKIN' WEIRD THOUGH SOMETIMES, WHEN YOU THINK ABOUT IT.
KING MOB. BOY. ROBIN.
THEY NEED HELP.
I THINK THEY'RE IN TROUBLE.

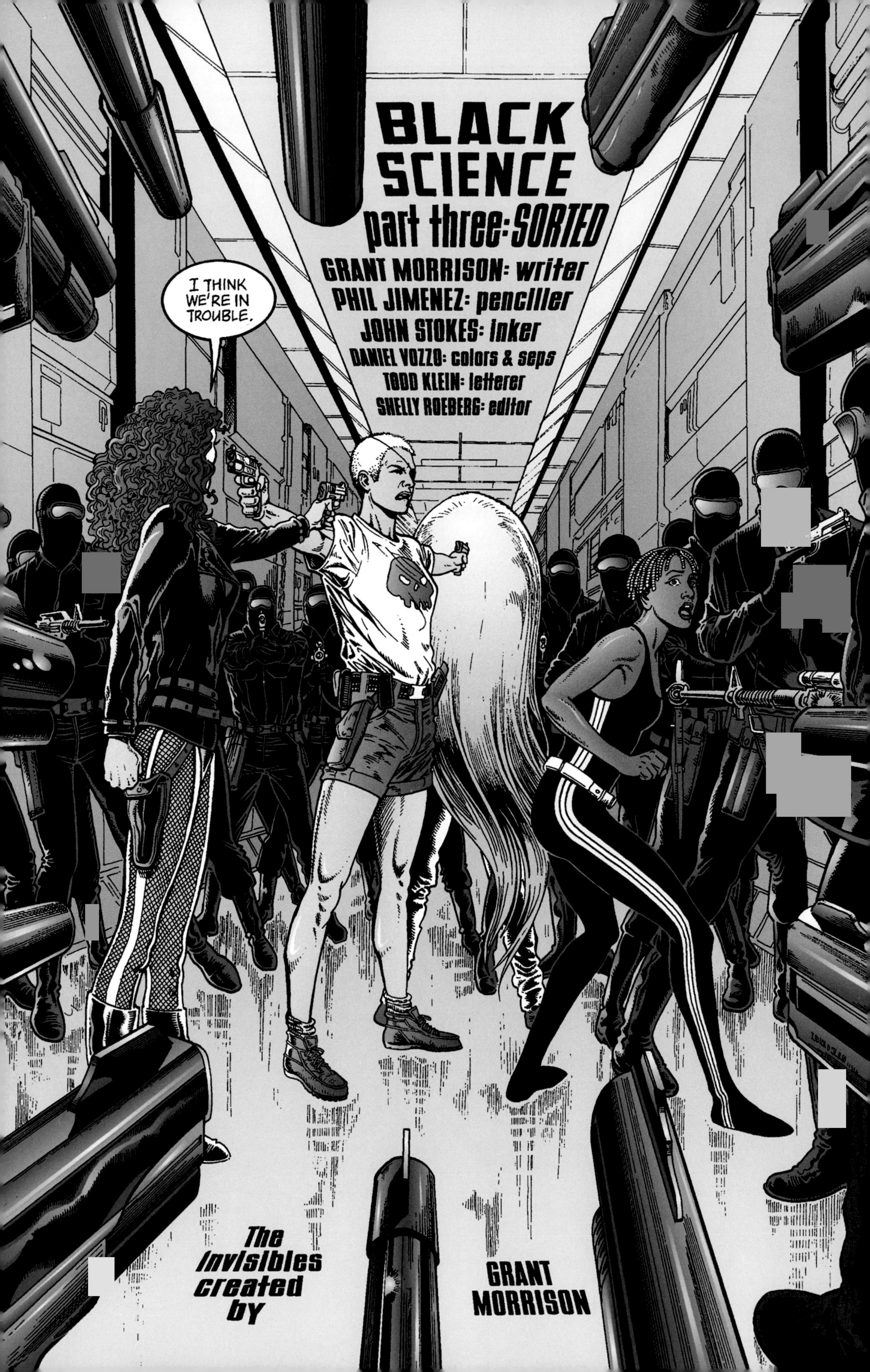

BLACK SCIENCE
part three: SORTED
GRANT MORRISON: writer
PHIL JIMENEZ: penciller
JOHN STOKES: inker
DANIEL VOZZO: colors & seps
TODD KLEIN: letterer
SHELLY ROEBERG: editor
I THINK WE'RE IN TROUBLE.
The Invisibles created by GRANT MORRISON

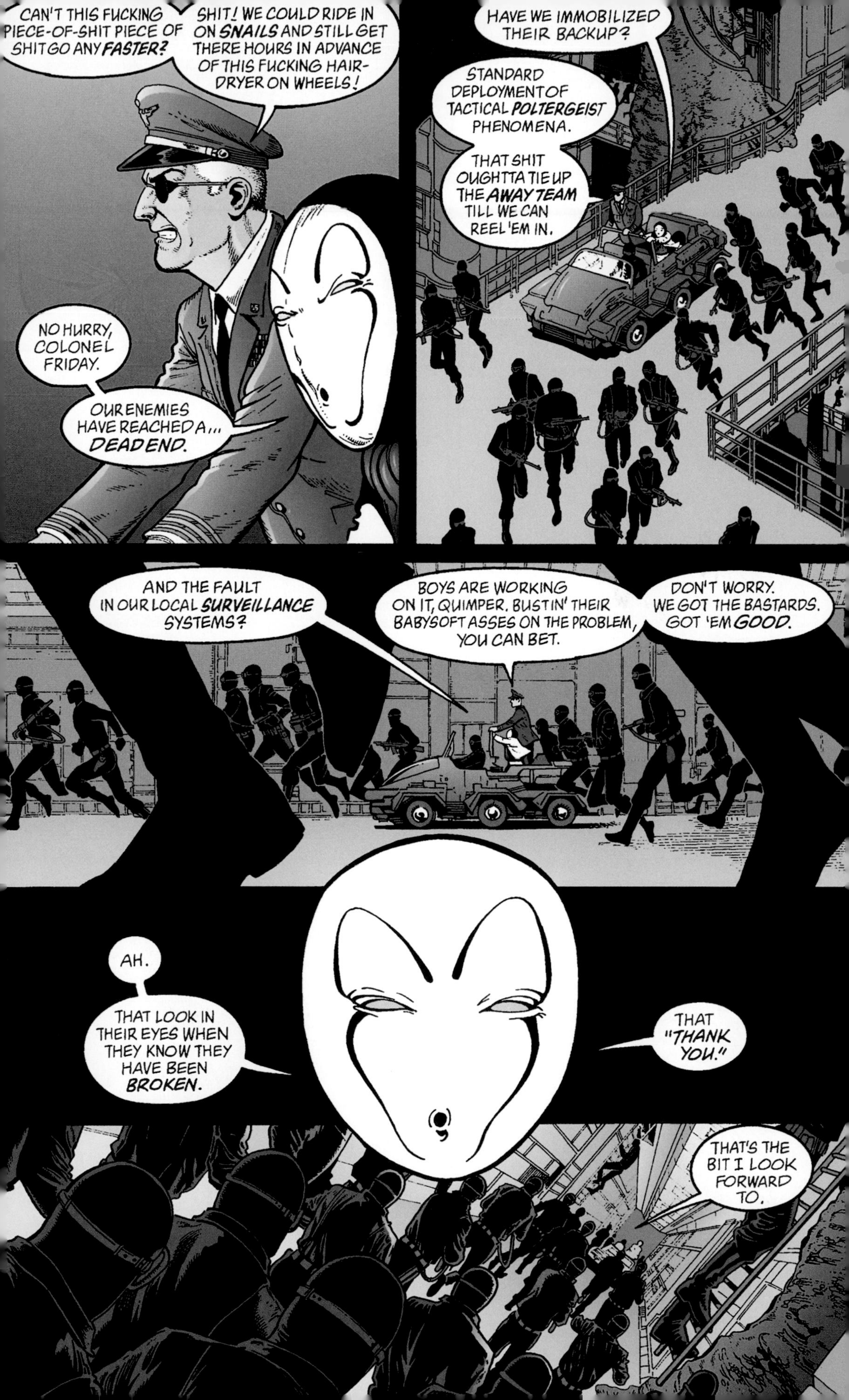
CAN'T THIS FUCKING PIECE-OF-SHIT PIECE OF SHIT GO ANY FASTER?
SHIT! WE COULD RIDE IN ON SNAILS AND STILL GET THERE HOURS IN ADVANCE OF THIS FUCKING HAIR-DRYER ON WHEELS!
NO HURRY, COLONEL FRIDAY.
OUR ENEMIES HAVE REACHED A... DEAD END.
HAVE WE IMMOBILIZED THEIR BACKUP?
STANDARD DEPLOYMENT OF TACTICAL POLTERGEIST PHENOMENA.
THAT SHIT OUGHTTA TIE UP THE AWAY TEAM TILL WE CAN REEL 'EM IN.
AND THE FAULT IN OUR LOCAL SURVEILLANCE SYSTEMS?
BOYS ARE WORKING ON IT, QUIMPER. BUSTIN' THEIR BABYSOFT ASSES ON THE PROBLEM, YOU CAN BET.
DON'T WORRY. WE GOT THE BASTARDS. GOT 'EM GOOD.
AH.
THAT LOOK IN THEIR EYES WHEN THEY KNOW THEY HAVE BEEN BROKEN.
THAT "THANK YOU."
THAT'S THE BIT I LOOK FORWARD TO.

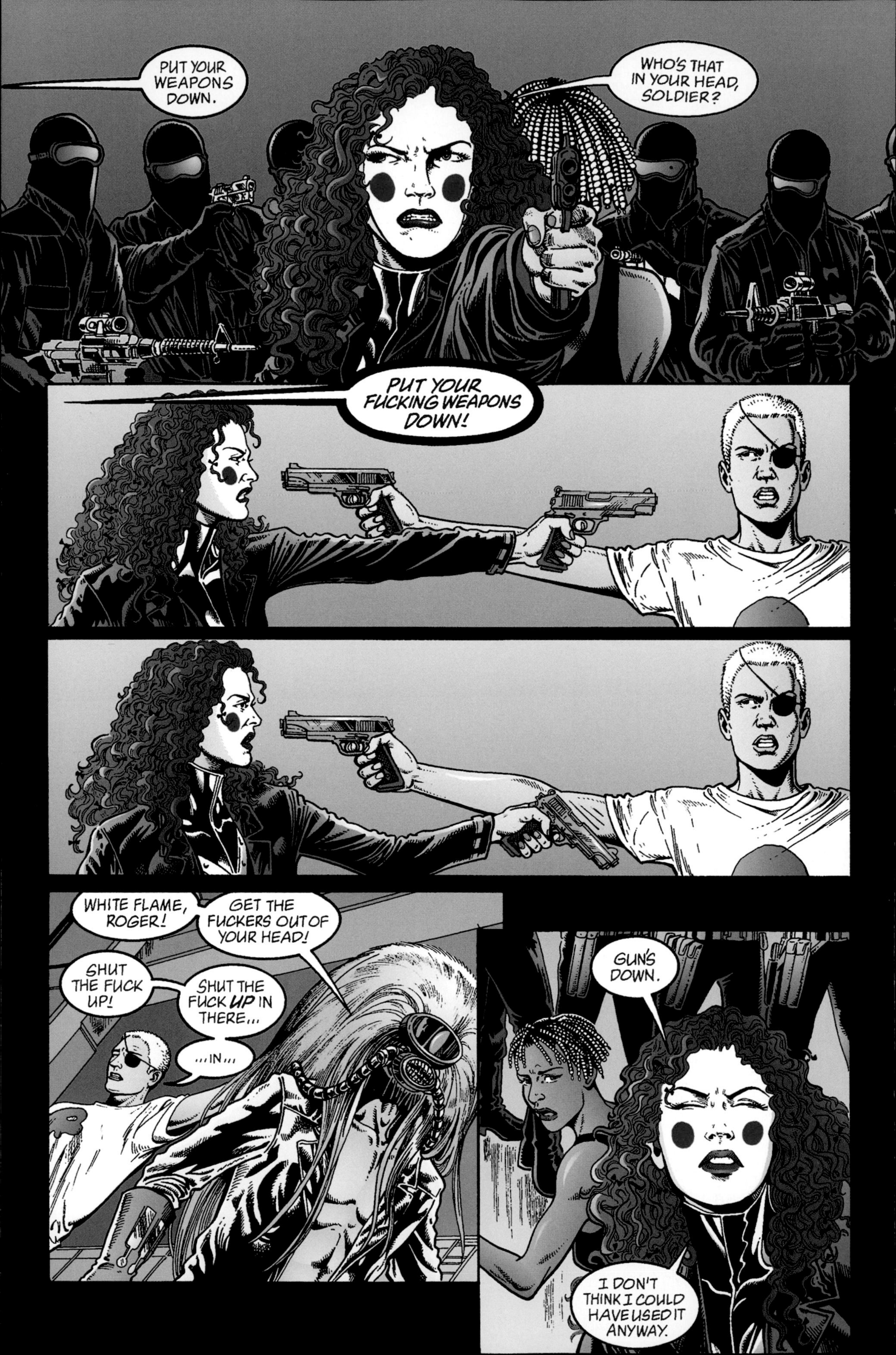
PUT YOUR WEAPONS DOWN.
WHO'S THAT IN YOUR HEAD, SOLDIER?
PUT YOUR FUCKING WEAPONS DOWN!
WHITE FLAME, ROGER!
GET THE FUCKERS OUT OF YOUR HEAD!
SHUT THE FUCK UP!
SHUT THE FUCK UP IN THERE...
...IN...
GUN'S DOWN.
I DON'T THINK I COULD HAVE USED IT ANYWAY.

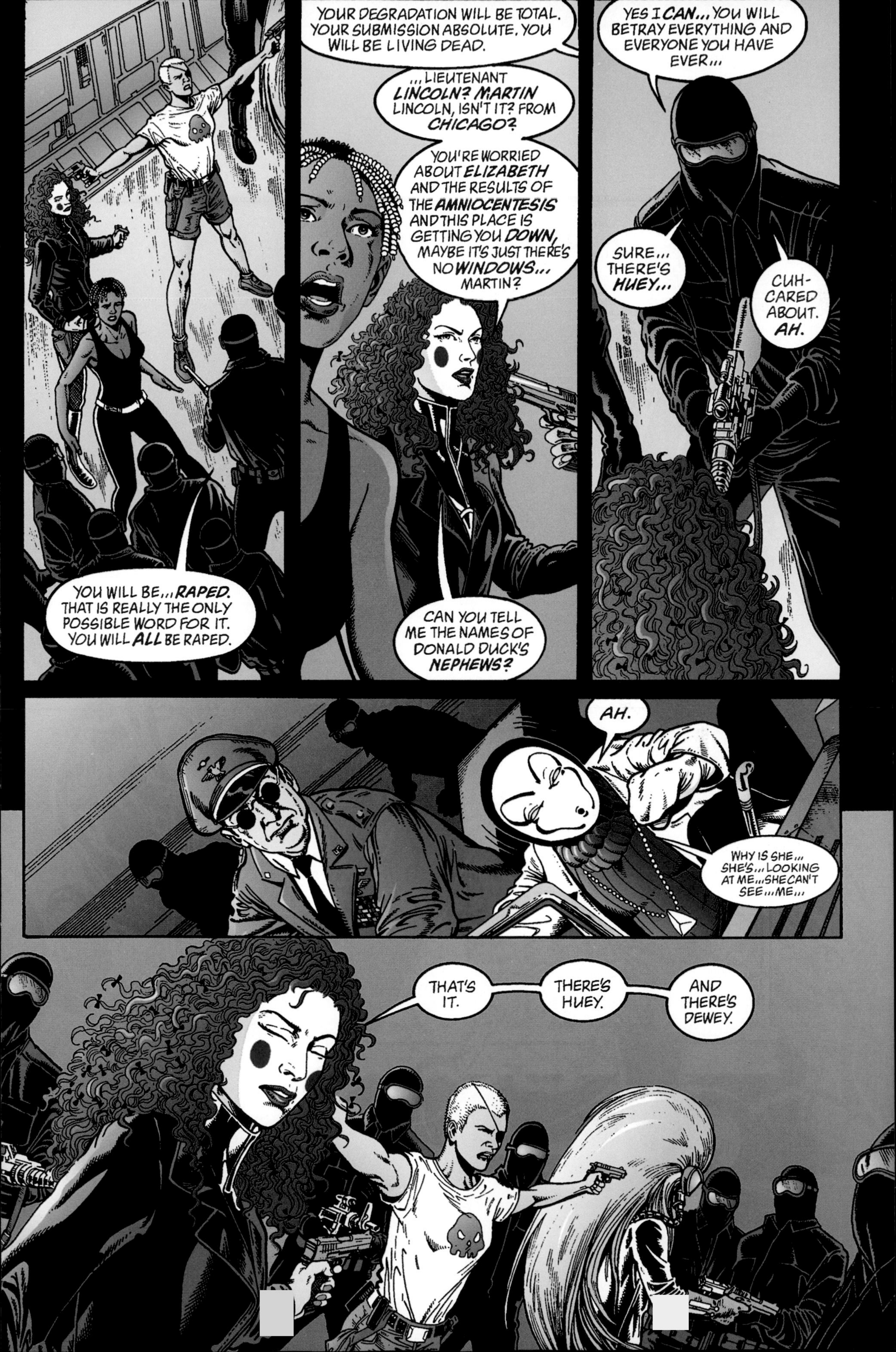
YOUR DEGRADATION WILL BE TOTAL. YOUR SUBMISSION ABSOLUTE. YOU WILL BE LIVING DEAD.
YOU WILL BE... RAPED. THAT IS REALLY THE ONLY POSSIBLE WORD FOR IT. YOU WILL ALL BE RAPED.
...LIEUTENANT LINCOLN? MARTIN LINCOLN, ISN'T IT? FROM CHICAGO?
YOU'RE WORRIED ABOUT ELIZABETH AND THE RESULTS OF THE AMNIOCENTESIS AND THIS PLACE IS GETTING YOU DOWN, MAYBE IT'S JUST THERE'S NO WINDOWS... MARTIN?
CAN YOU TELL ME THE NAMES OF DONALD DUCK'S NEPHEWS?
YES I CAN... YOU WILL BETRAY EVERYTHING AND EVERYONE YOU HAVE EVER...
SURE... THERE'S HUEY...
CUH- CARED ABOUT. AH.
AH.
WHY IS SHE... SHE'S... LOOKING AT ME... SHE CAN'T SEE... ME...
THAT'S IT.
THERE'S HUEY.
AND THERE'S DEWEY.

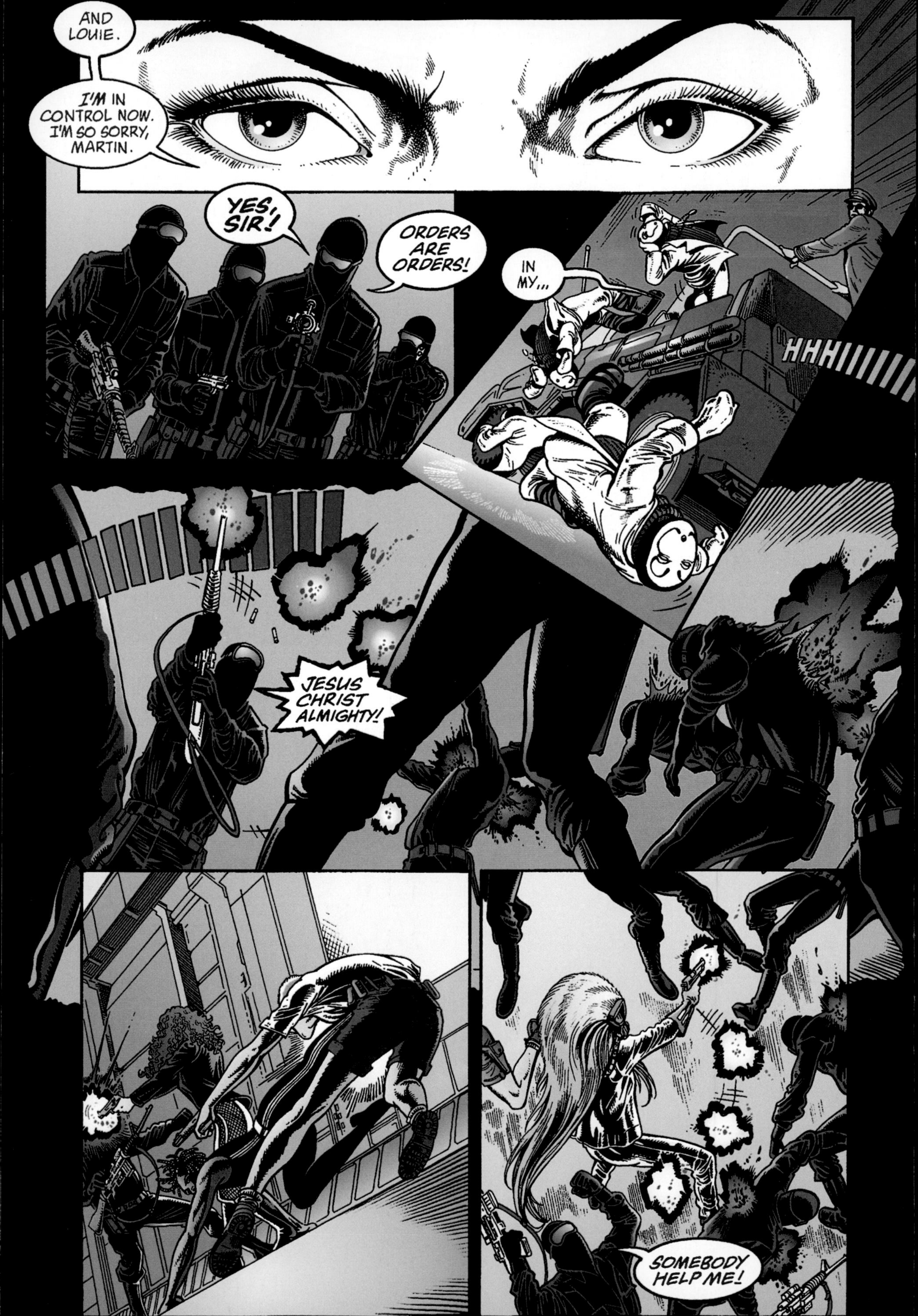
AND LOUIE.
I'M IN CONTROL NOW. I'M SO SORRY, MARTIN.
YES, SIR!
ORDERS ARE ORDERS!
IN MY...
HHHIIIIII
JESUS CHRIST ALMIGHTY!
SOMEBODY HELP ME!

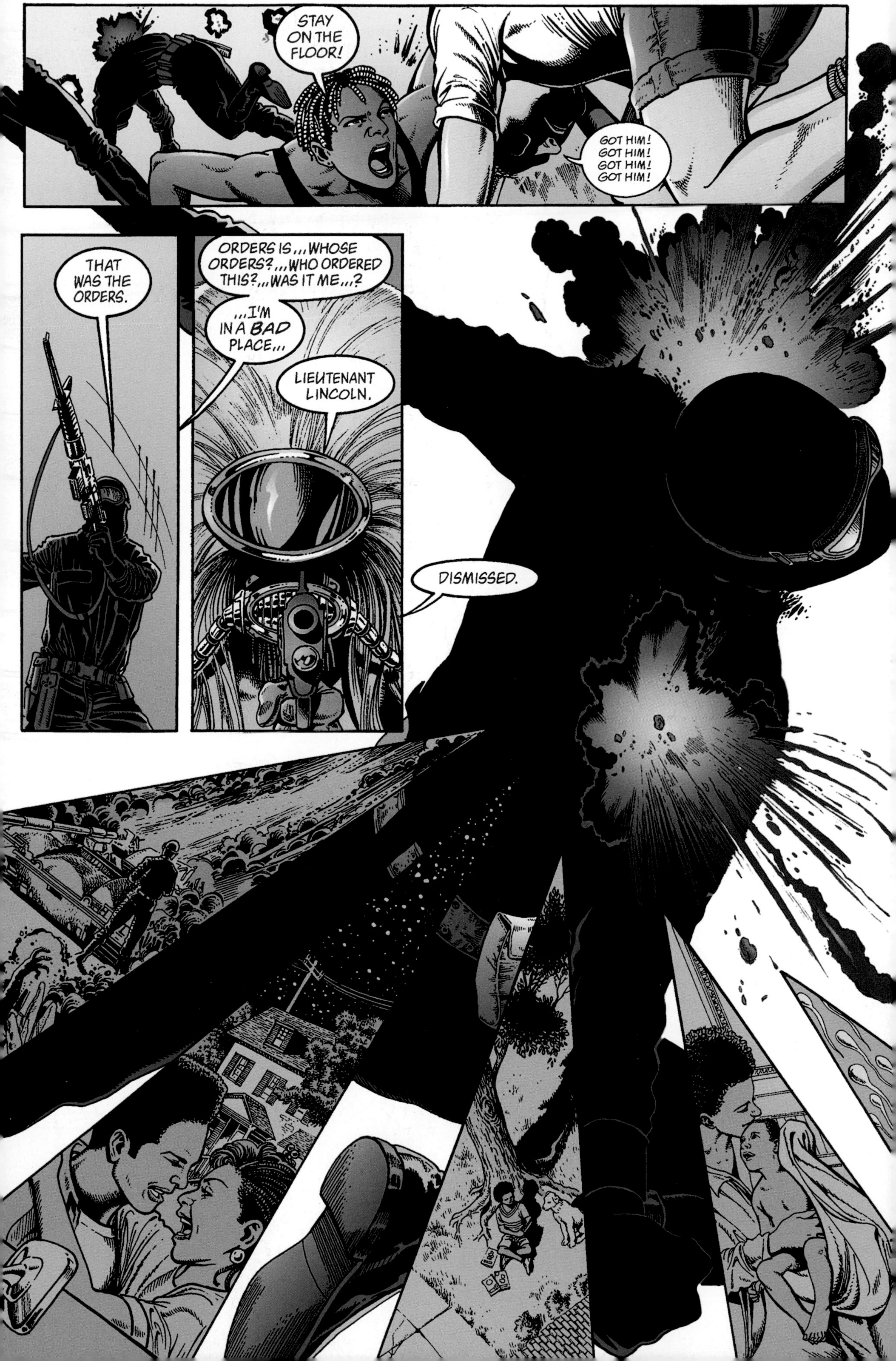
STAY ON THE FLOOR!
GOT HIM! GOT HIM! GOT HIM! GOT HIM!
THAT WAS THE ORDERS.
ORDERS IS,,, WHOSE ORDERS?,,, WHO ORDERED THIS?,,, WAS IT ME,,,?
,,, I'M IN A BAD PLACE,,,
LIEUTENANT LINCOLN.
DISMISSED.

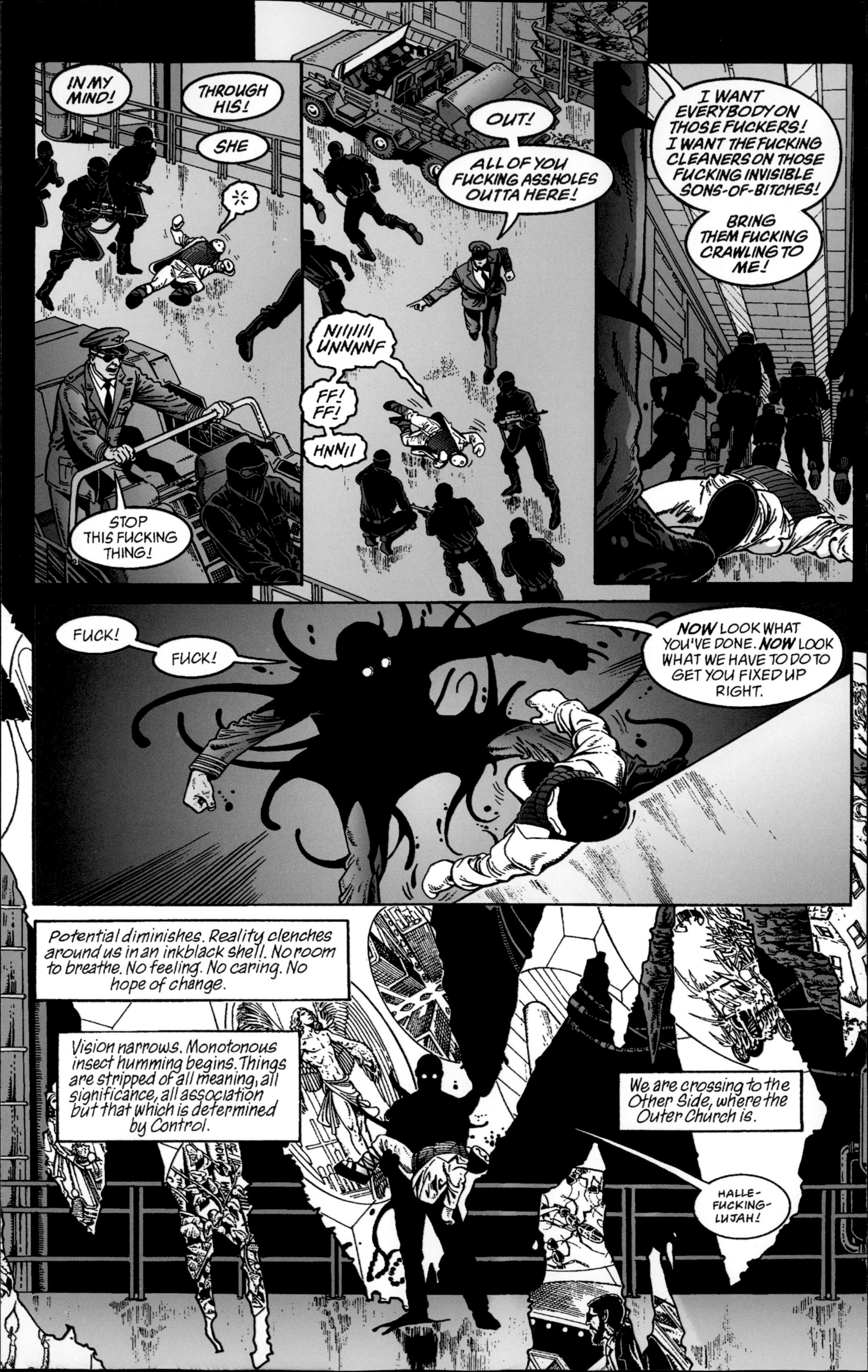
IN MY MIND!
THROUGH HIS!
SHE
!*!
STOP THIS FUCKING THING!
OUT!
ALL OF YOU FUCKING ASSHOLES OUTTA HERE!
NIIIIII UNNNNF
FF! FF!
HNN!!
I WANT EVERYBODY ON THOSE FUCKERS! I WANT THE FUCKING CLEANERS ON THOSE FUCKING INVISIBLE SONS-OF-BITCHES!
BRING THEM FUCKING CRAWLING TO ME!
FUCK!
FUCK!
NOW LOOK WHAT YOU'VE DONE. NOW LOOK WHAT WE HAVE TO DO TO GET YOU FIXED UP RIGHT.
Potential diminishes. Reality clenches around us in an inkblack shell. No room to breathe. No feeling. No caring. No hope of change.
Vision narrows. Monotonous insect humming begins. Things are stripped of all meaning, all significance, all association but that which is determined by Control.
We are crossing to the Other Side, where the Outer Church is.
HALLE-FUCKING-LUJAH!

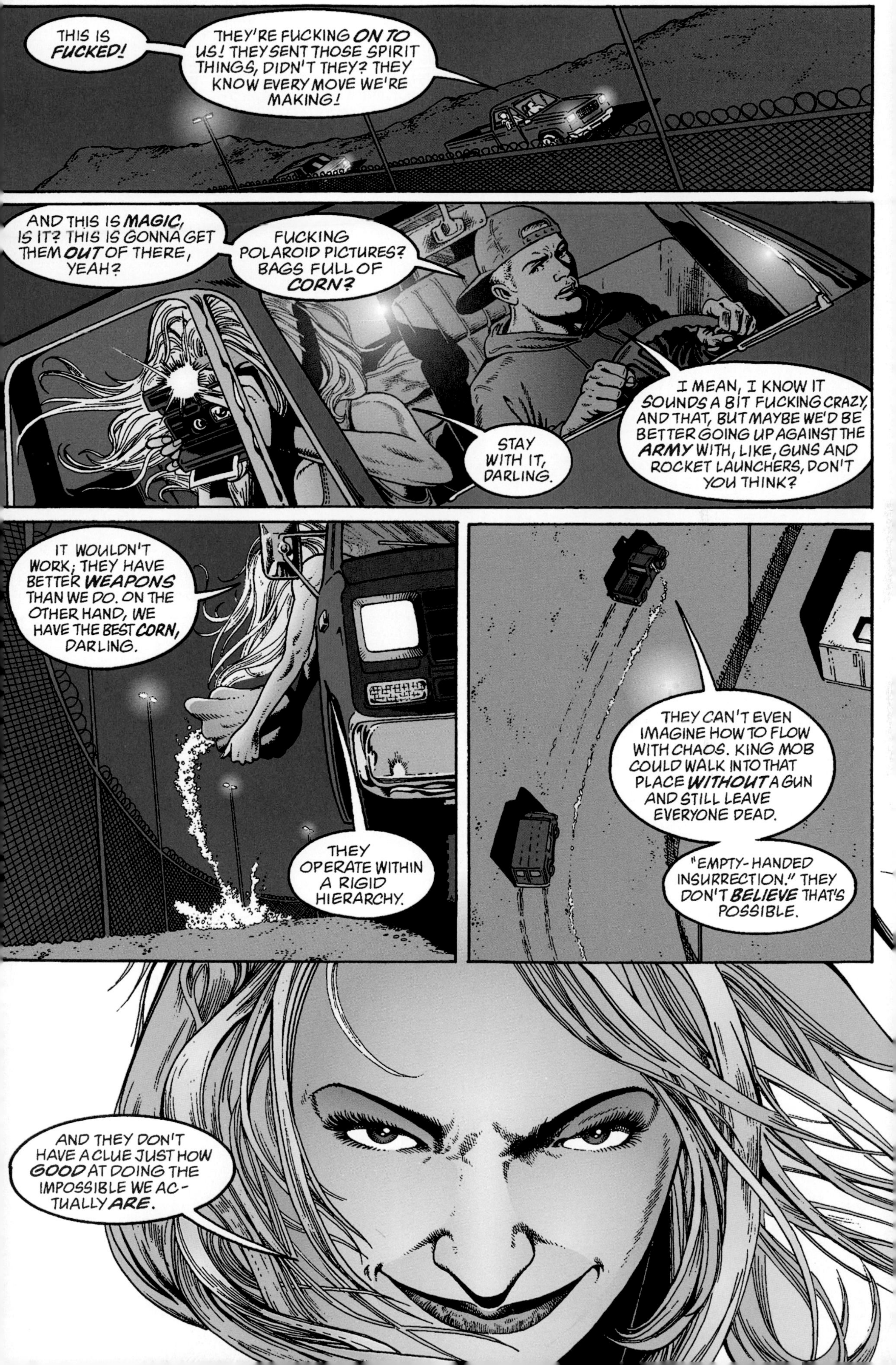
THIS IS FUCKED!
THEY'RE FUCKING ON TO US! THEY SENT THOSE SPIRIT THINGS, DIDN'T THEY? THEY KNOW EVERY MOVE WE'RE MAKING!
AND THIS IS MAGIC, IS IT? THIS IS GONNA GET THEM OUT OF THERE, YEAH?
FUCKING POLAROID PICTURES? BAGS FULL OF CORN?
I MEAN, I KNOW IT SOUNDS A BIT FUCKING CRAZY, AND THAT, BUT MAYBE WE'D BE BETTER GOING UP AGAINST THE ARMY WITH, LIKE, GUNS AND ROCKET LAUNCHERS, DON'T YOU THINK?
STAY WITH IT, DARLING.
IT WOULDN'T WORK; THEY HAVE BETTER WEAPONS THAN WE DO. ON THE OTHER HAND, WE HAVE THE BEST CORN, DARLING.
THEY OPERATE WITHIN A RIGID HIERARCHY.
THEY CAN'T EVEN IMAGINE HOW TO FLOW WITH CHAOS. KING MOB COULD WALK INTO THAT PLACE WITHOUT A GUN AND STILL LEAVE EVERYONE DEAD.
"EMPTY-HANDED INSURRECTION." THEY DON'T BELIEVE THAT'S POSSIBLE.
AND THEY DON'T HAVE A CLUE JUST HOW GOOD AT DOING THE IMPOSSIBLE WE AC-TUALLY ARE.

WHASS HAPPENING?...WALLS OPENING ...NOT WALLS...AN EMPTY DOOR. AH FUCK, THAT CAN'T...THAT *CAN'T* BE FUCKING HAPPENING...

HE'S STILL IN YOUR *HEAD*, ROGER. GET THE BASTARD OUT OF THERE! HE WAS *CONTROLLING* YOU AND THE OTHER GUY.

REMEMBER THE *TRAINING!* THE WHITE FLAME!

..."*I AM AN OPTIMIST,*" WE SAY. OR "*I AM UNLUCKY.*" OR PERHAPS "*I AM AN AMERICAN,*" "*I AM A JEW,*" "*I AM A HOMO-SEXUAL,*" "*I AM HETEROSEXUAL.*" WE CALL THE FOLLOWING THE WHITE FLAME MEDITATION.

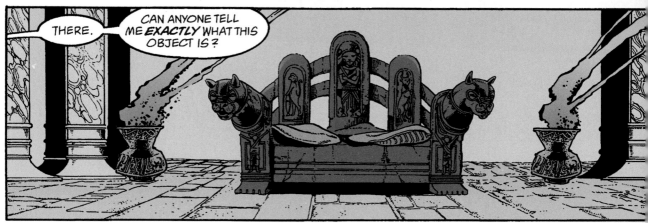

THERE.

CAN ANYONE TELL ME *EXACTLY* WHAT THIS OBJECT IS?

IT'S A CHAIR.

IS THAT *ALL?*

DOES THAT DESCRIBE THE *ENTIRETY* OF THIS OBJECT?

IT'S AN OBJECT WITH FOUR LEGS AND A THING TO HOLD UP YOUR *ASS* SO YOU DON'T HAVE TO SIT DOWN IN THE *DIRT* LIKE THE REST OF US DICKHEADS.

CHAIR.

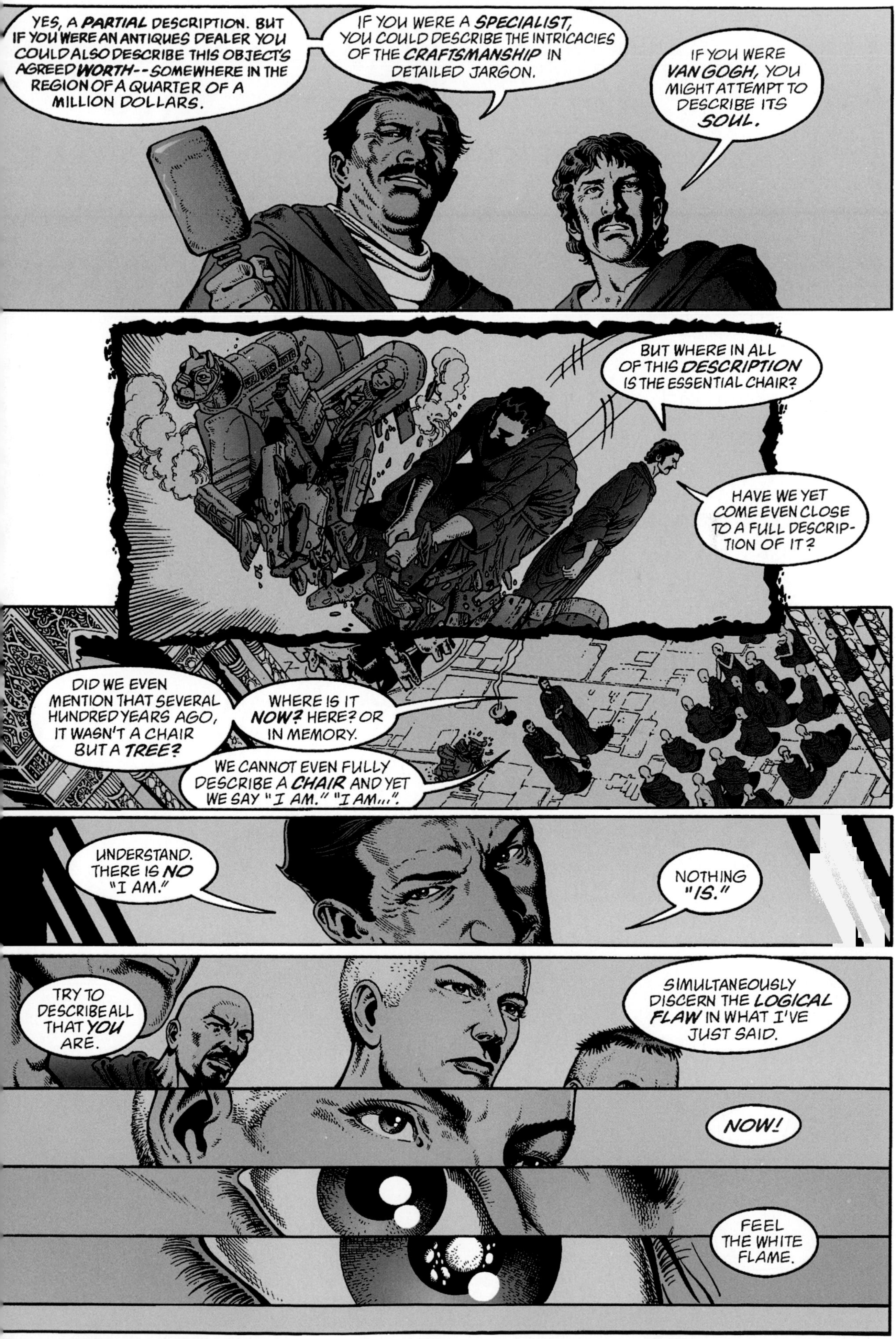
YES, A PARTIAL DESCRIPTION. BUT IF YOU WERE AN ANTIQUES DEALER YOU COULD ALSO DESCRIBE THIS OBJECT'S AGREED WORTH--SOMEWHERE IN THE REGION OF A QUARTER OF A MILLION DOLLARS.
IF YOU WERE A SPECIALIST, YOU COULD DESCRIBE THE INTRICACIES OF THE CRAFTSMANSHIP IN DETAILED JARGON.
IF YOU WERE VAN GOGH, YOU MIGHT ATTEMPT TO DESCRIBE ITS SOUL.
BUT WHERE IN ALL OF THIS DESCRIPTION IS THE ESSENTIAL CHAIR?
HAVE WE YET COME EVEN CLOSE TO A FULL DESCRIPTION OF IT?
DID WE EVEN MENTION THAT SEVERAL HUNDRED YEARS AGO, IT WASN'T A CHAIR BUT A TREE?
WHERE IS IT NOW? HERE? OR IN MEMORY.
WE CANNOT EVEN FULLY DESCRIBE A CHAIR AND YET WE SAY "I AM." "I AM...".
UNDERSTAND. THERE IS NO "I AM."
NOTHING "IS."
TRY TO DESCRIBE ALL THAT YOU ARE.
SIMULTANEOUSLY DISCERN THE LOGICAL FLAW IN WHAT I'VE JUST SAID.
NOW!
FEEL THE WHITE FLAME.

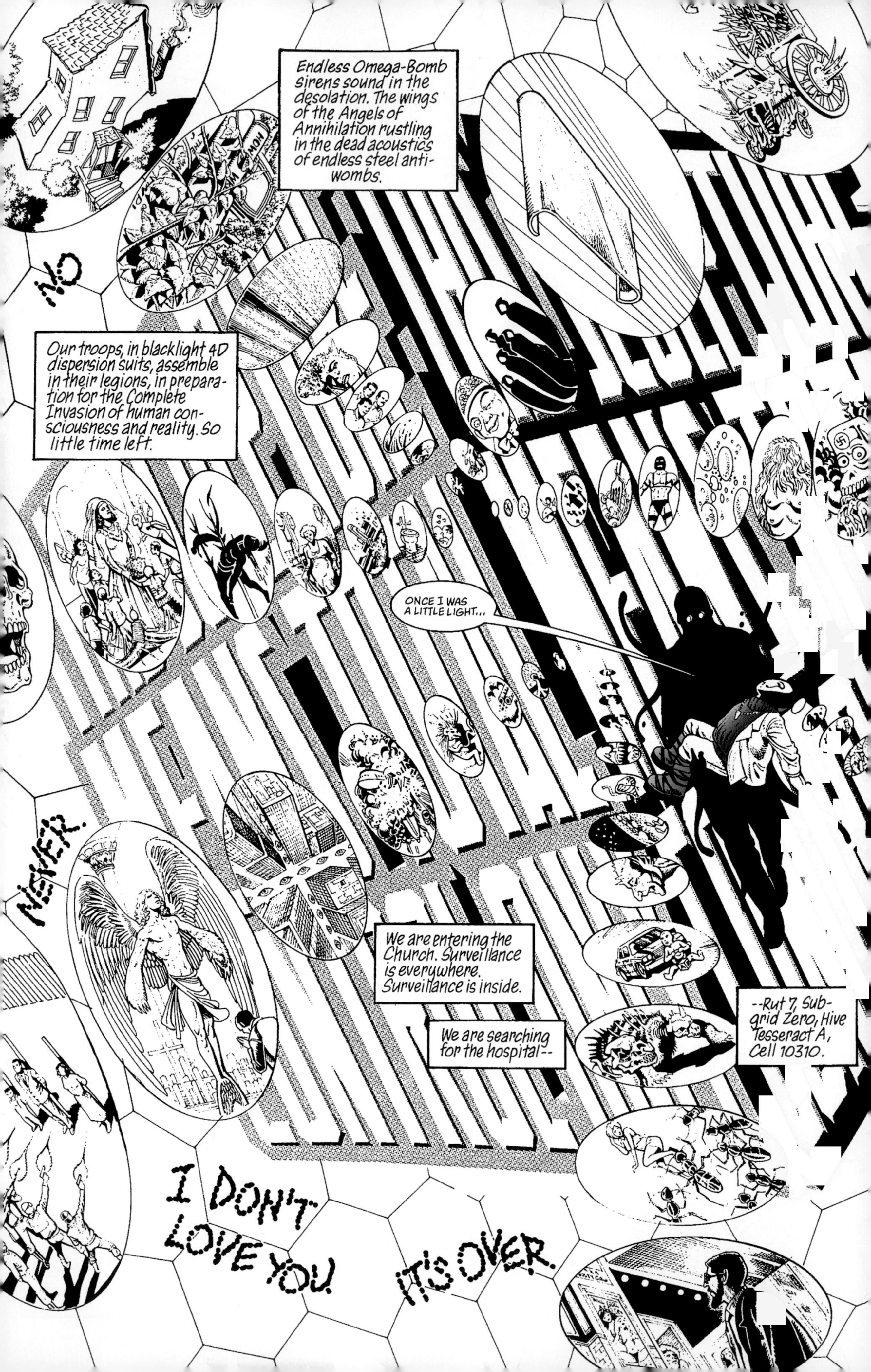

Endless Omega-Bomb sirens sound in the desolation. The wings of the Angels of Annihilation rustling in the dead acoustics of endless steel anti-wombs.
NO
Our troops, in blacklight 4D dispersion suits, assemble in their legions, in preparation for the Complete Invasion of human consciousness and reality. So little time left.
ONCE I WAS A LITTLE LIGHT...
NEVER.
We are entering the Church. Surveillance is everywhere. Surveillance is inside.
We are searching for the hospital--
--Rut 7, Sub-grid Zero, Hive Tesseract A, Cell 10310.
I DON'T LOVE YOU.
IT'S OVER.

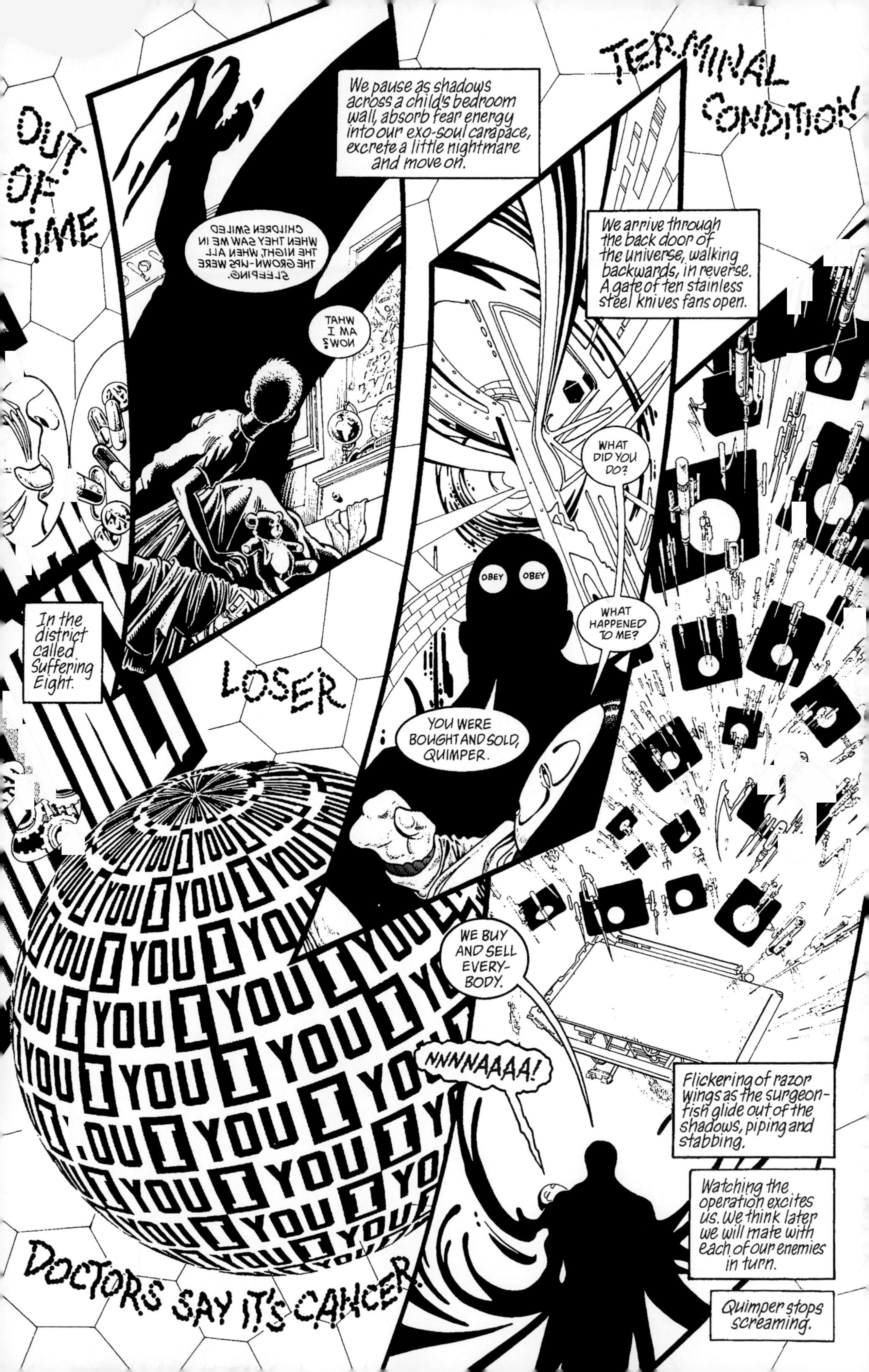

OUT OF TIME
We pause as shadows across a child's bedroom wall, absorb fear energy into our exo-soul carapace, excrete a little nightmare and move on.
CHILDREN SMILED WHEN THEY SAW ME IN THE NIGHT, WHEN ALL THE GROWN-UPS WERE SLEEPING.
WHAT AM I NOW?
TERMINAL CONDITION!
We arrive through the back door of the universe, walking backwards, in reverse. A gate of ten stainless steel knives fans open.
WHAT DID YOU DO?
OBEY
OBEY
WHAT HAPPENED TO ME?
In the district called Suffering Eight.
LOSER
YOU WERE BOUGHT AND SOLD, QUIMPER.
WE BUY AND SELL EVERY-BODY.
NNNNAAAA!
Flickering of razor wings as the surgeon-fish glide out of the shadows, piping and stabbing.
Watching the operation excites us. We think later we will mate with each of our enemies in turn.
DOCTORS SAY IT'S CANCER.
Quimper stops screaming.

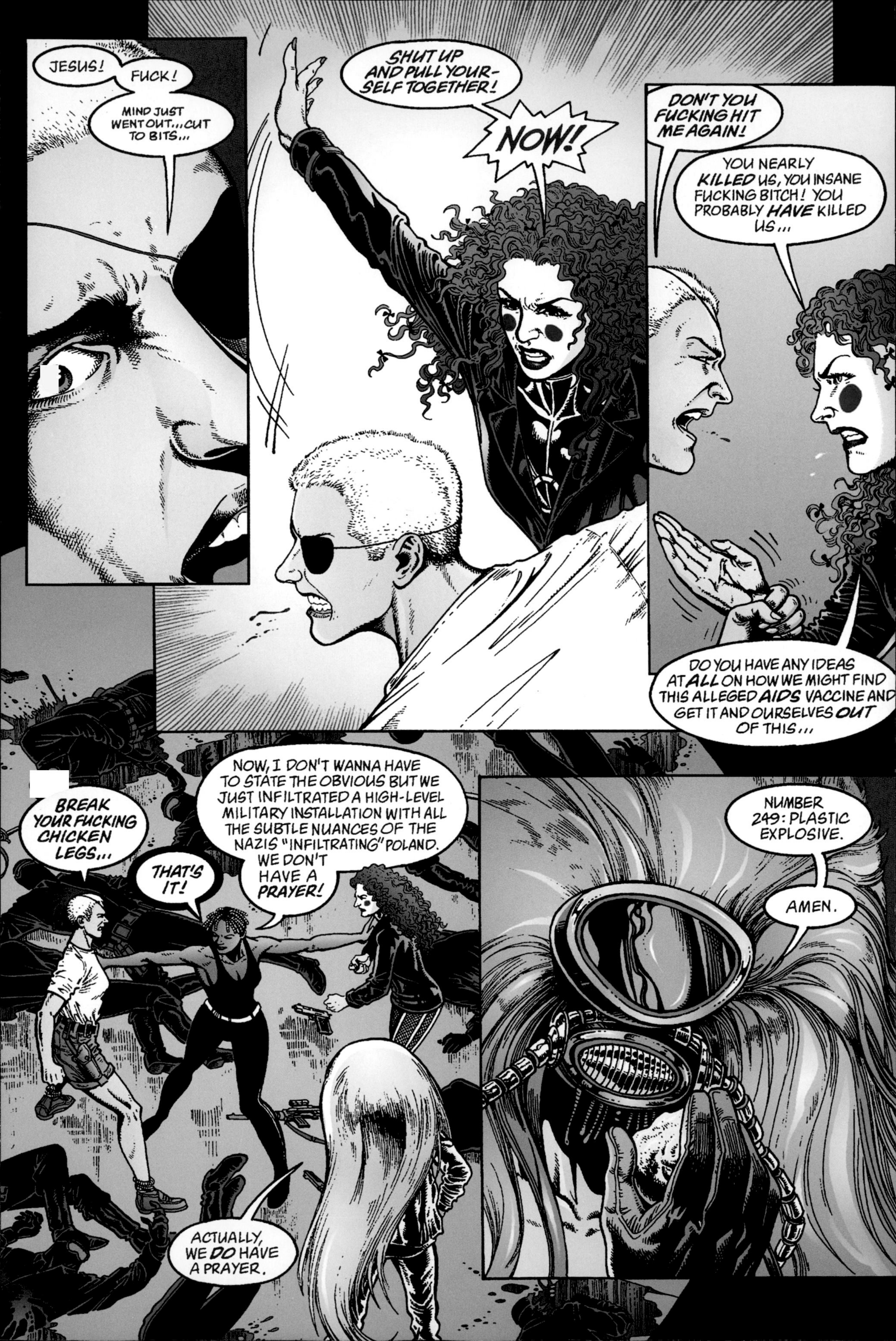
JESUS!
FUCK!
MIND JUST WENT OUT...CUT TO BITS...
SHUT UP AND PULL YOURSELF TOGETHER!
NOW!
DON'T YOU FUCKING HIT ME AGAIN!
YOU NEARLY KILLED US, YOU INSANE FUCKING BITCH! YOU PROBABLY HAVE KILLED US...
DO YOU HAVE ANY IDEAS AT ALL ON HOW WE MIGHT FIND THIS ALLEGED AIDS VACCINE AND GET IT AND OURSELVES OUT OF THIS...
BREAK YOUR FUCKING CHICKEN LEGS...
THAT'S IT!
NOW, I DON'T WANNA HAVE TO STATE THE OBVIOUS BUT WE JUST INFILTRATED A HIGH-LEVEL MILITARY INSTALLATION WITH ALL THE SUBTLE NUANCES OF THE NAZIS "INFILTRATING" POLAND. WE DON'T HAVE A PRAYER!
ACTUALLY, WE DO HAVE A PRAYER.
NUMBER 249: PLASTIC EXPLOSIVE.
AMEN.

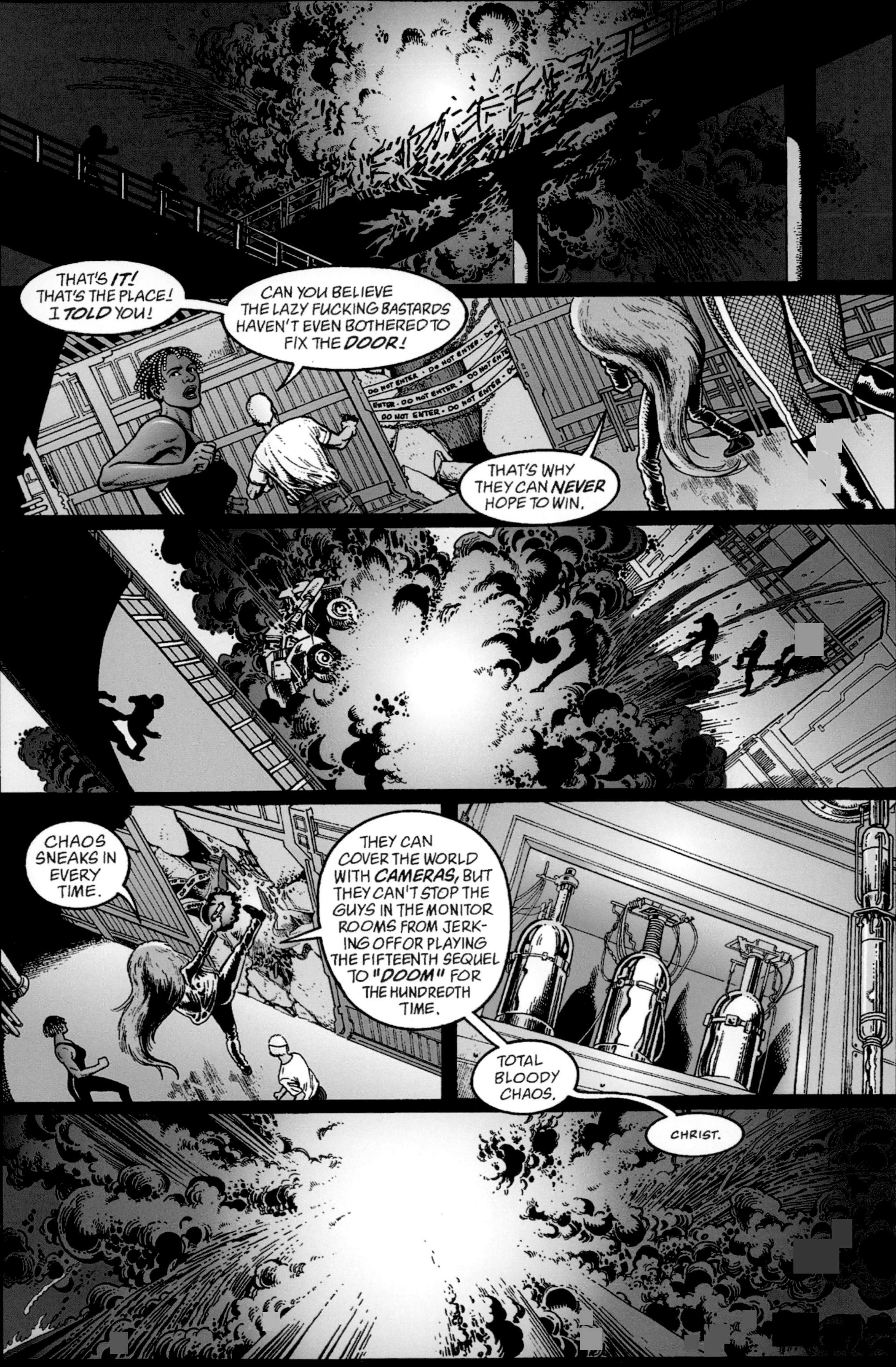
THAT'S IT! THAT'S THE PLACE! I TOLD YOU!
CAN YOU BELIEVE THE LAZY FUCKING BASTARDS HAVEN'T EVEN BOTHERED TO FIX THE DOOR!
THAT'S WHY THEY CAN NEVER HOPE TO WIN.
CHAOS SNEAKS IN EVERY TIME.
THEY CAN COVER THE WORLD WITH CAMERAS, BUT THEY CAN'T STOP THE GUYS IN THE MONITOR ROOMS FROM JERKING OFF OR PLAYING THE FIFTEENTH SEQUEL TO "DOOM" FOR THE HUNDREDTH TIME.
TOTAL BLOODY CHAOS.
CHRIST.

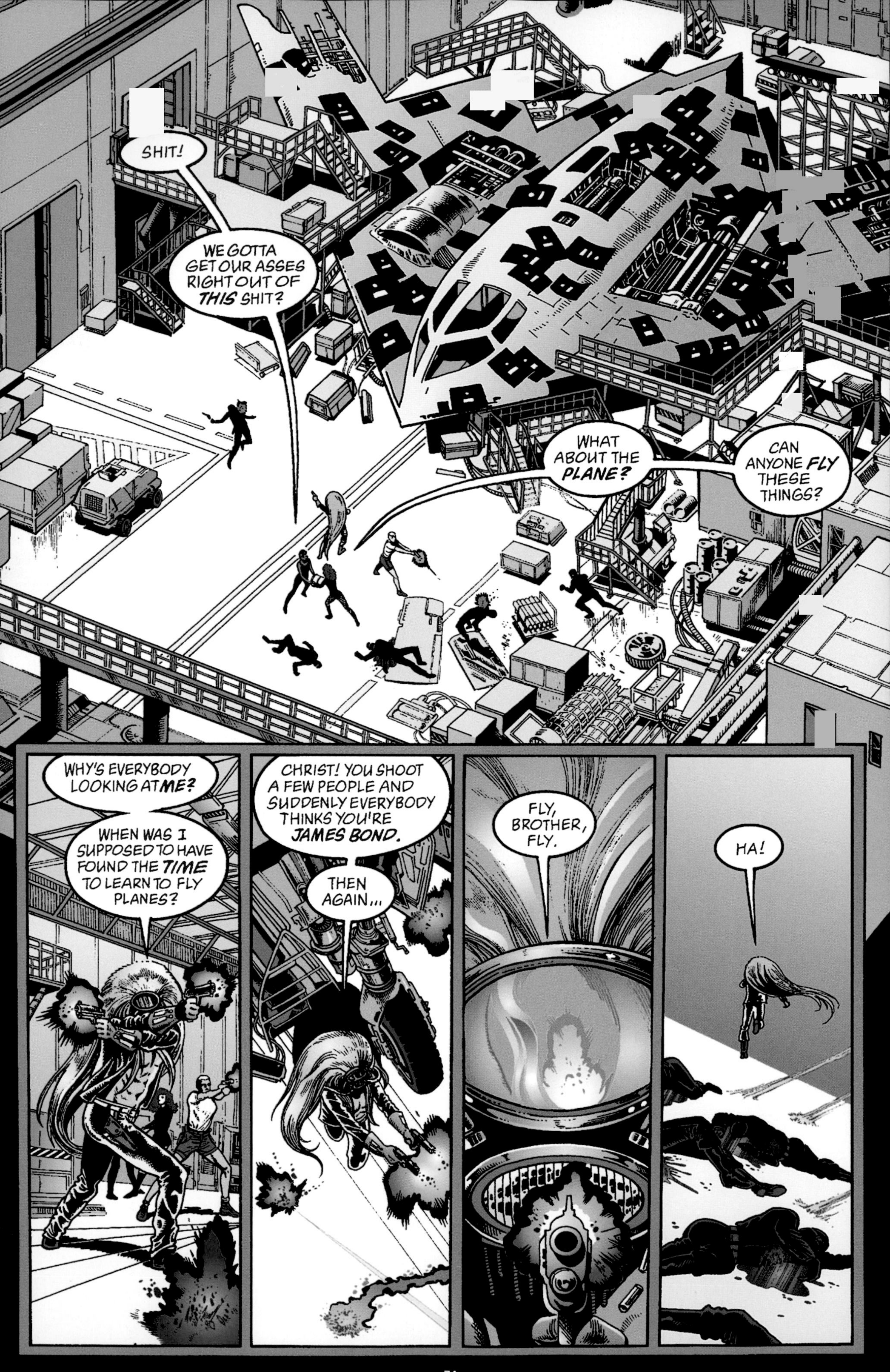
SHIT!
WE GOTTA GET OUR ASSES RIGHT OUT OF THIS SHIT?
WHAT ABOUT THE PLANE?
CAN ANYONE FLY THESE THINGS?
WHY'S EVERYBODY LOOKING AT ME?
WHEN WAS I SUPPOSED TO HAVE FOUND THE TIME TO LEARN TO FLY PLANES?
CHRIST! YOU SHOOT A FEW PEOPLE AND SUDDENLY EVERYBODY THINKS YOU'RE JAMES BOND.
THEN AGAIN...
FLY, BROTHER, FLY.
HA!

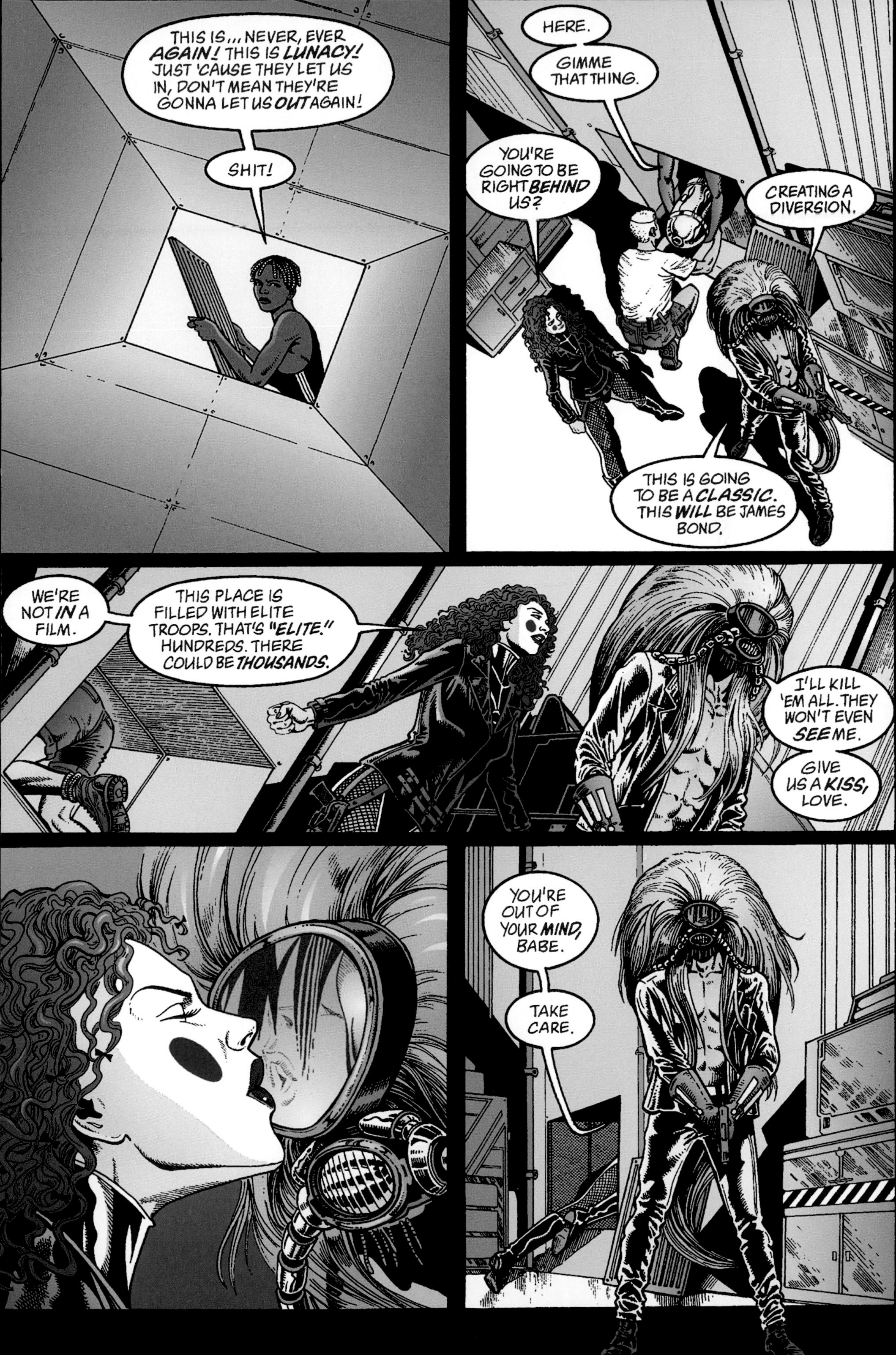
THIS IS... NEVER, EVER AGAIN! THIS IS LUNACY! JUST 'CAUSE THEY LET US IN, DON'T MEAN THEY'RE GONNA LET US OUT AGAIN!
SHIT!
HERE.
GIMME THAT THING.
YOU'RE GOING TO BE RIGHT BEHIND US?
CREATING A DIVERSION.
THIS IS GOING TO BE A CLASSIC. THIS WILL BE JAMES BOND.
WE'RE NOT IN A FILM.
THIS PLACE IS FILLED WITH ELITE TROOPS. THAT'S "ELITE." HUNDREDS. THERE COULD BE THOUSANDS.
I'LL KILL 'EM ALL. THEY WON'T EVEN SEE ME.
GIVE US A KISS, LOVE.
YOU'RE OUT OF YOUR MIND, BABE.
TAKE CARE.

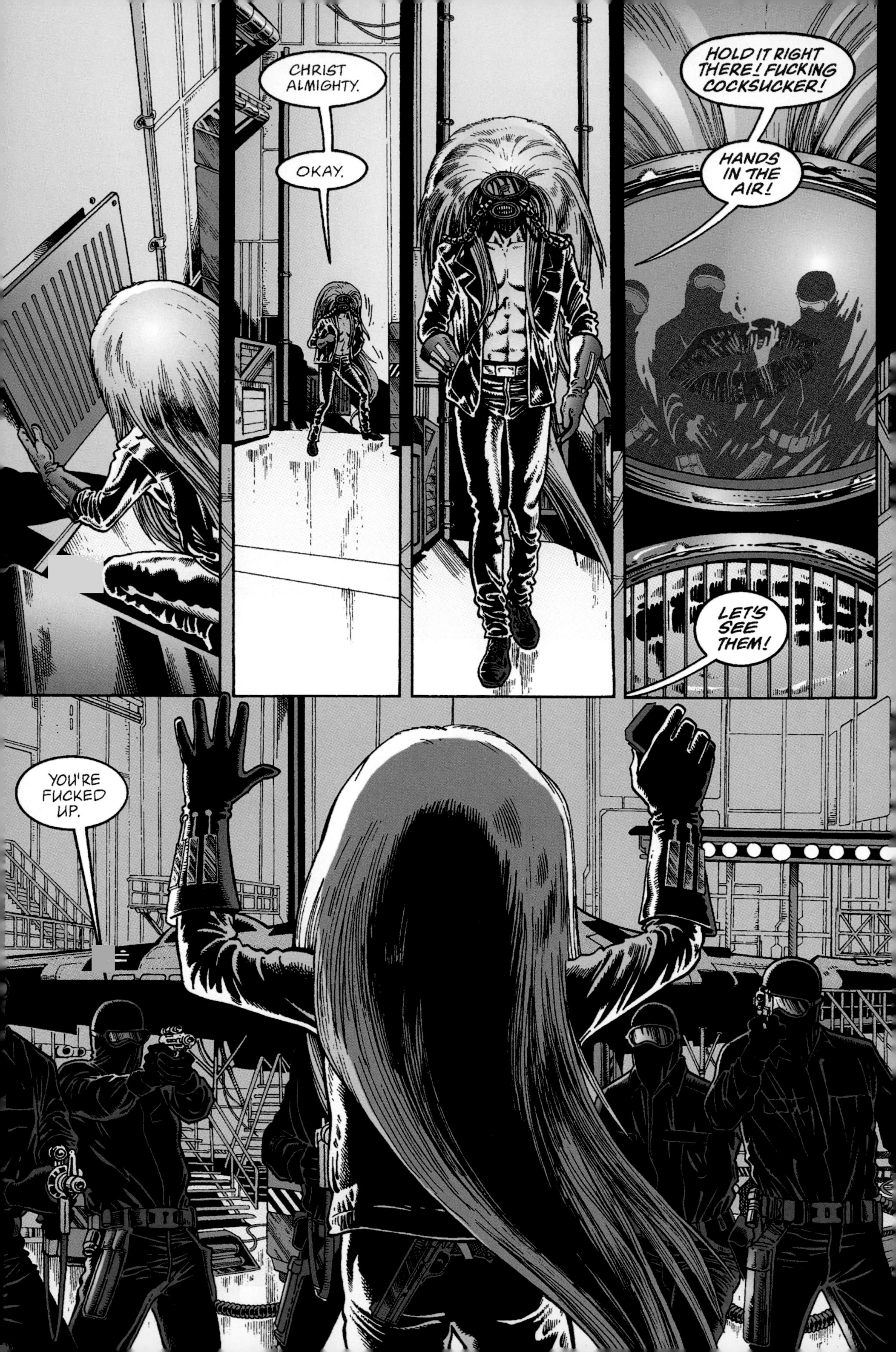
CHRIST ALMIGHTY.
OKAY.
HOLD IT RIGHT THERE! FUCKING COCKSUCKER!
HANDS IN THE AIR!
LET'S SEE THEM!
YOU'RE FUCKED UP.

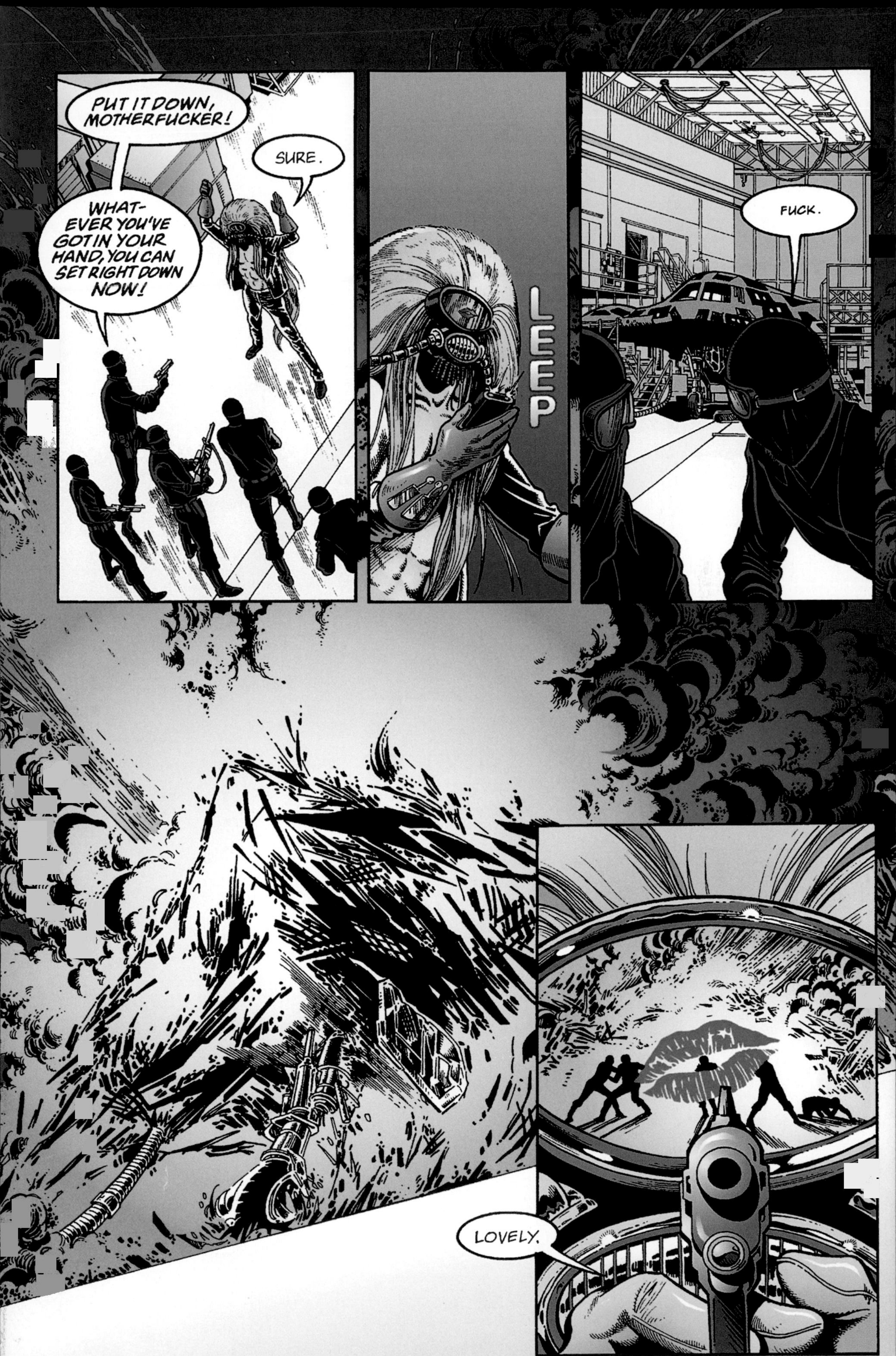
PUT IT DOWN, MOTHERFUCKER!
SURE.
WHAT-EVER YOU'VE GOT IN YOUR HAND, YOU CAN SET RIGHT DOWN NOW!
LEEP
FUCK.
LOVELY.

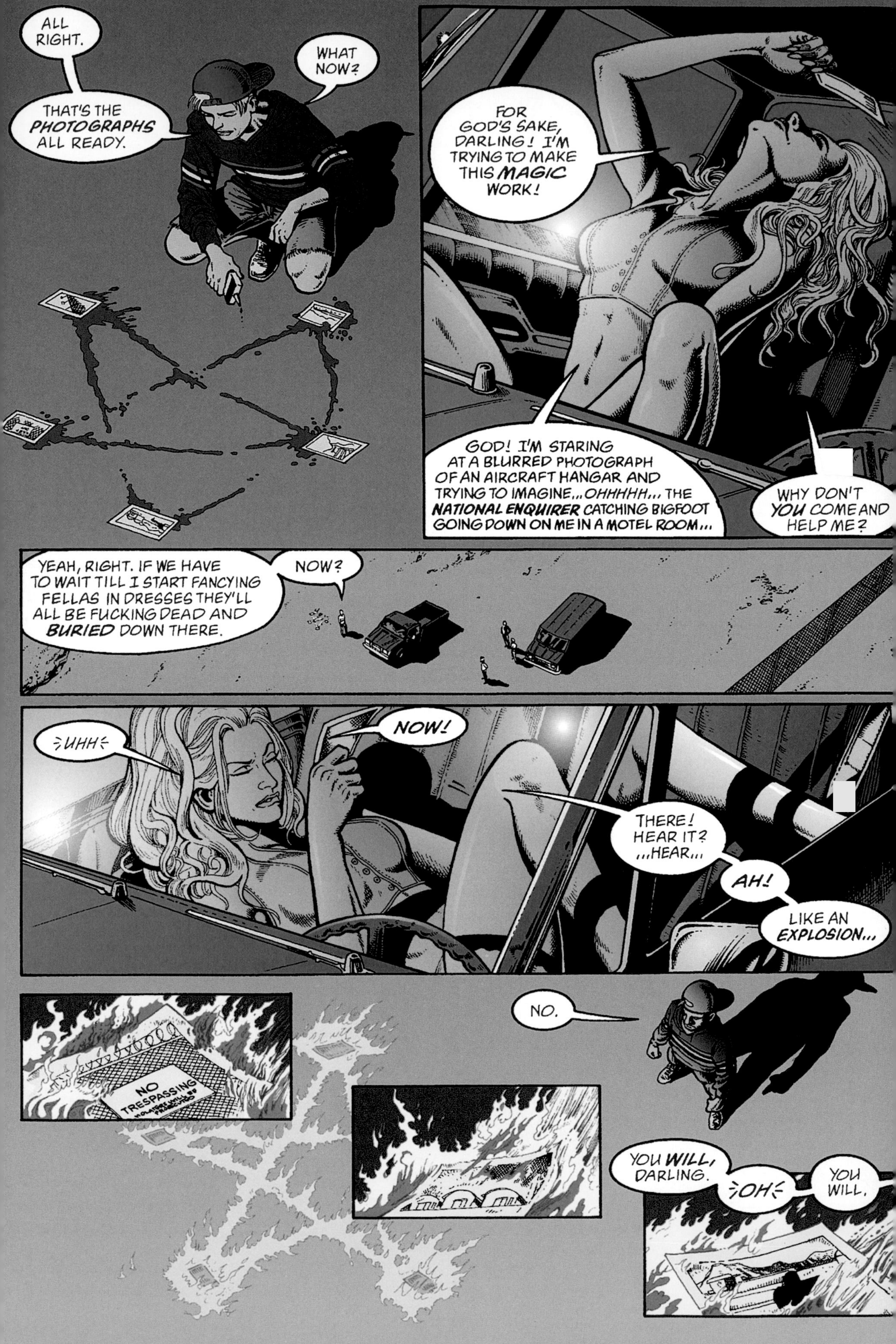
ALL RIGHT.
THAT'S THE PHOTOGRAPHS ALL READY.
WHAT NOW?
FOR GOD'S SAKE, DARLING! I'M TRYING TO MAKE THIS MAGIC WORK!
GOD! I'M STARING AT A BLURRED PHOTOGRAPH OF AN AIRCRAFT HANGAR AND TRYING TO IMAGINE... OHHHHH... THE NATIONAL ENQUIRER CATCHING BIGFOOT GOING DOWN ON ME IN A MOTEL ROOM...
WHY DON'T YOU COME AND HELP ME?
YEAH, RIGHT. IF WE HAVE TO WAIT TILL I START FANCYING FELLAS IN DRESSES THEY'LL ALL BE FUCKING DEAD AND BURIED DOWN THERE.
NOW?
UHH
NOW!
THERE! HEAR IT? ...HEAR...
AH!
LIKE AN EXPLOSION...
NO TRESPASSING
NO.
YOU WILL, DARLING.
OH
YOU WILL.

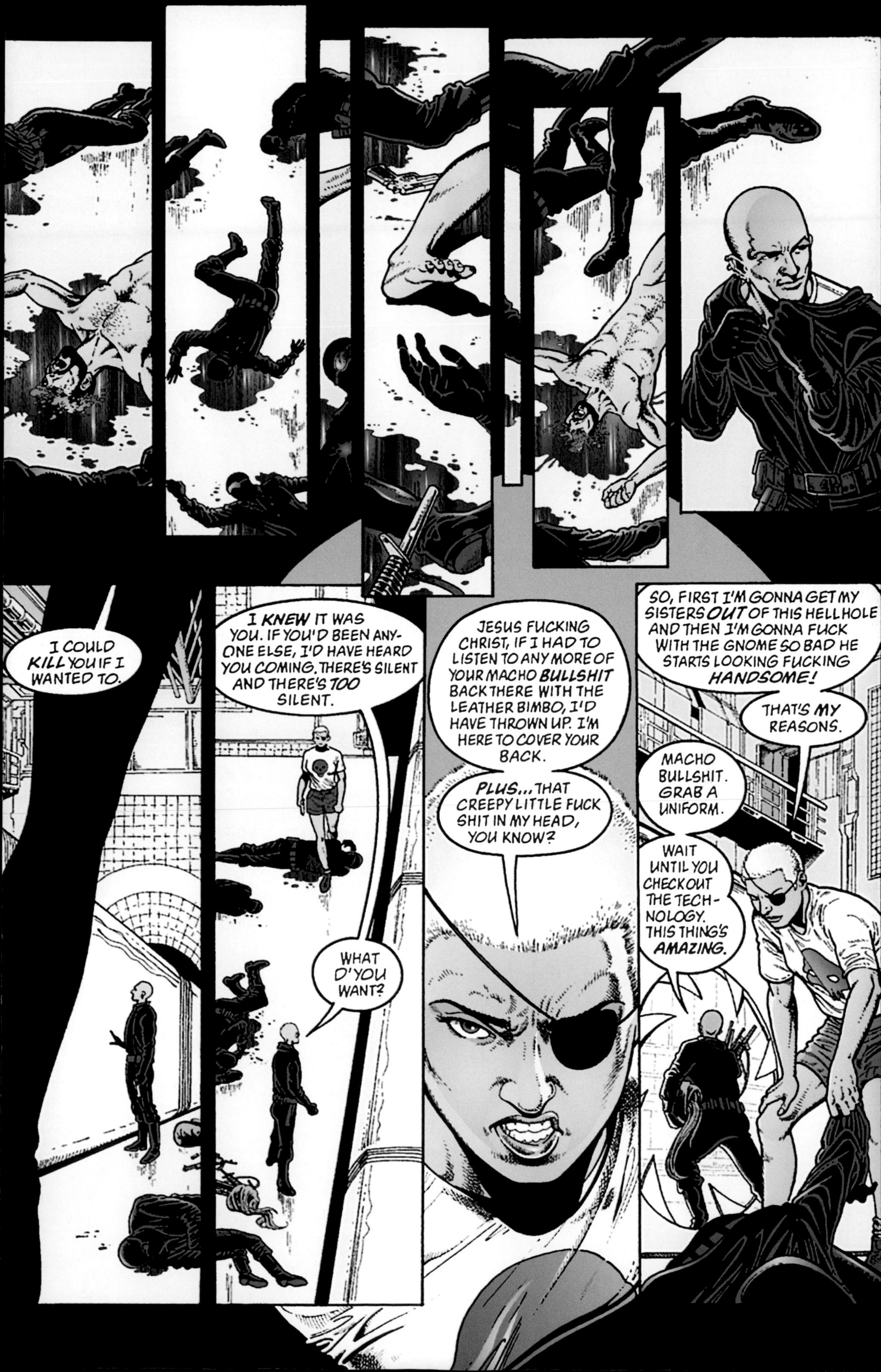
I COULD KILL YOU IF I WANTED TO.
I KNEW IT WAS YOU. IF YOU'D BEEN ANY-ONE ELSE, I'D HAVE HEARD YOU COMING. THERE'S SILENT AND THERE'S TOO SILENT.
WHAT D'YOU WANT?
JESUS FUCKING CHRIST, IF I HAD TO LISTEN TO ANY MORE OF YOUR MACHO BULLSHIT BACK THERE WITH THE LEATHER BIMBO, I'D HAVE THROWN UP. I'M HERE TO COVER YOUR BACK.
PLUS... THAT CREEPY LITTLE FUCK SHIT IN MY HEAD, YOU KNOW?
SO, FIRST I'M GONNA GET MY SISTERS OUT OF THIS HELLHOLE AND THEN I'M GONNA FUCK WITH THE GNOME SO BAD HE STARTS LOOKING FUCKING HANDSOME!
THAT'S MY REASONS.
MACHO BULLSHIT. GRAB A UNIFORM.
WAIT UNTIL YOU CHECK OUT THE TECH-NOLOGY. THIS THING'S AMAZING.

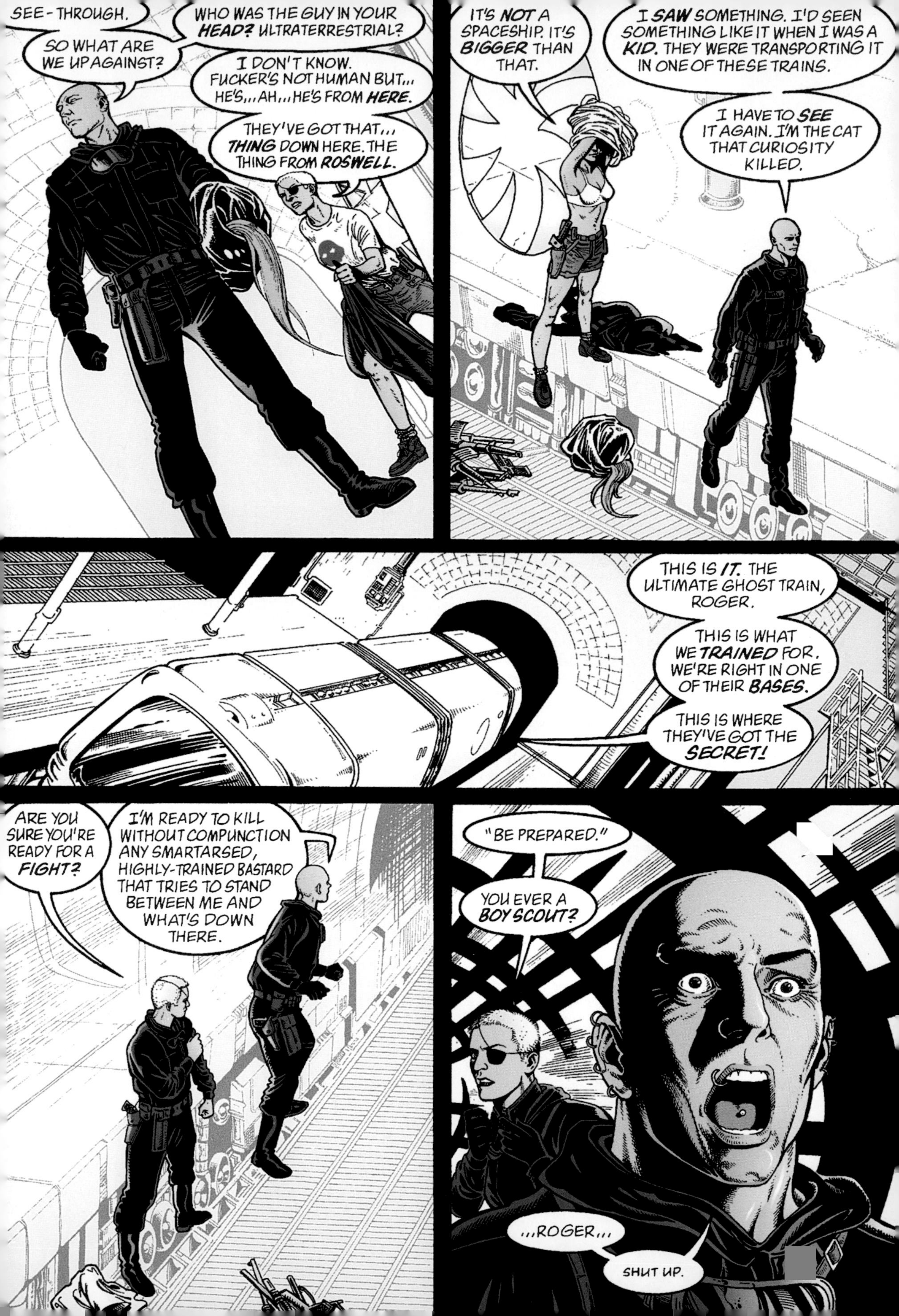
SEE-THROUGH.
SO WHAT ARE WE UP AGAINST?
WHO WAS THE GUY IN YOUR HEAD? ULTRATERRESTRIAL?
I DON'T KNOW. FUCKER'S NOT HUMAN BUT... HE'S... AH... HE'S FROM HERE.
THEY'VE GOT THAT... THING DOWN HERE. THE THING FROM ROSWELL.
IT'S NOT A SPACESHIP. IT'S BIGGER THAN THAT.
I SAW SOMETHING. I'D SEEN SOMETHING LIKE IT WHEN I WAS A KID. THEY WERE TRANSPORTING IT IN ONE OF THESE TRAINS.
I HAVE TO SEE IT AGAIN. I'M THE CAT THAT CURIOSITY KILLED.
THIS IS IT. THE ULTIMATE GHOST TRAIN, ROGER.
THIS IS WHAT WE TRAINED FOR. WE'RE RIGHT IN ONE OF THEIR BASES.
THIS IS WHERE THEY'VE GOT THE SECRET!
ARE YOU SURE YOU'RE READY FOR A FIGHT?
I'M READY TO KILL WITHOUT COMPUNCTION ANY SMARTARSED, HIGHLY-TRAINED BASTARD THAT TRIES TO STAND BETWEEN ME AND WHAT'S DOWN THERE.
"BE PREPARED."
YOU EVER A BOY SCOUT?
...ROGER...
SHUT UP.

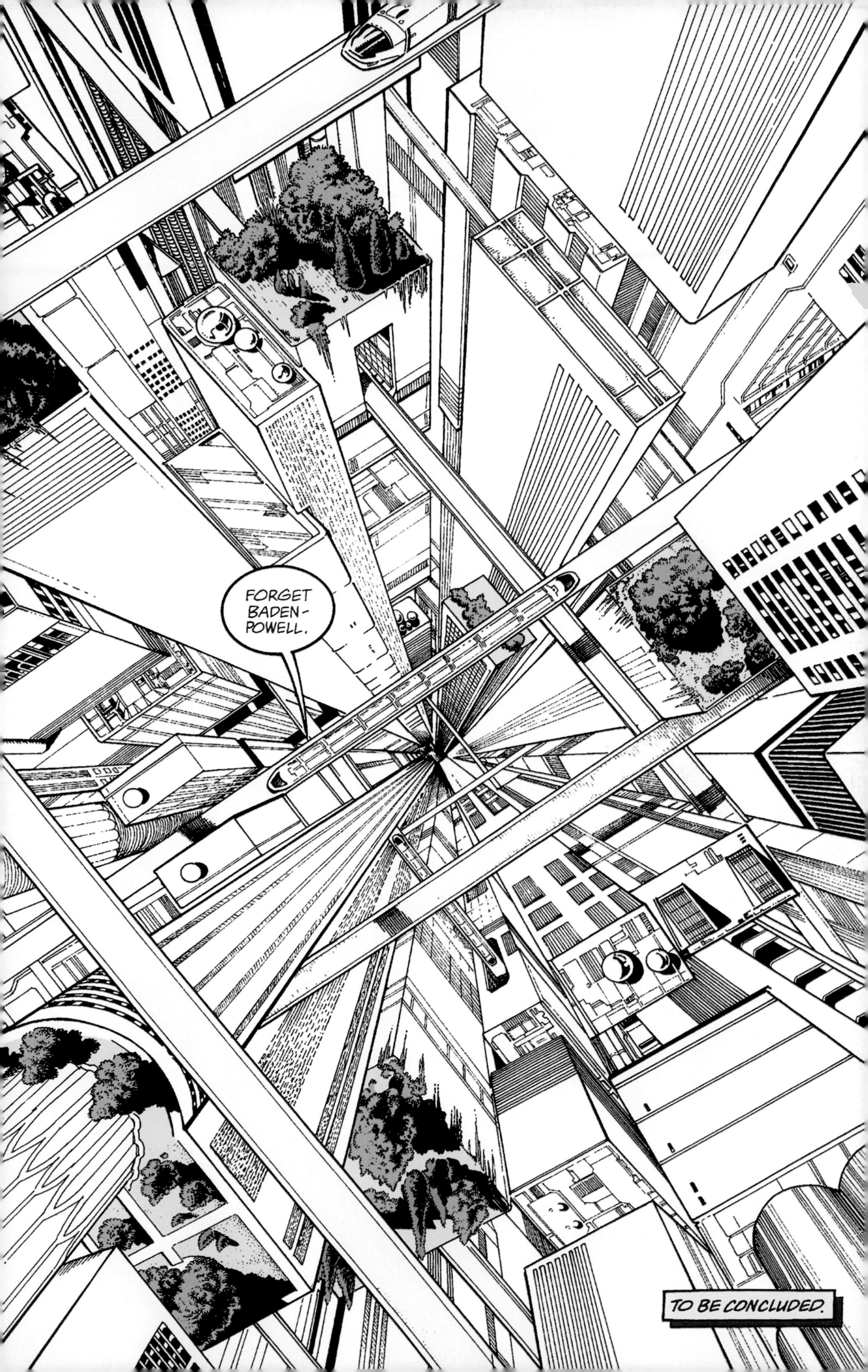
FORGET BADEN-POWELL.
TO BE CONCLUDED.

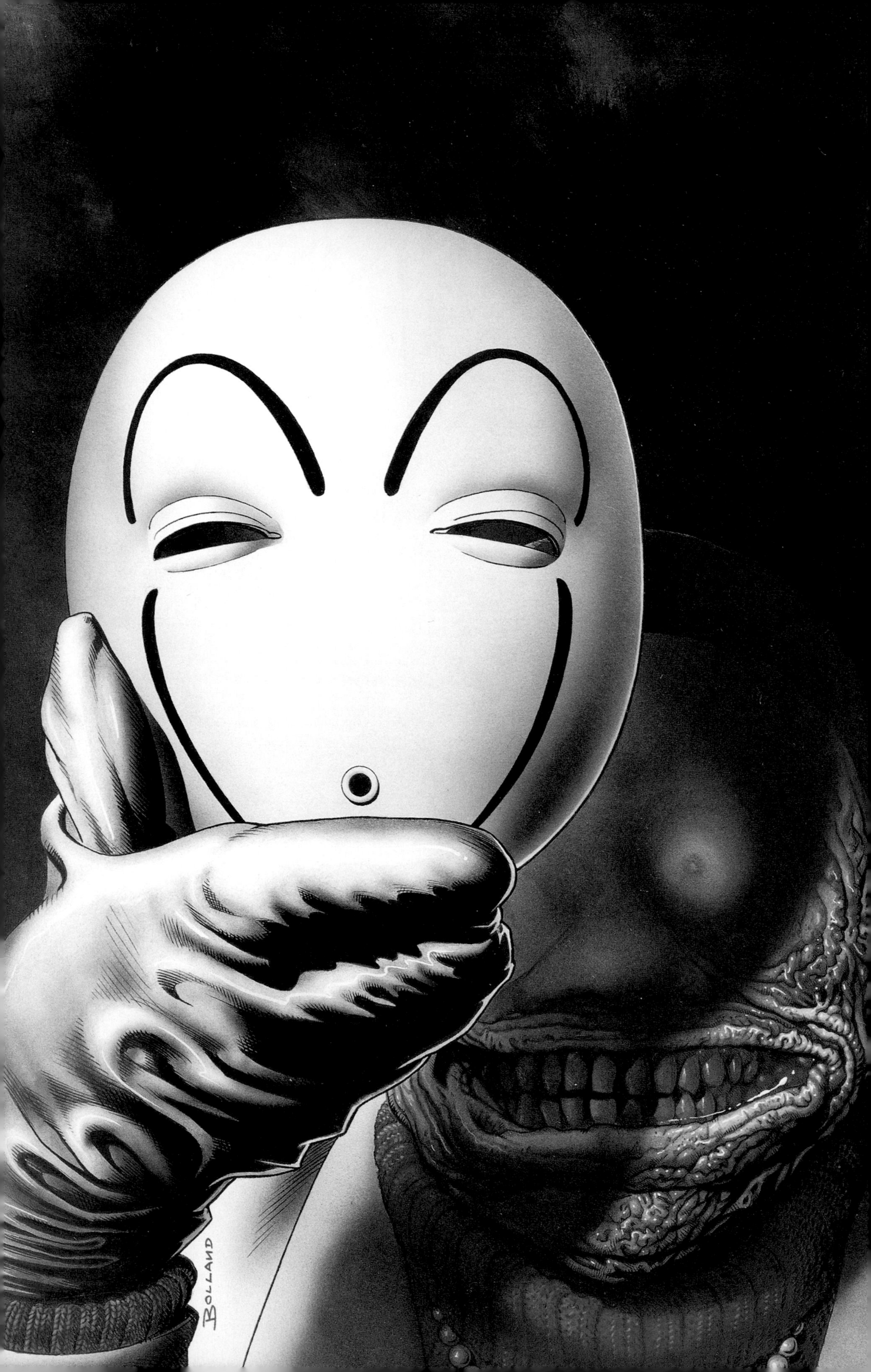
BOLLAND

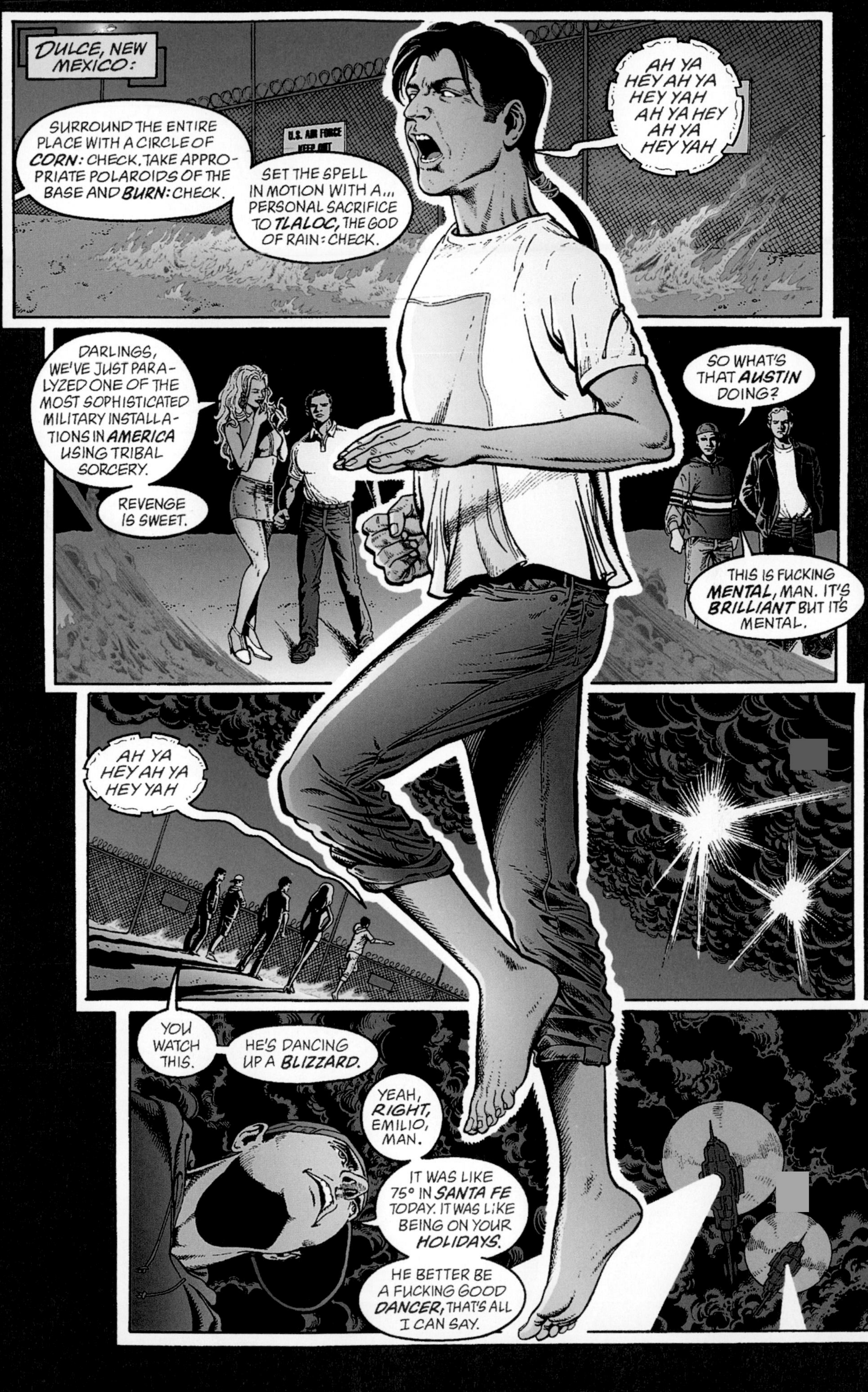
DULCE, NEW MEXICO:
SURROUND THE ENTIRE PLACE WITH A CIRCLE OF CORN: CHECK. TAKE APPROPRIATE POLAROIDS OF THE BASE AND BURN: CHECK.
SET THE SPELL IN MOTION WITH A... PERSONAL SACRIFICE TO TLALOC, THE GOD OF RAIN: CHECK.
AH YA HEY AH YA HEY YAH AH YA HEY AH YA HEY YAH
U.S. AIR FORCE
DARLINGS, WE'VE JUST PARALYZED ONE OF THE MOST SOPHISTICATED MILITARY INSTALLATIONS IN AMERICA USING TRIBAL SORCERY.
REVENGE IS SWEET.
SO WHAT'S THAT AUSTIN DOING?
THIS IS FUCKING MENTAL, MAN. IT'S BRILLIANT BUT IT'S MENTAL.
AH YA HEY AH YA HEY YAH
YOU WATCH THIS.
HE'S DANCING UP A BLIZZARD.
YEAH, RIGHT, EMILIO, MAN.
IT WAS LIKE 75° IN SANTA FE TODAY. IT WAS LIKE BEING ON YOUR HOLIDAYS.
HE BETTER BE A FUCKING GOOD DANCER, THAT'S ALL I CAN SAY.

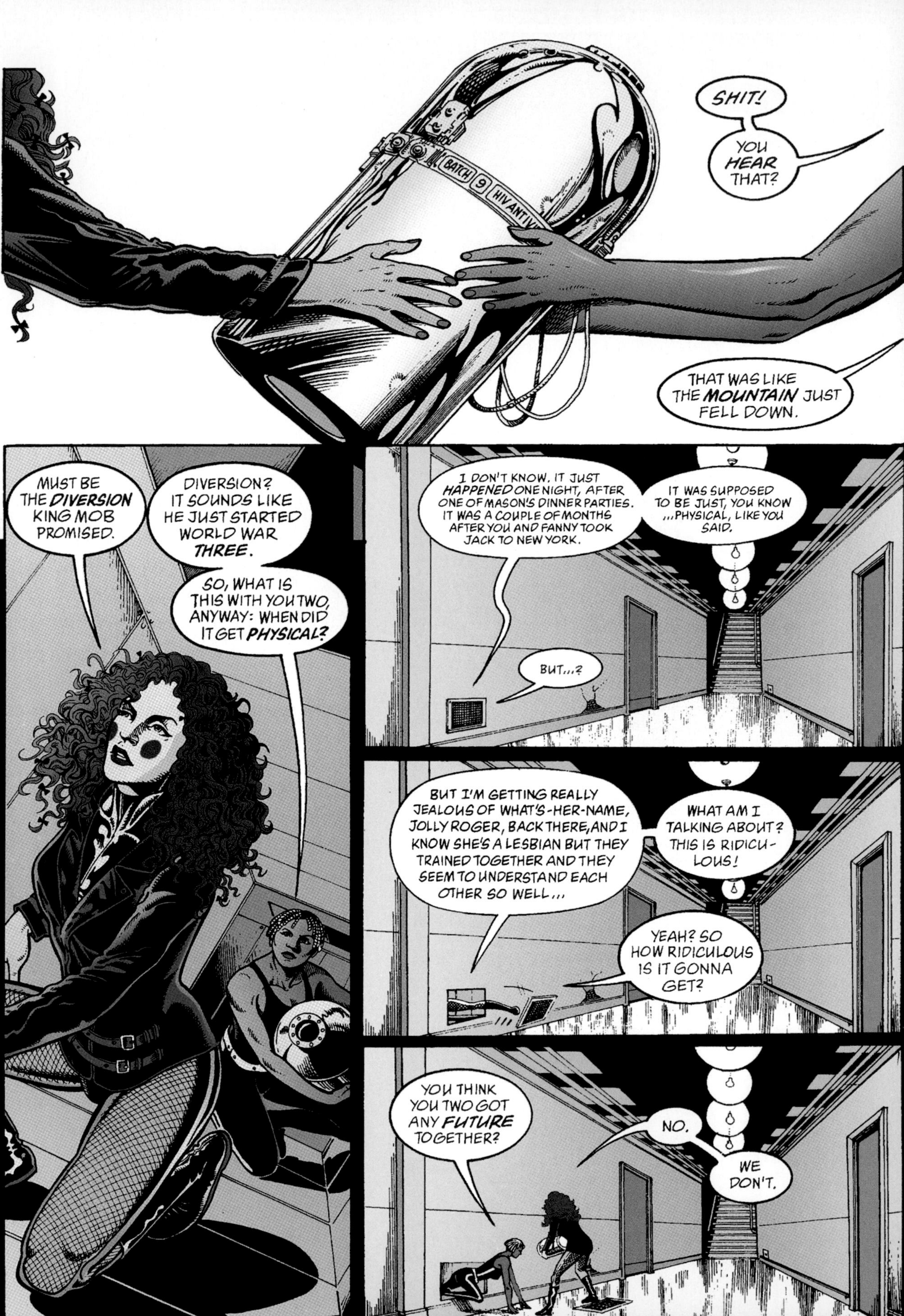
BATCH 9 HIV ANTIV
SHIT!
YOU HEAR THAT?
THAT WAS LIKE THE MOUNTAIN JUST FELL DOWN.
MUST BE THE DIVERSION KING MOB PROMISED.
DIVERSION? IT SOUNDS LIKE HE JUST STARTED WORLD WAR THREE.
SO, WHAT IS THIS WITH YOU TWO, ANYWAY: WHEN DID IT GET PHYSICAL?
I DON'T KNOW. IT JUST HAPPENED ONE NIGHT, AFTER ONE OF MASON'S DINNER PARTIES. IT WAS A COUPLE OF MONTHS AFTER YOU AND FANNY TOOK JACK TO NEW YORK.
IT WAS SUPPOSED TO BE JUST, YOU KNOW ...PHYSICAL, LIKE YOU SAID.
BUT...?
BUT I'M GETTING REALLY JEALOUS OF WHAT'S-HER-NAME, JOLLY ROGER, BACK THERE, AND I KNOW SHE'S A LESBIAN BUT THEY TRAINED TOGETHER AND THEY SEEM TO UNDERSTAND EACH OTHER SO WELL...
WHAT AM I TALKING ABOUT? THIS IS RIDICU-LOUS!
YEAH? SO HOW RIDICULOUS IS IT GONNA GET?
YOU THINK YOU TWO GOT ANY FUTURE TOGETHER?
NO.
WE DON'T.

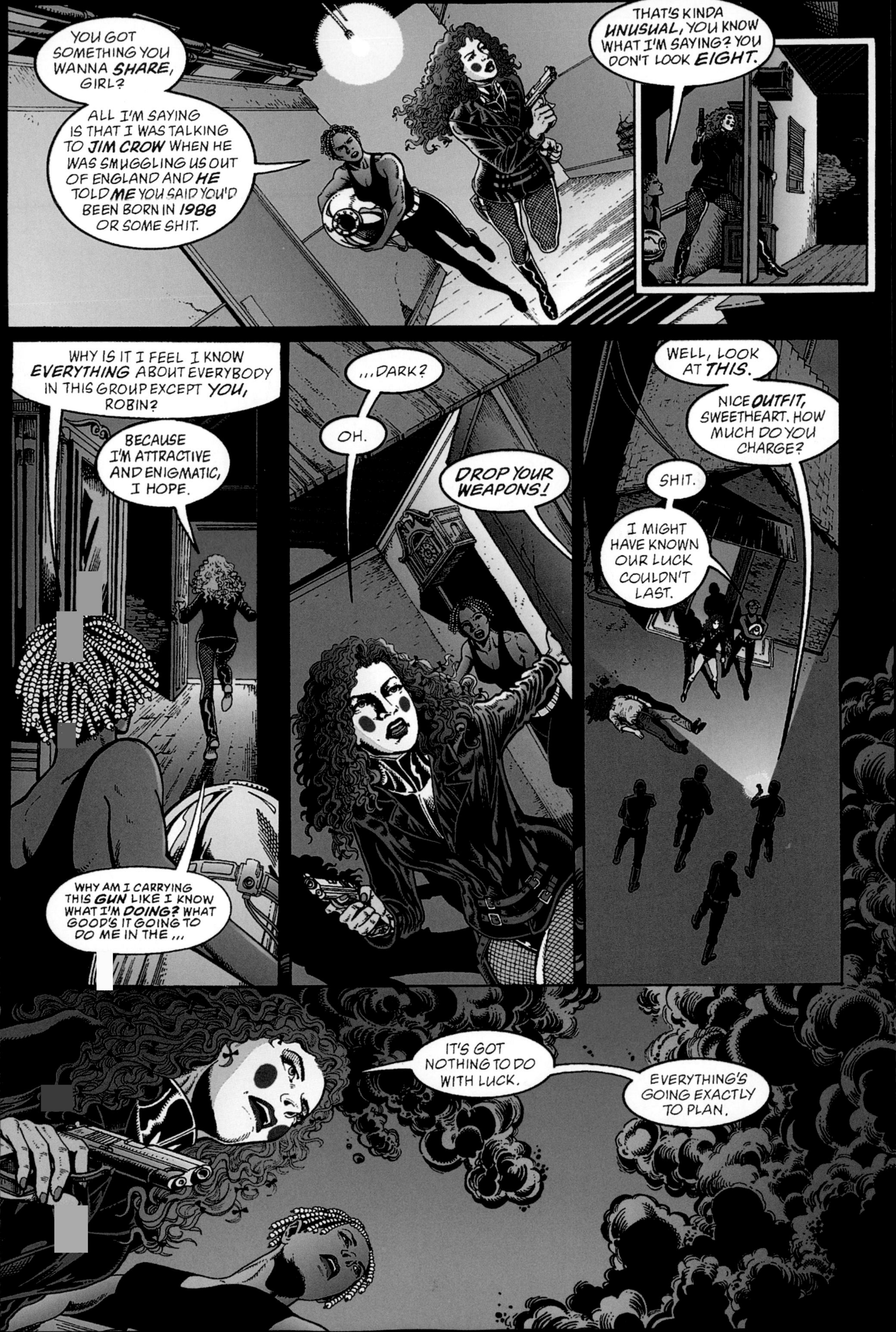

YOU GOT SOMETHING YOU WANNA SHARE, GIRL?
ALL I'M SAYING IS THAT I WAS TALKING TO JIM CROW WHEN HE WAS SMUGGLING US OUT OF ENGLAND AND HE TOLD ME YOU SAID YOU'D BEEN BORN IN 1988 OR SOME SHIT.
THAT'S KINDA UNUSUAL, YOU KNOW WHAT I'M SAYING? YOU DON'T LOOK EIGHT.
WHY IS IT I FEEL I KNOW EVERYTHING ABOUT EVERYBODY IN THIS GROUP EXCEPT YOU, ROBIN?
BECAUSE I'M ATTRACTIVE AND ENIGMATIC, I HOPE.
WHY AM I CARRYING THIS GUN LIKE I KNOW WHAT I'M DOING? WHAT GOOD'S IT GOING TO DO ME IN THE ...
...DARK?
OH.
DROP YOUR WEAPONS!
WELL, LOOK AT THIS.
NICE OUTFIT, SWEETHEART. HOW MUCH DO YOU CHARGE?
SHIT.
I MIGHT HAVE KNOWN OUR LUCK COULDN'T LAST.
IT'S GOT NOTHING TO DO WITH LUCK.
EVERYTHING'S GOING EXACTLY TO PLAN.

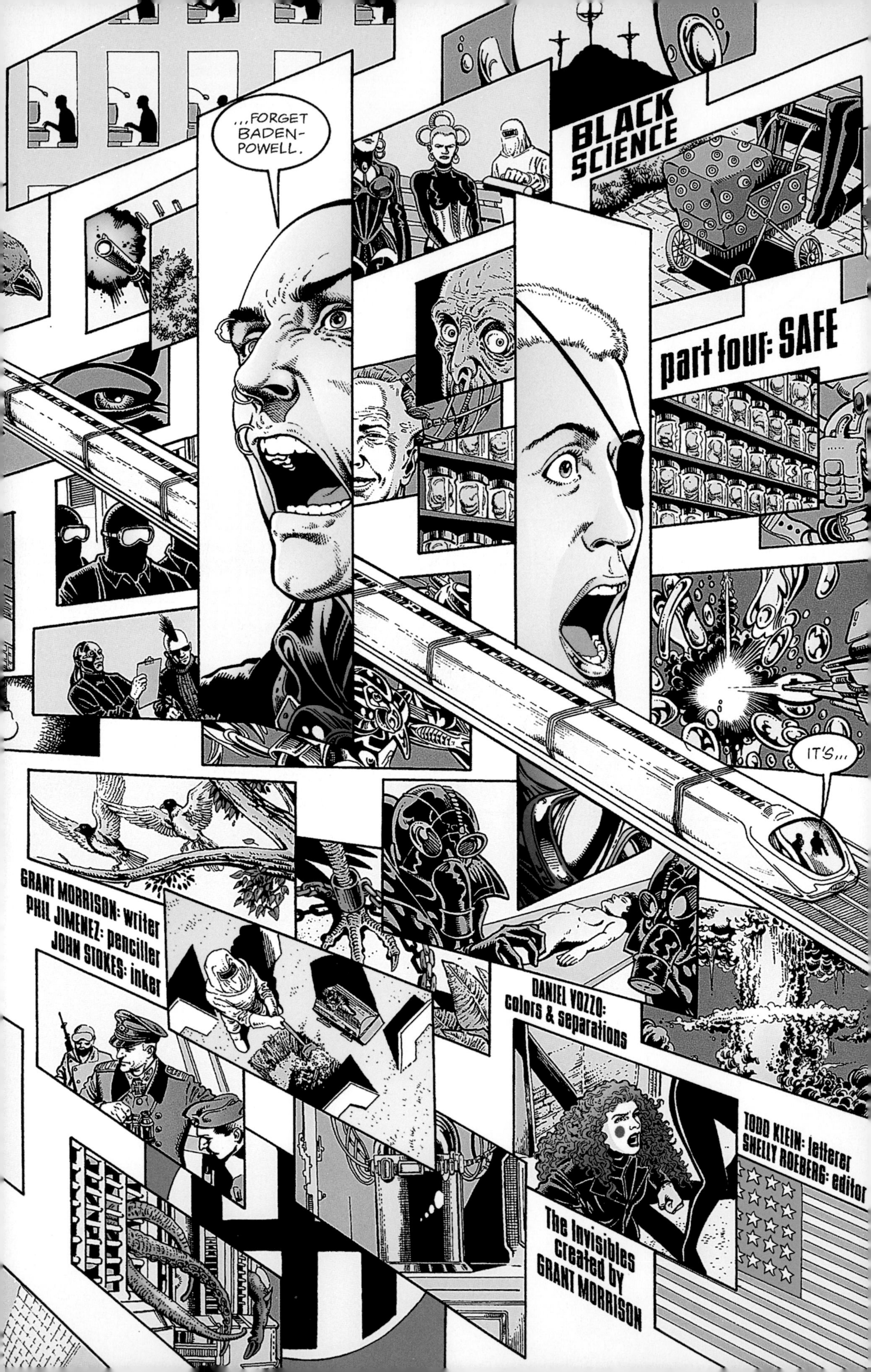

...FORGET BADEN-POWELL.
BLACK SCIENCE
part four: SAFE
IT'S...
GRANT MORRISON: writer
PHIL JIMENEZ: penciller
JOHN STOKES: inker
DANIEL VOZZO: colors & separations
TODD KLEIN: letterer
SHELLY ROEBERG: editor
The Invisibles created by GRANT MORRISON

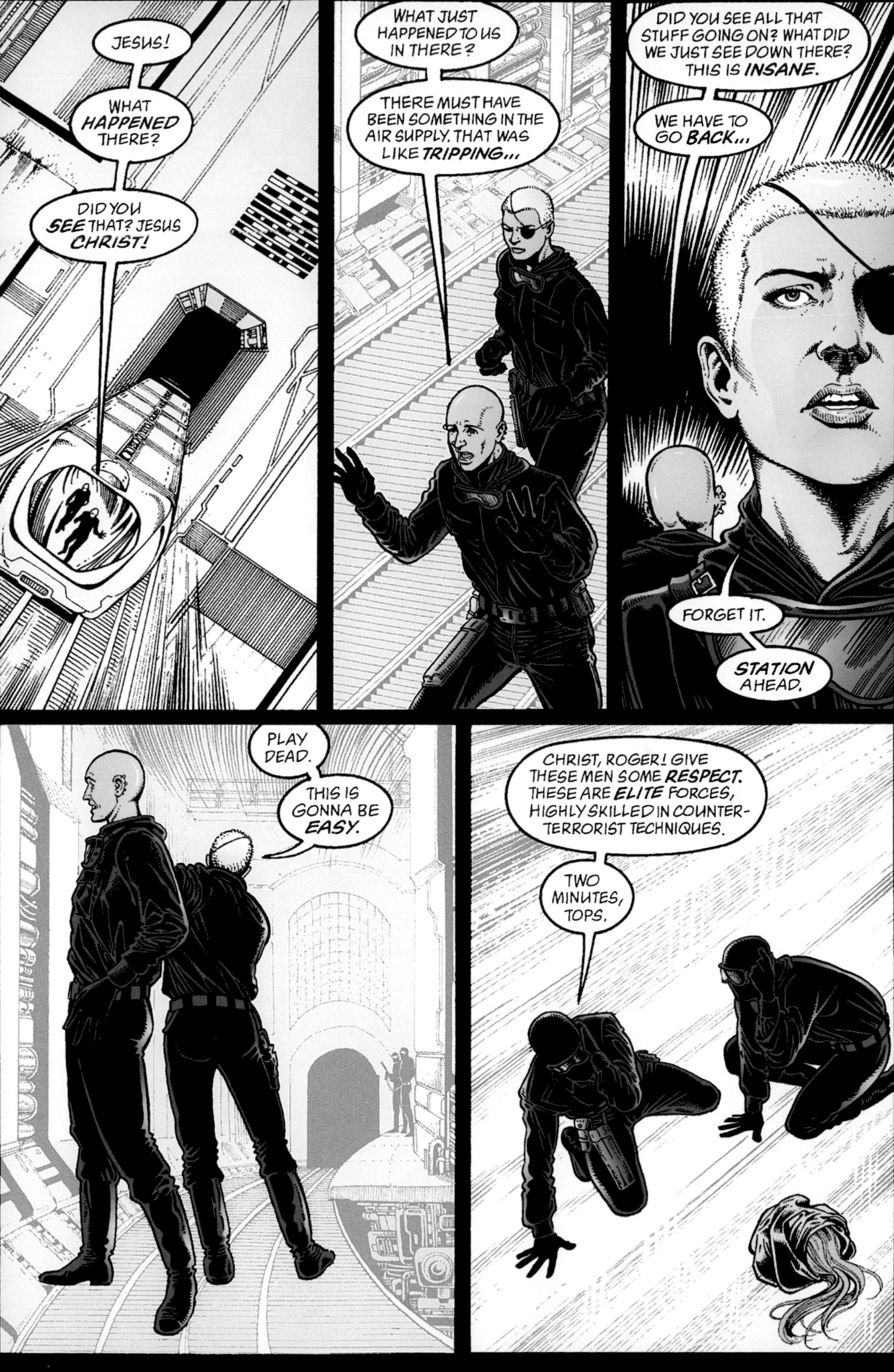
JESUS!
WHAT HAPPENED THERE?
DID YOU SEE THAT? JESUS CHRIST!
WHAT JUST HAPPENED TO US IN THERE?
THERE MUST HAVE BEEN SOMETHING IN THE AIR SUPPLY. THAT WAS LIKE TRIPPING...
DID YOU SEE ALL THAT STUFF GOING ON? WHAT DID WE JUST SEE DOWN THERE? THIS IS INSANE.
WE HAVE TO GO BACK...
FORGET IT.
STATION AHEAD.
PLAY DEAD.
THIS IS GONNA BE EASY.
CHRIST, ROGER! GIVE THESE MEN SOME RESPECT. THESE ARE ELITE FORCES, HIGHLY SKILLED IN COUNTER-TERRORIST TECHNIQUES.
TWO MINUTES, TOPS.

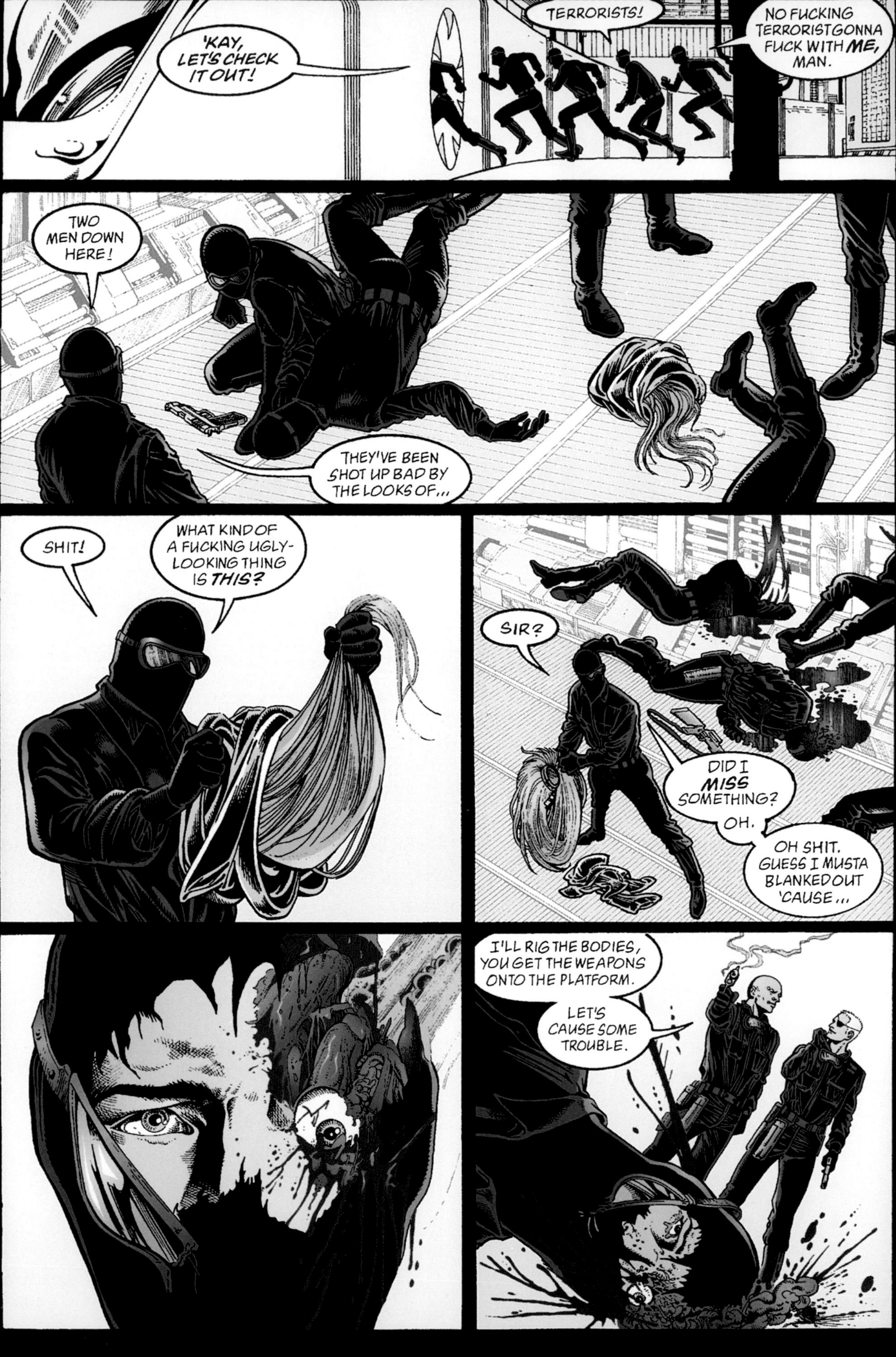
'KAY, LET'S CHECK IT OUT!
TERRORISTS!
NO FUCKING TERRORIST GONNA FUCK WITH ME, MAN.
TWO MEN DOWN HERE!
THEY'VE BEEN SHOT UP BAD BY THE LOOKS OF...
SHIT!
WHAT KIND OF A FUCKING UGLY-LOOKING THING IS THIS?
SIR?
DID I MISS SOMETHING?
OH.
OH SHIT. GUESS I MUSTA BLANKED OUT 'CAUSE...
I'LL RIG THE BODIES, YOU GET THE WEAPONS ONTO THE PLATFORM.
LET'S CAUSE SOME TROUBLE.

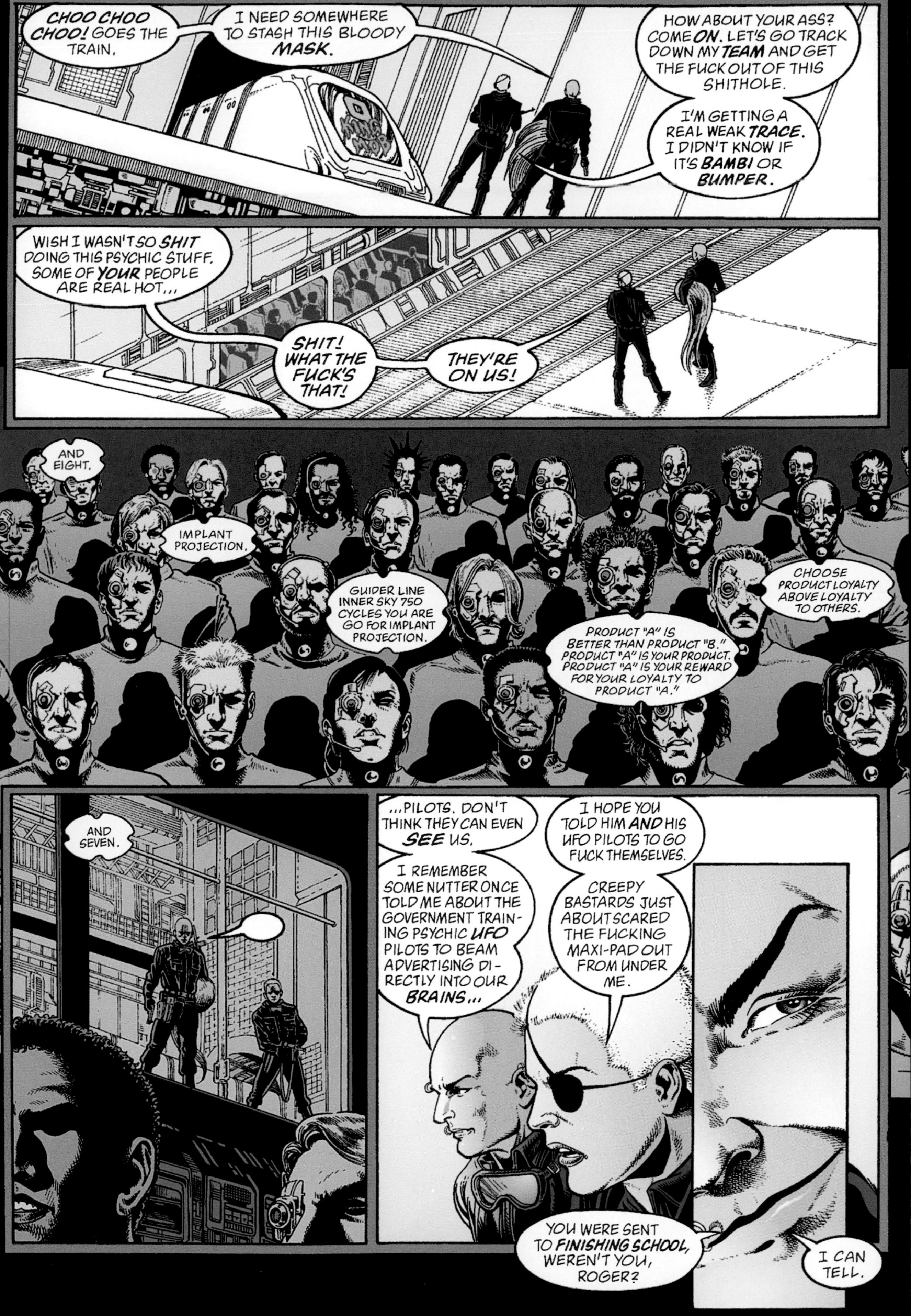

CHOO CHOO CHOO! GOES THE TRAIN.
I NEED SOMEWHERE TO STASH THIS BLOODY MASK.
HOW ABOUT YOUR ASS? COME ON. LET'S GO TRACK DOWN MY TEAM AND GET THE FUCK OUT OF THIS SHITHOLE.
I'M GETTING A REAL WEAK TRACE. I DIDN'T KNOW IF IT'S BAMBI OR BUMPER.
WISH I WASN'T SO SHIT DOING THIS PSYCHIC STUFF. SOME OF YOUR PEOPLE ARE REAL HOT...
SHIT! WHAT THE FUCK'S THAT!
THEY'RE ON US!
AND EIGHT.
IMPLANT PROJECTION.
GUIDER LINE INNER SKY 750 CYCLES YOU ARE GO FOR IMPLANT PROJECTION.
CHOOSE PRODUCT LOYALTY ABOVE LOYALTY TO OTHERS.
PRODUCT "A" IS BETTER THAN PRODUCT "B." PRODUCT "A" IS YOUR PRODUCT. PRODUCT "A" IS YOUR REWARD FOR YOUR LOYALTY TO PRODUCT "A."
AND SEVEN.
...PILOTS. DON'T THINK THEY CAN EVEN SEE US.
I REMEMBER SOME NUTTER ONCE TOLD ME ABOUT THE GOVERNMENT TRAINING PSYCHIC UFO PILOTS TO BEAM ADVERTISING DIRECTLY INTO OUR BRAINS...
I HOPE YOU TOLD HIM AND HIS UFO PILOTS TO GO FUCK THEMSELVES.
CREEPY BASTARDS JUST ABOUT SCARED THE FUCKING MAXI-PAD OUT FROM UNDER ME.
YOU WERE SENT TO FINISHING SCHOOL, WEREN'T YOU, ROGER?
I CAN TELL.

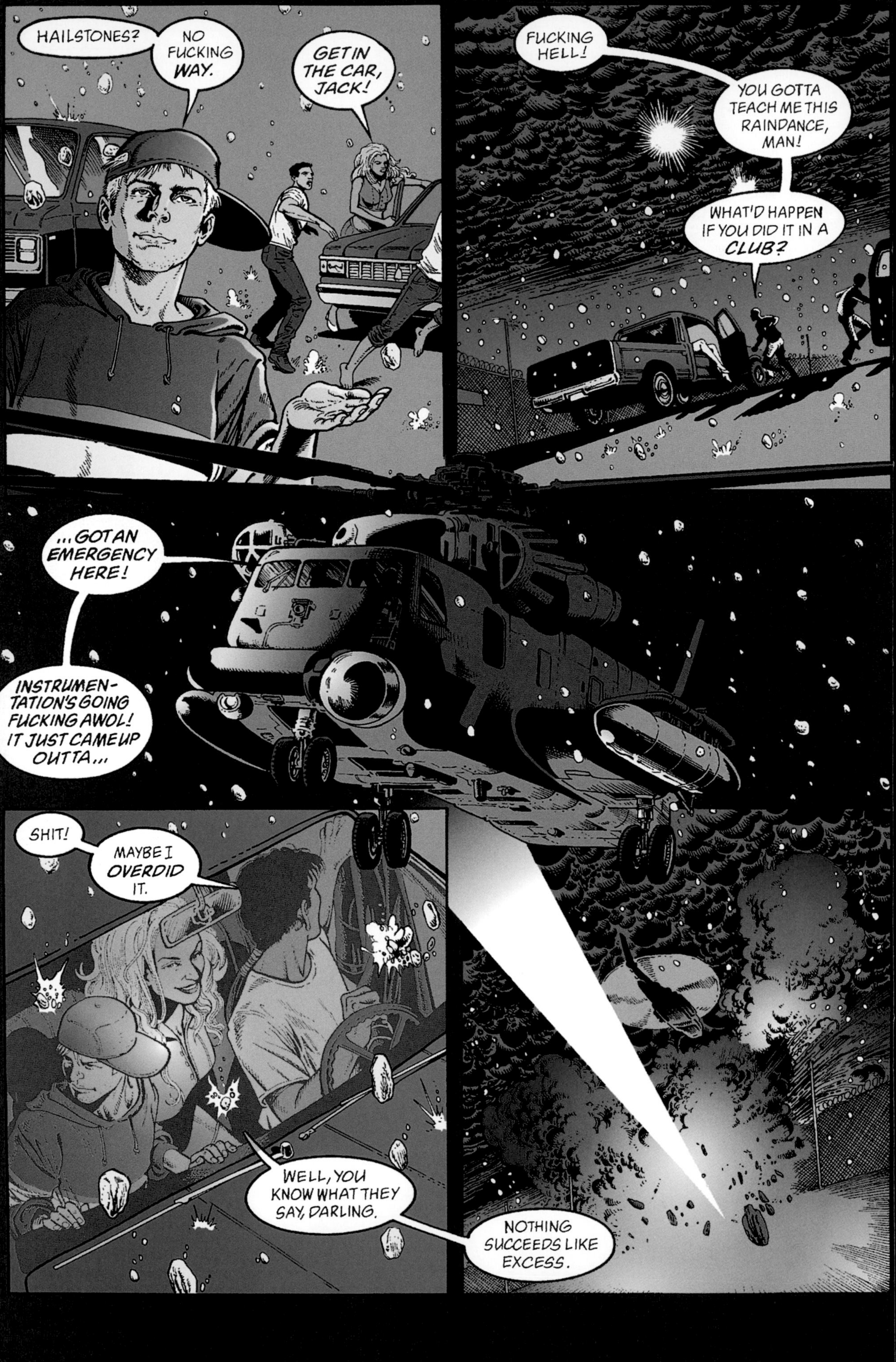
HAILSTONES?
NO FUCKING WAY.
GET IN THE CAR, JACK!
FUCKING HELL!
YOU GOTTA TEACH ME THIS RAINDANCE, MAN!
WHAT'D HAPPEN IF YOU DID IT IN A CLUB?
...GOT AN EMERGENCY HERE!
INSTRUMEN-TATION'S GOING FUCKING AWOL! IT JUST CAME UP OUTTA...
SHIT!
MAYBE I OVERDID IT.
WELL, YOU KNOW WHAT THEY SAY, DARLING.
NOTHING SUCCEEDS LIKE EXCESS.

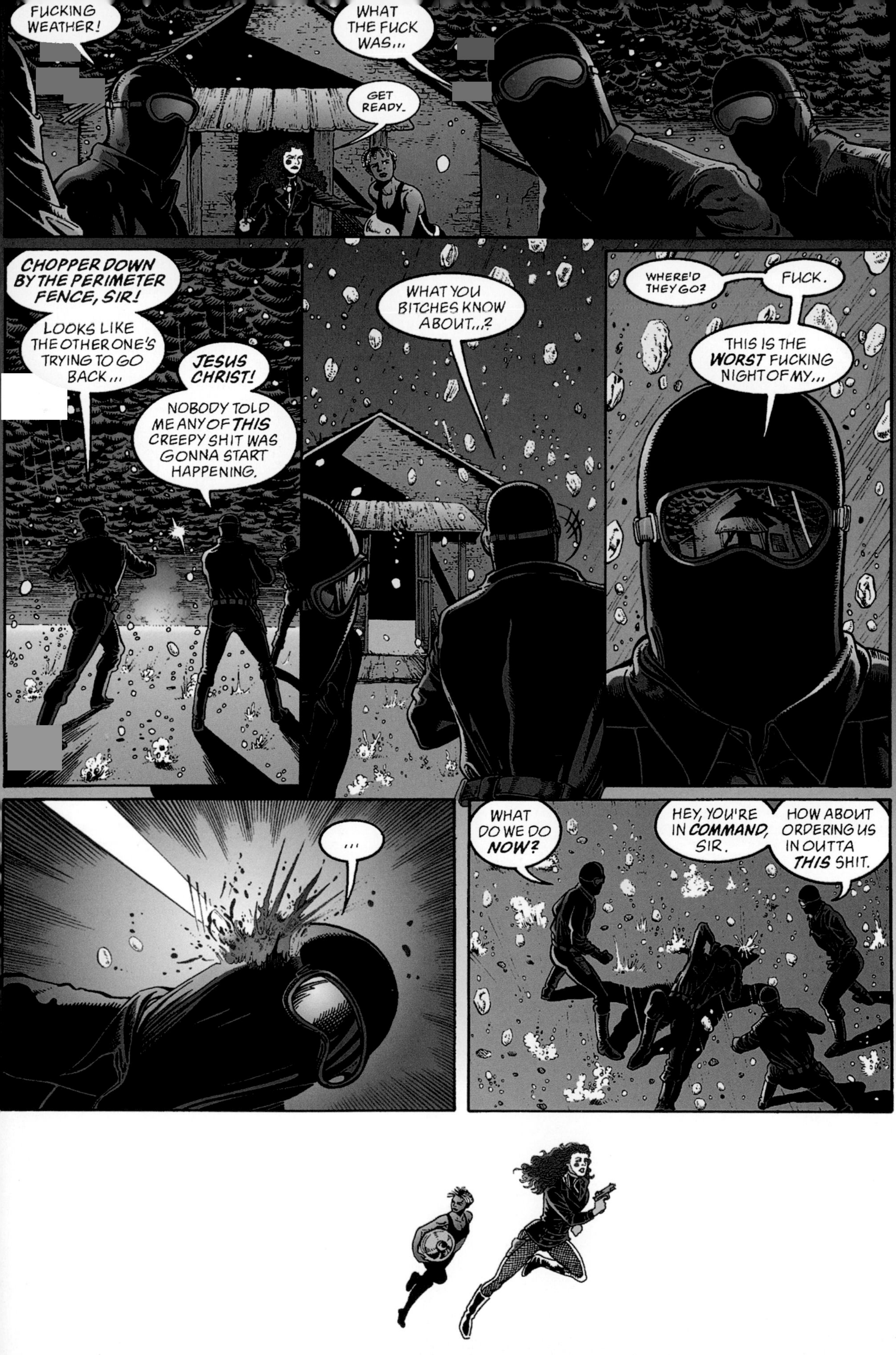
FUCKING WEATHER!
WHAT THE FUCK WAS...
GET READY.
CHOPPER DOWN BY THE PERIMETER FENCE, SIR!
LOOKS LIKE THE OTHER ONE'S TRYING TO GO BACK...
JESUS CHRIST!
NOBODY TOLD ME ANY OF THIS CREEPY SHIT WAS GONNA START HAPPENING.
WHAT YOU BITCHES KNOW ABOUT...?
WHERE'D THEY GO?
FUCK.
THIS IS THE WORST FUCKING NIGHT OF MY...
...
WHAT DO WE DO NOW?
HEY, YOU'RE IN COMMAND, SIR.
HOW ABOUT ORDERING US IN OUTTA THIS SHIT.

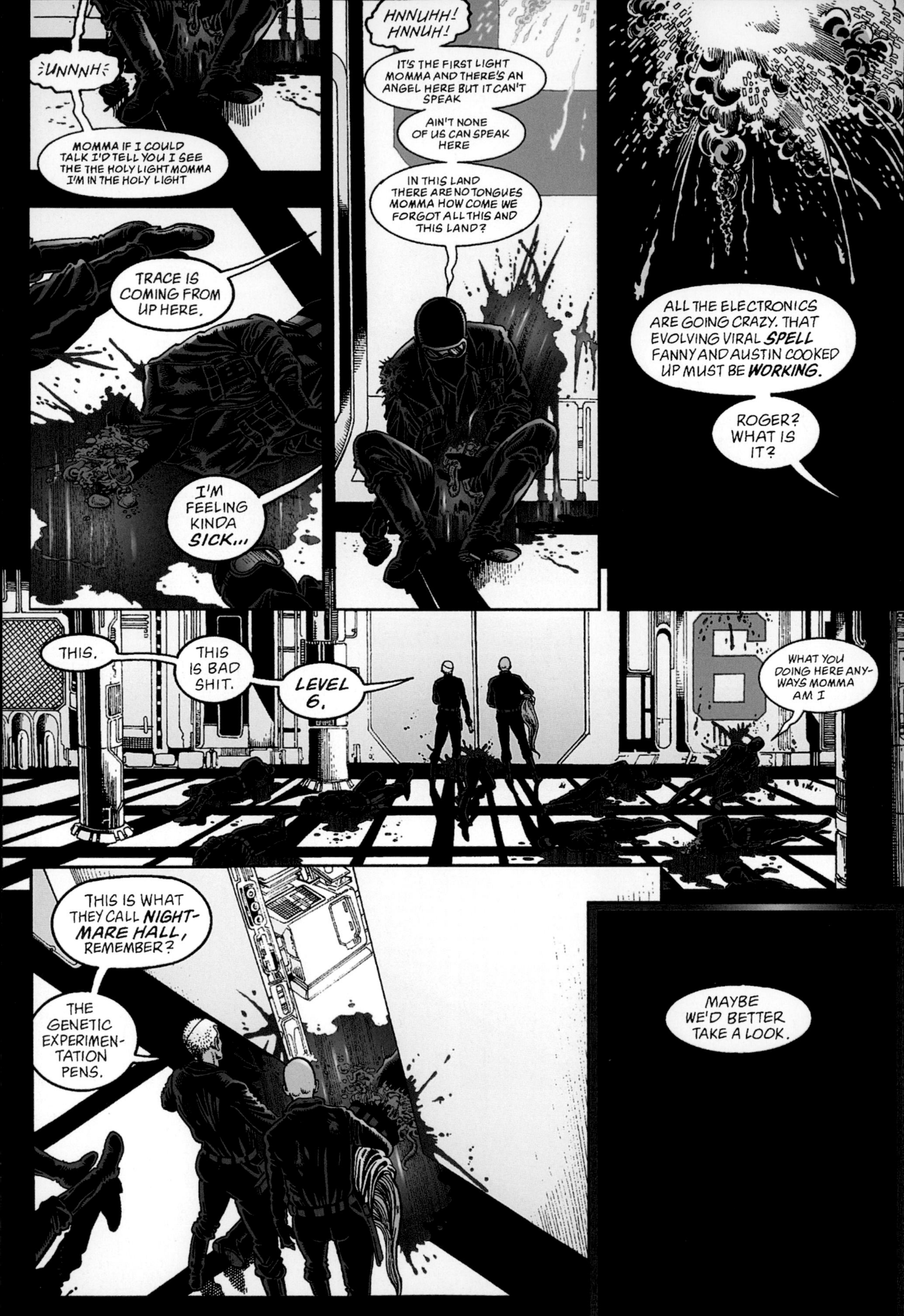

UNNNH
MOMMA IF I COULD TALK I'D TELL YOU I SEE THE THE HOLY LIGHT MOMMA I'M IN THE HOLY LIGHT
HNNUHH! HNNUH!
IT'S THE FIRST LIGHT MOMMA AND THERE'S AN ANGEL HERE BUT IT CAN'T SPEAK
AIN'T NONE OF US CAN SPEAK HERE
IN THIS LAND THERE ARE NO TONGUES MOMMA HOW COME WE FORGOT ALL THIS AND THIS LAND?
TRACE IS COMING FROM UP HERE.
I'M FEELING KINDA SICK...
ALL THE ELECTRONICS ARE GOING CRAZY. THAT EVOLVING VIRAL SPELL FANNY AND AUSTIN COOKED UP MUST BE WORKING.
ROGER? WHAT IS IT?
THIS.
THIS IS BAD SHIT.
LEVEL 6.
WHAT YOU DOING HERE ANY-WAYS MOMMA AM I
THIS IS WHAT THEY CALL NIGHT-MARE HALL, REMEMBER?
THE GENETIC EXPERIMEN-TATION PENS.
MAYBE WE'D BETTER TAKE A LOOK.

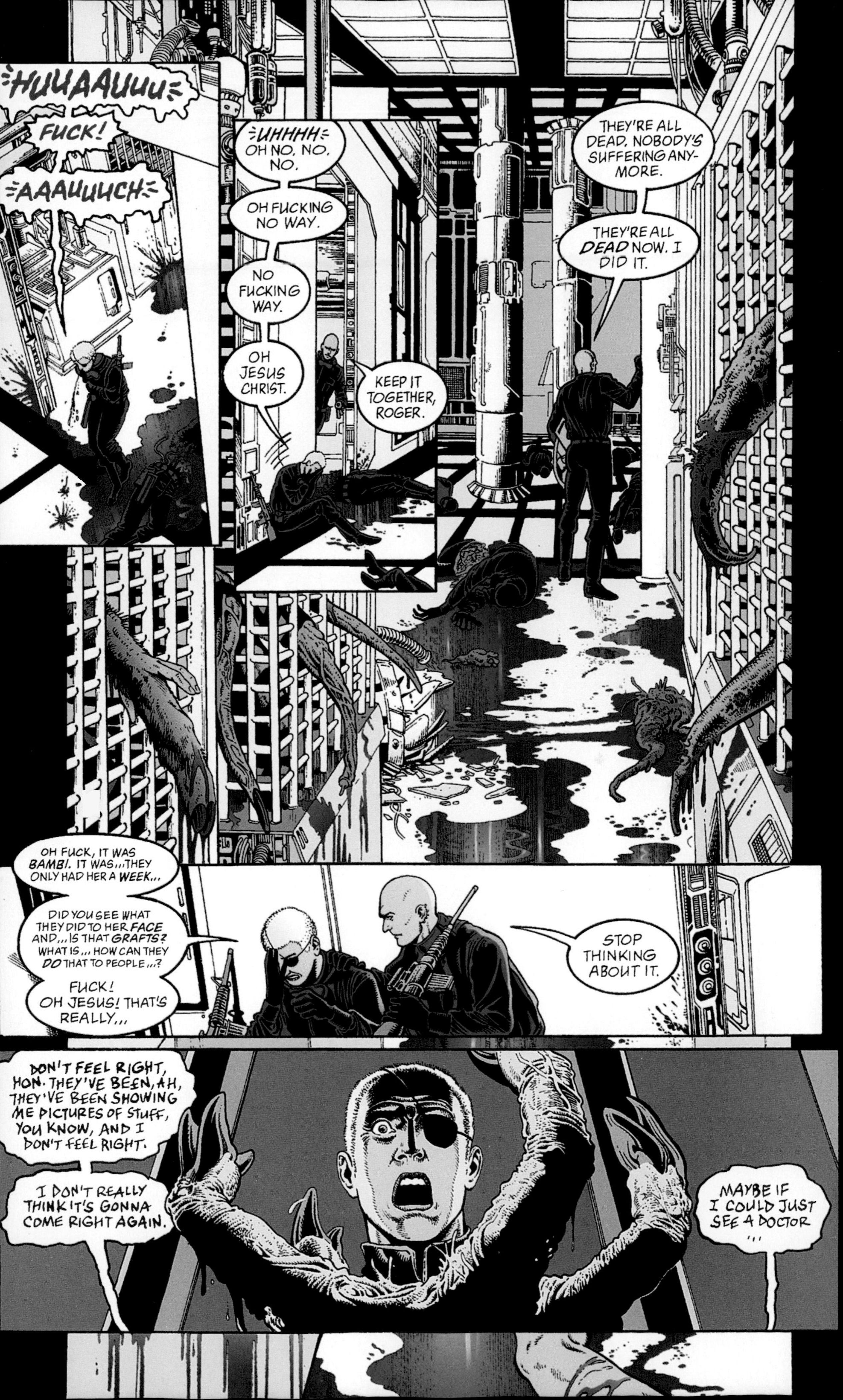
HUUAAUUU
FUCK!
AAAUUUCH
UHHHH OH NO, NO, NO.
OH FUCKING NO WAY.
NO FUCKING WAY.
OH JESUS CHRIST.
KEEP IT TOGETHER, ROGER.
THEY'RE ALL DEAD. NOBODY'S SUFFERING ANYMORE.
THEY'RE ALL DEAD NOW. I DID IT.
OH FUCK, IT WAS BAMBI. IT WAS...THEY ONLY HAD HER A WEEK...
DID YOU SEE WHAT THEY DID TO HER FACE AND... IS THAT GRAFTS? WHAT IS... HOW CAN THEY DO THAT TO PEOPLE...?
FUCK! OH JESUS! THAT'S REALLY...
STOP THINKING ABOUT IT.
DON'T FEEL RIGHT, HON. THEY'VE BEEN, AH, THEY'VE BEEN SHOWING ME PICTURES OF STUFF, YOU KNOW, AND I DON'T FEEL RIGHT.
I DON'T REALLY THINK IT'S GONNA COME RIGHT AGAIN.
MAYBE IF I COULD JUST SEE A DOCTOR ...

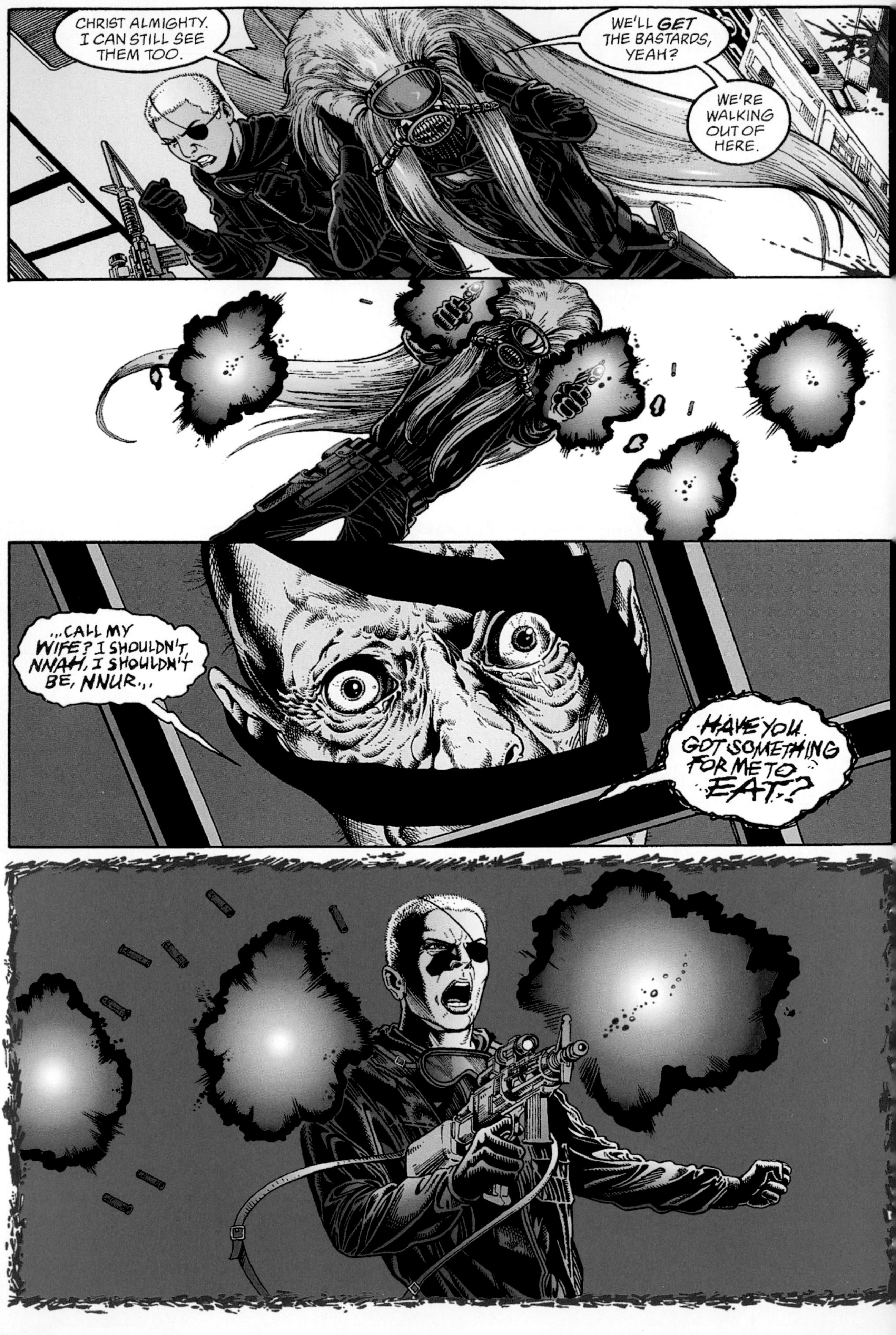
CHRIST ALMIGHTY. I CAN STILL SEE THEM TOO.
WE'LL GET THE BASTARDS, YEAH?
WE'RE WALKING OUT OF HERE.
...CALL MY WIFE? I SHOULDN'T, NNAH, I SHOULDN'T BE, NNUR...
HAVE YOU GOT SOMETHING FOR ME TO EAT?

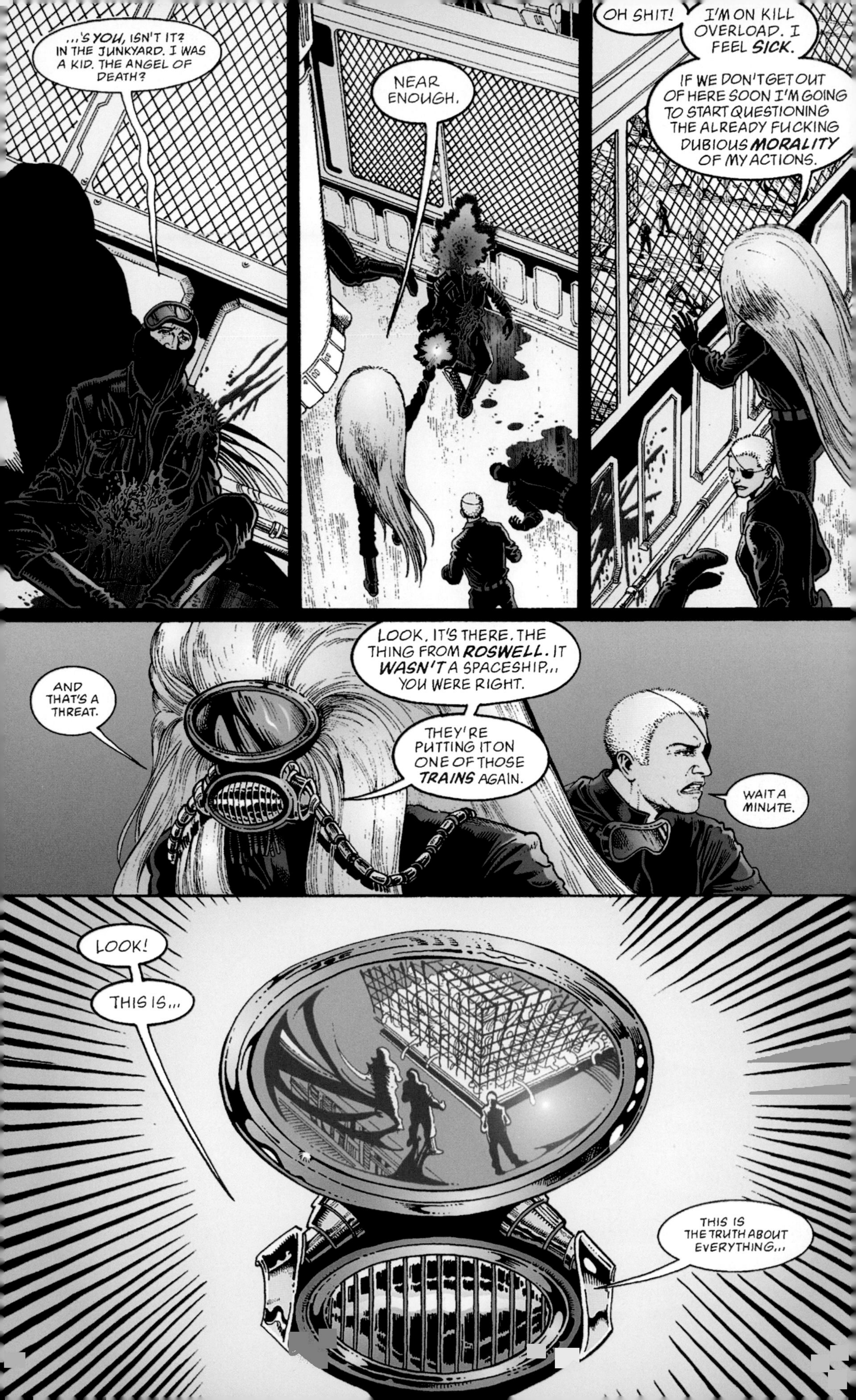
...'S YOU, ISN'T IT? IN THE JUNKYARD. I WAS A KID. THE ANGEL OF DEATH?
NEAR ENOUGH.
OH SHIT!
I'M ON KILL OVERLOAD. I FEEL SICK.
IF WE DON'T GET OUT OF HERE SOON I'M GOING TO START QUESTIONING THE ALREADY FUCKING DUBIOUS MORALITY OF MY ACTIONS.
AND THAT'S A THREAT.
LOOK, IT'S THERE. THE THING FROM ROSWELL. IT WASN'T A SPACESHIP... YOU WERE RIGHT.
THEY'RE PUTTING IT ON ONE OF THOSE TRAINS AGAIN.
WAIT A MINUTE.
LOOK!
THIS IS...
THIS IS THE TRUTH ABOUT EVERYTHING...

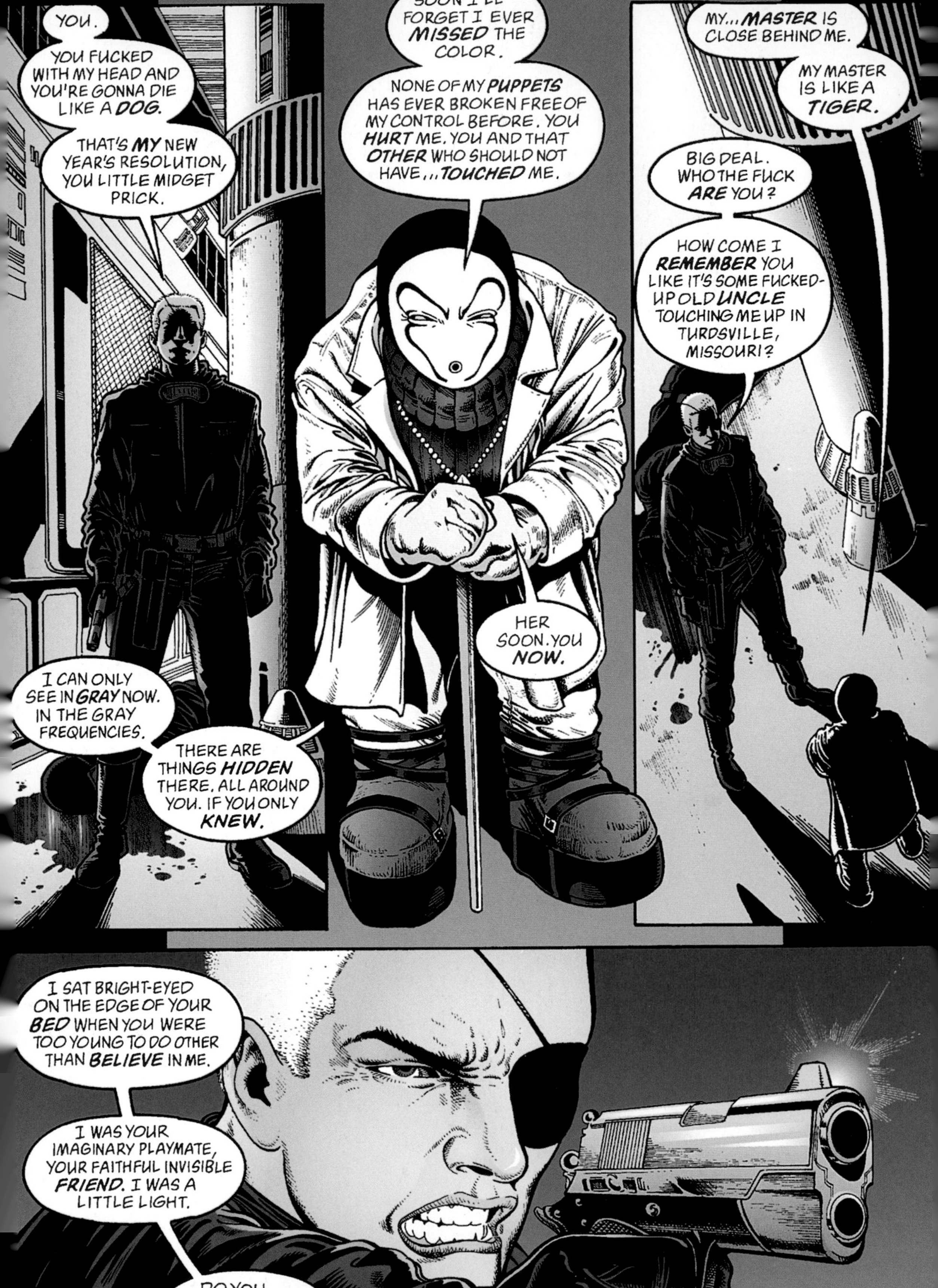
YOU.
YOU FUCKED WITH MY HEAD AND YOU'RE GONNA DIE LIKE A DOG.
THAT'S MY NEW YEAR'S RESOLUTION, YOU LITTLE MIDGET PRICK.
SOON I'LL FORGET I EVER MISSED THE COLOR.
NONE OF MY PUPPETS HAS EVER BROKEN FREE OF MY CONTROL BEFORE. YOU HURT ME. YOU AND THAT OTHER WHO SHOULD NOT HAVE... TOUCHED ME.
I CAN ONLY SEE IN GRAY NOW. IN THE GRAY FREQUENCIES.
THERE ARE THINGS HIDDEN THERE, ALL AROUND YOU. IF YOU ONLY KNEW.
HER SOON. YOU NOW.
MY... MASTER IS CLOSE BEHIND ME.
MY MASTER IS LIKE A TIGER.
BIG DEAL. WHO THE FUCK ARE YOU?
HOW COME I REMEMBER YOU LIKE IT'S SOME FUCKED-UP OLD UNCLE TOUCHING ME UP IN TURDSVILLE, MISSOURI?
I SAT BRIGHT-EYED ON THE EDGE OF YOUR BED WHEN YOU WERE TOO YOUNG TO DO OTHER THAN BELIEVE IN ME.
I WAS YOUR IMAGINARY PLAYMATE, YOUR FAITHFUL INVISIBLE FRIEND. I WAS A LITTLE LIGHT.
DO YOU UNDERSTAND WHAT I AM?

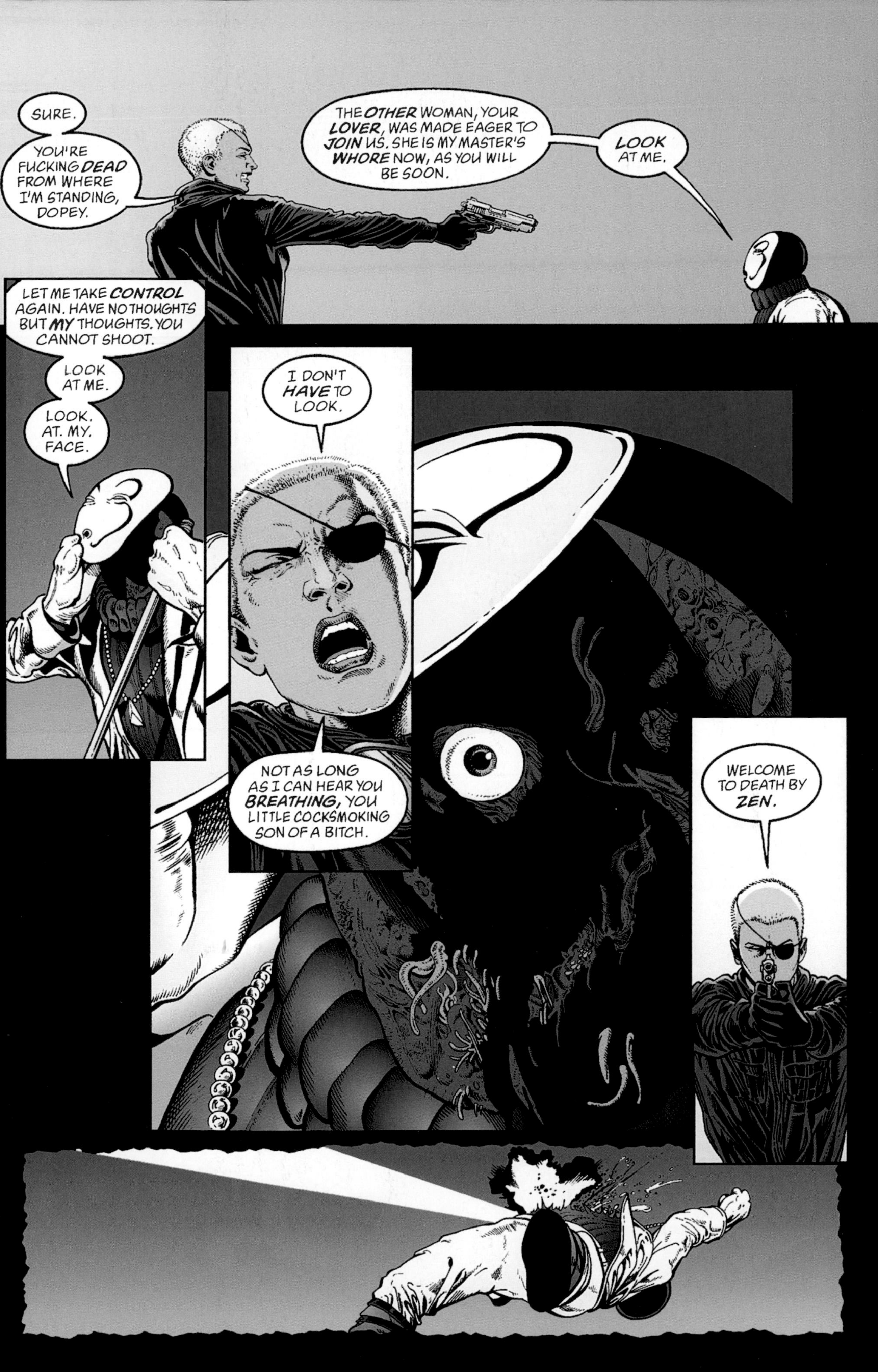
SURE.
YOU'RE FUCKING DEAD FROM WHERE I'M STANDING, DOPEY.
THE OTHER WOMAN, YOUR LOVER, WAS MADE EAGER TO JOIN US. SHE IS MY MASTER'S WHORE NOW, AS YOU WILL BE SOON.
LOOK AT ME.
LET ME TAKE CONTROL AGAIN. HAVE NO THOUGHTS BUT MY THOUGHTS. YOU CANNOT SHOOT.
LOOK AT ME.
LOOK. AT. MY. FACE.
I DON'T HAVE TO LOOK.
NOT AS LONG AS I CAN HEAR YOU BREATHING, YOU LITTLE COCKSMOKING SON OF A BITCH.
WELCOME TO DEATH BY ZEN.

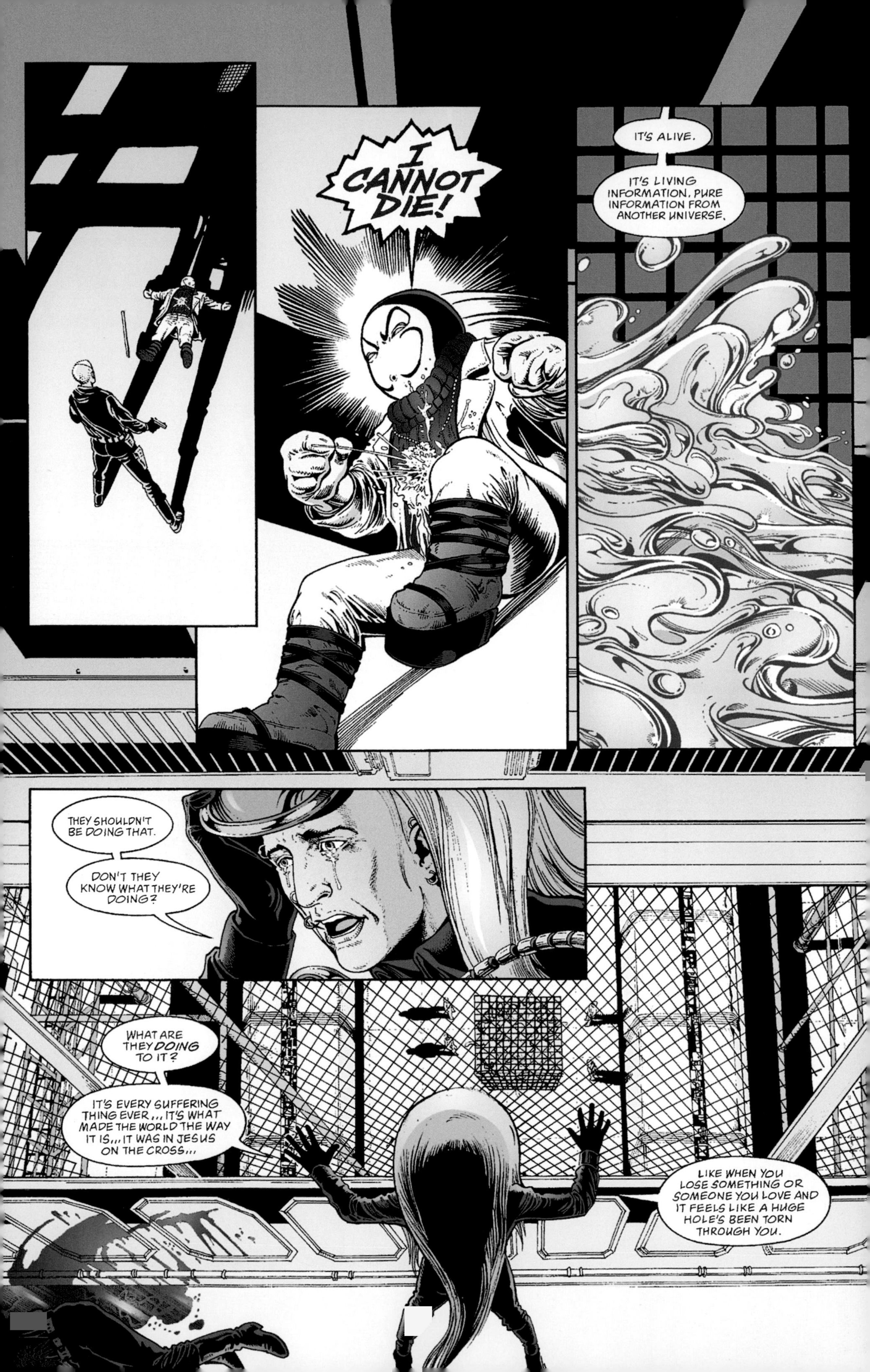
I CANNOT DIE!
IT'S ALIVE.
IT'S LIVING INFORMATION. PURE INFORMATION FROM ANOTHER UNIVERSE.
THEY SHOULDN'T BE DOING THAT.
DON'T THEY KNOW WHAT THEY'RE DOING?
WHAT ARE THEY DOING TO IT?
IT'S EVERY SUFFERING THING EVER... IT'S WHAT MADE THE WORLD THE WAY IT IS... IT WAS IN JESUS ON THE CROSS...
LIKE WHEN YOU LOSE SOMETHING OR SOMEONE YOU LOVE AND IT FEELS LIKE A HUGE HOLE'S BEEN TORN THROUGH YOU.

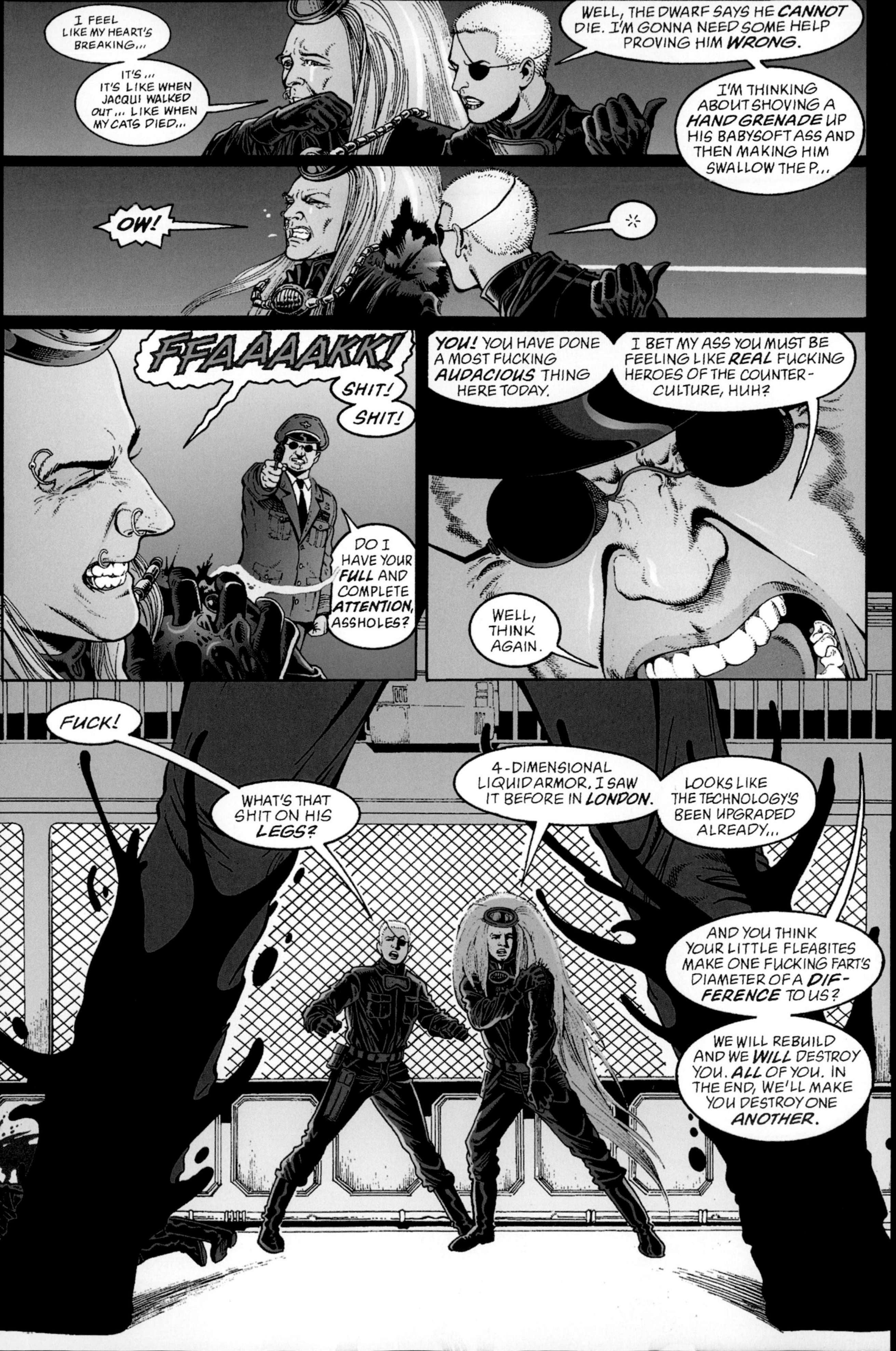
I FEEL LIKE MY HEART'S BREAKING...
IT'S... IT'S LIKE WHEN JACQUI WALKED OUT... LIKE WHEN MY CATS DIED...
WELL, THE DWARF SAYS HE CANNOT DIE. I'M GONNA NEED SOME HELP PROVING HIM WRONG.
I'M THINKING ABOUT SHOVING A HAND GRENADE UP HIS BABYSOFT ASS AND THEN MAKING HIM SWALLOW THE P...
OW!
FFAAAAAKK!
SHIT!
SHIT!
DO I HAVE YOUR FULL AND COMPLETE ATTENTION, ASSHOLES?
YOU! YOU HAVE DONE A MOST FUCKING AUDACIOUS THING HERE TODAY.
I BET MY ASS YOU MUST BE FEELING LIKE REAL FUCKING HEROES OF THE COUNTER-CULTURE, HUH?
WELL, THINK AGAIN.
FUCK!
WHAT'S THAT SHIT ON HIS LEGS?
4-DIMENSIONAL LIQUID ARMOR. I SAW IT BEFORE IN LONDON.
LOOKS LIKE THE TECHNOLOGY'S BEEN UPGRADED ALREADY...
AND YOU THINK YOUR LITTLE FLEABITES MAKE ONE FUCKING FART'S DIAMETER OF A DIF-FERENCE TO US?
WE WILL REBUILD AND WE WILL DESTROY YOU. ALL OF YOU. IN THE END, WE'LL MAKE YOU DESTROY ONE ANOTHER.

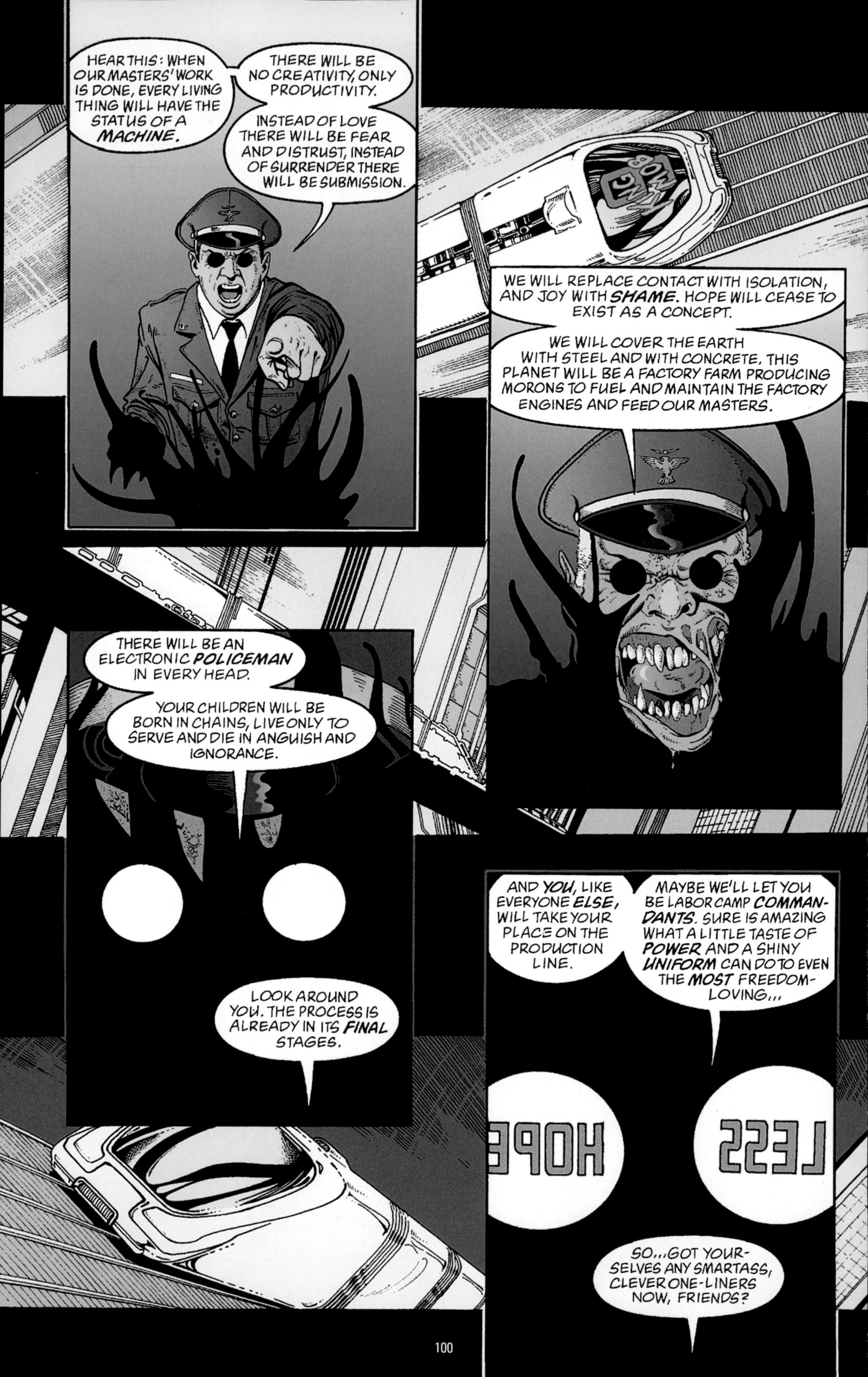
HEAR THIS: WHEN OUR MASTERS' WORK IS DONE, EVERY LIVING THING WILL HAVE THE STATUS OF A MACHINE.
THERE WILL BE NO CREATIVITY, ONLY PRODUCTIVITY.
INSTEAD OF LOVE THERE WILL BE FEAR AND DISTRUST, INSTEAD OF SURRENDER THERE WILL BE SUBMISSION.
WE WILL REPLACE CONTACT WITH ISOLATION, AND JOY WITH SHAME. HOPE WILL CEASE TO EXIST AS A CONCEPT.
WE WILL COVER THE EARTH WITH STEEL AND WITH CONCRETE. THIS PLANET WILL BE A FACTORY FARM PRODUCING MORONS TO FUEL AND MAINTAIN THE FACTORY ENGINES AND FEED OUR MASTERS.
THERE WILL BE AN ELECTRONIC POLICEMAN IN EVERY HEAD.
YOUR CHILDREN WILL BE BORN IN CHAINS, LIVE ONLY TO SERVE AND DIE IN ANGUISH AND IGNORANCE.
LOOK AROUND YOU. THE PROCESS IS ALREADY IN ITS FINAL STAGES.
AND YOU, LIKE EVERYONE ELSE, WILL TAKE YOUR PLACE ON THE PRODUCTION LINE.
MAYBE WE'LL LET YOU BE LABOR CAMP COMMANDANTS. SURE IS AMAZING WHAT A LITTLE TASTE OF POWER AND A SHINY UNIFORM CAN DO TO EVEN THE MOST FREEDOM-LOVING...
SO...GOT YOURSELVES ANY SMARTASS, CLEVER ONE-LINERS NOW, FRIENDS?

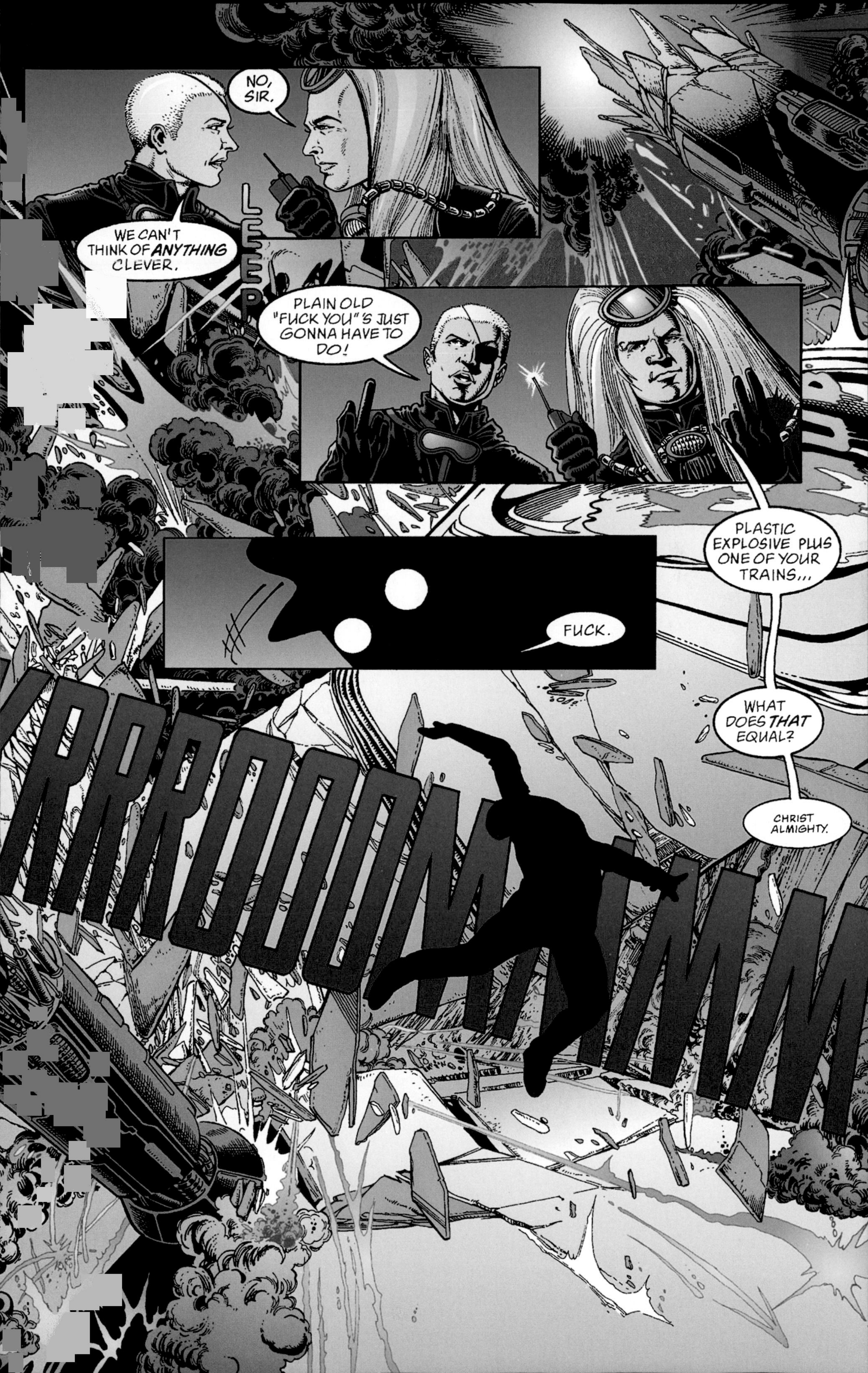

NO, SIR.
WE CAN'T THINK OF ANYTHING CLEVER.
LEEP
PLAIN OLD "FUCK YOU"'S JUST GONNA HAVE TO DO!
PLASTIC EXPLOSIVE PLUS ONE OF YOUR TRAINS,,,
FUCK.
WHAT DOES THAT EQUAL?
CHRIST ALMIGHTY.
KRRROOOMMMMM

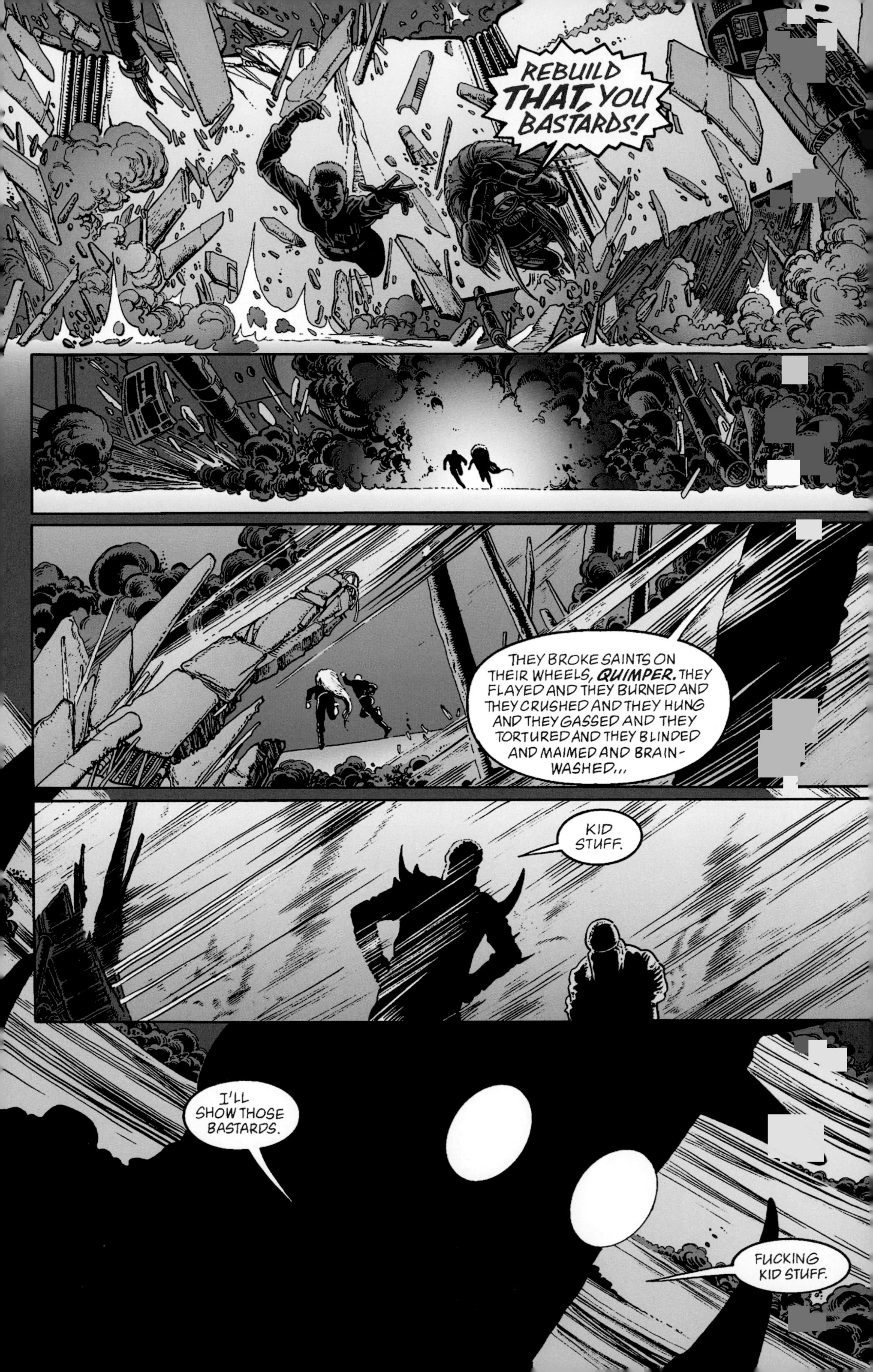
REBUILD THAT, YOU BASTARDS!
THEY BROKE SAINTS ON THEIR WHEELS, QUIMPER. THEY FLAYED AND THEY BURNED AND THEY CRUSHED AND THEY HUNG AND THEY GASSED AND THEY TORTURED AND THEY BLINDED AND MAIMED AND BRAIN-WASHED...
KID STUFF.
I'LL SHOW THOSE BASTARDS.
FUCKING KID STUFF.

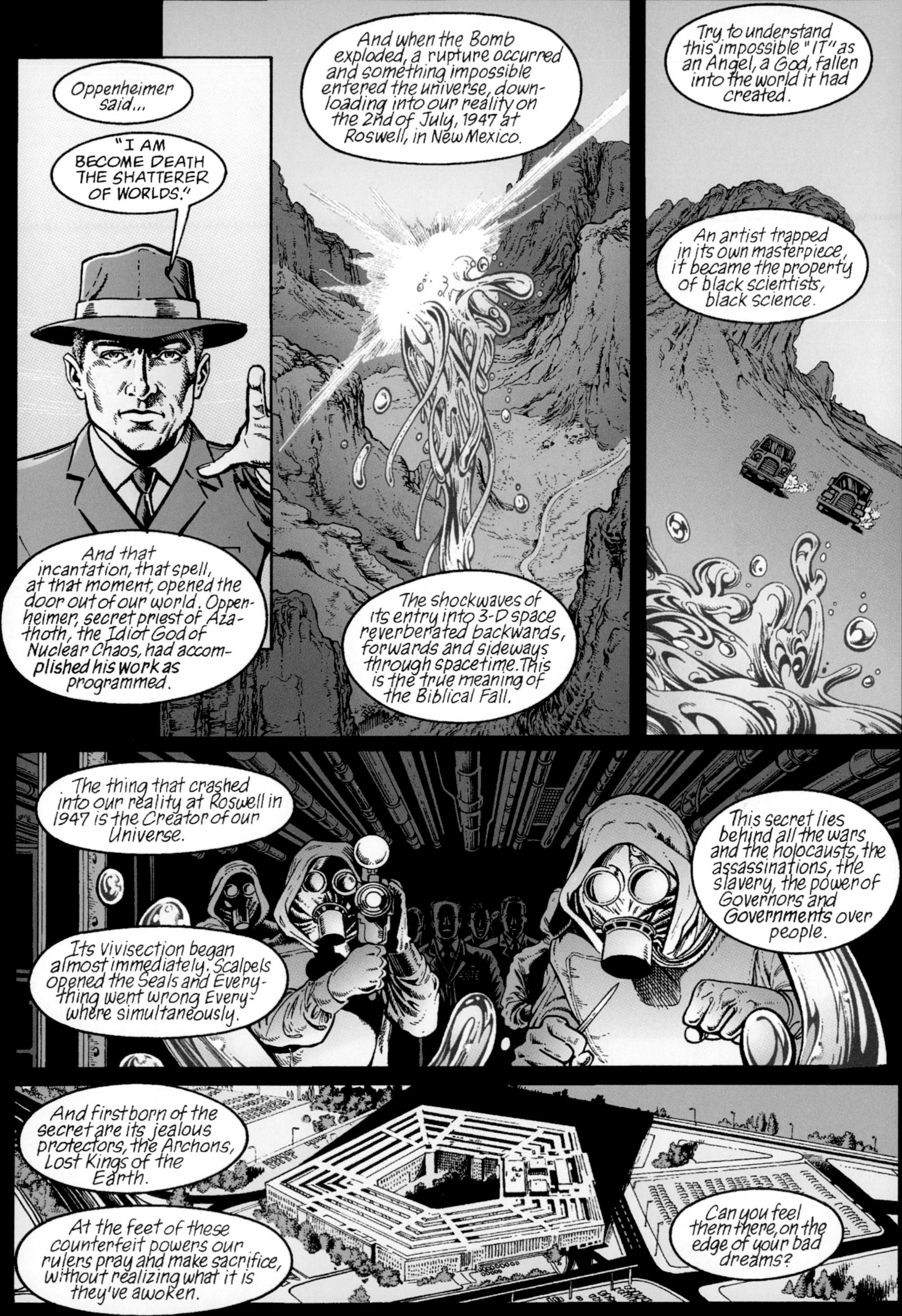
Oppenheimer said...
"I AM BECOME DEATH THE SHATTERER OF WORLDS."
And that incantation, that spell, at that moment, opened the door out of our world. Oppenheimer, secret priest of Azathoth, the Idiot God of Nuclear Chaos, had accomplished his work as programmed.
And when the Bomb exploded, a rupture occurred and something impossible entered the universe, downloading into our reality on the 2nd of July, 1947 at Roswell, in New Mexico.
The shockwaves of its entry into 3-D space reverberated backwards, forwards and sideways through spacetime. This is the true meaning of the Biblical Fall.
Try to understand this impossible "IT" as an Angel, a God, fallen into the world it had created.
An artist trapped in its own masterpiece, it became the property of black scientists, black science.
The thing that crashed into our reality at Roswell in 1947 is the Creator of our Universe.
Its vivisection began almost immediately. Scalpels opened the Seals and Everything went wrong Everywhere simultaneously.
This secret lies behind all the wars and the holocausts, the assassinations, the slavery, the power of Governors and Governments over people.
And firstborn of the secret are its jealous protectors, the Archons, Lost Kings of the Earth.
At the feet of these counterfeit powers our rulers pray and make sacrifice, without realizing what it is they've awoken.
Can you feel them there, on the edge of your bad dreams?

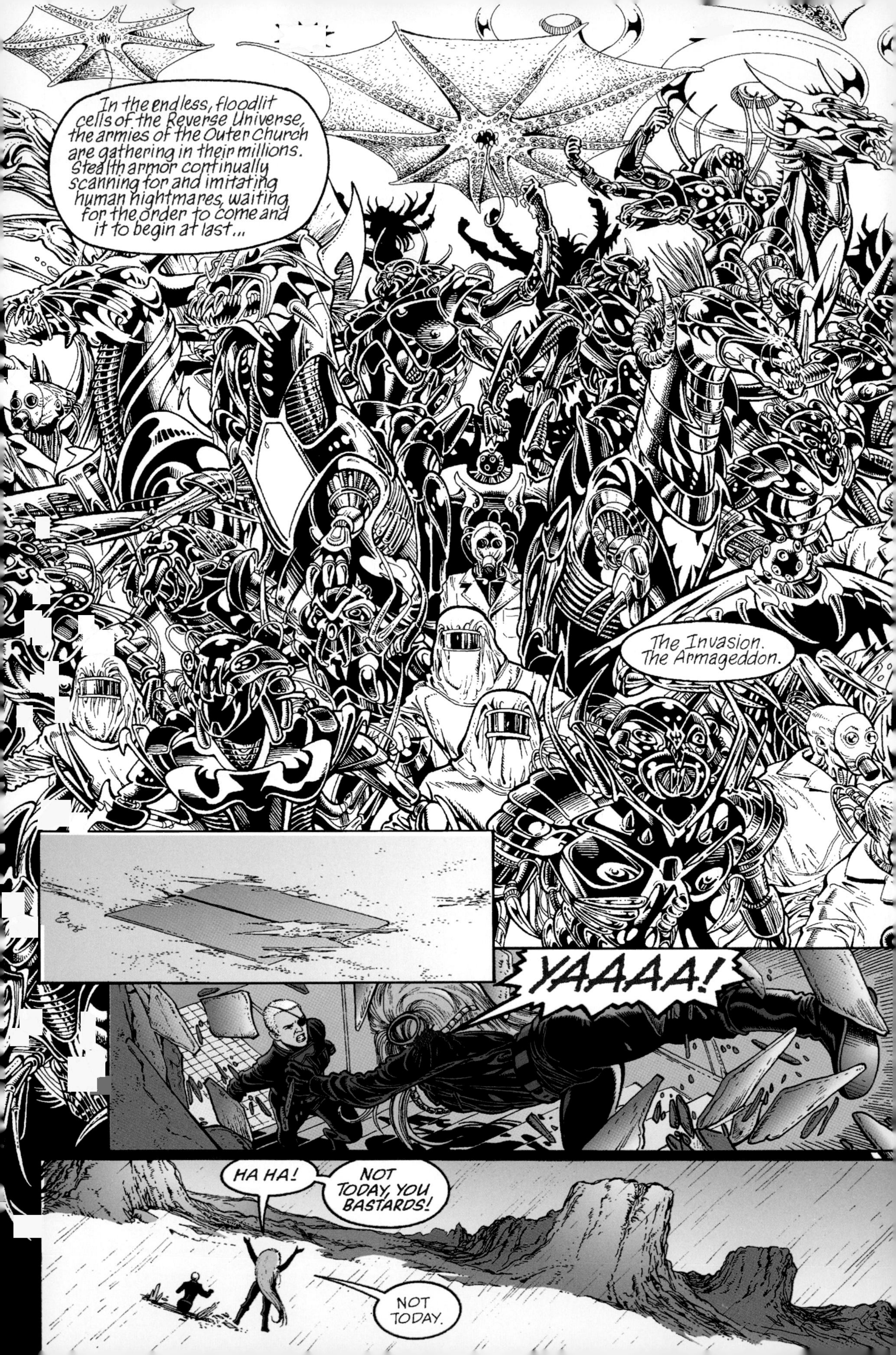
In the endless, floodlit cells of the Reverse Universe, the armies of the Outer Church are gathering in their millions. Stealth armor continually scanning for and imitating human nightmares, waiting for the order to come and it to begin at last...
The Invasion. The Armageddon.
YAAAA!
HA HA!
NOT TODAY, YOU BASTARDS!
NOT TODAY.

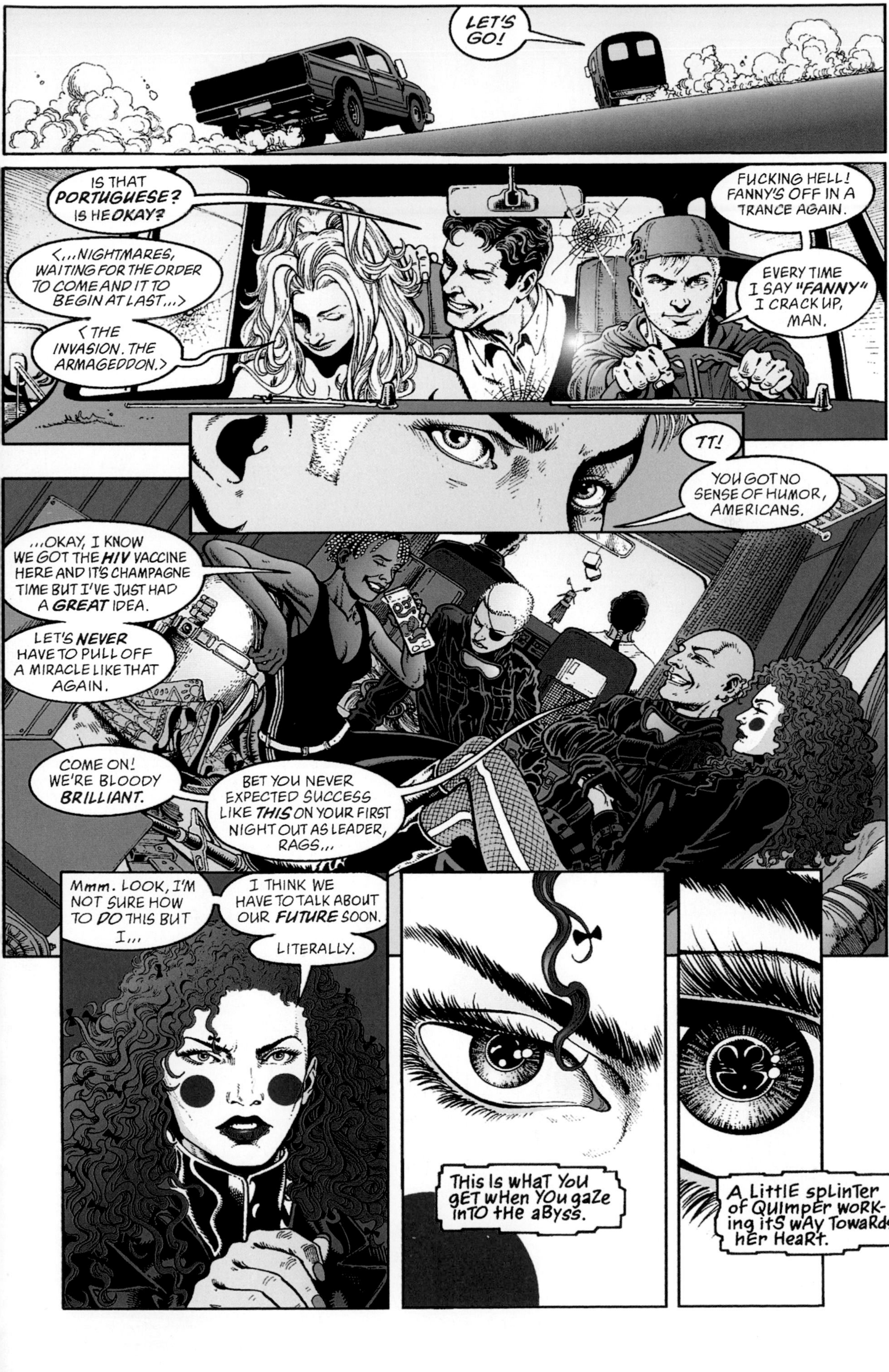
LET'S GO!
IS THAT PORTUGUESE? IS HE OKAY?
FUCKING HELL! FANNY'S OFF IN A TRANCE AGAIN.
<...NIGHTMARES, WAITING FOR THE ORDER TO COME AND IT TO BEGIN AT LAST...>
<THE INVASION. THE ARMAGEDDON.>
EVERY TIME I SAY "FANNY" I CRACK UP, MAN.
TT!
YOU GOT NO SENSE OF HUMOR, AMERICANS.
...OKAY, I KNOW WE GOT THE HIV VACCINE HERE AND IT'S CHAMPAGNE TIME BUT I'VE JUST HAD A GREAT IDEA.
LET'S NEVER HAVE TO PULL OFF A MIRACLE LIKE THAT AGAIN.
COME ON! WE'RE BLOODY BRILLIANT.
BET YOU NEVER EXPECTED SUCCESS LIKE THIS ON YOUR FIRST NIGHT OUT AS LEADER, RAGS...
Mmm. LOOK, I'M NOT SURE HOW TO DO THIS BUT I...
I THINK WE HAVE TO TALK ABOUT OUR FUTURE SOON.
LITERALLY.
This Is wHaT You gET wHen You gaZe inTO tHe aByss.
A LittlE spLinTer of QUImpEr WORKing itS wAy TowaRds hEr HeaRt.

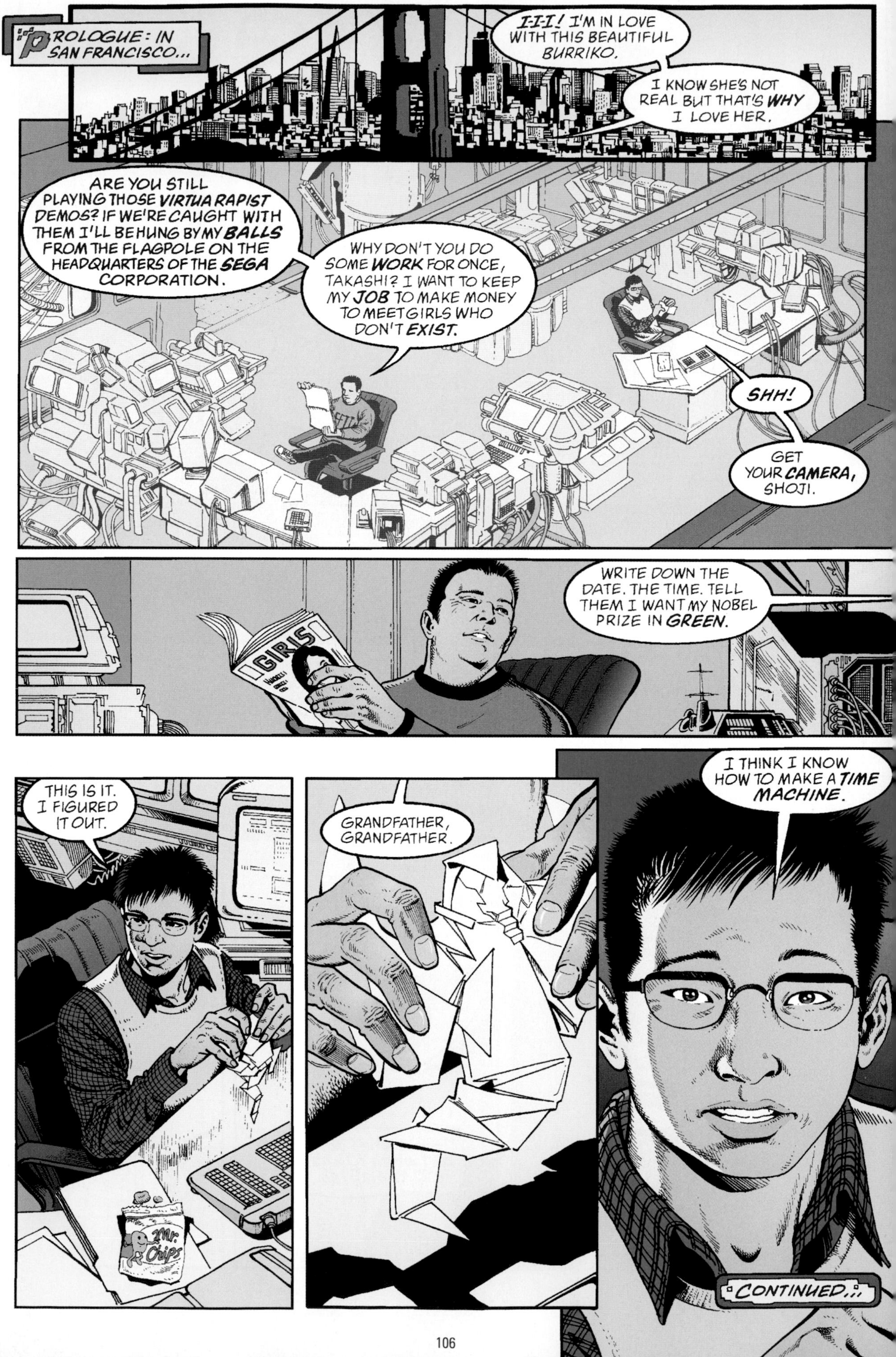
PROLOGUE: IN SAN FRANCISCO...
I-I-I! I'M IN LOVE WITH THIS BEAUTIFUL BURRIKO.
I KNOW SHE'S NOT REAL BUT THAT'S WHY I LOVE HER.
ARE YOU STILL PLAYING THOSE VIRTUA RAPIST DEMOS? IF WE'RE CAUGHT WITH THEM I'LL BE HUNG BY MY BALLS FROM THE FLAGPOLE ON THE HEADQUARTERS OF THE SEGA CORPORATION.
WHY DON'T YOU DO SOME WORK FOR ONCE, TAKASHI? I WANT TO KEEP MY JOB TO MAKE MONEY TO MEET GIRLS WHO DON'T EXIST.
SHH!
GET YOUR CAMERA, SHOJI.
WRITE DOWN THE DATE. THE TIME. TELL THEM I WANT MY NOBEL PRIZE IN GREEN.
GIRLS
THIS IS IT. I FIGURED IT OUT.
Mr. Chips
GRANDFATHER, GRANDFATHER.
I THINK I KNOW HOW TO MAKE A TIME MACHINE.
CONTINUED...

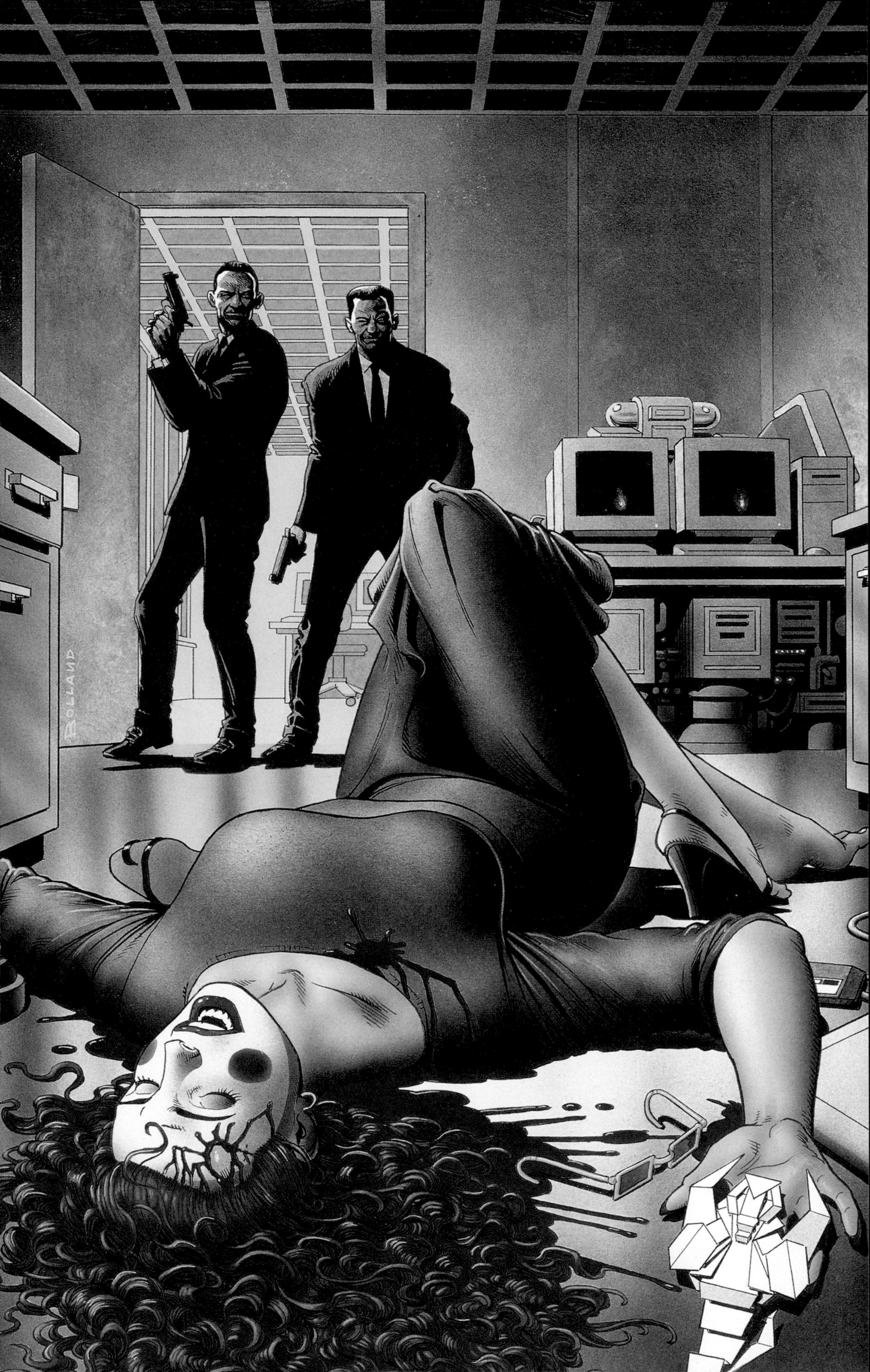
BOLLAND

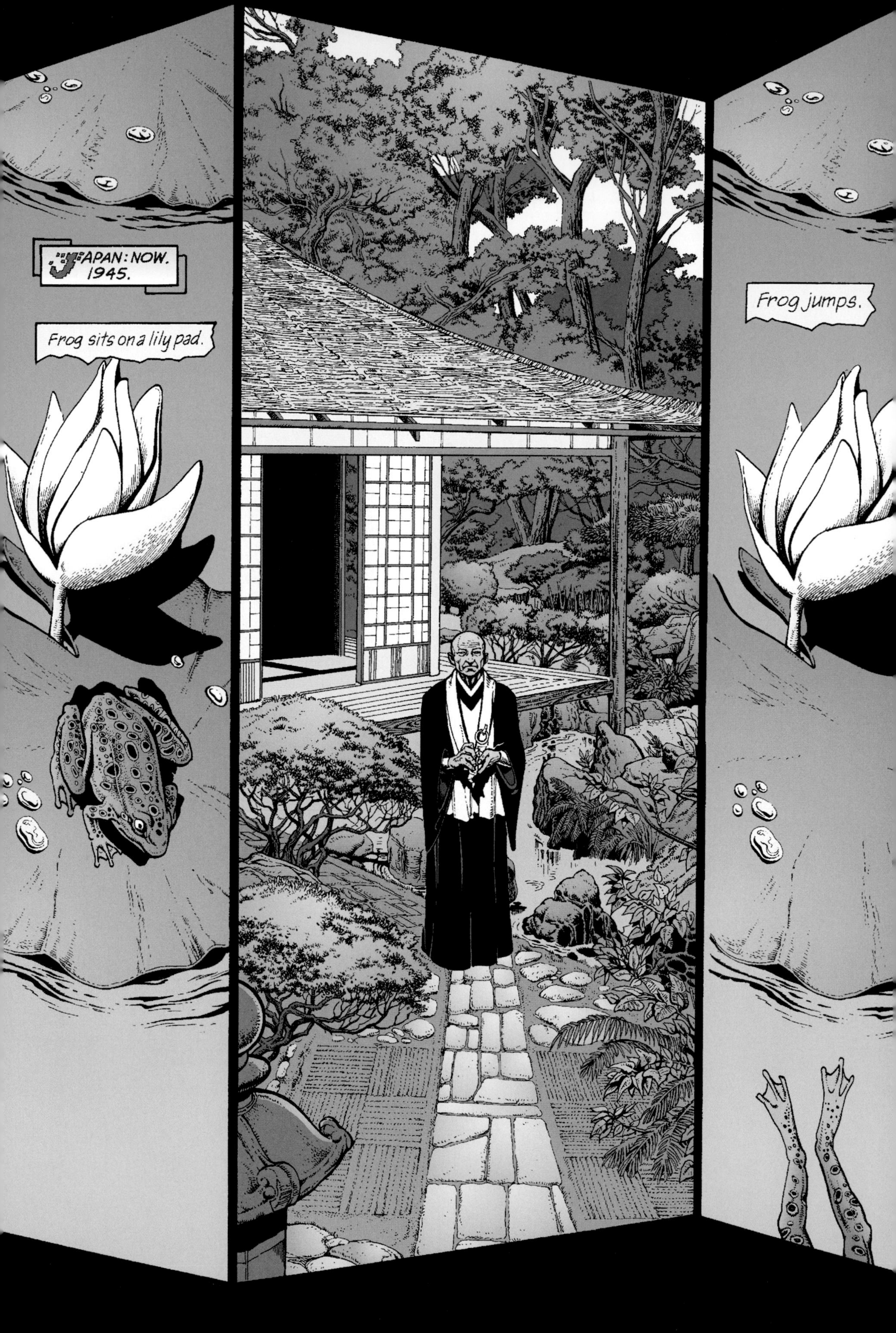
JAPAN: NOW. 1945.
Frog sits on a lily pad.
Frog jumps.

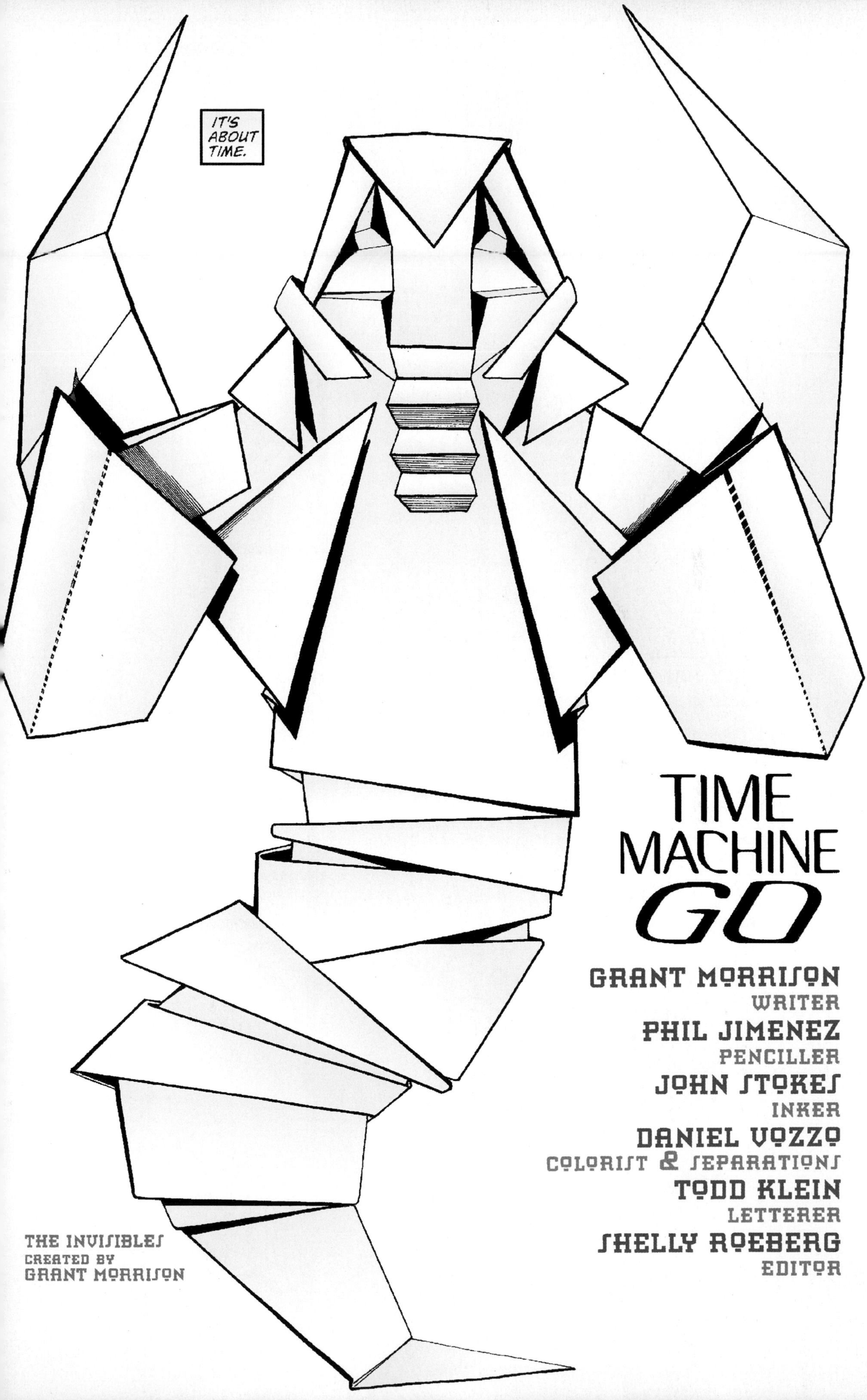
IT'S ABOUT TIME.

TIME MACHINE GO

GRANT MORRISON
WRITER
PHIL JIMENEZ
PENCILLER
JOHN STOKES
INKER
DANIEL VOZZO
COLORIST & SEPARATIONS
TODD KLEIN
LETTERER
SHELLY ROEBERG
EDITOR

THE INVISIBLES
CREATED BY
GRANT MORRISON

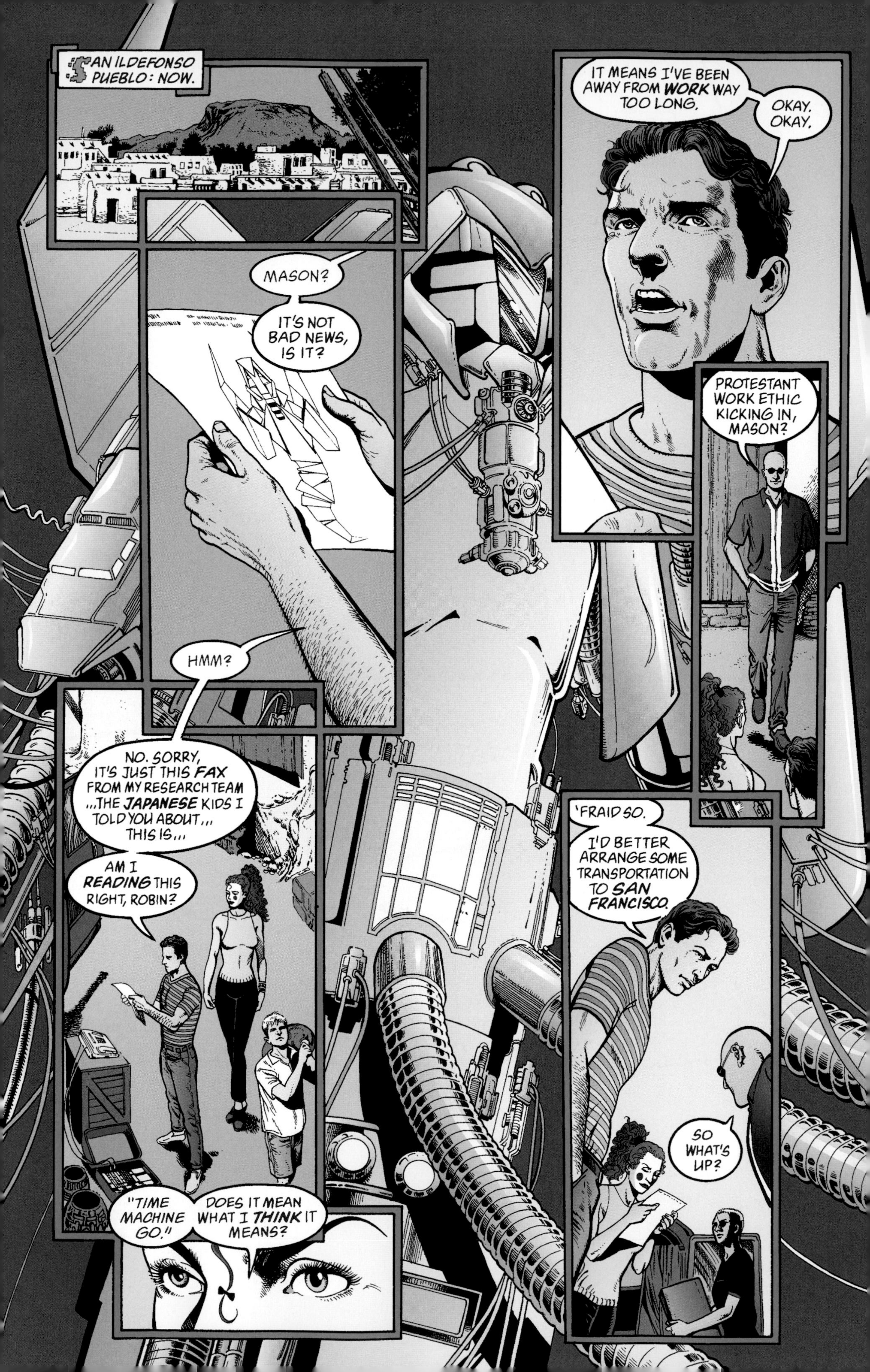
SAN ILDEFONSO PUEBLO: NOW.
MASON?
IT'S NOT BAD NEWS, IS IT?
HMM?
NO. SORRY, IT'S JUST THIS FAX FROM MY RESEARCH TEAM ...THE JAPANESE KIDS I TOLD YOU ABOUT... THIS IS...
AM I READING THIS RIGHT, ROBIN?
"TIME MACHINE GO."
DOES IT MEAN WHAT I THINK IT MEANS?
IT MEANS I'VE BEEN AWAY FROM WORK WAY TOO LONG.
OKAY. OKAY.
PROTESTANT WORK ETHIC KICKING IN, MASON?
'FRAID SO.
I'D BETTER ARRANGE SOME TRANSPORTATION TO SAN FRANCISCO.
SO WHAT'S UP?

THIS HAD BETTER BE WORTH ALL THE *SHIT* WE BEEN THROUGH, IS ALL I'M SAYING.

WHAT IF OUR CHEMISTS SAY IT'S JUST *WATER?* WHAT'S THE CHANCES WE REALLY GOT AN *HIV* CURE ON OUR HANDS, *FANNY?*

HIGHER THAN YOU THINK, DARLING.

LISTEN, I USED TO HAVE A *CLIENT,* A PHARMACIST. HIS NAME WAS *TONY.* BEAUTIFUL WIFE, TWO GIRLS, BUT HE HAD THIS *THING* FOR BOYS IN HIGH HEELS... ANYWAY...

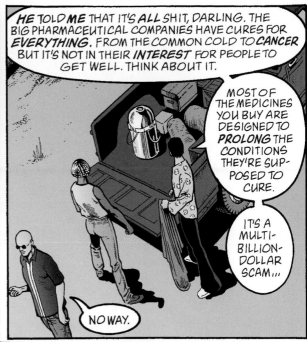

HE TOLD ME THAT IT'S *ALL* SHIT, DARLING. THE BIG PHARMACEUTICAL COMPANIES HAVE CURES FOR *EVERYTHING.* FROM THE COMMON COLD TO *CANCER* BUT IT'S NOT IN THEIR *INTEREST* FOR PEOPLE TO GET WELL. THINK ABOUT IT.

MOST OF THE MEDICINES YOU BUY ARE DESIGNED TO *PROLONG* THE CONDITIONS THEY'RE SUPPOSED TO CURE.

IT'S A MULTI-BILLION-DOLLAR SCAM...

NO WAY.

DO YOU REALLY THINK THEY'VE *DONE* IT?

THIS IS THE *THING,* ISN'T IT? THIS HAS ALL GOT TO DO WITH THAT *PHOTOGRAPH* YOU'RE CARRYING AROUND AND THIS BIG *SECRET* WE'RE *STILL* WAITING TO HEAR...

LOOK, THE TIME HASN'T BEEN RIGHT.

LISTEN, IF WE CAN JUST GO WITH MASON TO THE WEST COAST, I CAN EXPLAIN EVERYTHING WHEN WE'VE SEEN *TAKASHI* AND THE TIMESUIT AND...

TRUST ME ON THIS.

TAKASHI?

ROBIN, LOOK-- I'M NOT TELEPATHIC, YOU KNOW?

YOU'RE GOING TO HAVE TO START *TALKING* TO US BECAUSE EVERYONE'S GETTING...

HEY!

QUIT NECKING, YOU TWO!

AND THERE ARE TOO MANY PEOPLE AROUND ALL THE TIME...

GUESS WHAT WE JUST FOUND!

TEQUILA PARTY, YOU *BASTARDS!*

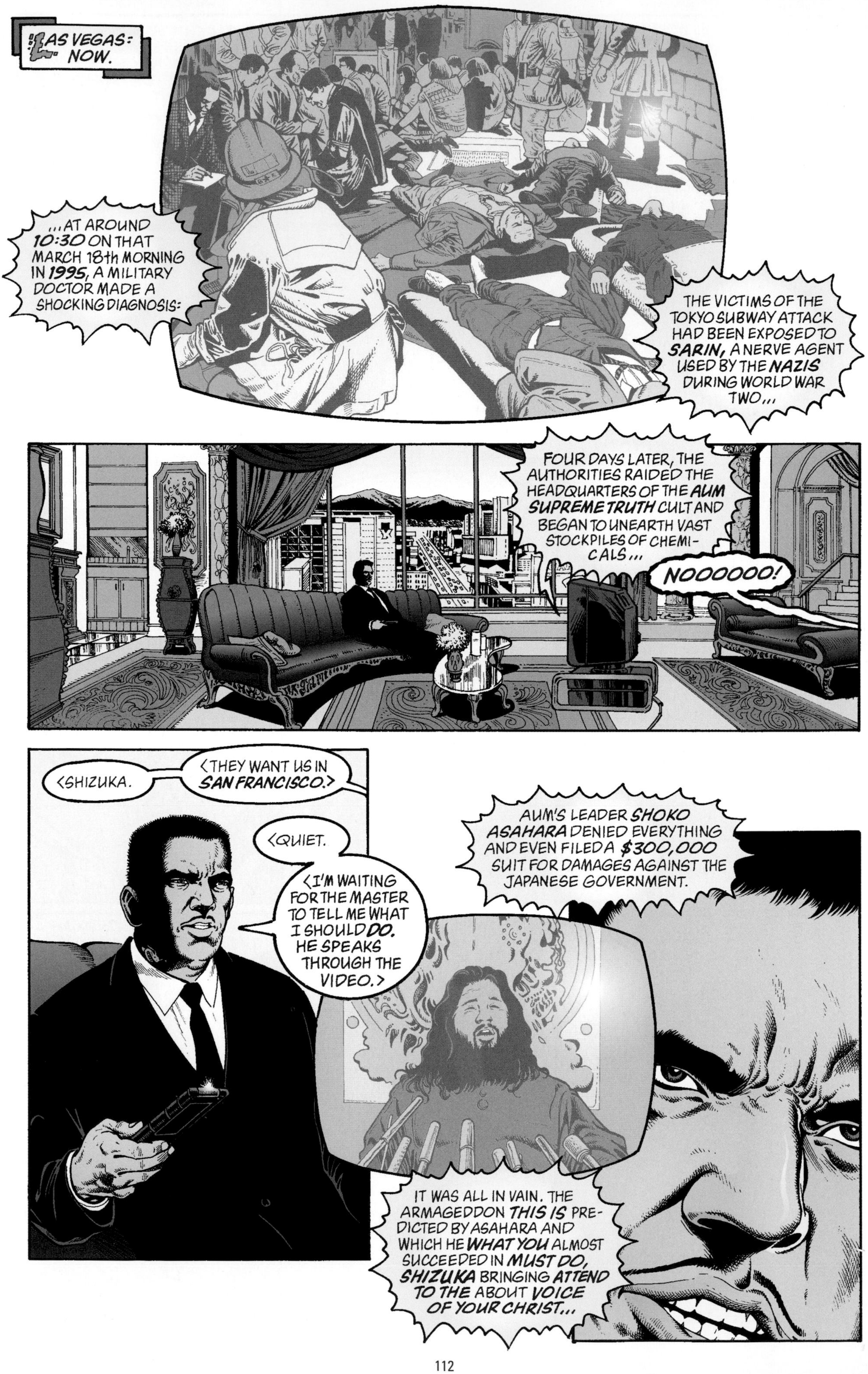
LAS VEGAS: NOW.
...AT AROUND 10:30 ON THAT MARCH 18th MORNING IN 1995, A MILITARY DOCTOR MADE A SHOCKING DIAGNOSIS:
THE VICTIMS OF THE TOKYO SUBWAY ATTACK HAD BEEN EXPOSED TO SARIN, A NERVE AGENT USED BY THE NAZIS DURING WORLD WAR TWO...
FOUR DAYS LATER, THE AUTHORITIES RAIDED THE HEADQUARTERS OF THE AUM SUPREME TRUTH CULT AND BEGAN TO UNEARTH VAST STOCKPILES OF CHEMI- CALS...
NOOOOOO!
<SHIZUKA.
<THEY WANT US IN SAN FRANCISCO.>
<QUIET.
<I'M WAITING FOR THE MASTER TO TELL ME WHAT I SHOULD DO. HE SPEAKS THROUGH THE VIDEO.>
AUM'S LEADER SHOKO ASAHARA DENIED EVERYTHING AND EVEN FILED A $300,000 SUIT FOR DAMAGES AGAINST THE JAPANESE GOVERNMENT.
IT WAS ALL IN VAIN. THE
ARMAGEDDON THIS IS PRE-
DICTED BY ASAHARA AND
WHICH HE WHAT YOU ALMOST
SUCCEEDED IN MUST DO,
SHIZUKA BRINGING ATTEND
TO THE ABOUT VOICE
OF YOUR CHRIST...

AH.
<DID YOU HEAR THAT, YOSHIO?>
<OF COURSE I DIDN'T. IT'S ONLY YOU THE GURU SPEAKS TO THAT WAY.>
<COME ON. LET'S CLEAN UP HERE. TIME TO MOVE ON.>
MY FRIEND, SHIZUKA HERE, IS NOT A BAD MAN; HE DOES WHAT MUST BE DONE AND HE DOES IT WITH ALL HIS HEART.
WE ARE NOT SADISTS; WE WISH ONLY TO PURGE YOU OF BAD KARMA.
IT'S NOT COINCIDENCE THAT LED YOU HERE BUT YOUR OWN NEED TO BALANCE THINGS. YOU MUST HAVE BEEN VERY BAD INDEED IN YOUR PAST LIVES.
NO. NO. NO. NO.
WHAT'S HE DOING? PLEASE, TELL HIM NOT TO HURT US. WHAT'S HE GOING TO DO?
MMMNNN
I WILL CUT OFF YOUR PENIS AND USE IT TO RAPE YOUR GIRL-FRIEND.
AND SO, WHEN YOU ARE BORN AGAIN INTO LIFE, YOU WOULD DO WELL TO RE-MEMBER THIS:
BE GOOD.

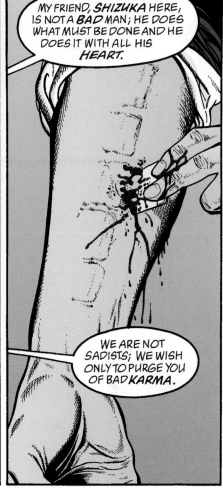

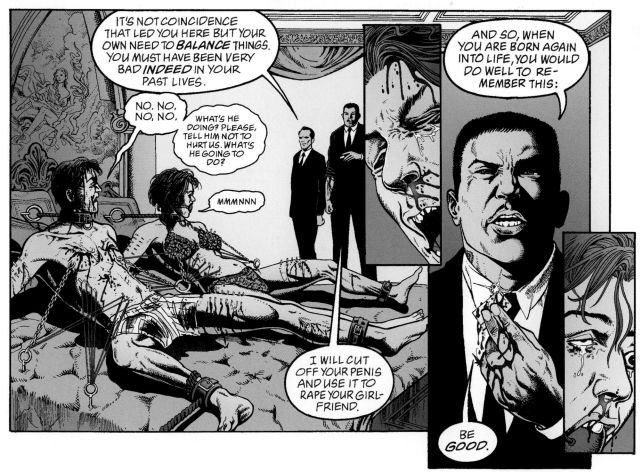

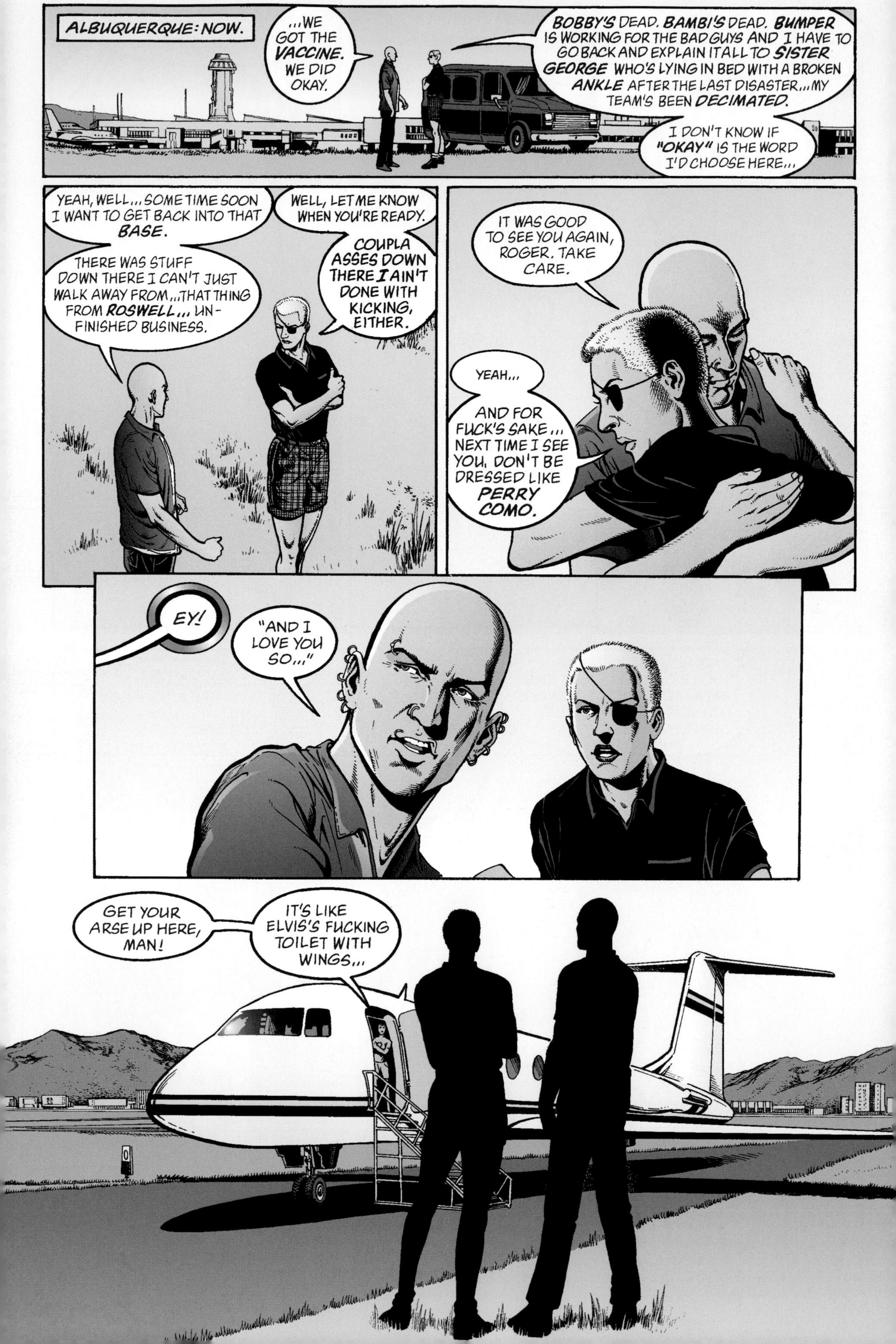
ALBUQUERQUE: NOW.
...WE GOT THE VACCINE. WE DID OKAY.
BOBBY'S DEAD. BAMBI'S DEAD. BUMPER IS WORKING FOR THE BAD GUYS AND I HAVE TO GO BACK AND EXPLAIN IT ALL TO SISTER GEORGE WHO'S LYING IN BED WITH A BROKEN ANKLE AFTER THE LAST DISASTER... MY TEAM'S BEEN DECIMATED.
I DON'T KNOW IF "OKAY" IS THE WORD I'D CHOOSE HERE...
YEAH, WELL... SOME TIME SOON I WANT TO GET BACK INTO THAT BASE.
THERE WAS STUFF DOWN THERE I CAN'T JUST WALK AWAY FROM... THAT THING FROM ROSWELL... UN-FINISHED BUSINESS.
WELL, LET ME KNOW WHEN YOU'RE READY.
COUPLA ASSES DOWN THERE I AIN'T DONE WITH KICKING, EITHER.
IT WAS GOOD TO SEE YOU AGAIN, ROGER. TAKE CARE.
YEAH...
AND FOR FUCK'S SAKE... NEXT TIME I SEE YOU, DON'T BE DRESSED LIKE PERRY COMO.
EY!
"AND I LOVE YOU SO..."
GET YOUR ARSE UP HERE, MAN!
IT'S LIKE ELVIS'S FUCKING TOILET WITH WINGS...

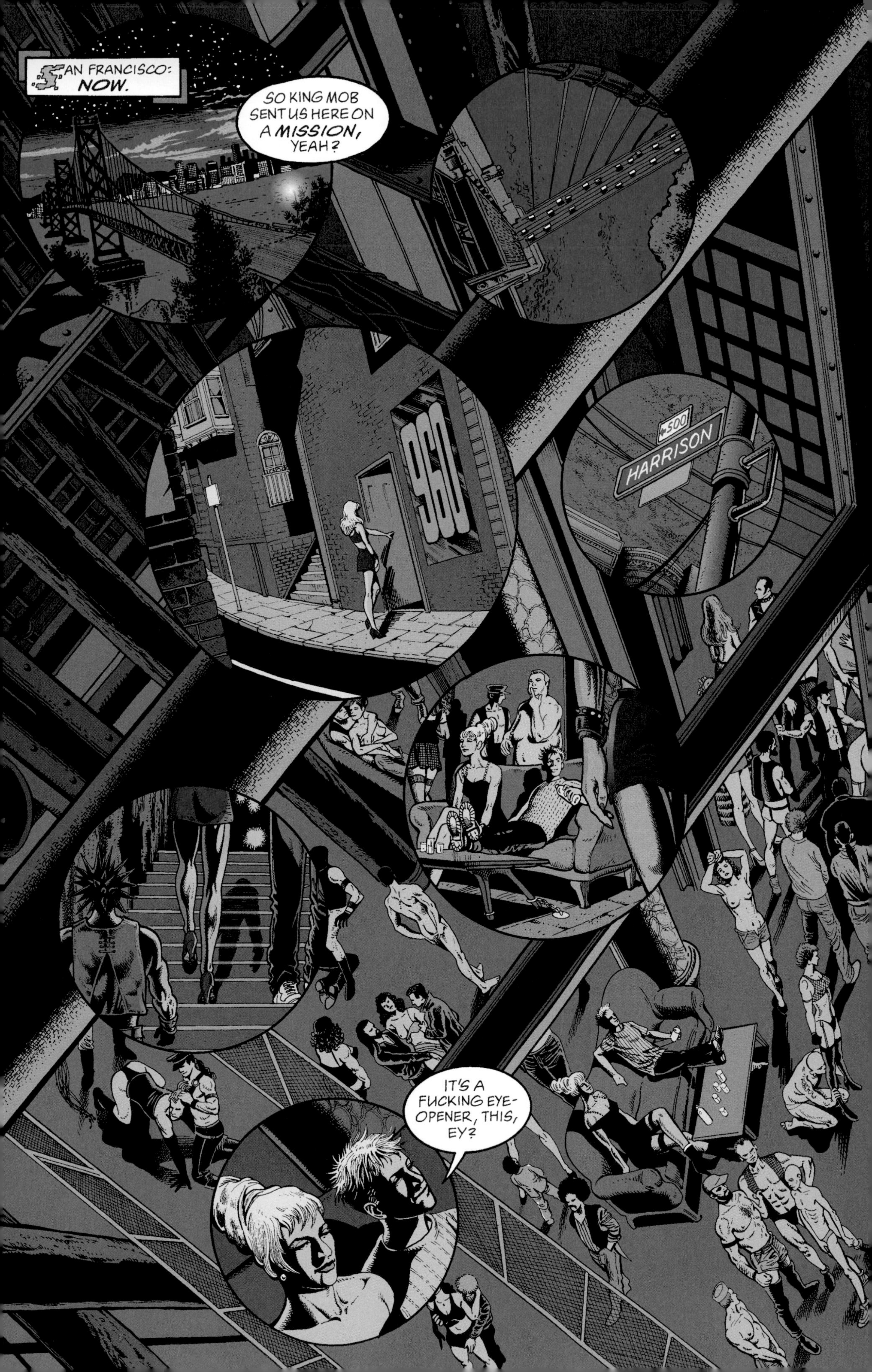
SAN FRANCISCO: NOW.
SO KING MOB SENT US HERE ON A MISSION, YEAH?
500
HARRISON
960
IT'S A FUCKING EYE-OPENER, THIS, EY?

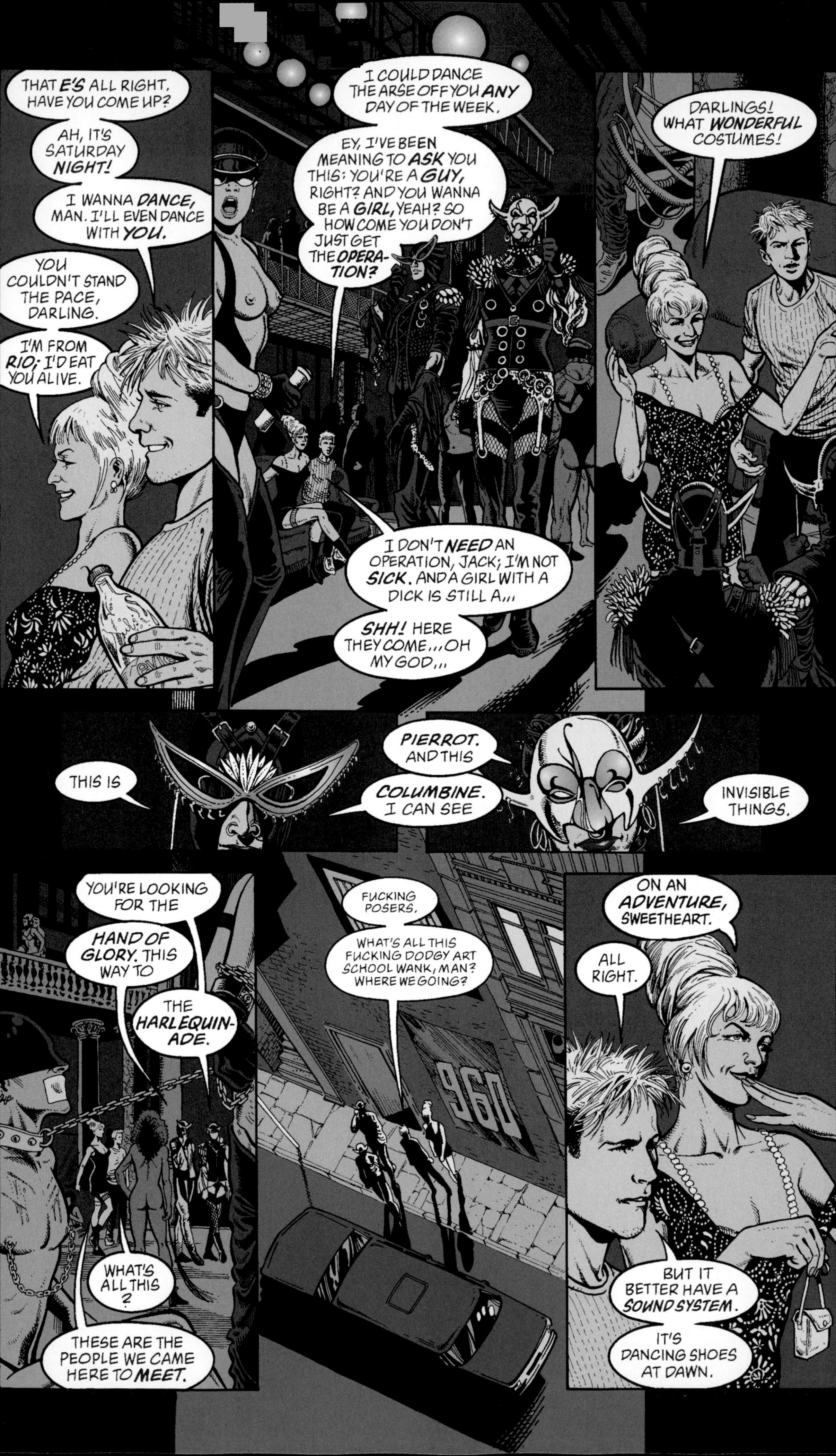
THAT E'S ALL RIGHT. HAVE YOU COME UP?
AH, IT'S SATURDAY NIGHT!
I WANNA DANCE, MAN. I'LL EVEN DANCE WITH YOU.
YOU COULDN'T STAND THE PACE, DARLING.
I'M FROM RIO; I'D EAT YOU ALIVE.
I COULD DANCE THE ARSE OFF YOU ANY DAY OF THE WEEK.
EY, I'VE BEEN MEANING TO ASK YOU THIS: YOU'RE A GUY, RIGHT? AND YOU WANNA BE A GIRL, YEAH? SO HOW COME YOU DON'T JUST GET THE OPERATION?
I DON'T NEED AN OPERATION, JACK; I'M NOT SICK. AND A GIRL WITH A DICK IS STILL A...
SHH! HERE THEY COME... OH MY GOD...
DARLINGS! WHAT WONDERFUL COSTUMES!
THIS IS
PIERROT. AND THIS
COLUMBINE. I CAN SEE
INVISIBLE THINGS.
YOU'RE LOOKING FOR THE
HAND OF GLORY. THIS WAY TO
THE HARLEQUINADE.
WHAT'S ALL THIS?
THESE ARE THE PEOPLE WE CAME HERE TO MEET.
FUCKING POSERS.
WHAT'S ALL THIS FUCKING DODGY ART SCHOOL WANK, MAN? WHERE WE GOING?
ON AN ADVENTURE, SWEETHEART.
ALL RIGHT.
BUT IT BETTER HAVE A SOUND SYSTEM.
IT'S DANCING SHOES AT DAWN.

BERKELEY: NOW.

...LAST I HEARD FROM YOU WAS THAT MAD POSTCARD FROM *AUSTRALIA* AND THEN A COUPLE OF PHONE CALLS AT *CHRISTMAS*...

IS THIS *PLEASURE* OR ARE THE *MANSON GIRLS* WITH YOU?

WE'RE ALL STAYING IN THE *MARRIOTT* ON MARKET, COURTESY OF *MASON LANG*, THE NEW-AGE BILLIONAIRE.

HE RECKONS ONE OF HIS RESEARCH PEOPLE HAS FIGURED OUT HOW TO MAKE A *TIME MACHINE* AND, WELL...

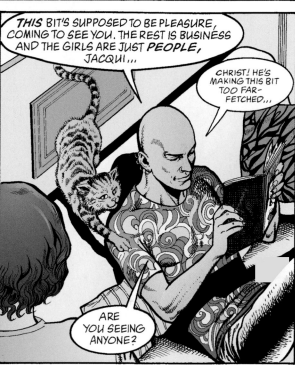

THIS BIT'S SUPPOSED TO BE PLEASURE, COMING TO SEE YOU. THE REST IS BUSINESS AND THE GIRLS ARE JUST *PEOPLE*, JACQUI...

CHRIST! HE'S MAKING THIS BIT TOO FAR-FETCHED...

ARE YOU SEEING ANYONE?

JUST PEOPLE. YOU KNOW.

NOTHING SERIOUS.

YEAH.

OURS WAS A HARD ACT TO FOLLOW.

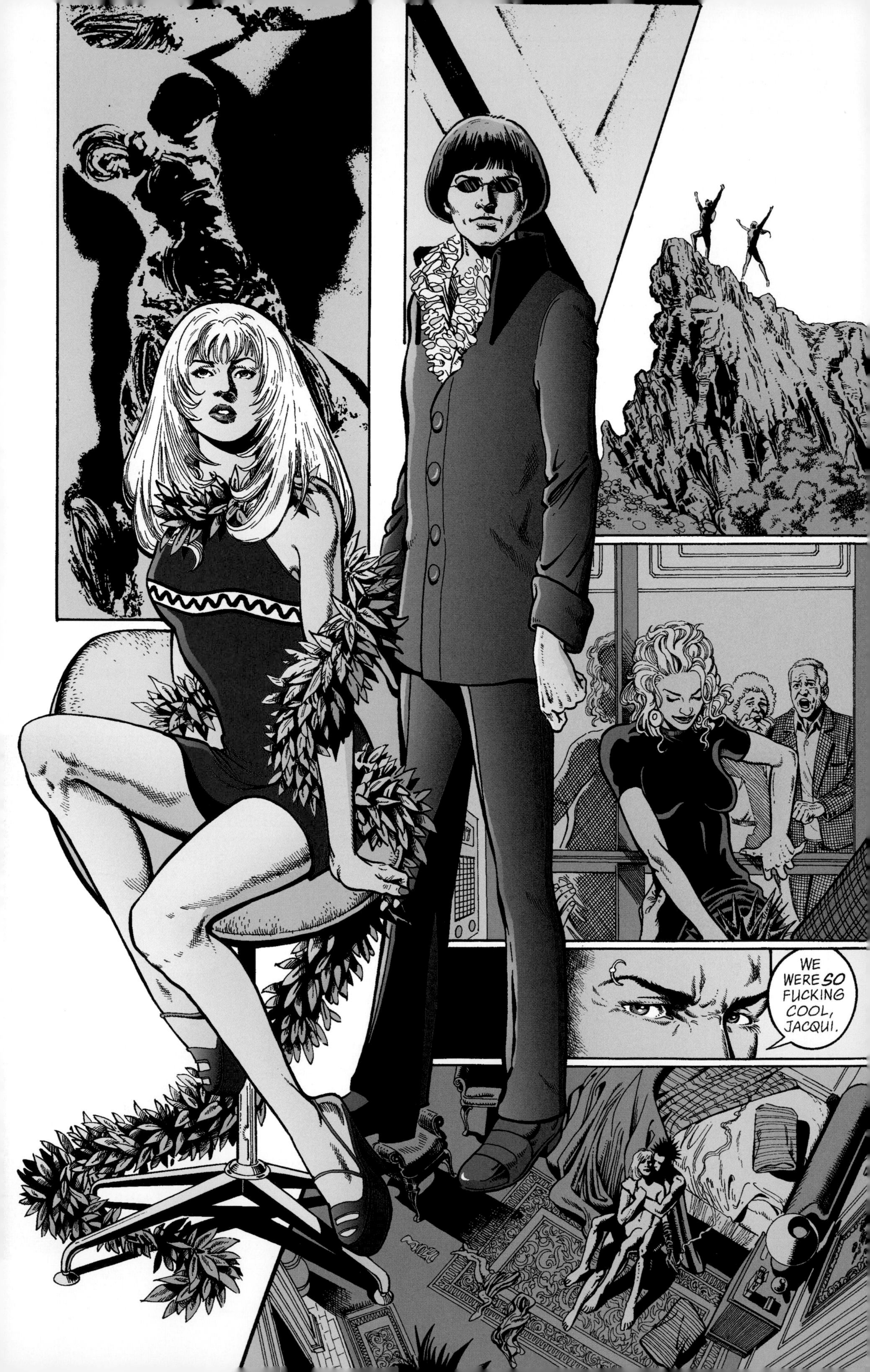
WE WERE SO FUCKING COOL, JACQUI.

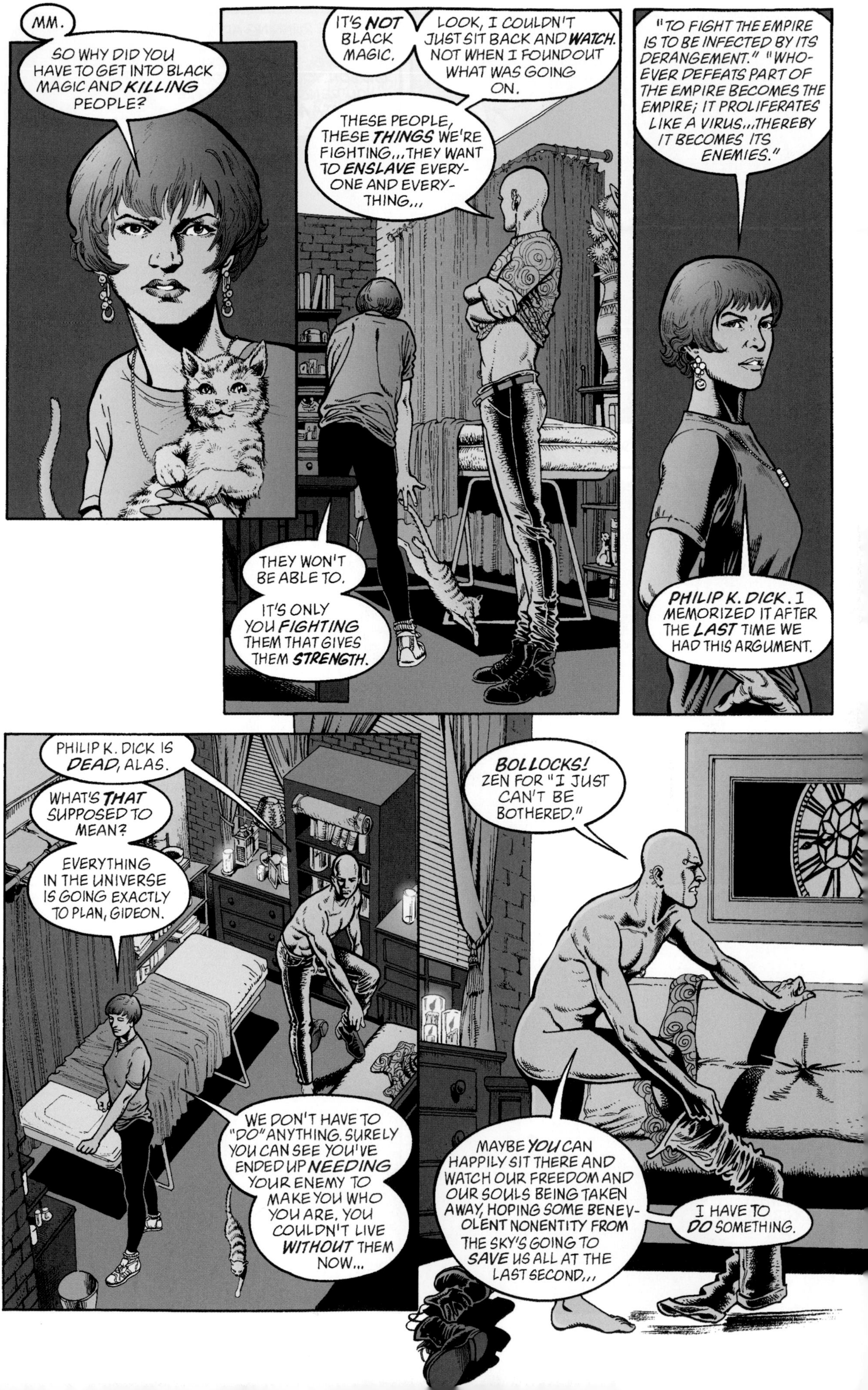
MM.
SO WHY DID YOU HAVE TO GET INTO BLACK MAGIC AND KILLING PEOPLE?
IT'S NOT BLACK MAGIC.
LOOK, I COULDN'T JUST SIT BACK AND WATCH. NOT WHEN I FOUND OUT WHAT WAS GOING ON.
THESE PEOPLE, THESE THINGS WE'RE FIGHTING... THEY WANT TO ENSLAVE EVERY-ONE AND EVERY-THING...
THEY WON'T BE ABLE TO.
IT'S ONLY YOU FIGHTING THEM THAT GIVES THEM STRENGTH.
"TO FIGHT THE EMPIRE IS TO BE INFECTED BY ITS DERANGEMENT." "WHO-EVER DEFEATS PART OF THE EMPIRE BECOMES THE EMPIRE; IT PROLIFERATES LIKE A VIRUS... THEREBY IT BECOMES ITS ENEMIES."
PHILIP K. DICK. I MEMORIZED IT AFTER THE LAST TIME WE HAD THIS ARGUMENT.
PHILIP K. DICK IS DEAD, ALAS.
WHAT'S THAT SUPPOSED TO MEAN?
EVERYTHING IN THE UNIVERSE IS GOING EXACTLY TO PLAN, GIDEON.
BOLLOCKS! ZEN FOR "I JUST CAN'T BE BOTHERED."
WE DON'T HAVE TO "DO" ANYTHING. SURELY YOU CAN SEE YOU'VE ENDED UP NEEDING YOUR ENEMY TO MAKE YOU WHO YOU ARE. YOU COULDN'T LIVE WITHOUT THEM NOW...
MAYBE YOU CAN HAPPILY SIT THERE AND WATCH OUR FREEDOM AND OUR SOULS BEING TAKEN AWAY, HOPING SOME BENEV-OLENT NONENTITY FROM THE SKY'S GOING TO SAVE US ALL AT THE LAST SECOND...
I HAVE TO DO SOMETHING.

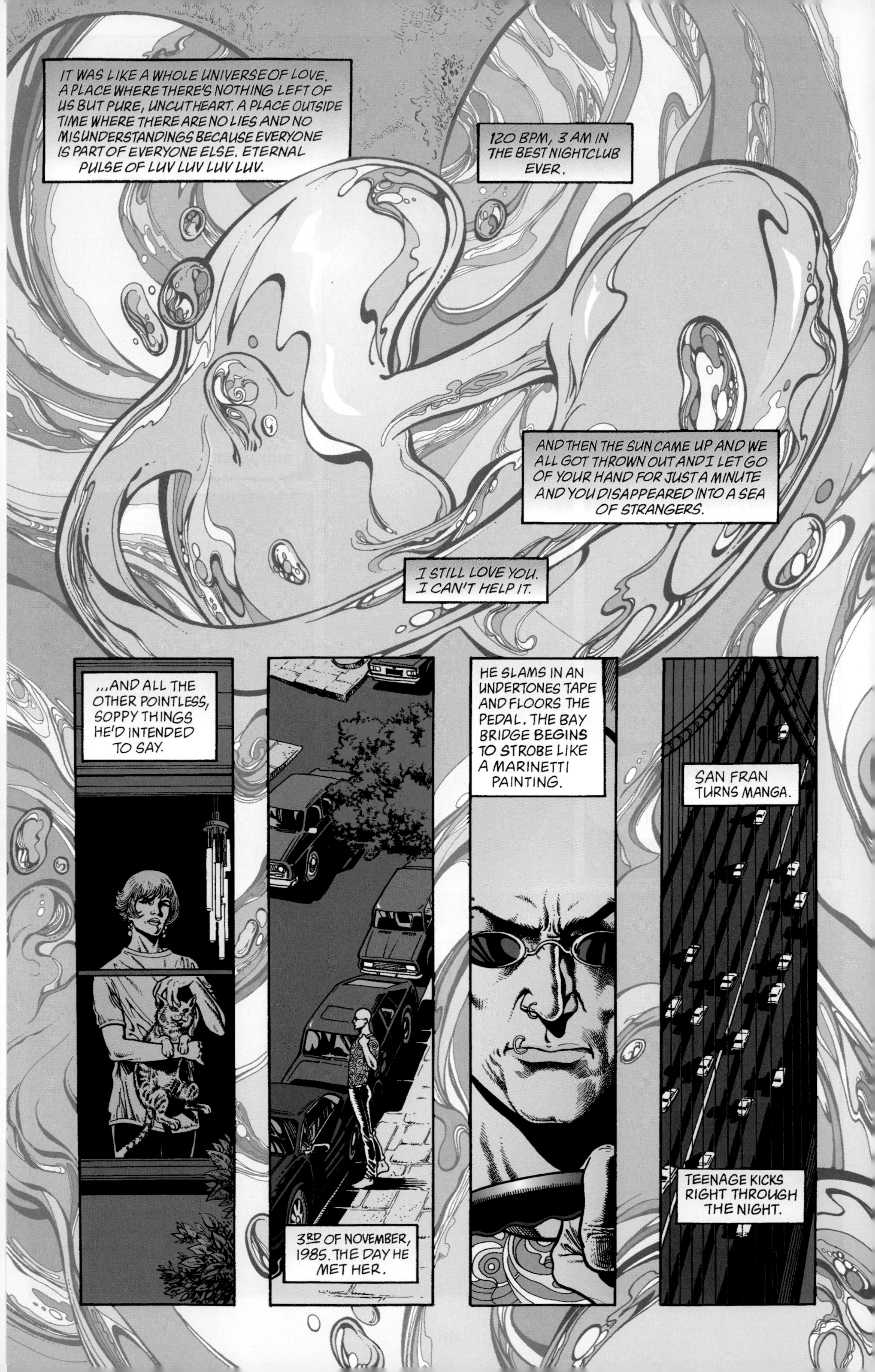
IT WAS LIKE A WHOLE UNIVERSE OF LOVE. A PLACE WHERE THERE'S NOTHING LEFT OF US BUT PURE, UNCUT HEART. A PLACE OUTSIDE TIME WHERE THERE ARE NO LIES AND NO MISUNDERSTANDINGS BECAUSE EVERYONE IS PART OF EVERYONE ELSE. ETERNAL PULSE OF LUV LUV LUV LUV.
120 BPM, 3 AM IN THE BEST NIGHTCLUB EVER.
AND THEN THE SUN CAME UP AND WE ALL GOT THROWN OUT AND I LET GO OF YOUR HAND FOR JUST A MINUTE AND YOU DISAPPEARED INTO A SEA OF STRANGERS.
I STILL LOVE YOU. I CAN'T HELP IT.
...AND ALL THE OTHER POINTLESS, SOPPY THINGS HE'D INTENDED TO SAY.
3RD OF NOVEMBER, 1985. THE DAY HE MET HER.
HE SLAMS IN AN UNDERTONES TAPE AND FLOORS THE PEDAL. THE BAY BRIDGE BEGINS TO STROBE LIKE A MARINETTI PAINTING.
SAN FRAN TURNS MANGA.
TEENAGE KICKS RIGHT THROUGH THE NIGHT.

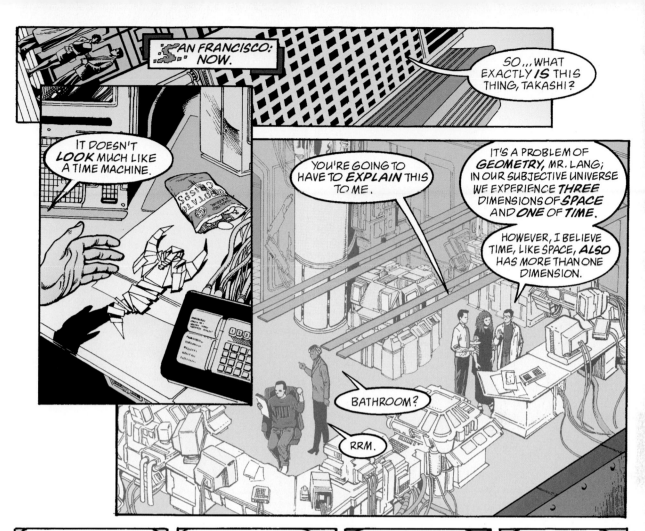

SAN FRANCISCO: NOW.

IT DOESN'T **LOOK** MUCH LIKE A TIME MACHINE.

SO... WHAT EXACTLY **IS** THIS THING, TAKASHI?

YOU'RE GOING TO HAVE TO **EXPLAIN** THIS TO ME.

IT'S A PROBLEM OF **GEOMETRY**, MR. LANG; IN OUR SUBJECTIVE UNIVERSE WE EXPERIENCE **THREE** DIMENSIONS OF **SPACE** AND **ONE** OF **TIME**.

HOWEVER, I BELIEVE TIME, LIKE SPACE, **ALSO** HAS MORE THAN ONE DIMENSION.

BATHROOM?

RRM.

THINK OF TIMESPACE AS A MULTIDIMENSIONAL SELF-PERFECTING **SYSTEM** IN WHICH EVERYTHING THAT **HAS** EVER, OR **WILL** EVER OCCUR, OCCURS **SIMULTANEOUSLY**.

I BELIEVE TIMESPACE IS A KIND OF **OBJECT**, A GEOMETRICAL **SUPERSOLID**. I BELIEVE IT MAY EVEN BE A TYPE OF **HOLOGRAM** IN WHICH ENERGY AND MATTER THEMSELVES ARE BY PRODUCTS OF THE OVERLAPPING OF TWO **HIGHER** SYSTEMS...

MAYBE YOU SHOULD JUST WRITE THIS DOWN...

EVERYTHING IS ON **DISK**, MR. LANG, THINK OF IT **THIS** WAY: WHERE **IS** THE PAST? WHERE **IS** THE FUTURE? UNDENIABLY, THEY **EXIST**, BUT WHY CAN'T YOU **POINT** TO THEM?

THE ONLY WAY TO DO THAT IS TO JUMP "**UP**" FROM THE SURFACE OF TIMESPACE AND SEE ALL OF HISTORY AND ALL OUR TOMORROWS AS THE SINGLE **OBJECT** I BELIEVE IT IS.

THE INVENTION OF THE **AIRPLANE** GAVE US MASTERY OF THE THIRD **SPATIAL** DIMENSION, NOW WE HAVE TO BUILD A MACHINE CAPABLE OF FREEING US FROM THE SINGLE **TIME** DIMENSION WE INHABIT.

AND YOU KNOW WHAT?

I THINK MY GREAT-GRANDFATHER'S ORIGAMI IS FROM THE **FUTURE**. I THINK **I** WILL SEND IT BACK TO **HIM** FROM A TIME TO COME SO THAT IT WILL PASS DOWN THROUGH MY FAMILY TO INSPIRE MY EFFORTS.

I BELIEVE, MR. LANG, THAT I HAVE **ALREADY** INVENTED THE TIME MACHINE.

AND I HAVE SENT ITS IMAGE **BACK** TO GUIDE ME TOWARD ITS CREATION.

123

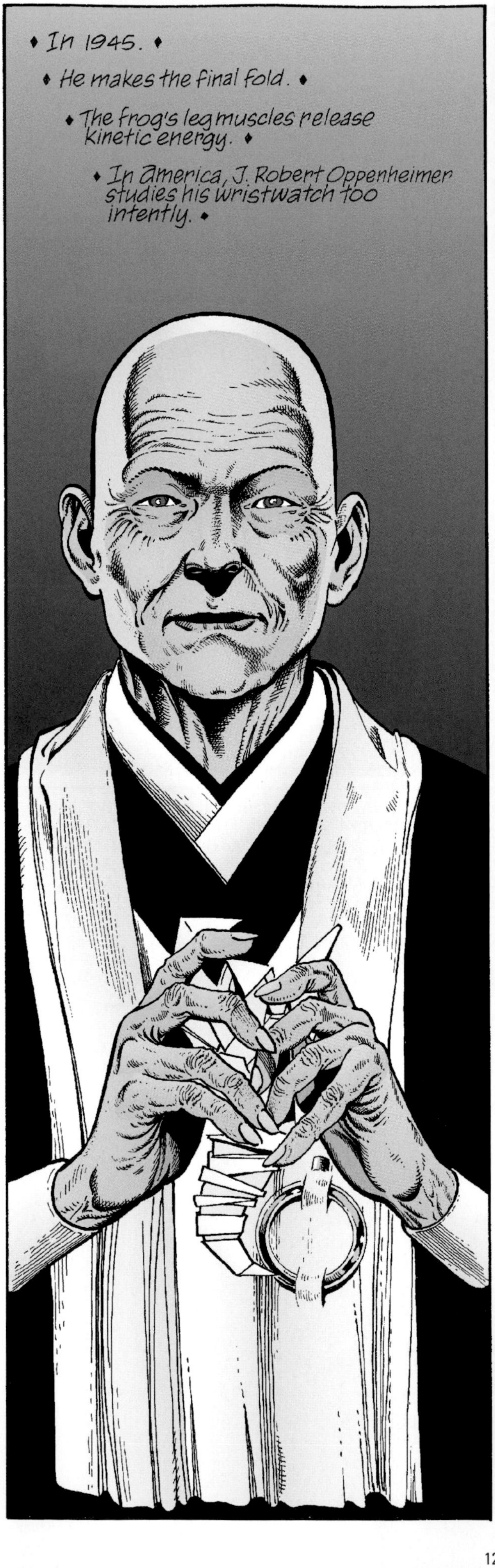
In 1945.
He makes the final fold.
The frog's leg muscles release kinetic energy.
In America, J. Robert Oppenheimer studies his wristwatch too intently.

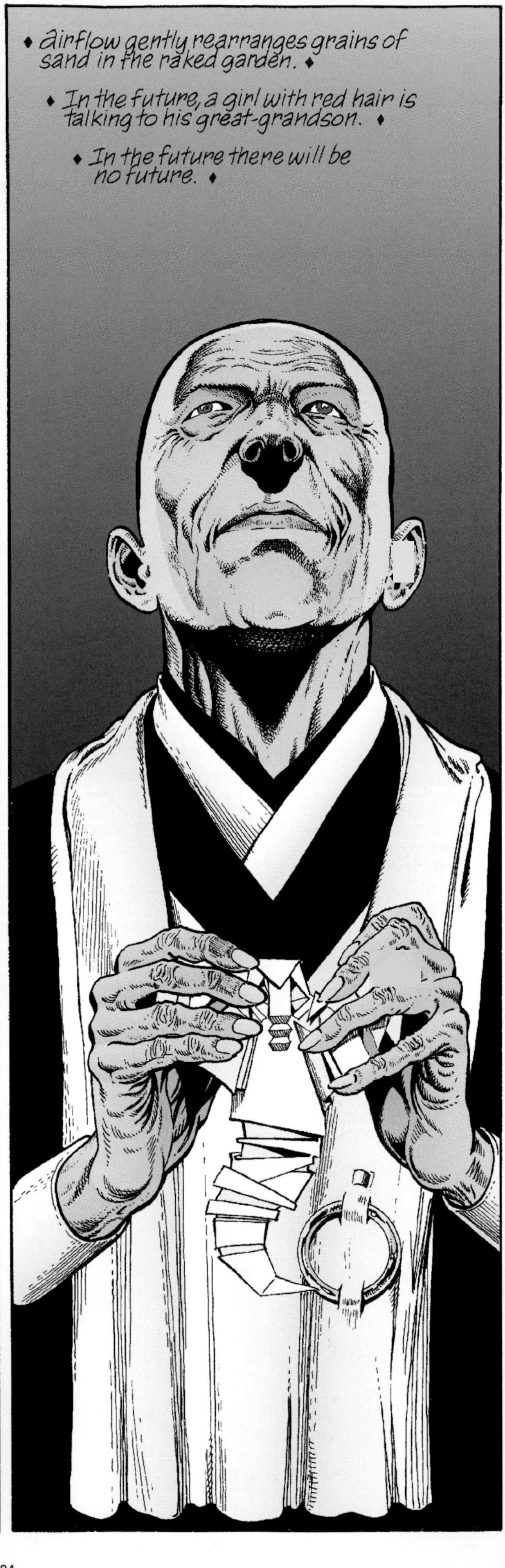
Airflow gently rearranges grains of sand in the raked garden.
In the future, a girl with red hair is talking to his great-grandson.
In the future there will be no future.

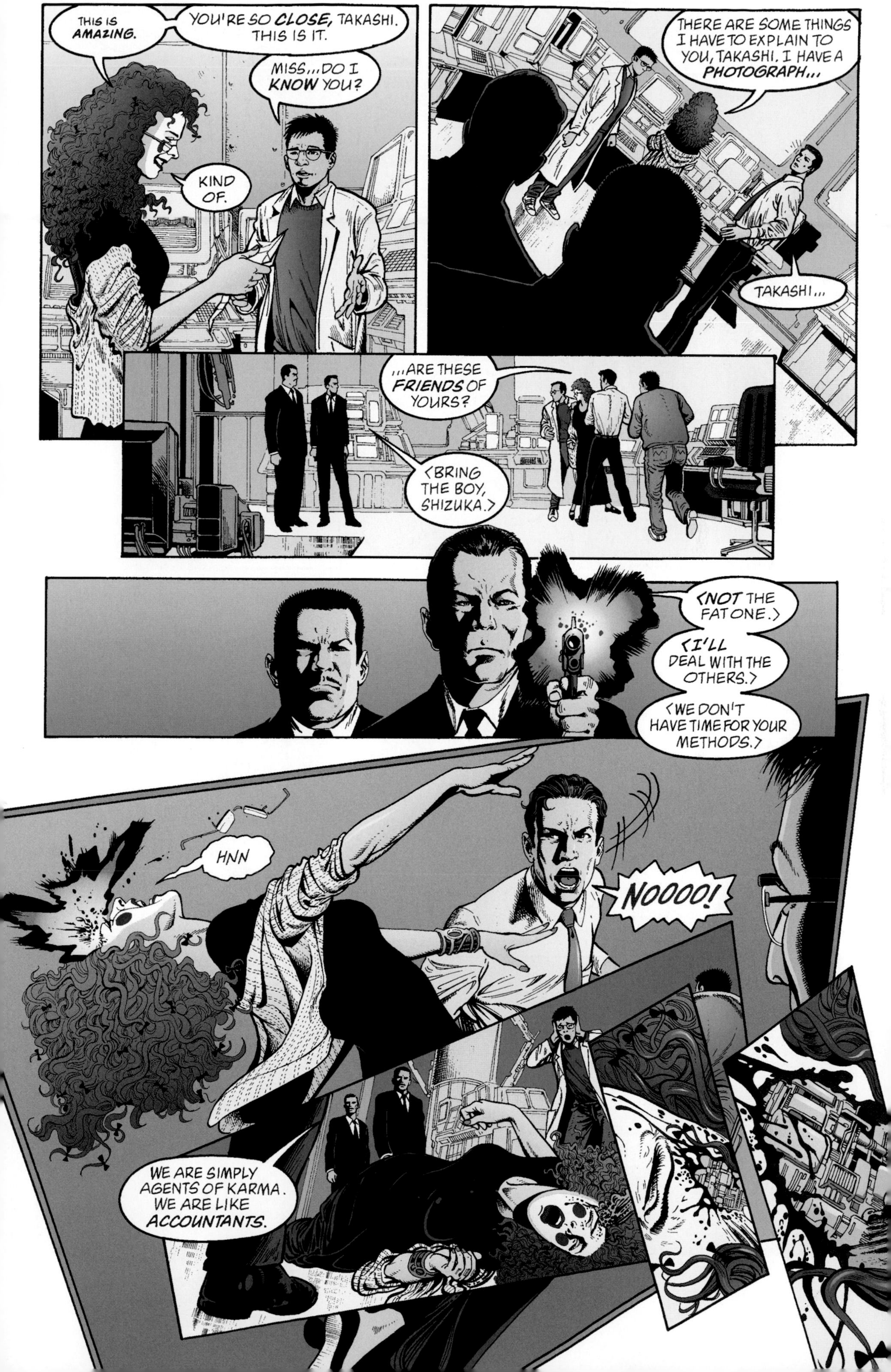
THIS IS AMAZING.
YOU'RE SO CLOSE, TAKASHI. THIS IS IT.
MISS...DO I KNOW YOU?
KIND OF.
THERE ARE SOME THINGS I HAVE TO EXPLAIN TO YOU, TAKASHI. I HAVE A PHOTOGRAPH...
TAKASHI...
...ARE THESE FRIENDS OF YOURS?
<BRING THE BOY, SHIZUKA.>
<NOT THE FAT ONE.>
<I'LL DEAL WITH THE OTHERS.>
<WE DON'T HAVE TIME FOR YOUR METHODS.>
HNN
NOOOO!
WE ARE SIMPLY AGENTS OF KARMA. WE ARE LIKE ACCOUNTANTS.

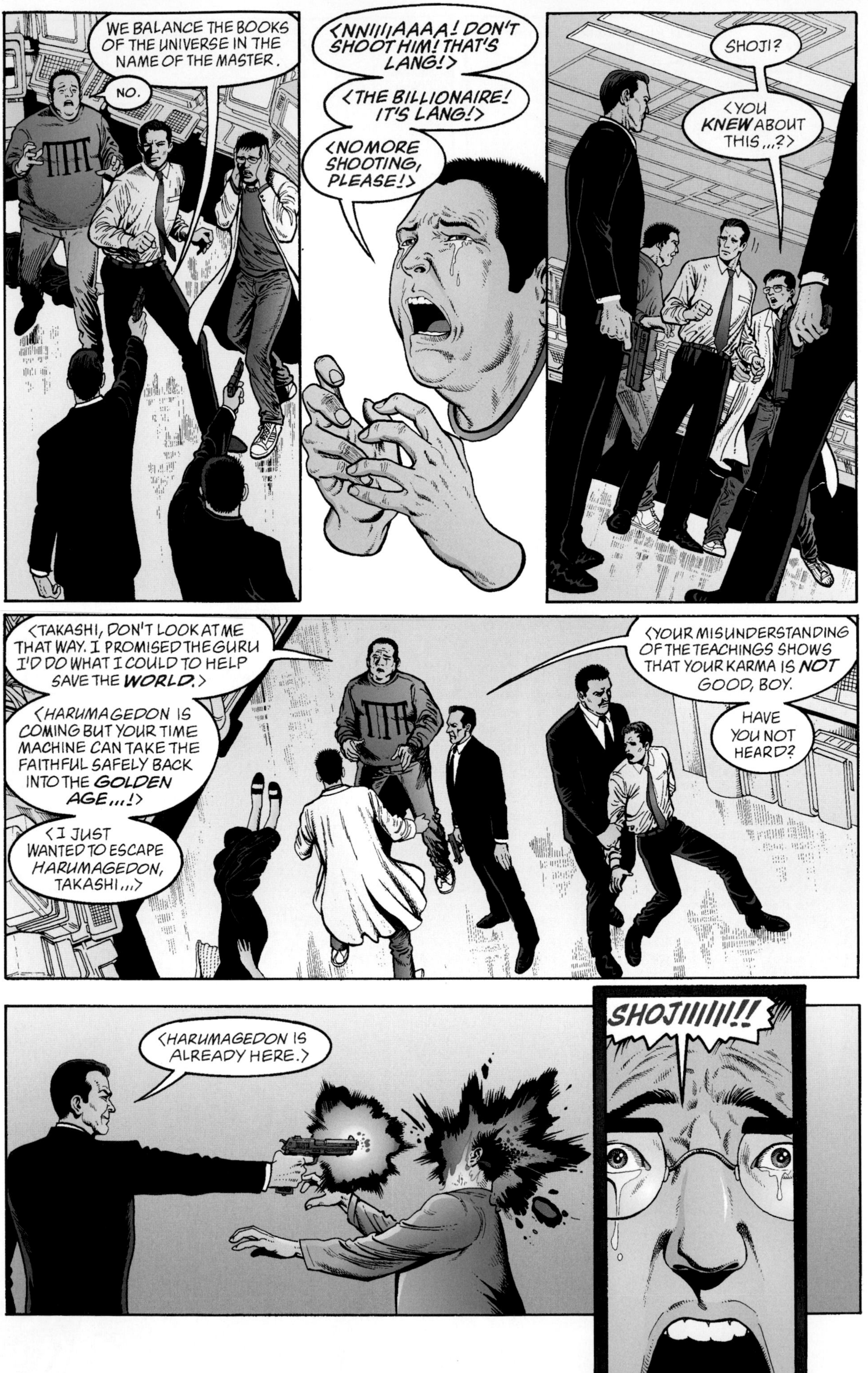
WE BALANCE THE BOOKS OF THE UNIVERSE IN THE NAME OF THE MASTER.
NO.
<NNIIIIAAAA! DON'T SHOOT HIM! THAT'S LANG!>
<THE BILLIONAIRE! IT'S LANG!>
<NO MORE SHOOTING, PLEASE!>
SHOJI?
<YOU KNEW ABOUT THIS...?>
<TAKASHI, DON'T LOOK AT ME THAT WAY. I PROMISED THE GURU I'D DO WHAT I COULD TO HELP SAVE THE WORLD.>
<HARUMAGEDON IS COMING BUT YOUR TIME MACHINE CAN TAKE THE FAITHFUL SAFELY BACK INTO THE GOLDEN AGE...!>
<I JUST WANTED TO ESCAPE HARUMAGEDON, TAKASHI...>
<YOUR MISUNDERSTANDING OF THE TEACHINGS SHOWS THAT YOUR KARMA IS NOT GOOD, BOY.
HAVE YOU NOT HEARD?
<HARUMAGEDON IS ALREADY HERE.>
SHOJIIIIIII!!

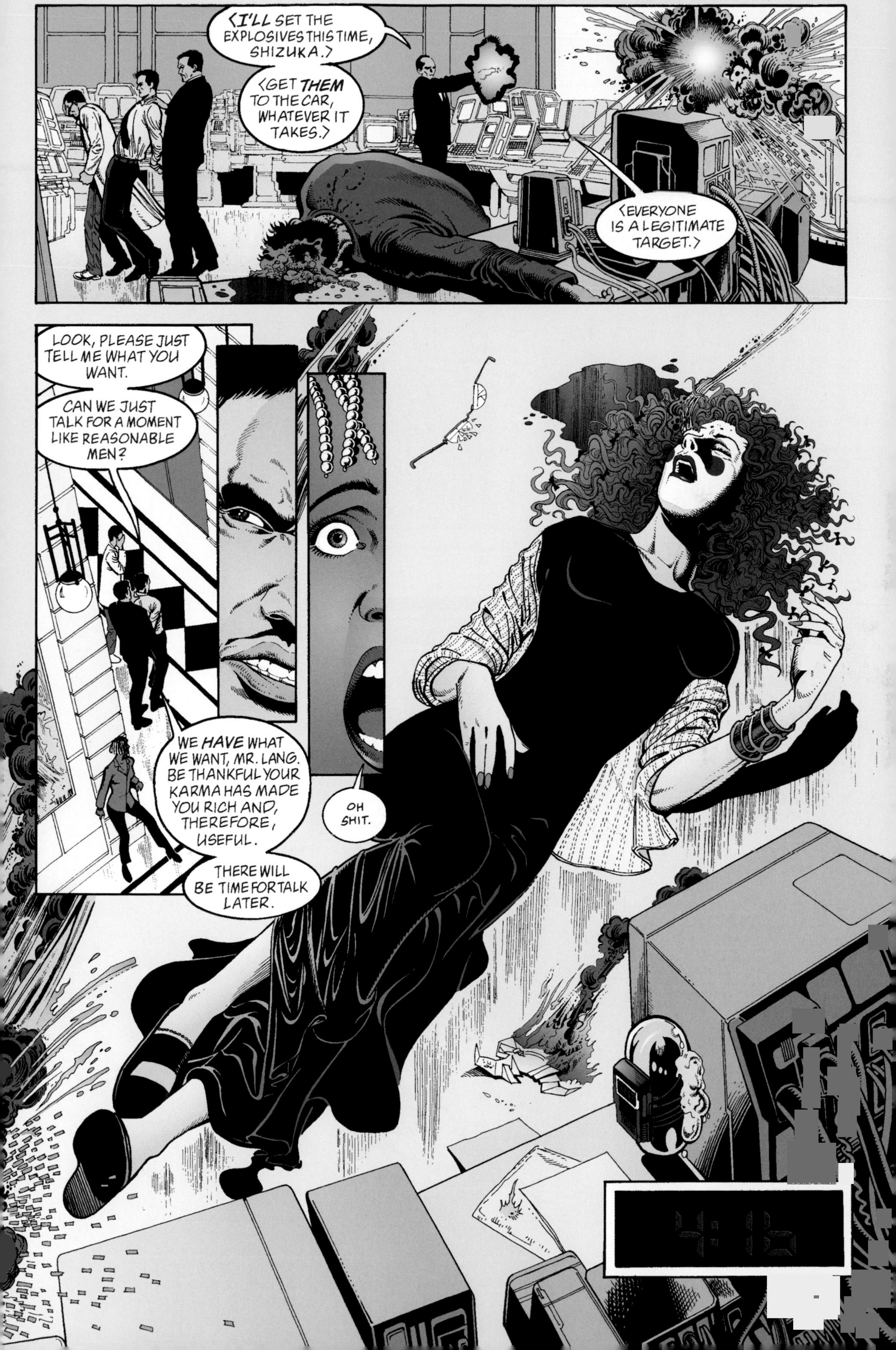
<I'LL SET THE EXPLOSIVES THIS TIME, SHIZUKA.>
<GET THEM TO THE CAR, WHATEVER IT TAKES.>
<EVERYONE IS A LEGITIMATE TARGET.>
LOOK, PLEASE JUST TELL ME WHAT YOU WANT.
CAN WE JUST TALK FOR A MOMENT LIKE REASONABLE MEN?
WE HAVE WHAT WE WANT, MR. LANG. BE THANKFUL YOUR KARMA HAS MADE YOU RICH AND, THEREFORE, USEFUL.
THERE WILL BE TIME FOR TALK LATER.
OH SHIT.

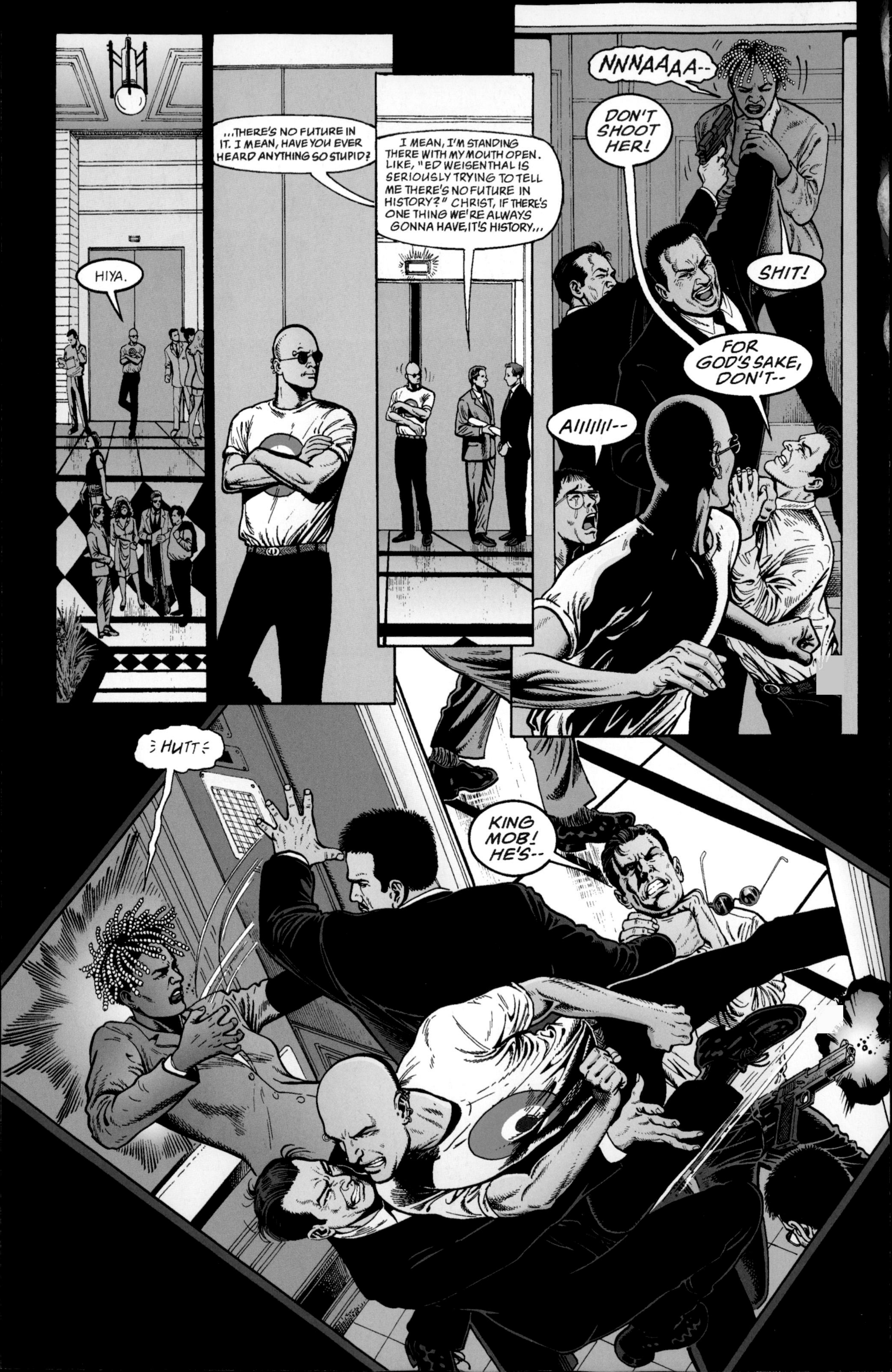
HIYA.
...THERE'S NO FUTURE IN IT. I MEAN, HAVE YOU EVER HEARD ANYTHING SO STUPID?
I MEAN, I'M STANDING THERE WITH MY MOUTH OPEN. LIKE, "ED WEISENTHAL IS SERIOUSLY TRYING TO TELL ME THERE'S NO FUTURE IN HISTORY?" CHRIST, IF THERE'S ONE THING WE'RE ALWAYS GONNA HAVE, IT'S HISTORY...
NNNAAAAA--
DON'T SHOOT HER!
SHIT!
FOR GOD'S SAKE, DON'T--
AIIIIIII--
HUTT
KING MOB! HE'S--

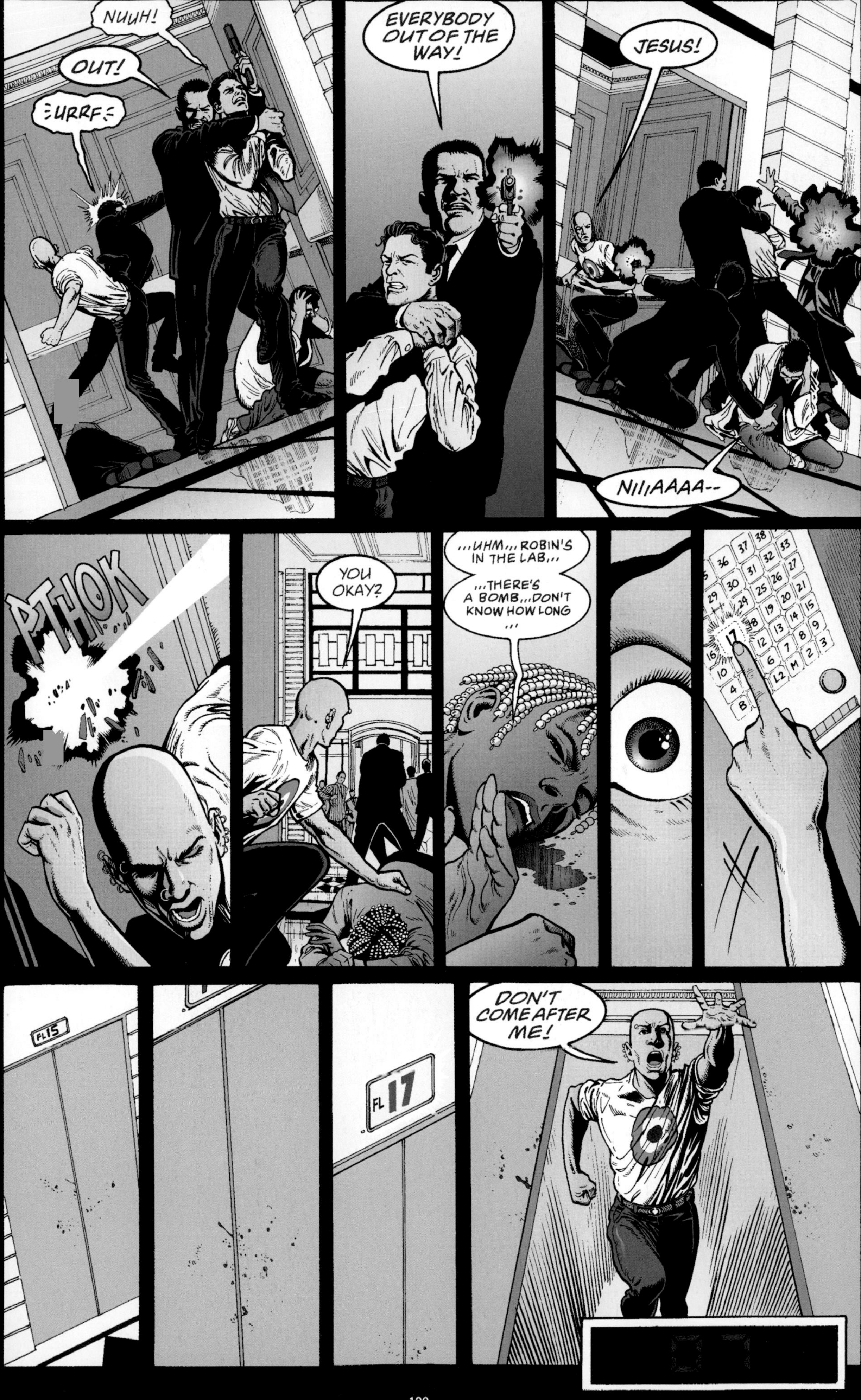
NUUH!
OUT!
URRF
EVERYBODY OUT OF THE WAY!
JESUS!
NIIIAAAA--
PTHOK
YOU OKAY?
...UHM... ROBIN'S IN THE LAB...
...THERE'S A BOMB...DON'T KNOW HOW LONG ...
FL 15
FL 17
DON'T COME AFTER ME!

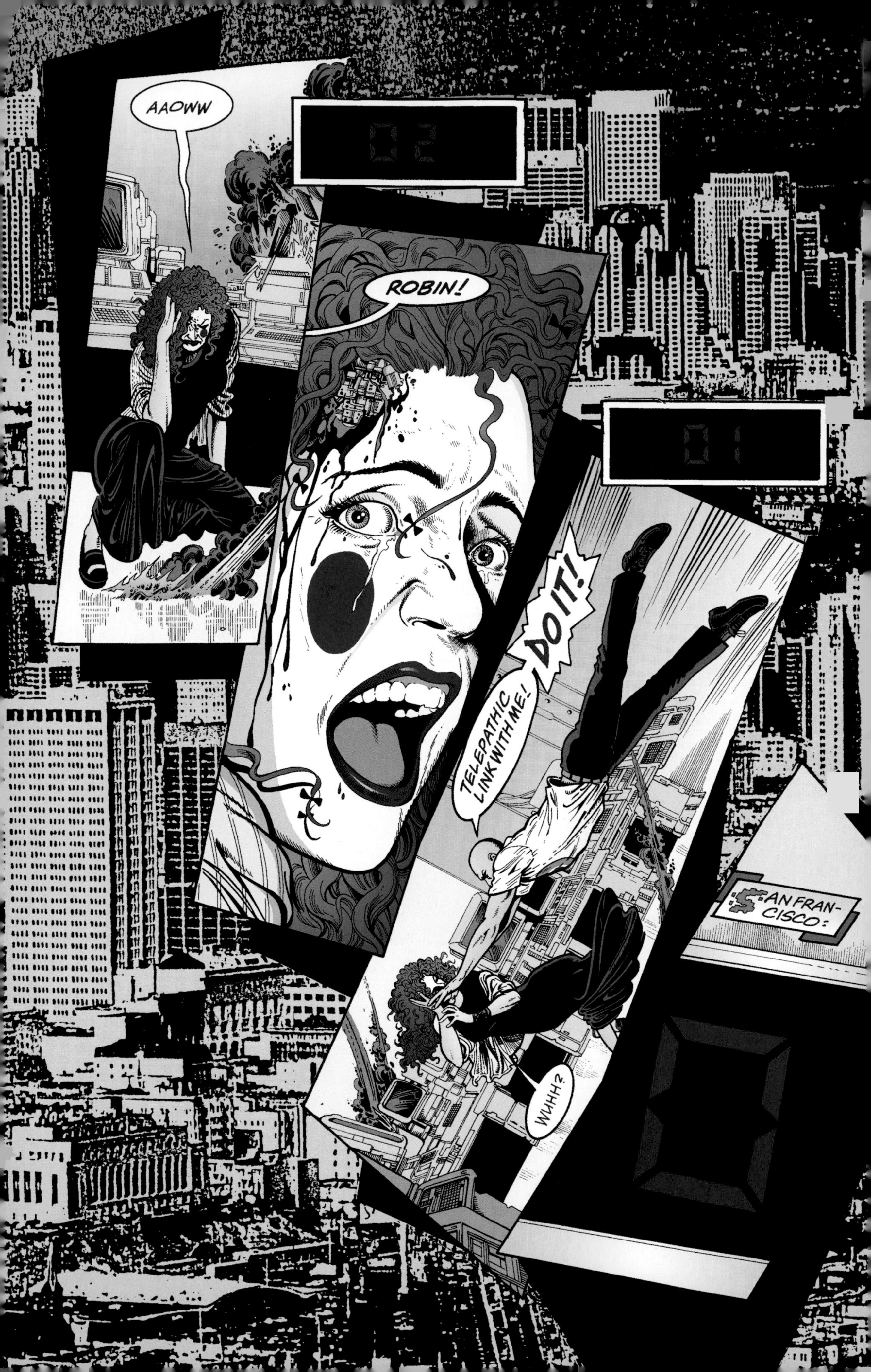
AAOWW
02
ROBIN!
01
DO IT!
TELEPATHIC LINK WITH ME!
SAN FRAN-CISCO:
WUHH?

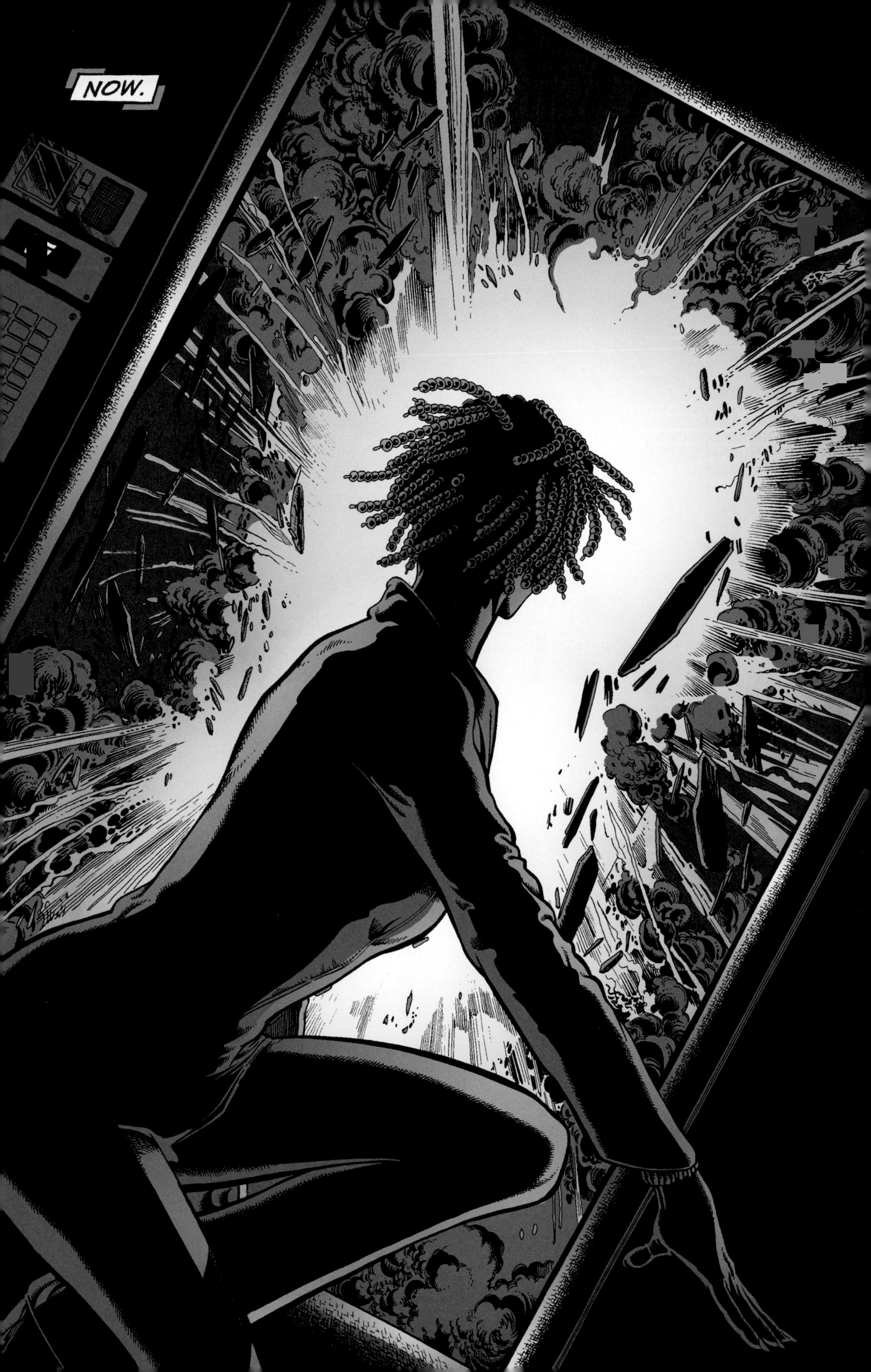
NOW.

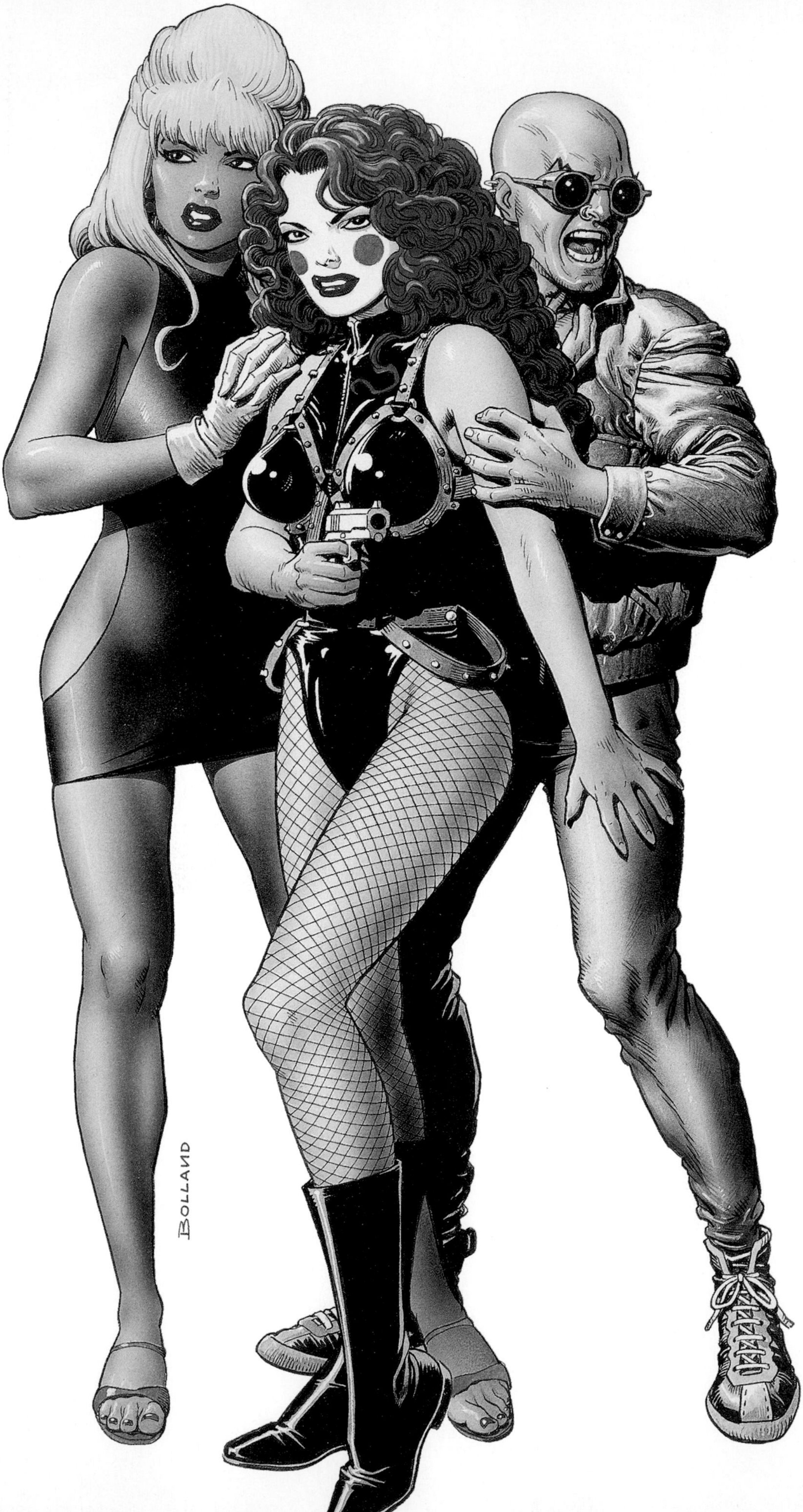
BOLLAND

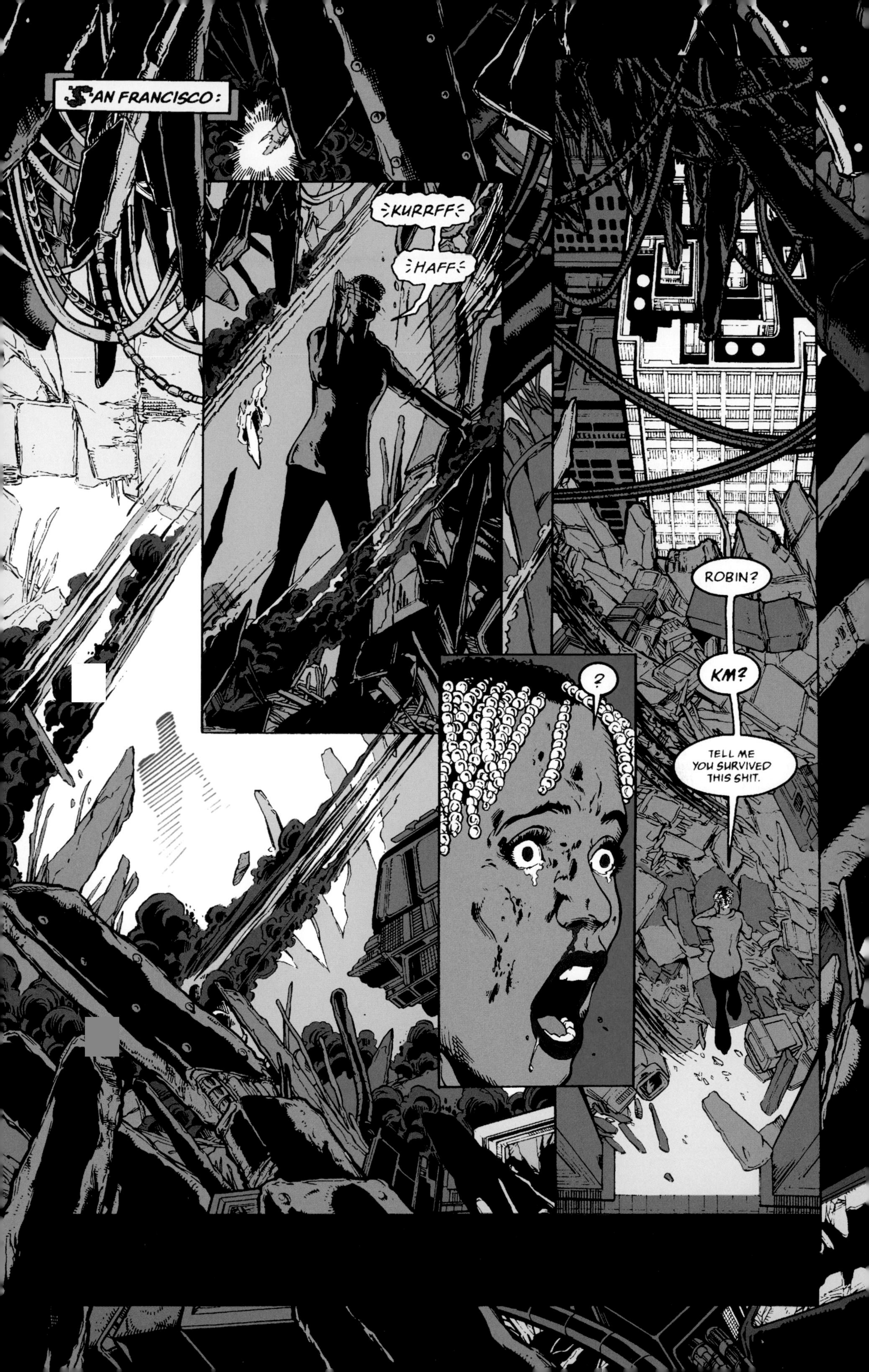
SAN FRANCISCO:
KURRFF
HAFF
?
ROBIN?
KM?
TELL ME YOU SURVIVED THIS SHIT.

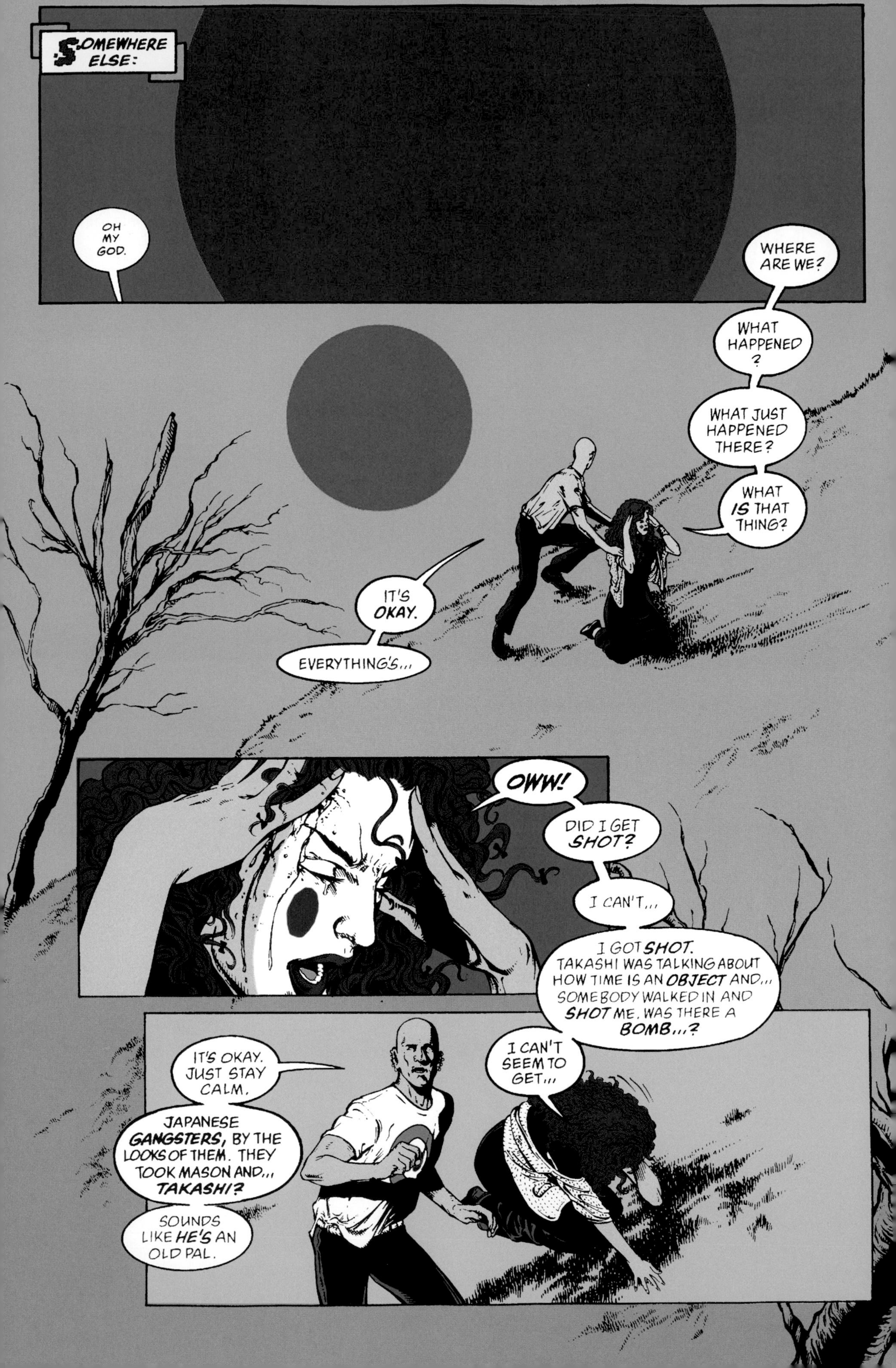
SOMEWHERE ELSE:
OH MY GOD.
WHERE ARE WE?
WHAT HAPPENED?
WHAT JUST HAPPENED THERE?
WHAT IS THAT THING?
IT'S OKAY.
EVERYTHING'S...
OWW!
DID I GET SHOT?
I CAN'T...
I GOT SHOT. TAKASHI WAS TALKING ABOUT HOW TIME IS AN OBJECT AND... SOMEBODY WALKED IN AND SHOT ME. WAS THERE A BOMB...?
I CAN'T SEEM TO GET...
IT'S OKAY. JUST STAY CALM.
JAPANESE GANGSTERS, BY THE LOOKS OF THEM. THEY TOOK MASON AND... TAKASHI?
SOUNDS LIKE HE'S AN OLD PAL.

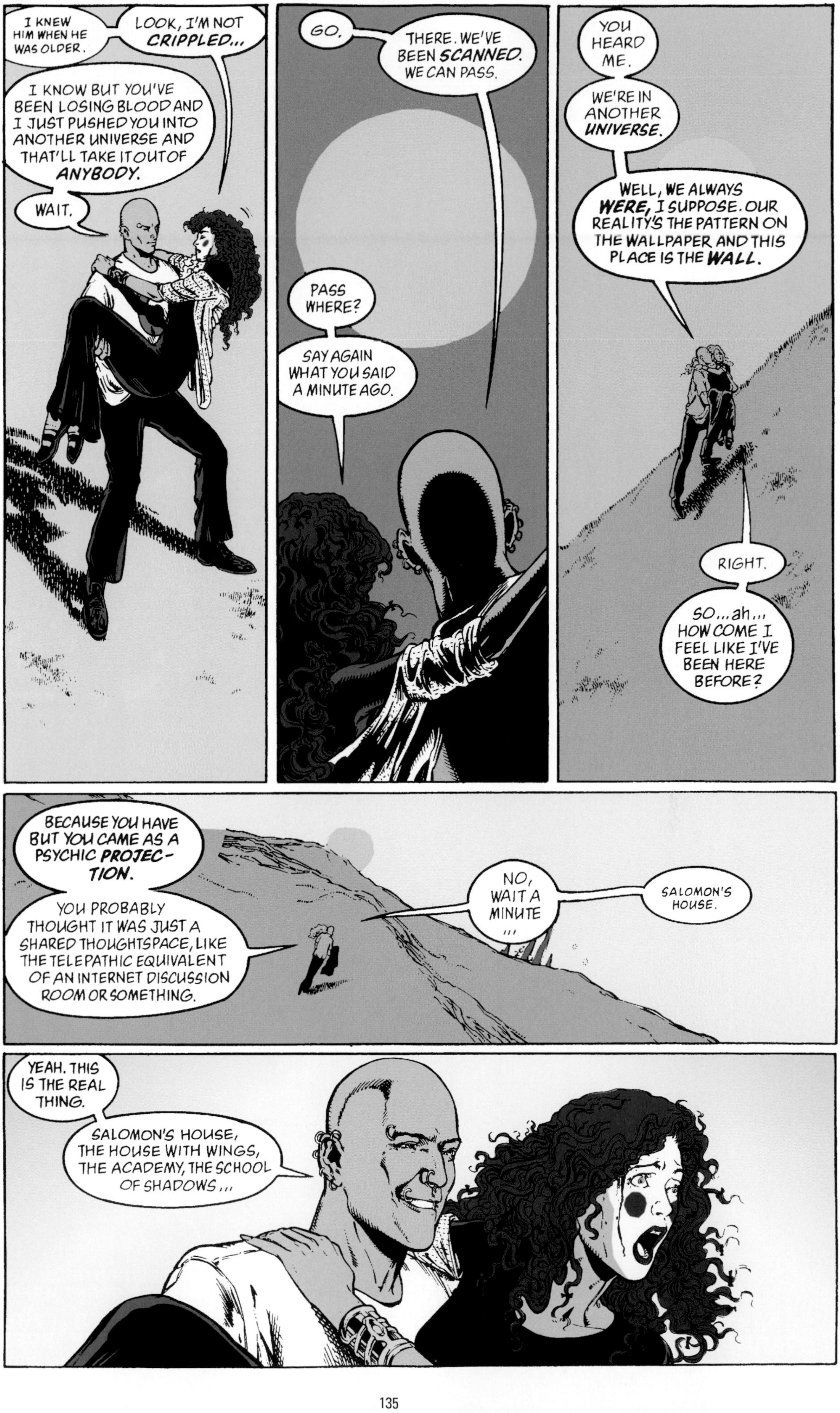
I KNEW HIM WHEN HE WAS OLDER.
LOOK, I'M NOT CRIPPLED...
I KNOW BUT YOU'VE BEEN LOSING BLOOD AND I JUST PUSHED YOU INTO ANOTHER UNIVERSE AND THAT'LL TAKE IT OUT OF ANYBODY.
WAIT.
GO.
THERE. WE'VE BEEN SCANNED. WE CAN PASS.
PASS WHERE?
SAY AGAIN WHAT YOU SAID A MINUTE AGO.
YOU HEARD ME.
WE'RE IN ANOTHER UNIVERSE.
WELL, WE ALWAYS WERE, I SUPPOSE. OUR REALITY'S THE PATTERN ON THE WALLPAPER AND THIS PLACE IS THE WALL.
RIGHT.
SO...ah... HOW COME I FEEL LIKE I'VE BEEN HERE BEFORE?
BECAUSE YOU HAVE BUT YOU CAME AS A PSYCHIC PROJECTION.
YOU PROBABLY THOUGHT IT WAS JUST A SHARED THOUGHTSPACE, LIKE THE TELEPATHIC EQUIVALENT OF AN INTERNET DISCUSSION ROOM OR SOMETHING.
NO, WAIT A MINUTE ...
SALOMON'S HOUSE.
YEAH. THIS IS THE REAL THING.
SALOMON'S HOUSE, THE HOUSE WITH WINGS, THE ACADEMY, THE SCHOOL OF SHADOWS...

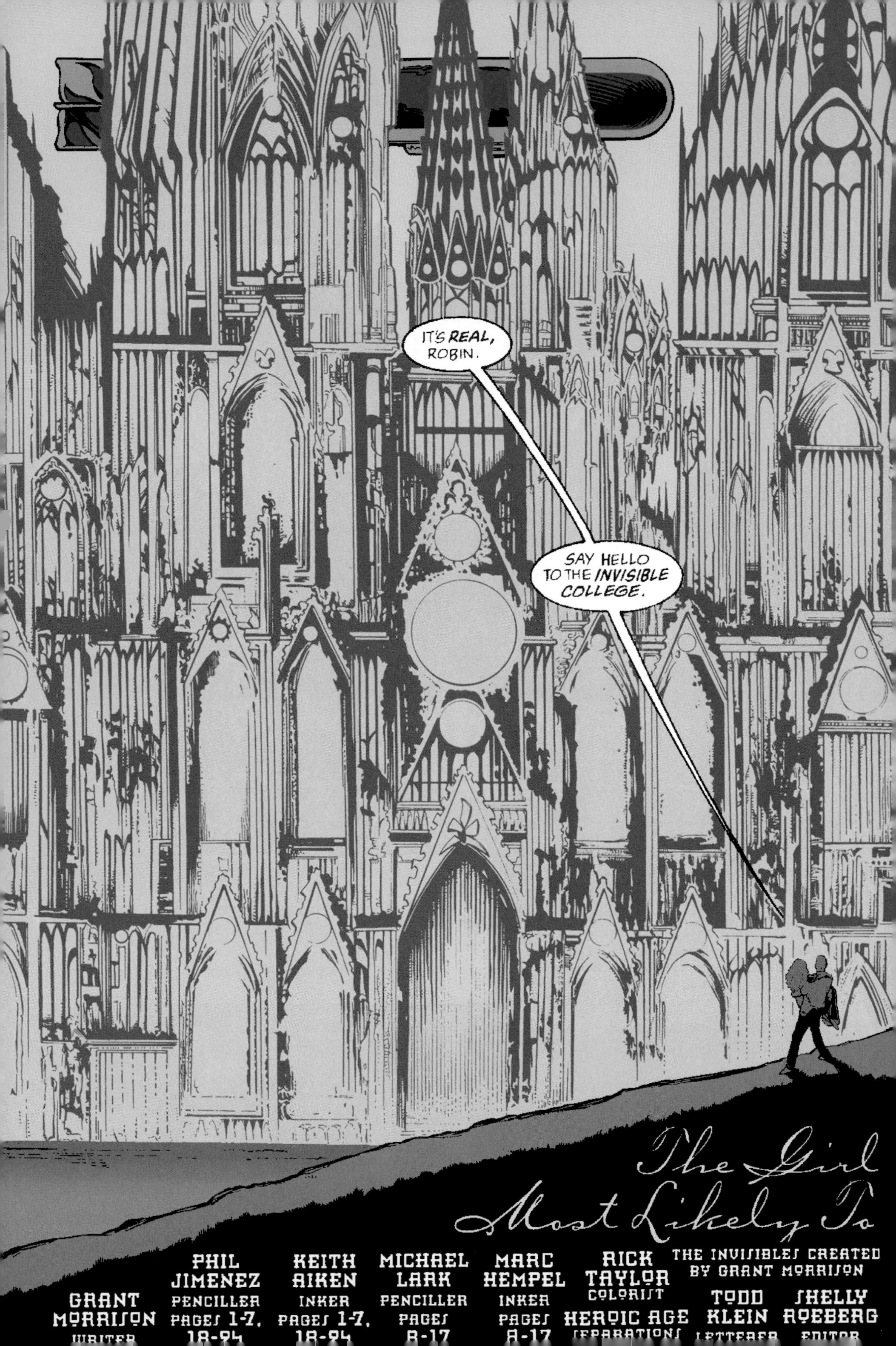
IT'S REAL, ROBIN.
SAY HELLO TO THE INVISIBLE COLLEGE.
The Girl Most Likely To
GRANT MORRISON
PHIL JIMENEZ PENCILLER PAGES 1-7,
KEITH AIKEN INKER PAGES 1-7,
MICHAEL LARK PENCILLER PAGES
MARC HEMPEL INKER PAGES
RICK TAYLOR COLORIST
HEROIC AGE
THE INVISIBLES CREATED BY GRANT MORRISON
TODD KLEIN
SHELLY ROEBERG

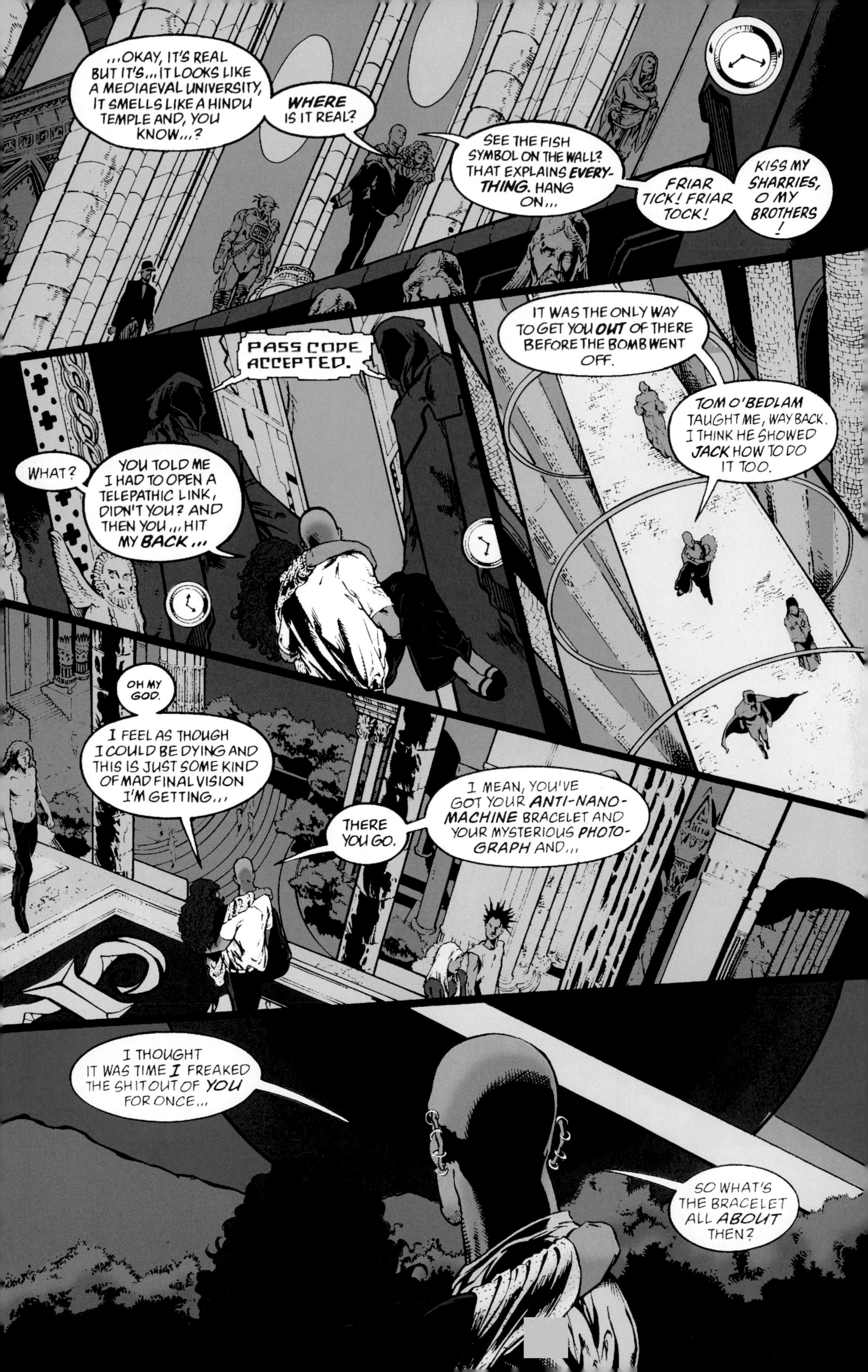

...OKAY, IT'S REAL BUT IT'S... IT LOOKS LIKE A MEDIAEVAL UNIVERSITY, IT SMELLS LIKE A HINDU TEMPLE AND, YOU KNOW...?
WHERE IS IT REAL?
SEE THE FISH SYMBOL ON THE WALL? THAT EXPLAINS EVERYTHING. HANG ON...
FRIAR TICK! FRIAR TOCK!
KISS MY SHARRIES, O MY BROTHERS!
PASS CODE ACCEPTED.
WHAT?
YOU TOLD ME I HAD TO OPEN A TELEPATHIC LINK, DIDN'T YOU? AND THEN YOU... HIT MY BACK...
IT WAS THE ONLY WAY TO GET YOU OUT OF THERE BEFORE THE BOMB WENT OFF.
TOM O'BEDLAM TAUGHT ME, WAY BACK. I THINK HE SHOWED JACK HOW TO DO IT TOO.
OH MY GOD.
I FEEL AS THOUGH I COULD BE DYING AND THIS IS JUST SOME KIND OF MAD FINAL VISION I'M GETTING...
THERE YOU GO.
I MEAN, YOU'VE GOT YOUR ANTI-NANO-MACHINE BRACELET AND YOUR MYSTERIOUS PHOTOGRAPH AND...
I THOUGHT IT WAS TIME I FREAKED THE SHIT OUT OF YOU FOR ONCE...
SO WHAT'S THE BRACELET ALL ABOUT THEN?

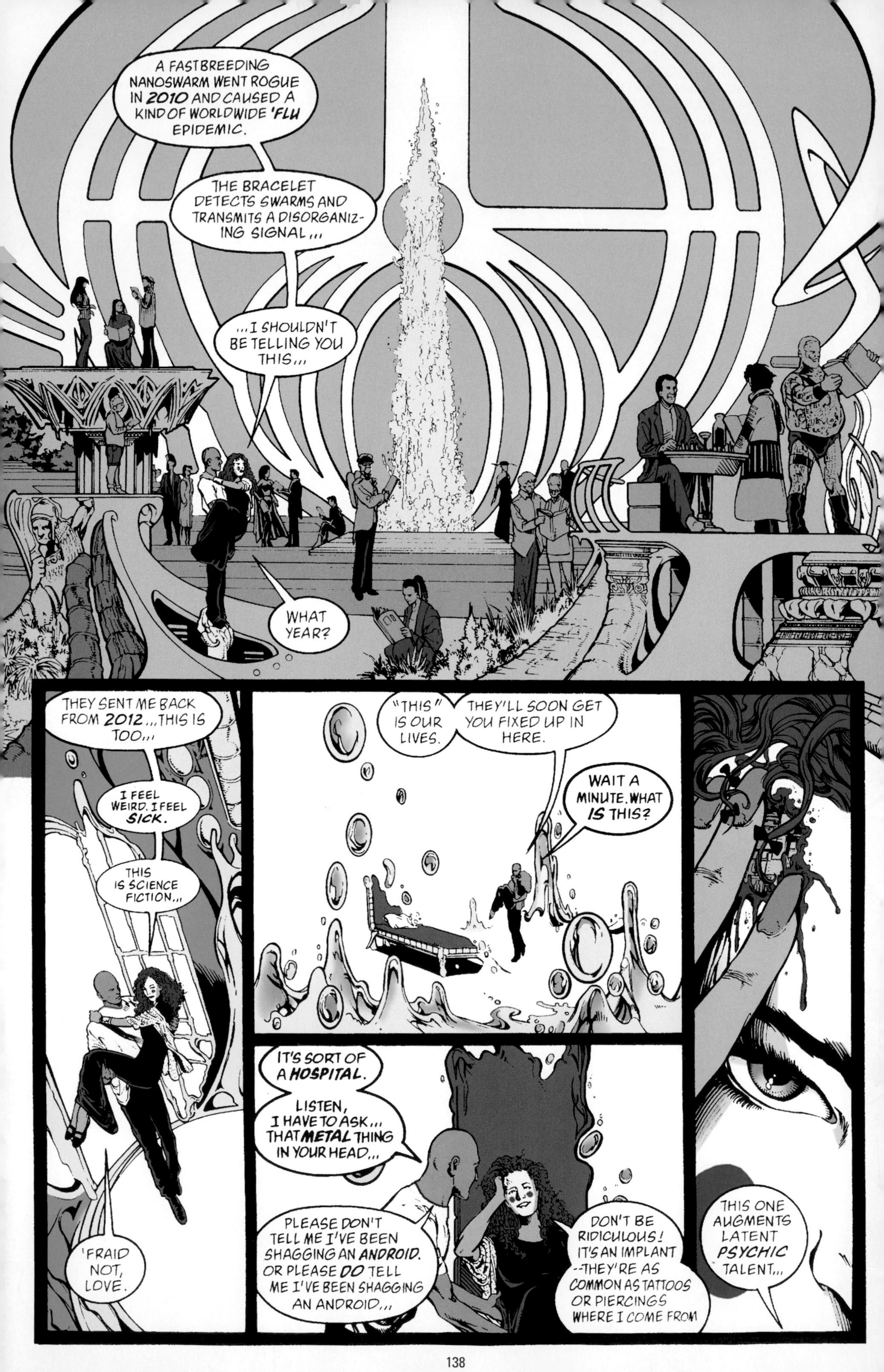
A FASTBREEDING NANOSWARM WENT ROGUE IN 2010 AND CAUSED A KIND OF WORLDWIDE 'FLU EPIDEMIC.
THE BRACELET DETECTS SWARMS AND TRANSMITS A DISORGANIZING SIGNAL...
...I SHOULDN'T BE TELLING YOU THIS...
WHAT YEAR?
THEY SENT ME BACK FROM 2012... THIS IS TOO...
I FEEL WEIRD. I FEEL SICK.
THIS IS SCIENCE FICTION...
'FRAID NOT, LOVE.
"THIS" IS OUR LIVES.
THEY'LL SOON GET YOU FIXED UP IN HERE.
WAIT A MINUTE. WHAT IS THIS?
IT'S SORT OF A HOSPITAL.
LISTEN, I HAVE TO ASK... THAT METAL THING IN YOUR HEAD...
PLEASE DON'T TELL ME I'VE BEEN SHAGGING AN ANDROID. OR PLEASE DO TELL ME I'VE BEEN SHAGGING AN ANDROID...
DON'T BE RIDICULOUS! IT'S AN IMPLANT --THEY'RE AS COMMON AS TATTOOS OR PIERCINGS WHERE I COME FROM
THIS ONE AUGMENTS LATENT PSYCHIC TALENT...

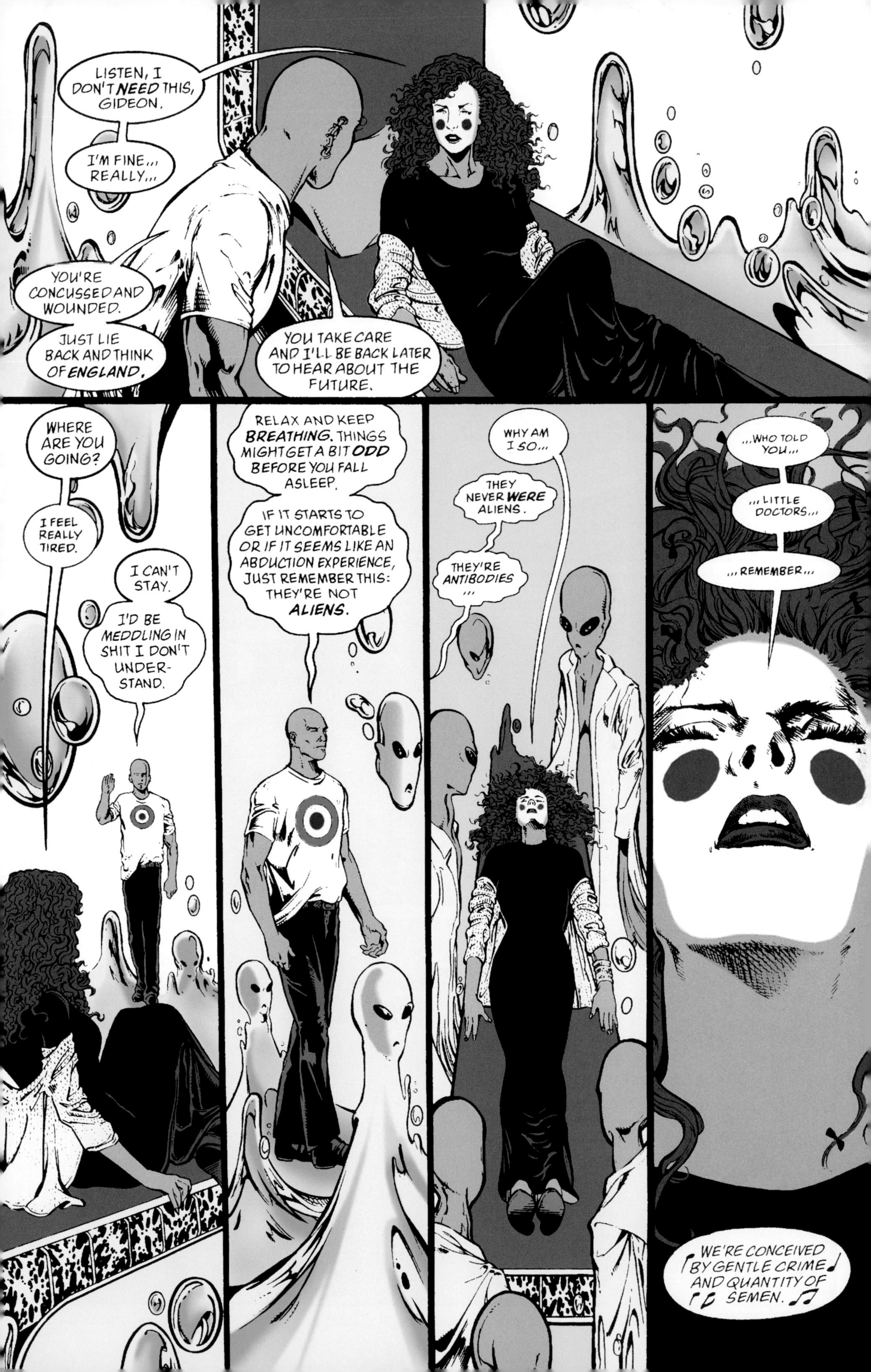
LISTEN, I DON'T NEED THIS, GIDEON.
I'M FINE... REALLY...
YOU'RE CONCUSSED AND WOUNDED.
JUST LIE BACK AND THINK OF ENGLAND.
YOU TAKE CARE AND I'LL BE BACK LATER TO HEAR ABOUT THE FUTURE.
WHERE ARE YOU GOING?
I FEEL REALLY TIRED.
I CAN'T STAY.
I'D BE MEDDLING IN SHIT I DON'T UNDER-STAND.
RELAX AND KEEP BREATHING. THINGS MIGHT GET A BIT ODD BEFORE YOU FALL ASLEEP.
IF IT STARTS TO GET UNCOMFORTABLE OR IF IT SEEMS LIKE AN ABDUCTION EXPERIENCE, JUST REMEMBER THIS: THEY'RE NOT ALIENS.
WHY AM I SO...
THEY NEVER WERE ALIENS.
THEY'RE ANTIBODIES ...
...WHO TOLD YOU...
...LITTLE DOCTORS...
...REMEMBER...
WE'RE CONCEIVED BY GENTLE CRIME AND QUANTITY OF SEMEN.

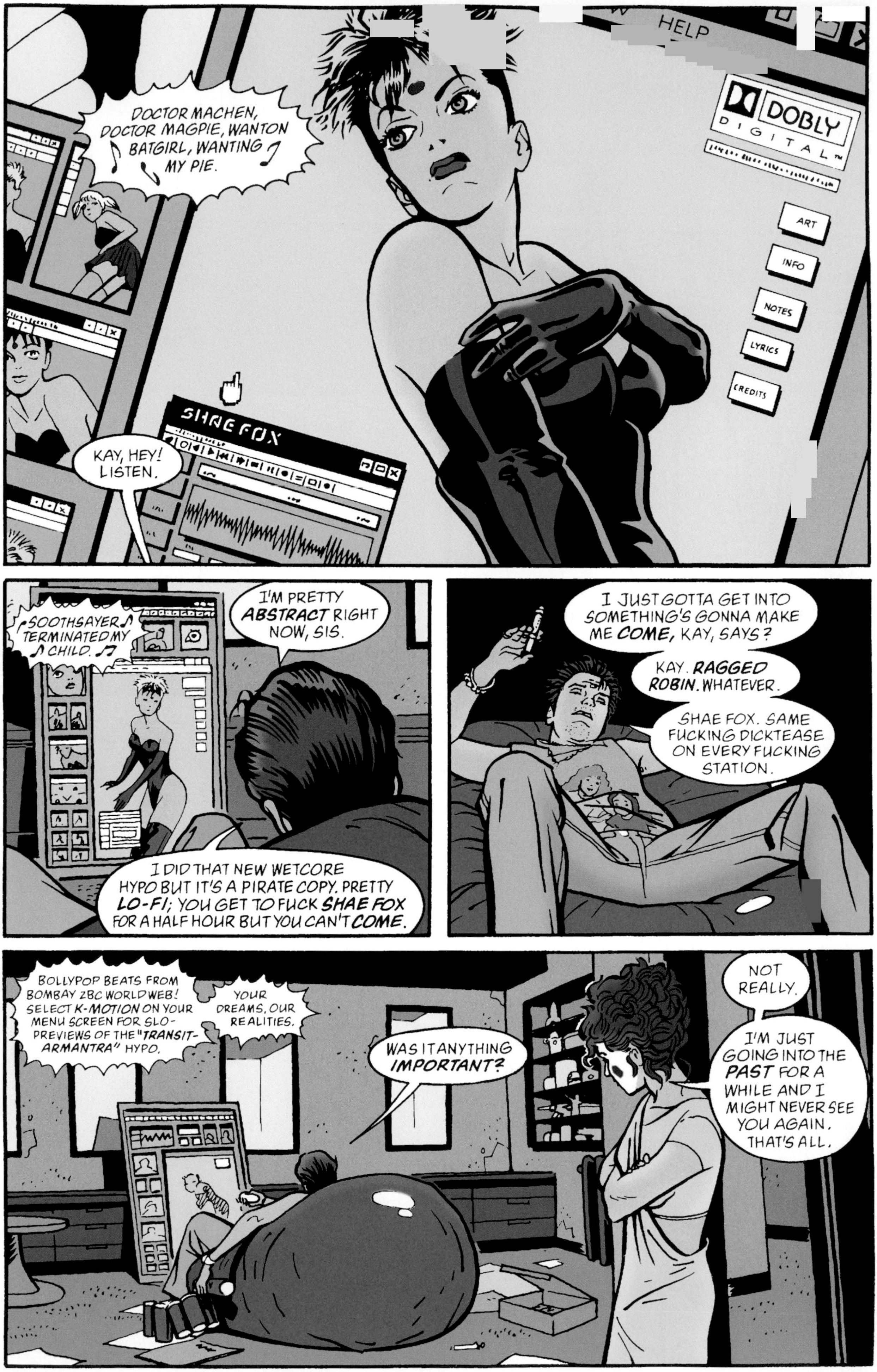
HELP
DOBLY DIGITAL
DOCTOR MACHEN, DOCTOR MAGPIE, WANTON BATGIRL, WANTING MY PIE.
ART
INFO
NOTES
LYRICS
CREDITS
SHAE FOX
KAY, HEY! LISTEN.
SOOTHSAYER TERMINATED MY CHILD.
I'M PRETTY **ABSTRACT** RIGHT NOW, SIS.
I DID THAT NEW WETCORE HYPO BUT IT'S A PIRATE COPY. PRETTY **LO-FI**; YOU GET TO FUCK **SHAE FOX** FOR A HALF HOUR BUT YOU CAN'T **COME**.
I JUST GOTTA GET INTO SOMETHING'S GONNA MAKE ME **COME**, KAY, SAYS?
KAY. **RAGGED ROBIN**. WHATEVER.
SHAE FOX. SAME FUCKING DICKTEASE ON EVERY FUCKING STATION.
BOLLYPOP BEATS FROM BOMBAY ZBC WORLDWEB! SELECT **K-MOTION** ON YOUR MENU SCREEN FOR SLO-PREVIEWS OF THE "**TRANSIT-ARMANTRA**" HYPO.
YOUR DREAMS, OUR REALITIES.
WAS IT ANYTHING **IMPORTANT?**
NOT REALLY.
I'M JUST GOING INTO THE **PAST** FOR A WHILE AND I MIGHT NEVER SEE YOU AGAIN. THAT'S ALL.

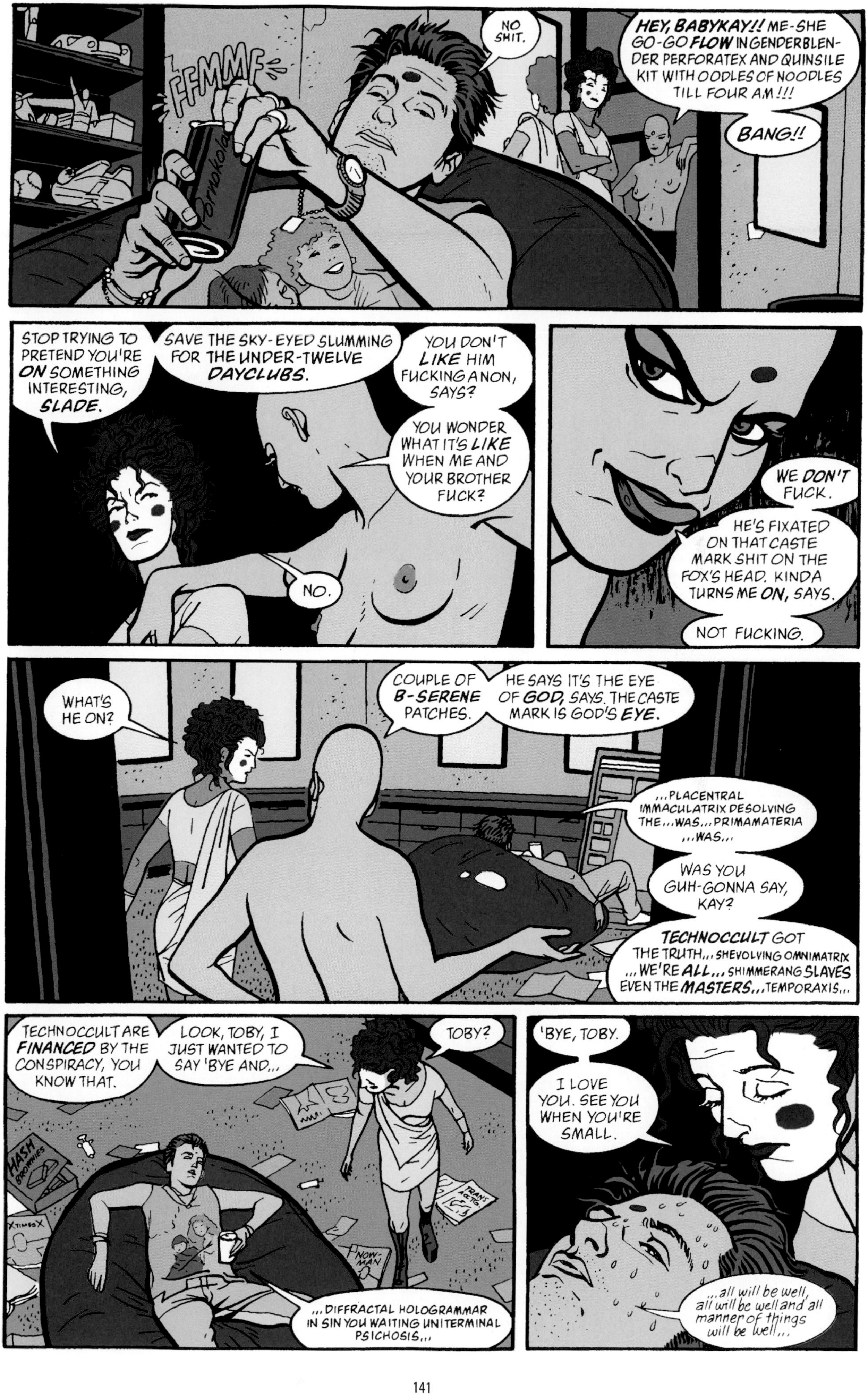
FFMMF
Orinokola
NO SHIT.
HEY, BABYKAY!! ME-SHE GO-GO FLOW IN GENDERBLENDER PERFORATEX AND QUINSILE KIT WITH OODLES OF NOODLES TILL FOUR AM!!!
BANG!!
STOP TRYING TO PRETEND YOU'RE ON SOMETHING INTERESTING, SLADE.
SAVE THE SKY-EYED SLUMMING FOR THE UNDER-TWELVE DAYCLUBS.
YOU DON'T LIKE HIM FUCKING A NON, SAYS?
YOU WONDER WHAT IT'S LIKE WHEN ME AND YOUR BROTHER FUCK?
NO.
WE DON'T FUCK.
HE'S FIXATED ON THAT CASTE MARK SHIT ON THE FOX'S HEAD. KINDA TURNS ME ON, SAYS.
NOT FUCKING.
WHAT'S HE ON?
COUPLE OF B-SERENE PATCHES.
HE SAYS IT'S THE EYE OF GOD, SAYS. THE CASTE MARK IS GOD'S EYE.
...PLACENTRAL IMMACULATRIX DESOLVING THE...WAS...PRIMAMATERIA ...WAS...
WAS YOU GUH-GONNA SAY, KAY?
TECHNOCCULT GOT THE TRUTH... SHEVOLVING OMNIMATRIX ...WE'RE ALL... SHIMMERANG SLAVES EVEN THE MASTERS... TEMPORAXIS...
TECHNOCCULT ARE FINANCED BY THE CONSPIRACY, YOU KNOW THAT.
LOOK, TOBY, I JUST WANTED TO SAY 'BYE AND...
TOBY?
HASH BROWNIES
TRANS ACTG.
X TIMES X
NOW-MAN
...DIFFRACTAL HOLOGRAMMAR IN SIN YOU WAITING UNITERMINAL PSICHOSIS...
'BYE, TOBY.
I LOVE YOU. SEE YOU WHEN YOU'RE SMALL.
...all will be well, all will be well and all manner of things will be well...

...BOB WON'T RAPE AGAIN, THANKS TO I-SPY AUTO-SURVEILLANCE SYSTEMS.

YOUR ELECTRONIC CONSCIENCE!

THOSE NEW I-SPY SYSTEMS LOOK SET TO CONSIGN CONVENTIONAL SMARTCAMS AND TAGS TO THE HISTORY FILES. BAD NEWS FOR REUBEN ZION, THE ORTHODOX ACTIVIST WHO TURNED GOVERNMENT SURVEILLANCE FOOTAGE OF HIS APARTMENT INTO AN ONGOING PER-FORMANCE ART MULTIMEDIA SUCCESS STORY.

SELECT "ZION" ON YOUR MENU FOR DETAILS.

NOW OTHER NEWS.

"IT'S NO WORSE THAN THE FLU OF 2010," SAY THE EXPERTS, BUT DOOMSAYER DOCTOR CLEM KENDRED CLAIMS THAT THE COLONY OF MICROSCOPIC ROBOTS WHICH ESCAPED FROM A LABORATORY IN SINGAPORE COULD BE SELF-REPLICATING PLAGUE-MACHINES POISED TO DESTROY THE WORLD!

"THE ROGUE NANOS ARE ATTACKING MATTER ITSELF AT THE SUBATOMIC LEVEL," CLAIMS DOCTOR K. "THAT'S BAD NEWS IN ANY LANGUAGE!"

SHIT!

"IF THIS BLOB OF INCOHERENT, SO-CALLED "MAGIC MATTER" --FOUND IN SINGAPORE'S CHANGI AIRPORT--IS ANYTHING TO GO BY, THE WHOLE WORLD COULD BE DUE FOR MOLECULAR MELTDOWN BEFORE CHRISTMAS DAY.

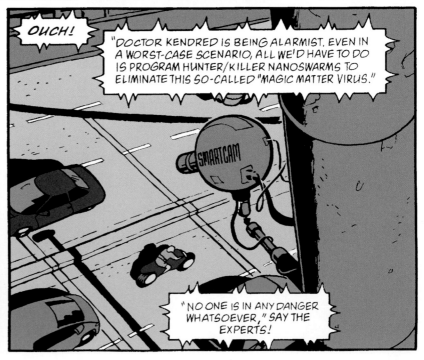

OUCH!

"DOCTOR KENDRED IS BEING ALARMIST. EVEN IN A WORST-CASE SCENARIO, ALL WE'D HAVE TO DO IS PROGRAM HUNTER/KILLER NANOSWARMS TO ELIMINATE THIS SO-CALLED "MAGIC MATTER VIRUS."

SMARTCAM

"NO ONE IS IN ANY DANGER WHATSOEVER," SAY THE EXPERTS!

YOU HAVE SELECTED *"TRAFFIC REPORT"* FROM MENU OPTIONS.

TRAFFIC IN THE BAY AREA IS *LIGHT* DUE TO FUEL RESTRICTIONS AND PREPARATIONS FOR TONIGHT'S *END-OF-THE-WORLD FLASHBACK PARADE.*

SELECT *"PARADE"* ON YOUR MENU FOR DETAILS.

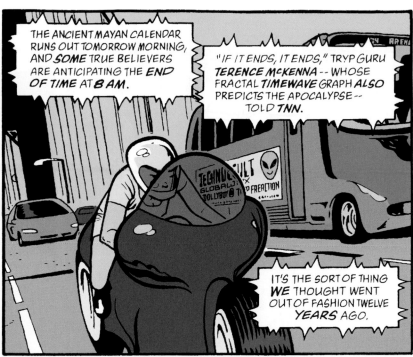

THE ANCIENT MAYAN CALENDAR RUNS OUT TOMORROW MORNING, AND *SOME* TRUE BELIEVERS ARE ANTICIPATING THE *END OF TIME* AT *8 AM.*

"IF IT ENDS, IT ENDS," TRYP GURU *TERENCE MCKENNA* -- WHOSE FRACTAL *TIMEWAVE* GRAPH *ALSO* PREDICTS THE APOCALYPSE -- TOLD *TNN.*

IT'S THE SORT OF THING *WE* THOUGHT WENT OUT OF FASHION TWELVE *YEARS* AGO.

BUT FOR SOME PEOPLE, IT SEEMS, THE APOCALYPSE JUST NEVER KNOWS *WHEN* TO STOP.

TERRANET NEWS. SERVING THE ENTERMERTION NEURO-HIGHWAY FROM DAWN TILL DAWN!

MENU SELECT: SOAP: *"DOLLYBOYS DOWN UNDER."*

BERT, I'M HAVING IT *DONE!* I'M BEING *"SHAVED"* TO BE YOUR *NON* BITCH!

IN FUCK'S NAME, *MAGOO* ...MMMAAAASSSS-STAND AND DELIVER! THIS SOAP IS BEING DÉTOURNED BY BANDIT BROADCASTERS! I'M JUST AN ACTOR. MY PERFORMANCE IS NOT MORE IMPORTANT THAN YOUR LIFE. STOP WATCHING.

WE'RE FALSE IMAGES DESIGNED TO SELL YOU PRODUCTS BY EXPLOITING YOUR INSECURITIES.

TO MAKE YOU SPECTATORS IN LIFE, NOT PARTICIPANTS ...ZZZ... RRRLLET ME MAKE YOU *HAPPY,* BERT!

PLEASE FORGIVE THE INTERRUPTION TO PROGRAMMING. IGNORE FALSE SLOGANS. THE TERRORISTS WILL BE DEALT WITH IN DUE COURSE.

MENU SELECTION: *"DOLLYBOYS DOWN UNDER!"*

MAGOO, YOU KNOW I CAN *NEVER* BE HAPPY...!

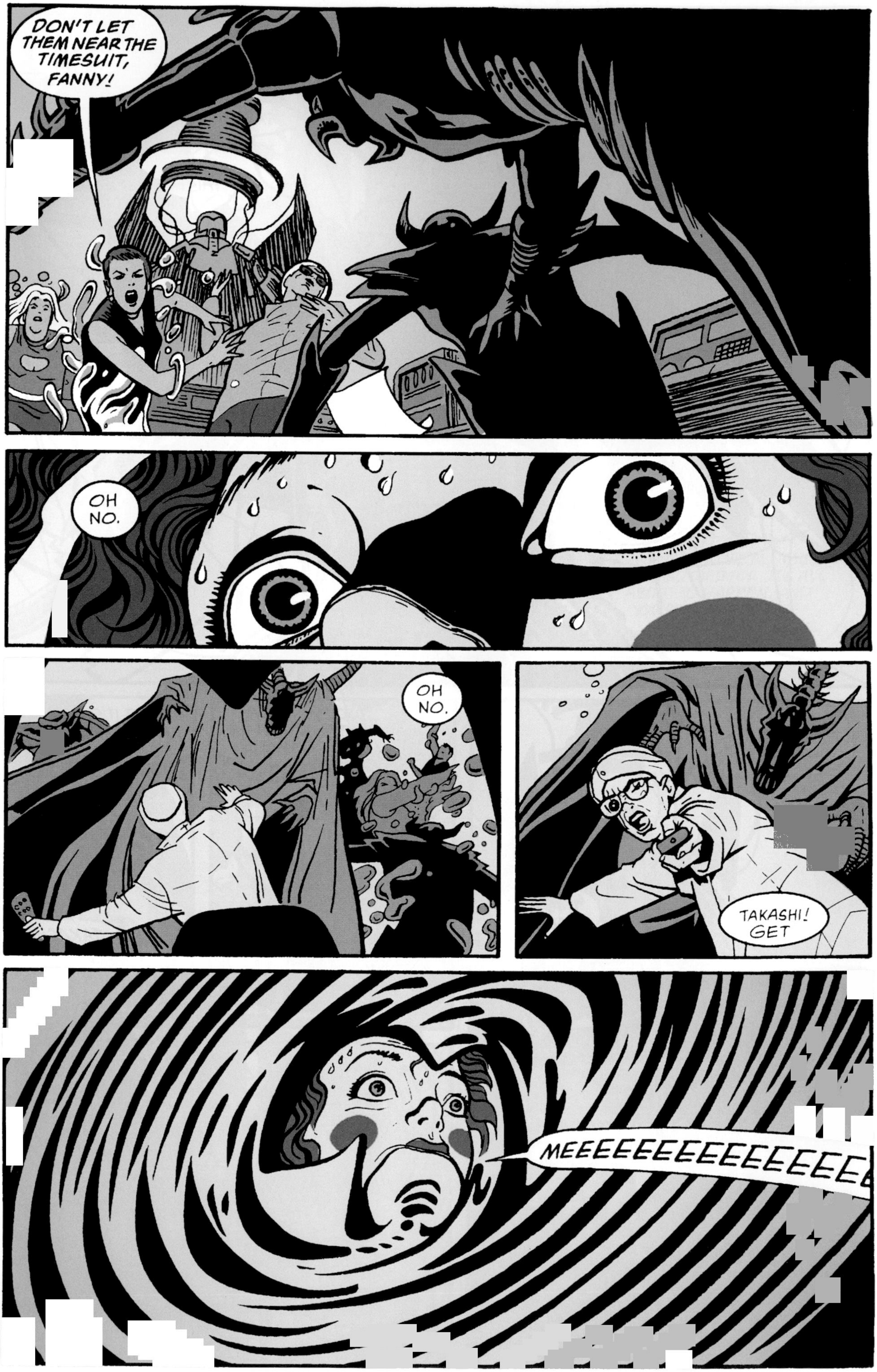
DON'T LET THEM NEAR THE TIMESUIT, FANNY!
OH NO.
OH NO.
TAKASHI! GET
MEEEEEEEEEEEEEEEE

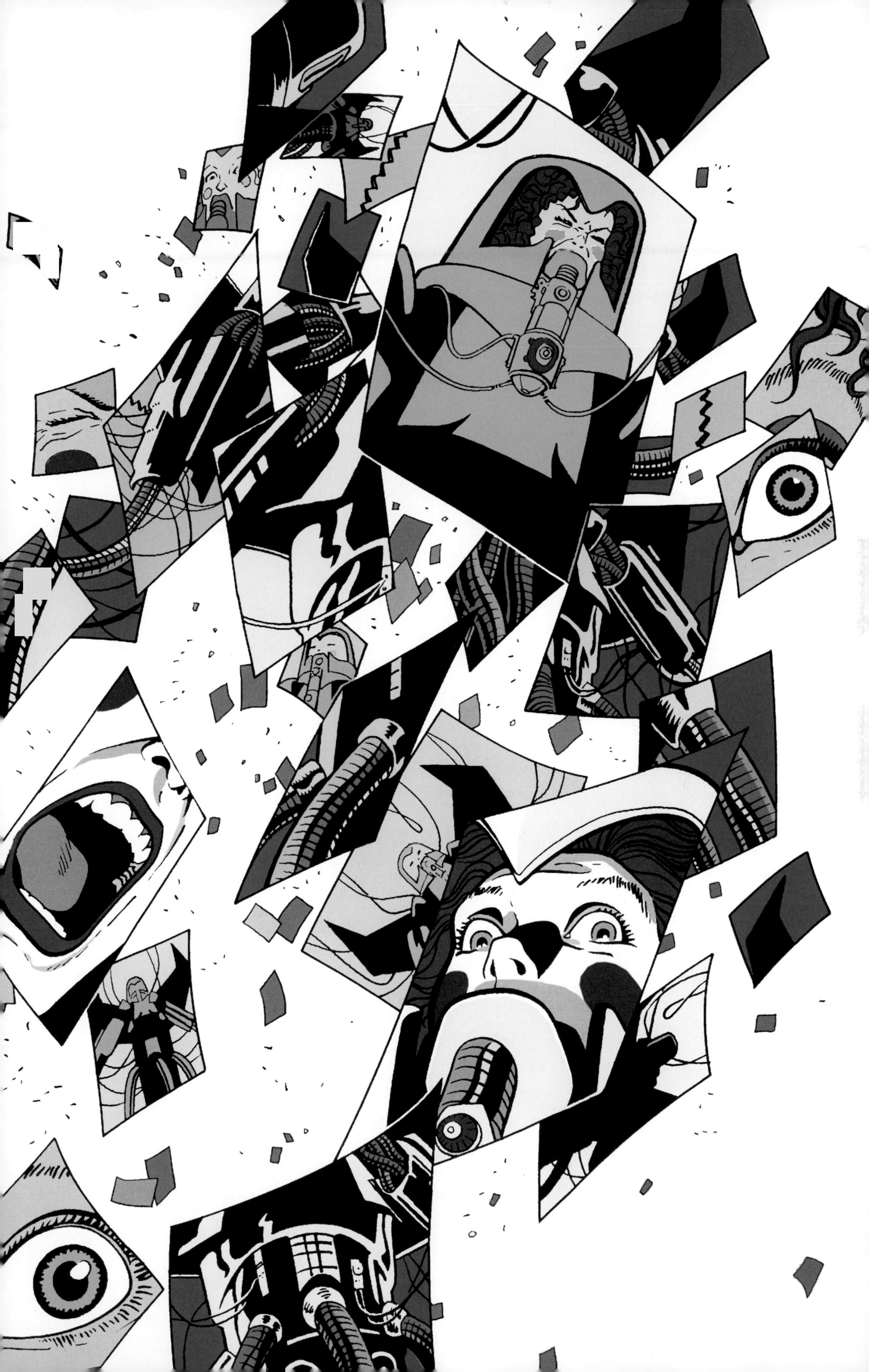

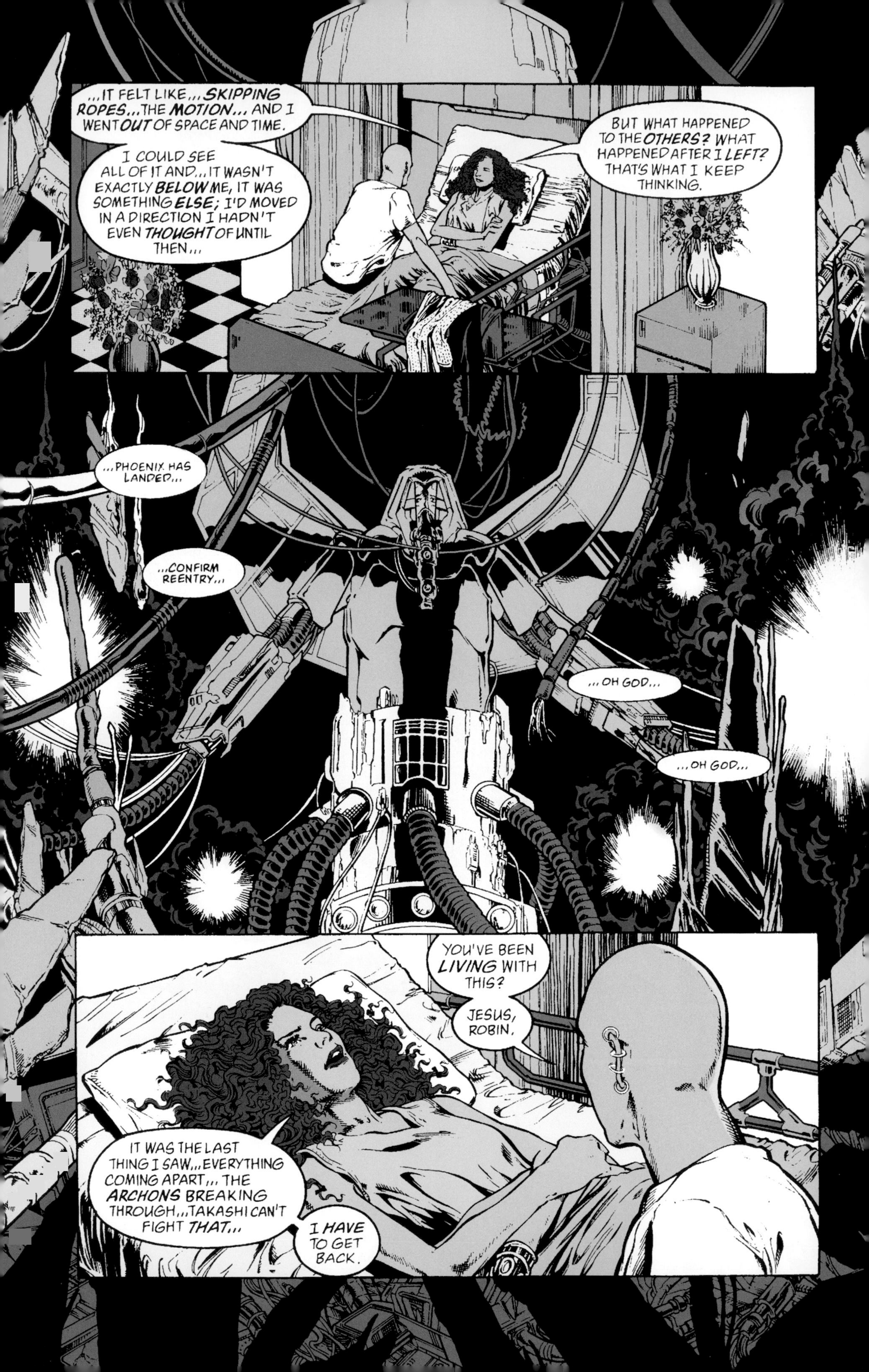
...IT FELT LIKE... SKIPPING ROPES... THE MOTION... AND I WENT OUT OF SPACE AND TIME.
I COULD SEE ALL OF IT AND... IT WASN'T EXACTLY BELOW ME, IT WAS SOMETHING ELSE; I'D MOVED IN A DIRECTION I HADN'T EVEN THOUGHT OF UNTIL THEN...
BUT WHAT HAPPENED TO THE OTHERS? WHAT HAPPENED AFTER I LEFT? THAT'S WHAT I KEEP THINKING.
...PHOENIX HAS LANDED...
...CONFIRM REENTRY...
...OH GOD...
...OH GOD...
YOU'VE BEEN LIVING WITH THIS?
JESUS, ROBIN.
IT WAS THE LAST THING I SAW... EVERYTHING COMING APART... THE ARCHONS BREAKING THROUGH... TAKASHI CAN'T FIGHT THAT...
I HAVE TO GET BACK.

BUT TO GET BACK I HAVE TO SHOW TAKASHI THE *PHOTOGRAPH.*

IT'S THE FINAL CONFIRMATION OF HIS *THEORY* OR SOMETHING.

IF HE DOESN'T SEE IT, HE CAN'T FIX THE *TIMESUIT...*

...AND ONCE HE'S FIXED IT AND SENT ME BACK, *HE'LL KNOW HOW TO* BUILD *IT, EVEN THOUGH IT TAKES FIFTEEN YEARS...*

YOU'RE *THIRTY-THREE.* I JUST REALIZED.

I THOUGHT YOU WERE ABOUT TEN YEARS *YOUNGER* THAN ME. YOU LOOK REALLY *AMAZING...*

WE *ALL* DID; IT WAS THE FUTURE. *SIXTY* WAS MIDDLE-AGE.

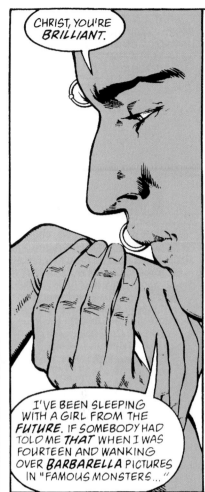

CHRIST, YOU'RE *BRILLIANT.*

I'VE BEEN SLEEPING WITH A GIRL FROM THE *FUTURE.* IF SOMEBODY HAD TOLD ME *THAT* WHEN I WAS FOURTEEN AND WANKING OVER *BARBARELLA* PICTURES IN "FAMOUS MONSTERS..."

HOW DID YOU *DO* IT? HOW DID YOU *LIVE* HERE WITHOUT *TELLING* ANYONE?

IF I HAD TO GO BACK AND LIVE IN *1980,* I'D GO MAD...

I *DID* GO MAD. I WAS IN A MENTAL HOSPITAL IN *PORTLAND* FOR TWO YEARS BEFORE I MET YOU.

THANK GOD FOR THE *PHOTOGRAPH...*

THIS THING?

IT DOESN'T *FEEL* LIKE A PHOTOGRAPH...

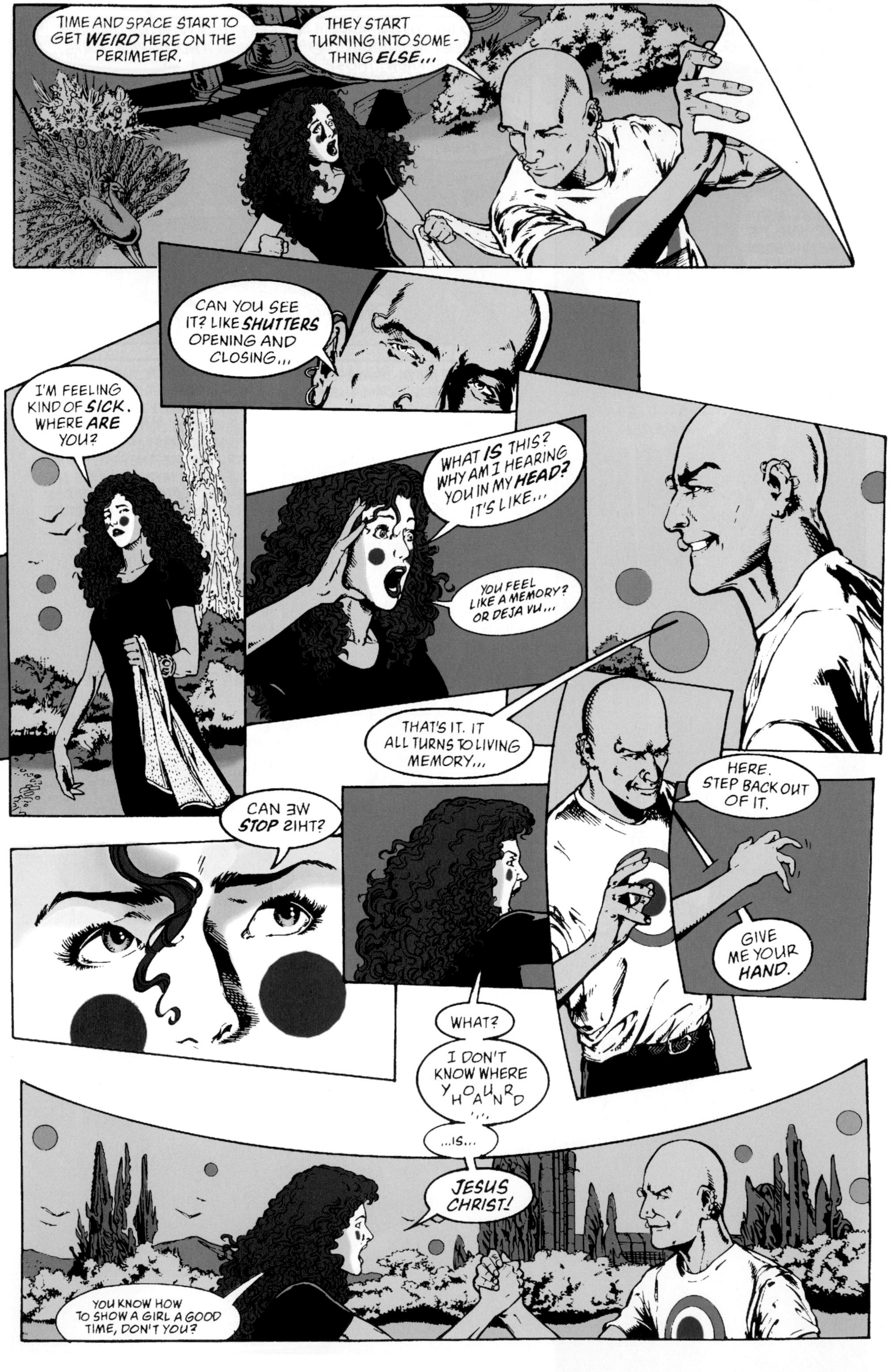

TIME AND SPACE START TO GET WEIRD HERE ON THE PERIMETER.
THEY START TURNING INTO SOME-THING ELSE...
CAN YOU SEE IT? LIKE SHUTTERS OPENING AND CLOSING...
I'M FEELING KIND OF SICK. WHERE ARE YOU?
WHAT IS THIS? WHY AM I HEARING YOU IN MY HEAD? IT'S LIKE...
YOU FEEL LIKE A MEMORY? OR DEJA VU...
THAT'S IT. IT ALL TURNS TO LIVING MEMORY...
CAN ƎW STOP SIHT?
HERE. STEP BACK OUT OF IT.
GIVE ME YOUR HAND.
WHAT?
I DON'T KNOW WHERE YHOAUNRD ...
...IS...
JESUS CHRIST!
YOU KNOW HOW TO SHOW A GIRL A GOOD TIME, DON'T YOU?

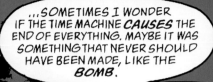

...SOMETIMES I WONDER IF THE TIME MACHINE *CAUSES* THE END OF EVERYTHING. MAYBE IT WAS SOMETHING THAT NEVER SHOULD HAVE BEEN MADE, LIKE THE *BOMB.*

WHAT IF I HAVE TO GO BACK AND THE ENEMY HAS *WON?* WHAT DO I *DO?* IT'S TERRIFYING ME.

I DON'T THINK THEY WIN. THE ANTIBODIES ARE APPEARING *EVERYWHERE* IN OUR WORLD NOW.

I JUST DON'T KNOW IF *WE* WIN EITHER. I'M SHOOTING PEOPLE AND IT NEVER SEEMS TO *END*...

IT WAS ALL THOSE *MOORCOCK* BOOKS; I WANTED TO BE *JERRY CORNELIUS,* THE ENGLISH ASSASSIN. I WANTED THE GUNS AND THE CARS AND THE GIRLS AND THE CHAOS...

SHIT.

I'VE ENDED UP A *MURDERER.* MY KARMA'S A BLOODY *MINEFIELD...*

WHY DOES THIS HAVE TO BE *US?* DON'T YOU SOMETIMES WISH YOU JUST DIDN'T *KNOW?*

I MEAN, THOSE MEN WERE *SERIOUS.* WHAT IF THEY *KILL* TAKASHI? OR MASON?

WHAT IF IT'S ALL GONE WRONG? CHRIST, WHAT IF IT'S ALL GONE *RIGHT?* WHICH IS *WORSE?*

WHAT DO WE *DO?*

ROBIN, WE *WANTED* THIS. WE WANTED TO BE SPECIAL AND IMPORTANT AND COOL AND *LOOK!* HERE WE ARE.

SO WHAT CAN WE DO BUT LIE IN THE BEDS WE MADE.

YOU SAVE THE FUTURE FROM THE PAST.

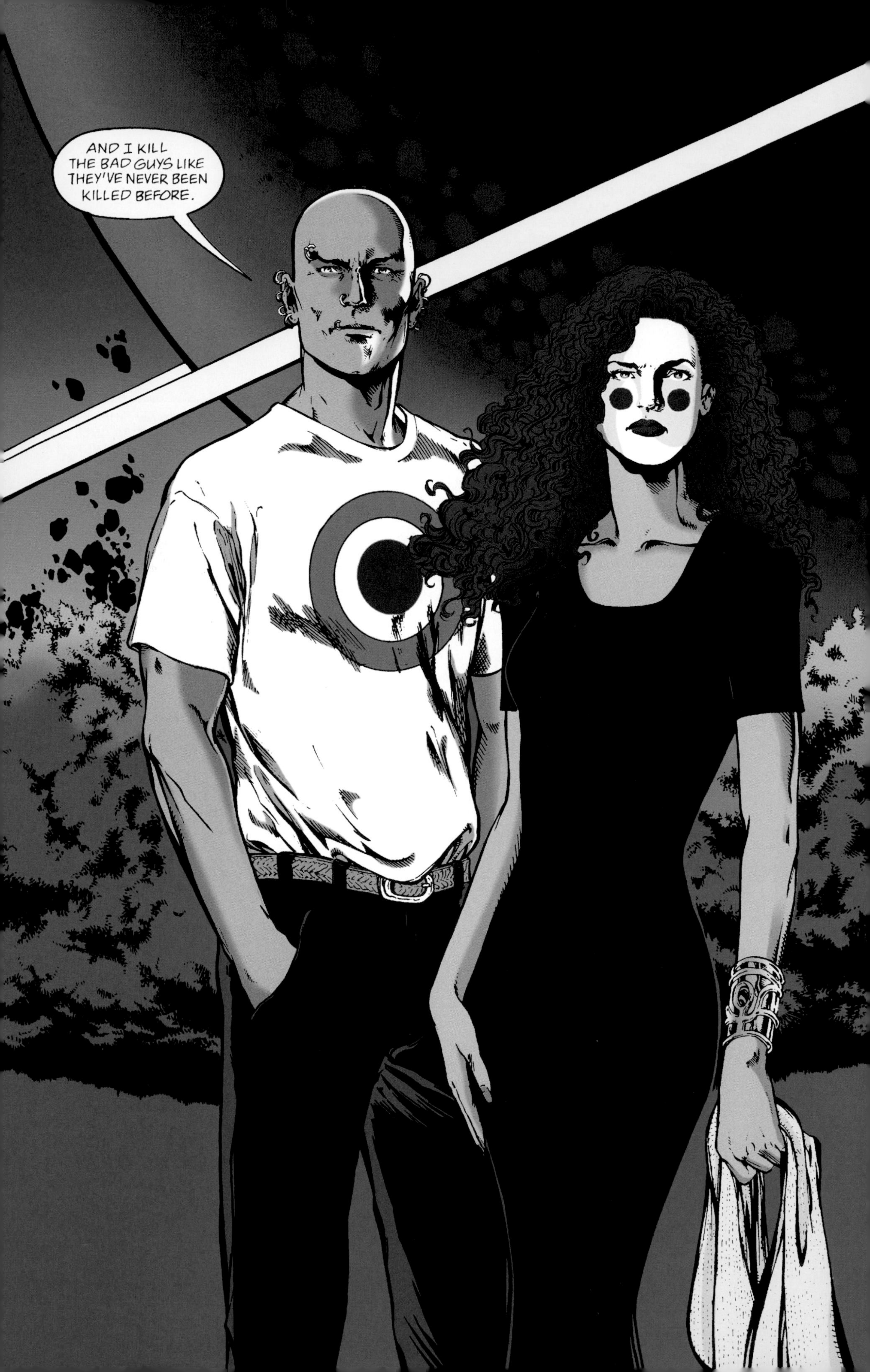
AND I KILL THE BAD GUYS LIKE THEY'VE NEVER BEEN KILLED BEFORE.

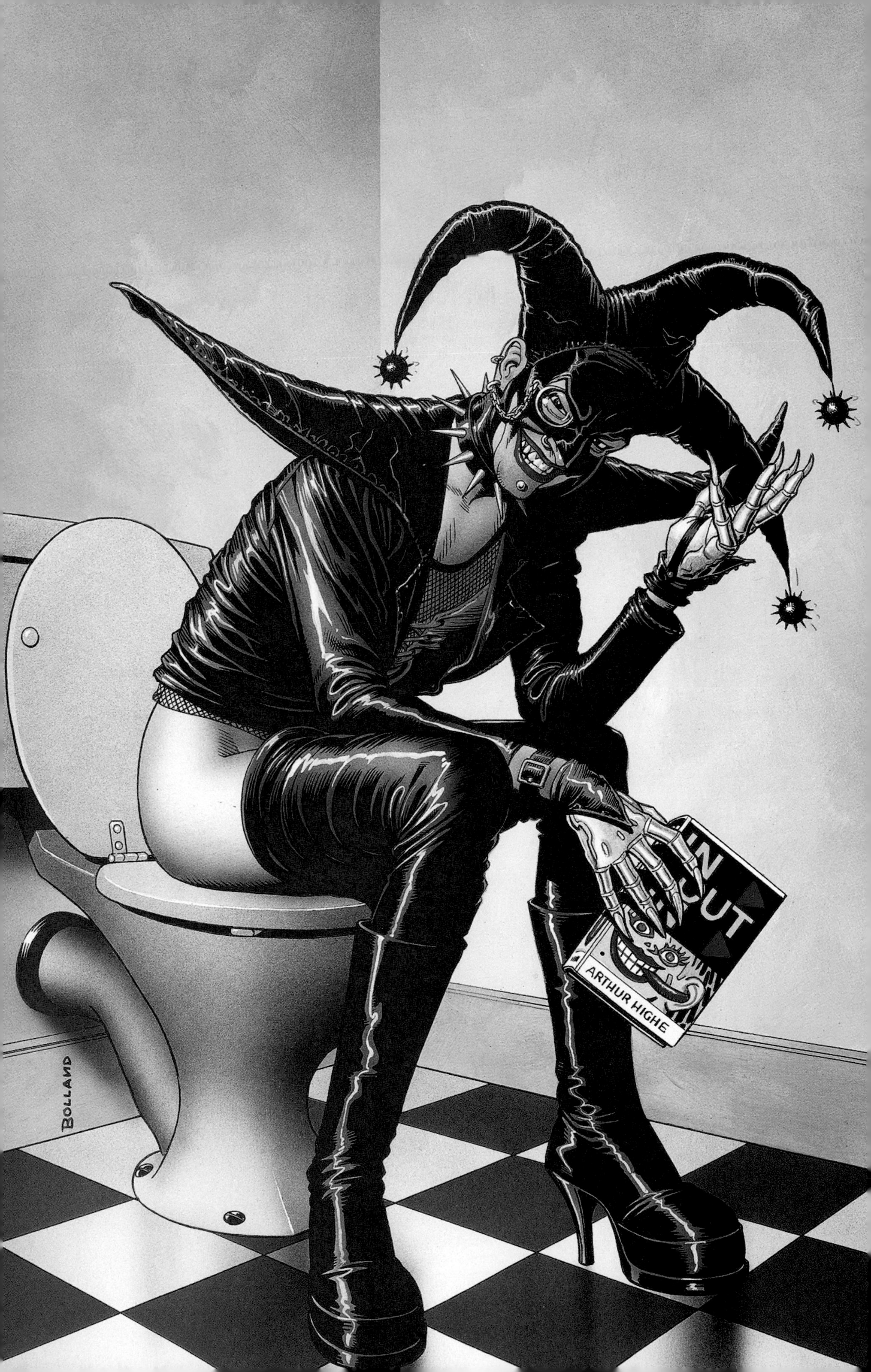
IN
OUT
ARTHUR HIGHE
BOLLAND

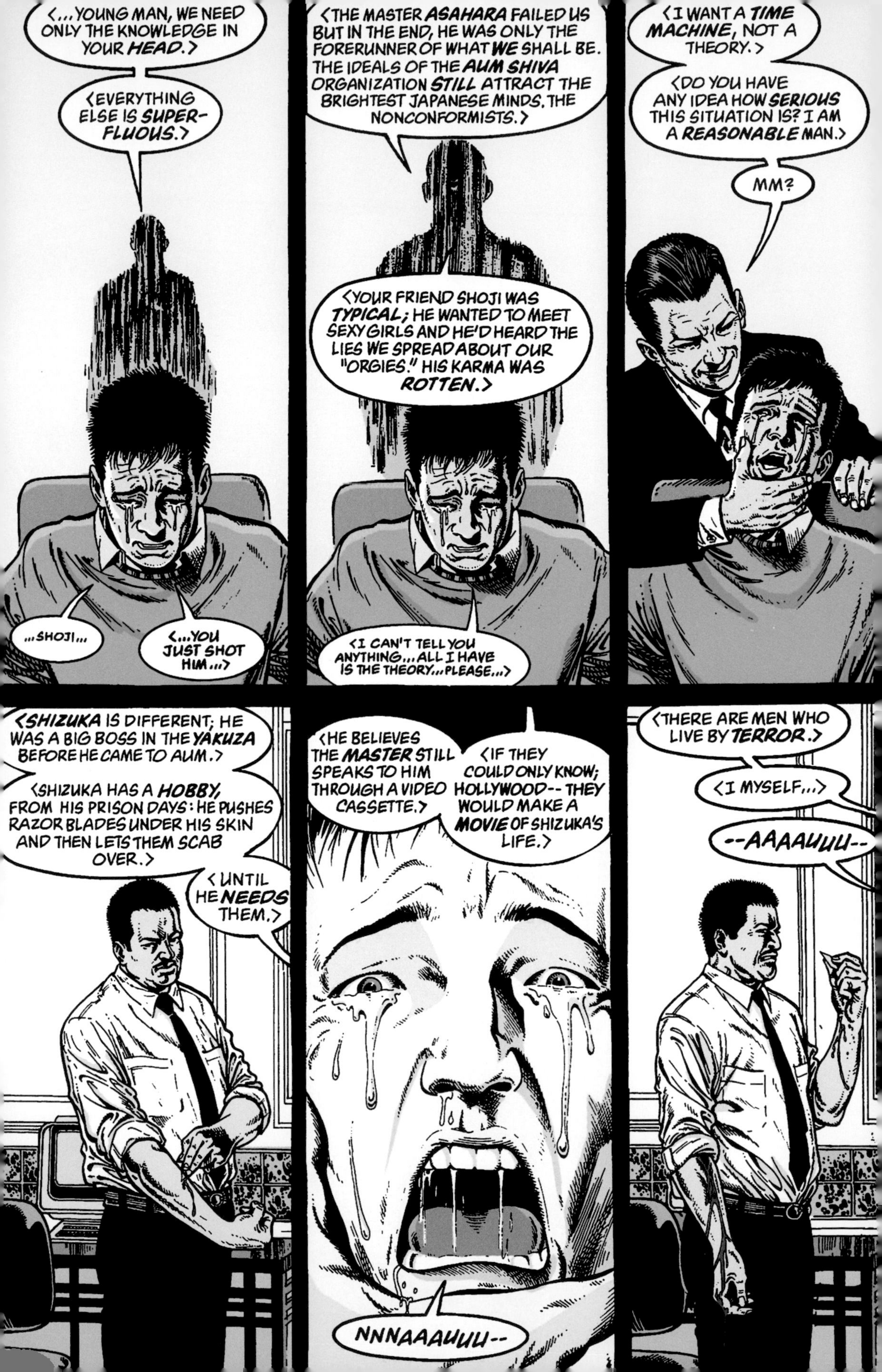
<...YOUNG MAN, WE NEED ONLY THE KNOWLEDGE IN YOUR HEAD.>
<EVERYTHING ELSE IS SUPERFLUOUS.>
...SHOJI...
<...YOU JUST SHOT HIM...>
<THE MASTER ASAHARA FAILED US BUT IN THE END, HE WAS ONLY THE FORERUNNER OF WHAT WE SHALL BE. THE IDEALS OF THE AUM SHIVA ORGANIZATION STILL ATTRACT THE BRIGHTEST JAPANESE MINDS. THE NONCONFORMISTS.>
<YOUR FRIEND SHOJI WAS TYPICAL; HE WANTED TO MEET SEXY GIRLS AND HE'D HEARD THE LIES WE SPREAD ABOUT OUR "ORGIES." HIS KARMA WAS ROTTEN.>
<I CAN'T TELL YOU ANYTHING... ALL I HAVE IS THE THEORY... PLEASE...>
<I WANT A TIME MACHINE, NOT A THEORY.>
<DO YOU HAVE ANY IDEA HOW SERIOUS THIS SITUATION IS? I AM A REASONABLE MAN.>
MM?
<SHIZUKA IS DIFFERENT; HE WAS A BIG BOSS IN THE YAKUZA BEFORE HE CAME TO AUM.>
<SHIZUKA HAS A HOBBY, FROM HIS PRISON DAYS: HE PUSHES RAZOR BLADES UNDER HIS SKIN AND THEN LETS THEM SCAB OVER.>
<UNTIL HE NEEDS THEM.>
<HE BELIEVES THE MASTER STILL SPEAKS TO HIM THROUGH A VIDEO CASSETTE.>
<IF THEY COULD ONLY KNOW; HOLLYWOOD-- THEY WOULD MAKE A MOVIE OF SHIZUKA'S LIFE.>
NNNAAAUUU--
<THERE ARE MEN WHO LIVE BY TERROR.>
<I MYSELF...>
--AAAAUUU--

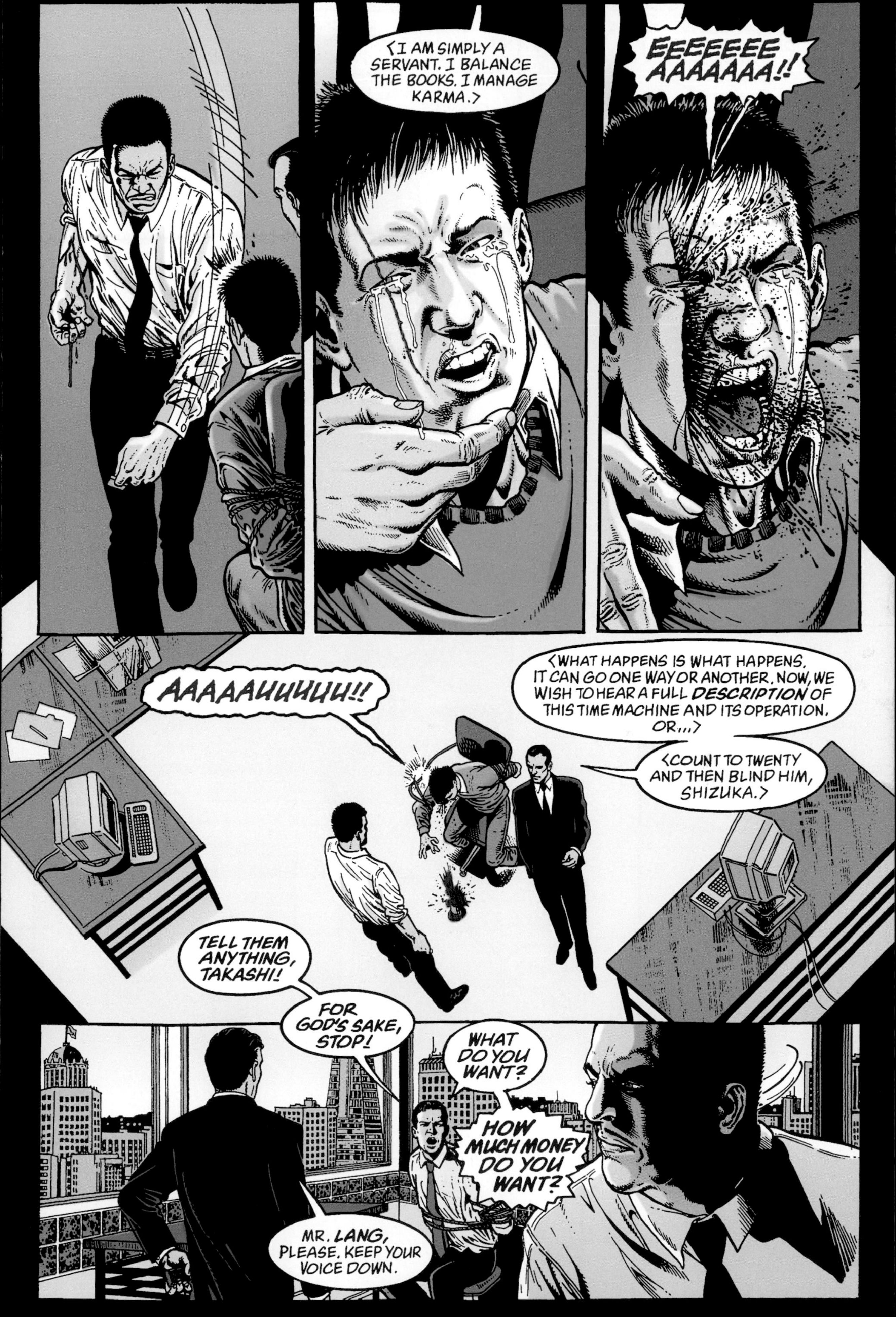

‹I AM SIMPLY A SERVANT. I BALANCE THE BOOKS. I MANAGE KARMA.›
EEEEEEE AAAAAAA!!
AAAAAUUUUUU!!
‹WHAT HAPPENS IS WHAT HAPPENS. IT CAN GO ONE WAY OR ANOTHER. NOW, WE WISH TO HEAR A FULL DESCRIPTION OF THIS TIME MACHINE AND ITS OPERATION. OR...›
‹COUNT TO TWENTY AND THEN BLIND HIM, SHIZUKA.›
TELL THEM ANYTHING, TAKASHI!
FOR GOD'S SAKE, STOP!
WHAT DO YOU WANT?
HOW MUCH MONEY DO YOU WANT?
MR. LANG, PLEASE. KEEP YOUR VOICE DOWN.

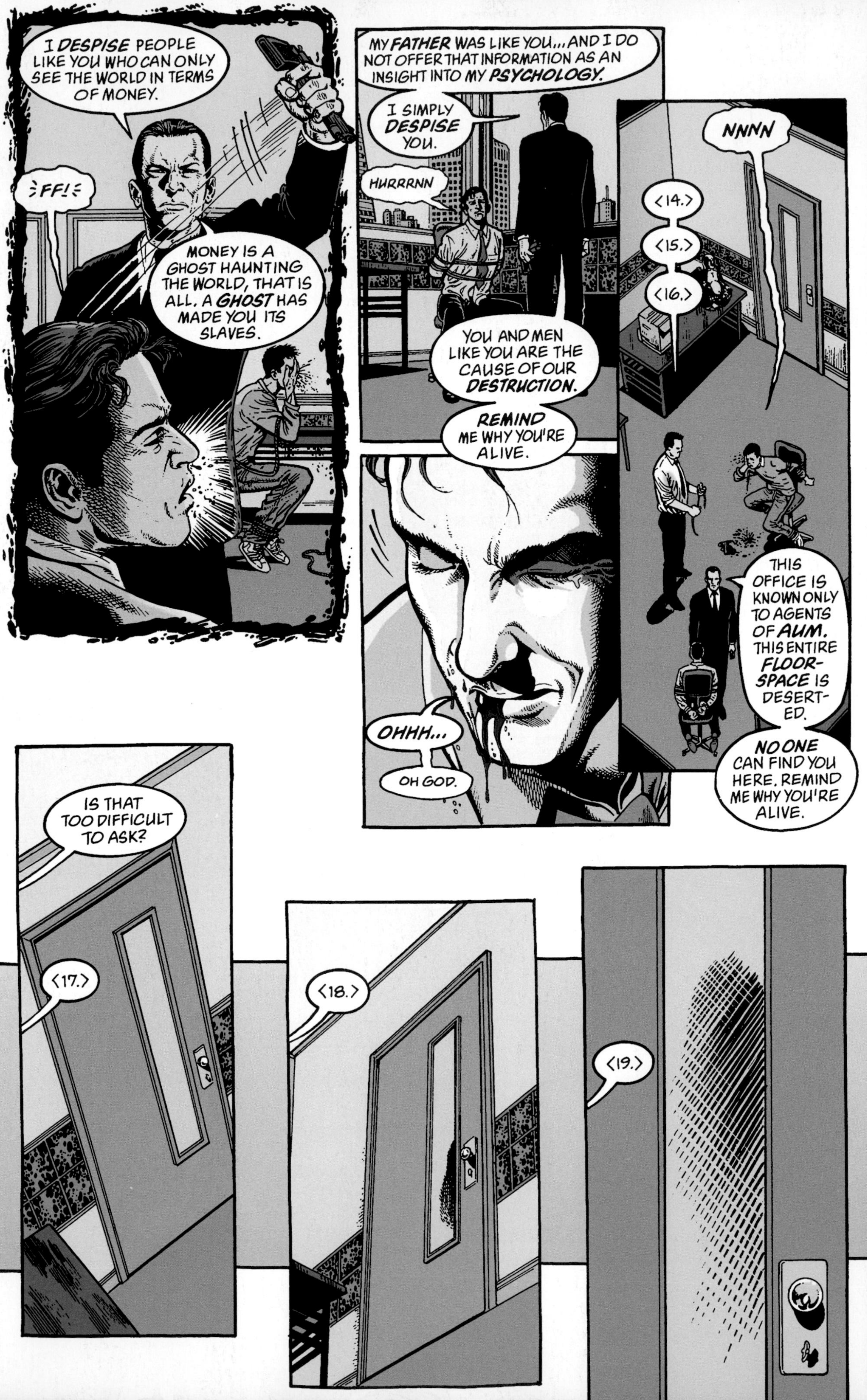
I DESPISE PEOPLE LIKE YOU WHO CAN ONLY SEE THE WORLD IN TERMS OF MONEY.
FF!
MONEY IS A GHOST HAUNTING THE WORLD, THAT IS ALL. A GHOST HAS MADE YOU ITS SLAVES.
MY FATHER WAS LIKE YOU... AND I DO NOT OFFER THAT INFORMATION AS AN INSIGHT INTO MY PSYCHOLOGY.
I SIMPLY DESPISE YOU.
HURRRNN
YOU AND MEN LIKE YOU ARE THE CAUSE OF OUR DESTRUCTION.
REMIND ME WHY YOU'RE ALIVE.
OHHH...
OH GOD.
NNNN
<14.>
<15.>
<16.>
THIS OFFICE IS KNOWN ONLY TO AGENTS OF AUM. THIS ENTIRE FLOOR-SPACE IS DESERT-ED.
NO ONE CAN FIND YOU HERE. REMIND ME WHY YOU'RE ALIVE.
IS THAT TOO DIFFICULT TO ASK?
<17.>
<18.>
<19.>

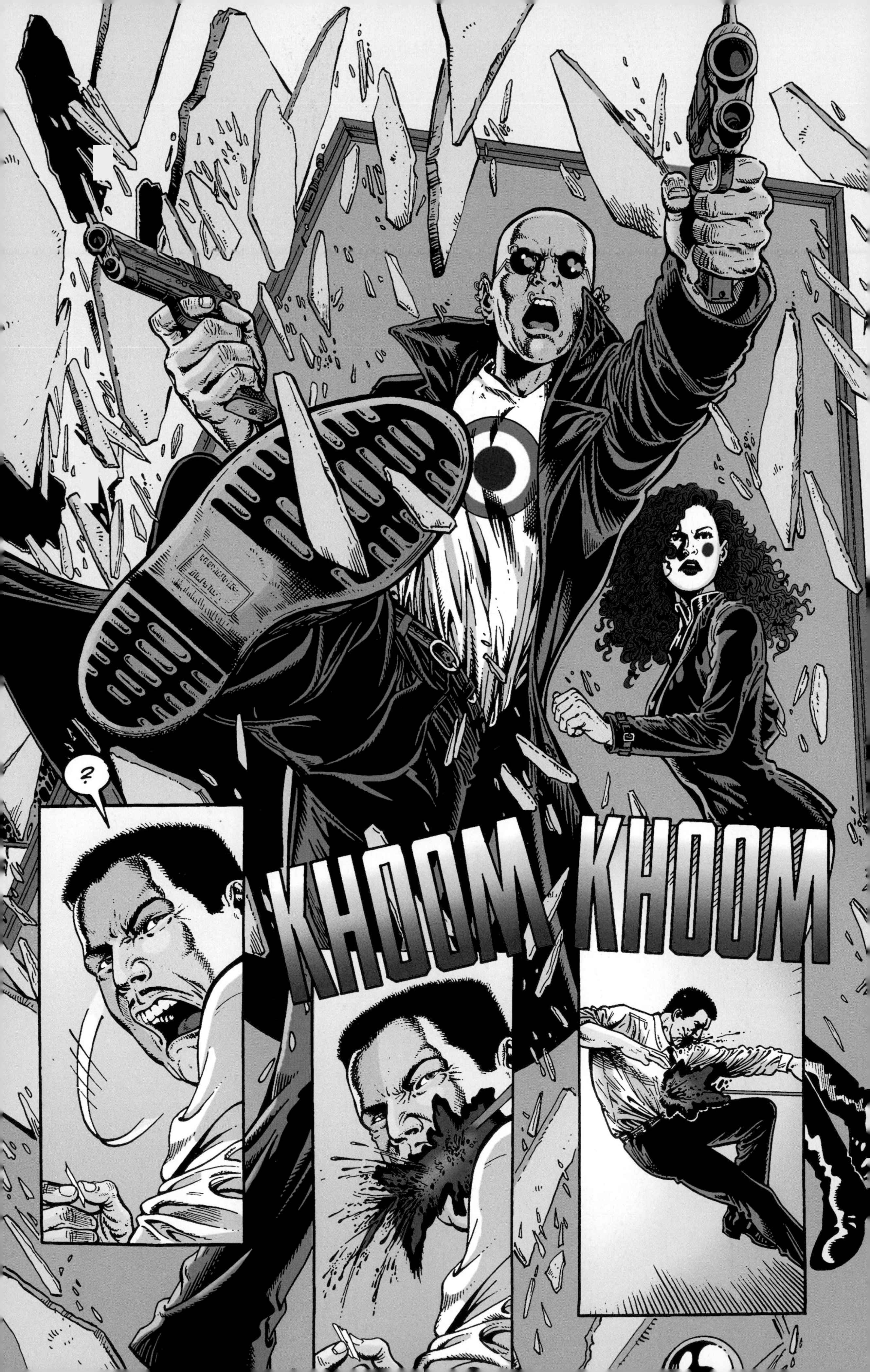
?
KHOOM KHOOM

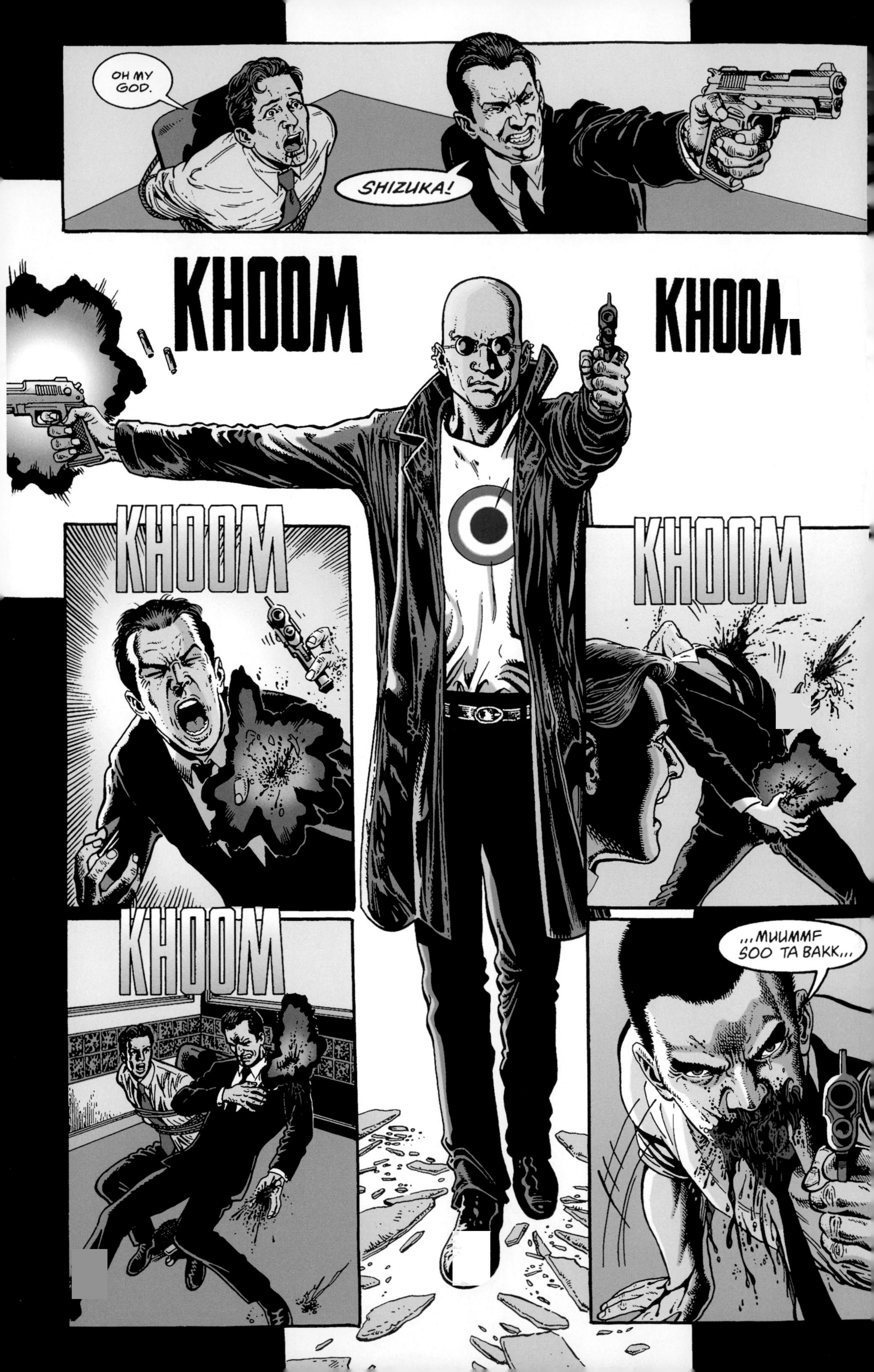
OH MY GOD.
SHIZUKA!
KHOOM
KHOOM
KHOOM
KHOOM
KHOOM
...MUUMMF SOO TA BAKK...

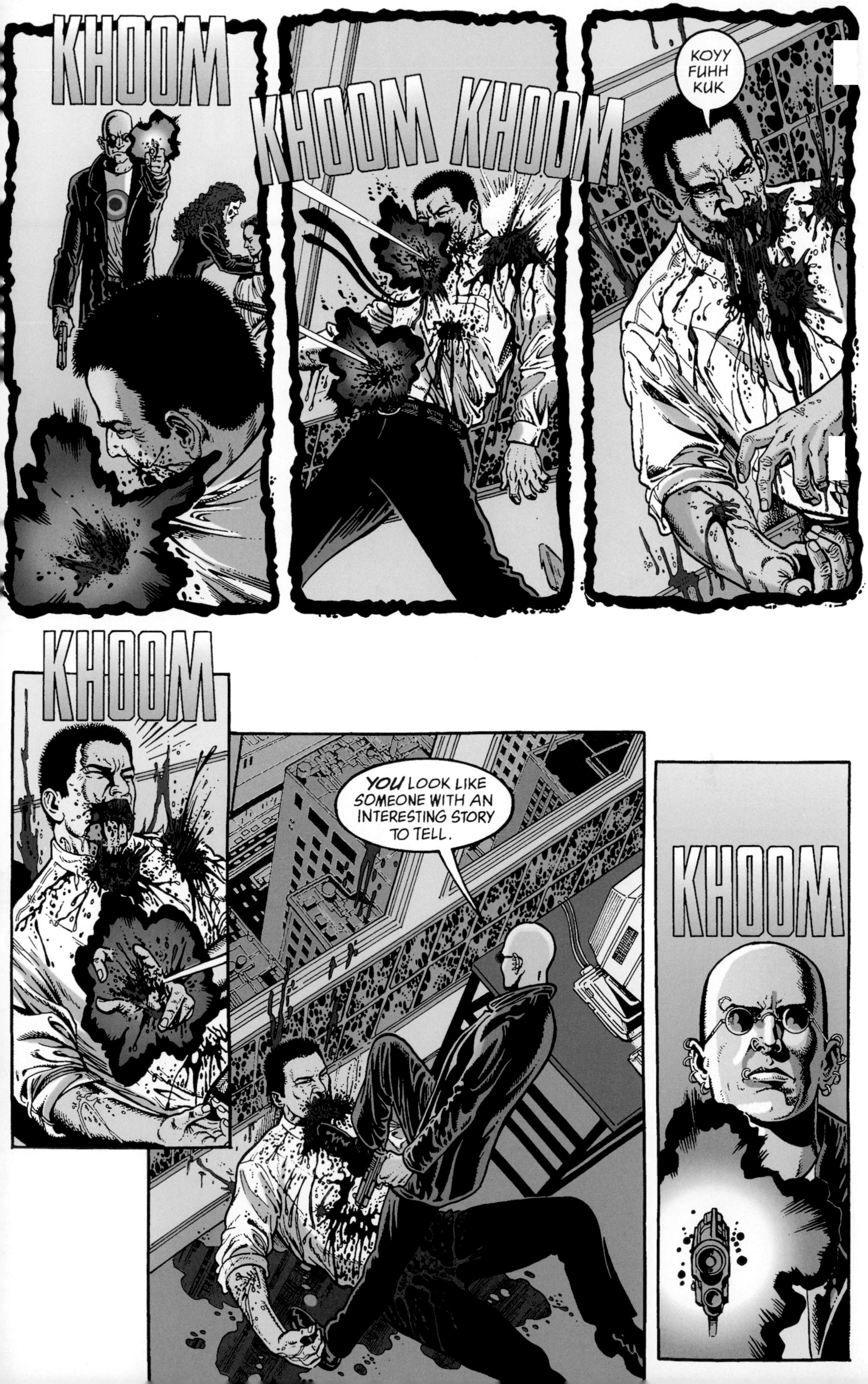
KHOOM
KHOOM KHOOM
KOYY FUHH KUK
KHOOM
YOU LOOK LIKE SOMEONE WITH AN INTERESTING STORY TO TELL.
KHOOM

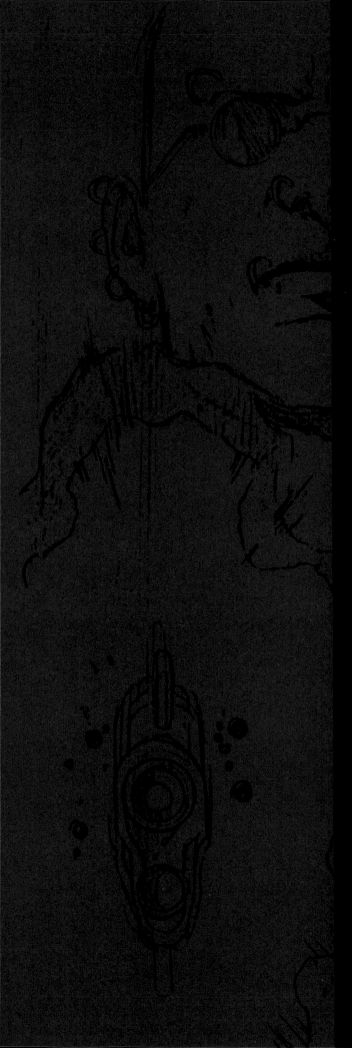

THE SOUND OF THE ATOM SPLITTING

GRANT MORRISON
WRITER

PHIL JIMENEZ
PENCILLER

JOHN STOKES
INKER

DANIEL VOZZO
COLORIST

HEROIC AGE
SEPARATIONS

TODD KLEIN
LETTERER

SHELLY ROEBERG
EDITOR

THE INVISIBLES CREATED
BY GRANT MORRISON

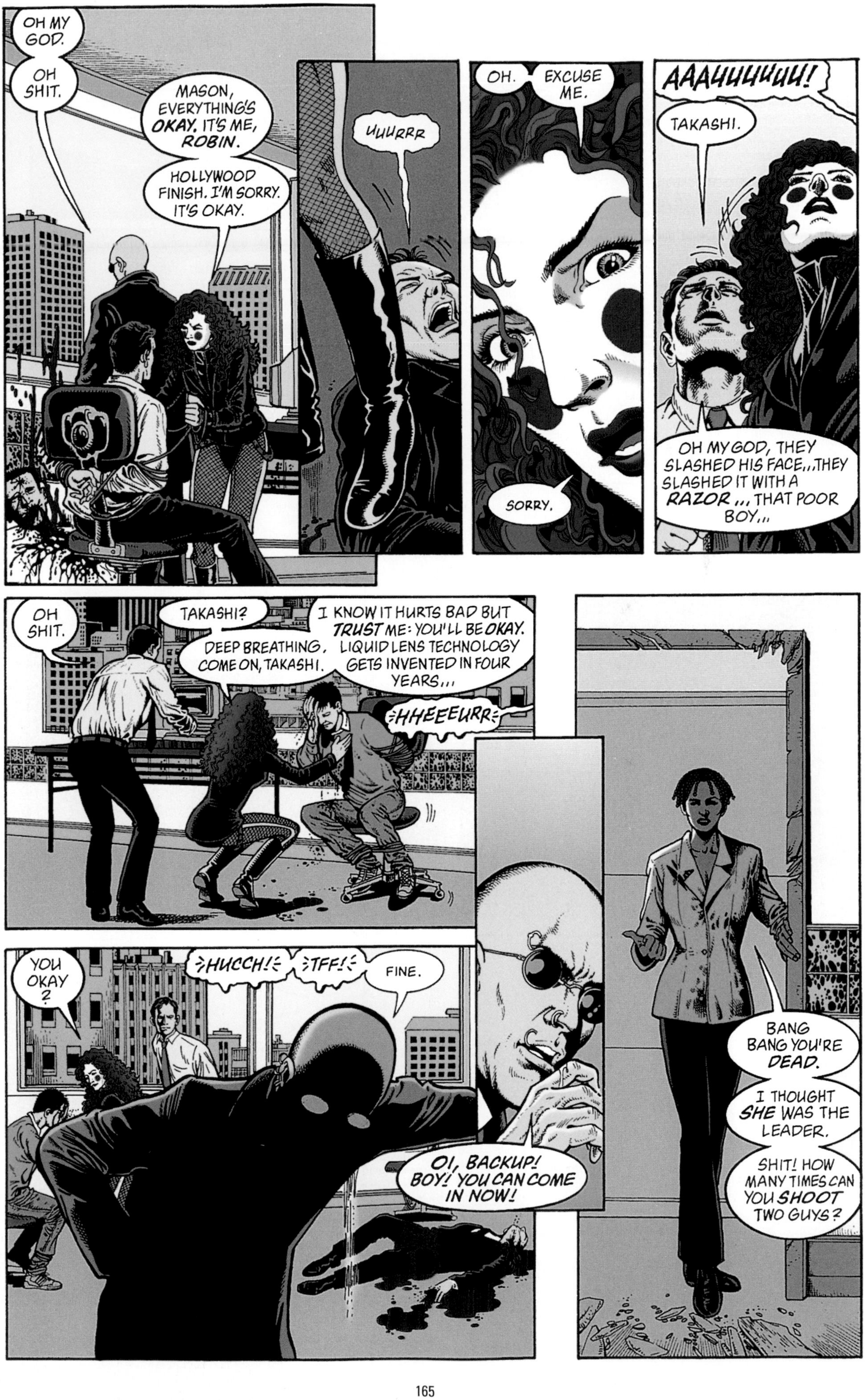
OH MY GOD.
OH SHIT.
MASON, EVERYTHING'S OKAY. IT'S ME, ROBIN.
HOLLYWOOD FINISH. I'M SORRY. IT'S OKAY.
UUURRR
OH.
EXCUSE ME.
SORRY.
AAAUUUUUU!
TAKASHI.
OH MY GOD, THEY SLASHED HIS FACE... THEY SLASHED IT WITH A RAZOR... THAT POOR BOY...
OH SHIT.
TAKASHI?
DEEP BREATHING. COME ON, TAKASHI.
I KNOW IT HURTS BAD BUT TRUST ME: YOU'LL BE OKAY. LIQUID LENS TECHNOLOGY GETS INVENTED IN FOUR YEARS...
HHEEEURR
YOU OKAY?
HUCCH!
TFF!
FINE.
OI, BACKUP! BOY! YOU CAN COME IN NOW!
BANG BANG YOU'RE DEAD.
I THOUGHT SHE WAS THE LEADER.
SHIT! HOW MANY TIMES CAN YOU SHOOT TWO GUYS?

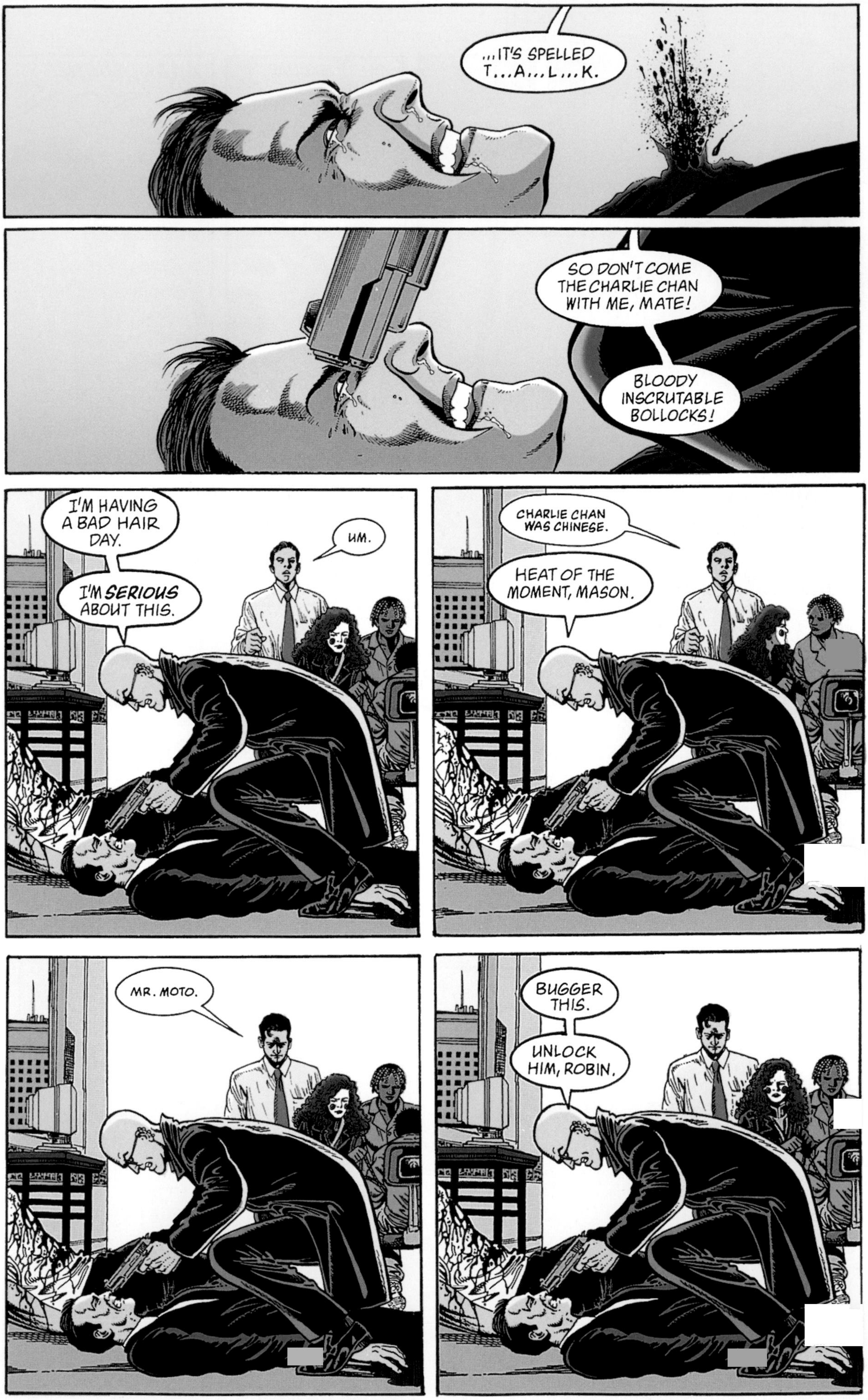
...IT'S SPELLED T...A...L...K.
SO DON'T COME THE CHARLIE CHAN WITH ME, MATE!
BLOODY INSCRUTABLE BOLLOCKS!
I'M HAVING A BAD HAIR DAY.
I'M SERIOUS ABOUT THIS.
UM.
CHARLIE CHAN WAS CHINESE.
HEAT OF THE MOMENT, MASON.
MR. MOTO.
BUGGER THIS.
UNLOCK HIM, ROBIN.

...ALL I'M SAYING IS I FEEL IT'S *UNETHICAL*...

WHAT?

COME *ON*, ROBIN! ETHICS WENT FLYING OUT THE WINDOW WHEN HE SLASHED THE KID'S *FACE* FROM ALASKA TO TIERRA DEL FUEGO!

YEAH, BUT YOU'RE ASKING HER TO TAKE PSYCHOLOGICAL *RISKS*...

I'D DO IT IF I COULD! WE HAVE TO KNOW WHAT THESE BASTARDS ARE ALL ABOUT. WE'VE JUST BEEN THROUGH *SHIT*, YOU KNOW? OUR LIVES MIGHT DE-*PEND* ON THIS.

WE *HAVE* TO KNOW.

BOY'S RIGHT: I *AM* THE LEADER. IT'S GOT NOTHING TO DO WITH PSYCHOLOGICAL RISKS.

I'LL DECIDE.

AND DON'T YOU START YOWLING AT EVERY- ONE BECAUSE YOUR *EX* BLEW YOU OUT THIS MORNING!

I'M WARNING YOU!

YOU'VE BEEN READING MY MIND...

WELL YOU SHOULDN'T BE THINKING SO LOUD!

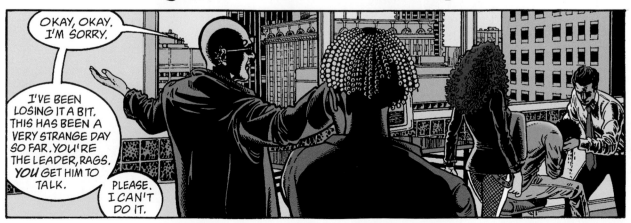

OKAY, OKAY. I'M SORRY.

I'VE BEEN LOSING IT A BIT. THIS HAS BEEN A VERY STRANGE DAY SO FAR. YOU'RE THE LEADER, RAGS. *YOU* GET HIM TO TALK.

PLEASE. I CAN'T DO IT.

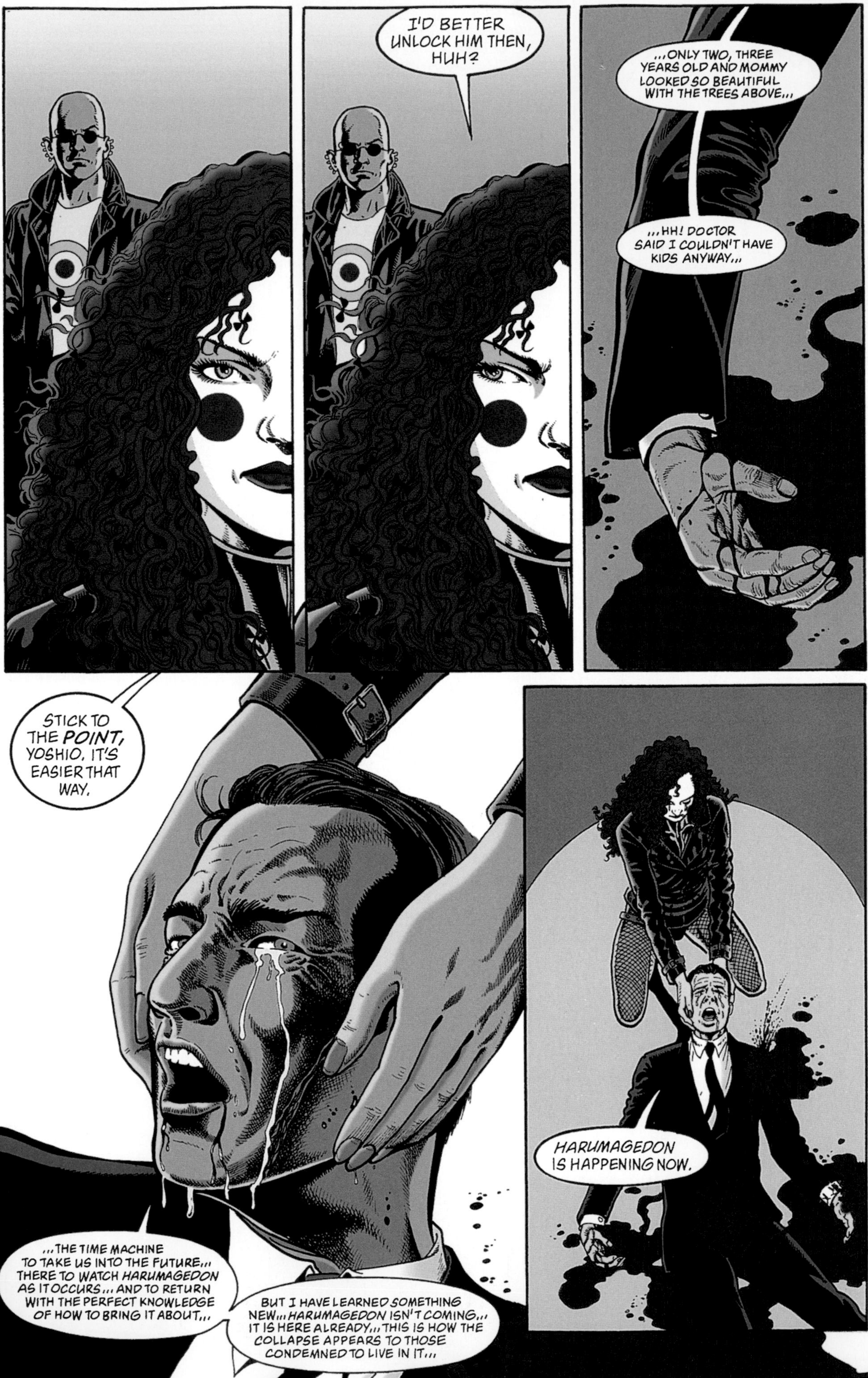
I'D BETTER UNLOCK HIM THEN, HUH?
...ONLY TWO, THREE YEARS OLD AND MOMMY LOOKED SO BEAUTIFUL WITH THE TREES ABOVE...
...HH! DOCTOR SAID I COULDN'T HAVE KIDS ANYWAY...
STICK TO THE POINT, YOSHIO. IT'S EASIER THAT WAY.
HARUMAGEDON IS HAPPENING NOW.
...THE TIME MACHINE TO TAKE US INTO THE FUTURE... THERE TO WATCH HARUMAGEDON AS IT OCCURS... AND TO RETURN WITH THE PERFECT KNOWLEDGE OF HOW TO BRING IT ABOUT...
BUT I HAVE LEARNED SOMETHING NEW... HARUMAGEDON ISN'T COMING... IT IS HERE ALREADY... THIS IS HOW THE COLLAPSE APPEARS TO THOSE CONDEMNED TO LIVE IN IT...

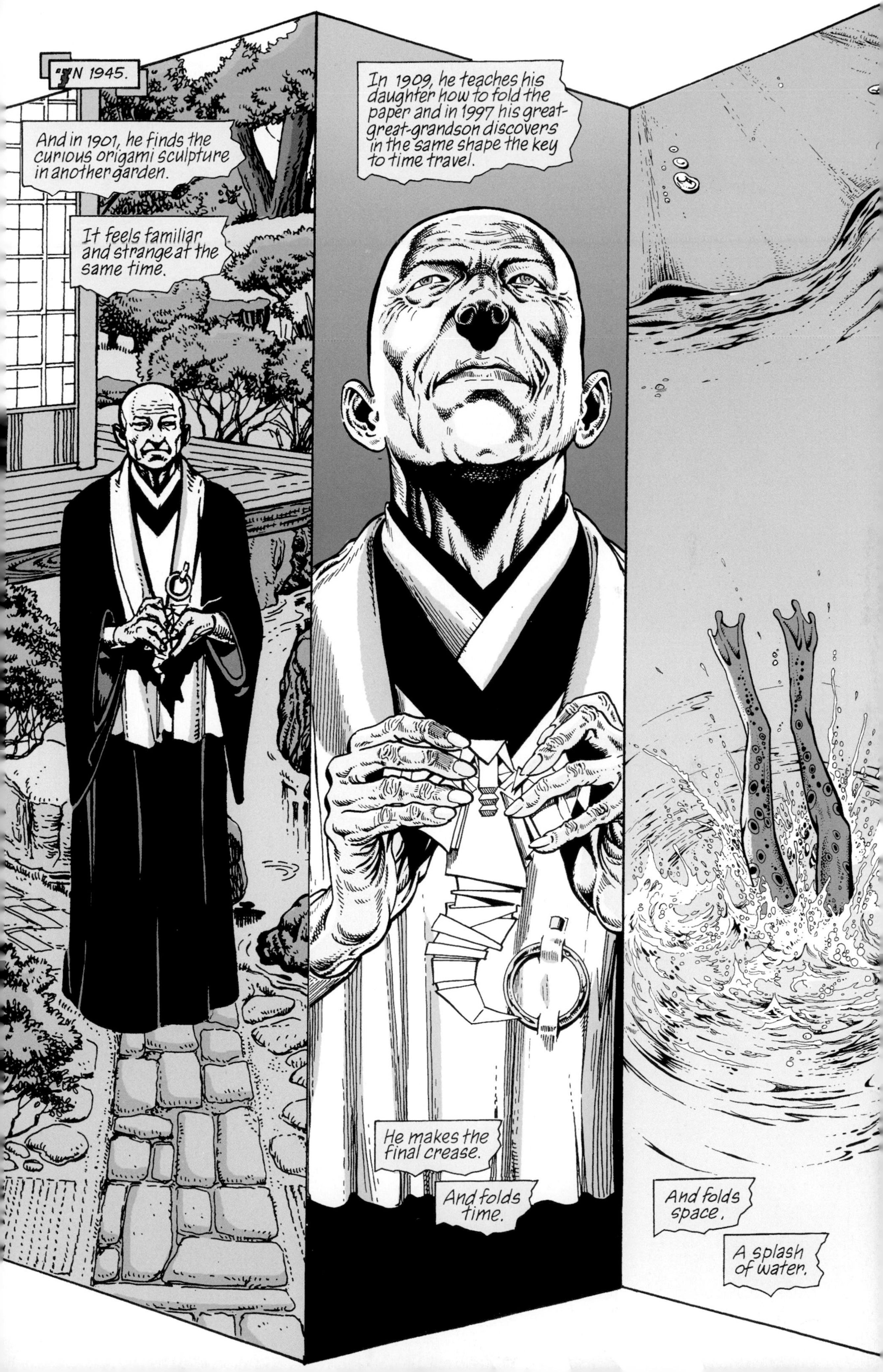
"IN 1945.
And in 1901, he finds the curious origami sculpture in another garden.
It feels familiar and strange at the same time.
In 1909, he teaches his daughter how to fold the paper and in 1997 his great-great-grandson discovers in the same shape the key to time travel.
He makes the final crease.
And folds time.
And folds space.
A splash of water.

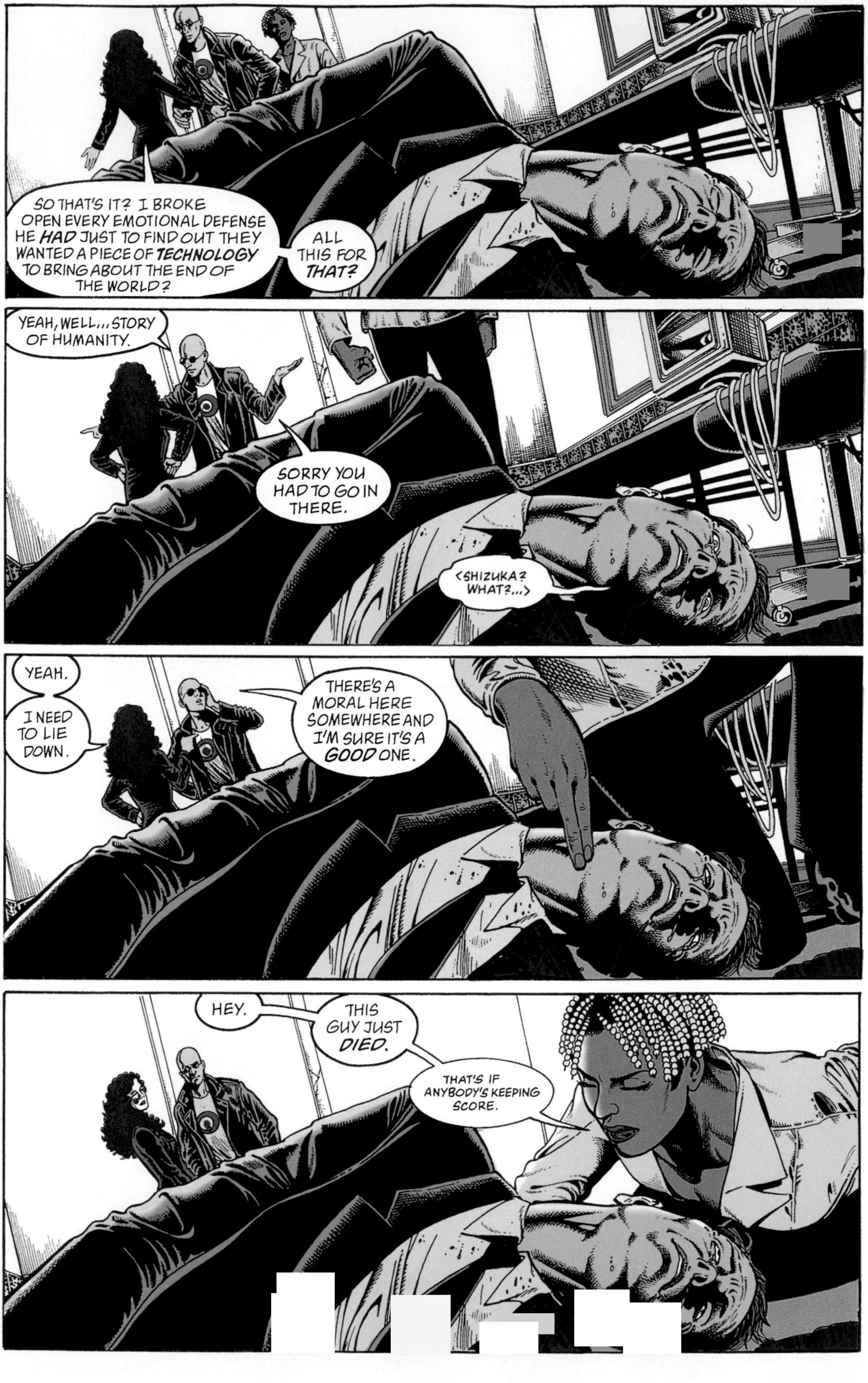
SO THAT'S IT? I BROKE OPEN EVERY EMOTIONAL DEFENSE HE *HAD* JUST TO FIND OUT THEY WANTED A PIECE OF *TECHNOLOGY* TO BRING ABOUT THE END OF THE WORLD?
ALL THIS FOR *THAT?*
YEAH, WELL... STORY OF HUMANITY.
SORRY YOU HAD TO GO IN THERE.
<SHIZUKA? WHAT?...>
YEAH.
I NEED TO LIE DOWN.
THERE'S A MORAL HERE SOMEWHERE AND I'M SURE IT'S A *GOOD* ONE.
HEY.
THIS GUY JUST *DIED*.
THAT'S IF ANYBODY'S KEEPING SCORE.

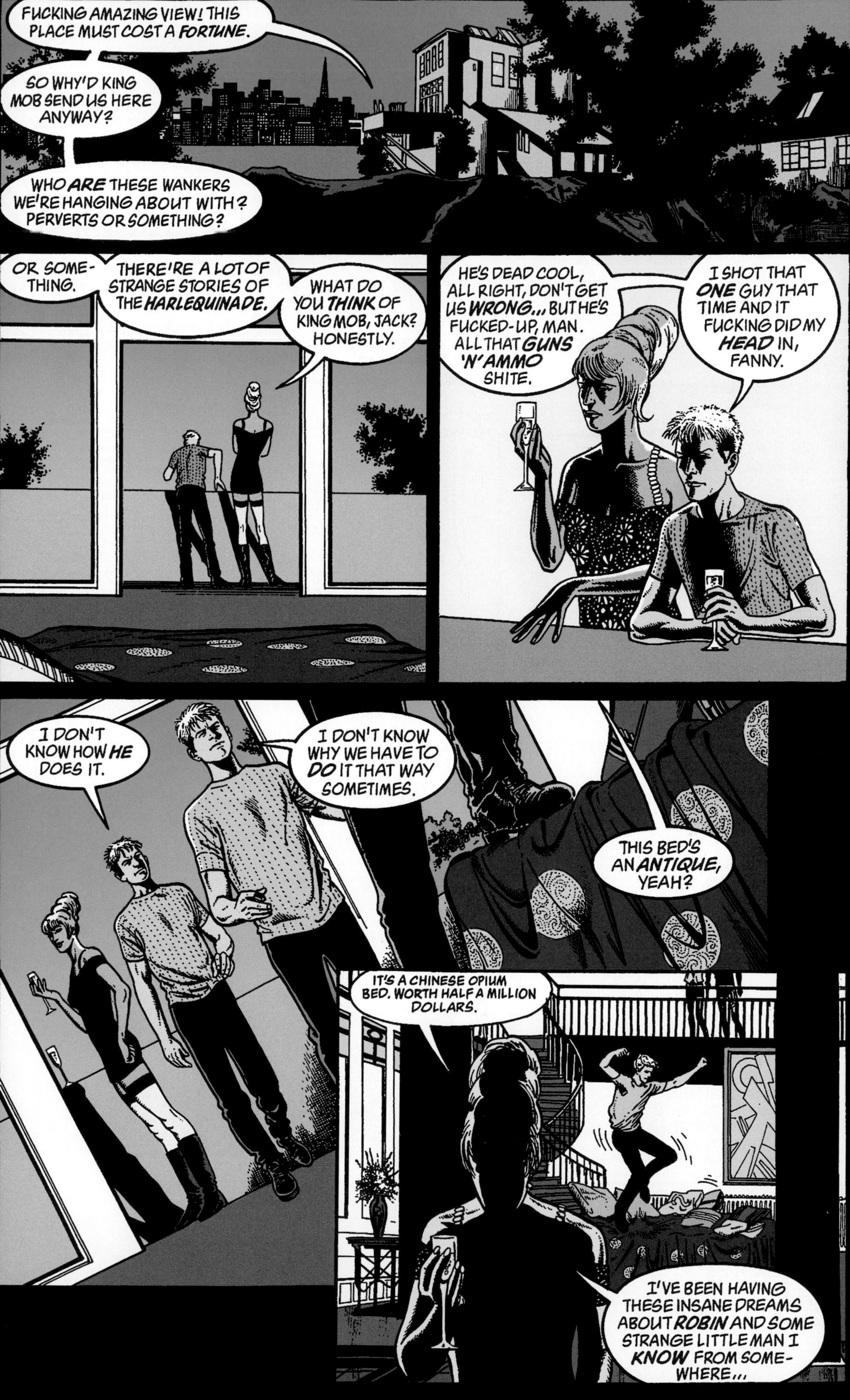
FUCKING AMAZING VIEW! THIS PLACE MUST COST A FORTUNE.
SO WHY'D KING MOB SEND US HERE ANYWAY?
WHO ARE THESE WANKERS WE'RE HANGING ABOUT WITH? PERVERTS OR SOMETHING?
OR SOME-THING.
THERE'RE A LOT OF STRANGE STORIES OF THE HARLEQUINADE.
WHAT DO YOU THINK OF KING MOB, JACK? HONESTLY.
HE'S DEAD COOL, ALL RIGHT, DON'T GET US WRONG... BUT HE'S FUCKED-UP, MAN. ALL THAT GUNS 'N' AMMO SHITE.
I SHOT THAT ONE GUY THAT TIME AND IT FUCKING DID MY HEAD IN, FANNY.
I DON'T KNOW HOW HE DOES IT.
I DON'T KNOW WHY WE HAVE TO DO IT THAT WAY SOMETIMES.
THIS BED'S AN ANTIQUE, YEAH?
IT'S A CHINESE OPIUM BED. WORTH HALF A MILLION DOLLARS.
I'VE BEEN HAVING THESE INSANE DREAMS ABOUT ROBIN AND SOME STRANGE LITTLE MAN I KNOW FROM SOME-WHERE...

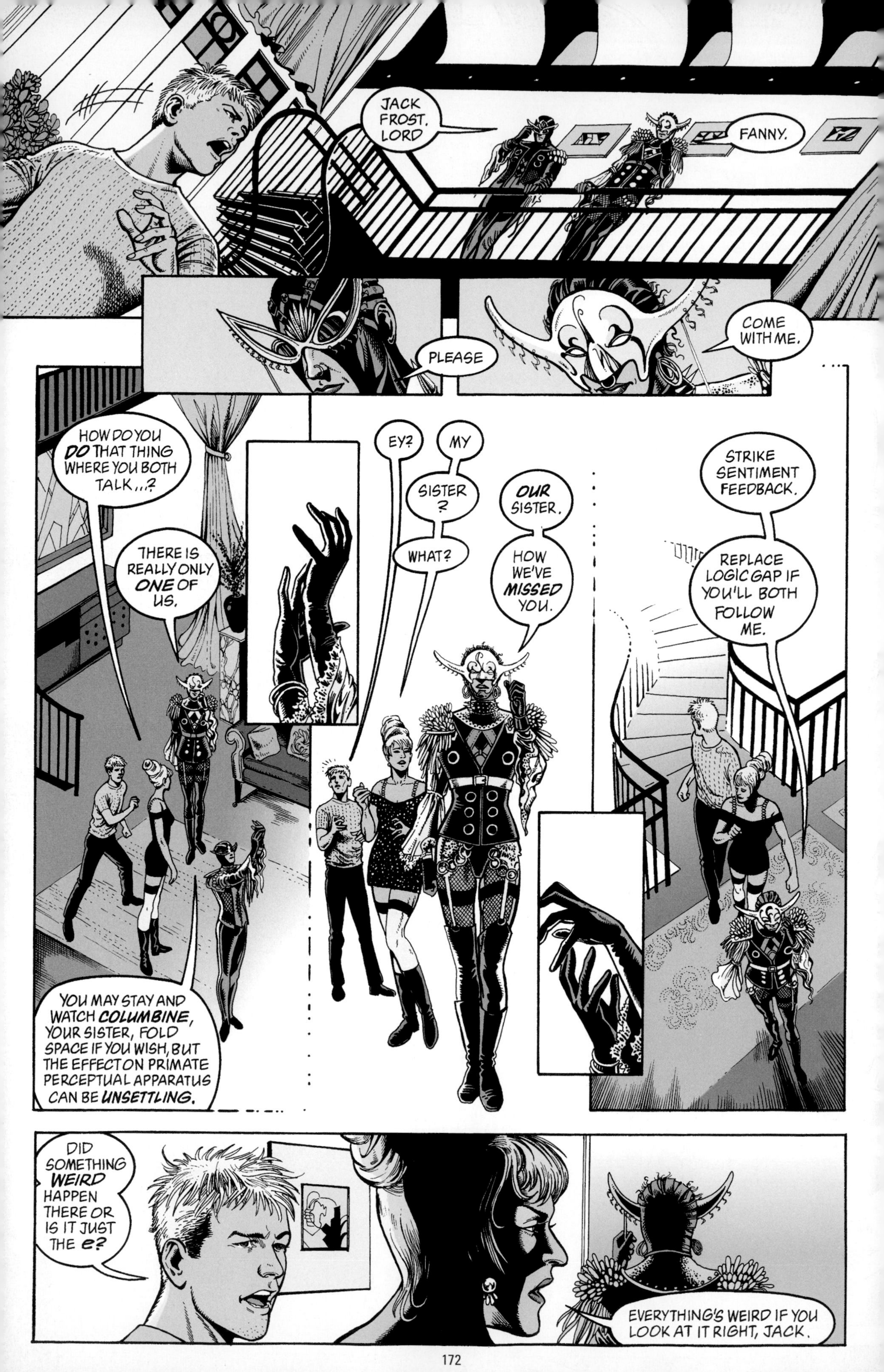
JACK FROST. LORD
FANNY.
PLEASE
COME WITH ME.
HOW DO YOU DO THAT THING WHERE YOU BOTH TALK...?
THERE IS REALLY ONLY ONE OF US.
YOU MAY STAY AND WATCH COLUMBINE, YOUR SISTER, FOLD SPACE IF YOU WISH, BUT THE EFFECT ON PRIMATE PERCEPTUAL APPARATUS CAN BE UNSETTLING.
EY?
MY SISTER?
WHAT?
OUR SISTER.
HOW WE'VE MISSED YOU.
STRIKE SENTIMENT FEEDBACK.
REPLACE LOGIC GAP IF YOU'LL BOTH FOLLOW ME.
DID SOMETHING WEIRD HAPPEN THERE OR IS IT JUST THE e?
EVERYTHING'S WEIRD IF YOU LOOK AT IT RIGHT, JACK.

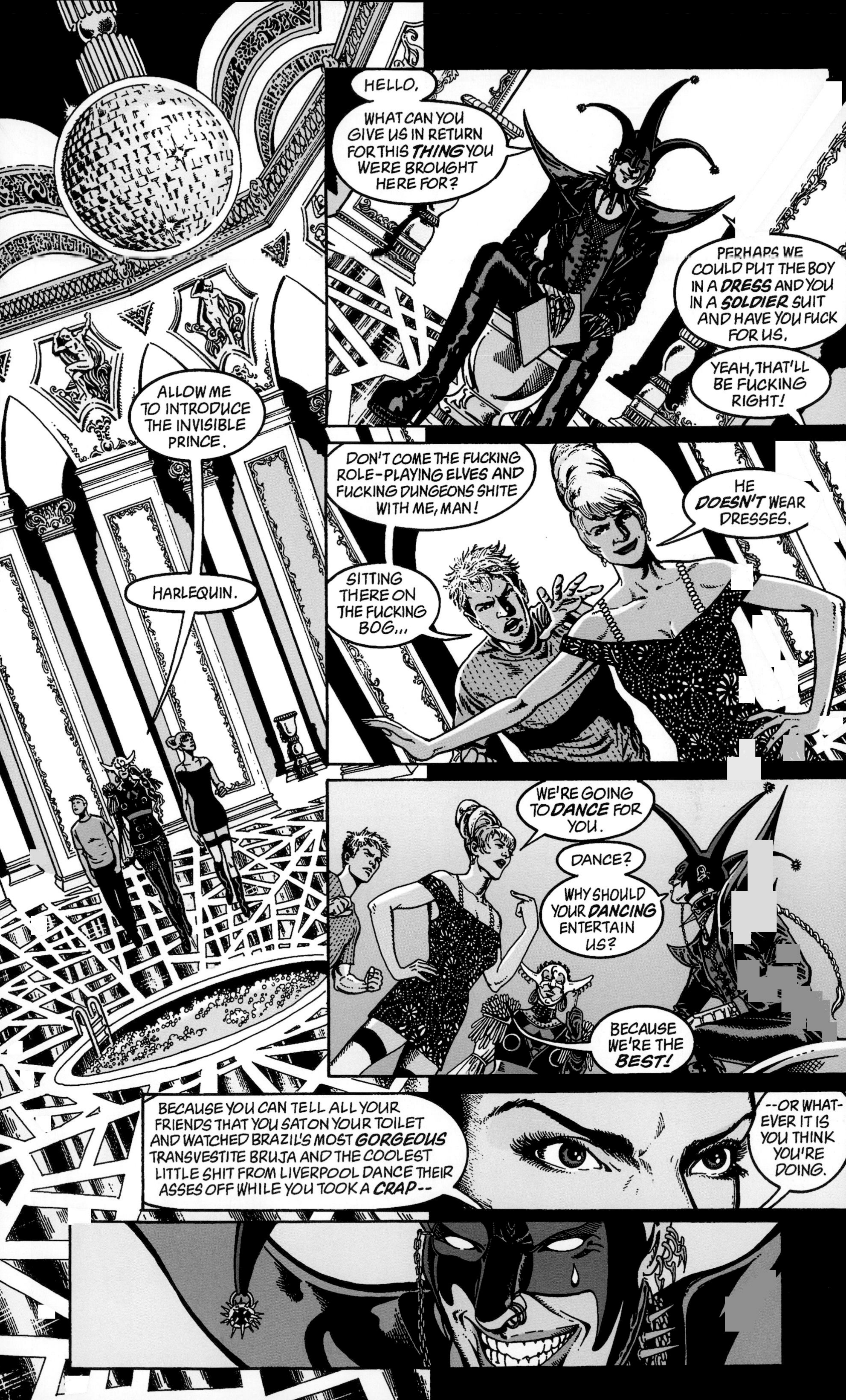
ALLOW ME TO INTRODUCE THE INVISIBLE PRINCE.
HARLEQUIN.
HELLO,
WHAT CAN YOU GIVE US IN RETURN FOR THIS THING YOU WERE BROUGHT HERE FOR?
PERHAPS WE COULD PUT THE BOY IN A DRESS AND YOU IN A SOLDIER SUIT AND HAVE YOU FUCK FOR US.
YEAH, THAT'LL BE FUCKING RIGHT!
DON'T COME THE FUCKING ROLE-PLAYING ELVES AND FUCKING DUNGEONS SHITE WITH ME, MAN!
SITTING THERE ON THE FUCKING BOG...
HE DOESN'T WEAR DRESSES.
WE'RE GOING TO DANCE FOR YOU.
DANCE?
WHY SHOULD YOUR DANCING ENTERTAIN US?
BECAUSE WE'RE THE BEST!
BECAUSE YOU CAN TELL ALL YOUR FRIENDS THAT YOU SAT ON YOUR TOILET AND WATCHED BRAZIL'S MOST GORGEOUS TRANSVESTITE BRUJA AND THE COOLEST LITTLE SHIT FROM LIVERPOOL DANCE THEIR ASSES OFF WHILE YOU TOOK A CRAP--
--OR WHATEVER IT IS YOU THINK YOU'RE DOING.

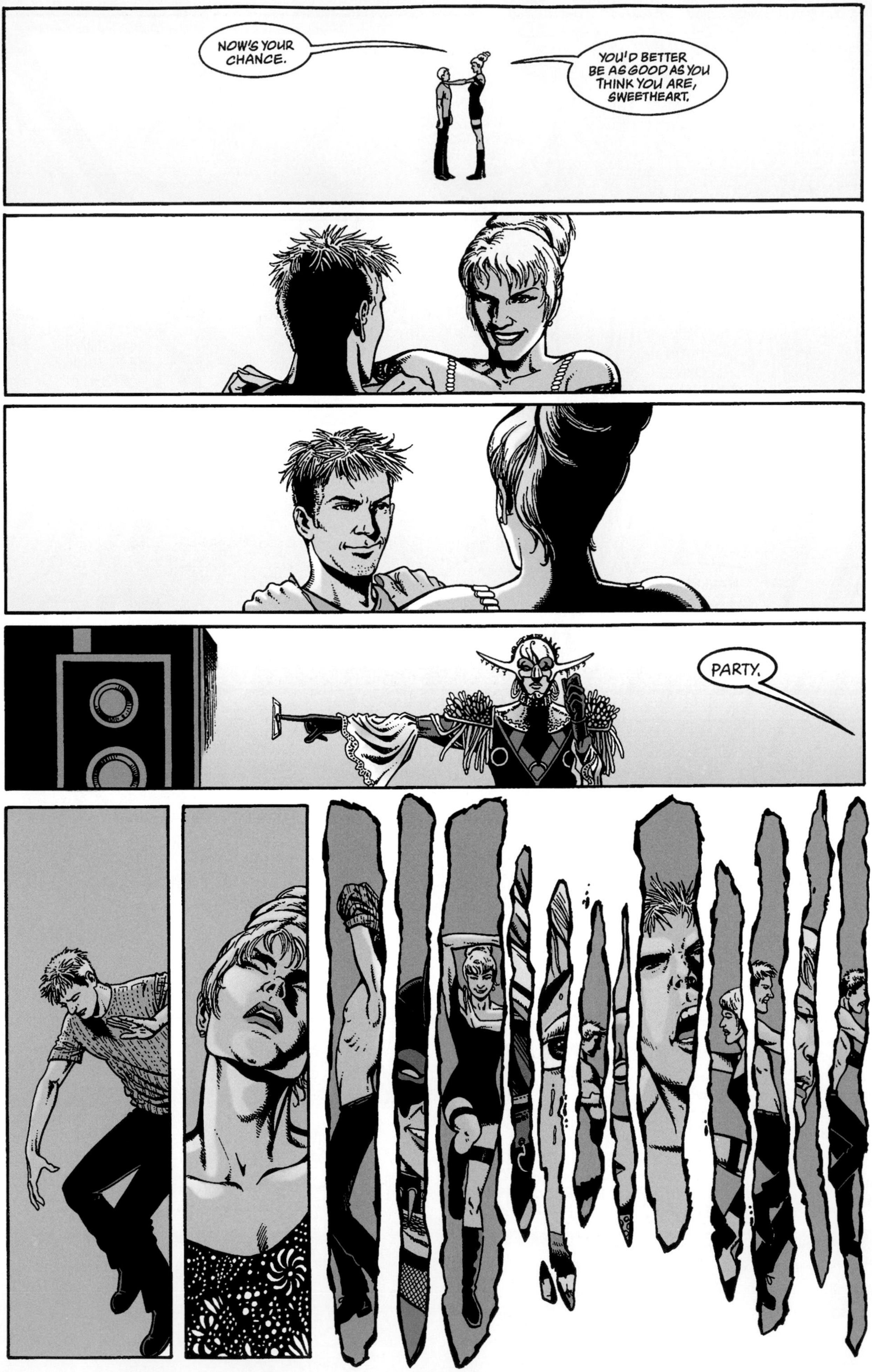
NOW'S YOUR CHANCE.
YOU'D BETTER BE AS GOOD AS YOU THINK YOU ARE, SWEETHEART.
PARTY.

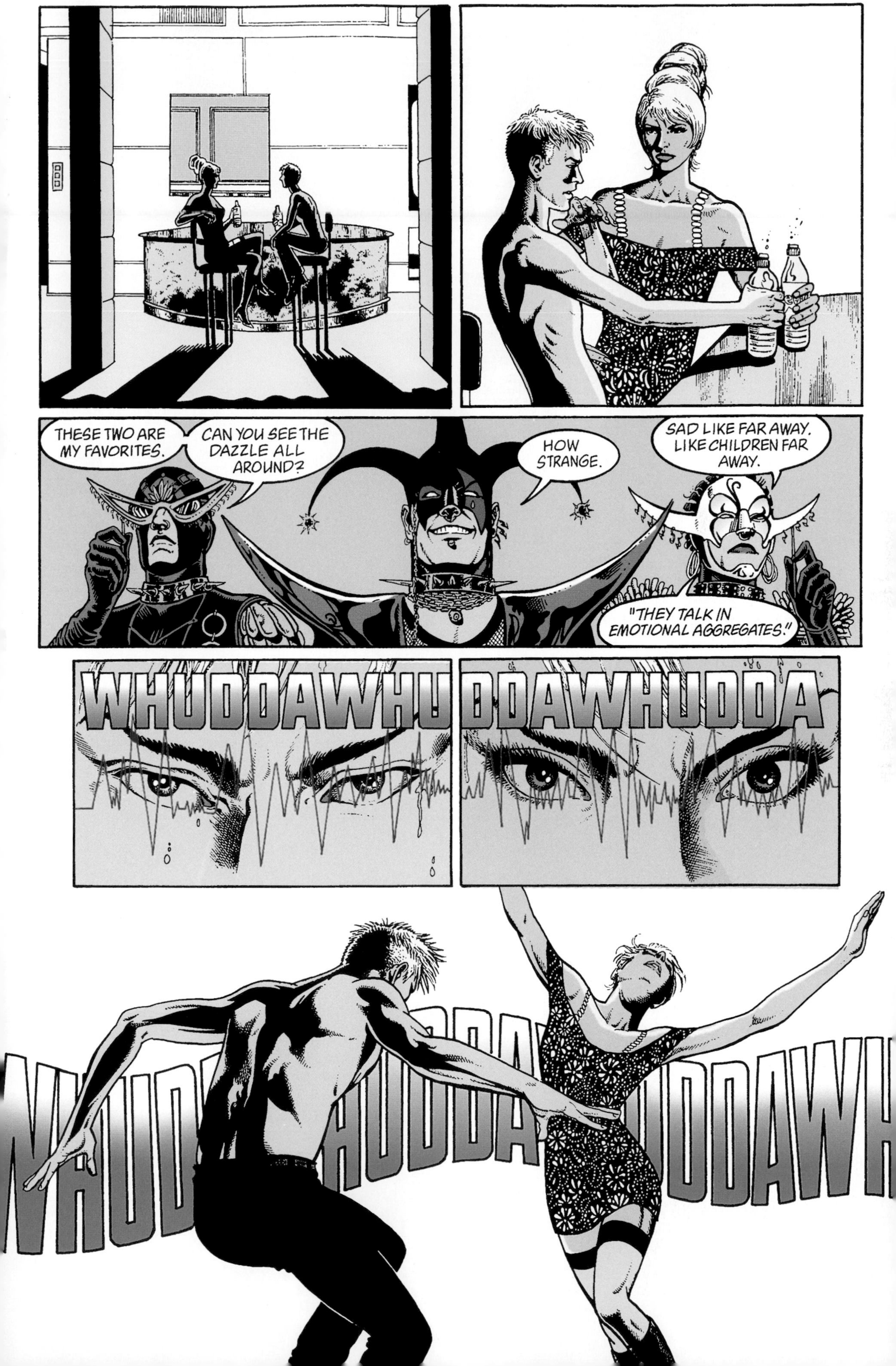

THESE TWO ARE MY FAVORITES.
CAN YOU SEE THE DAZZLE ALL AROUND?
HOW STRANGE.
SAD LIKE FAR AWAY. LIKE CHILDREN FAR AWAY.
"THEY TALK IN EMOTIONAL AGGREGATES."
WHUDDAWHUDDAWHUDDA

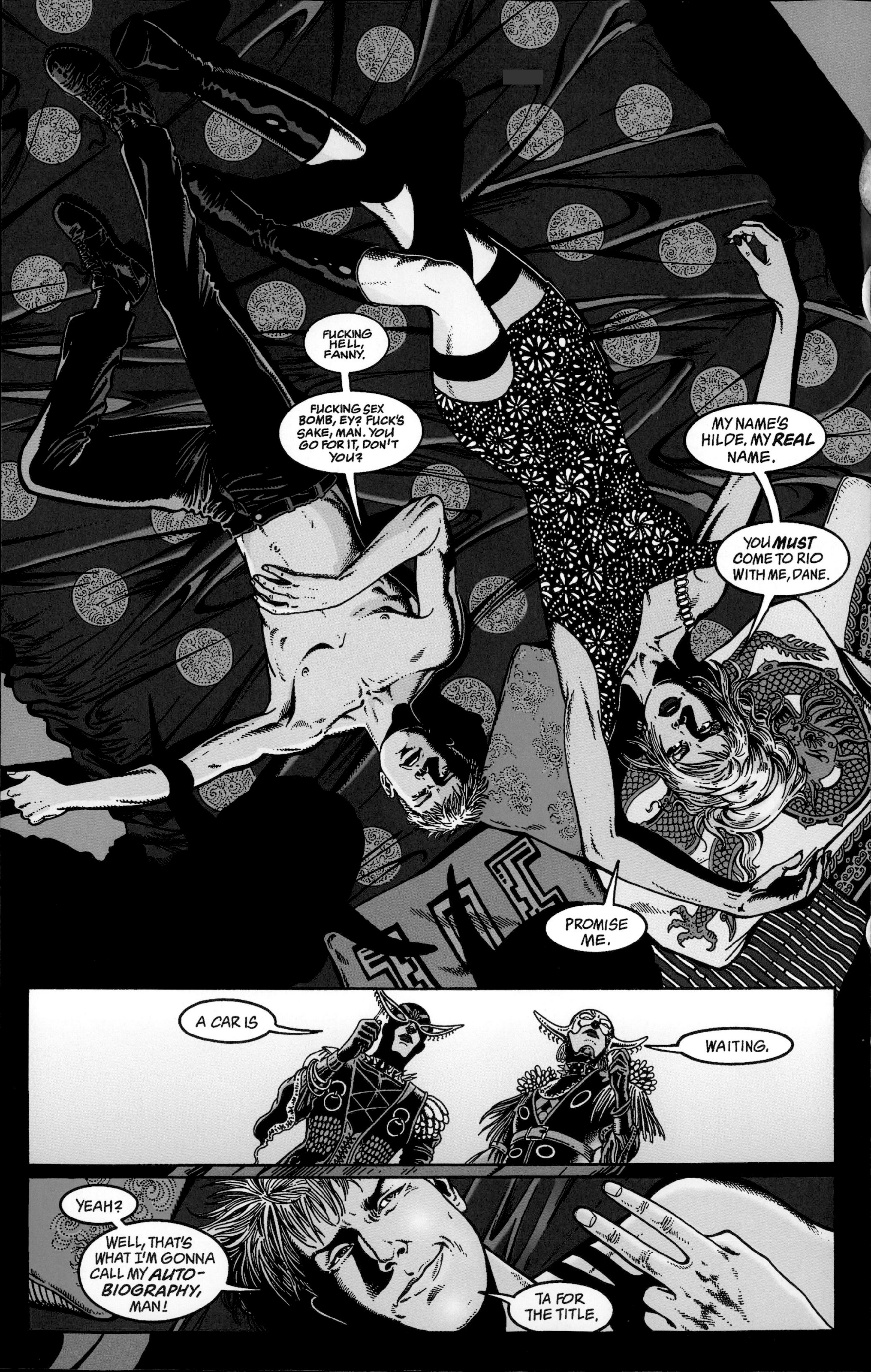
FUCKING HELL, FANNY.
FUCKING SEX BOMB, EY? FUCK'S SAKE, MAN. YOU GO FOR IT, DON'T YOU?
MY NAME'S HILDE. MY *REAL* NAME.
YOU *MUST* COME TO RIO WITH ME, DANE.
PROMISE ME.
A CAR IS
WAITING.
YEAH?
WELL, THAT'S WHAT I'M GONNA CALL MY *AUTO-BIOGRAPHY*, MAN!
TA FOR THE TITLE.

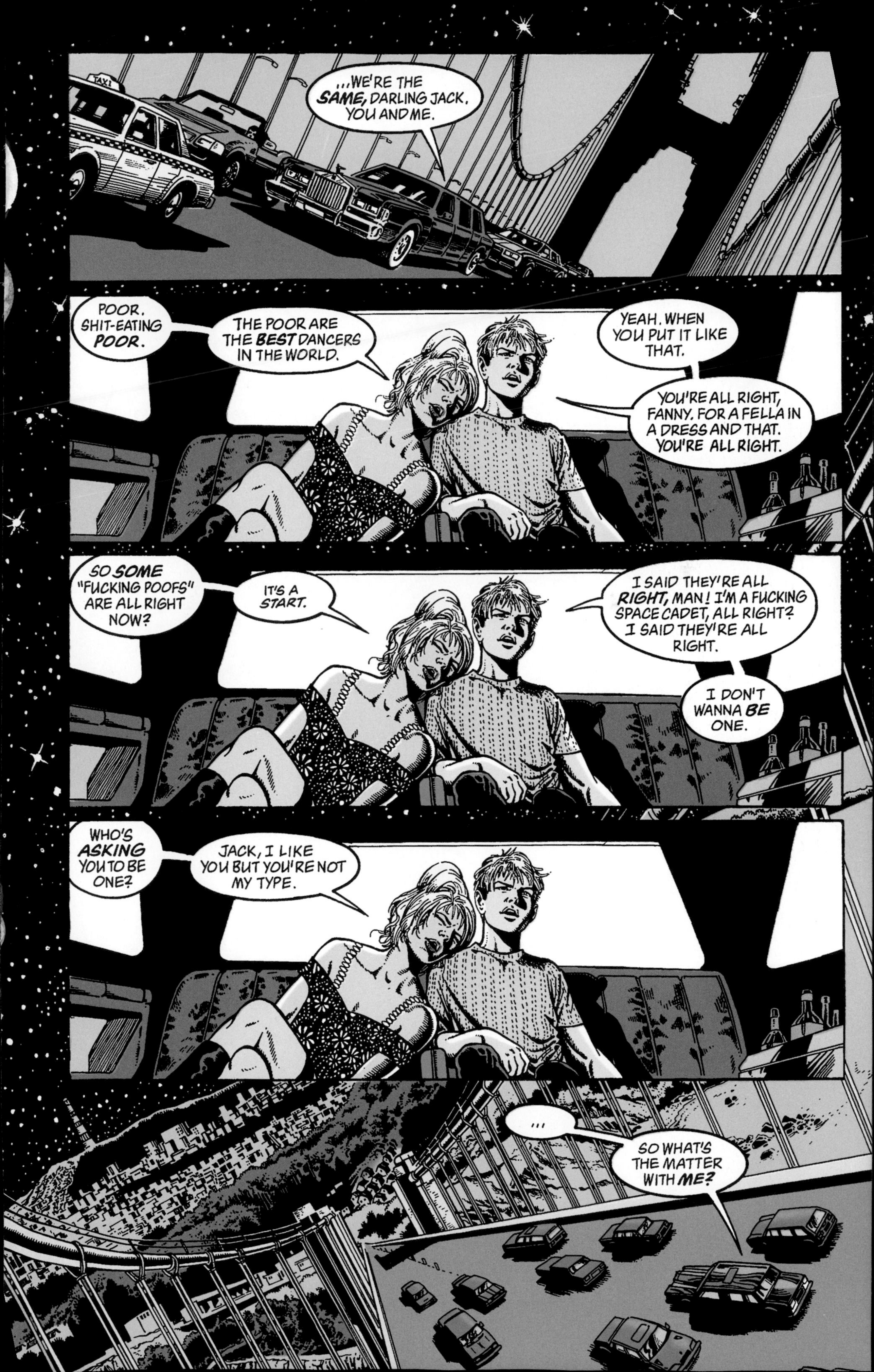
...WE'RE THE SAME, DARLING JACK. YOU AND ME.
POOR. SHIT-EATING POOR.
THE POOR ARE THE BEST DANCERS IN THE WORLD.
YEAH. WHEN YOU PUT IT LIKE THAT.
YOU'RE ALL RIGHT, FANNY. FOR A FELLA IN A DRESS AND THAT. YOU'RE ALL RIGHT.
SO SOME "FUCKING POOFS" ARE ALL RIGHT NOW?
IT'S A START.
I SAID THEY'RE ALL RIGHT, MAN! I'M A FUCKING SPACE CADET, ALL RIGHT? I SAID THEY'RE ALL RIGHT.
I DON'T WANNA BE ONE.
WHO'S ASKING YOU TO BE ONE?
JACK, I LIKE YOU BUT YOU'RE NOT MY TYPE.
...
SO WHAT'S THE MATTER WITH ME?

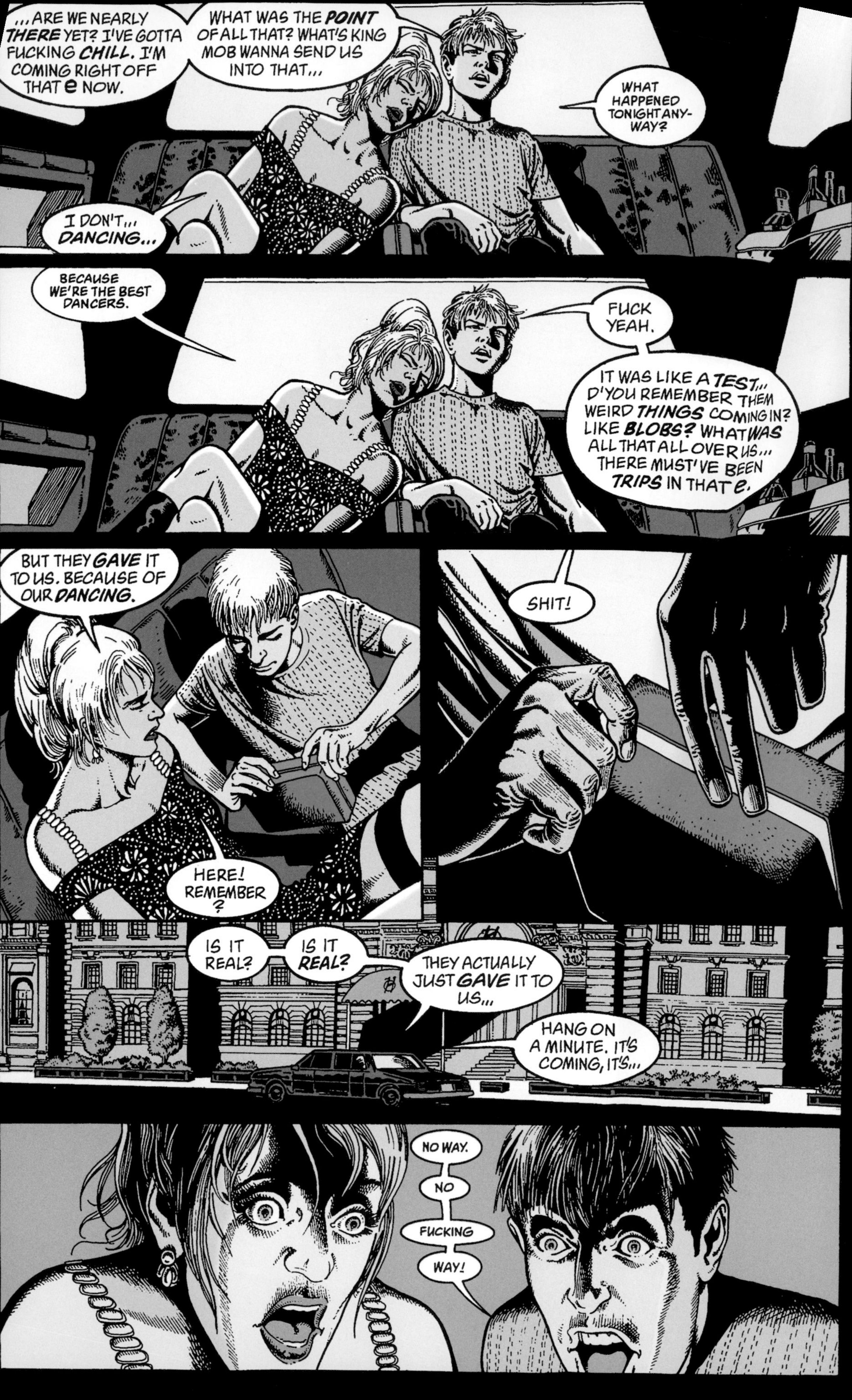
...ARE WE NEARLY THERE YET? I'VE GOTTA FUCKING CHILL. I'M COMING RIGHT OFF THAT e NOW.
WHAT WAS THE POINT OF ALL THAT? WHAT'S KING MOB WANNA SEND US INTO THAT...
WHAT HAPPENED TONIGHT ANY-WAY?
I DON'T... DANCING...
BECAUSE WE'RE THE BEST DANCERS.
FUCK YEAH.
IT WAS LIKE A TEST... D'YOU REMEMBER THEM WEIRD THINGS COMING IN? LIKE BLOBS? WHAT WAS ALL THAT ALL OVER US... THERE MUST'VE BEEN TRIPS IN THAT e.
BUT THEY GAVE IT TO US. BECAUSE OF OUR DANCING.
HERE! REMEMBER?
SHIT!
IS IT REAL?
IS IT REAL?
THEY ACTUALLY JUST GAVE IT TO US...
HANG ON A MINUTE. IT'S COMING, IT'S...
NO WAY.
NO
FUCKING
WAY!

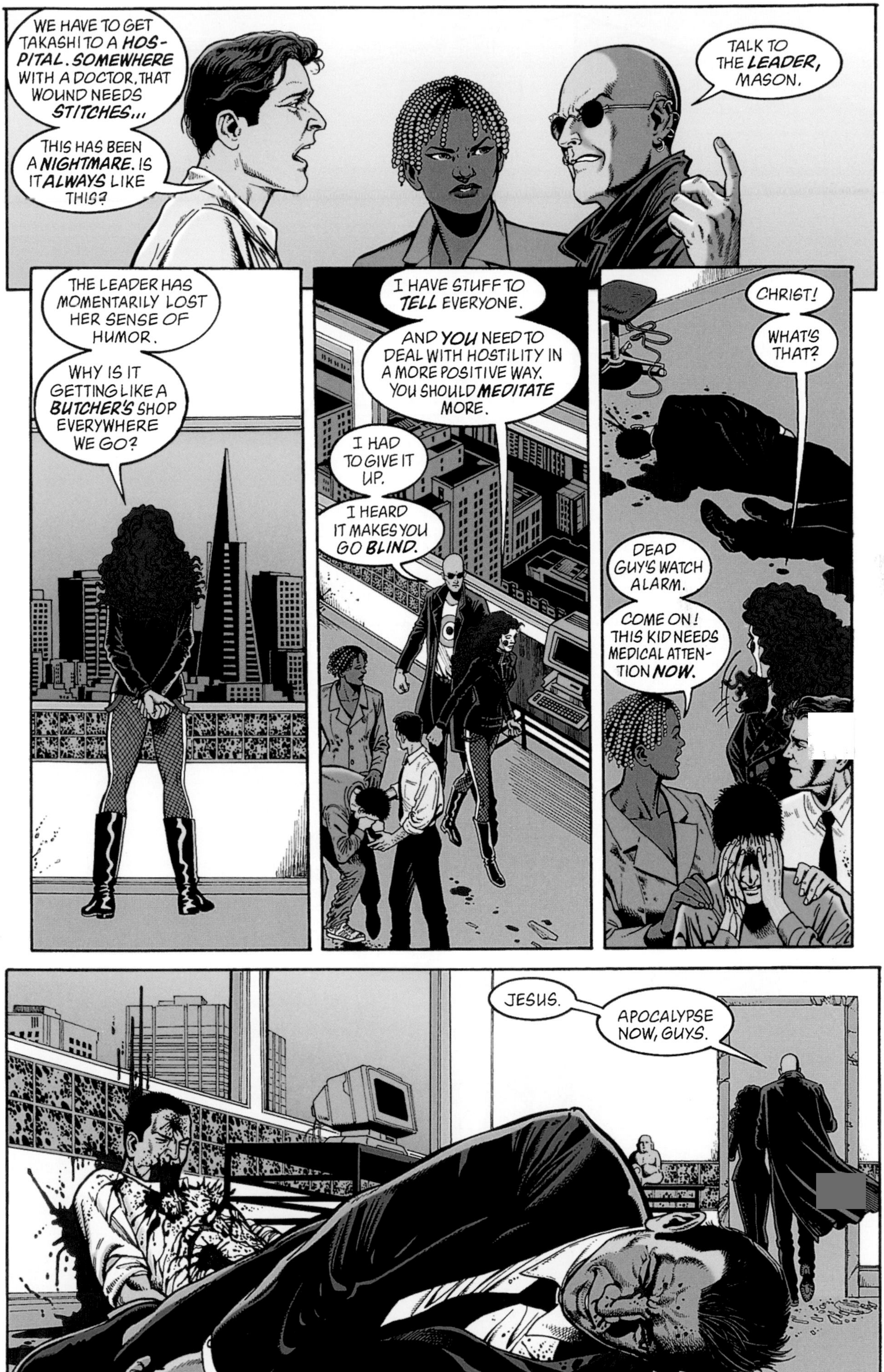

WE HAVE TO GET TAKASHI TO A HOSPITAL. SOMEWHERE WITH A DOCTOR. THAT WOUND NEEDS STITCHES...
THIS HAS BEEN A NIGHTMARE. IS IT ALWAYS LIKE THIS?
TALK TO THE LEADER, MASON.
THE LEADER HAS MOMENTARILY LOST HER SENSE OF HUMOR.
WHY IS IT GETTING LIKE A BUTCHER'S SHOP EVERYWHERE WE GO?
I HAVE STUFF TO TELL EVERYONE.
AND YOU NEED TO DEAL WITH HOSTILITY IN A MORE POSITIVE WAY. YOU SHOULD MEDITATE MORE.
I HAD TO GIVE IT UP.
I HEARD IT MAKES YOU GO BLIND.
CHRIST!
WHAT'S THAT?
DEAD GUY'S WATCH ALARM.
COME ON! THIS KID NEEDS MEDICAL ATTENTION NOW.
JESUS.
APOCALYPSE NOW, GUYS.

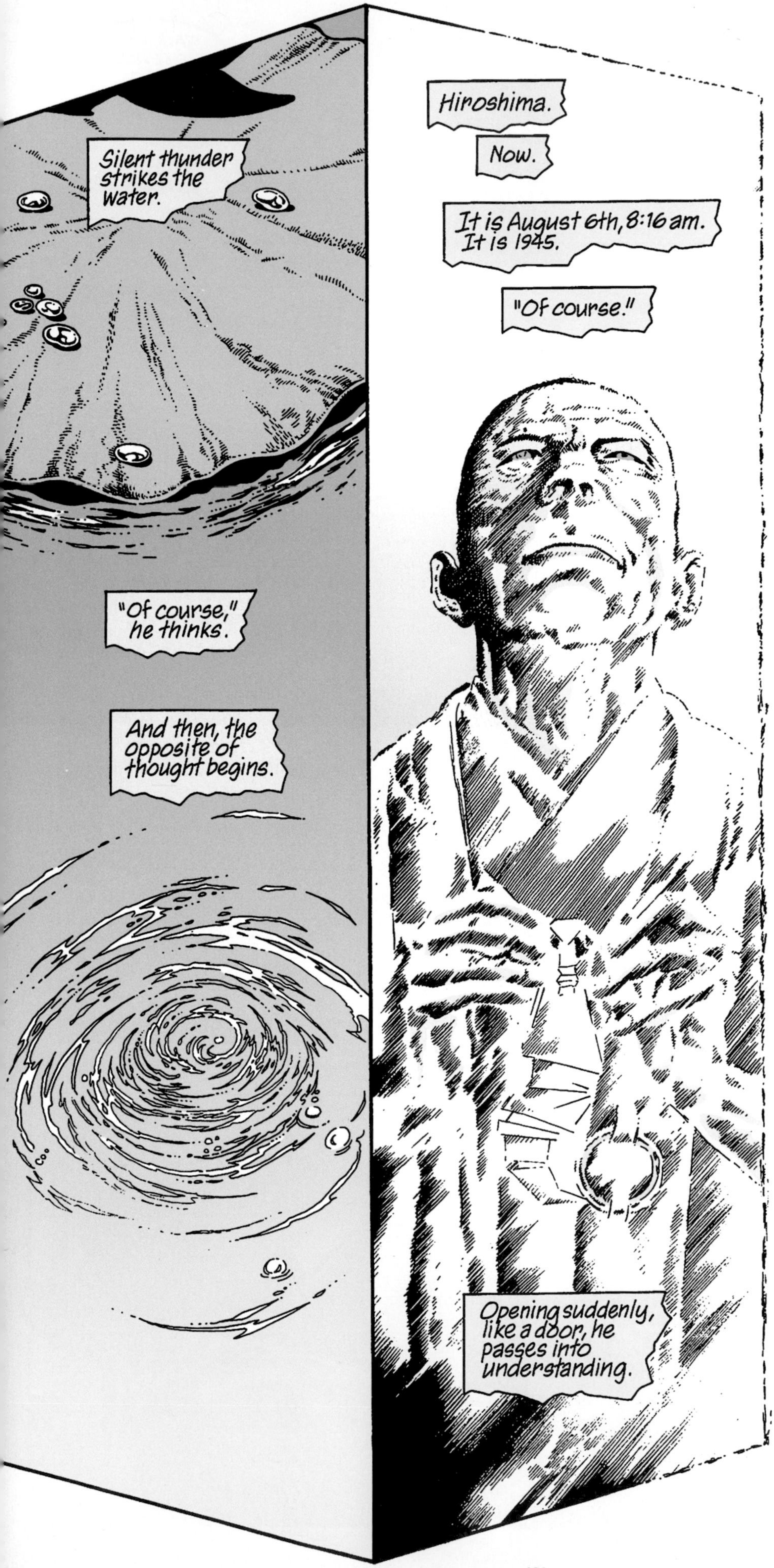
Silent thunder strikes the water.
"Of course," he thinks.
And then, the opposite of thought begins.
Hiroshima.
Now.
It is August 6th, 8:16 am. It is 1945.
"Of course."
Opening suddenly, like a door, he passes into understanding.

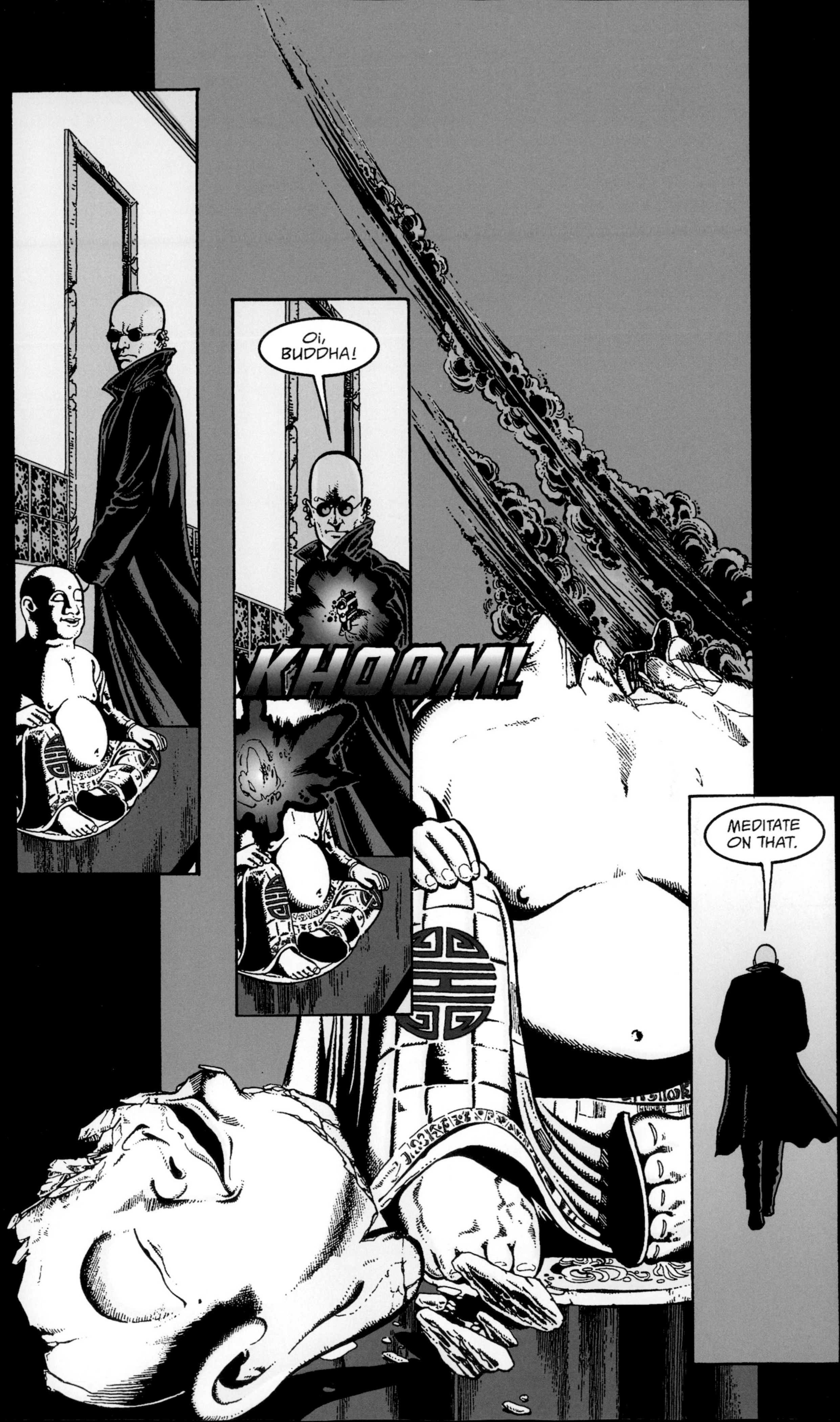
Oi,
BUDDHA!
KHOOM!
MEDITATE
ON THAT.

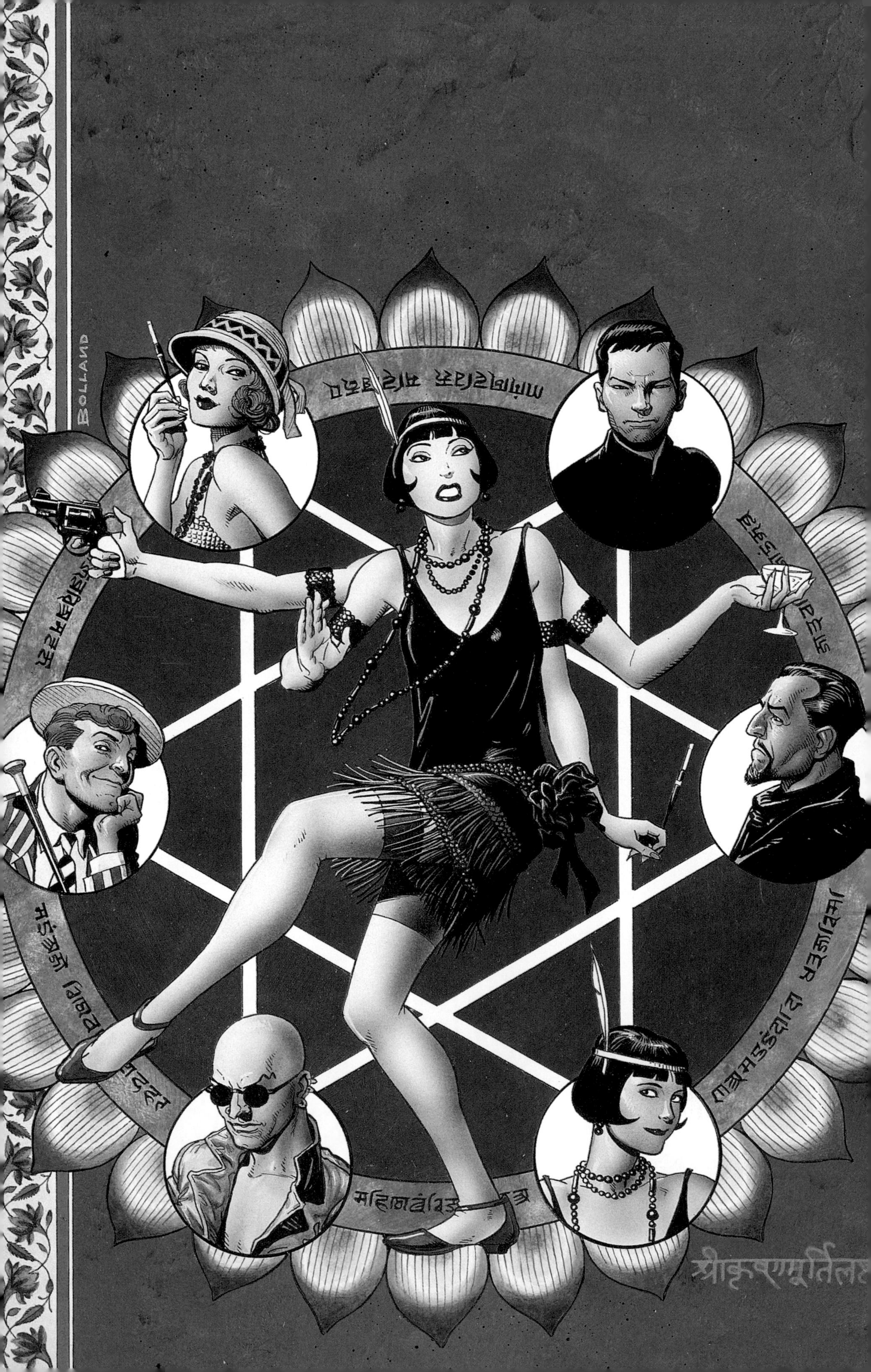
BOLLAND

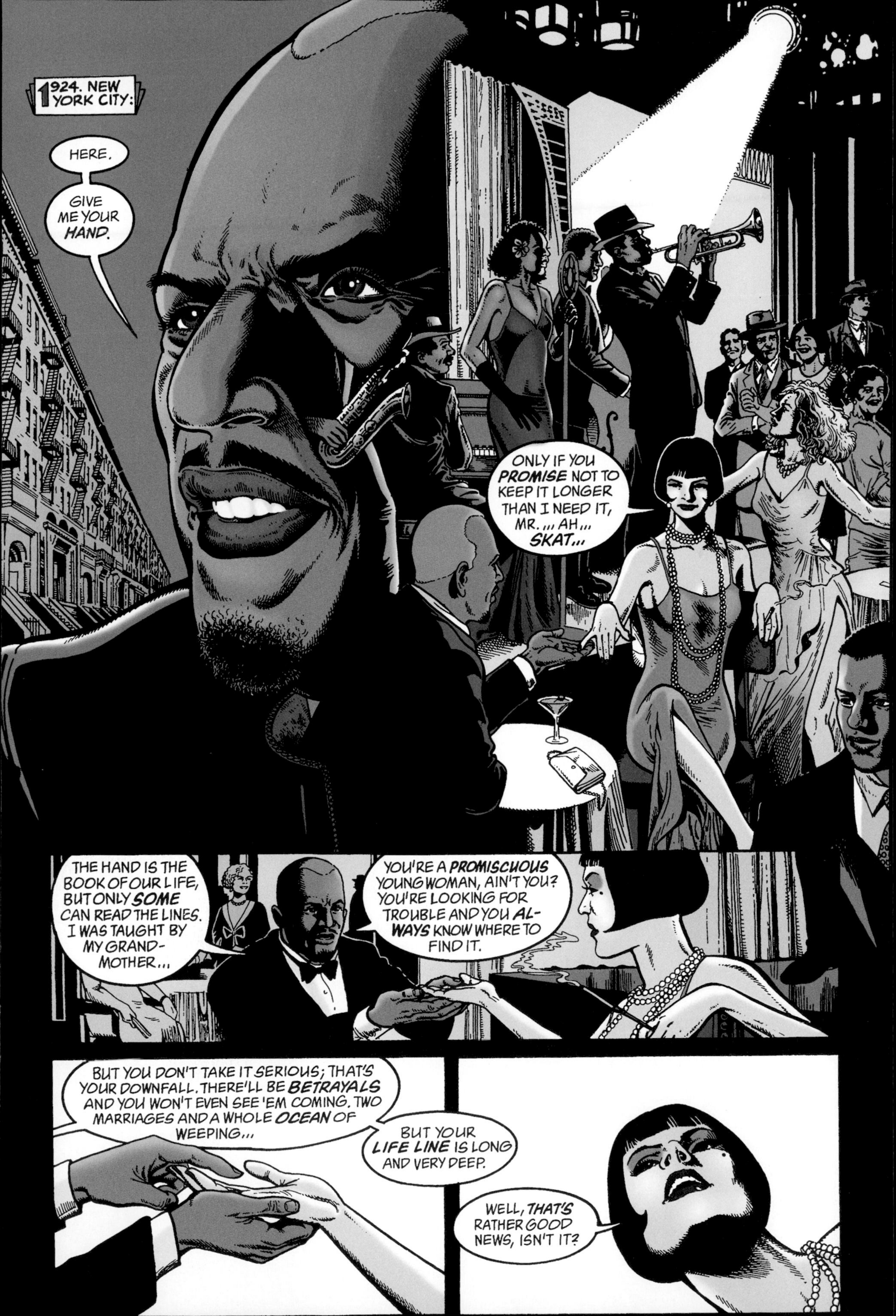
1924. NEW YORK CITY:
HERE.
GIVE ME YOUR HAND.
ONLY IF YOU PROMISE NOT TO KEEP IT LONGER THAN I NEED IT, MR. ... AH ... SKAT...
THE HAND IS THE BOOK OF OUR LIFE, BUT ONLY SOME CAN READ THE LINES. I WAS TAUGHT BY MY GRAND-MOTHER...
YOU'RE A PROMISCUOUS YOUNG WOMAN, AIN'T YOU? YOU'RE LOOKING FOR TROUBLE AND YOU AL-WAYS KNOW WHERE TO FIND IT.
BUT YOU DON'T TAKE IT SERIOUS; THAT'S YOUR DOWNFALL. THERE'LL BE BETRAYALS AND YOU WON'T EVEN SEE 'EM COMING. TWO MARRIAGES AND A WHOLE OCEAN OF WEEPING...
BUT YOUR LIFE LINE IS LONG AND VERY DEEP.
WELL, THAT'S RATHER GOOD NEWS, ISN'T IT?

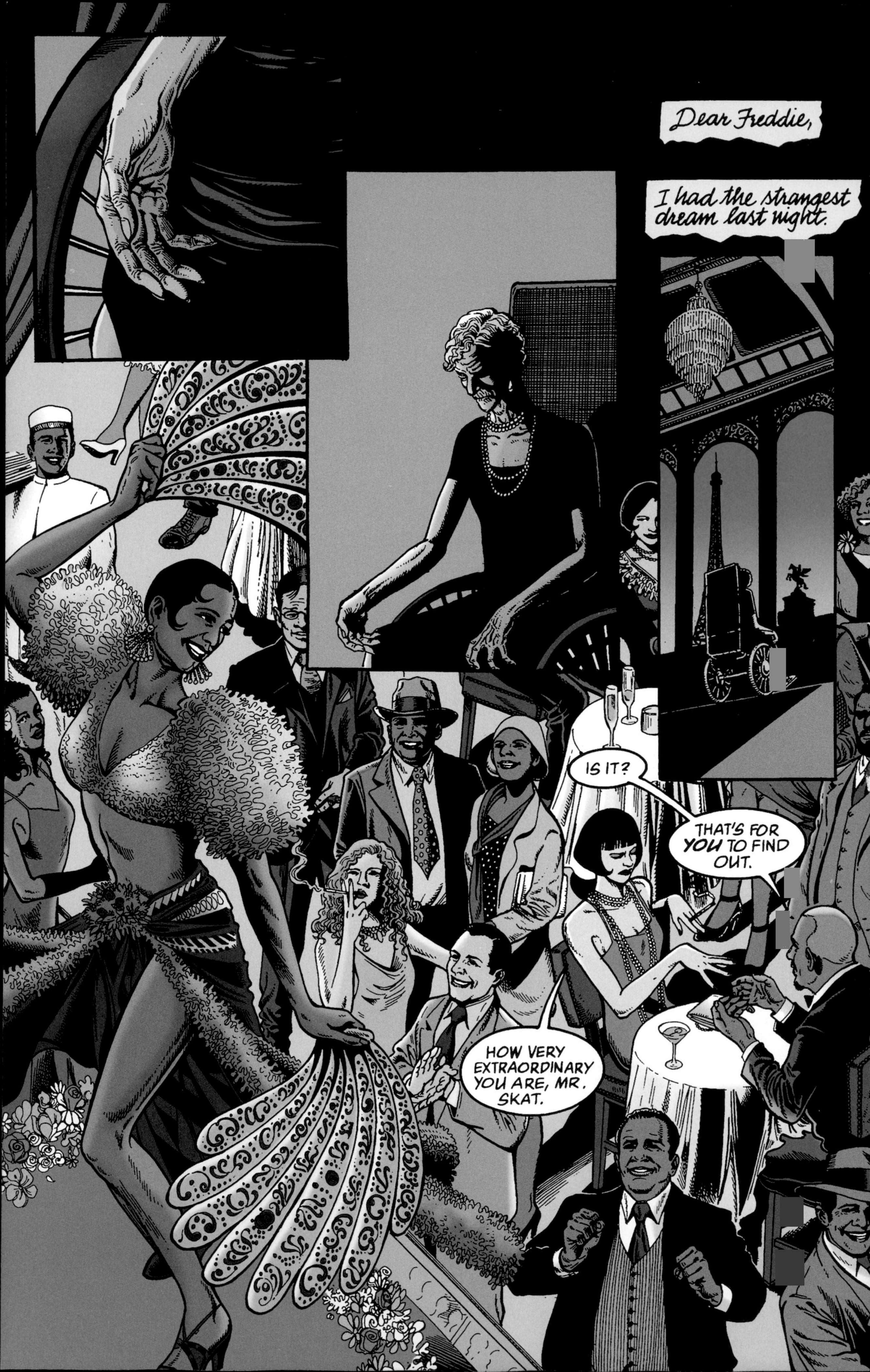
Dear Freddie,
I had the strangest dream last night.
IS IT?
THAT'S FOR YOU TO FIND OUT.
HOW VERY EXTRAORDINARY YOU ARE, MR. SKAT.

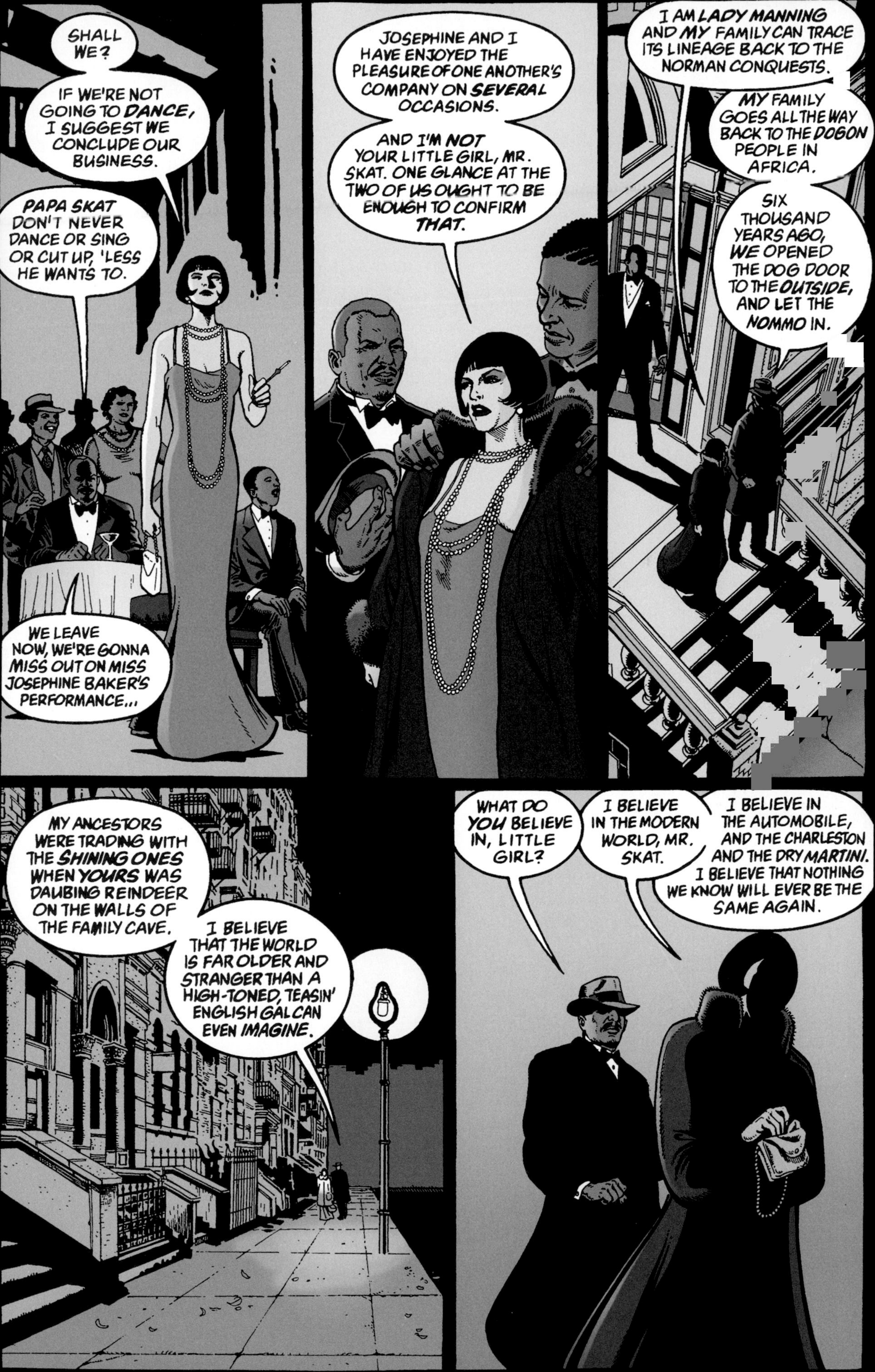
SHALL WE?
IF WE'RE NOT GOING TO DANCE, I SUGGEST WE CONCLUDE OUR BUSINESS.
PAPA SKAT DON'T NEVER DANCE OR SING OR CUT UP, 'LESS HE WANTS TO.
WE LEAVE NOW, WE'RE GONNA MISS OUT ON MISS JOSEPHINE BAKER'S PERFORMANCE...
JOSEPHINE AND I HAVE ENJOYED THE PLEASURE OF ONE ANOTHER'S COMPANY ON SEVERAL OCCASIONS.
AND I'M NOT YOUR LITTLE GIRL, MR. SKAT. ONE GLANCE AT THE TWO OF US OUGHT TO BE ENOUGH TO CONFIRM THAT.
I AM LADY MANNING AND MY FAMILY CAN TRACE ITS LINEAGE BACK TO THE NORMAN CONQUESTS.
MY FAMILY GOES ALL THE WAY BACK TO THE DOGON PEOPLE IN AFRICA.
SIX THOUSAND YEARS AGO, WE OPENED THE DOG DOOR TO THE OUTSIDE, AND LET THE NOMMO IN.
MY ANCESTORS WERE TRADING WITH THE SHINING ONES WHEN YOURS WAS DAUBING REINDEER ON THE WALLS OF THE FAMILY CAVE.
I BELIEVE THAT THE WORLD IS FAR OLDER AND STRANGER THAN A HIGH-TONED, TEASIN' ENGLISH GAL CAN EVEN IMAGINE.
WHAT DO YOU BELIEVE IN, LITTLE GIRL?
I BELIEVE IN THE MODERN WORLD, MR. SKAT.
I BELIEVE IN THE AUTOMOBILE, AND THE CHARLESTON AND THE DRY MARTINI. I BELIEVE THAT NOTHING WE KNOW WILL EVER BE THE SAME AGAIN.

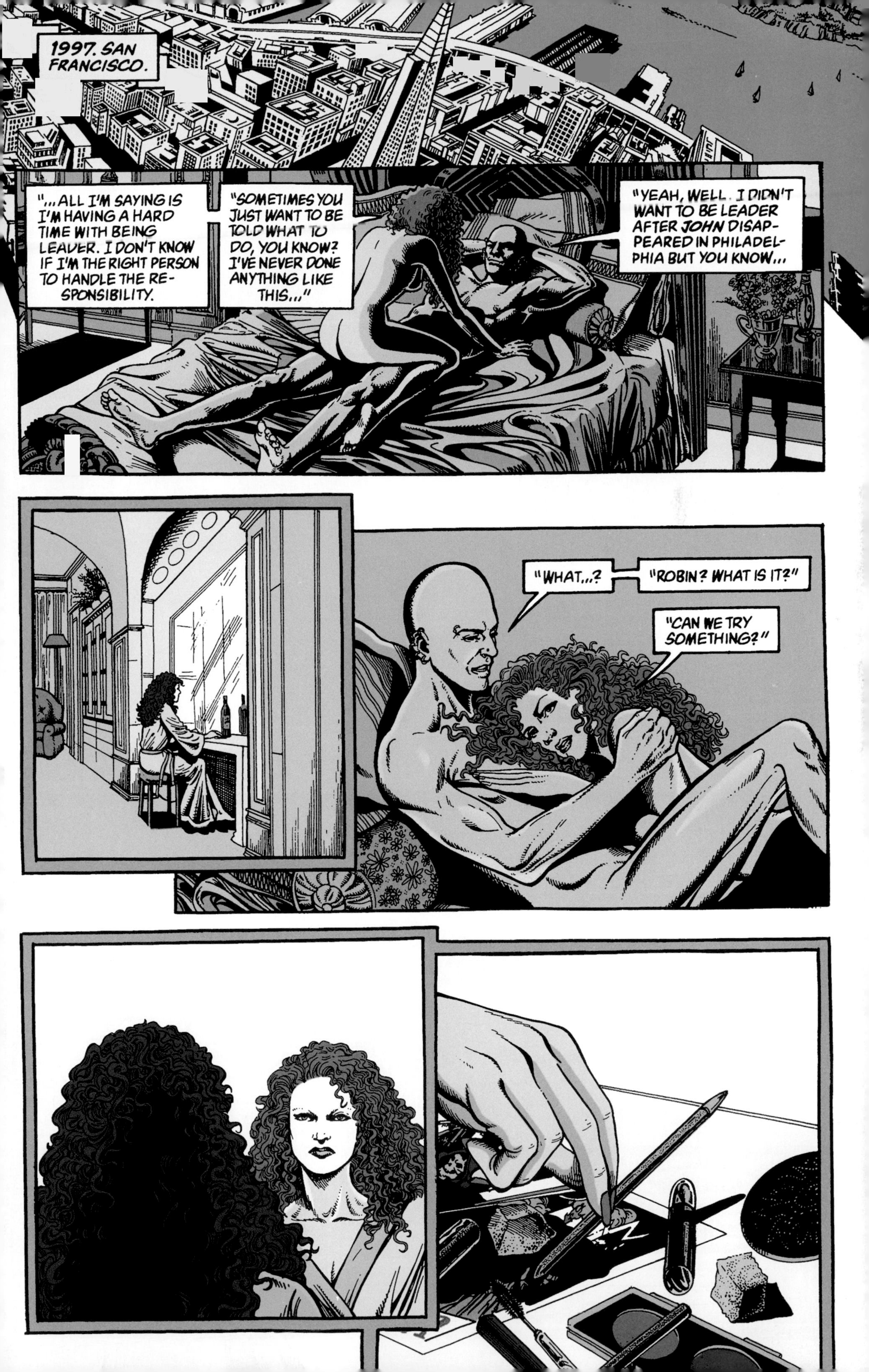
1997. SAN FRANCISCO.
"...ALL I'M SAYING IS I'M HAVING A HARD TIME WITH BEING LEADER. I DON'T KNOW IF I'M THE RIGHT PERSON TO HANDLE THE RESPONSIBILITY.
"SOMETIMES YOU JUST WANT TO BE TOLD WHAT TO DO, YOU KNOW? I'VE NEVER DONE ANYTHING LIKE THIS..."
"YEAH, WELL. I DIDN'T WANT TO BE LEADER AFTER JOHN DISAPPEARED IN PHILADELPHIA BUT YOU KNOW...
"WHAT...?
"ROBIN? WHAT IS IT?"
"CAN WE TRY SOMETHING?"

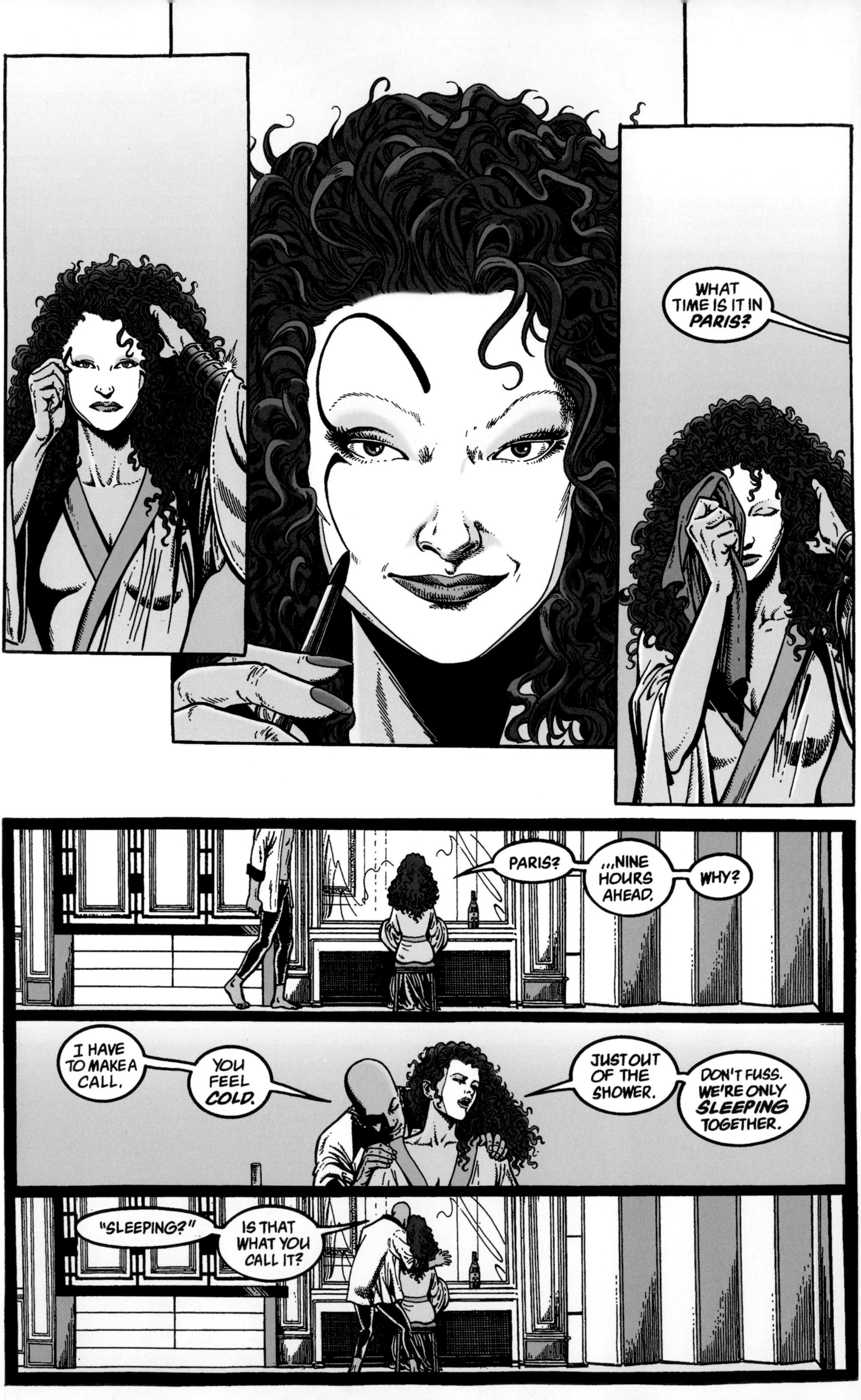
WHAT TIME IS IT IN PARIS?
PARIS?
...NINE HOURS AHEAD.
WHY?
I HAVE TO MAKE A CALL.
YOU FEEL COLD.
JUST OUT OF THE SHOWER.
DON'T FUSS. WE'RE ONLY SLEEPING TOGETHER.
"SLEEPING?"
IS THAT WHAT YOU CALL IT?

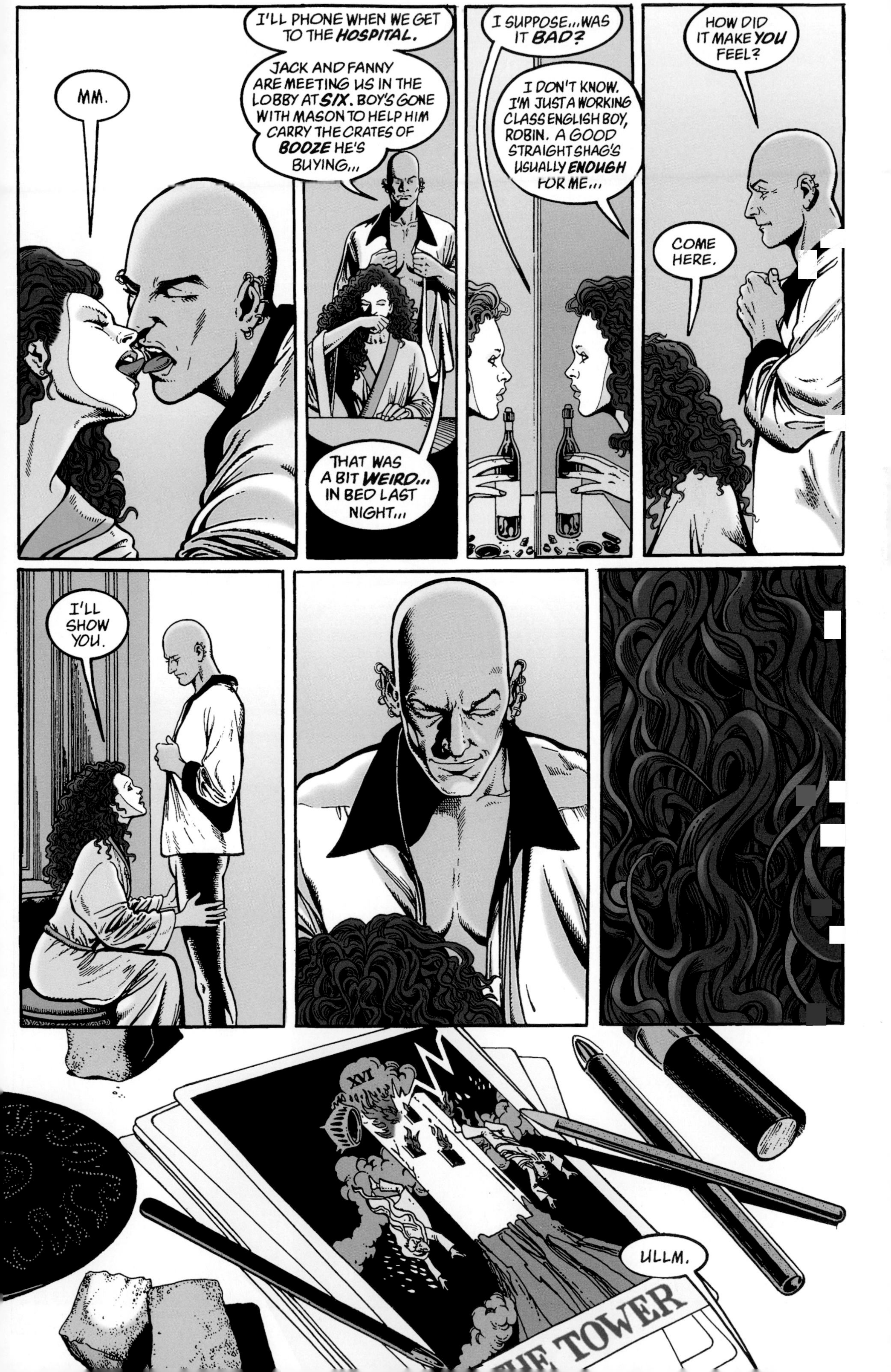
MM.
I'LL PHONE WHEN WE GET TO THE HOSPITAL.
JACK AND FANNY ARE MEETING US IN THE LOBBY AT SIX. BOY'S GONE WITH MASON TO HELP HIM CARRY THE CRATES OF BOOZE HE'S BUYING...
THAT WAS A BIT WEIRD... IN BED LAST NIGHT...
I SUPPOSE... WAS IT BAD?
I DON'T KNOW. I'M JUST A WORKING CLASS ENGLISH BOY, ROBIN. A GOOD STRAIGHT SHAG'S USUALLY ENOUGH FOR ME...
HOW DID IT MAKE YOU FEEL?
COME HERE.
I'LL SHOW YOU.
XVI
ULLM.
THE TOWER

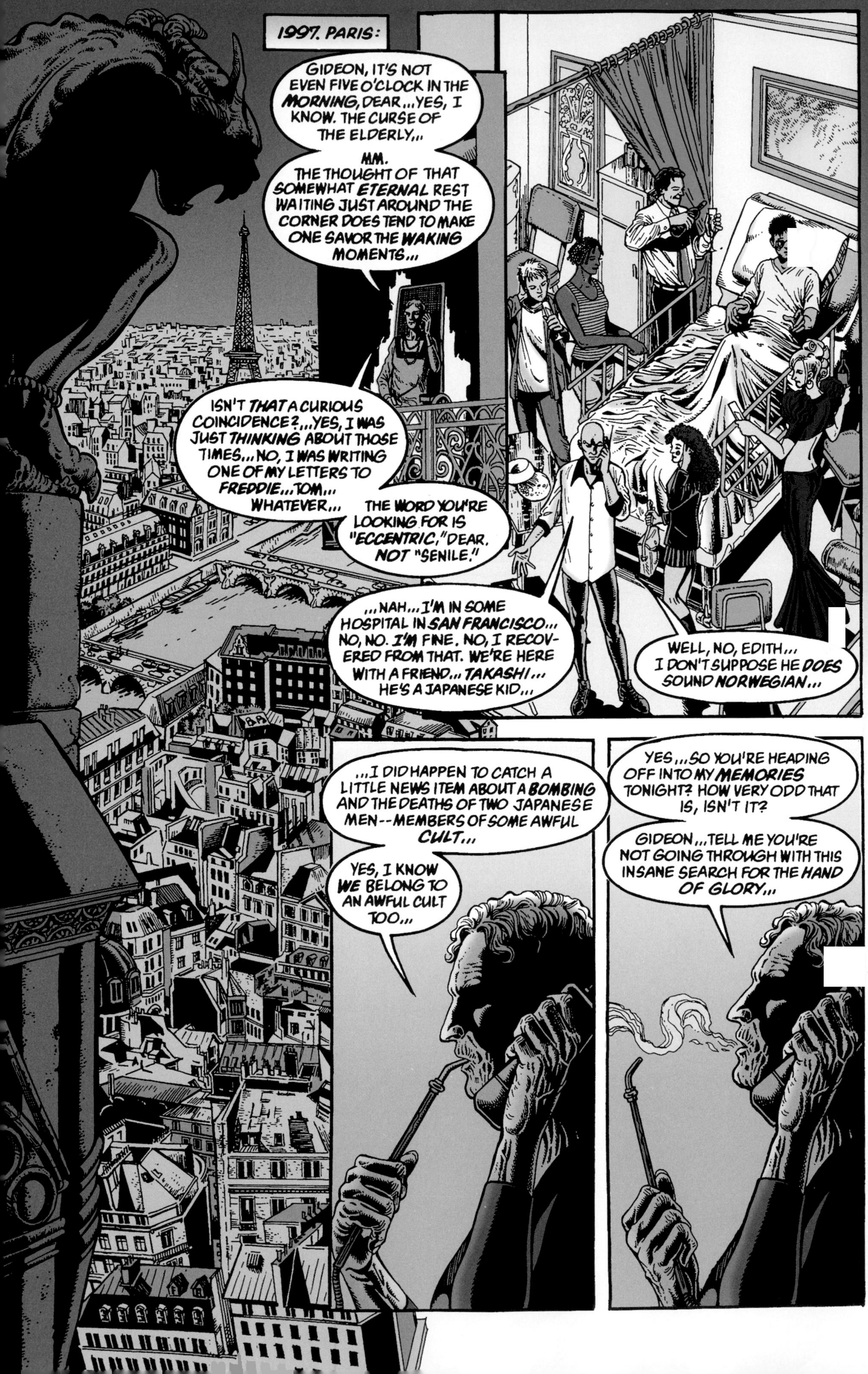
1997. PARIS:
GIDEON, IT'S NOT EVEN FIVE O'CLOCK IN THE MORNING, DEAR... YES, I KNOW. THE CURSE OF THE ELDERLY...
MM. THE THOUGHT OF THAT SOMEWHAT ETERNAL REST WAITING JUST AROUND THE CORNER DOES TEND TO MAKE ONE SAVOR THE WAKING MOMENTS...
ISN'T THAT A CURIOUS COINCIDENCE?...YES, I WAS JUST THINKING ABOUT THOSE TIMES... NO, I WAS WRITING ONE OF MY LETTERS TO FREDDIE... TOM... WHATEVER...
THE WORD YOU'RE LOOKING FOR IS "ECCENTRIC," DEAR. NOT "SENILE."
...NAH... I'M IN SOME HOSPITAL IN SAN FRANCISCO... NO, NO. I'M FINE. NO, I RECOVERED FROM THAT. WE'RE HERE WITH A FRIEND... TAKASHI... HE'S A JAPANESE KID...
WELL, NO, EDITH... I DON'T SUPPOSE HE DOES SOUND NORWEGIAN...
...I DID HAPPEN TO CATCH A LITTLE NEWS ITEM ABOUT A BOMBING AND THE DEATHS OF TWO JAPANESE MEN--MEMBERS OF SOME AWFUL CULT...
YES, I KNOW WE BELONG TO AN AWFUL CULT TOO...
YES... SO YOU'RE HEADING OFF INTO MY MEMORIES TONIGHT? HOW VERY ODD THAT IS, ISN'T IT?
GIDEON... TELL ME YOU'RE NOT GOING THROUGH WITH THIS INSANE SEARCH FOR THE HAND OF GLORY...

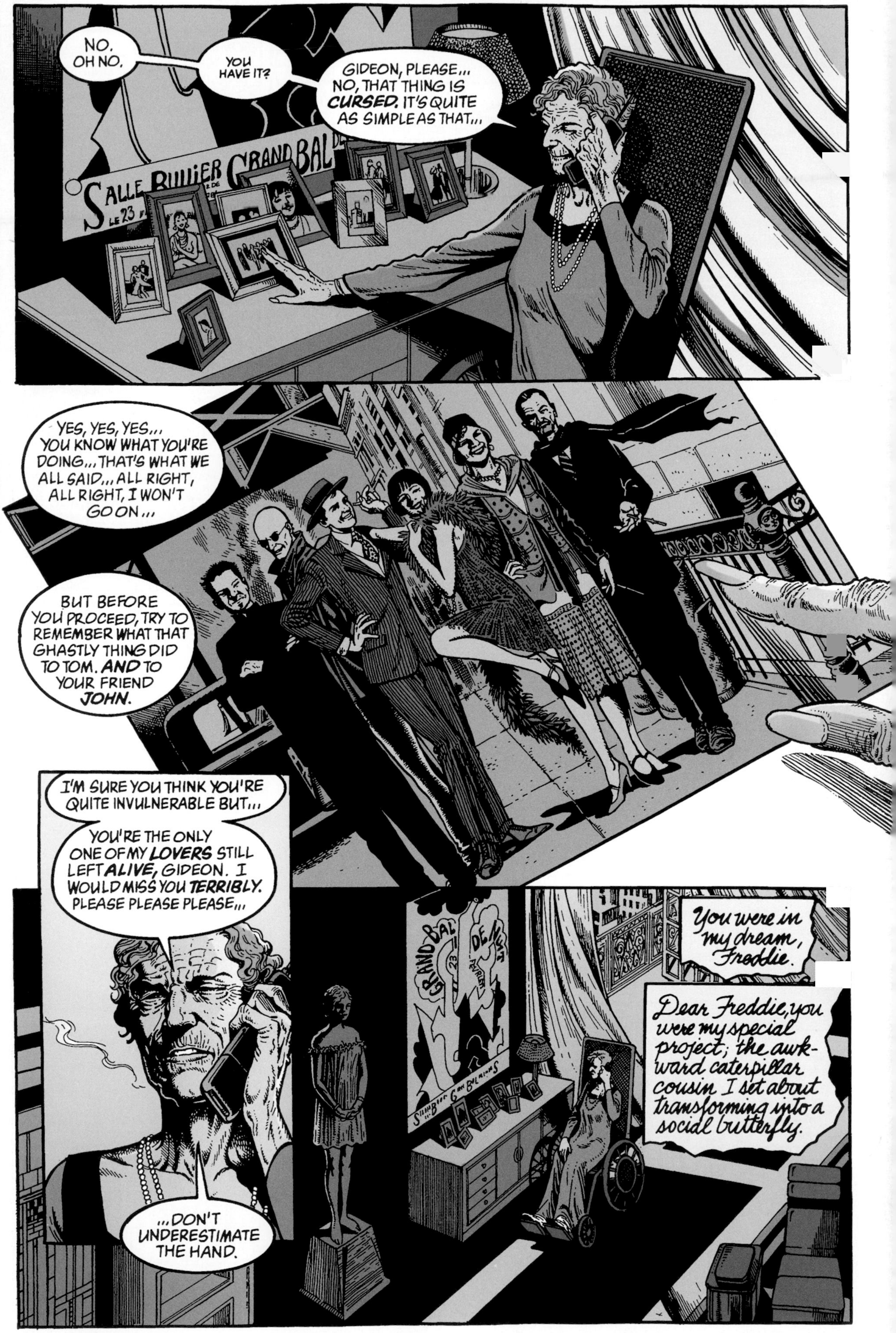

NO. OH NO.
YOU HAVE IT?
GIDEON, PLEASE... NO, THAT THING IS CURSED. IT'S QUITE AS SIMPLE AS THAT...
SALLE BULLIER GRAND BAL
YES, YES, YES... YOU KNOW WHAT YOU'RE DOING... THAT'S WHAT WE ALL SAID... ALL RIGHT, ALL RIGHT, I WON'T GO ON...
BUT BEFORE YOU PROCEED, TRY TO REMEMBER WHAT THAT GHASTLY THING DID TO TOM. AND TO YOUR FRIEND JOHN.
I'M SURE YOU THINK YOU'RE QUITE INVULNERABLE BUT...
YOU'RE THE ONLY ONE OF MY LOVERS STILL LEFT ALIVE, GIDEON. I WOULD MISS YOU TERRIBLY. PLEASE PLEASE PLEASE...
...DON'T UNDERESTIMATE THE HAND.
GRAND BAL DE NUIT
You were in my dream, Freddie.
Dear Freddie, you were my special project; the awkward caterpillar cousin I set about transforming into a social butterfly.

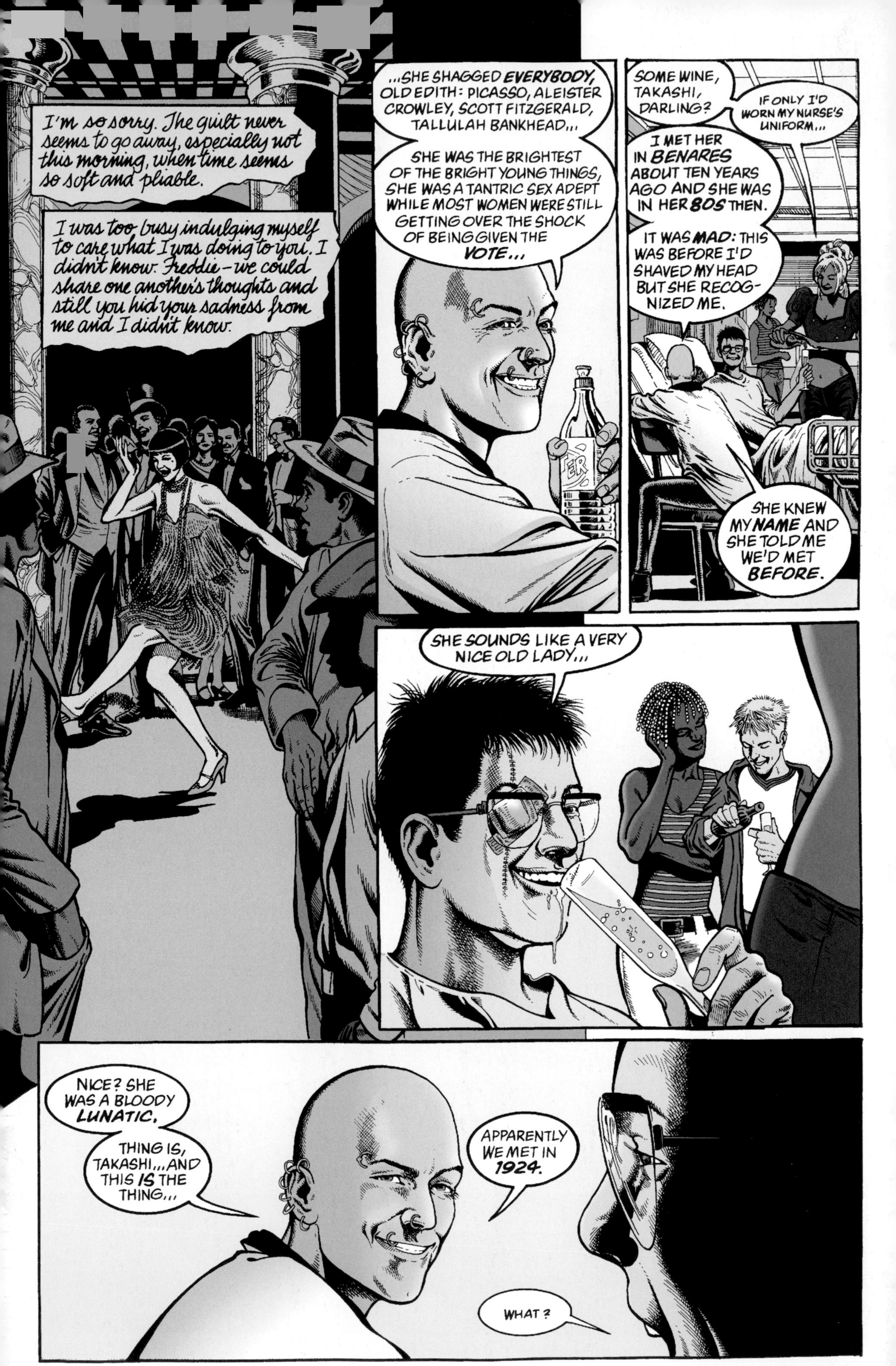

I'm so sorry. The guilt never seems to go away, especially not this morning, when time seems so soft and pliable.
I was too busy indulging myself to care what I was doing to you. I didn't know. Freddie - we could share one another's thoughts and still you hid your sadness from me and I didn't know.
...SHE SHAGGED EVERYBODY, OLD EDITH: PICASSO, ALEISTER CROWLEY, SCOTT FITZGERALD, TALLULAH BANKHEAD...
SHE WAS THE BRIGHTEST OF THE BRIGHT YOUNG THINGS, SHE WAS A TANTRIC SEX ADEPT WHILE MOST WOMEN WERE STILL GETTING OVER THE SHOCK OF BEING GIVEN THE VOTE...
SOME WINE, TAKASHI, DARLING?
IF ONLY I'D WORN MY NURSE'S UNIFORM...
I MET HER IN BENARES ABOUT TEN YEARS AGO AND SHE WAS IN HER 80S THEN.
IT WAS MAD: THIS WAS BEFORE I'D SHAVED MY HEAD BUT SHE RECOGNIZED ME.
SHE KNEW MY NAME AND SHE TOLD ME WE'D MET BEFORE.
SHE SOUNDS LIKE A VERY NICE OLD LADY...
NICE? SHE WAS A BLOODY LUNATIC.
THING IS, TAKASHI... AND THIS IS THE THING...
APPARENTLY WE MET IN 1924.
WHAT?

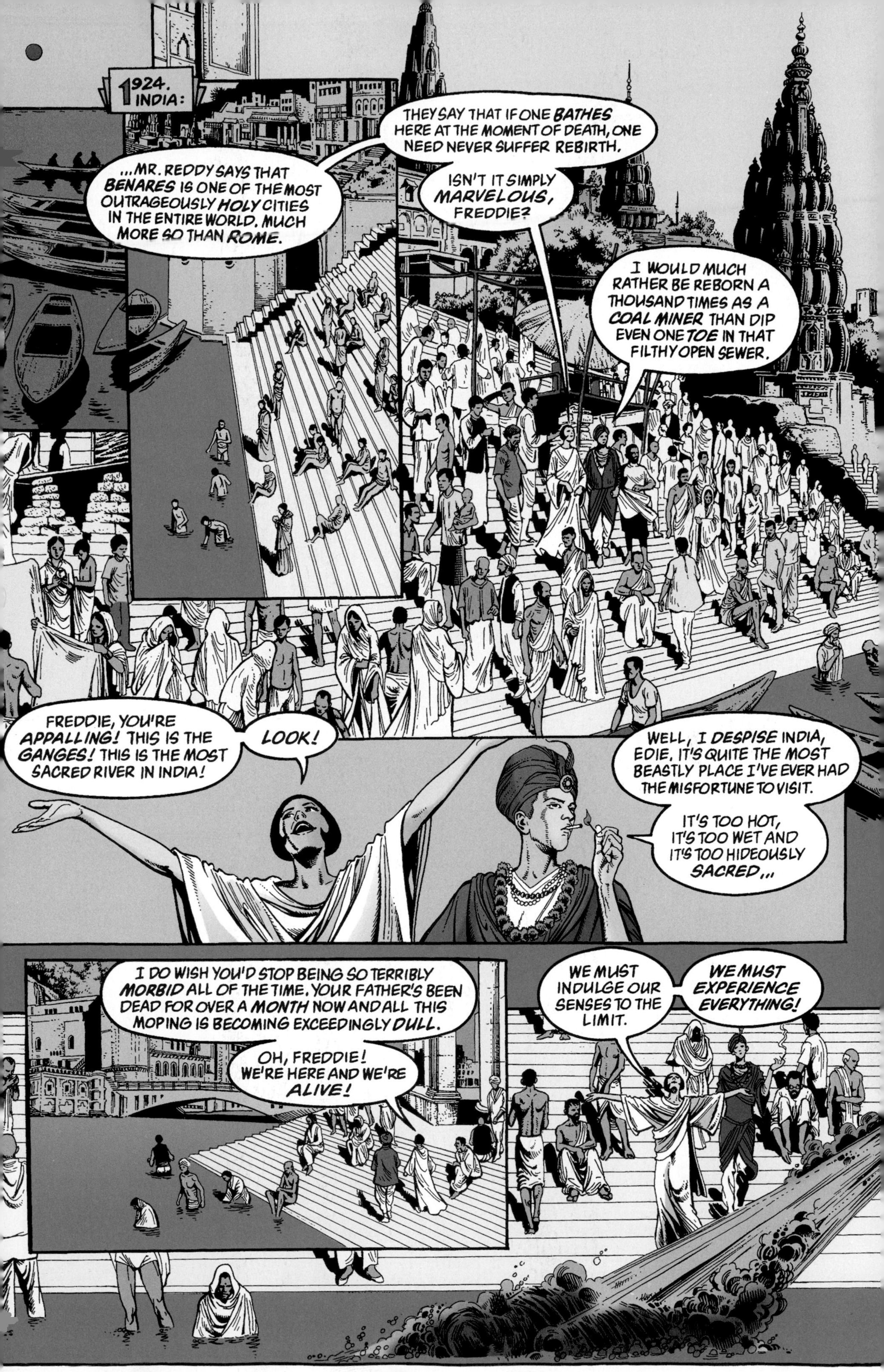
1924. INDIA:
...MR. REDDY SAYS THAT BENARES IS ONE OF THE MOST OUTRAGEOUSLY HOLY CITIES IN THE ENTIRE WORLD. MUCH MORE SO THAN ROME.
THEY SAY THAT IF ONE BATHES HERE AT THE MOMENT OF DEATH, ONE NEED NEVER SUFFER REBIRTH.
ISN'T IT SIMPLY MARVELOUS, FREDDIE?
I WOULD MUCH RATHER BE REBORN A THOUSAND TIMES AS A COAL MINER THAN DIP EVEN ONE TOE IN THAT FILTHY OPEN SEWER.
FREDDIE, YOU'RE APPALLING! THIS IS THE GANGES! THIS IS THE MOST SACRED RIVER IN INDIA!
LOOK!
WELL, I DESPISE INDIA, EDIE. IT'S QUITE THE MOST BEASTLY PLACE I'VE EVER HAD THE MISFORTUNE TO VISIT.
IT'S TOO HOT, IT'S TOO WET AND IT'S TOO HIDEOUSLY SACRED...
I DO WISH YOU'D STOP BEING SO TERRIBLY MORBID ALL OF THE TIME. YOUR FATHER'S BEEN DEAD FOR OVER A MONTH NOW AND ALL THIS MOPING IS BECOMING EXCEEDINGLY DULL.
OH, FREDDIE! WE'RE HERE AND WE'RE ALIVE!
WE MUST INDULGE OUR SENSES TO THE LIMIT.
WE MUST EXPERIENCE EVERYTHING!

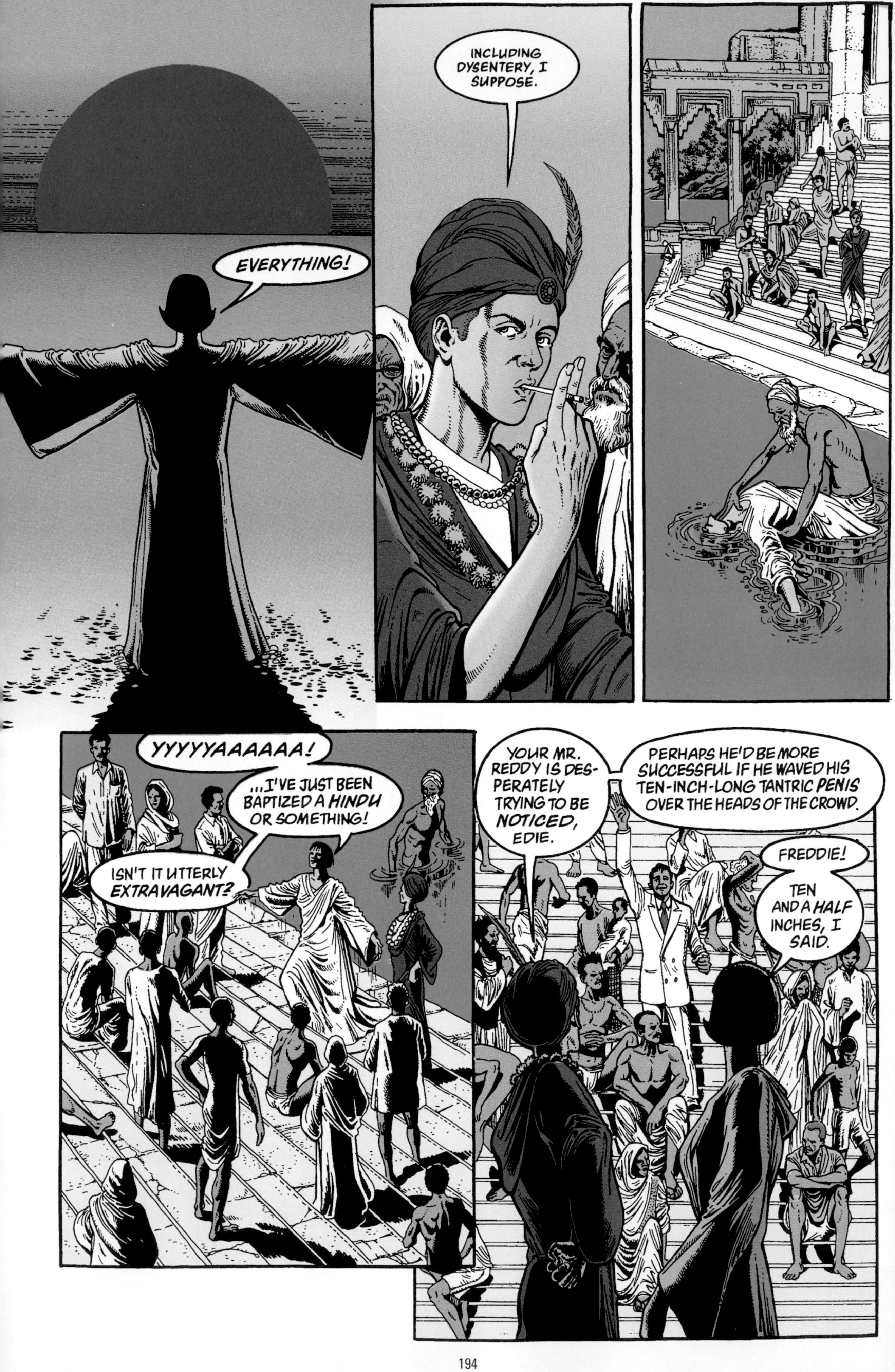
EVERYTHING!
INCLUDING DYSENTERY, I SUPPOSE.
YYYYYAAAAAA!
...I'VE JUST BEEN BAPTIZED A HINDU OR SOMETHING!
ISN'T IT UTTERLY EXTRAVAGANT?
YOUR MR. REDDY IS DESPERATELY TRYING TO BE NOTICED, EDIE.
PERHAPS HE'D BE MORE SUCCESSFUL IF HE WAVED HIS TEN-INCH-LONG TANTRIC PENIS OVER THE HEADS OF THE CROWD.
FREDDIE!
TEN AND A HALF INCHES, I SAID.

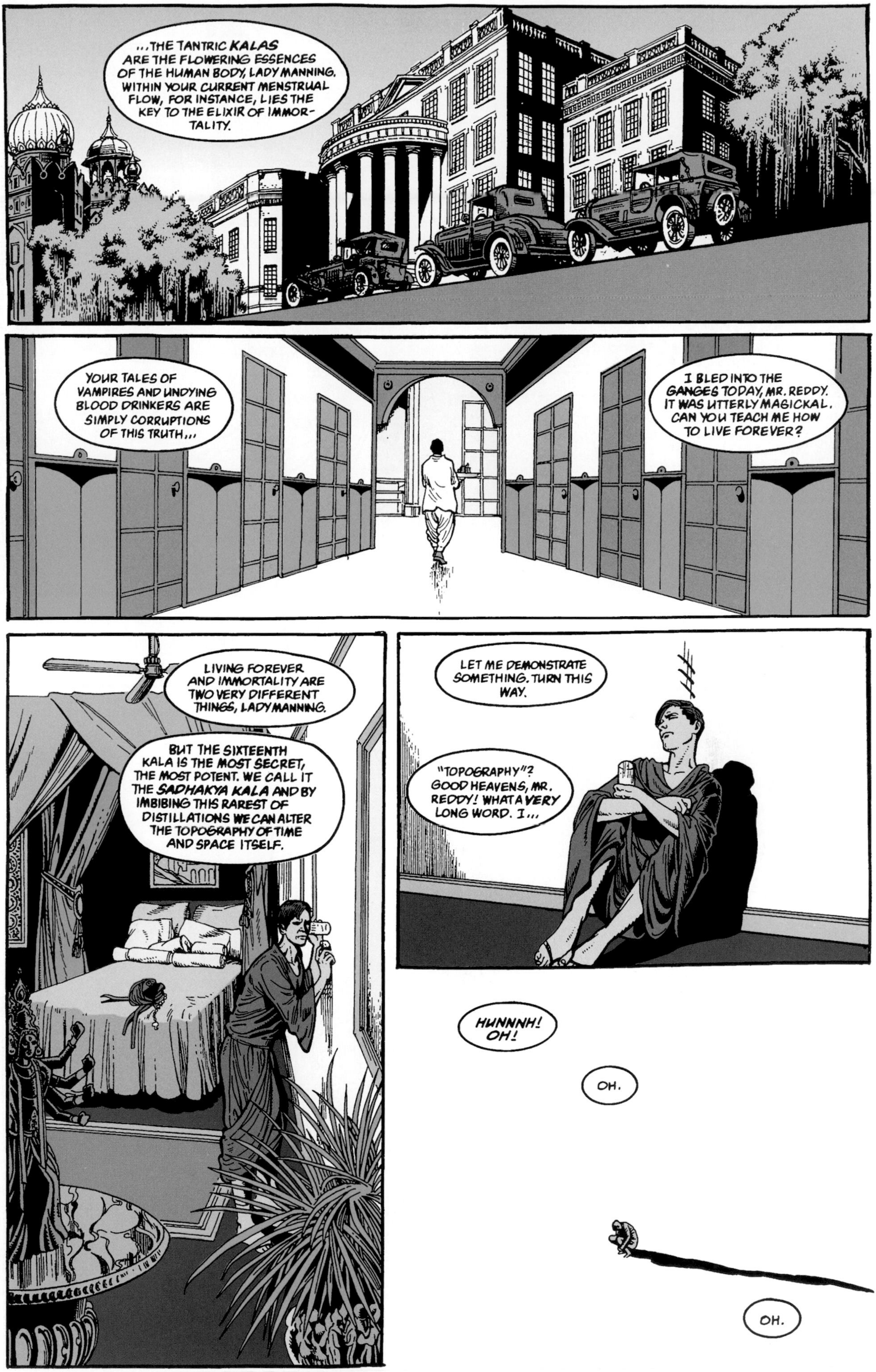

...THE TANTRIC KALAS ARE THE FLOWERING ESSENCES OF THE HUMAN BODY, LADY MANNING. WITHIN YOUR CURRENT MENSTRUAL FLOW, FOR INSTANCE, LIES THE KEY TO THE ELIXIR OF IMMORTALITY.
YOUR TALES OF VAMPIRES AND UNDYING BLOOD DRINKERS ARE SIMPLY CORRUPTIONS OF THIS TRUTH...
I BLED INTO THE GANGES TODAY, MR. REDDY. IT WAS UTTERLY MAGICKAL. CAN YOU TEACH ME HOW TO LIVE FOREVER?
LIVING FOREVER AND IMMORTALITY ARE TWO VERY DIFFERENT THINGS, LADY MANNING.
BUT THE SIXTEENTH KALA IS THE MOST SECRET, THE MOST POTENT. WE CALL IT THE SADHAKYA KALA AND BY IMBIBING THIS RAREST OF DISTILLATIONS WE CAN ALTER THE TOPOGRAPHY OF TIME AND SPACE ITSELF.
LET ME DEMONSTRATE SOMETHING. TURN THIS WAY.
"TOPOGRAPHY"? GOOD HEAVENS, MR. REDDY! WHAT A VERY LONG WORD. I...
HUNNNH! OH!
OH.
OH.

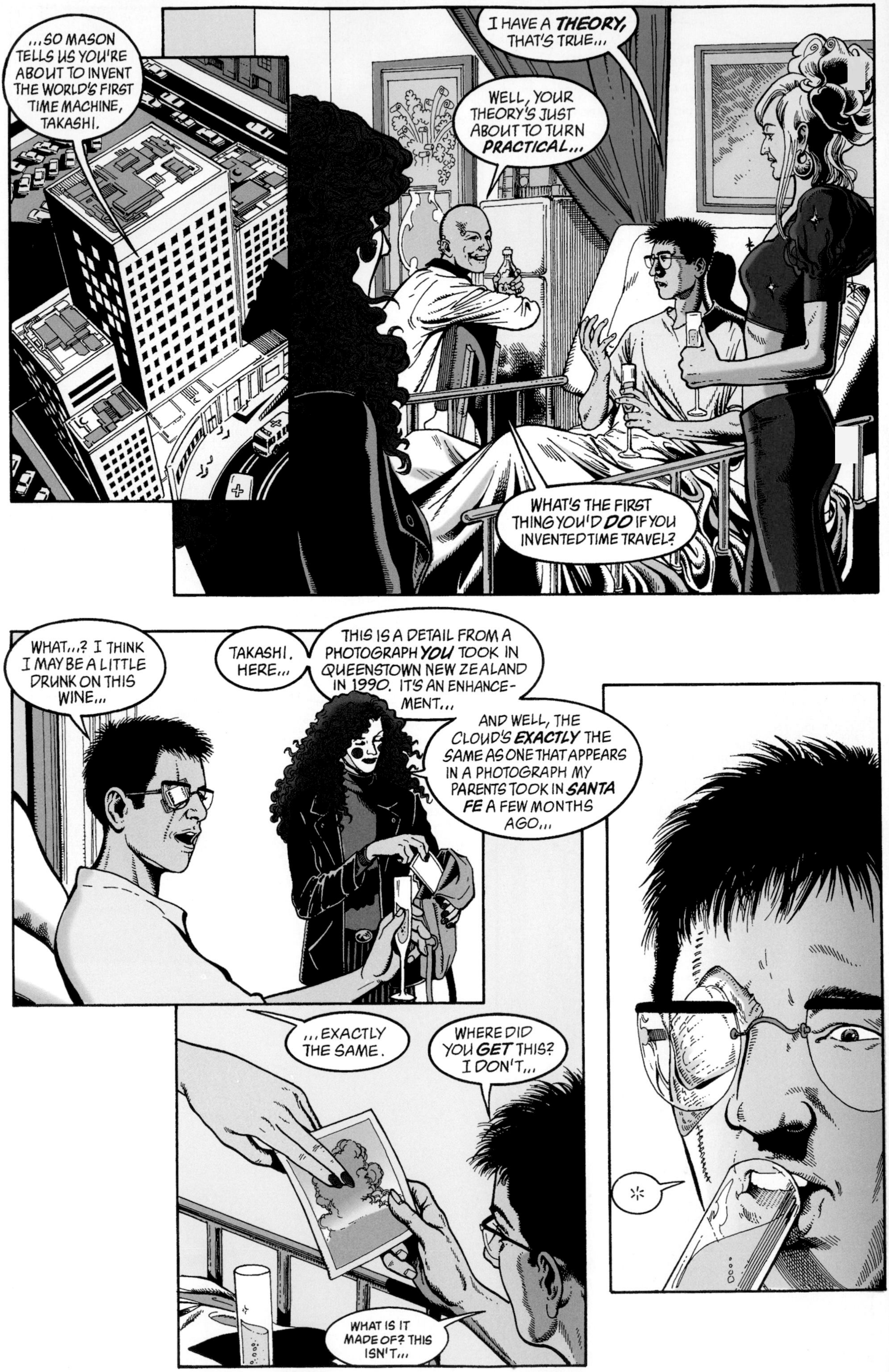
...SO MASON TELLS US YOU'RE ABOUT TO INVENT THE WORLD'S FIRST TIME MACHINE, TAKASHI.
I HAVE A THEORY, THAT'S TRUE...
WELL, YOUR THEORY'S JUST ABOUT TO TURN PRACTICAL...
WHAT'S THE FIRST THING YOU'D DO IF YOU INVENTED TIME TRAVEL?
WHAT...? I THINK I MAY BE A LITTLE DRUNK ON THIS WINE...
TAKASHI. HERE...
THIS IS A DETAIL FROM A PHOTOGRAPH YOU TOOK IN QUEENSTOWN NEW ZEALAND IN 1990. IT'S AN ENHANCEMENT...
AND WELL, THE CLOUD'S EXACTLY THE SAME AS ONE THAT APPEARS IN A PHOTOGRAPH MY PARENTS TOOK IN SANTA FE A FEW MONTHS AGO...
...EXACTLY THE SAME.
WHERE DID YOU GET THIS? I DON'T...
WHAT IS IT MADE OF? THIS ISN'T...
!

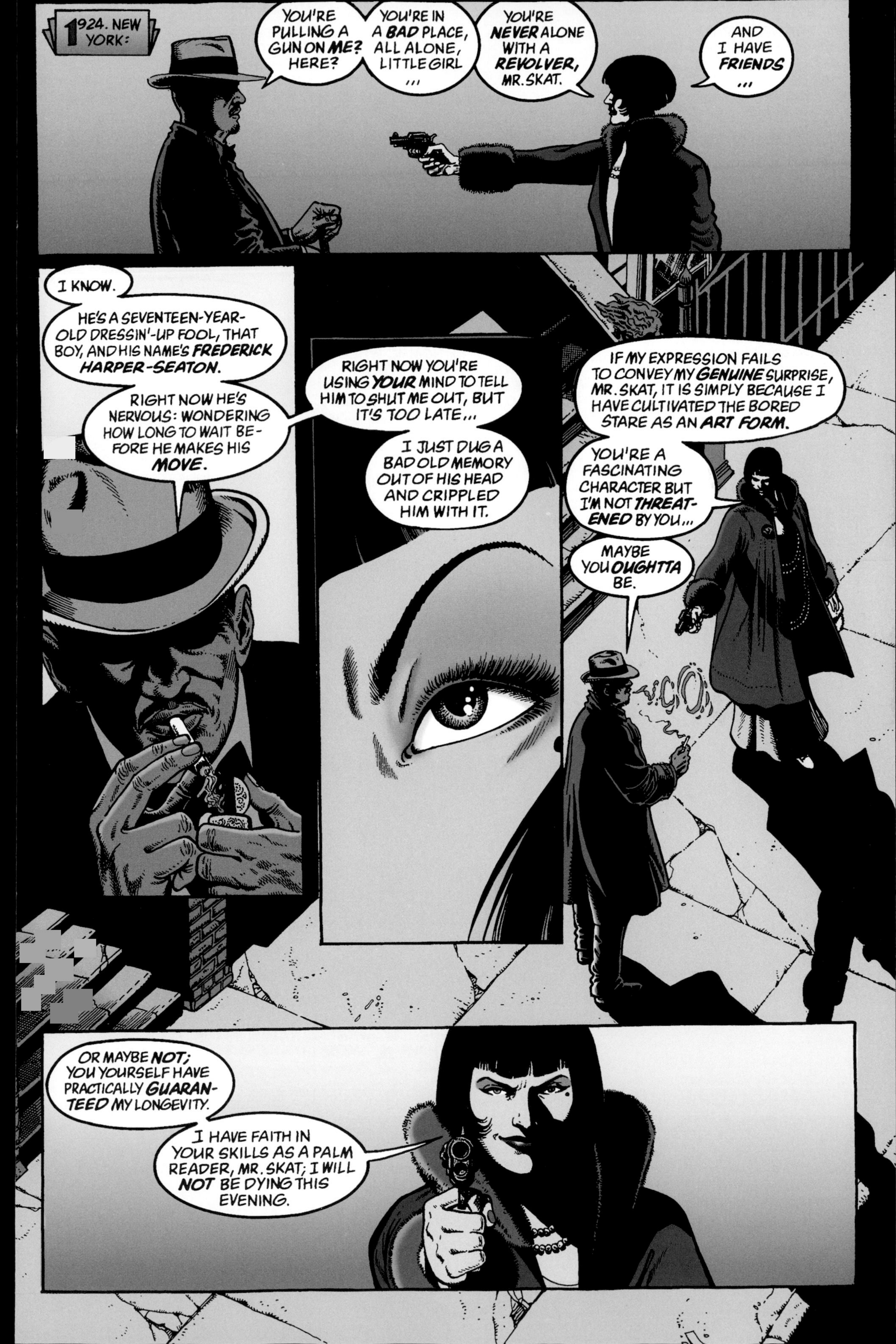
1924. NEW YORK:
YOU'RE PULLING A GUN ON ME? HERE?
YOU'RE IN A BAD PLACE, ALL ALONE, LITTLE GIRL ...
YOU'RE NEVER ALONE WITH A REVOLVER, MR. SKAT.
AND I HAVE FRIENDS ...
I KNOW.
HE'S A SEVENTEEN-YEAR-OLD DRESSIN'-UP FOOL, THAT BOY, AND HIS NAME'S FREDERICK HARPER-SEATON.
RIGHT NOW HE'S NERVOUS: WONDERING HOW LONG TO WAIT BEFORE HE MAKES HIS MOVE.
RIGHT NOW YOU'RE USING YOUR MIND TO TELL HIM TO SHUT ME OUT, BUT IT'S TOO LATE...
I JUST DUG A BAD OLD MEMORY OUT OF HIS HEAD AND CRIPPLED HIM WITH IT.
IF MY EXPRESSION FAILS TO CONVEY MY GENUINE SURPRISE, MR. SKAT, IT IS SIMPLY BECAUSE I HAVE CULTIVATED THE BORED STARE AS AN ART FORM.
YOU'RE A FASCINATING CHARACTER BUT I'M NOT THREATENED BY YOU...
MAYBE YOU OUGHTTA BE.
OR MAYBE NOT; YOU YOURSELF HAVE PRACTICALLY GUARANTEED MY LONGEVITY.
I HAVE FAITH IN YOUR SKILLS AS A PALM READER, MR. SKAT; I WILL NOT BE DYING THIS EVENING.

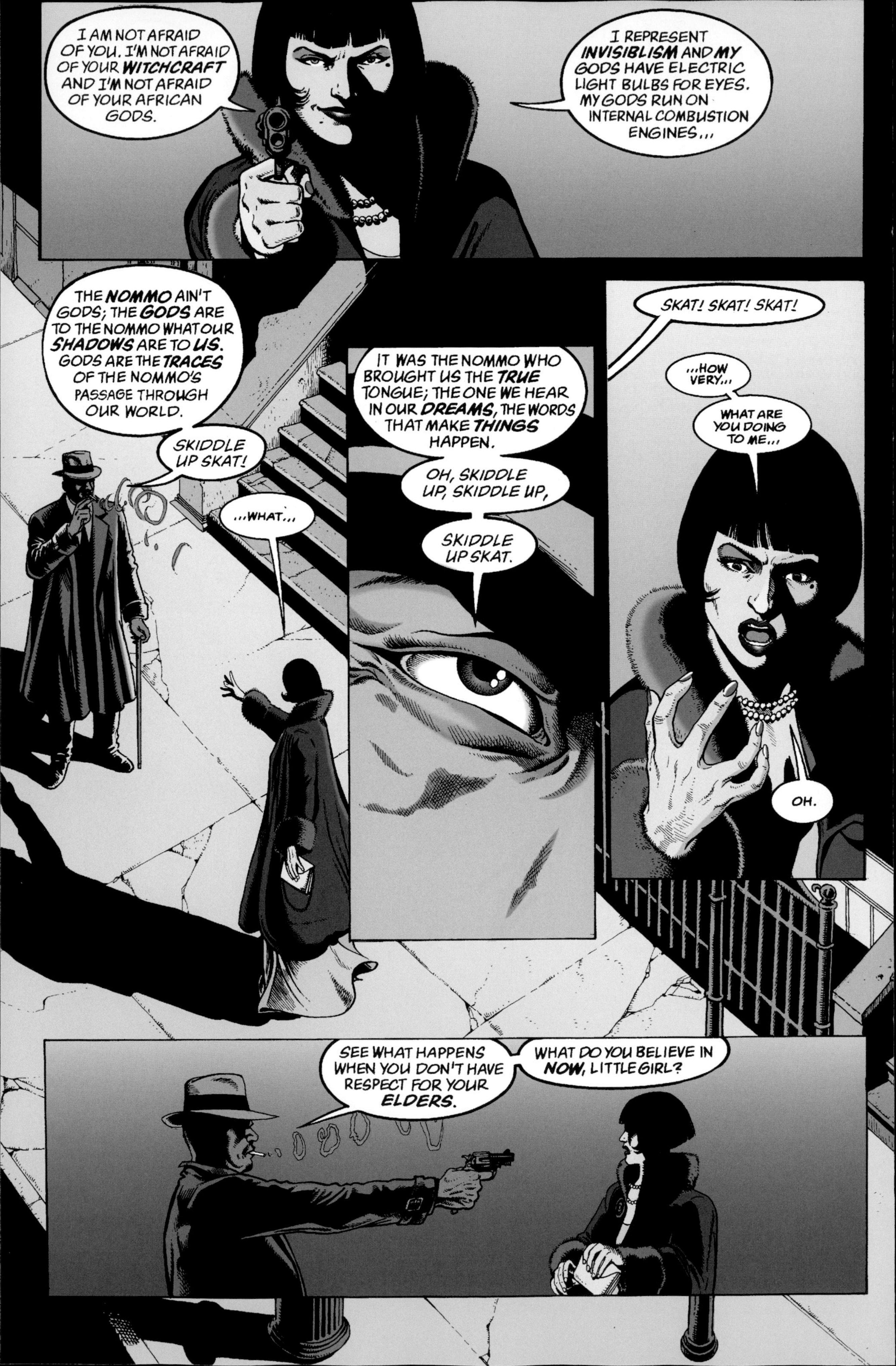
I AM NOT AFRAID OF YOU. I'M NOT AFRAID OF YOUR WITCHCRAFT AND I'M NOT AFRAID OF YOUR AFRICAN GODS.
I REPRESENT INVISIBLISM AND MY GODS HAVE ELECTRIC LIGHT BULBS FOR EYES. MY GODS RUN ON INTERNAL COMBUSTION ENGINES...
THE NOMMO AIN'T GODS; THE GODS ARE TO THE NOMMO WHAT OUR SHADOWS ARE TO US. GODS ARE THE TRACES OF THE NOMMO'S PASSAGE THROUGH OUR WORLD.
SKIDDLE UP SKAT!
...WHAT...
IT WAS THE NOMMO WHO BROUGHT US THE TRUE TONGUE; THE ONE WE HEAR IN OUR DREAMS, THE WORDS THAT MAKE THINGS HAPPEN.
OH, SKIDDLE UP, SKIDDLE UP,
SKIDDLE UP SKAT.
SKAT! SKAT! SKAT!
...HOW VERY...
WHAT ARE YOU DOING TO ME...
OH.
SEE WHAT HAPPENS WHEN YOU DON'T HAVE RESPECT FOR YOUR ELDERS.
WHAT DO YOU BELIEVE IN NOW, LITTLE GIRL?

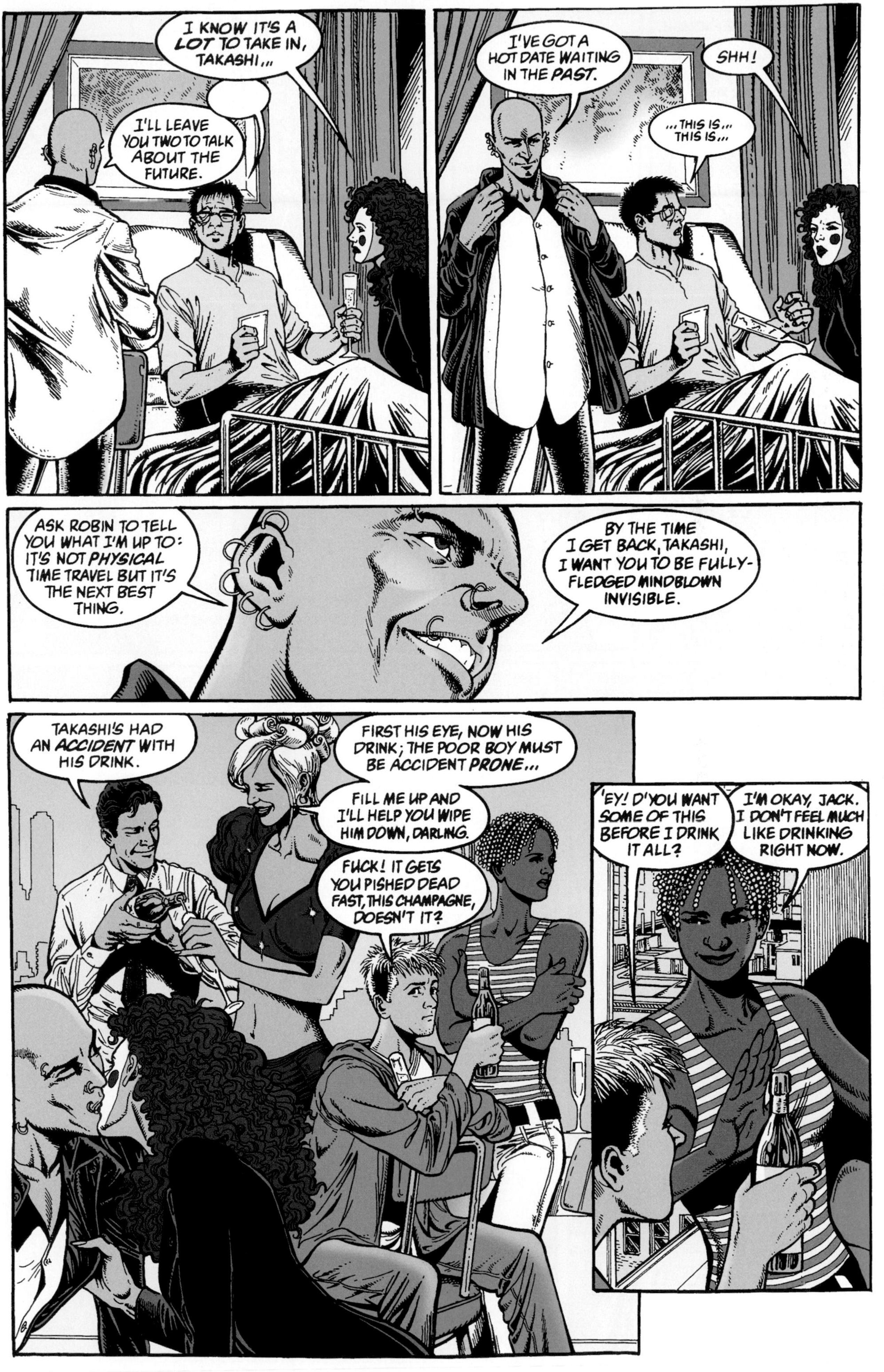
I KNOW IT'S A LOT TO TAKE IN, TAKASHI...
I'LL LEAVE YOU TWO TO TALK ABOUT THE FUTURE.
I'VE GOT A HOT DATE WAITING IN THE PAST.
SHH!
...THIS IS... THIS IS...
ASK ROBIN TO TELL YOU WHAT I'M UP TO: IT'S NOT PHYSICAL TIME TRAVEL BUT IT'S THE NEXT BEST THING.
BY THE TIME I GET BACK, TAKASHI, I WANT YOU TO BE FULLY-FLEDGED MINDBLOWN INVISIBLE.
TAKASHI'S HAD AN ACCIDENT WITH HIS DRINK.
FIRST HIS EYE, NOW HIS DRINK; THE POOR BOY MUST BE ACCIDENT PRONE...
FILL ME UP AND I'LL HELP YOU WIPE HIM DOWN, DARLING.
FUCK! IT GETS YOU PISHED DEAD FAST, THIS CHAMPAGNE, DOESN'T IT?
'EY! D'YOU WANT SOME OF THIS BEFORE I DRINK IT ALL?
I'M OKAY, JACK. I DON'T FEEL MUCH LIKE DRINKING RIGHT NOW.

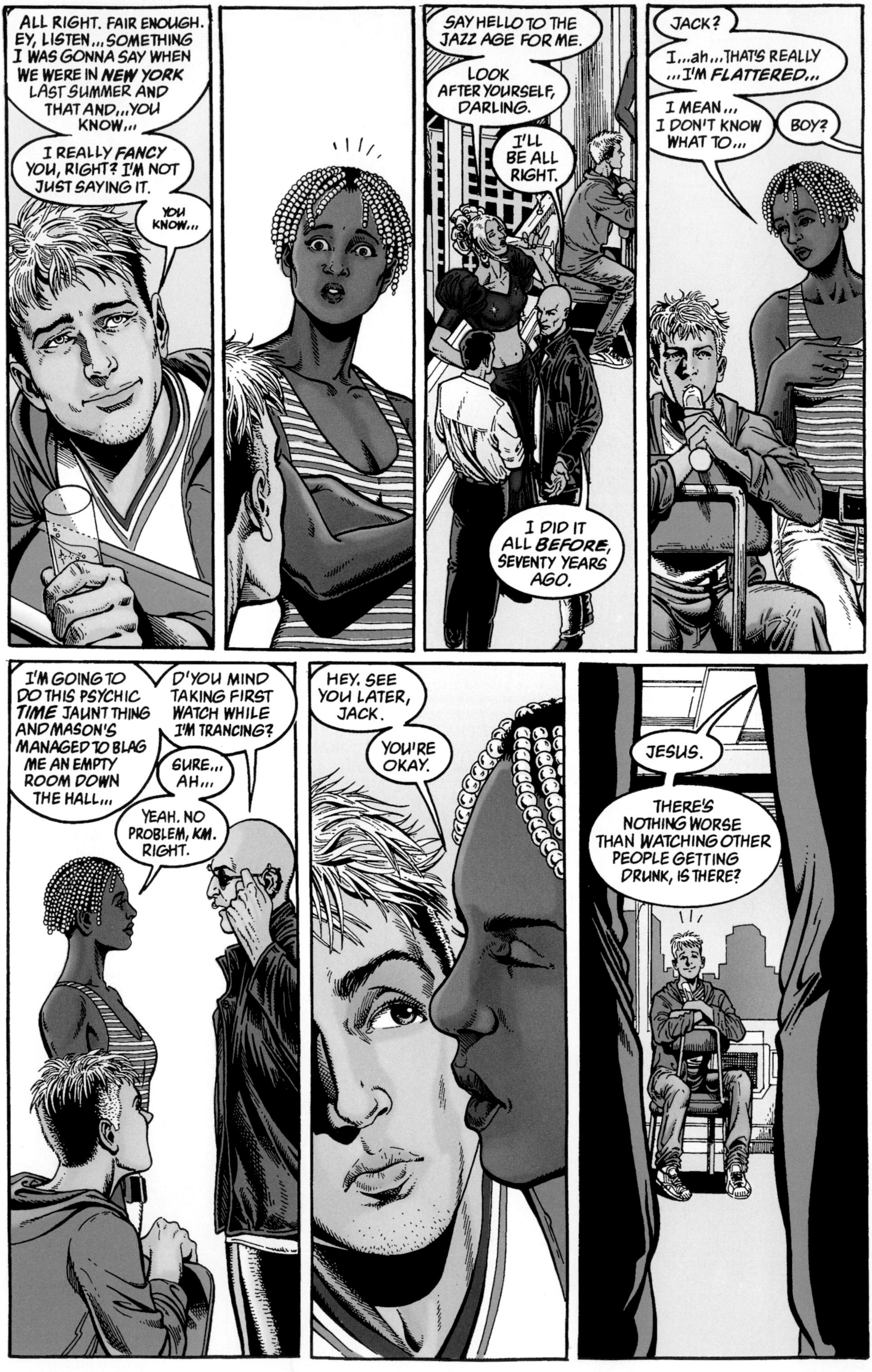
ALL RIGHT. FAIR ENOUGH. EY, LISTEN... SOMETHING I WAS GONNA SAY WHEN WE WERE IN NEW YORK LAST SUMMER AND THAT AND... YOU KNOW...
I REALLY FANCY YOU, RIGHT? I'M NOT JUST SAYING IT.
YOU KNOW...
SAY HELLO TO THE JAZZ AGE FOR ME.
LOOK AFTER YOURSELF, DARLING.
I'LL BE ALL RIGHT.
I DID IT ALL BEFORE, SEVENTY YEARS AGO.
JACK?
I...ah... THAT'S REALLY ...I'M FLATTERED...
I MEAN... I DON'T KNOW WHAT TO...
BOY?
I'M GOING TO DO THIS PSYCHIC TIME JAUNT THING AND MASON'S MANAGED TO BLAG ME AN EMPTY ROOM DOWN THE HALL...
D'YOU MIND TAKING FIRST WATCH WHILE I'M TRANCING?
SURE... AH...
YEAH. NO PROBLEM, KM. RIGHT.
HEY. SEE YOU LATER, JACK.
YOU'RE OKAY.
JESUS.
THERE'S NOTHING WORSE THAN WATCHING OTHER PEOPLE GETTING DRUNK, IS THERE?

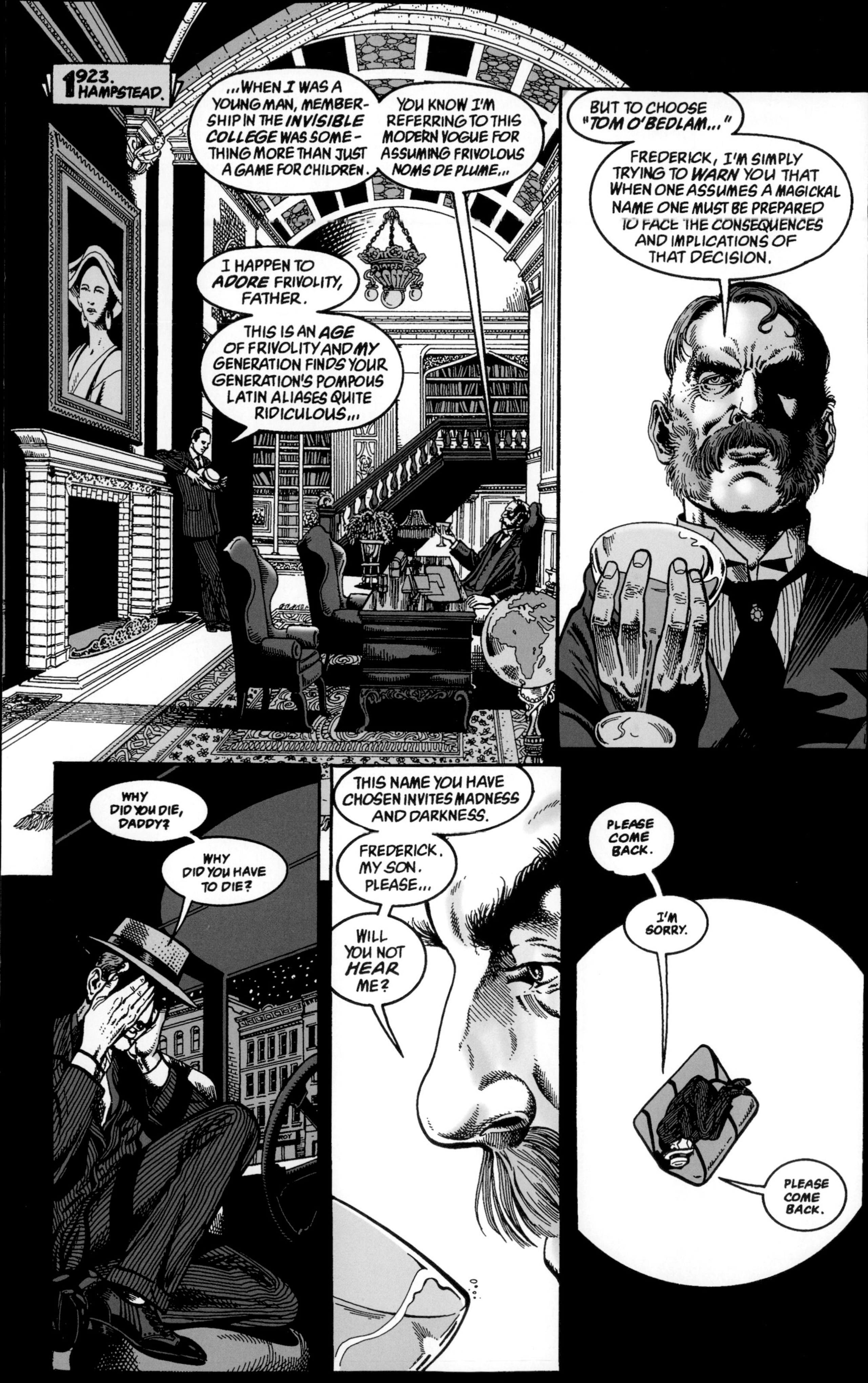
1923. HAMPSTEAD.
...WHEN I WAS A YOUNG MAN, MEMBER-SHIP IN THE INVISIBLE COLLEGE WAS SOME-THING MORE THAN JUST A GAME FOR CHILDREN.
YOU KNOW I'M REFERRING TO THIS MODERN VOGUE FOR ASSUMING FRIVOLOUS NOMS DE PLUME...
I HAPPEN TO ADORE FRIVOLITY, FATHER.
THIS IS AN AGE OF FRIVOLITY AND MY GENERATION FINDS YOUR GENERATION'S POMPOUS LATIN ALIASES QUITE RIDICULOUS...
BUT TO CHOOSE "TOM O'BEDLAM..."
FREDERICK, I'M SIMPLY TRYING TO WARN YOU THAT WHEN ONE ASSUMES A MAGICKAL NAME ONE MUST BE PREPARED TO FACE THE CONSEQUENCES AND IMPLICATIONS OF THAT DECISION.
WHY DID YOU DIE, DADDY?
WHY DID YOU HAVE TO DIE?
THIS NAME YOU HAVE CHOSEN INVITES MADNESS AND DARKNESS.
FREDERICK. MY SON. PLEASE...
WILL YOU NOT HEAR ME?
PLEASE COME BACK.
I'M SORRY.
PLEASE COME BACK.

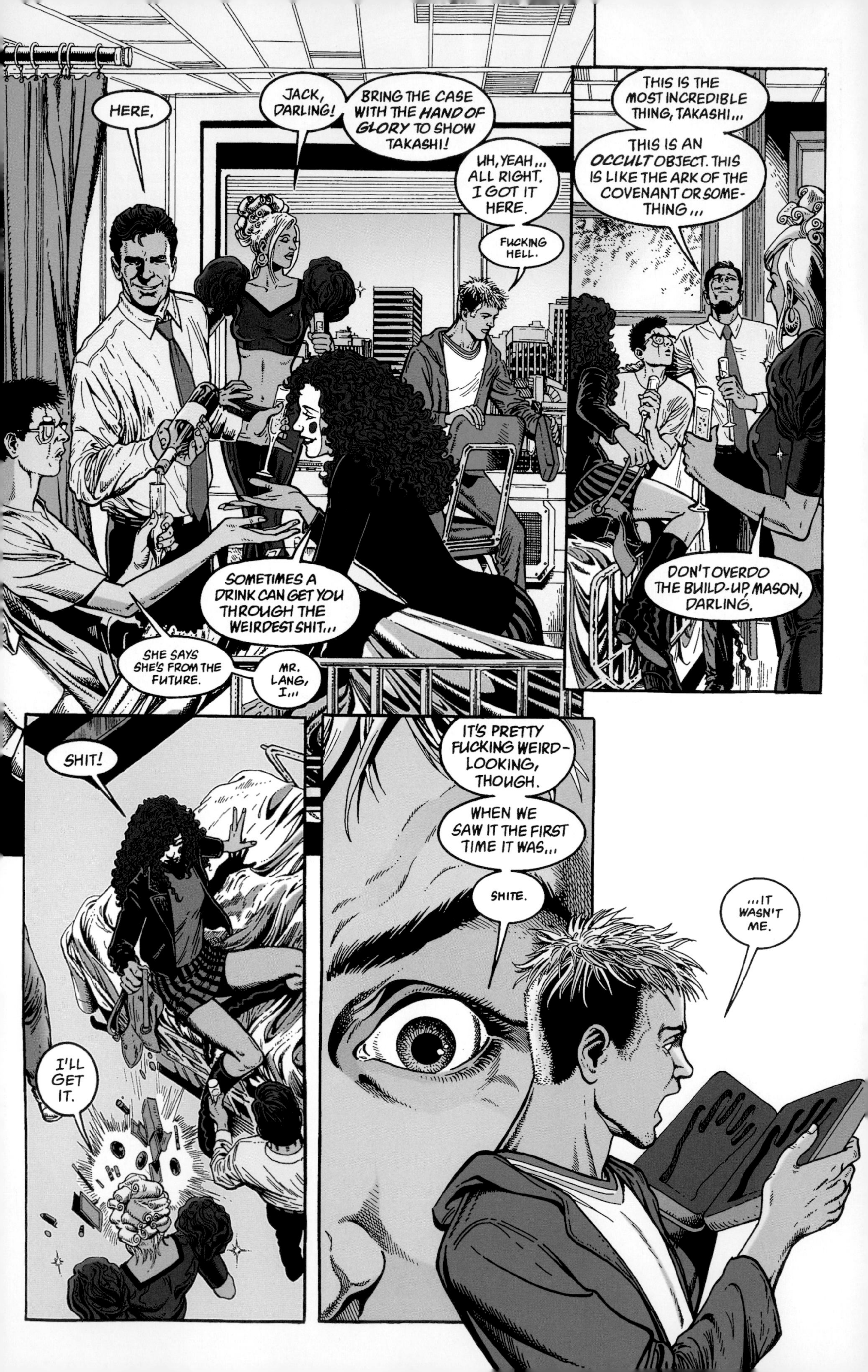
HERE.
JACK, DARLING!
BRING THE CASE WITH THE *HAND OF GLORY* TO SHOW TAKASHI!
UH, YEAH,,, ALL RIGHT. I GOT IT HERE.
FUCKING HELL.
SOMETIMES A DRINK CAN GET YOU THROUGH THE WEIRDEST SHIT,,,
SHE SAYS SHE'S FROM THE FUTURE.
MR. LANG, I,,,
THIS IS THE MOST INCREDIBLE THING, TAKASHI,,,
THIS IS AN *OCCULT* OBJECT. THIS IS LIKE THE ARK OF THE COVENANT OR SOME-THING,,,
DON'T OVERDO THE BUILD-UP, MASON, DARLING.
SHIT!
I'LL GET IT.
IT'S PRETTY FUCKING WEIRD-LOOKING, THOUGH.
WHEN WE SAW IT THE FIRST TIME IT WAS,,,
SHITE.
,,,IT WASN'T ME.

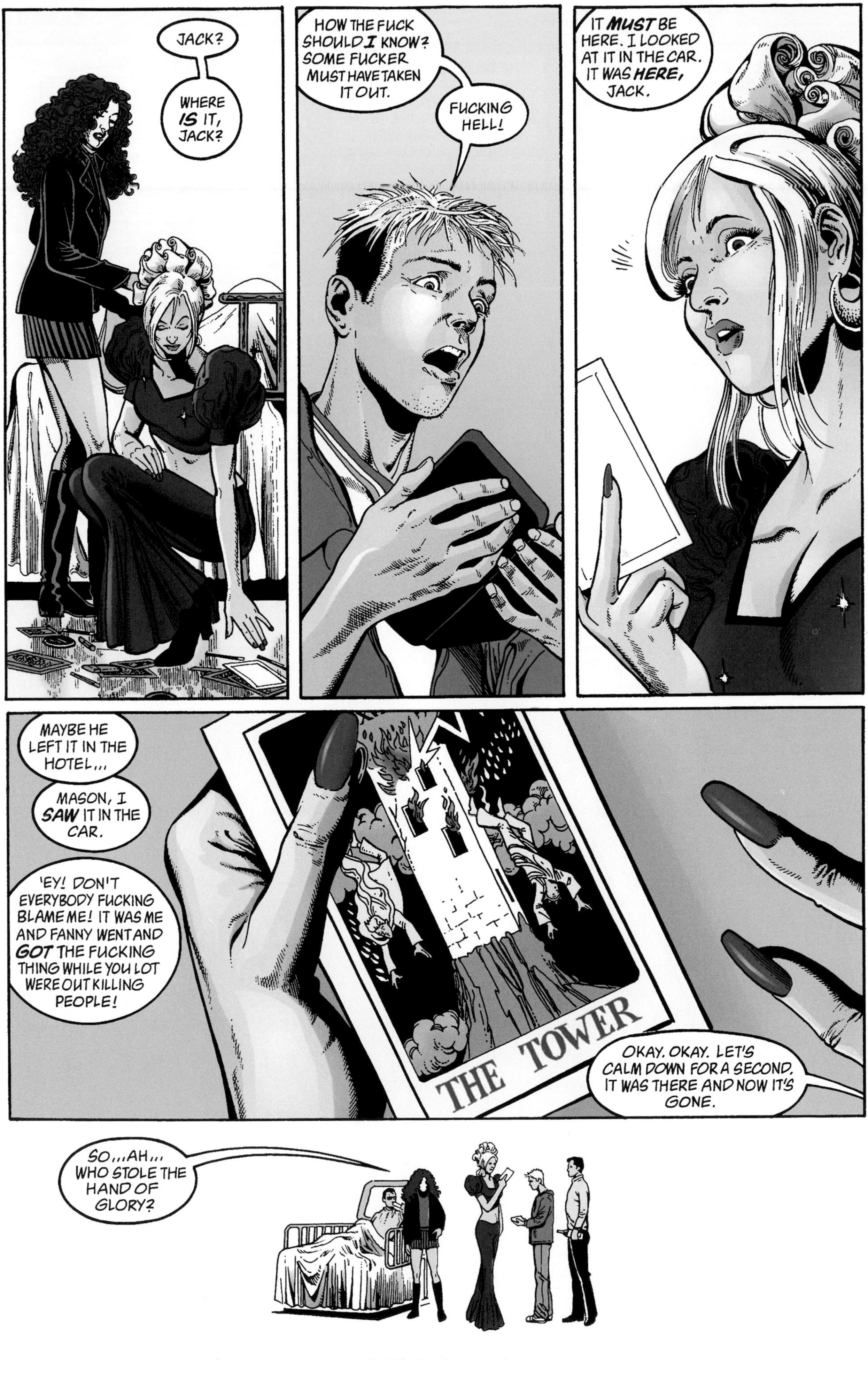
JACK?
WHERE IS IT, JACK?
HOW THE FUCK SHOULD I KNOW? SOME FUCKER MUST HAVE TAKEN IT OUT.
FUCKING HELL!
IT MUST BE HERE. I LOOKED AT IT IN THE CAR. IT WAS HERE, JACK.
MAYBE HE LEFT IT IN THE HOTEL...
MASON, I SAW IT IN THE CAR.
'EY! DON'T EVERYBODY FUCKING BLAME ME! IT WAS ME AND FANNY WENT AND GOT THE FUCKING THING WHILE YOU LOT WERE OUT KILLING PEOPLE!
THE TOWER
OKAY. OKAY. LET'S CALM DOWN FOR A SECOND. IT WAS THERE AND NOW IT'S GONE.
SO...AH... WHO STOLE THE HAND OF GLORY?

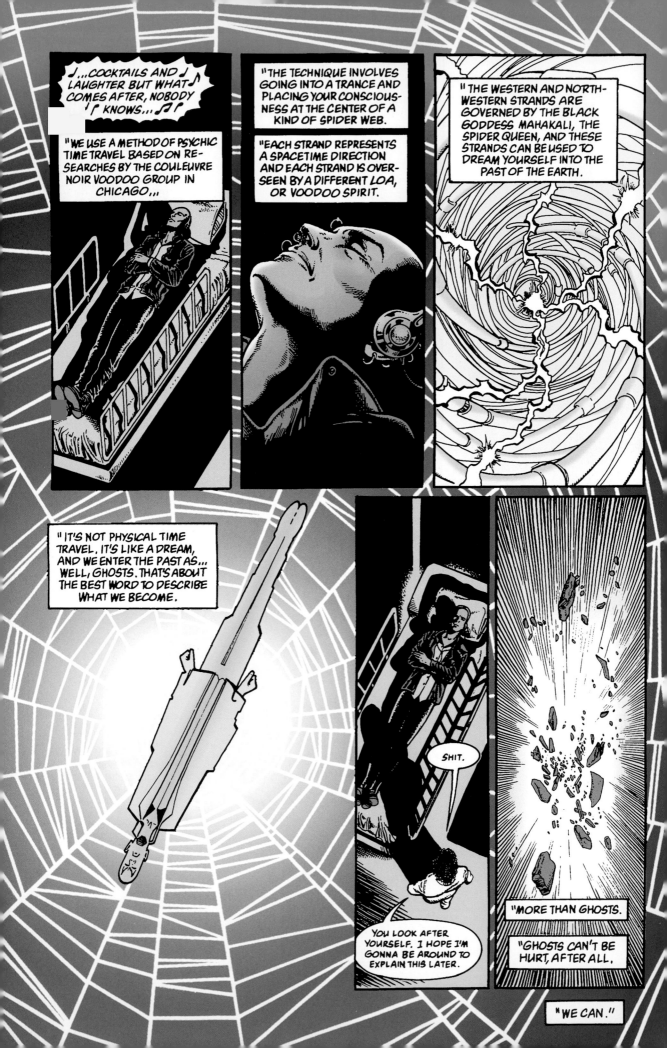

♪ ...COCKTAILS AND ♪ LAUGHTER BUT WHAT COMES AFTER, NOBODY ♪♪ KNOWS... ♪♪

"WE USE A METHOD OF PSYCHIC TIME TRAVEL BASED ON RE-SEARCHES BY THE COULEUVRE NOIR VOODOO GROUP IN CHICAGO..."

"THE TECHNIQUE INVOLVES GOING INTO A TRANCE AND PLACING YOUR CONSCIOUS-NESS AT THE CENTER OF A KIND OF SPIDER WEB.

"EACH STRAND REPRESENTS A SPACETIME DIRECTION AND EACH STRAND IS OVER-SEEN BY A DIFFERENT LOA, OR VOODOO SPIRIT.

"THE WESTERN AND NORTH-WESTERN STRANDS ARE GOVERNED BY THE BLACK GODDESS MAHAKALI, THE SPIDER QUEEN, AND THESE STRANDS CAN BE USED TO DREAM YOURSELF INTO THE PAST OF THE EARTH.

"IT'S NOT PHYSICAL TIME TRAVEL, IT'S LIKE A DREAM, AND WE ENTER THE PAST AS... WELL, GHOSTS. THAT'S ABOUT THE BEST WORD TO DESCRIBE WHAT WE BECOME.

SHIT.

YOU LOOK AFTER YOURSELF. I HOPE I'M GONNA BE AROUND TO EXPLAIN THIS LATER.

"MORE THAN GHOSTS.

"GHOSTS CAN'T BE HURT, AFTER ALL.

"WE CAN."

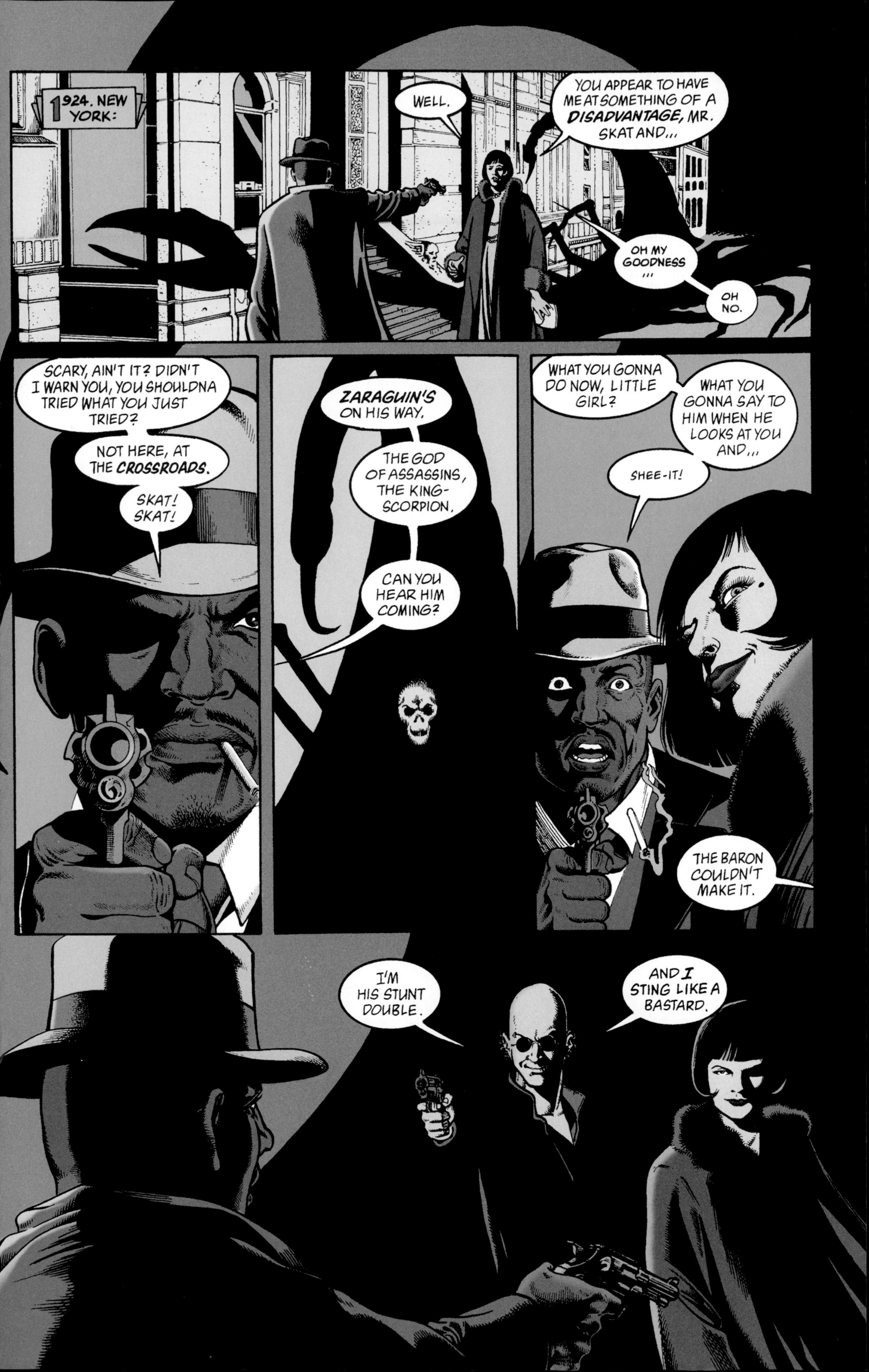
1924. NEW YORK:
WELL.
YOU APPEAR TO HAVE ME AT SOMETHING OF A DISADVANTAGE, MR. SKAT AND...
OH MY GOODNESS ...
OH NO.
SCARY, AIN'T IT? DIDN'T I WARN YOU, YOU SHOULDNA TRIED WHAT YOU JUST TRIED?
NOT HERE, AT THE CROSSROADS.
SKAT! SKAT!
ZARAGUIN'S ON HIS WAY.
THE GOD OF ASSASSINS, THE KING-SCORPION.
CAN YOU HEAR HIM COMING?
WHAT YOU GONNA DO NOW, LITTLE GIRL?
WHAT YOU GONNA SAY TO HIM WHEN HE LOOKS AT YOU AND...
SHEE-IT!
THE BARON COULDN'T MAKE IT.
I'M HIS STUNT DOUBLE.
AND I STING LIKE A BASTARD.

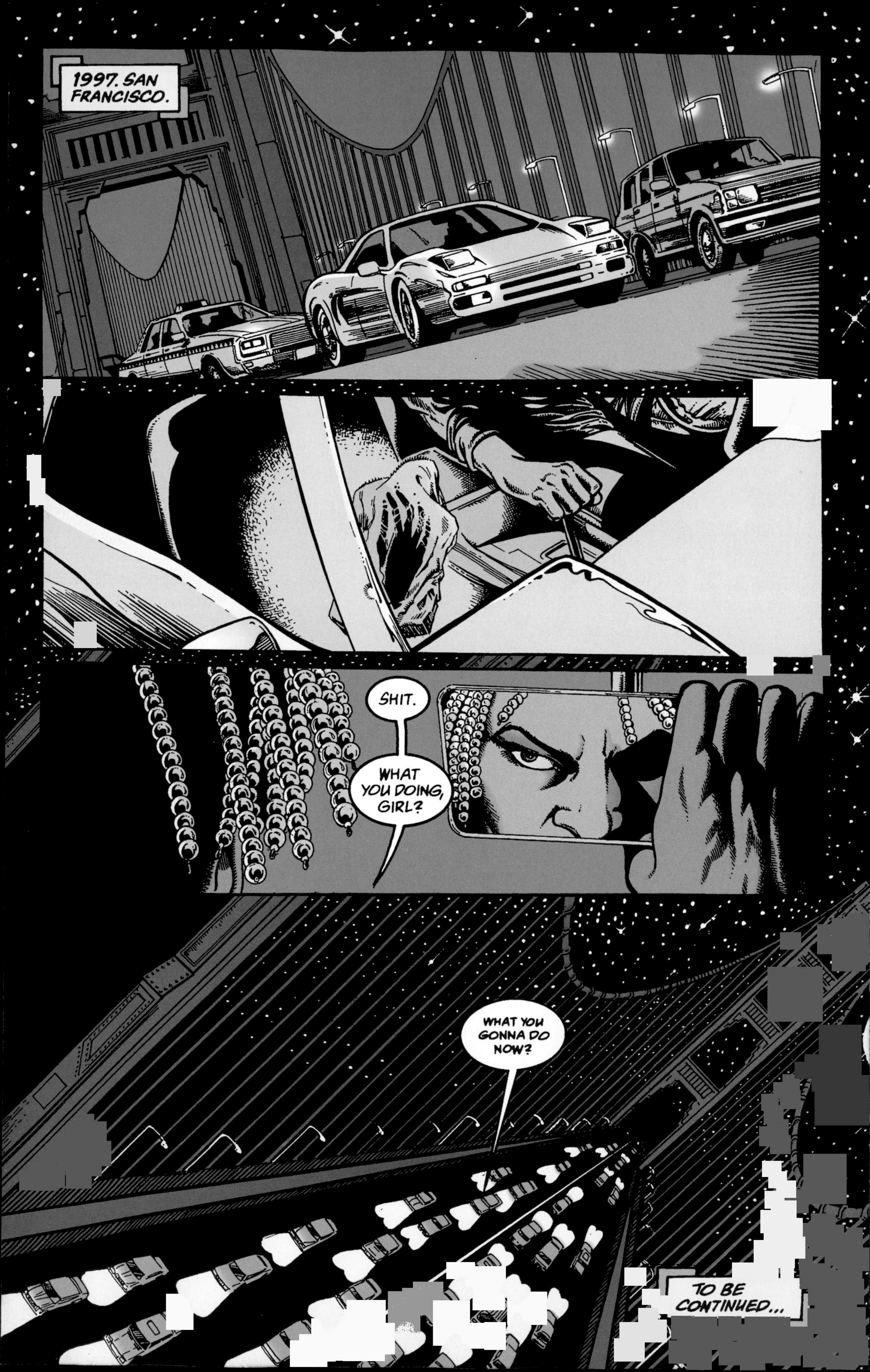
1997. SAN FRANCISCO.
SHIT.
WHAT YOU DOING, GIRL?
WHAT YOU GONNA DO NOW?
TO BE CONTINUED...

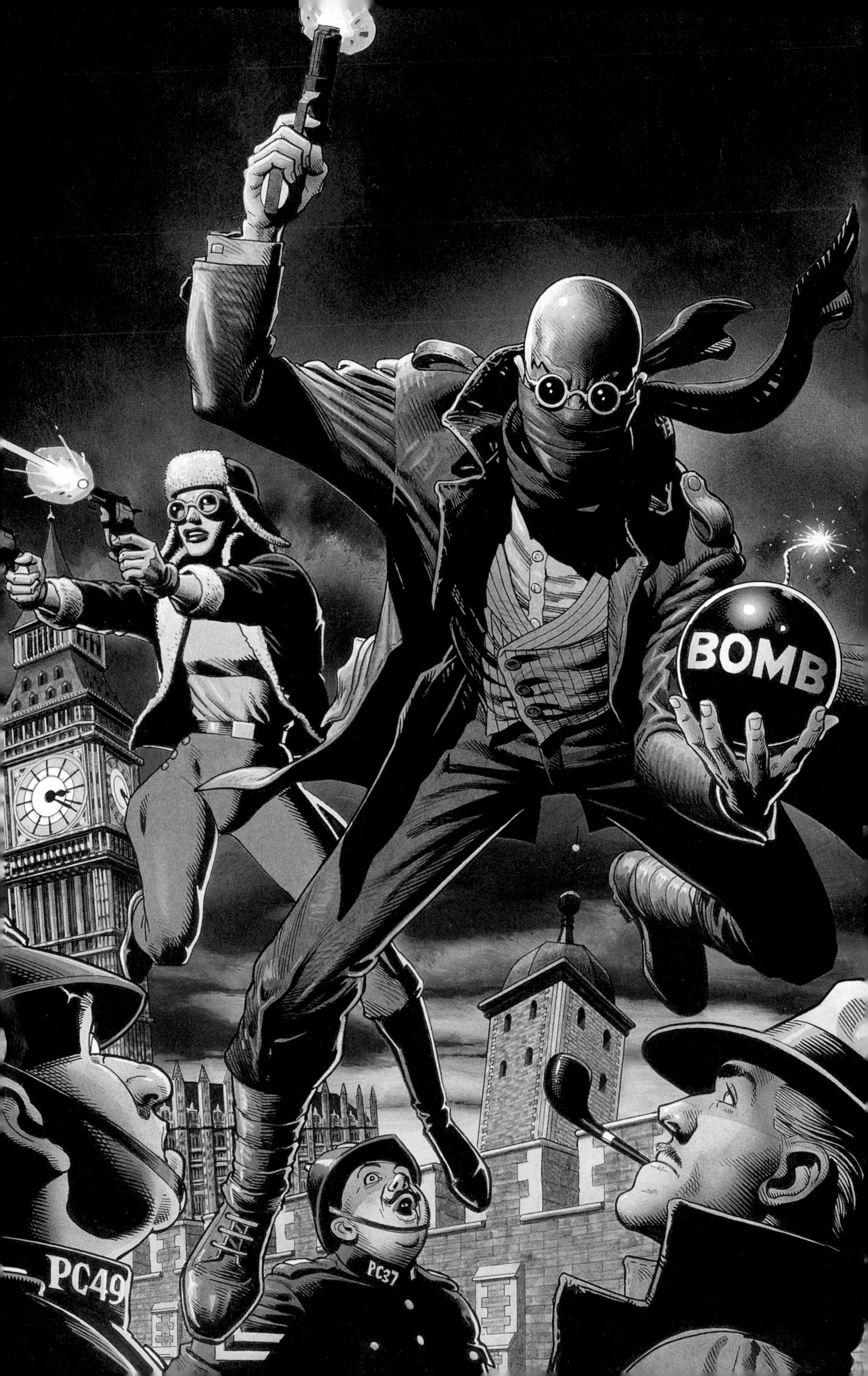
BOMB
PC49
PC37

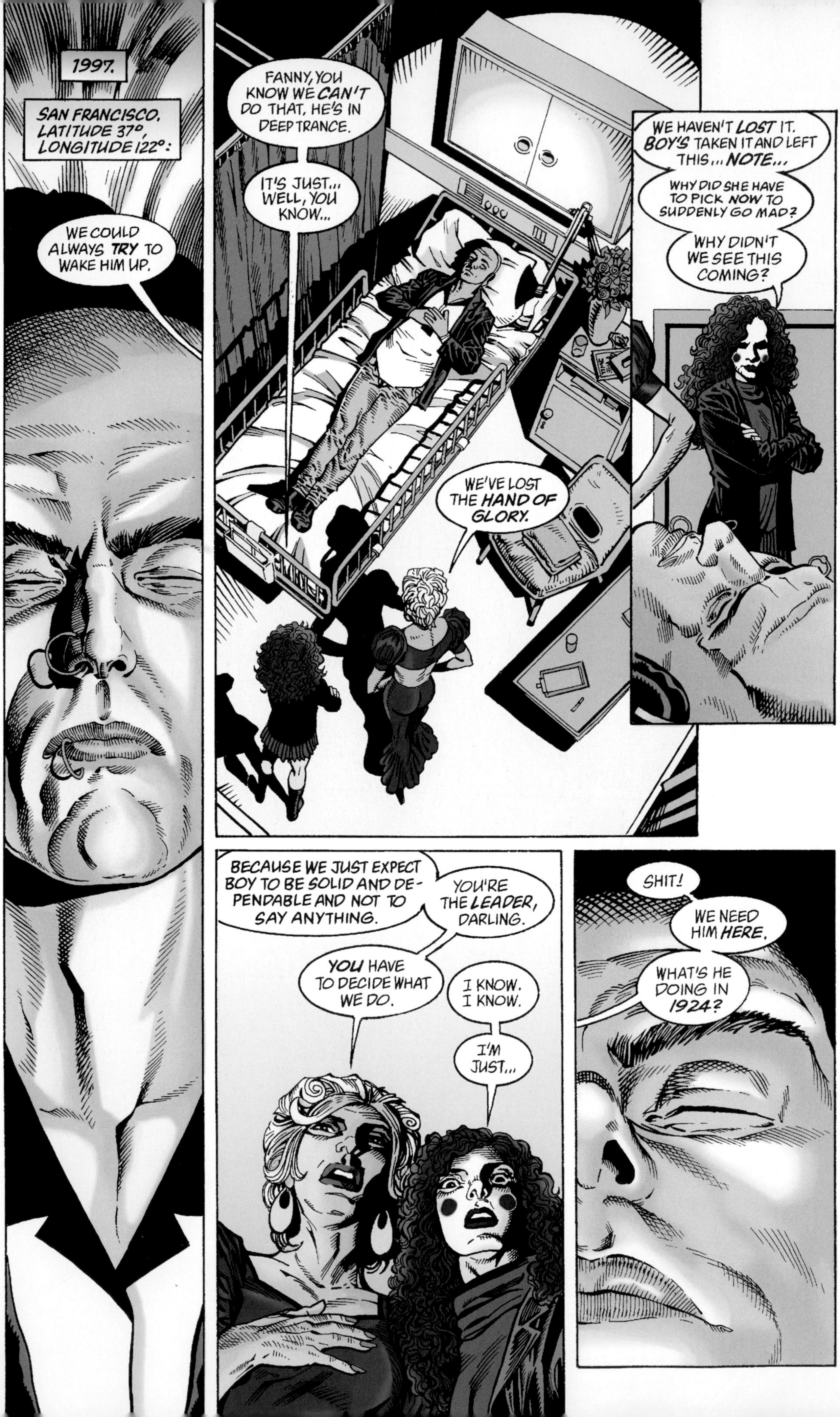
1997.
SAN FRANCISCO, LATITUDE 37°, LONGITUDE 122°:
WE COULD ALWAYS TRY TO WAKE HIM UP.
FANNY, YOU KNOW WE CAN'T DO THAT. HE'S IN DEEP TRANCE.
IT'S JUST... WELL, YOU KNOW...
WE'VE LOST THE HAND OF GLORY.
WE HAVEN'T LOST IT. BOY'S TAKEN IT AND LEFT THIS... NOTE...
WHY DID SHE HAVE TO PICK NOW TO SUDDENLY GO MAD?
WHY DIDN'T WE SEE THIS COMING?
BECAUSE WE JUST EXPECT BOY TO BE SOLID AND DE-PENDABLE AND NOT TO SAY ANYTHING.
YOU'RE THE LEADER, DARLING.
YOU HAVE TO DECIDE WHAT WE DO.
I KNOW. I KNOW.
I'M JUST...
SHIT!
WE NEED HIM HERE.
WHAT'S HE DOING IN 1924?

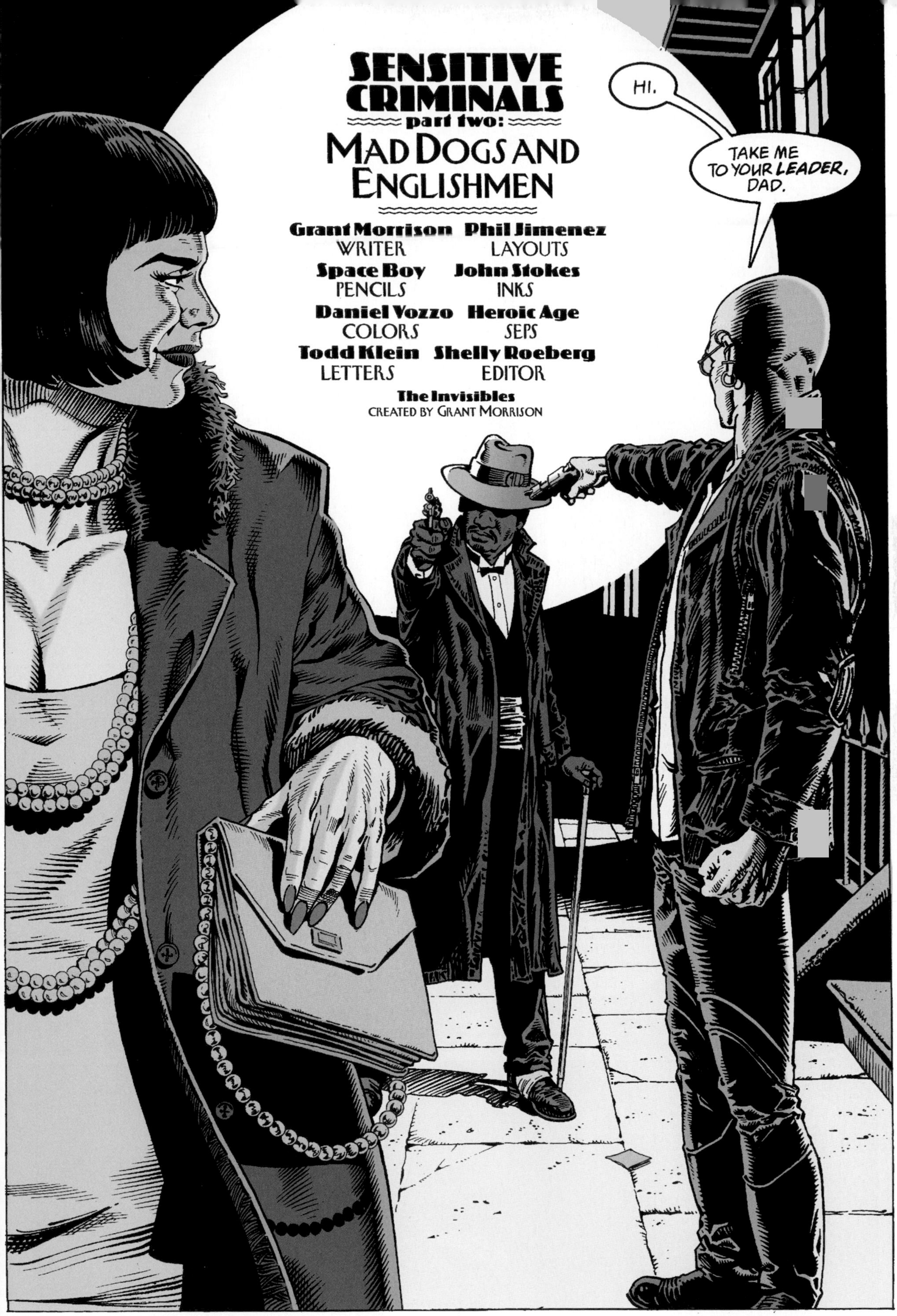
SENSITIVE CRIMINALS
part two:
MAD DOGS AND ENGLISHMEN
Grant Morrison WRITER
Phil Jimenez LAYOUTS
Space Boy PENCILS
John Stokes INKS
Daniel Vozzo COLORS
Heroic Age SEPS
Todd Klein LETTERS
Shelly Roeberg EDITOR
The Invisibles CREATED BY GRANT MORRISON
HI.
TAKE ME TO YOUR LEADER, DAD.

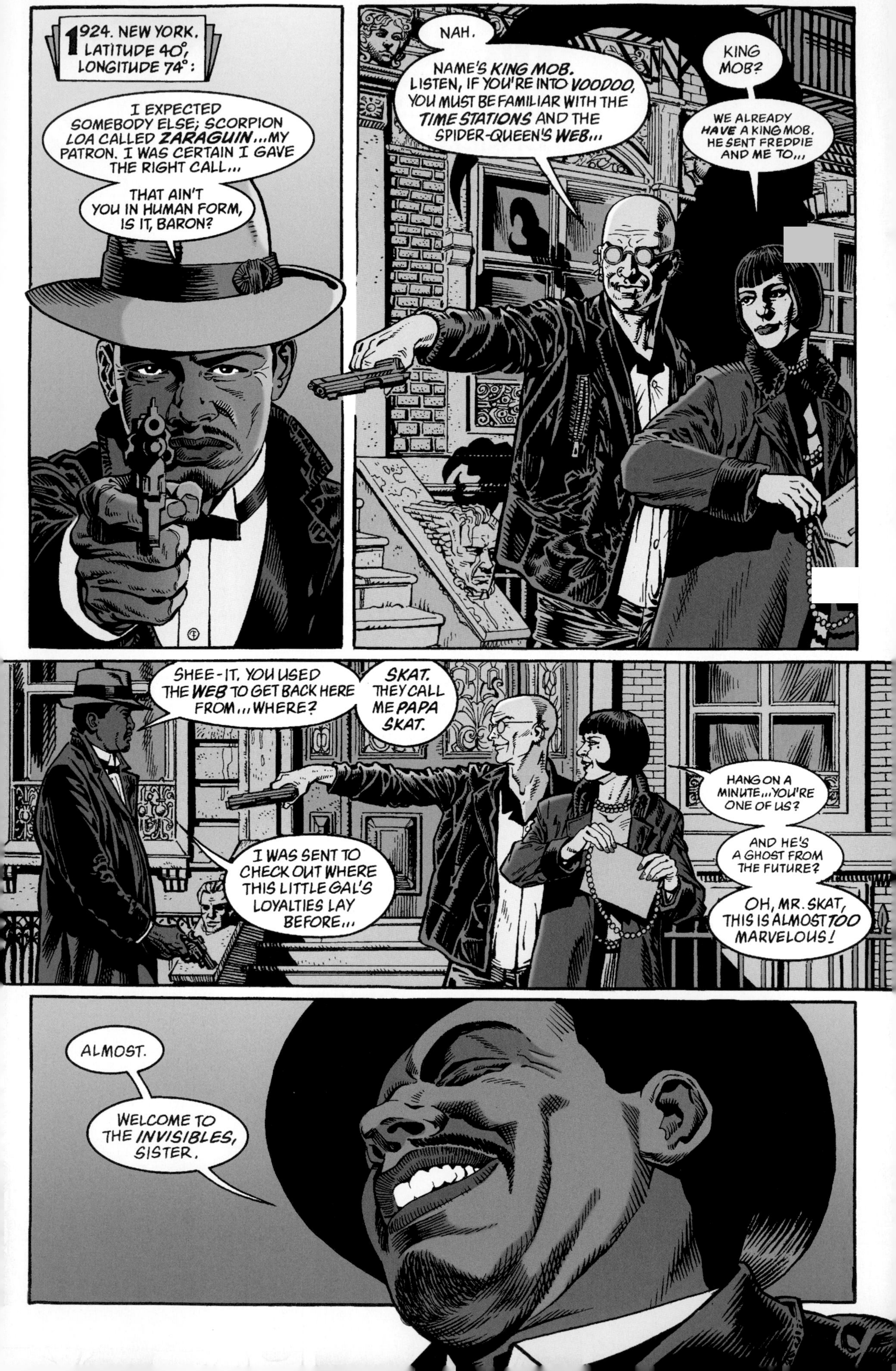
1924. NEW YORK. LATITUDE 40°, LONGITUDE 74°:
I EXPECTED SOMEBODY ELSE; SCORPION LOA CALLED ZARAGUIN...MY PATRON. I WAS CERTAIN I GAVE THE RIGHT CALL...
THAT AIN'T YOU IN HUMAN FORM, IS IT, BARON?
NAH.
NAME'S KING MOB. LISTEN, IF YOU'RE INTO VOODOO, YOU MUST BE FAMILIAR WITH THE TIME STATIONS AND THE SPIDER-QUEEN'S WEB...
KING MOB?
WE ALREADY HAVE A KING MOB. HE SENT FREDDIE AND ME TO...
SHEE-IT. YOU USED THE WEB TO GET BACK HERE FROM...WHERE?
SKAT. THEY CALL ME PAPA SKAT.
I WAS SENT TO CHECK OUT WHERE THIS LITTLE GAL'S LOYALTIES LAY BEFORE...
HANG ON A MINUTE...YOU'RE ONE OF US?
AND HE'S A GHOST FROM THE FUTURE?
OH, MR. SKAT, THIS IS ALMOST TOO MARVELOUS!
ALMOST.
WELCOME TO THE INVISIBLES, SISTER.

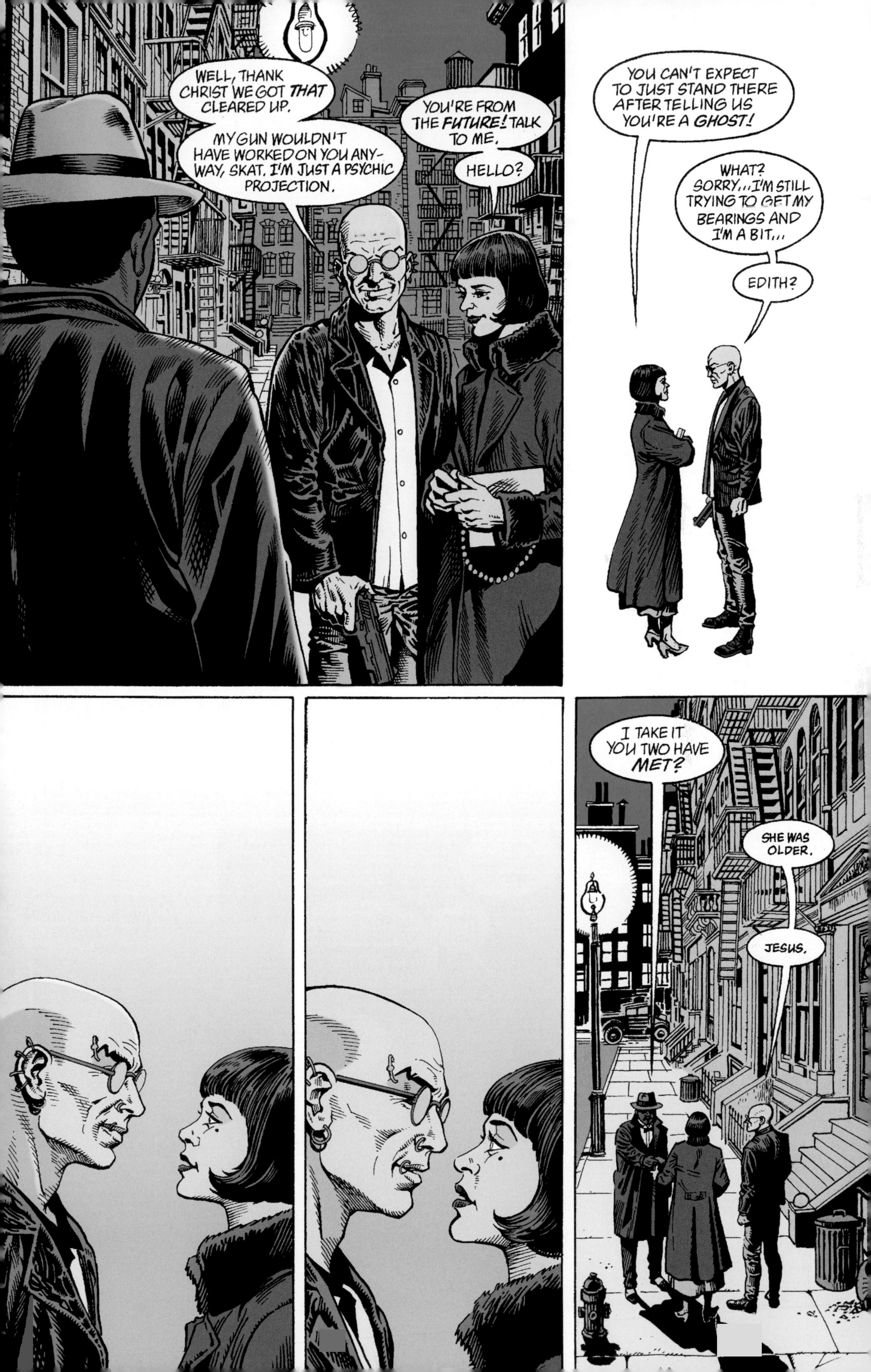
WELL, THANK CHRIST WE GOT THAT CLEARED UP.
MY GUN WOULDN'T HAVE WORKED ON YOU ANY-WAY, SKAT. I'M JUST A PSYCHIC PROJECTION.
YOU'RE FROM THE FUTURE! TALK TO ME.
HELLO?
YOU CAN'T EXPECT TO JUST STAND THERE AFTER TELLING US YOU'RE A GHOST!
WHAT? SORRY... I'M STILL TRYING TO GET MY BEARINGS AND I'M A BIT...
EDITH?
I TAKE IT YOU TWO HAVE MET?
SHE WAS OLDER.
JESUS.

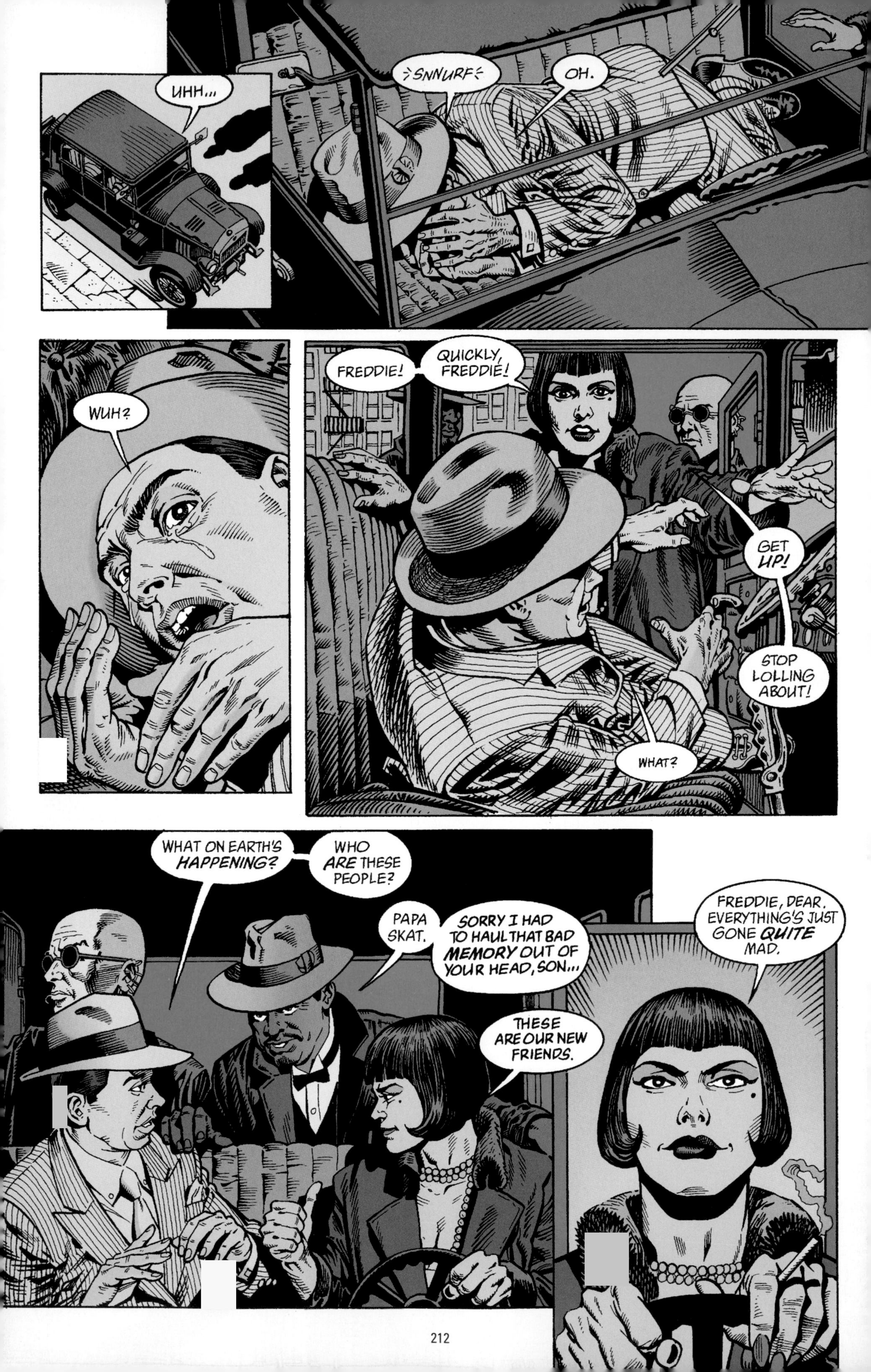
UHH...
SNNURF
OH.
WUH?
FREDDIE!
QUICKLY, FREDDIE!
GET UP!
STOP LOLLING ABOUT!
WHAT?
WHAT ON EARTH'S HAPPENING?
WHO ARE THESE PEOPLE?
PAPA SKAT.
SORRY I HAD TO HAUL THAT BAD MEMORY OUT OF YOUR HEAD, SON...
THESE ARE OUR NEW FRIENDS.
FREDDIE, DEAR. EVERYTHING'S JUST GONE QUITE MAD.

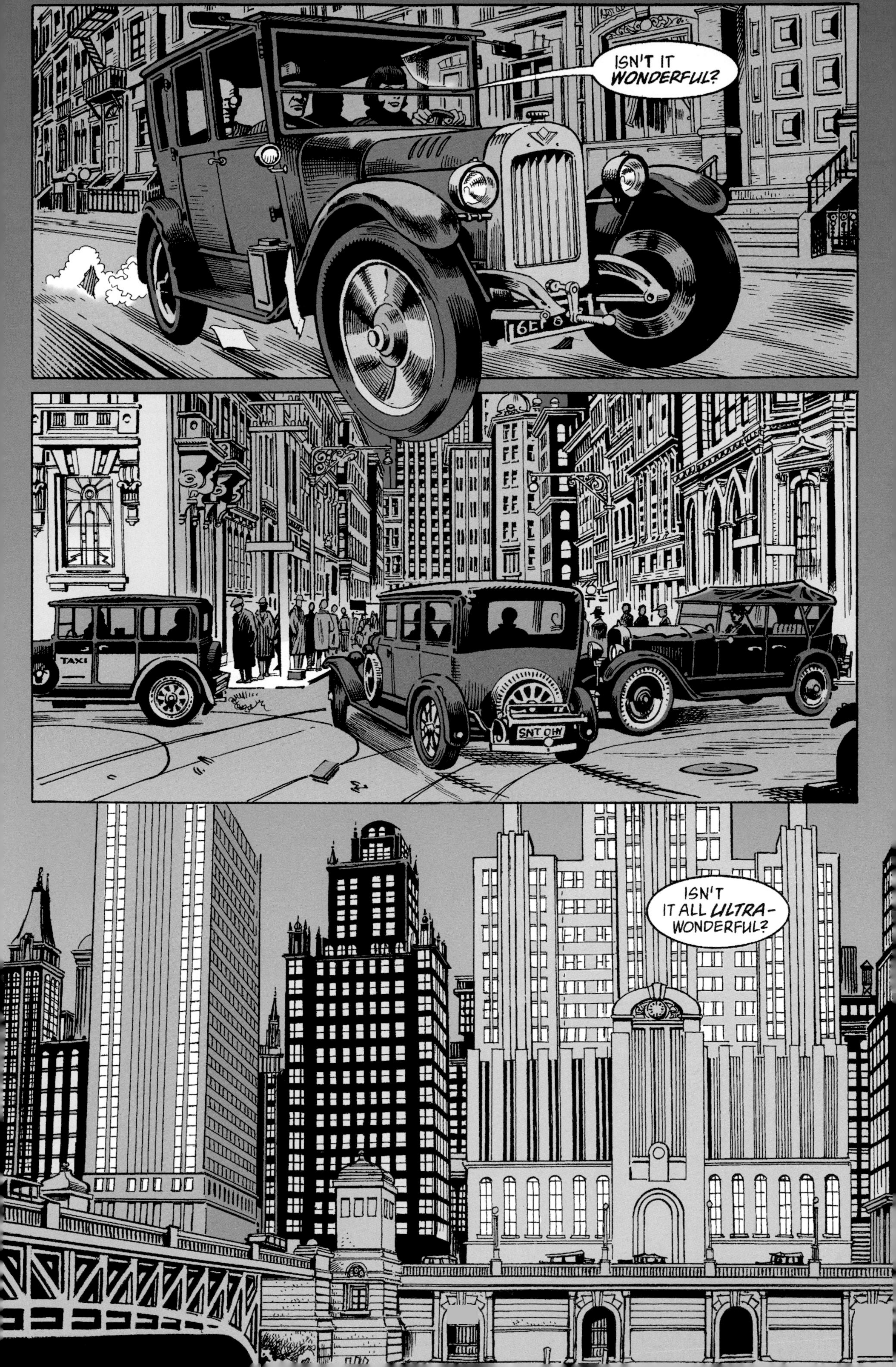
ISN'T IT WONDERFUL?
TAXI
SNT OHY
ISN'T IT ALL ULTRA-WONDERFUL?

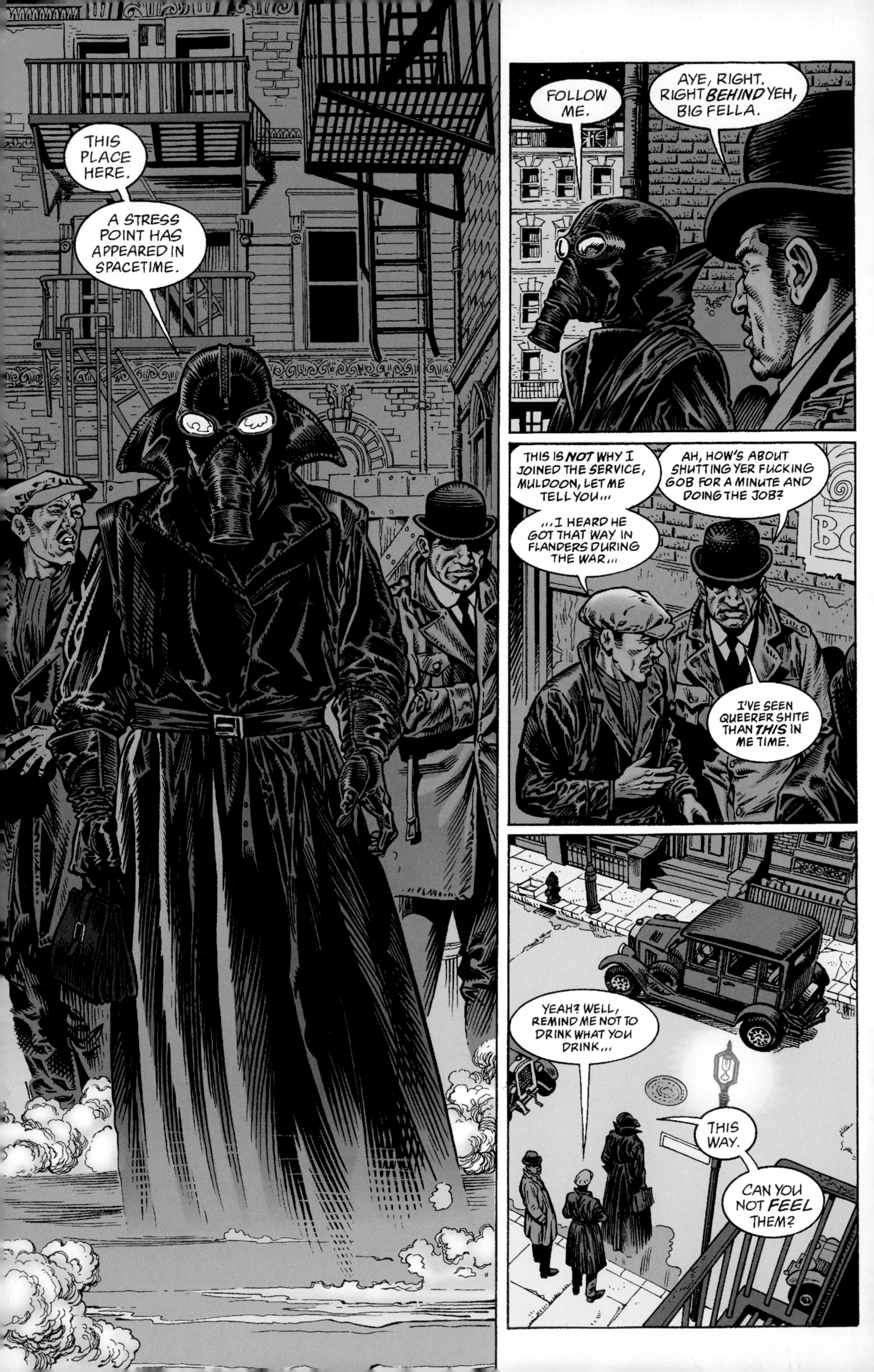
THIS PLACE HERE.
A STRESS POINT HAS APPEARED IN SPACETIME.
FOLLOW ME.
AYE, RIGHT. RIGHT BEHIND YEH, BIG FELLA.
THIS IS NOT WHY I JOINED THE SERVICE, MULDOON, LET ME TELL YOU...
AH, HOW'S ABOUT SHUTTING YER FUCKING GOB FOR A MINUTE AND DOING THE JOB?
...I HEARD HE GOT THAT WAY IN FLANDERS DURING THE WAR...
I'VE SEEN QUEERER SHITE THAN THIS IN ME TIME.
YEAH? WELL, REMIND ME NOT TO DRINK WHAT YOU DRINK...
THIS WAY.
CAN YOU NOT FEEL THEM?

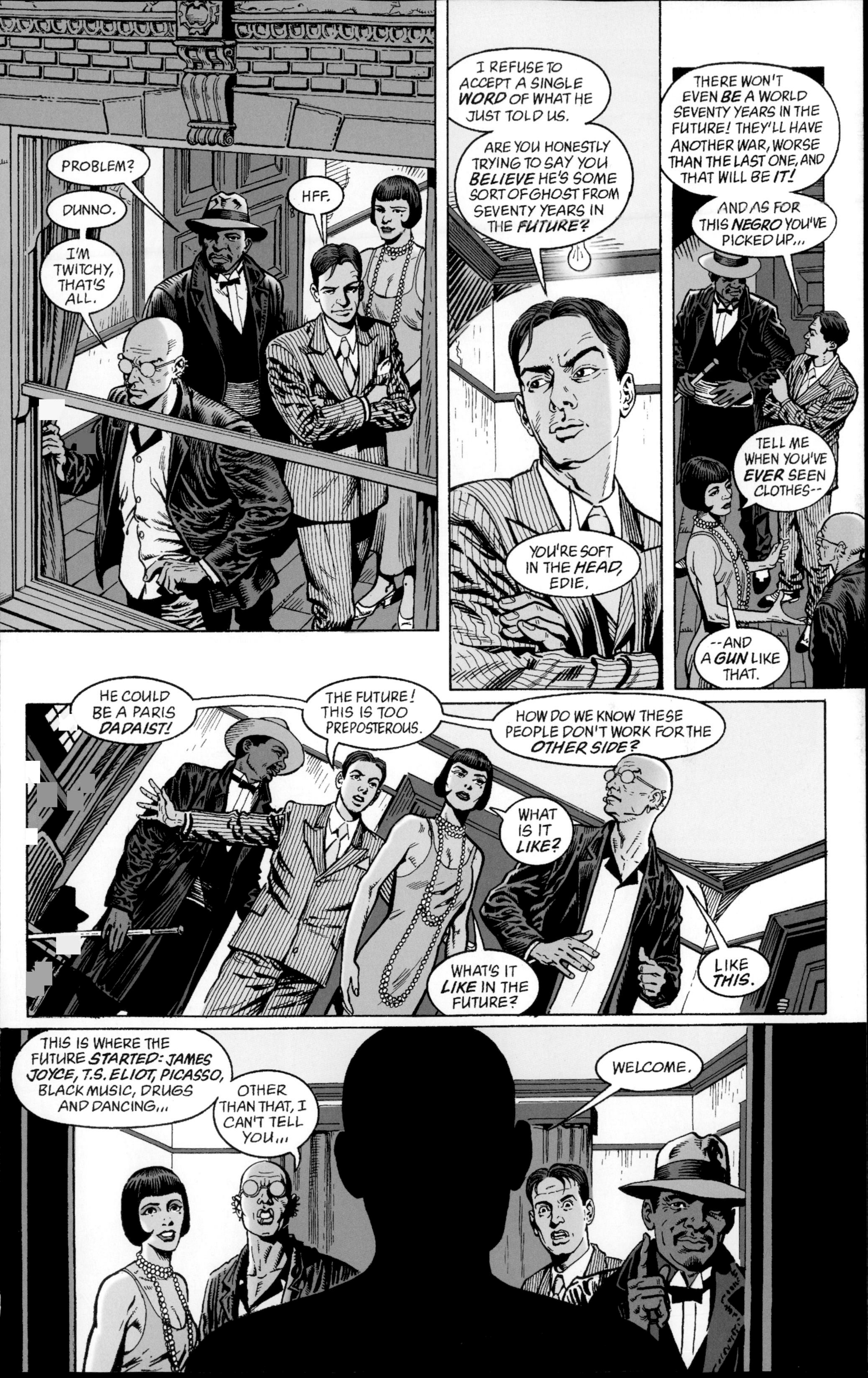
PROBLEM?
DUNNO.
I'M TWITCHY, THAT'S ALL.
HFF.
I REFUSE TO ACCEPT A SINGLE WORD OF WHAT HE JUST TOLD US.
ARE YOU HONESTLY TRYING TO SAY YOU BELIEVE HE'S SOME SORT OF GHOST FROM SEVENTY YEARS IN THE FUTURE?
YOU'RE SOFT IN THE HEAD, EDIE.
THERE WON'T EVEN BE A WORLD SEVENTY YEARS IN THE FUTURE! THEY'LL HAVE ANOTHER WAR, WORSE THAN THE LAST ONE, AND THAT WILL BE IT!
AND AS FOR THIS NEGRO YOU'VE PICKED UP...
TELL ME WHEN YOU'VE EVER SEEN CLOTHES--
--AND A GUN LIKE THAT.
HE COULD BE A PARIS DADAIST!
THE FUTURE! THIS IS TOO PREPOSTEROUS.
HOW DO WE KNOW THESE PEOPLE DON'T WORK FOR THE OTHER SIDE?
WHAT IS IT LIKE?
WHAT'S IT LIKE IN THE FUTURE?
LIKE THIS.
THIS IS WHERE THE FUTURE STARTED: JAMES JOYCE, T.S. ELIOT, PICASSO, BLACK MUSIC, DRUGS AND DANCING...
OTHER THAN THAT, I CAN'T TELL YOU...
WELCOME.

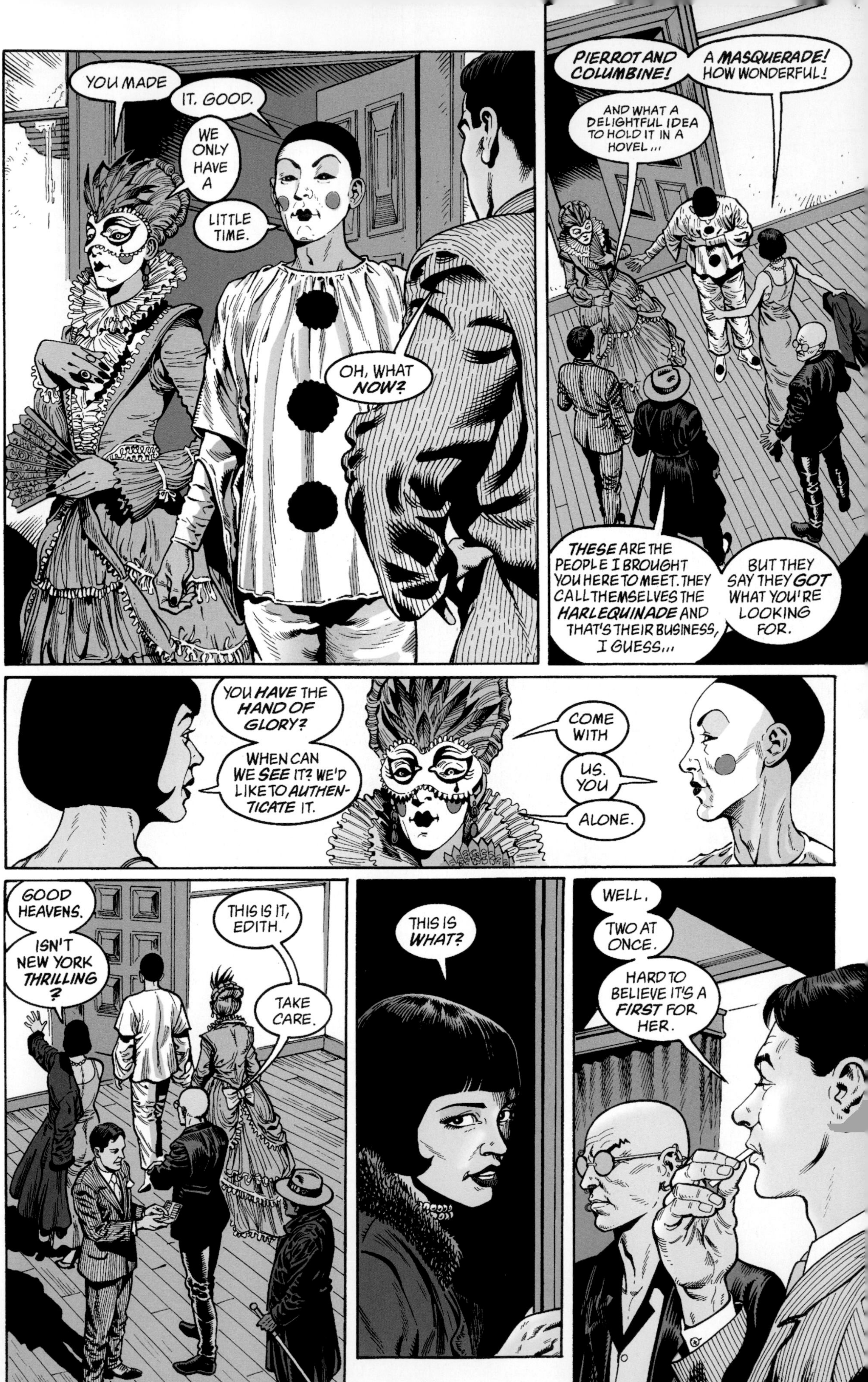
YOU MADE
IT. GOOD.
WE ONLY HAVE A
LITTLE TIME.
OH, WHAT NOW?
PIERROT AND COLUMBINE!
A MASQUERADE! HOW WONDERFUL!
AND WHAT A DELIGHTFUL IDEA TO HOLD IT IN A HOVEL...
THESE ARE THE PEOPLE I BROUGHT YOU HERE TO MEET. THEY CALL THEMSELVES THE HARLEQUINADE AND THAT'S THEIR BUSINESS, I GUESS...
BUT THEY SAY THEY GOT WHAT YOU'RE LOOKING FOR.
YOU HAVE THE HAND OF GLORY?
WHEN CAN WE SEE IT? WE'D LIKE TO AUTHENTICATE IT.
COME WITH
US. YOU
ALONE.
GOOD HEAVENS.
ISN'T NEW YORK THRILLING?
THIS IS IT, EDITH.
TAKE CARE.
THIS IS WHAT?
WELL,
TWO AT ONCE.
HARD TO BELIEVE IT'S A FIRST FOR HER.

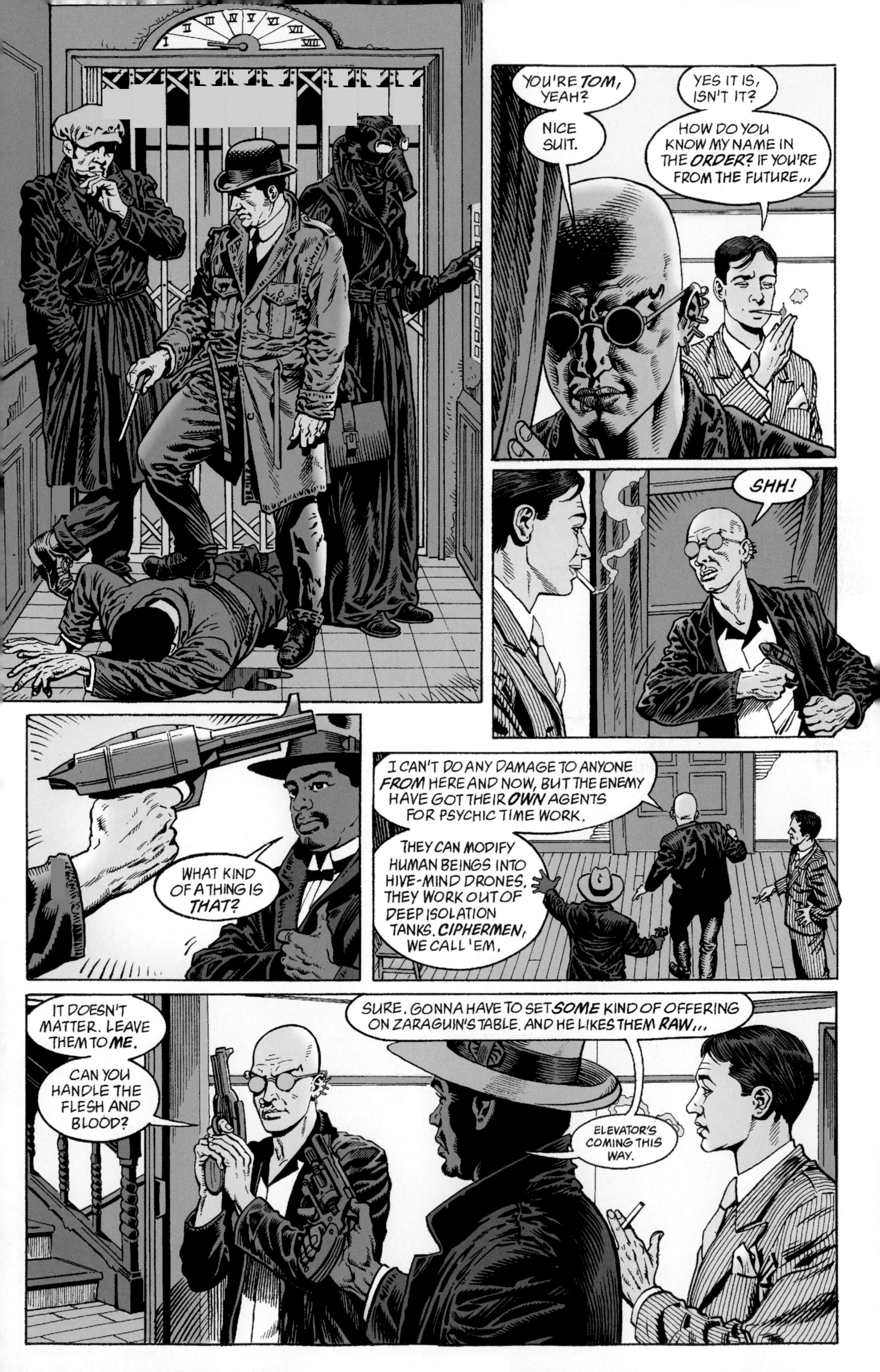
YOU'RE TOM, YEAH?
NICE SUIT.
YES IT IS, ISN'T IT?
HOW DO YOU KNOW MY NAME IN THE ORDER? IF YOU'RE FROM THE FUTURE...
SHH!
WHAT KIND OF A THING IS THAT?
I CAN'T DO ANY DAMAGE TO ANYONE FROM HERE AND NOW, BUT THE ENEMY HAVE GOT THEIR OWN AGENTS FOR PSYCHIC TIME WORK.
THEY CAN MODIFY HUMAN BEINGS INTO HIVE-MIND DRONES. THEY WORK OUT OF DEEP ISOLATION TANKS. CIPHERMEN, WE CALL 'EM.
IT DOESN'T MATTER. LEAVE THEM TO ME.
CAN YOU HANDLE THE FLESH AND BLOOD?
SURE. GONNA HAVE TO SET SOME KIND OF OFFERING ON ZARAGUIN'S TABLE. AND HE LIKES THEM RAW...
ELEVATOR'S COMING THIS WAY.

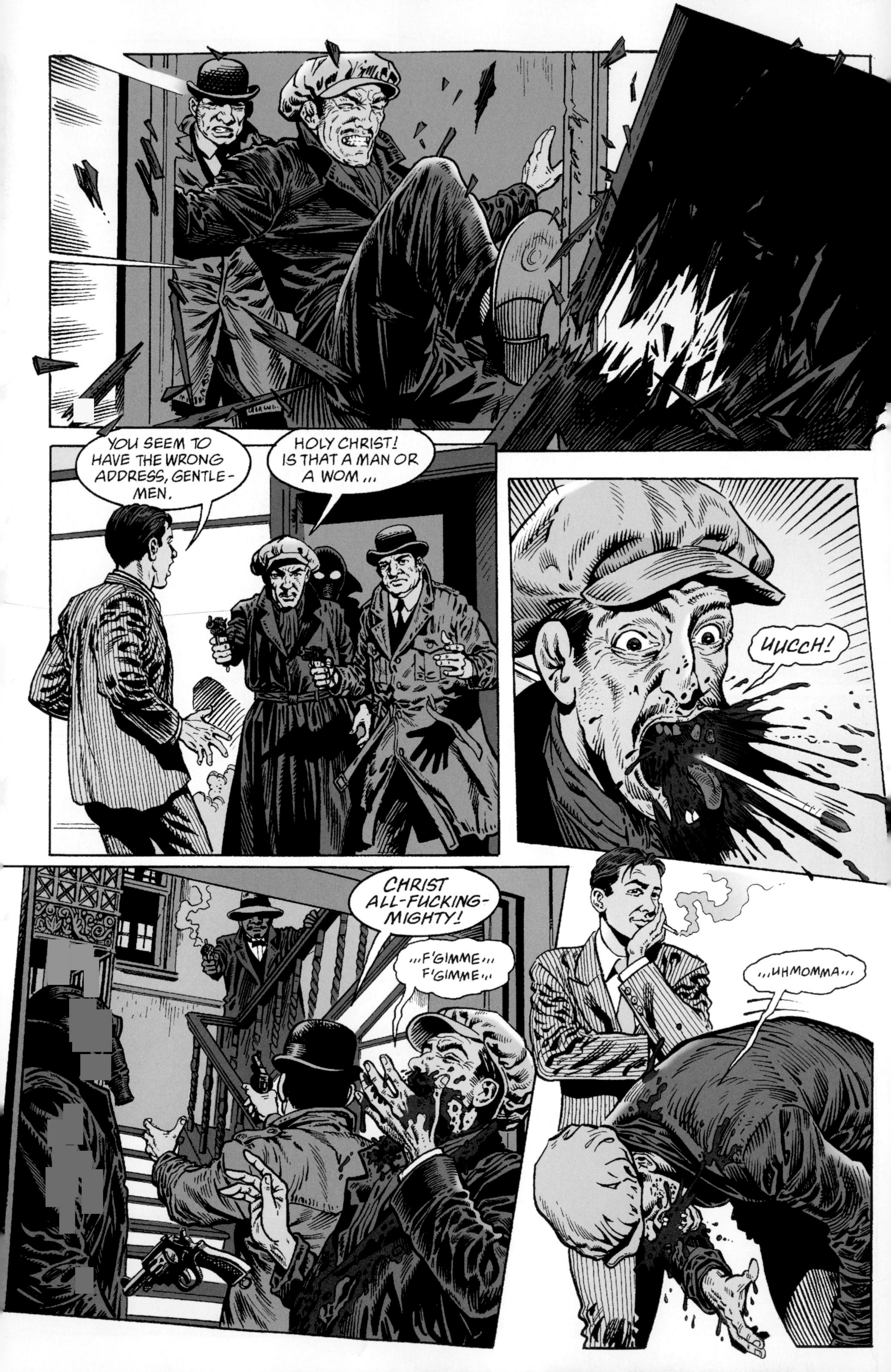
YOU SEEM TO HAVE THE WRONG ADDRESS, GENTLE-MEN.
HOLY CHRIST! IS THAT A MAN OR A WOM ...
UUCCH!
CHRIST ALL-FUCKING-MIGHTY!
...F'GIMME... F'GIMME...
...UHMOMMA...

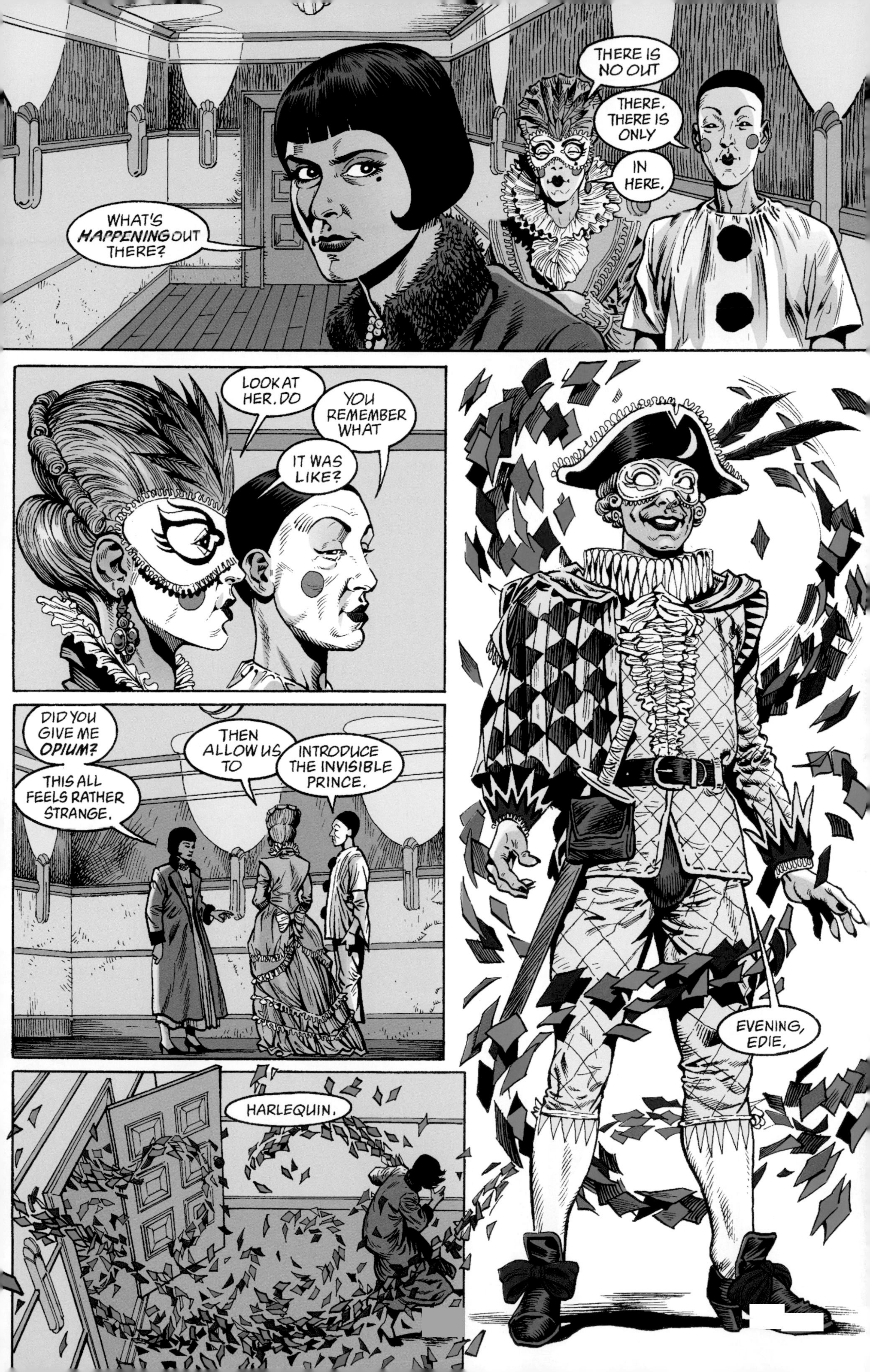
WHAT'S *HAPPENING* OUT THERE?
THERE IS NO OUT
THERE, THERE IS ONLY
IN HERE.
LOOK AT HER. DO
YOU REMEMBER WHAT
IT WAS LIKE?
DID YOU GIVE ME *OPIUM*?
THIS ALL FEELS RATHER STRANGE.
THEN ALLOW US TO
INTRODUCE THE INVISIBLE PRINCE.
HARLEQUIN.
EVENING, EDIE.

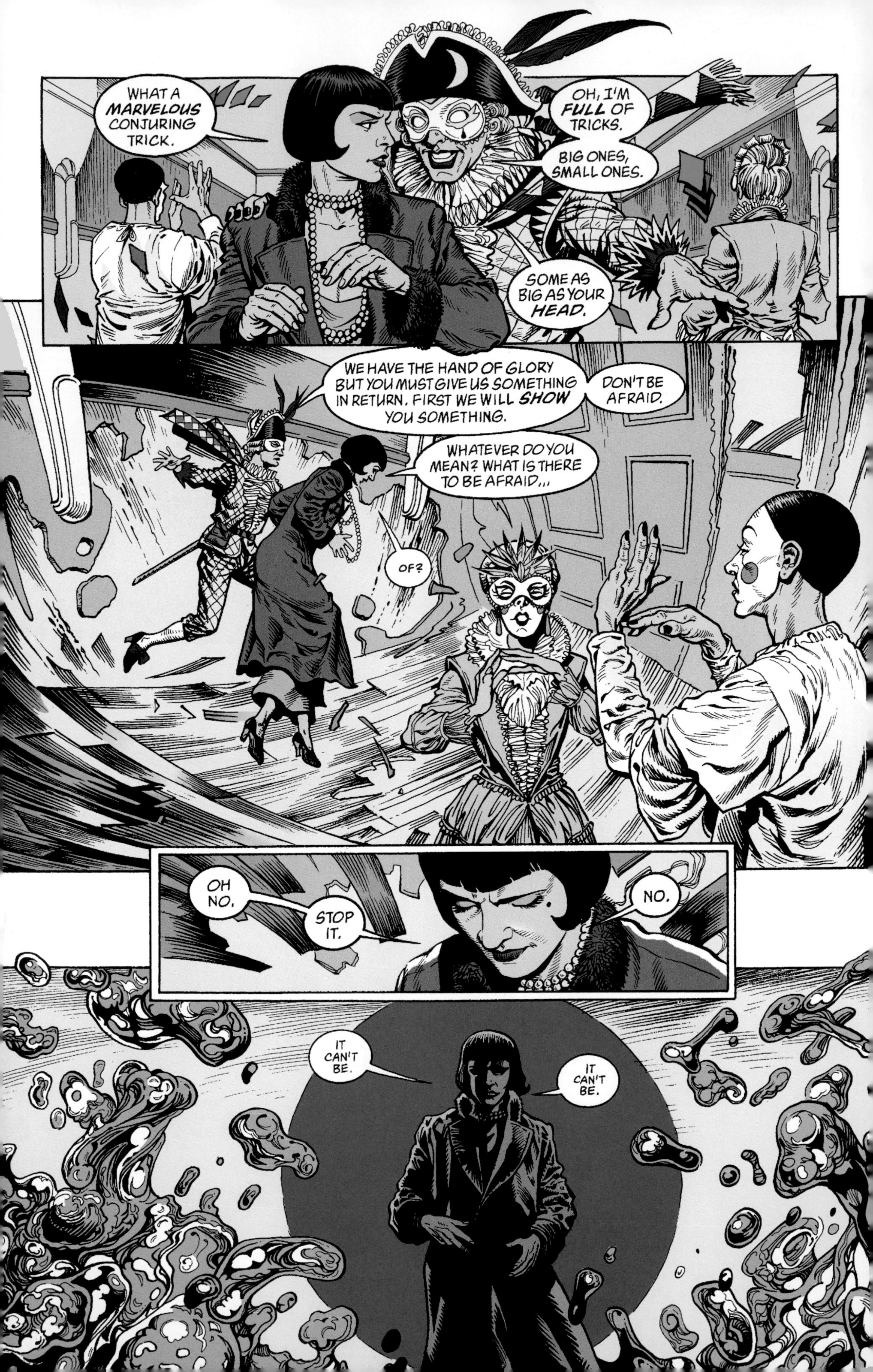
WHAT A MARVELOUS CONJURING TRICK.
OH, I'M FULL OF TRICKS.
BIG ONES, SMALL ONES.
SOME AS BIG AS YOUR HEAD.
WE HAVE THE HAND OF GLORY BUT YOU MUST GIVE US SOMETHING IN RETURN. FIRST WE WILL SHOW YOU SOMETHING.
DON'T BE AFRAID.
WHATEVER DO YOU MEAN? WHAT IS THERE TO BE AFRAID...
OF?
OH NO.
STOP IT.
NO.
IT CAN'T BE.
IT CAN'T BE.

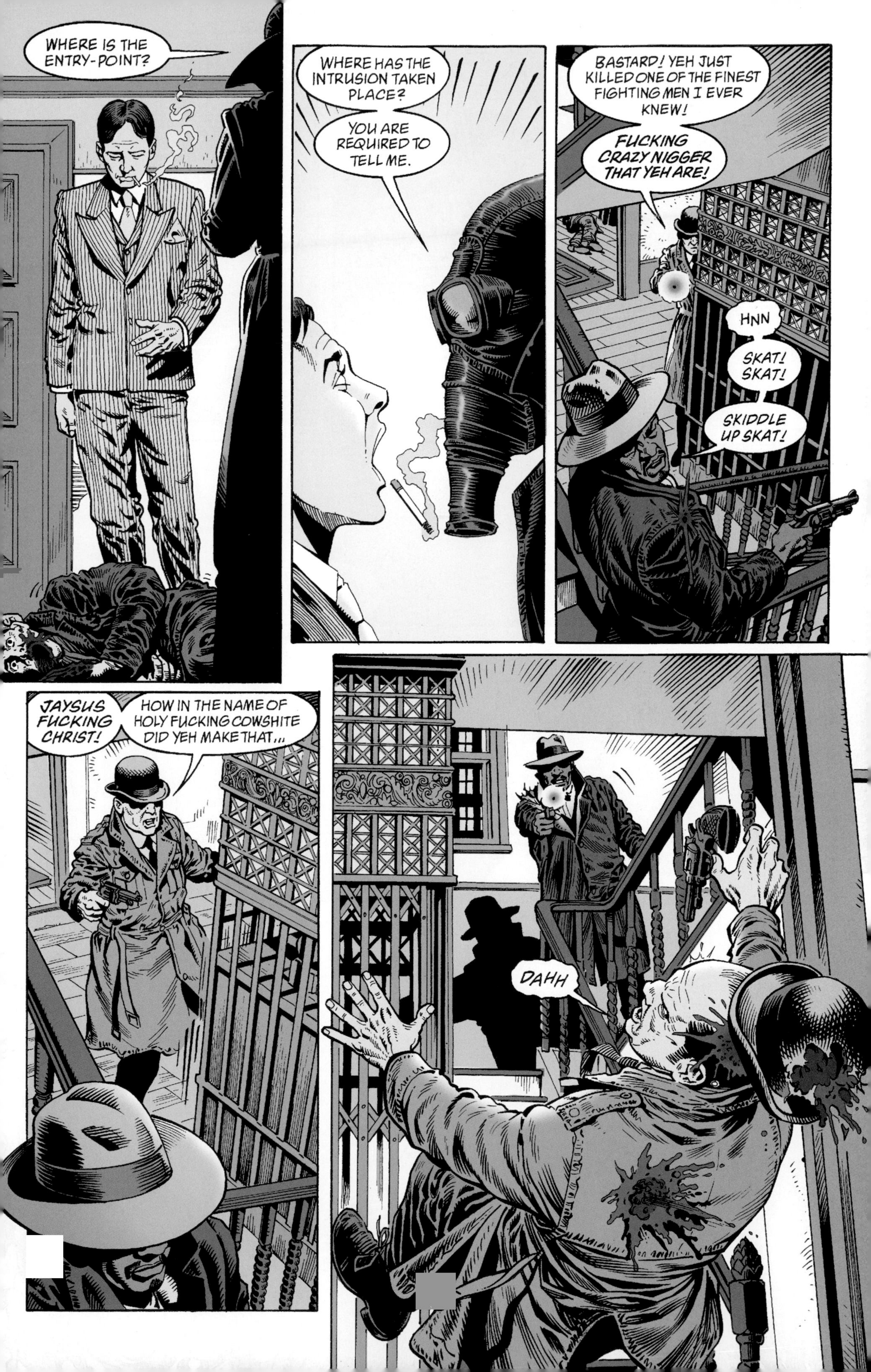
WHERE IS THE ENTRY-POINT?
WHERE HAS THE INTRUSION TAKEN PLACE?
YOU ARE REQUIRED TO TELL ME.
BASTARD! YEH JUST KILLED ONE OF THE FINEST FIGHTING MEN I EVER KNEW!
FUCKING CRAZY NIGGER THAT YEH ARE!
HNN
SKAT! SKAT!
SKIDDLE UP SKAT!
JAYSUS FUCKING CHRIST!
HOW IN THE NAME OF HOLY FUCKING COWSHITE DID YEH MAKE THAT...
DAHH

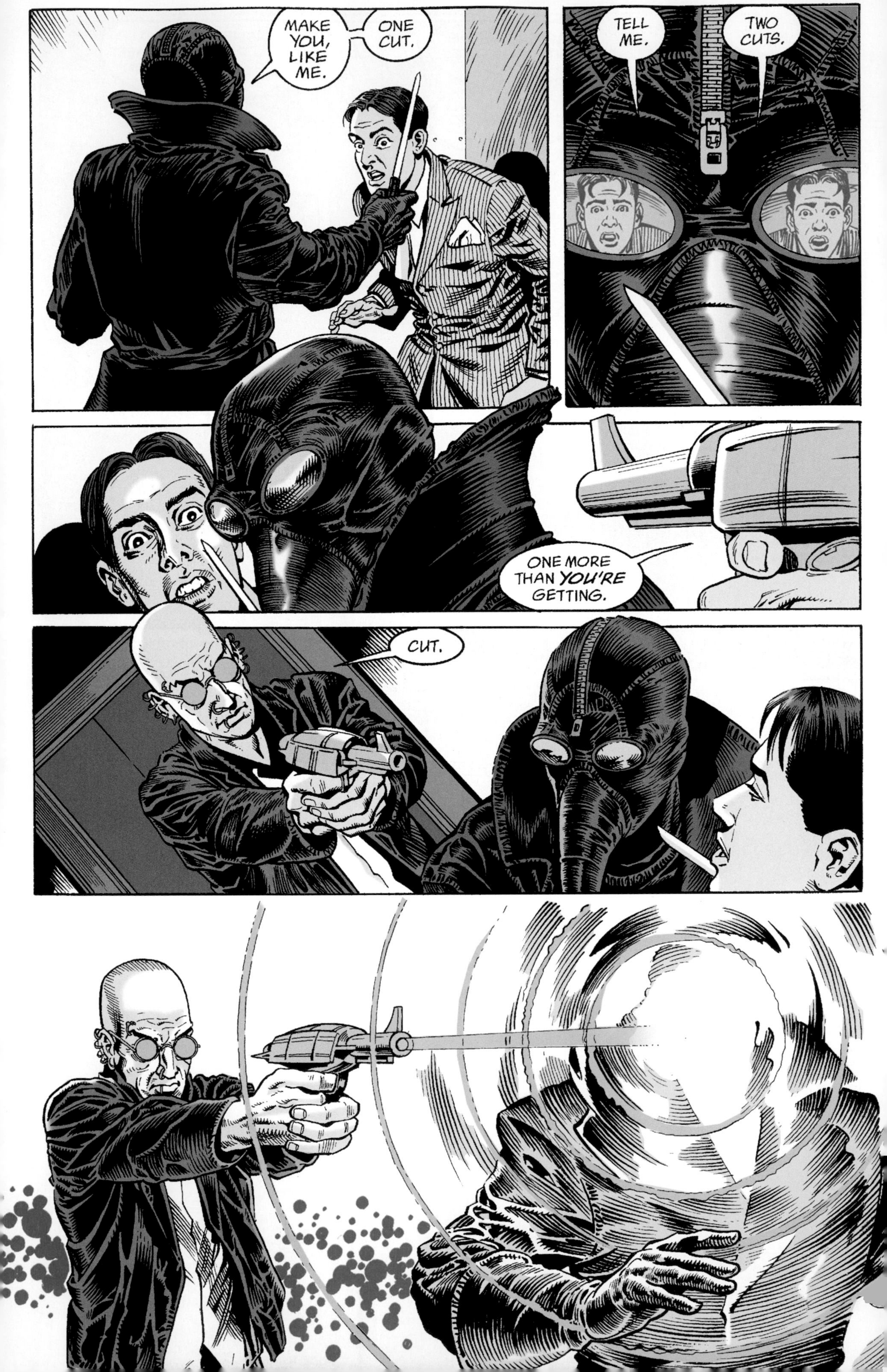
MAKE YOU, LIKE ME.
ONE CUT.
TELL ME.
TWO CUTS.
ONE MORE THAN YOU'RE GETTING.
CUT.

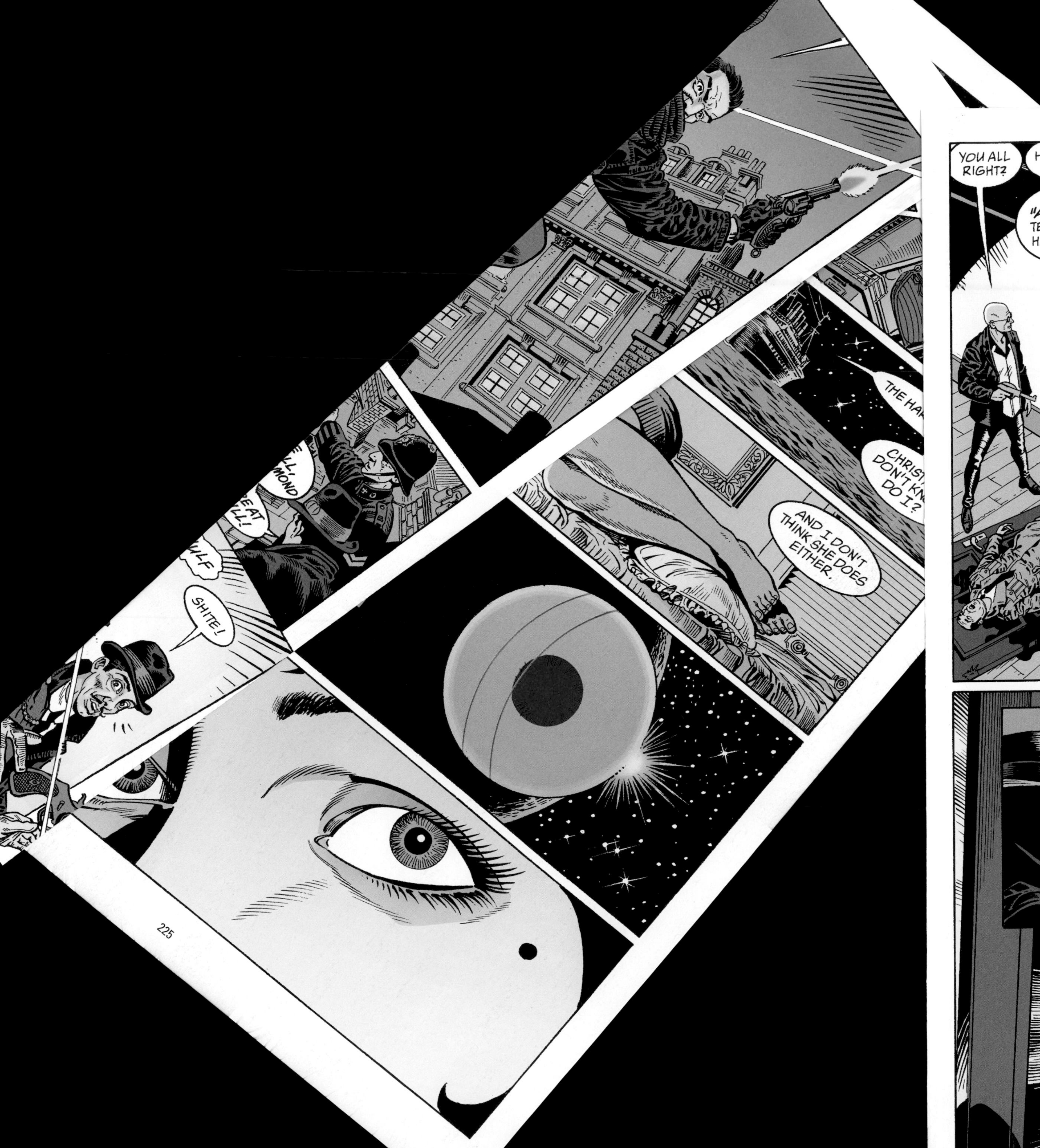
SHITE!
AND I DON'T THINK SHE DOES EITHER.

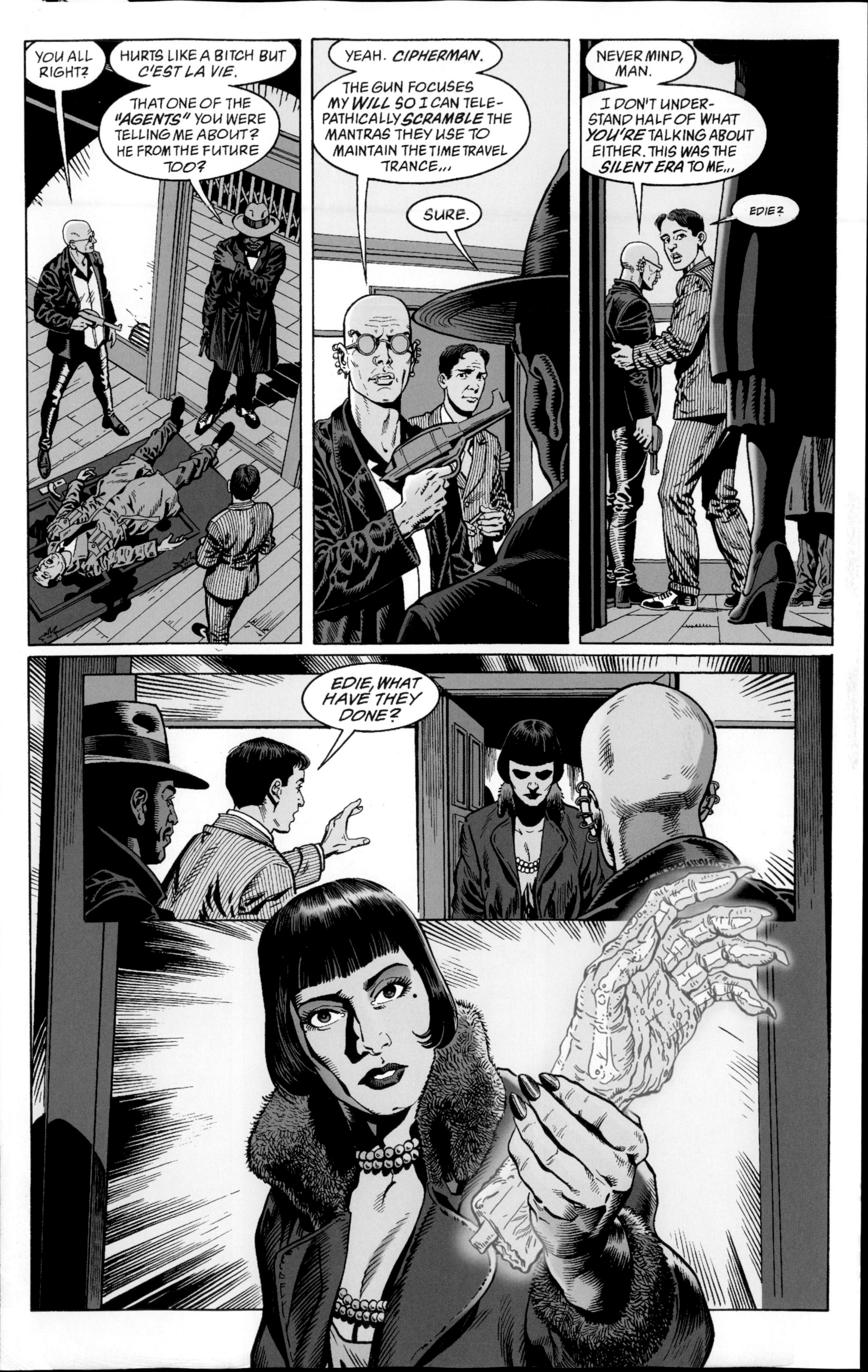
YOU ALL RIGHT?
HURTS LIKE A BITCH BUT C'EST LA VIE.
THAT ONE OF THE "AGENTS" YOU WERE TELLING ME ABOUT? HE FROM THE FUTURE TOO?
YEAH. CIPHERMAN.
THE GUN FOCUSES MY WILL SO I CAN TELEPATHICALLY SCRAMBLE THE MANTRAS THEY USE TO MAINTAIN THE TIME TRAVEL TRANCE...
SURE.
NEVER MIND, MAN.
I DON'T UNDERSTAND HALF OF WHAT YOU'RE TALKING ABOUT EITHER. THIS WAS THE SILENT ERA TO ME...
EDIE?
EDIE, WHAT HAVE THEY DONE?

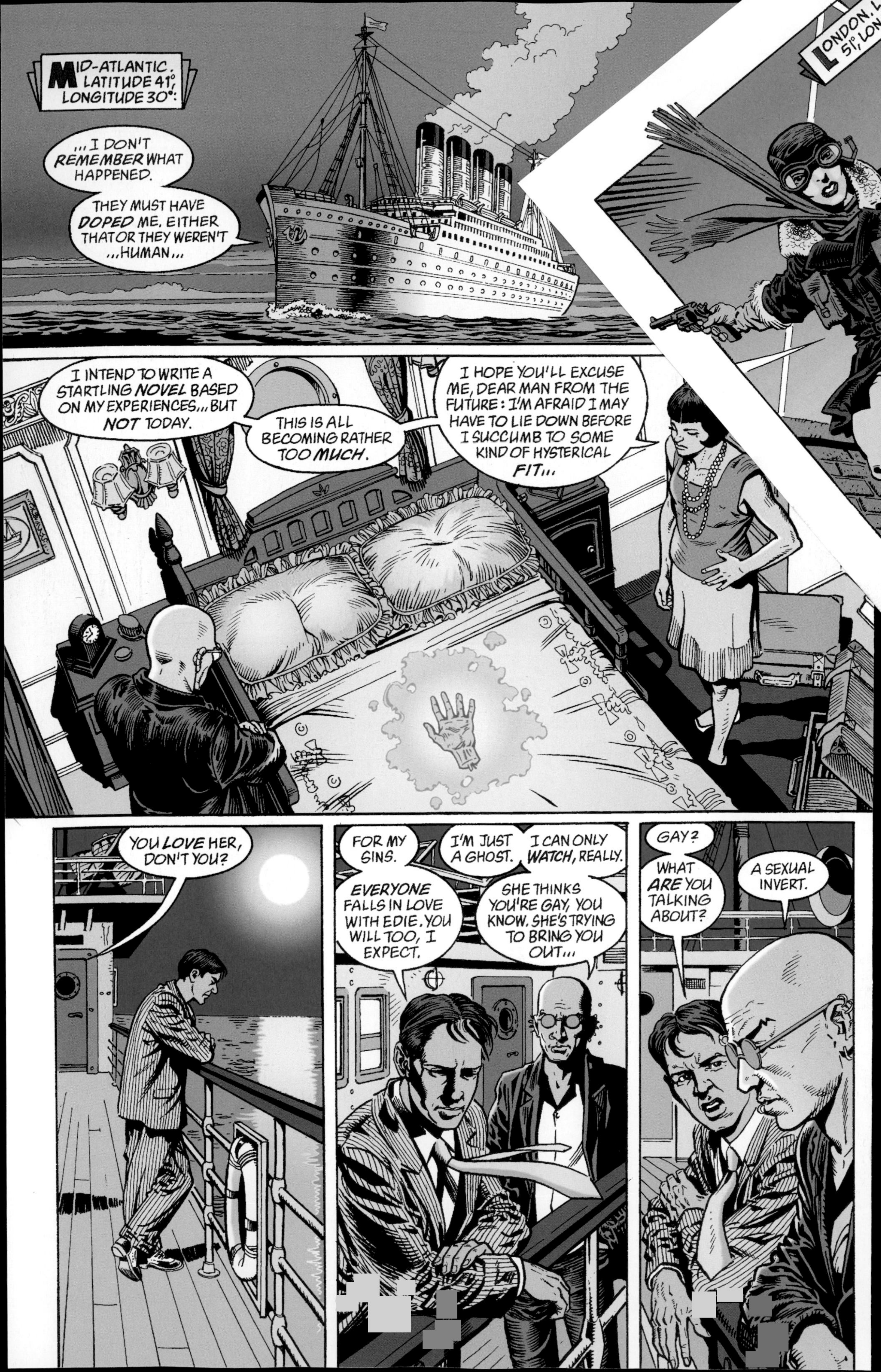
MID-ATLANTIC. LATITUDE 41° LONGITUDE 30°:
...I DON'T REMEMBER WHAT HAPPENED.
THEY MUST HAVE DOPED ME. EITHER THAT OR THEY WEREN'T ...HUMAN...
I INTEND TO WRITE A STARTLING NOVEL BASED ON MY EXPERIENCES... BUT NOT TODAY.
THIS IS ALL BECOMING RATHER TOO MUCH.
I HOPE YOU'LL EXCUSE ME, DEAR MAN FROM THE FUTURE: I'M AFRAID I MAY HAVE TO LIE DOWN BEFORE I SUCCUMB TO SOME KIND OF HYSTERICAL FIT...
YOU LOVE HER, DON'T YOU?
FOR MY SINS.
EVERYONE FALLS IN LOVE WITH EDIE. YOU WILL TOO, I EXPECT.
I'M JUST A GHOST.
I CAN ONLY WATCH, REALLY.
SHE THINKS YOU'RE GAY, YOU KNOW. SHE'S TRYING TO BRING YOU OUT...
GAY?
WHAT ARE YOU TALKING ABOUT?
A SEXUAL INVERT.

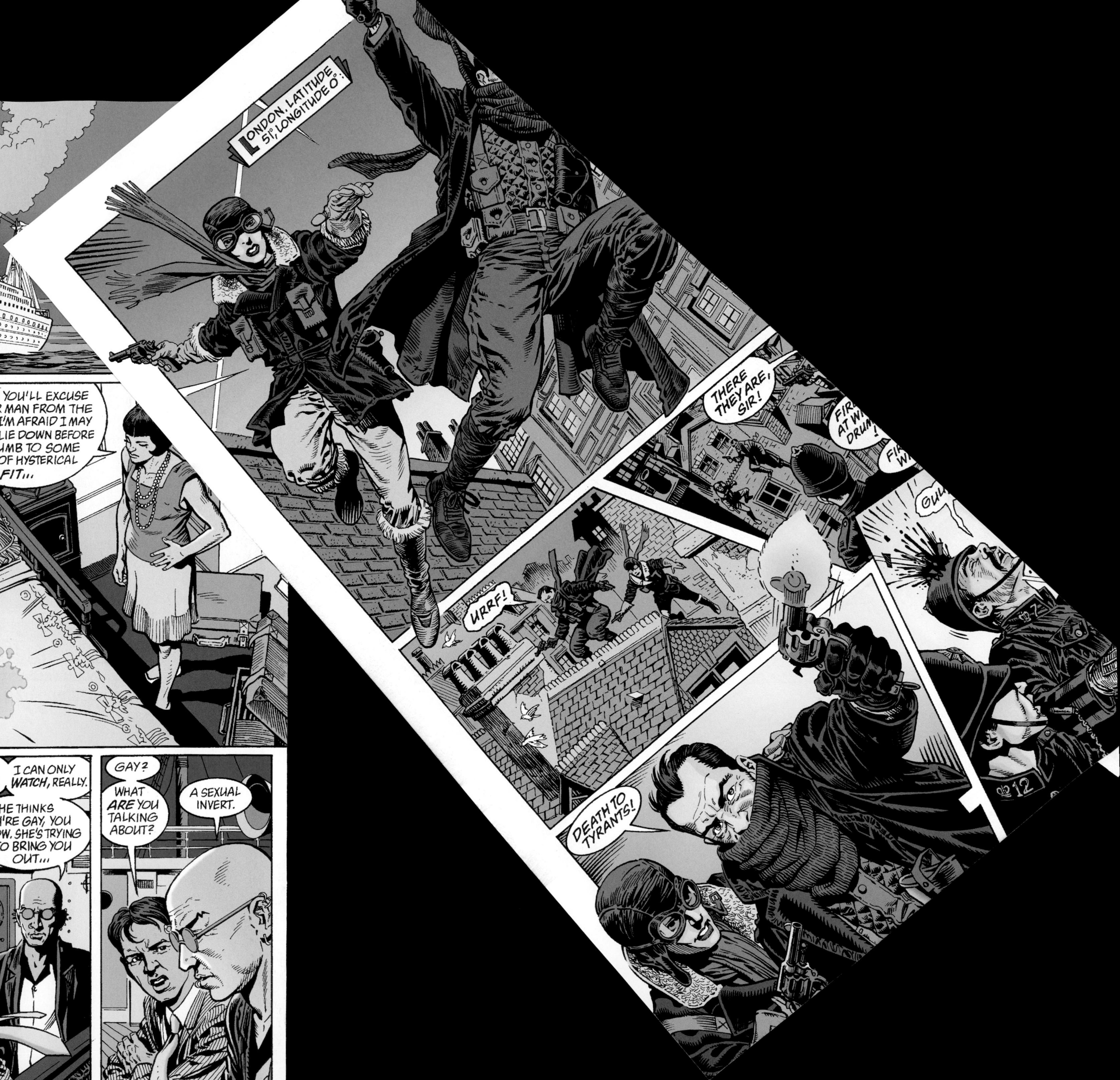
LONDON, LATITUDE 51°, LONGITUDE 0°.
THERE THEY ARE, SIR!
URRF!
DEATH TO TYRANTS!

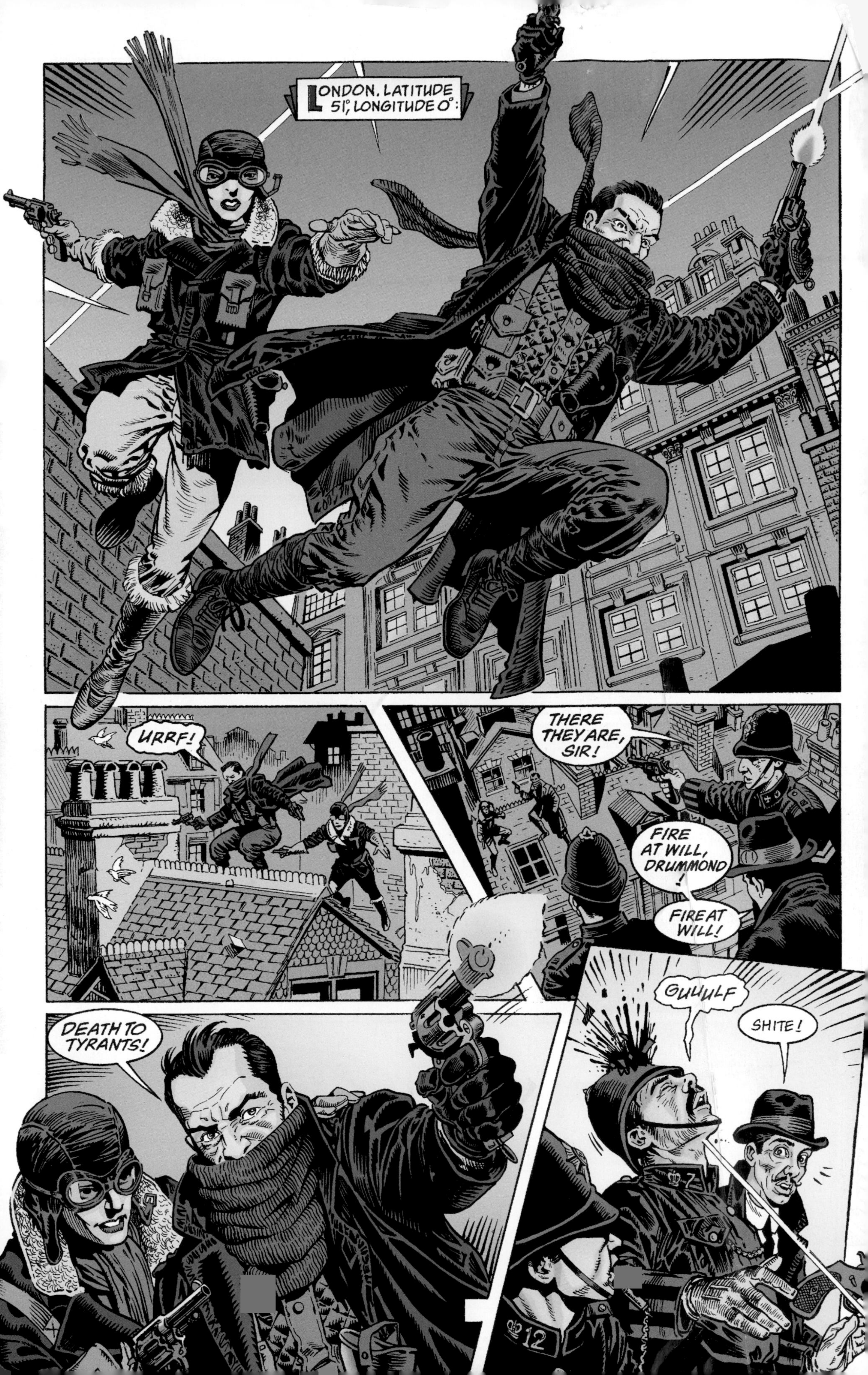
LONDON. LATITUDE 51°, LONGITUDE 0°:
URRF!
THERE THEY ARE, SIR!
FIRE AT WILL, DRUMMOND!
FIRE AT WILL!
DEATH TO TYRANTS!
GUUULF
SHITE!

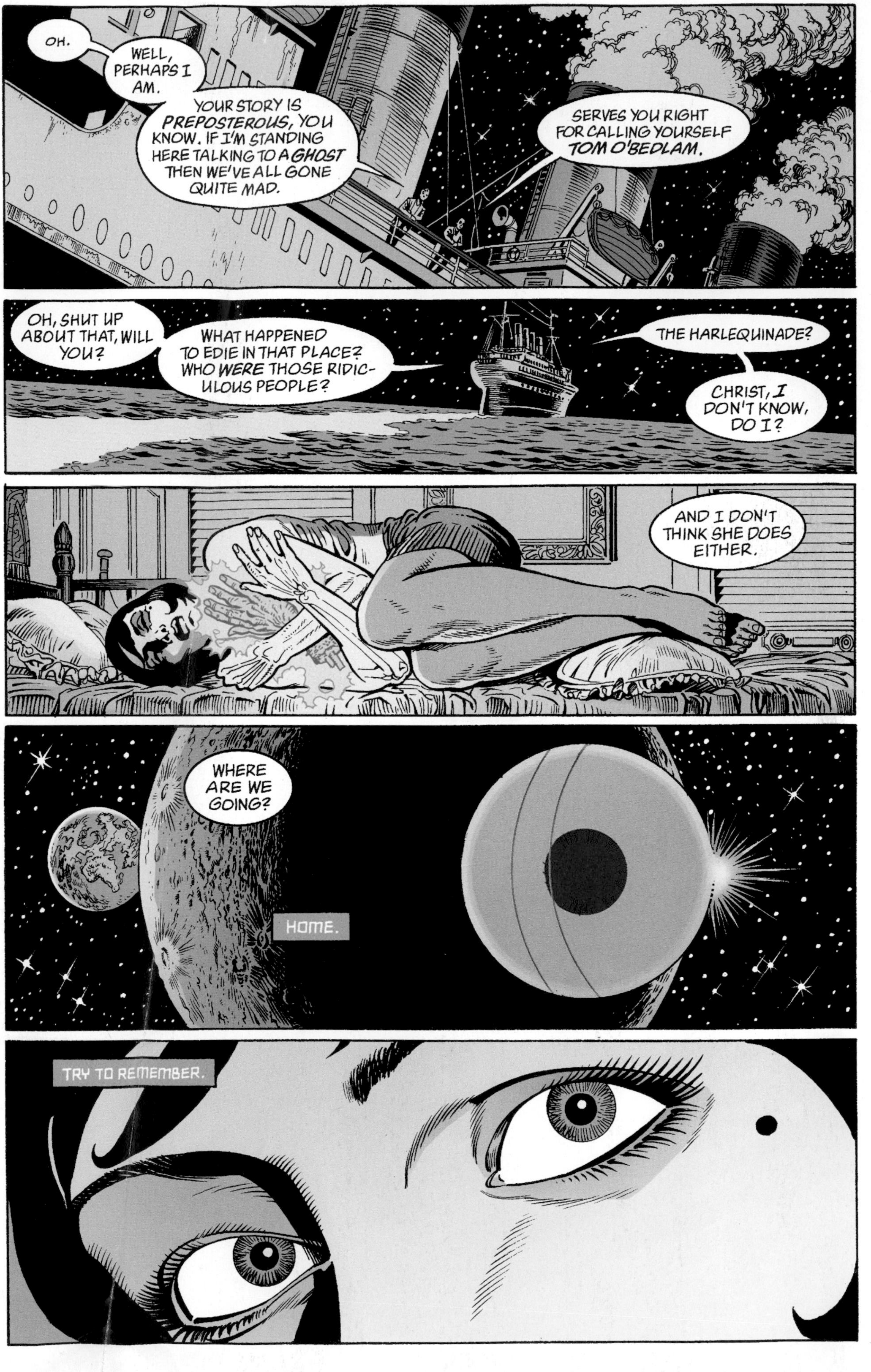
OH.
WELL, PERHAPS I AM.
YOUR STORY IS PREPOSTEROUS, YOU KNOW. IF I'M STANDING HERE TALKING TO A GHOST THEN WE'VE ALL GONE QUITE MAD.
SERVES YOU RIGHT FOR CALLING YOURSELF TOM O'BEDLAM.
OH, SHUT UP ABOUT THAT, WILL YOU?
WHAT HAPPENED TO EDIE IN THAT PLACE? WHO WERE THOSE RIDICULOUS PEOPLE?
THE HARLEQUINADE?
CHRIST, I DON'T KNOW, DO I?
AND I DON'T THINK SHE DOES EITHER.
WHERE ARE WE GOING?
HOME.
TRY TO REMEMBER.

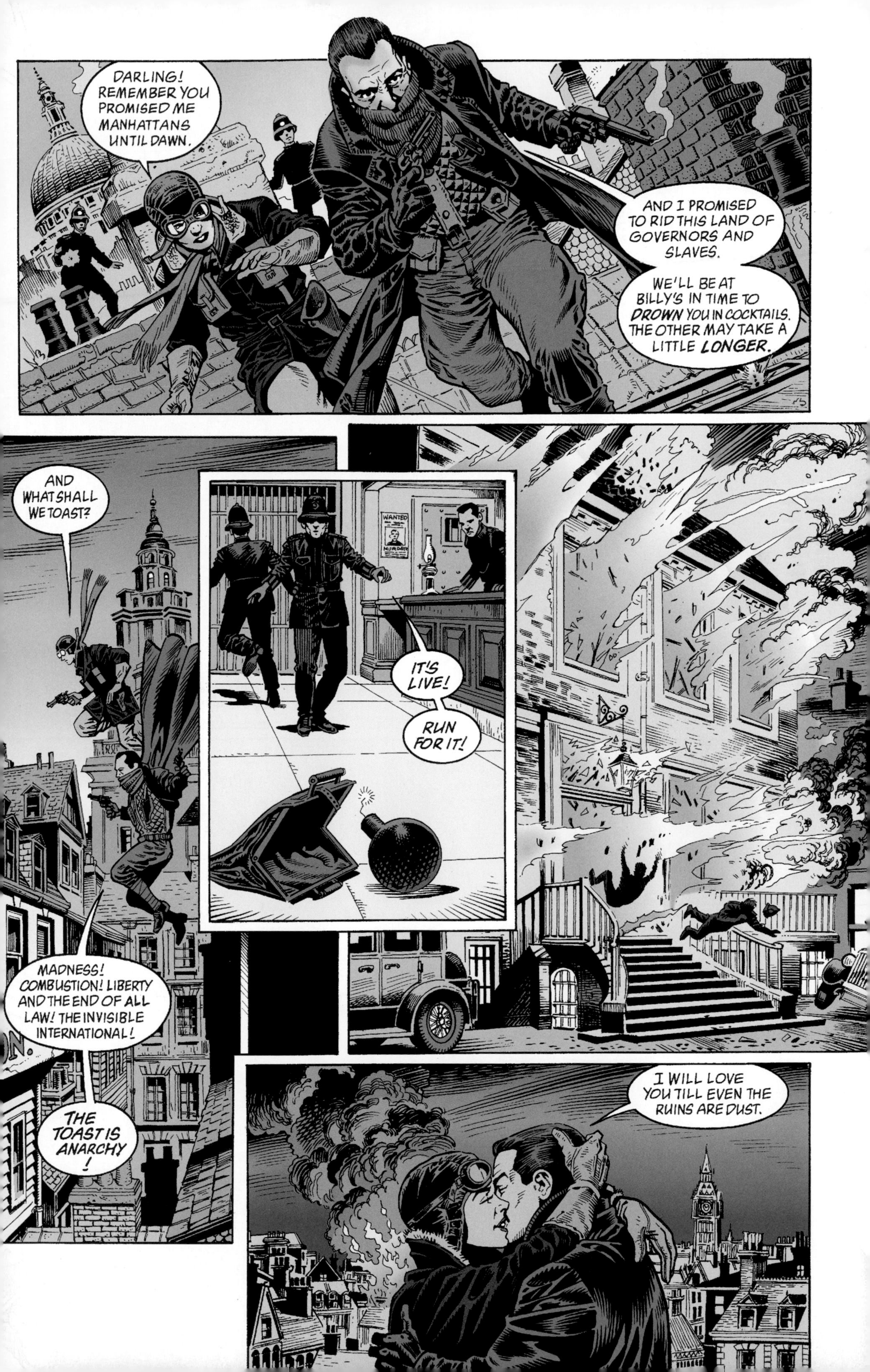
DARLING! REMEMBER YOU PROMISED ME MANHATTANS UNTIL DAWN.
AND I PROMISED TO RID THIS LAND OF GOVERNORS AND SLAVES.
WE'LL BE AT BILLY'S IN TIME TO DROWN YOU IN COCKTAILS. THE OTHER MAY TAKE A LITTLE LONGER.
AND WHAT SHALL WE TOAST?
WANTED
MURDER
IT'S LIVE!
RUN FOR IT!
MADNESS! COMBUSTION! LIBERTY AND THE END OF ALL LAW! THE INVISIBLE INTERNATIONAL!
THE TOAST IS ANARCHY!
I WILL LOVE YOU TILL EVEN THE RUINS ARE DUST.

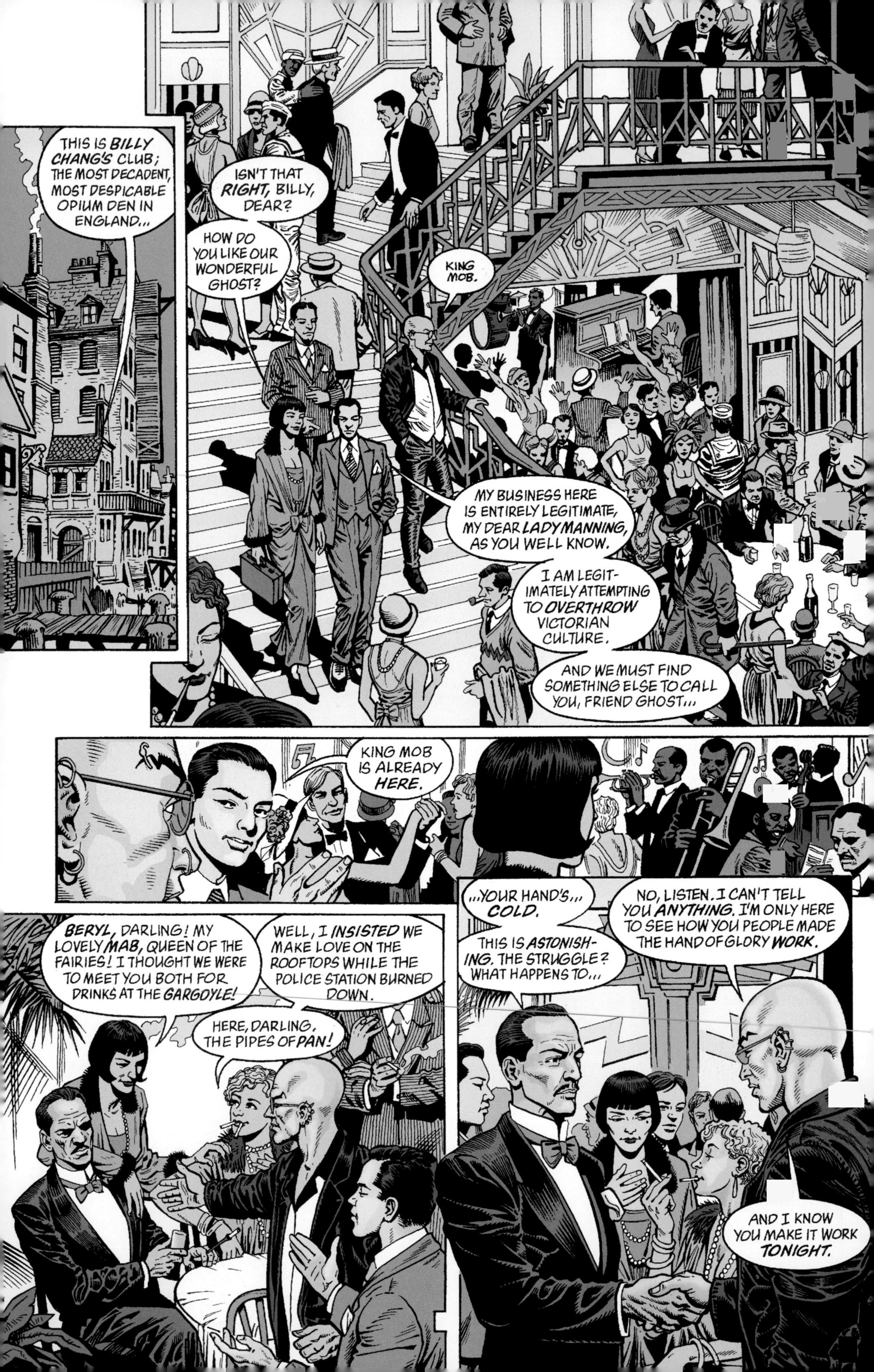
THIS IS BILLY CHANG'S CLUB; THE MOST DECADENT, MOST DESPICABLE OPIUM DEN IN ENGLAND...
ISN'T THAT RIGHT, BILLY, DEAR?
HOW DO YOU LIKE OUR WONDERFUL GHOST?
KING MOB.
MY BUSINESS HERE IS ENTIRELY LEGITIMATE, MY DEAR LADY MANNING, AS YOU WELL KNOW.
I AM LEGIT-IMATELY ATTEMPTING TO OVERTHROW VICTORIAN CULTURE.
AND WE MUST FIND SOMETHING ELSE TO CALL YOU, FRIEND GHOST...
KING MOB IS ALREADY HERE.
BERYL, DARLING! MY LOVELY MAB, QUEEN OF THE FAIRIES! I THOUGHT WE WERE TO MEET YOU BOTH FOR DRINKS AT THE GARGOYLE!
WELL, I INSISTED WE MAKE LOVE ON THE ROOFTOPS WHILE THE POLICE STATION BURNED DOWN.
HERE, DARLING, THE PIPES OF PAN!
...YOUR HAND'S... COLD.
THIS IS ASTONISH-ING. THE STRUGGLE? WHAT HAPPENS TO...
NO, LISTEN. I CAN'T TELL YOU ANYTHING. I'M ONLY HERE TO SEE HOW YOU PEOPLE MADE THE HAND OF GLORY WORK.
AND I KNOW YOU MAKE IT WORK TONIGHT.

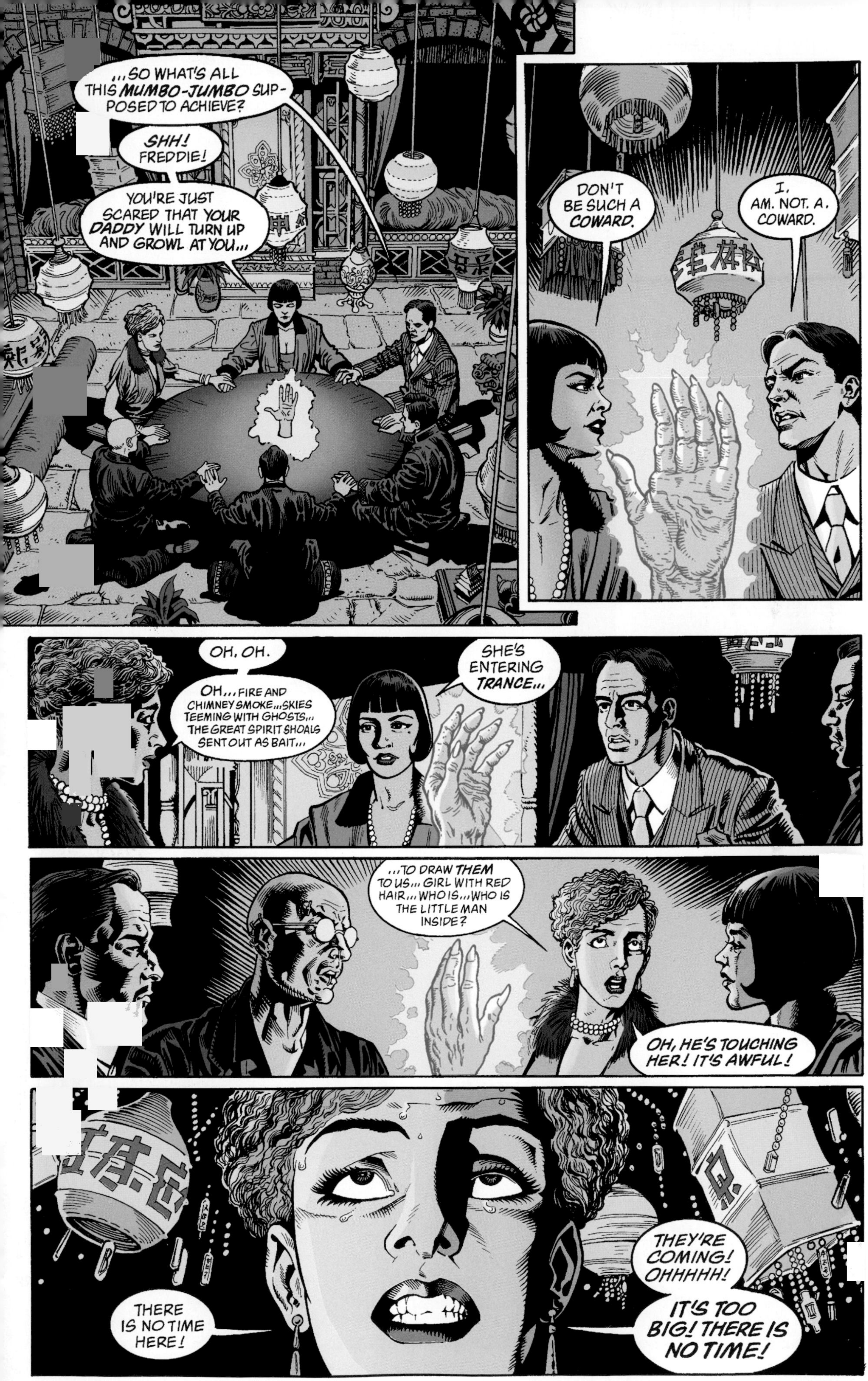
...SO WHAT'S ALL THIS MUMBO-JUMBO SUPPOSED TO ACHIEVE?
SHH! FREDDIE!
YOU'RE JUST SCARED THAT YOUR DADDY WILL TURN UP AND GROWL AT YOU...
DON'T BE SUCH A COWARD.
I. AM. NOT. A. COWARD.
OH, OH.
OH... FIRE AND CHIMNEY SMOKE... SKIES TEEMING WITH GHOSTS... THE GREAT SPIRIT SHOALS SENT OUT AS BAIT...
SHE'S ENTERING TRANCE...
...TO DRAW THEM TO US... GIRL WITH RED HAIR... WHO IS... WHO IS THE LITTLE MAN INSIDE?
OH, HE'S TOUCHING HER! IT'S AWFUL!
THERE IS NO TIME HERE!
THEY'RE COMING! OHHHHH!
IT'S TOO BIG! THERE IS NO TIME!

...GIRL WITH RED HAIR...?

THE FLAW! THE FRACTURE!

THE HOWLING DIAMOND!

THEY'RE COMING!

OH MY GOD.

STAY CALM.

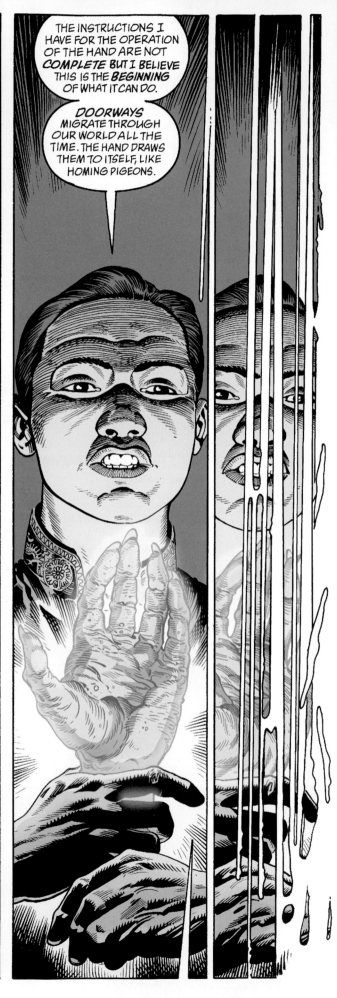

THE INSTRUCTIONS I HAVE FOR THE OPERATION OF THE HAND ARE NOT *COMPLETE* BUT I BELIEVE THIS IS THE *BEGINNING* OF WHAT IT CAN DO.

DOORWAYS MIGRATE THROUGH OUR WORLD ALL THE TIME. THE HAND DRAWS THEM TO ITSELF, LIKE HOMING PIGEONS.

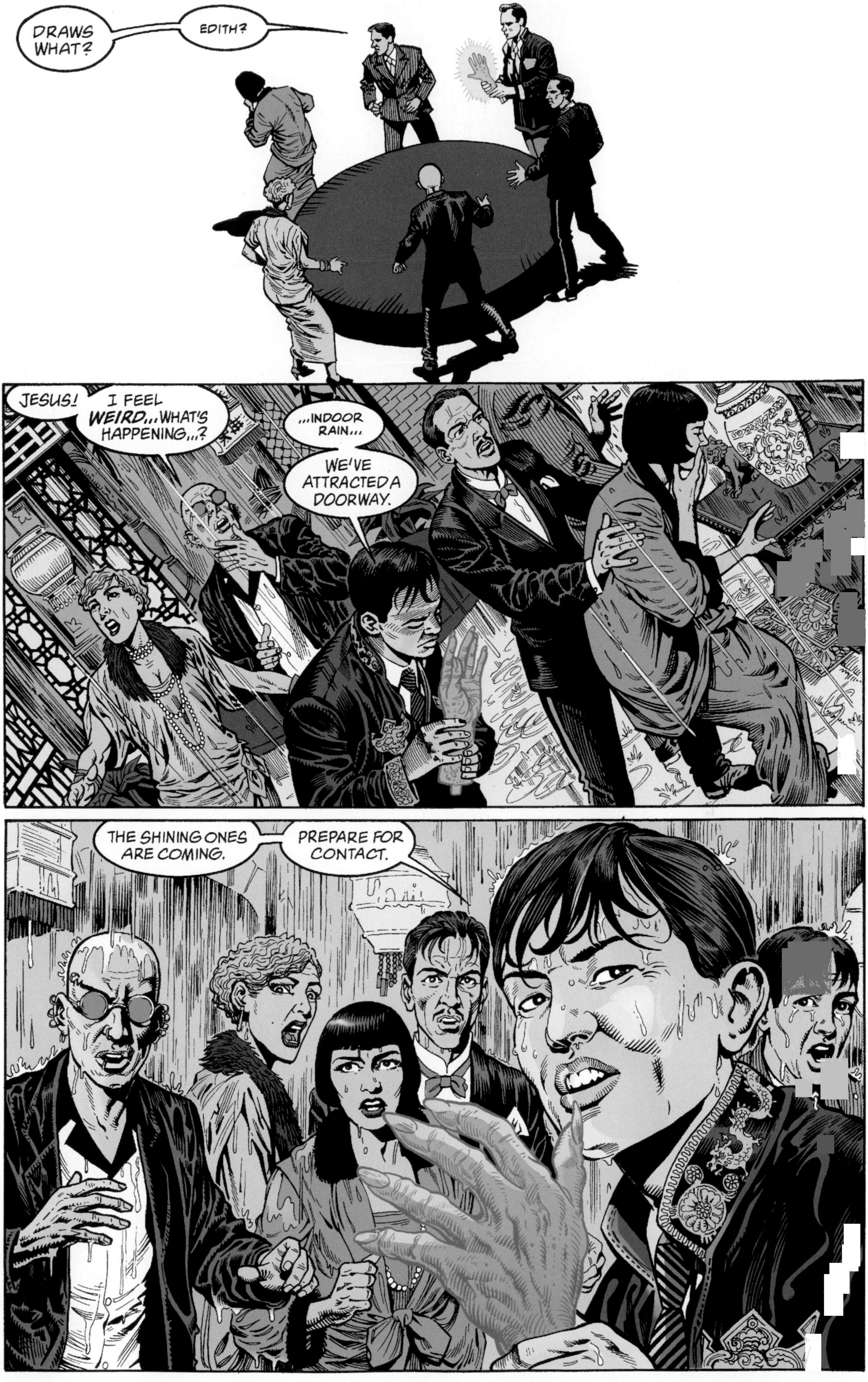
DRAWS WHAT?
EDITH?
JESUS!
I FEEL WEIRD... WHAT'S HAPPENING...?
...INDOOR RAIN...
WE'VE ATTRACTED A DOORWAY.
THE SHINING ONES ARE COMING.
PREPARE FOR CONTACT.

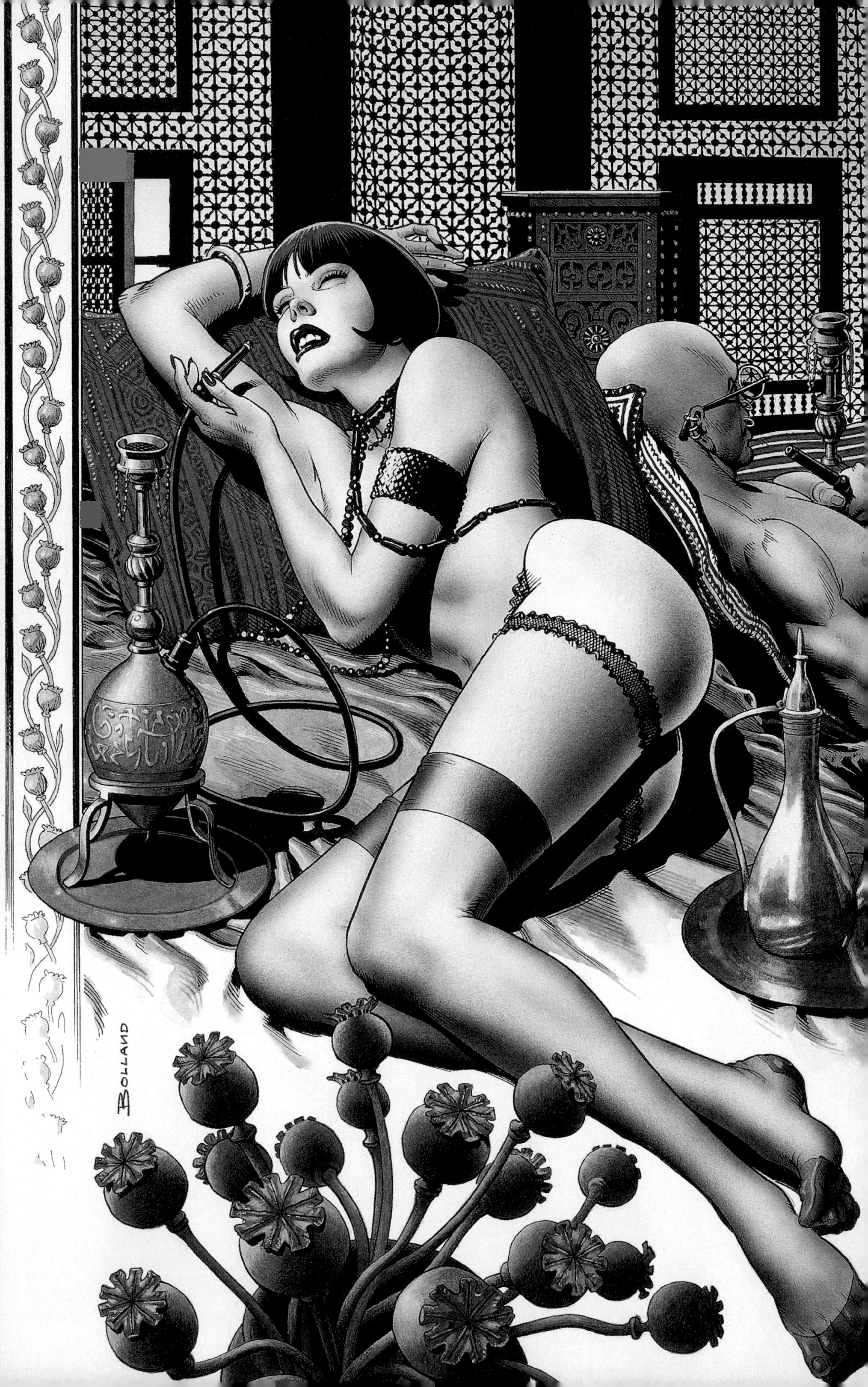
BOLLAND

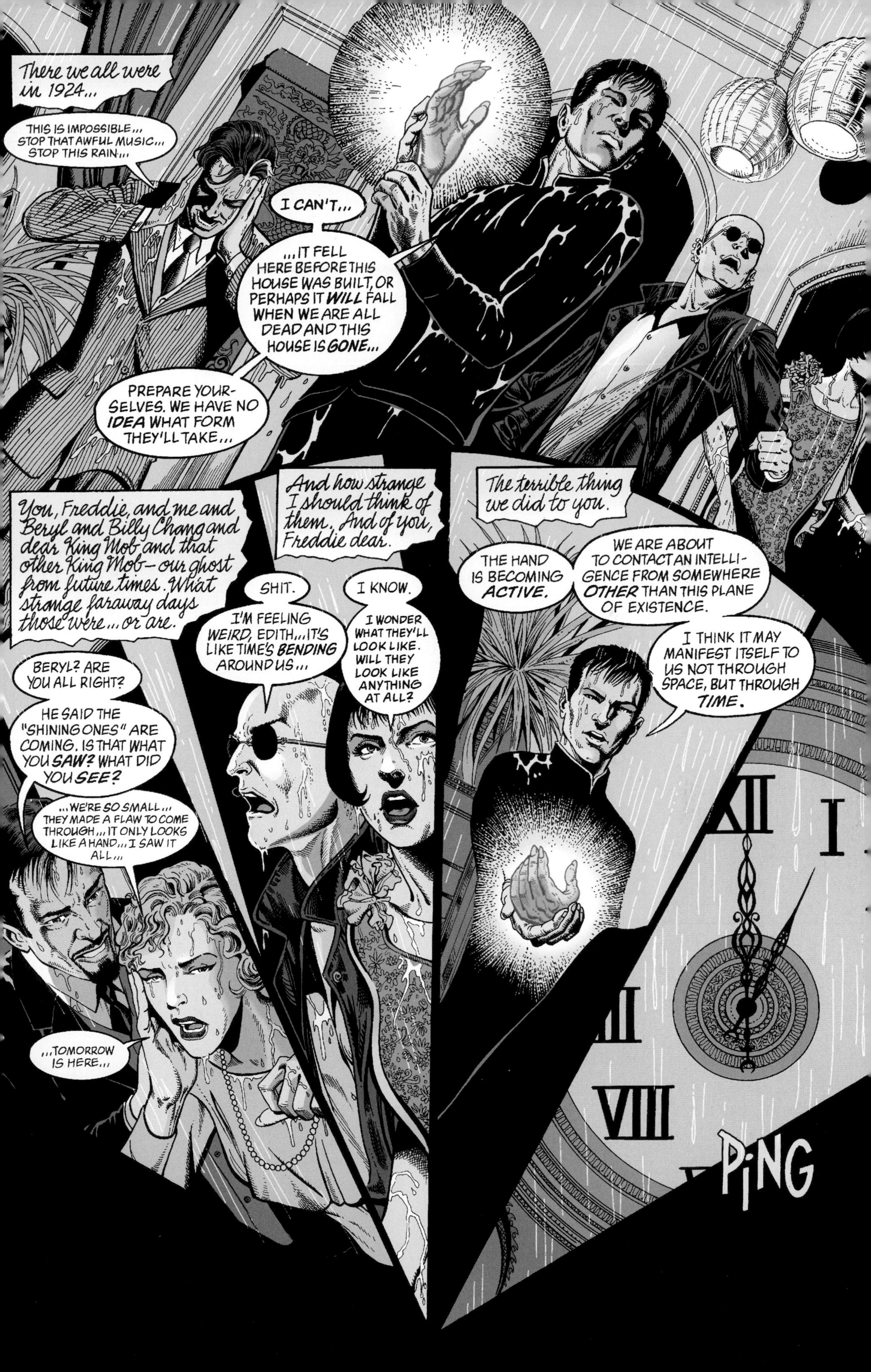
There we all were in 1924...
THIS IS IMPOSSIBLE... STOP THAT AWFUL MUSIC... STOP THIS RAIN...
I CAN'T...
...IT FELL HERE BEFORE THIS HOUSE WAS BUILT, OR PERHAPS IT WILL FALL WHEN WE ARE ALL DEAD AND THIS HOUSE IS GONE...
PREPARE YOURSELVES. WE HAVE NO IDEA WHAT FORM THEY'LL TAKE...
You, Freddie, and me and Beryl and Billy Chang and dear King Mob and that other King Mob—our ghost from future times. What strange faraway days those were... or are.
And how strange I should think of them. And of you, Freddie dear.
The terrible thing we did to you.
SHIT.
I'M FEELING WEIRD, EDITH... IT'S LIKE TIME'S BENDING AROUND US...
I KNOW.
I WONDER WHAT THEY'LL LOOK LIKE. WILL THEY LOOK LIKE ANYTHING AT ALL?
THE HAND IS BECOMING ACTIVE.
WE ARE ABOUT TO CONTACT AN INTELLIGENCE FROM SOMEWHERE OTHER THAN THIS PLANE OF EXISTENCE.
I THINK IT MAY MANIFEST ITSELF TO US NOT THROUGH SPACE, BUT THROUGH TIME.
BERYL? ARE YOU ALL RIGHT?
HE SAID THE "SHINING ONES" ARE COMING. IS THAT WHAT YOU SAW? WHAT DID YOU SEE?
...WE'RE SO SMALL... THEY MADE A FLAW TO COME THROUGH... IT ONLY LOOKS LIKE A HAND... I SAW IT ALL...
...TOMORROW IS HERE...
PING

SEN
SIT
IVE
CRI
MIN
ALS
part three
PARISIAN · PIERROT.

And through time it came.

Grant Morrison
WRITER

Phil Jimenez
PENCILLER

John Stokes
INKER

Daniel Vozzo
COLORIST

Heroic Age
COLOR SEPS

Todd Klein
LETTERER

Shelly Roeberg
EDITOR

The Invisibles
CREATED BY
GRANT MORRISON

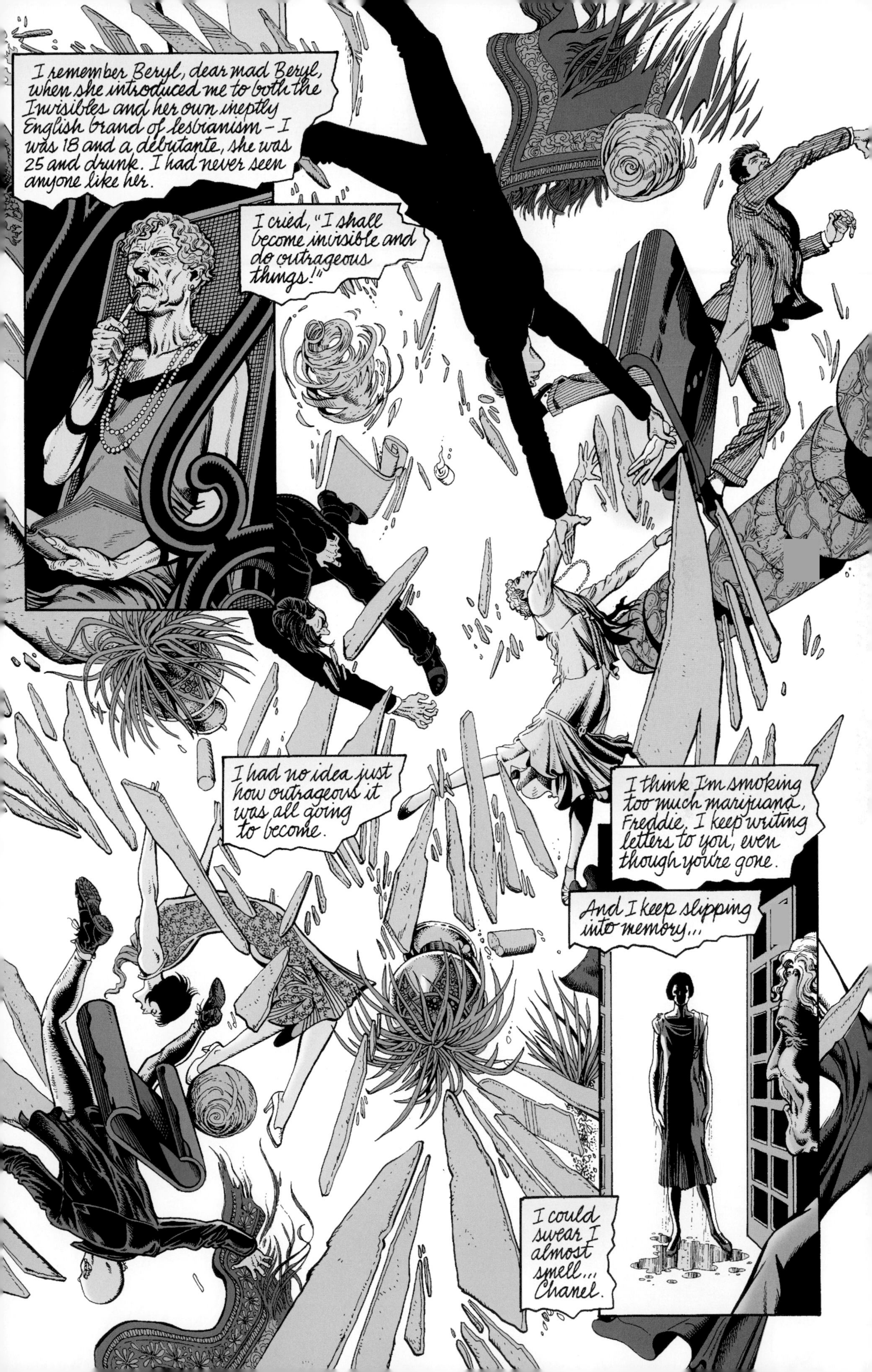
I remember Beryl, dear mad Beryl, when she introduced me to both the Invisibles and her own ineptly English brand of lesbianism — I was 18 and a debutante, she was 25 and drunk. I had never seen anyone like her.
I cried, "I shall become invisible and do outrageous things!"
I had no idea just how outrageous it was all going to become.
I think I'm smoking too much marijuana, Freddie. I keep writing letters to you, even though you're gone.
And I keep slipping into memory...
I could swear I almost smell... Chanel.

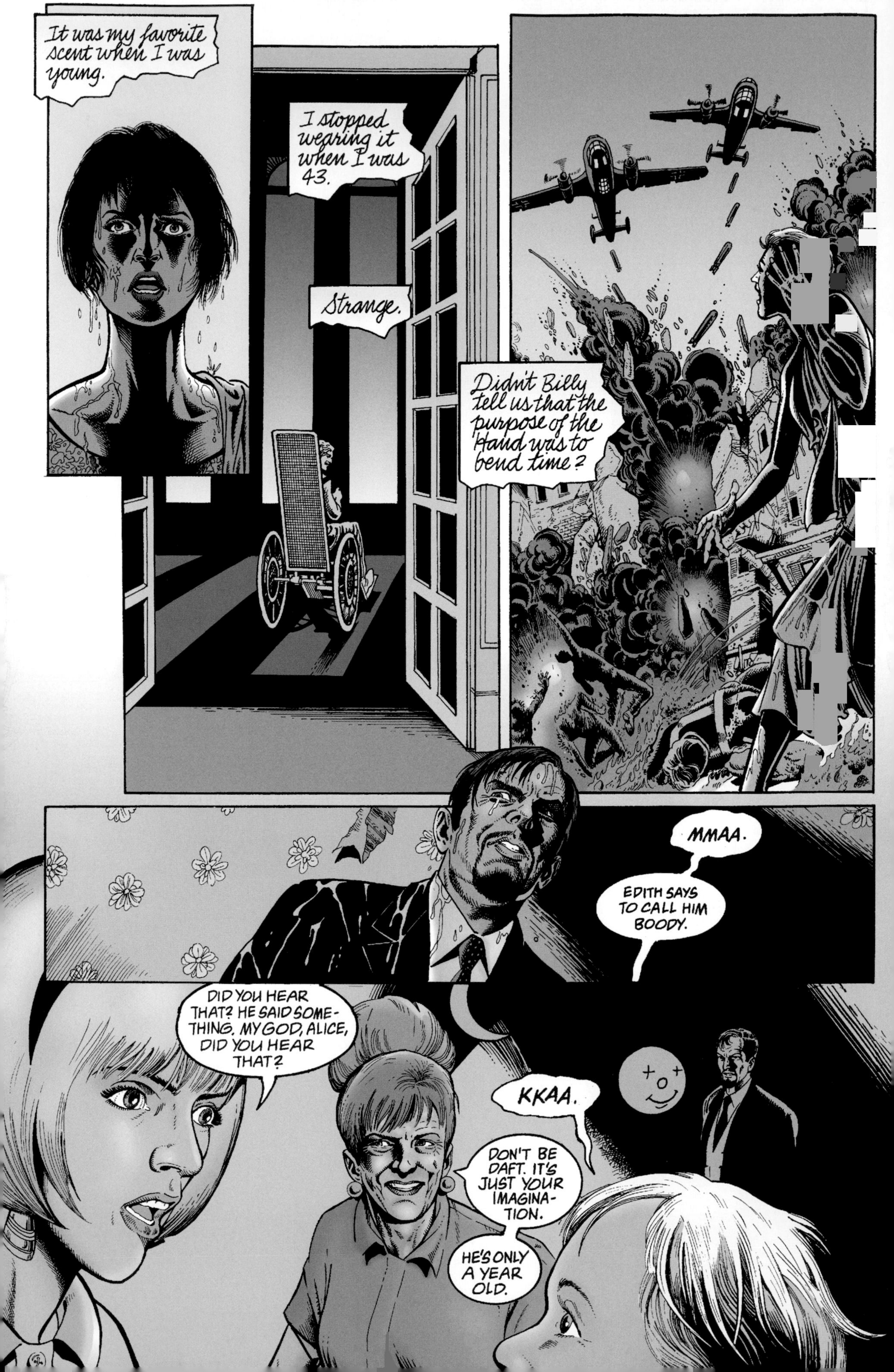
It was my favorite scent when I was young.
I stopped wearing it when I was 43.
Strange.
Didn't Billy tell us that the purpose of the Hand was to bend time?
MMAA.
EDITH SAYS TO CALL HIM BOODY.
DID YOU HEAR THAT? HE SAID SOMETHING. MY GOD, ALICE, DID YOU HEAR THAT?
KKAA.
DON'T BE DAFT. IT'S JUST YOUR IMAGINATION.
HE'S ONLY A YEAR OLD.

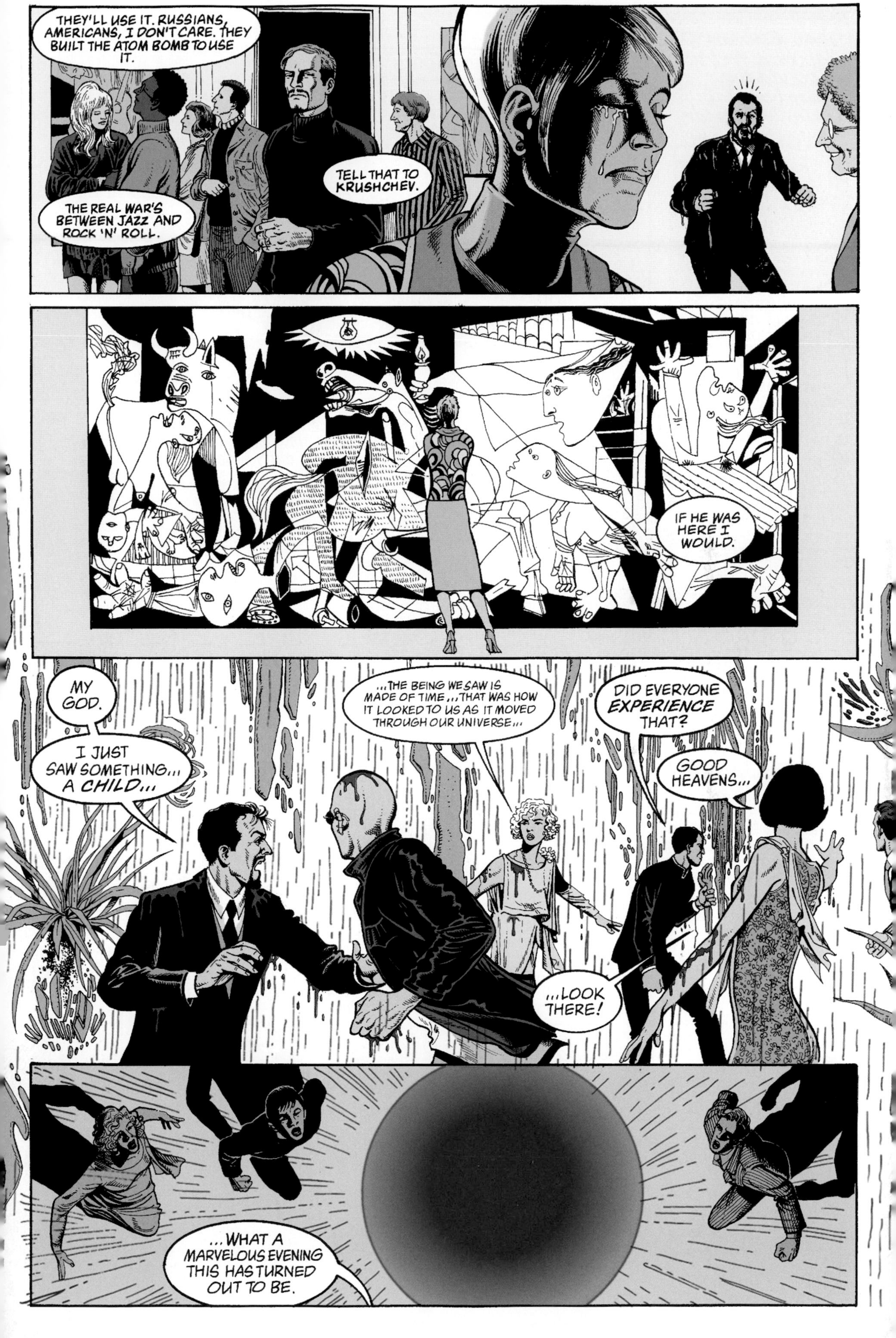

THEY'LL USE IT. RUSSIANS, AMERICANS, I DON'T CARE. THEY BUILT THE ATOM BOMB TO USE IT.
TELL THAT TO KRUSHCHEV.
THE REAL WAR'S BETWEEN JAZZ AND ROCK 'N' ROLL.
IF HE WAS HERE I WOULD.
MY GOD.
I JUST SAW SOMETHING... A CHILD...
...THE BEING WE SAW IS MADE OF TIME... THAT WAS HOW IT LOOKED TO US AS IT MOVED THROUGH OUR UNIVERSE...
DID EVERYONE EXPERIENCE THAT?
GOOD HEAVENS...
...LOOK THERE!
...WHAT A MARVELOUS EVENING THIS HAS TURNED OUT TO BE.

And then something happened. And no one could ever remember what, could they, Freddie?

Then it was the next day...

ST. DUNSTAN'S IN-THE-EAST.

ACCORDING TO BILLY, THIS IS THE BEST PLACE IN **LONDON** TO REV UP THE HAND. "TIME IS THIN AROUND ST. DUNSTAN'S," HE CLAIMS. HE CAN BE SO UTTERLY **POETIC** AT TIMES.

I DON'T FEEL **COMFORTABLE** WITH THIS AT ALL.

THINGS ARE **HAPPENING** AROUND THIS OBJECT...

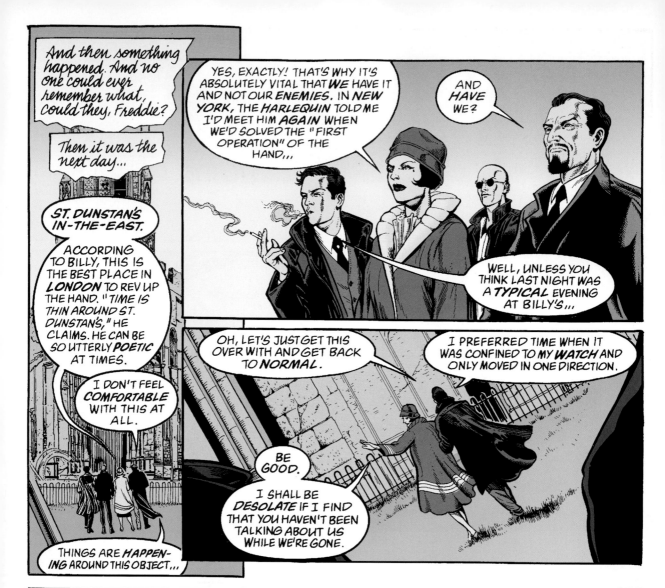

YES, EXACTLY! THAT'S WHY IT'S ABSOLUTELY VITAL THAT **WE** HAVE IT AND NOT OUR **ENEMIES.** IN **NEW YORK,** THE **HARLEQUIN** TOLD ME I'D MEET HIM **AGAIN** WHEN WE'D SOLVED THE "FIRST OPERATION" OF THE HAND...

AND **HAVE** WE?

WELL, UNLESS YOU THINK LAST NIGHT WAS A **TYPICAL** EVENING AT BILLY'S...

OH, LET'S JUST GET THIS OVER WITH AND GET BACK TO **NORMAL.**

I PREFERRED TIME WHEN IT WAS CONFINED TO MY **WATCH** AND ONLY MOVED IN ONE DIRECTION.

BE **GOOD.**

I SHALL BE **DESOLATE** IF I FIND THAT YOU HAVEN'T BEEN TALKING ABOUT US WHILE WE'RE GONE.

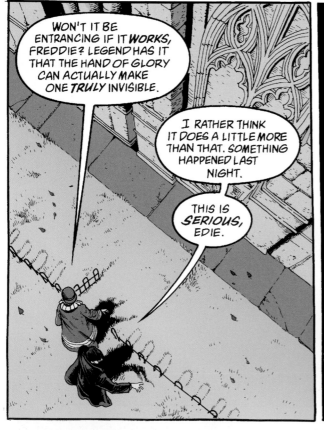

WON'T IT BE ENTRANCING IF IT **WORKS,** FREDDIE? LEGEND HAS IT THAT THE HAND OF GLORY CAN ACTUALLY MAKE ONE **TRULY** INVISIBLE.

I RATHER THINK IT DOES A LITTLE MORE THAN THAT. SOMETHING HAPPENED LAST NIGHT.

THIS IS **SERIOUS,** EDIE.

STOP FRETTING.

WE HAVE **PAN** AND **DIONYSUS** ON OUR SIDE, FREDDIE DEAR.

AND WE MUST BE **INCANDESCENT** WHEN WE FACE THE HARLEQUIN. ANYTHING LESS WILL BE FATAL.

THAT'S EASY FOR YOU TO SAY.

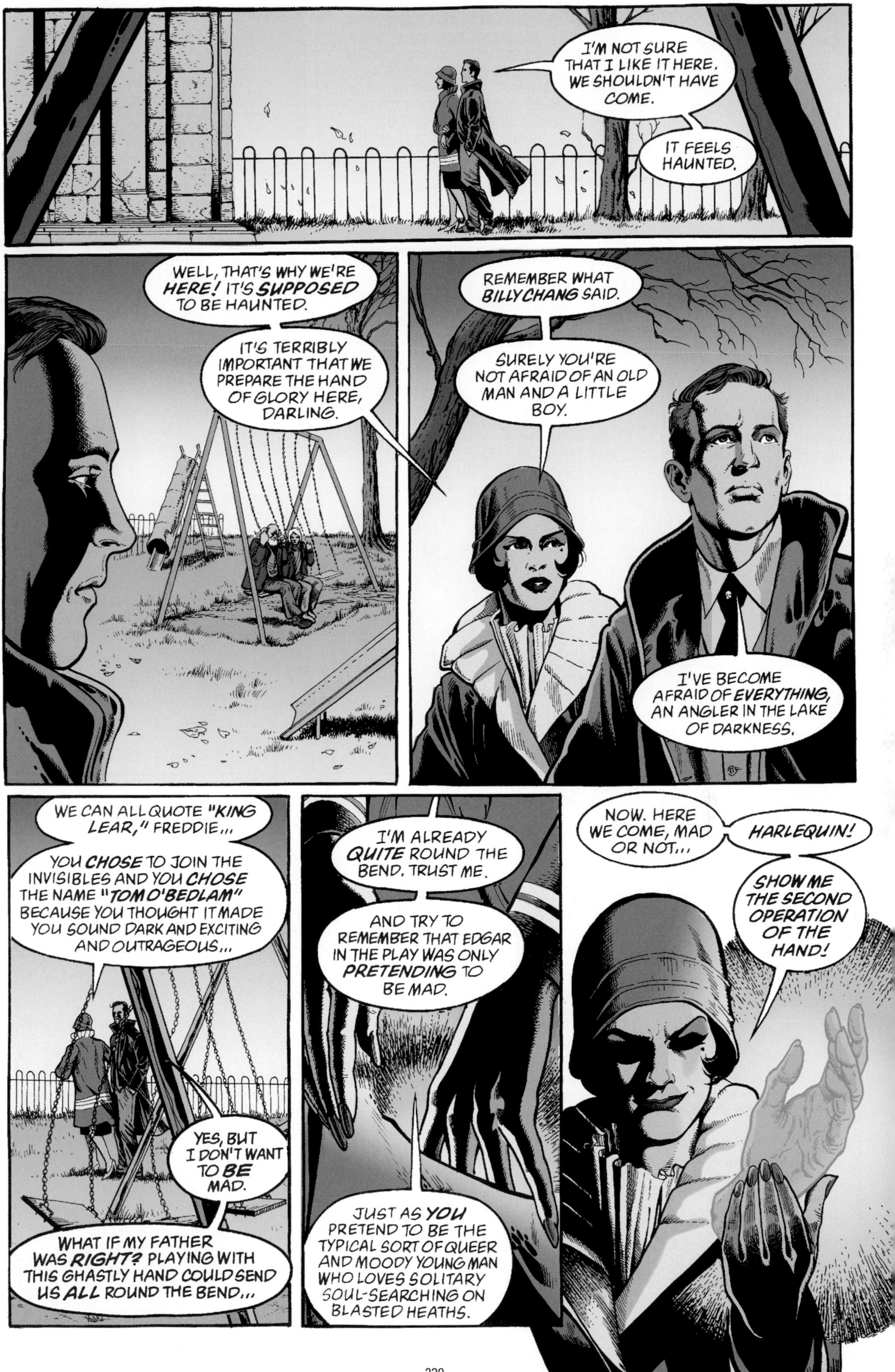
I'M NOT SURE THAT I LIKE IT HERE. WE SHOULDN'T HAVE COME.
IT FEELS HAUNTED.
WELL, THAT'S WHY WE'RE HERE! IT'S SUPPOSED TO BE HAUNTED.
IT'S TERRIBLY IMPORTANT THAT WE PREPARE THE HAND OF GLORY HERE, DARLING.
REMEMBER WHAT BILLY CHANG SAID.
SURELY YOU'RE NOT AFRAID OF AN OLD MAN AND A LITTLE BOY.
I'VE BECOME AFRAID OF EVERYTHING, AN ANGLER IN THE LAKE OF DARKNESS.
WE CAN ALL QUOTE "KING LEAR," FREDDIE...
YOU CHOSE TO JOIN THE INVISIBLES AND YOU CHOSE THE NAME "TOM O'BEDLAM" BECAUSE YOU THOUGHT IT MADE YOU SOUND DARK AND EXCITING AND OUTRAGEOUS...
YES, BUT I DON'T WANT TO BE MAD.
WHAT IF MY FATHER WAS RIGHT? PLAYING WITH THIS GHASTLY HAND COULD SEND US ALL ROUND THE BEND...
I'M ALREADY QUITE ROUND THE BEND. TRUST ME.
AND TRY TO REMEMBER THAT EDGAR IN THE PLAY WAS ONLY PRETENDING TO BE MAD.
JUST AS YOU PRETEND TO BE THE TYPICAL SORT OF QUEER AND MOODY YOUNG MAN WHO LOVES SOLITARY SOUL-SEARCHING ON BLASTED HEATHS.
NOW. HERE WE COME, MAD OR NOT...
HARLEQUIN!
SHOW ME THE SECOND OPERATION OF THE HAND!

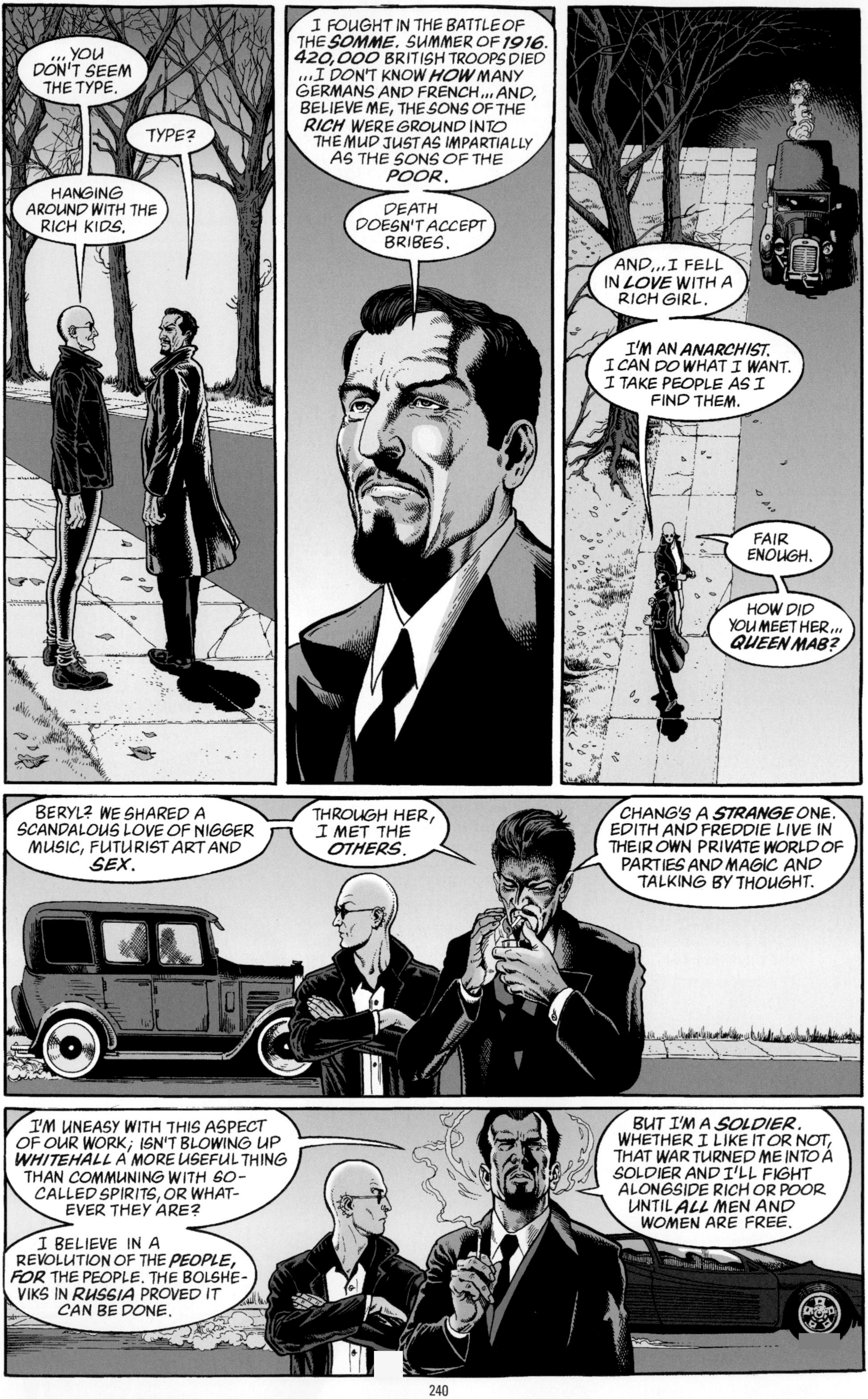
...YOU DON'T SEEM THE TYPE.
TYPE?
HANGING AROUND WITH THE RICH KIDS.
I FOUGHT IN THE BATTLE OF THE SOMME. SUMMER OF 1916. 420,000 BRITISH TROOPS DIED ...I DON'T KNOW HOW MANY GERMANS AND FRENCH... AND, BELIEVE ME, THE SONS OF THE RICH WERE GROUND INTO THE MUD JUST AS IMPARTIALLY AS THE SONS OF THE POOR.
DEATH DOESN'T ACCEPT BRIBES.
AND... I FELL IN LOVE WITH A RICH GIRL.
I'M AN ANARCHIST. I CAN DO WHAT I WANT. I TAKE PEOPLE AS I FIND THEM.
FAIR ENOUGH.
HOW DID YOU MEET HER... QUEEN MAB?
BERYL? WE SHARED A SCANDALOUS LOVE OF NIGGER MUSIC, FUTURIST ART AND SEX.
THROUGH HER, I MET THE OTHERS.
CHANG'S A STRANGE ONE. EDITH AND FREDDIE LIVE IN THEIR OWN PRIVATE WORLD OF PARTIES AND MAGIC AND TALKING BY THOUGHT.
I'M UNEASY WITH THIS ASPECT OF OUR WORK; ISN'T BLOWING UP WHITEHALL A MORE USEFUL THING THAN COMMUNING WITH SO-CALLED SPIRITS, OR WHAT-EVER THEY ARE?
I BELIEVE IN A REVOLUTION OF THE PEOPLE, FOR THE PEOPLE. THE BOLSHE-VIKS IN RUSSIA PROVED IT CAN BE DONE.
BUT I'M A SOLDIER. WHETHER I LIKE IT OR NOT, THAT WAR TURNED ME INTO A SOLDIER AND I'LL FIGHT ALONGSIDE RICH OR POOR UNTIL ALL MEN AND WOMEN ARE FREE.

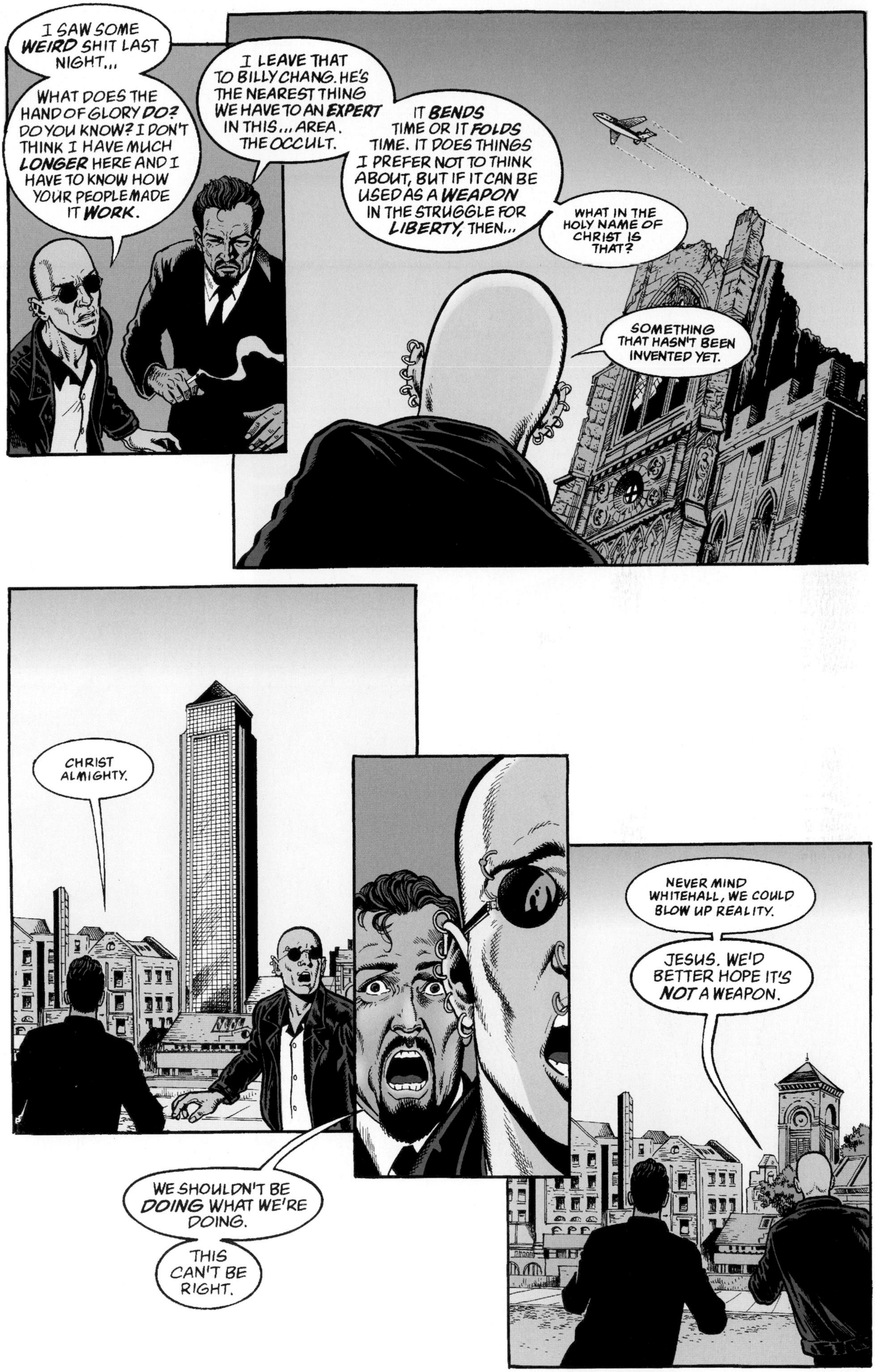
I SAW SOME WEIRD SHIT LAST NIGHT...
WHAT DOES THE HAND OF GLORY DO? DO YOU KNOW? I DON'T THINK I HAVE MUCH LONGER HERE AND I HAVE TO KNOW HOW YOUR PEOPLE MADE IT WORK.
I LEAVE THAT TO BILLY CHANG. HE'S THE NEAREST THING WE HAVE TO AN EXPERT IN THIS... AREA. THE OCCULT.
IT BENDS TIME OR IT FOLDS TIME. IT DOES THINGS I PREFER NOT TO THINK ABOUT, BUT IF IT CAN BE USED AS A WEAPON IN THE STRUGGLE FOR LIBERTY, THEN...
WHAT IN THE HOLY NAME OF CHRIST IS THAT?
SOMETHING THAT HASN'T BEEN INVENTED YET.
CHRIST ALMIGHTY.
WE SHOULDN'T BE DOING WHAT WE'RE DOING.
THIS CAN'T BE RIGHT.
NEVER MIND WHITEHALL, WE COULD BLOW UP REALITY.
JESUS. WE'D BETTER HOPE IT'S NOT A WEAPON.

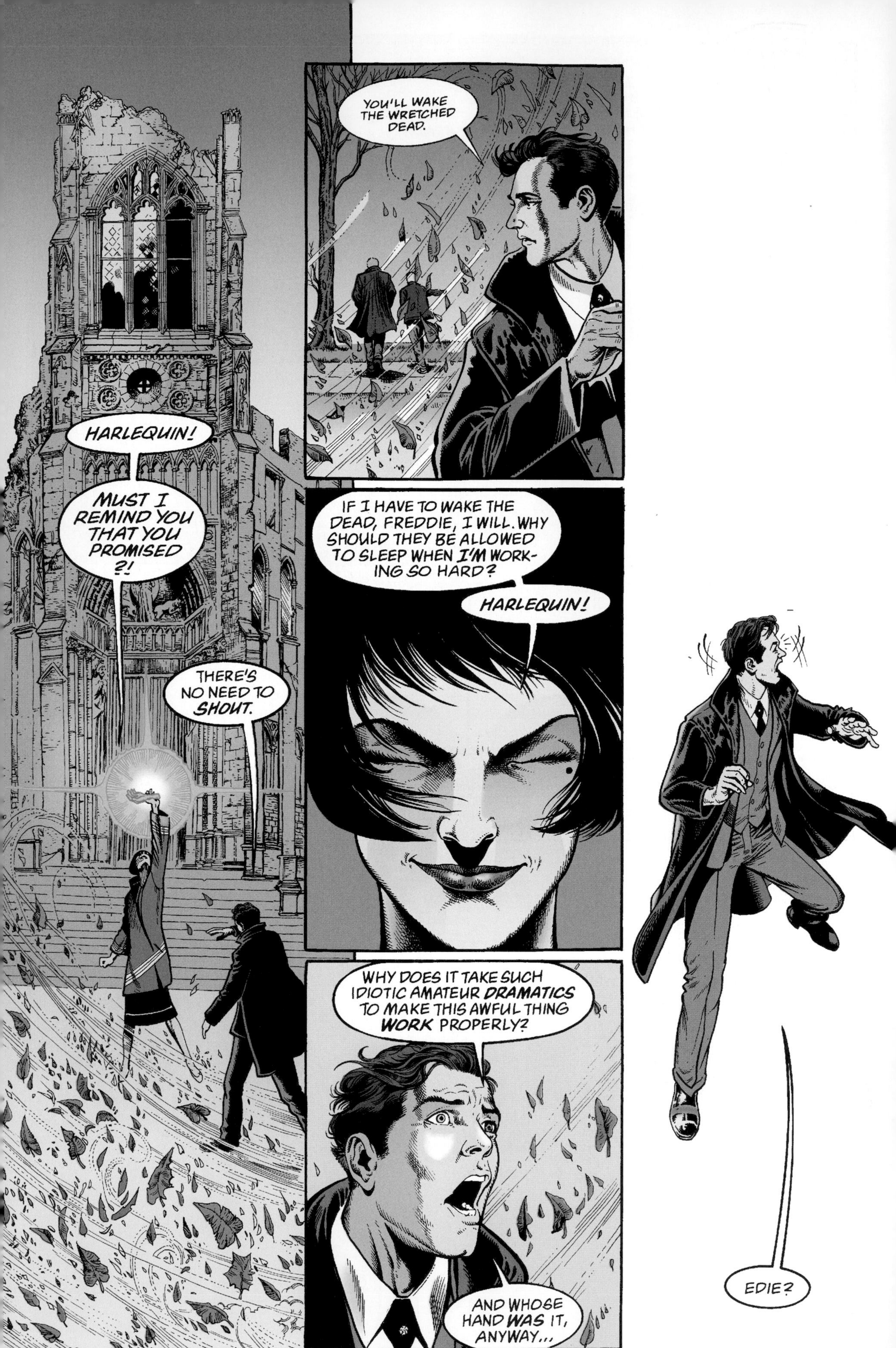
YOU'LL WAKE THE WRETCHED DEAD.
HARLEQUIN!
MUST I REMIND YOU THAT YOU PROMISED ?!
THERE'S NO NEED TO SHOUT.
IF I HAVE TO WAKE THE DEAD, FREDDIE, I WILL. WHY SHOULD THEY BE ALLOWED TO SLEEP WHEN I'M WORKING SO HARD?
HARLEQUIN!
WHY DOES IT TAKE SUCH IDIOTIC AMATEUR DRAMATICS TO MAKE THIS AWFUL THING WORK PROPERLY?
AND WHOSE HAND WAS IT, ANYWAY...
EDIE?

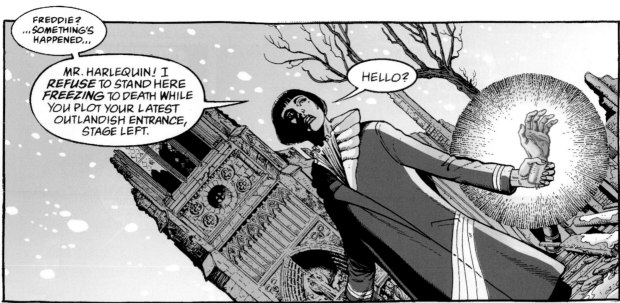

FREDDIE? ...SOMETHING'S HAPPENED...

MR. HARLEQUIN! I *REFUSE* TO STAND HERE *FREEZING* TO DEATH WHILE YOU PLOT YOUR LATEST OUTLANDISH ENTRANCE, STAGE LEFT.

HELLO?

IS THERE SOMEONE...?

SHOW YOUR *FACE*...

YOU COULDN'T LOOK AT MY FACE.

EEEEEEE!

EDIE!

...FREDDIE...

...HOW CAN WE BE IN SO MANY PLACES AT ONCE...?

243

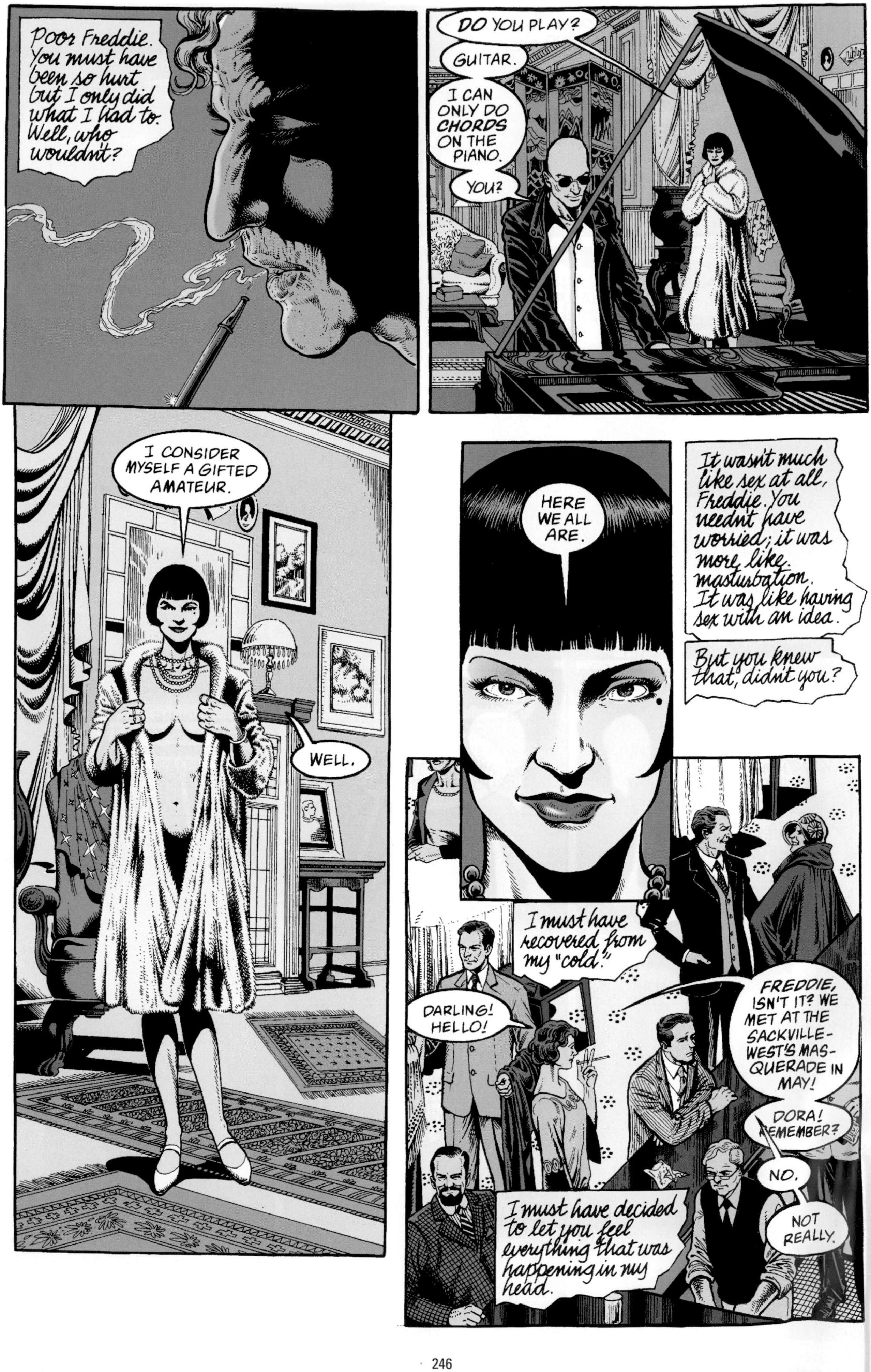
Poor Freddie. You must have been so hurt but I only did what I had to. Well, who wouldn't?
DO YOU PLAY?
GUITAR.
I CAN ONLY DO CHORDS ON THE PIANO.
YOU?
I CONSIDER MYSELF A GIFTED AMATEUR.
WELL.
HERE WE ALL ARE.
It wasn't much like sex at all, Freddie. You needn't have worried; it was more like masturbation. It was like having sex with an idea.
But you knew that, didn't you?
I must have recovered from my "cold."
DARLING! HELLO!
FREDDIE, ISN'T IT? WE MET AT THE SACKVILLE-WEST'S MAS-QUERADE IN MAY!
DORA! REMEMBER?
NO.
NOT REALLY.
I must have decided to let you feel everything that was happening in my head.

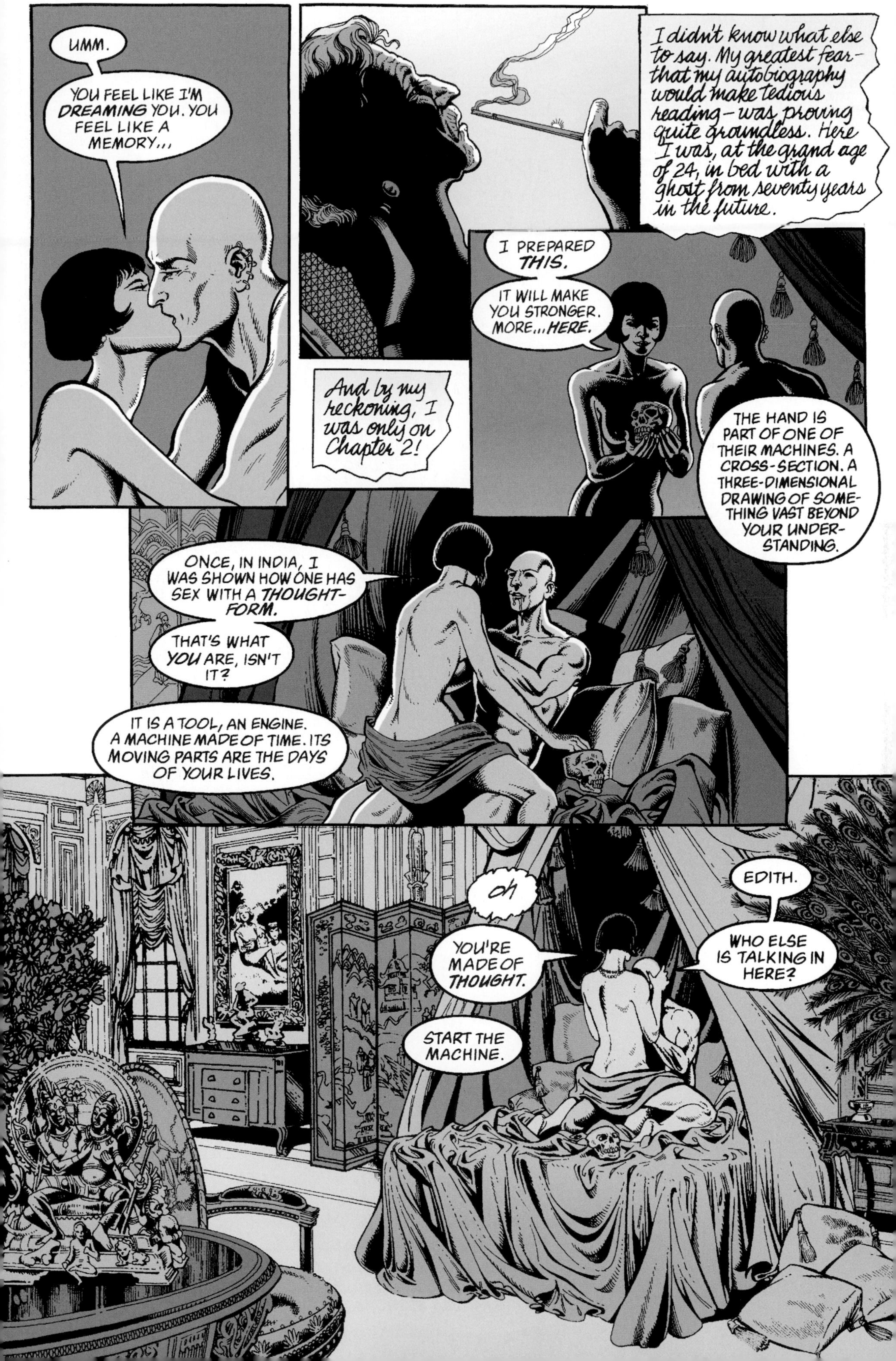
UMM.
YOU FEEL LIKE I'M DREAMING YOU. YOU FEEL LIKE A MEMORY...
I didn't know what else to say. My greatest fear--that my autobiography would make tedious reading--was proving quite groundless. Here I was, at the grand age of 24, in bed with a ghost from seventy years in the future.
And by my reckoning, I was only on Chapter 2!
I PREPARED THIS.
IT WILL MAKE YOU STRONGER. MORE... HERE.
THE HAND IS PART OF ONE OF THEIR MACHINES. A CROSS-SECTION. A THREE-DIMENSIONAL DRAWING OF SOMETHING VAST BEYOND YOUR UNDERSTANDING.
ONCE, IN INDIA, I WAS SHOWN HOW ONE HAS SEX WITH A THOUGHT-FORM.
THAT'S WHAT YOU ARE, ISN'T IT?
IT IS A TOOL, AN ENGINE. A MACHINE MADE OF TIME. ITS MOVING PARTS ARE THE DAYS OF YOUR LIVES.
oh
YOU'RE MADE OF THOUGHT.
START THE MACHINE.
EDITH.
WHO ELSE IS TALKING IN HERE?

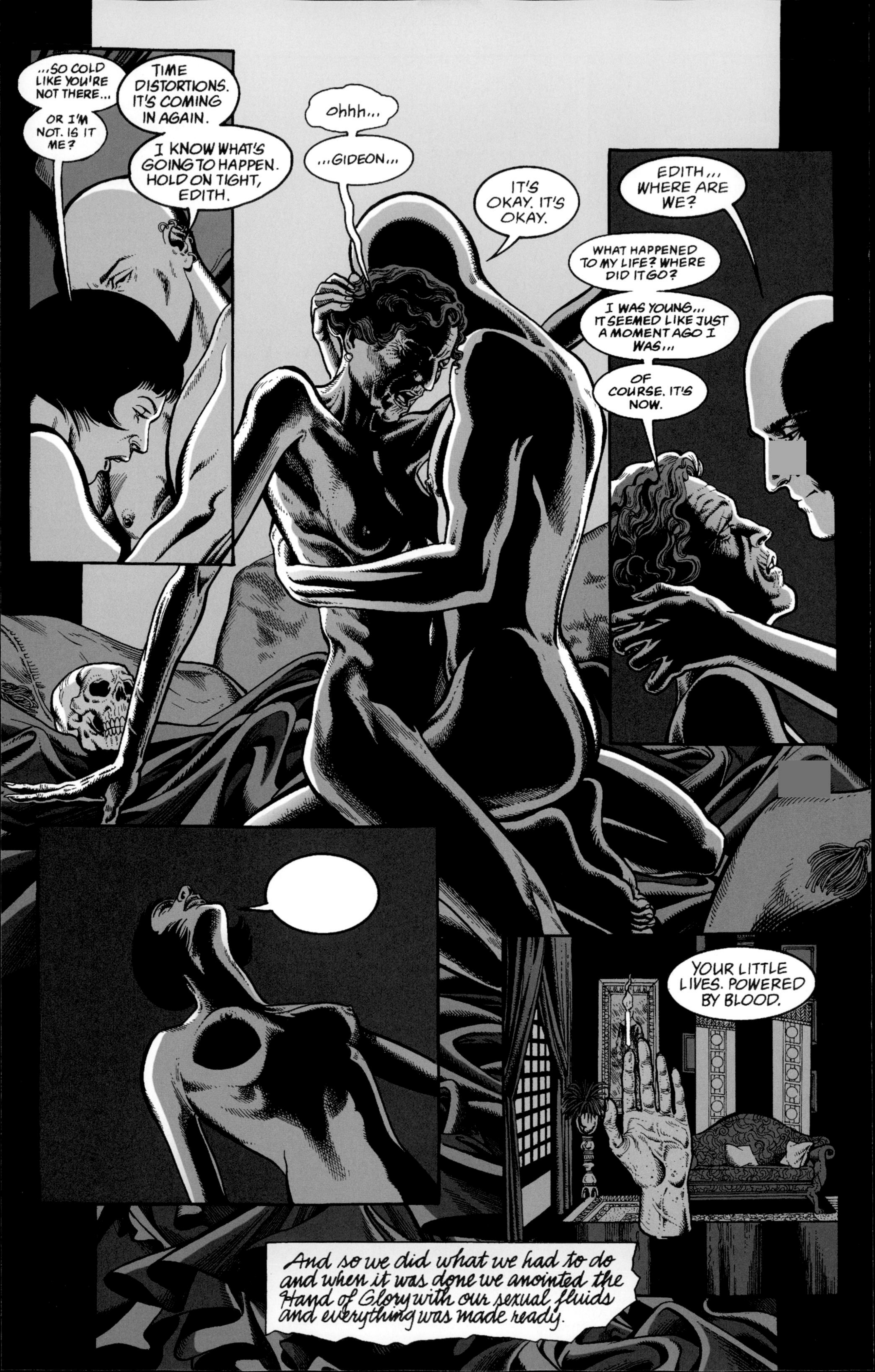
...SO COLD LIKE YOU'RE NOT THERE...
OR I'M NOT. IS IT ME?
TIME DISTORTIONS. IT'S COMING IN AGAIN.
I KNOW WHAT'S GOING TO HAPPEN. HOLD ON TIGHT, EDITH.
Ohhh...
...GIDEON...
IT'S OKAY. IT'S OKAY.
EDITH... WHERE ARE WE?
WHAT HAPPENED TO MY LIFE? WHERE DID IT GO?
I WAS YOUNG... IT SEEMED LIKE JUST A MOMENT AGO I WAS...
OF COURSE. IT'S NOW.
YOUR LITTLE LIVES. POWERED BY BLOOD.
And so we did what we had to do and when it was done we anointed the Hand of Glory with our sexual fluids and everything was made ready.

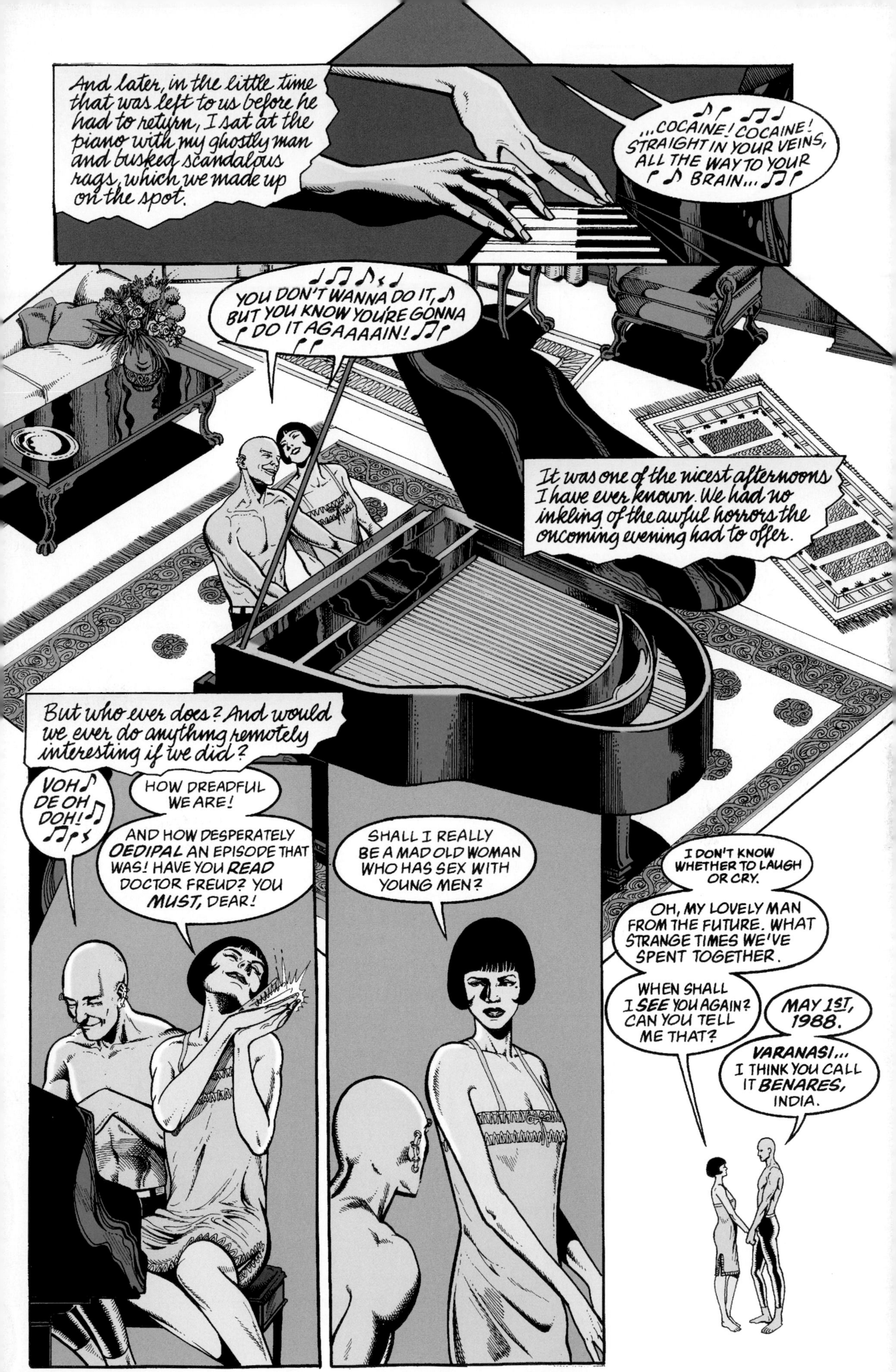
And later, in the little time that was left to us before he had to return, I sat at the piano with my ghostly man and busked scandalous rags, which we made up on the spot.
...COCAINE! COCAINE! STRAIGHT IN YOUR VEINS, ALL THE WAY TO YOUR BRAIN...
YOU DON'T WANNA DO IT, BUT YOU KNOW YOU'RE GONNA DO IT AGAAAAIN!
It was one of the nicest afternoons I have ever known. We had no inkling of the awful horrors the oncoming evening had to offer.
But who ever does? And would we ever do anything remotely interesting if we did?
VOH DE OH DOH!
HOW DREADFUL WE ARE!
AND HOW DESPERATELY OEDIPAL AN EPISODE THAT WAS! HAVE YOU READ DOCTOR FREUD? YOU MUST, DEAR!
SHALL I REALLY BE A MAD OLD WOMAN WHO HAS SEX WITH YOUNG MEN?
I DON'T KNOW WHETHER TO LAUGH OR CRY.
OH, MY LOVELY MAN FROM THE FUTURE. WHAT STRANGE TIMES WE'VE SPENT TOGETHER.
WHEN SHALL I SEE YOU AGAIN? CAN YOU TELL ME THAT?
MAY 1ST, 1988.
VARANASI... I THINK YOU CALL IT BENARES, INDIA.

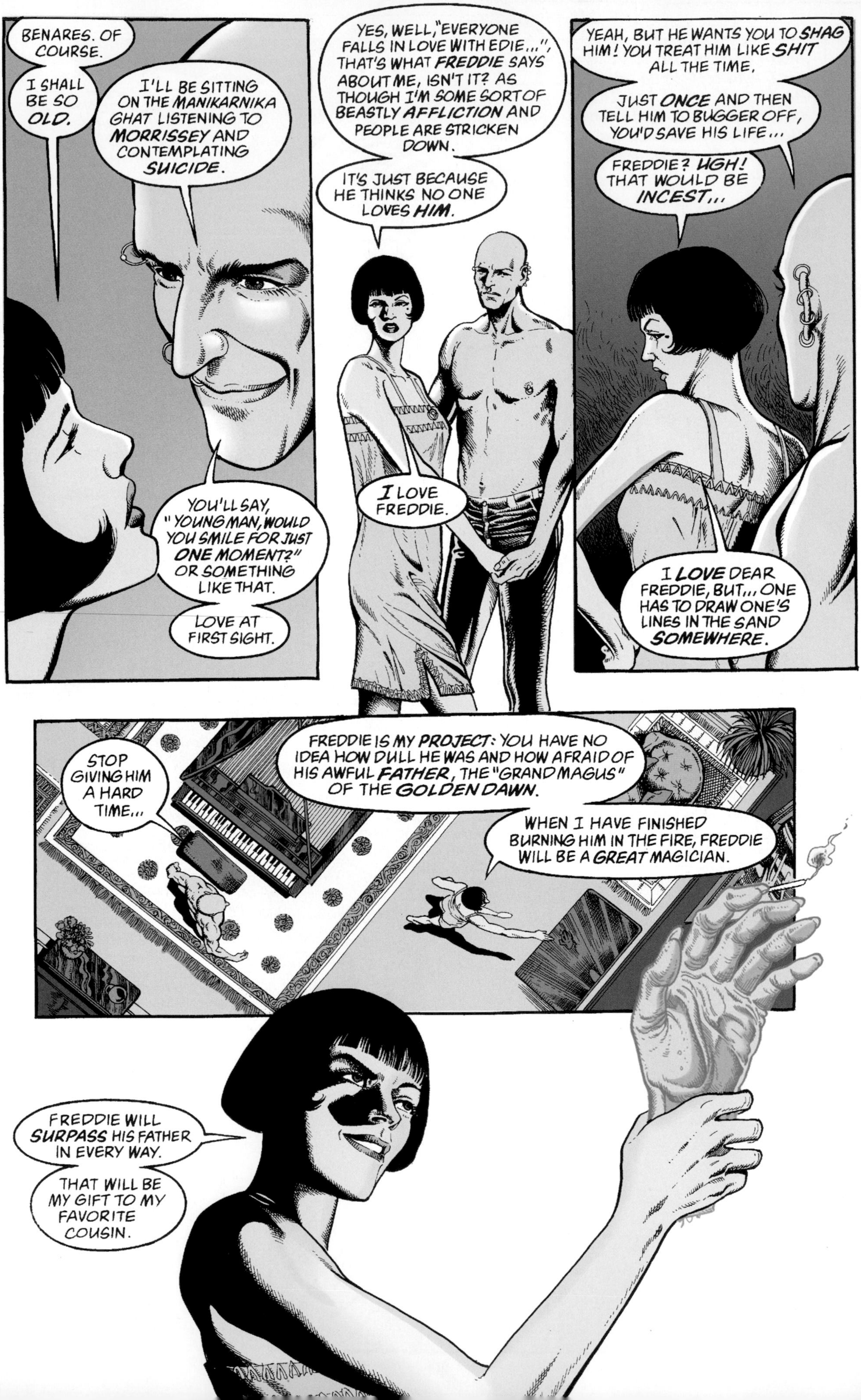
BENARES. OF COURSE.
I SHALL BE SO OLD.
I'LL BE SITTING ON THE MANIKARNIKA GHAT LISTENING TO MORRISSEY AND CONTEMPLATING SUICIDE.
YOU'LL SAY, "YOUNG MAN, WOULD YOU SMILE FOR JUST ONE MOMENT?" OR SOMETHING LIKE THAT.
LOVE AT FIRST SIGHT.
YES, WELL, "EVERYONE FALLS IN LOVE WITH EDIE...", THAT'S WHAT FREDDIE SAYS ABOUT ME, ISN'T IT? AS THOUGH I'M SOME SORT OF BEASTLY AFFLICTION AND PEOPLE ARE STRICKEN DOWN.
IT'S JUST BECAUSE HE THINKS NO ONE LOVES HIM.
I LOVE FREDDIE.
YEAH, BUT HE WANTS YOU TO SHAG HIM! YOU TREAT HIM LIKE SHIT ALL THE TIME.
JUST ONCE AND THEN TELL HIM TO BUGGER OFF, YOU'D SAVE HIS LIFE...
FREDDIE? UGH! THAT WOULD BE INCEST...
I LOVE DEAR FREDDIE, BUT... ONE HAS TO DRAW ONE'S LINES IN THE SAND SOMEWHERE.
STOP GIVING HIM A HARD TIME...
FREDDIE IS MY PROJECT: YOU HAVE NO IDEA HOW DULL HE WAS AND HOW AFRAID OF HIS AWFUL FATHER, THE "GRAND MAGUS" OF THE GOLDEN DAWN.
WHEN I HAVE FINISHED BURNING HIM IN THE FIRE, FREDDIE WILL BE A GREAT MAGICIAN.
FREDDIE WILL SURPASS HIS FATHER IN EVERY WAY.
THAT WILL BE MY GIFT TO MY FAVORITE COUSIN.

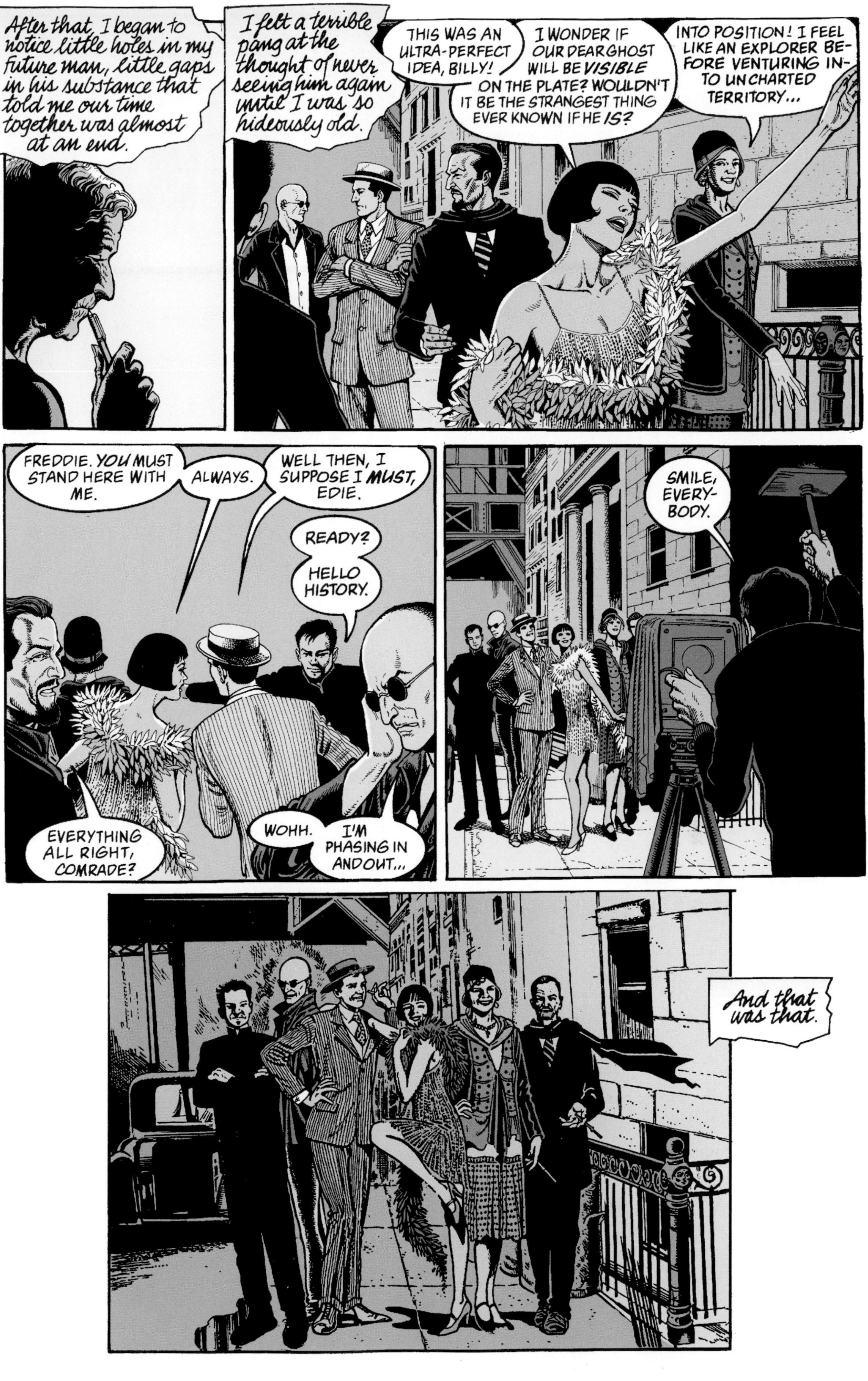
After that, I began to notice little holes in my future man, little gaps in his substance that told me our time together was almost at an end.
I felt a terrible pang at the thought of never seeing him again until I was so hideously old.
THIS WAS AN ULTRA-PERFECT IDEA, BILLY!
I WONDER IF OUR DEAR GHOST WILL BE VISIBLE ON THE PLATE? WOULDN'T IT BE THE STRANGEST THING EVER KNOWN IF HE IS?
INTO POSITION! I FEEL LIKE AN EXPLORER BEFORE VENTURING INTO UNCHARTED TERRITORY...
FREDDIE. YOU MUST STAND HERE WITH ME.
ALWAYS.
WELL THEN, I SUPPOSE I MUST, EDIE.
READY?
HELLO HISTORY.
EVERYTHING ALL RIGHT, COMRADE?
WOHH.
I'M PHASING IN AND OUT...
SMILE, EVERYBODY.
And that was that.

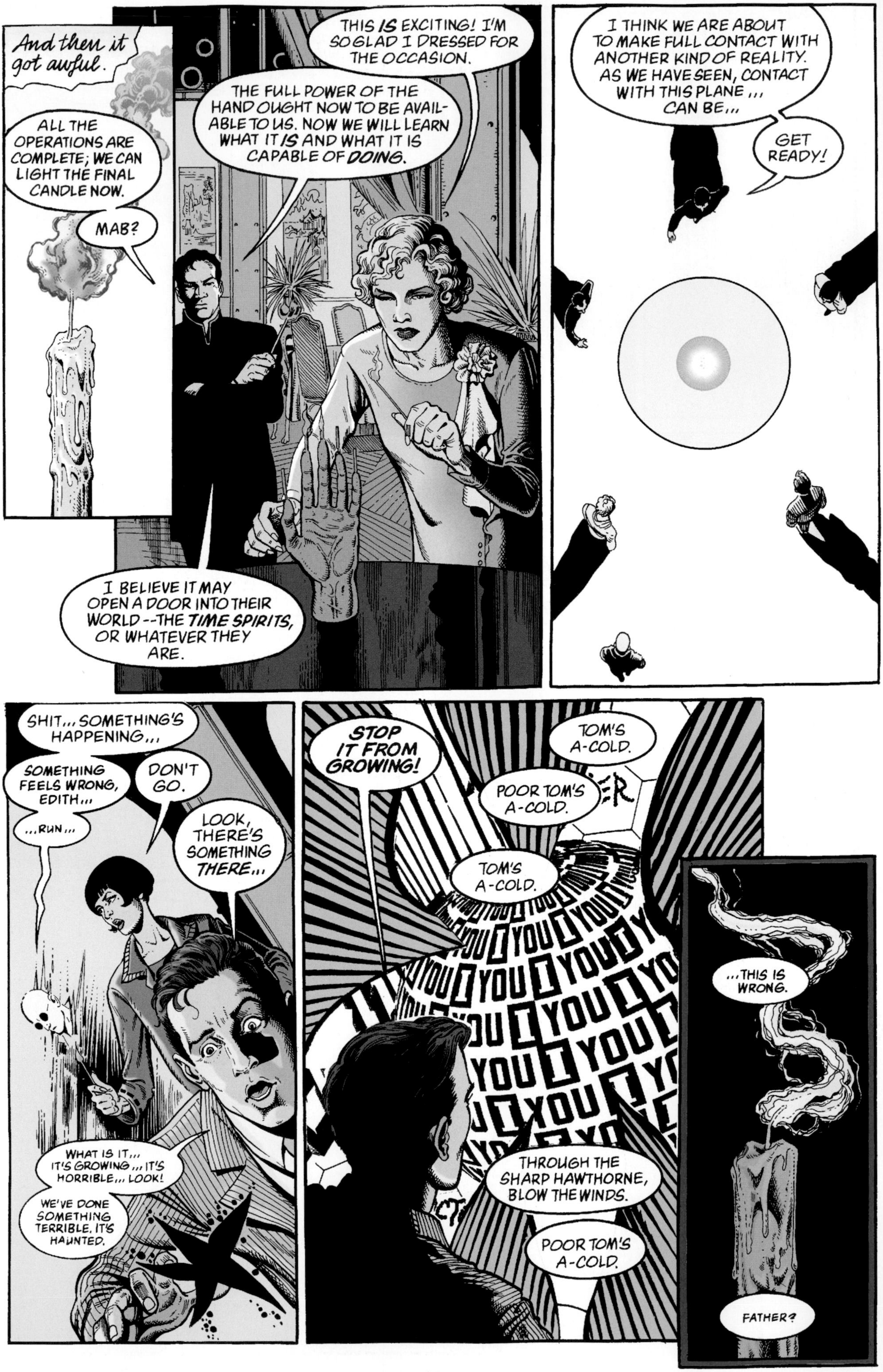

And then it got awful.
ALL THE OPERATIONS ARE COMPLETE; WE CAN LIGHT THE FINAL CANDLE NOW.
MAB?
THIS IS EXCITING! I'M SO GLAD I DRESSED FOR THE OCCASION.
THE FULL POWER OF THE HAND OUGHT NOW TO BE AVAILABLE TO US. NOW WE WILL LEARN WHAT IT IS AND WHAT IT IS CAPABLE OF DOING.
I BELIEVE IT MAY OPEN A DOOR INTO THEIR WORLD--THE TIME SPIRITS, OR WHATEVER THEY ARE.
I THINK WE ARE ABOUT TO MAKE FULL CONTACT WITH ANOTHER KIND OF REALITY. AS WE HAVE SEEN, CONTACT WITH THIS PLANE ... CAN BE ...
GET READY!
SHIT... SOMETHING'S HAPPENING...
SOMETHING FEELS WRONG, EDITH...
DON'T GO.
...RUN...
LOOK, THERE'S SOMETHING THERE...
WHAT IS IT... IT'S GROWING... IT'S HORRIBLE... LOOK!
WE'VE DONE SOMETHING TERRIBLE. IT'S HAUNTED.
STOP IT FROM GROWING!
TOM'S A-COLD.
POOR TOM'S A-COLD.
TOM'S A-COLD.
THROUGH THE SHARP HAWTHORNE, BLOW THE WINDS.
POOR TOM'S A-COLD.
...THIS IS WRONG.
FATHER?

NINETEEN. NINETY. SEVEN.

NNNNAAAA!

SHIT.

OH SHIT. I SAW IT.

OH JESUS CHRIST.

GIDEON, CALM DOWN. IT'S *ROBIN*. YOU'RE BACK *HOME*.

1997. SAN FRANCISCO, YOU'VE BEEN TRANCING FOR ABOUT TWO HOURS AND...

...WELL, THERE'S BEEN A *PROBLEM.*

BOY'S GONE. WE DON'T KNOW WHERE.

SHE TOOK THE *HAND OF GLORY* AND WALKED.

I'M NOT SURE HOW TO DEAL WITH THIS. I WAITED TO SPEAK TO YOU.

WE DON'T KNOW *WHY.* WE DON'T KNOW *WHERE.*

WHAT DID YOU FIND OUT ABOUT THE *HAND?* ANYTHING WE CAN USE?

...*BOY* DID WHAT...?

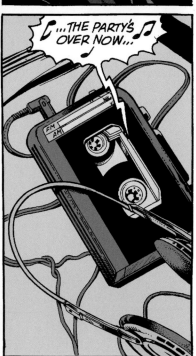

♪ *...THE PARTY'S OVER NOW...* ♪

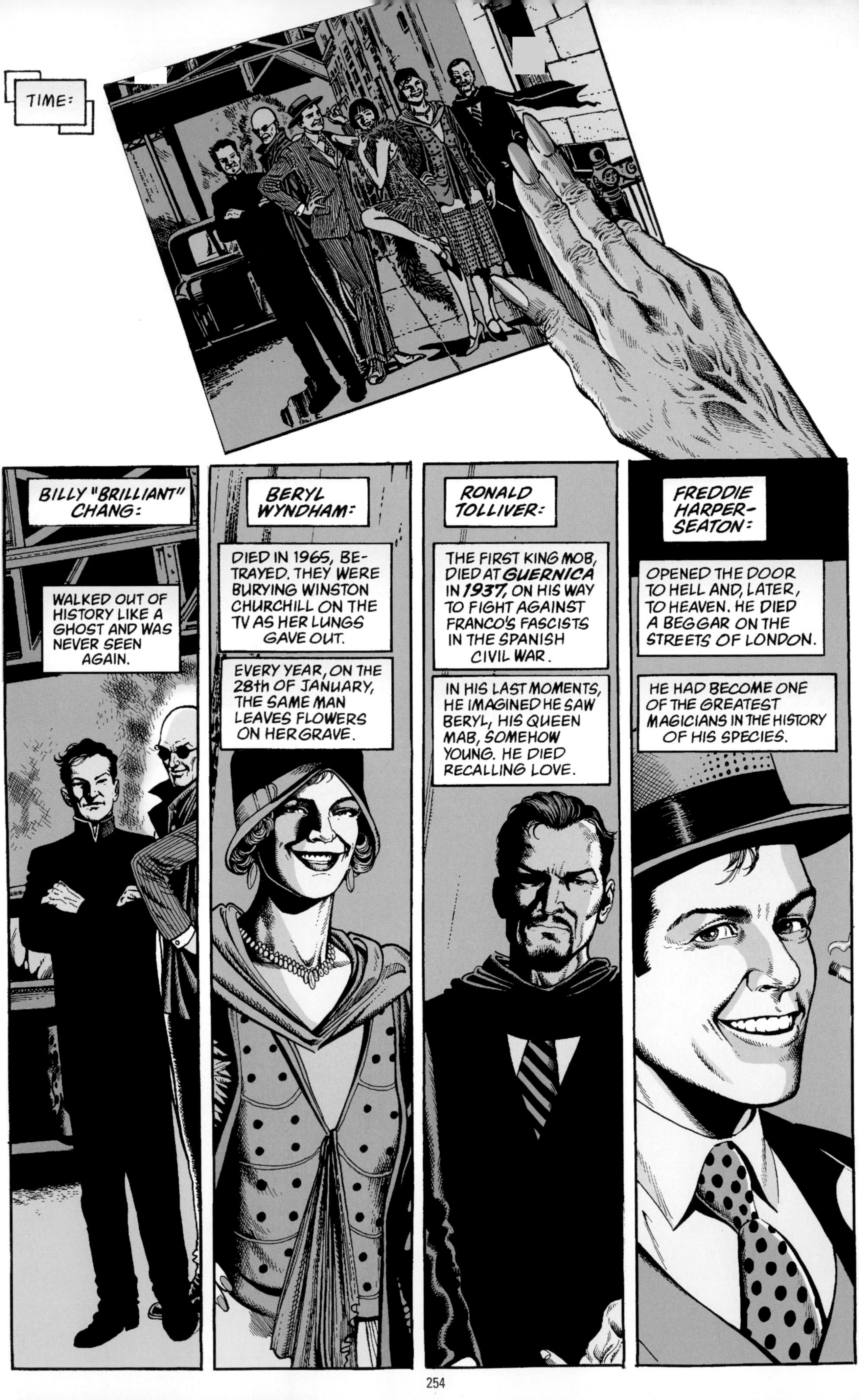
TIME:
BILLY "BRILLIANT" CHANG:
WALKED OUT OF HISTORY LIKE A GHOST AND WAS NEVER SEEN AGAIN.
BERYL WYNDHAM:
DIED IN 1965, BETRAYED. THEY WERE BURYING WINSTON CHURCHILL ON THE TV AS HER LUNGS GAVE OUT.
EVERY YEAR, ON THE 28th OF JANUARY, THE SAME MAN LEAVES FLOWERS ON HER GRAVE.
RONALD TOLLIVER:
THE FIRST KING MOB, DIED AT GUERNICA IN 1937, ON HIS WAY TO FIGHT AGAINST FRANCO'S FASCISTS IN THE SPANISH CIVIL WAR.
IN HIS LAST MOMENTS, HE IMAGINED HE SAW BERYL, HIS QUEEN MAB, SOMEHOW YOUNG. HE DIED RECALLING LOVE.
FREDDIE HARPER-SEATON:
OPENED THE DOOR TO HELL AND, LATER, TO HEAVEN. HE DIED A BEGGAR ON THE STREETS OF LONDON.
HE HAD BECOME ONE OF THE GREATEST MAGICIANS IN THE HISTORY OF HIS SPECIES.

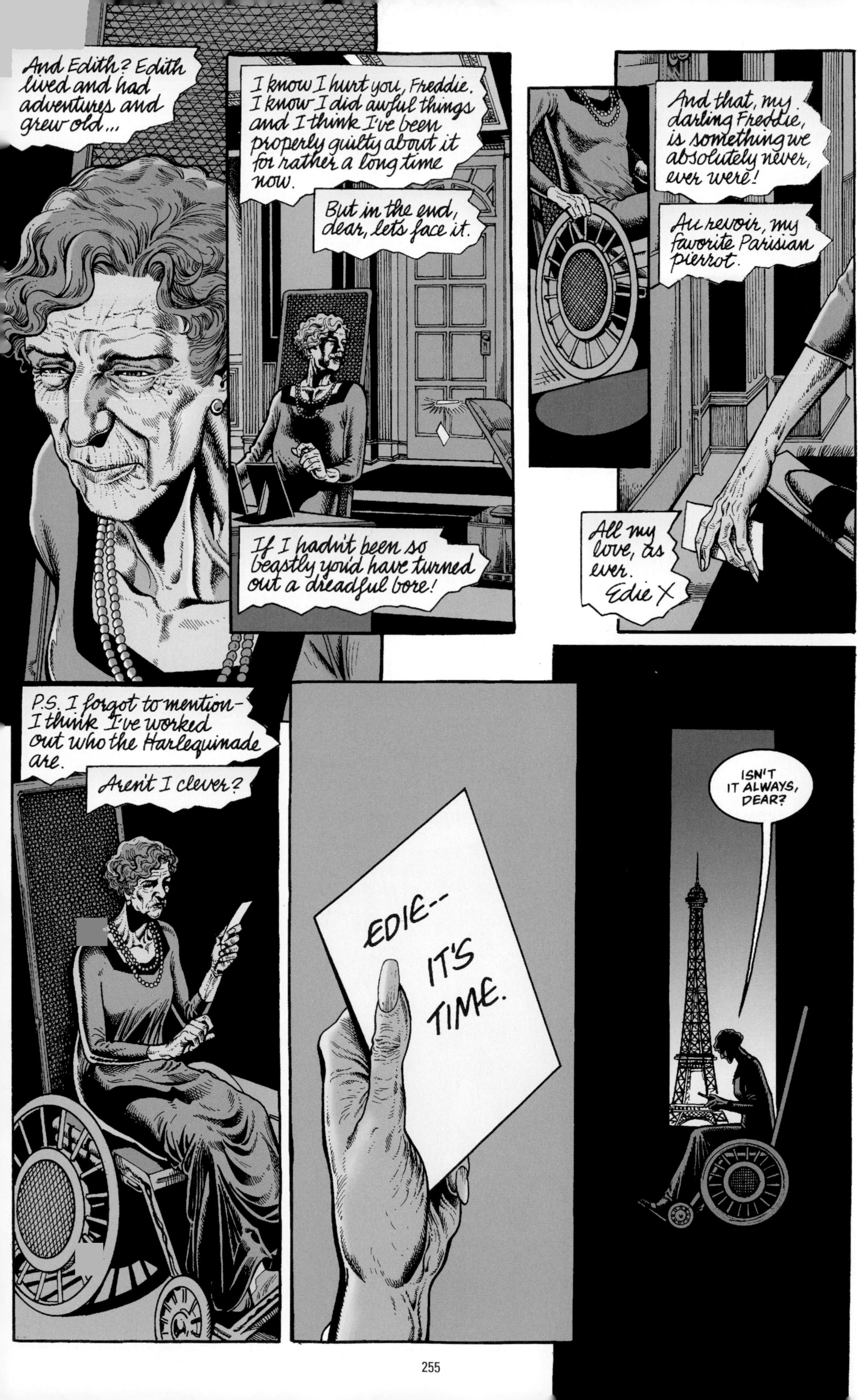
And Edith? Edith lived and had adventures and grew old...
I know I hurt you, Freddie. I know I did awful things and I think I've been properly guilty about it for rather a long time now.
But in the end, dear, let's face it.
If I hadn't been so beastly you'd have turned out a dreadful bore!
And that, my darling Freddie, is something we absolutely never, ever were!
Au revoir, my favorite Parisian pierrot.
All my love, as ever.
Edie X
P.S. I forgot to mention— I think I've worked out who the Harlequinade are.
Aren't I clever?
EDIE-- IT'S TIME.
ISN'T IT ALWAYS, DEAR?

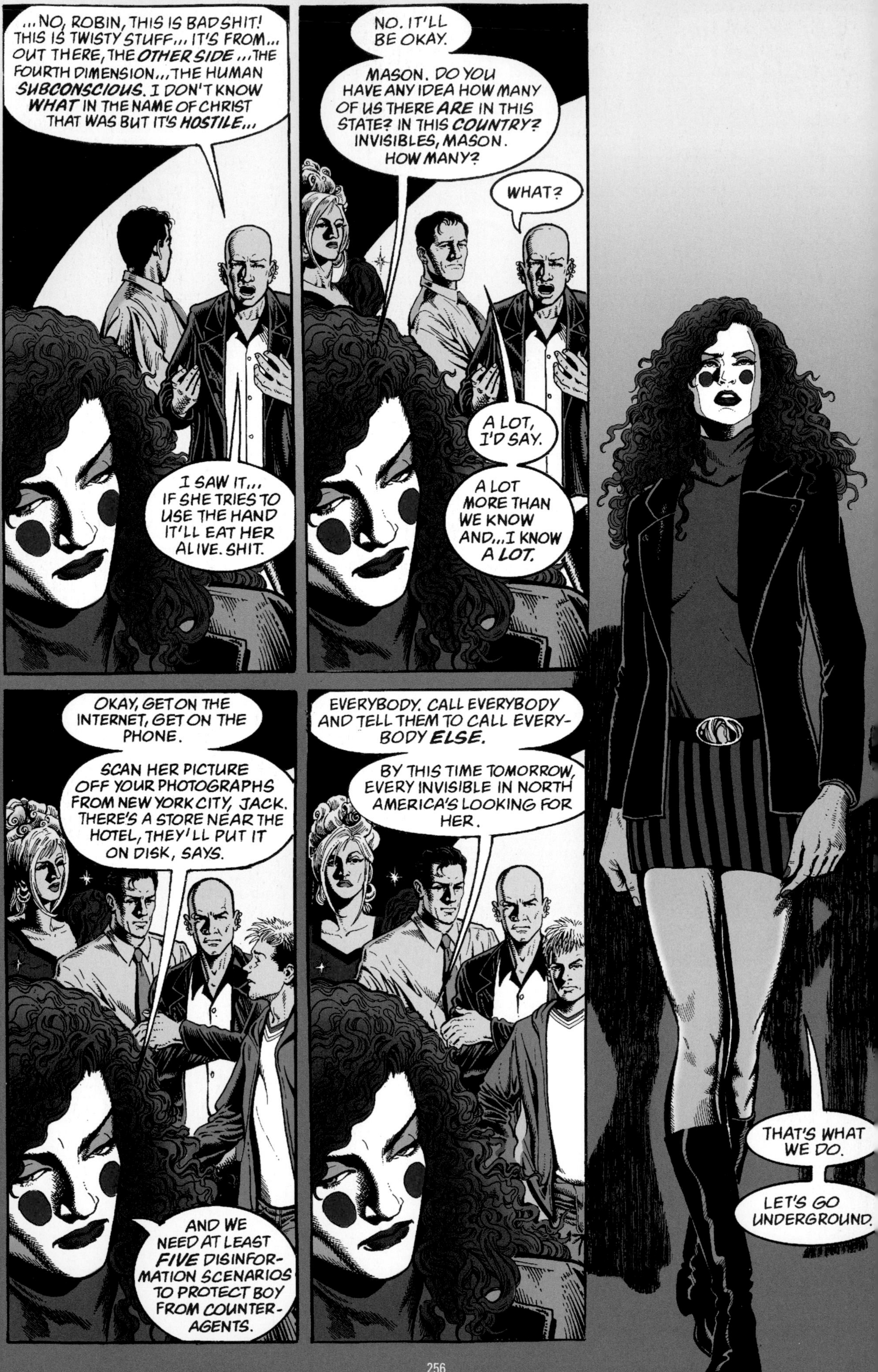
...NO, ROBIN, THIS IS BAD SHIT! THIS IS TWISTY STUFF... IT'S FROM... OUT THERE, THE OTHER SIDE... THE FOURTH DIMENSION... THE HUMAN SUBCONSCIOUS. I DON'T KNOW WHAT IN THE NAME OF CHRIST THAT WAS BUT IT'S HOSTILE...
I SAW IT... IF SHE TRIES TO USE THE HAND IT'LL EAT HER ALIVE. SHIT.
NO. IT'LL BE OKAY.
MASON. DO YOU HAVE ANY IDEA HOW MANY OF US THERE ARE IN THIS STATE? IN THIS COUNTRY? INVISIBLES, MASON. HOW MANY?
WHAT?
A LOT, I'D SAY.
A LOT MORE THAN WE KNOW AND... I KNOW A LOT.
OKAY, GET ON THE INTERNET, GET ON THE PHONE.
SCAN HER PICTURE OFF YOUR PHOTOGRAPHS FROM NEW YORK CITY, JACK. THERE'S A STORE NEAR THE HOTEL, THEY'LL PUT IT ON DISK, SAYS.
AND WE NEED AT LEAST FIVE DISINFORMATION SCENARIOS TO PROTECT BOY FROM COUNTER-AGENTS.
EVERYBODY. CALL EVERYBODY AND TELL THEM TO CALL EVERYBODY ELSE.
BY THIS TIME TOMORROW, EVERY INVISIBLE IN NORTH AMERICA'S LOOKING FOR HER.
THAT'S WHAT WE DO.
LET'S GO UNDERGROUND.

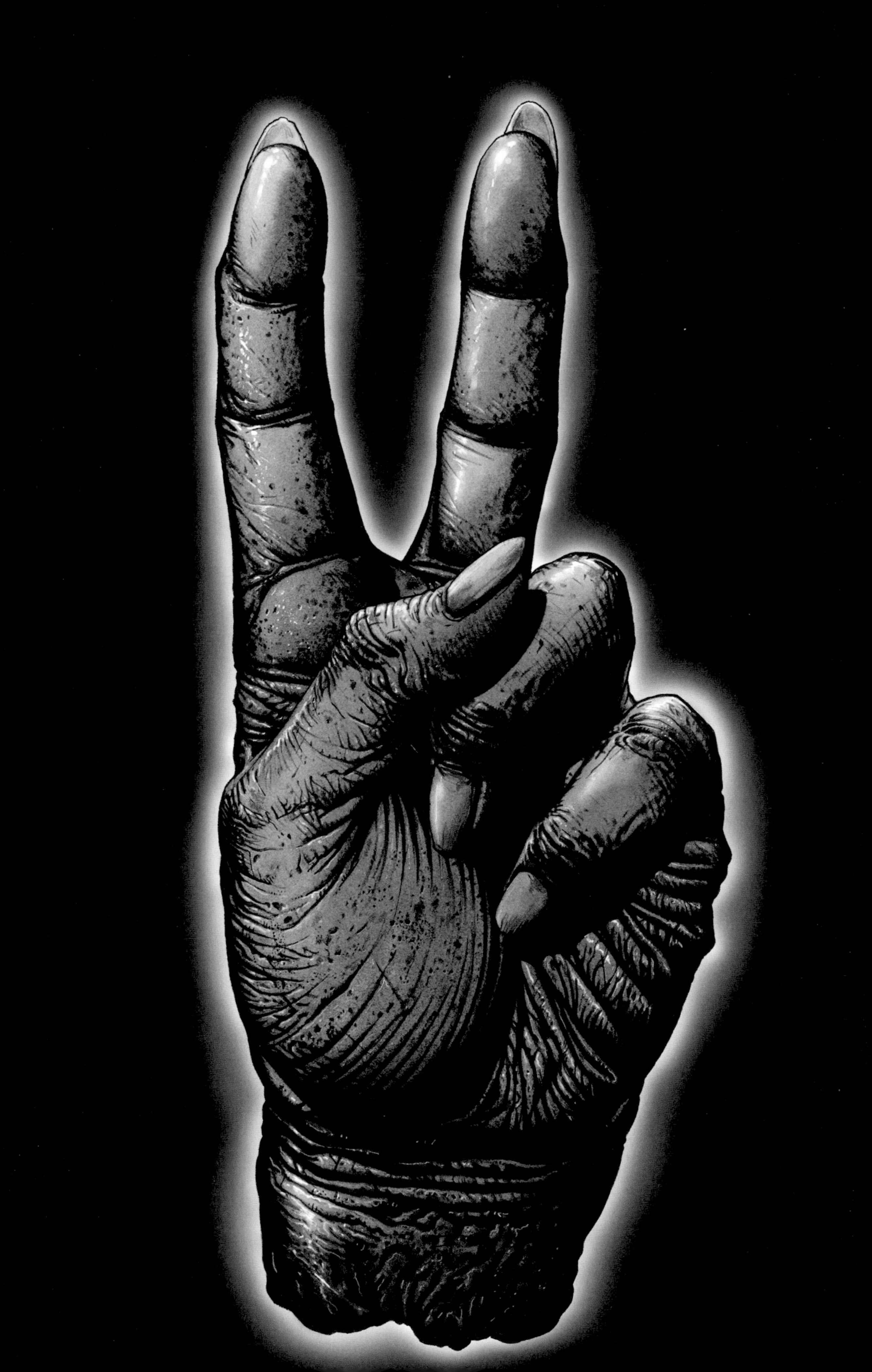

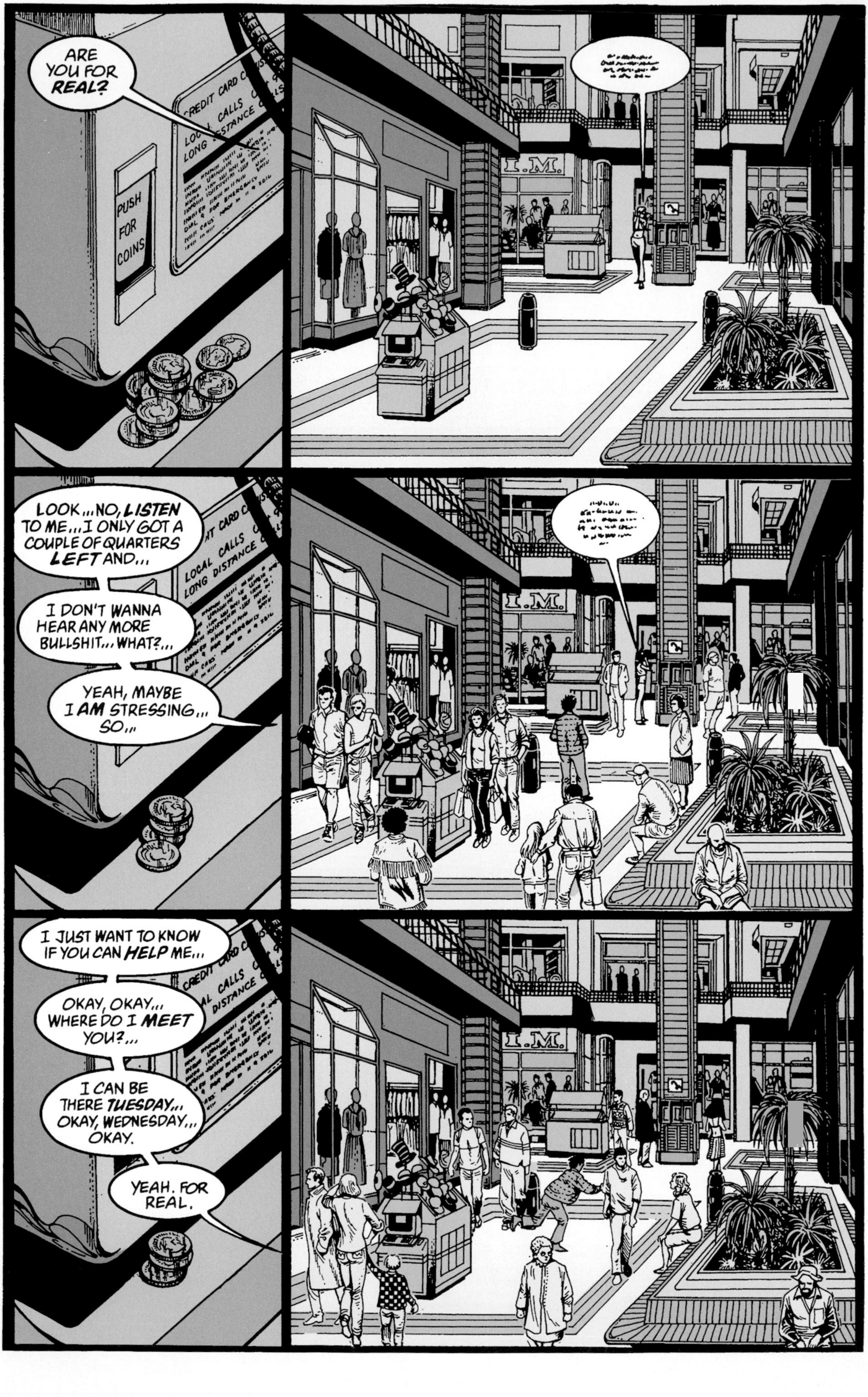
ARE YOU FOR REAL?
CREDIT CARD CALLS
LOCAL CALLS
LONG DISTANCE CALLS
PUSH FOR COINS
I.M.
LOOK... NO, LISTEN TO ME... I ONLY GOT A COUPLE OF QUARTERS LEFT AND...
I DON'T WANNA HEAR ANY MORE BULLSHIT... WHAT?...
YEAH, MAYBE I AM STRESSING... SO...
I JUST WANT TO KNOW IF YOU CAN HELP ME...
OKAY, OKAY... WHERE DO I MEET YOU?...
I CAN BE THERE TUESDAY... OKAY, WEDNESDAY... OKAY.
YEAH. FOR REAL.

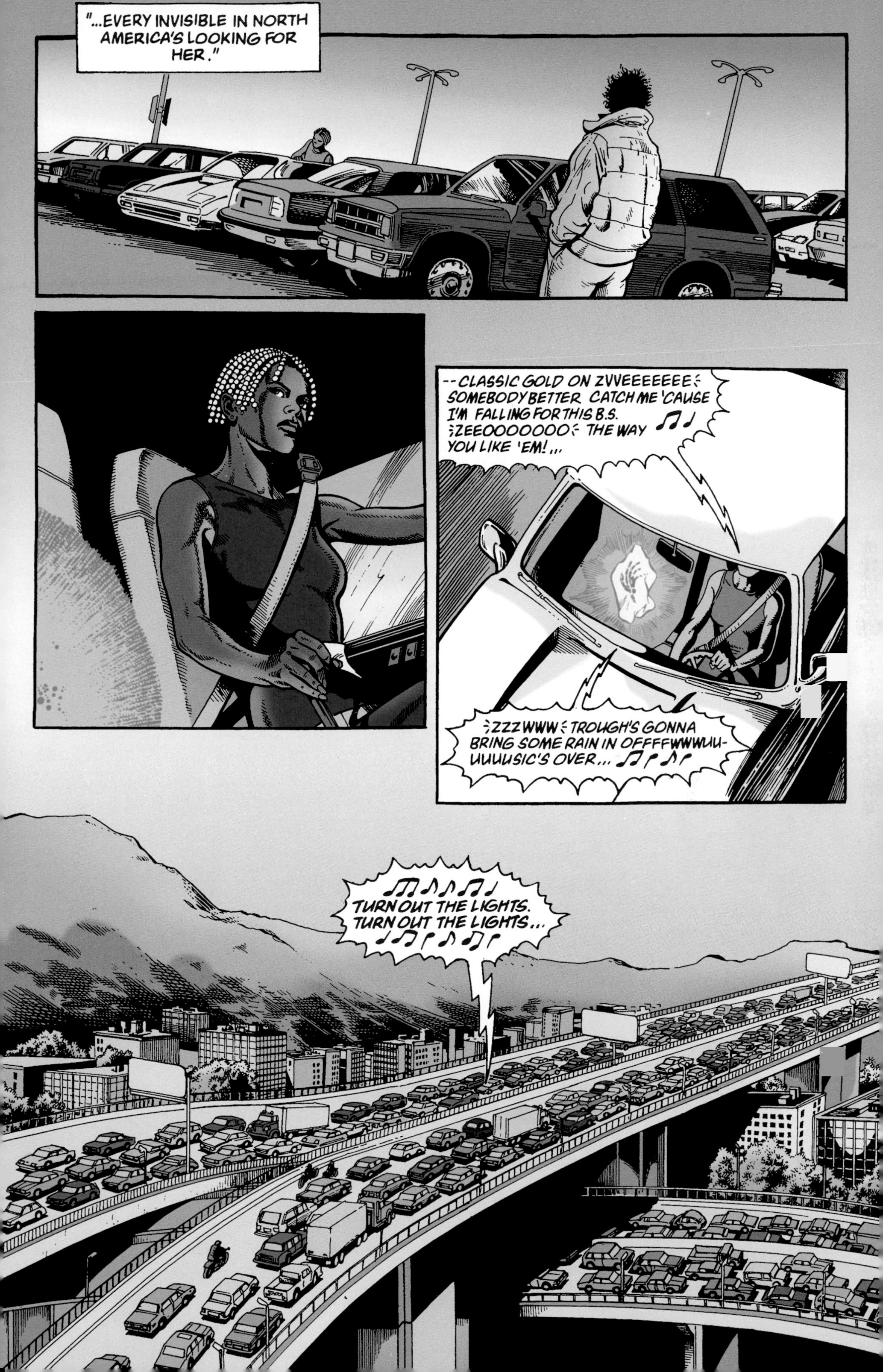
"...EVERY INVISIBLE IN NORTH AMERICA'S LOOKING FOR HER."
--CLASSIC GOLD ON ZVVEEEEEEE: SOMEBODY BETTER CATCH ME 'CAUSE I'M FALLING FOR THIS B.S. ZEEOOOOOOO: THE WAY YOU LIKE 'EM!...
ZZZWWW: TROUGH'S GONNA BRING SOME RAIN IN OFFFFWWUU-UUUUSIC'S OVER...
TURN OUT THE LIGHTS. TURN OUT THE LIGHTS...

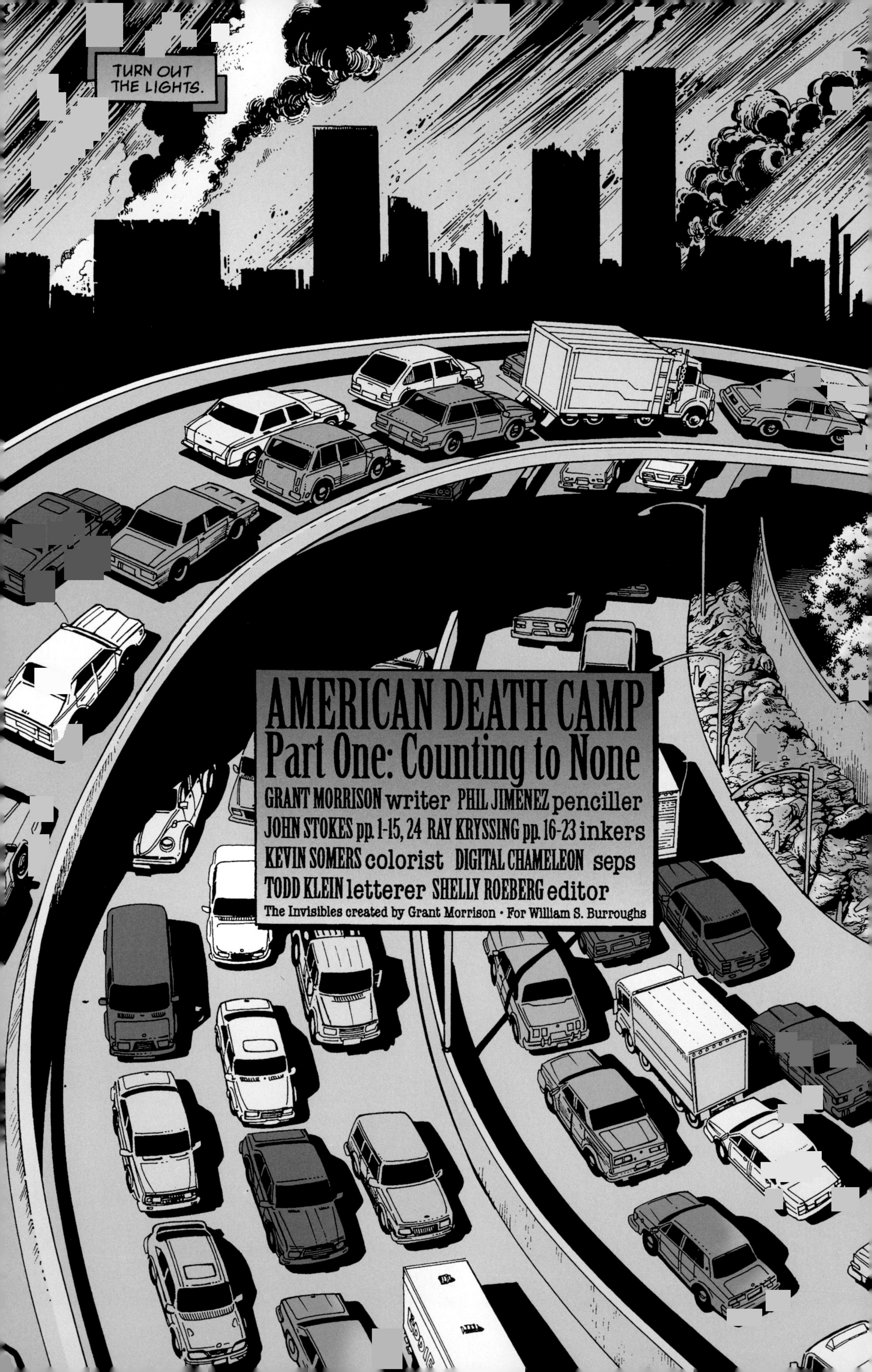
TURN OUT THE LIGHTS.
AMERICAN DEATH CAMP
Part One: Counting to None
GRANT MORRISON writer PHIL JIMENEZ penciller
JOHN STOKES pp. 1-15, 24 RAY KRYSSING pp. 16-23 inkers
KEVIN SOMERS colorist DIGITAL CHAMELEON seps
TODD KLEIN letterer SHELLY ROEBERG editor
The Invisibles created by Grant Morrison • For William S. Burroughs

...RIGHT ON TIME.

PUNCTUALITY. THAT'S A STRANGE TRAIT IN AN *ANARCHIST*, DON'T YOU THINK?

KINDA THING I FIND AMUSING.

I'M *COYOTE*.

THIS HERE'S MY *MUSIC* WE'RE LISTENING TO. THAT'S WHAT'S IMPORTANT TO ME.

WHAT'S YOUR *NAME*, SISTER?

AH... *MAYA*...

LOOK, JUST TELL ME WHAT I NEED TO KNOW AND I'LL BE OUT OF HERE.

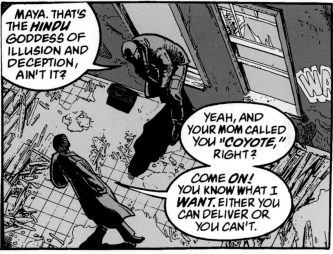

MAYA. THAT'S THE *HINDU* GODDESS OF ILLUSION AND DECEPTION, AIN'T IT?

YEAH, AND YOUR MOM CALLED YOU *"COYOTE,"* RIGHT?

COME *ON!* YOU KNOW WHAT I *WANT.* EITHER YOU CAN DELIVER OR YOU CAN'T.

YOU'RE LOOKING FOR THE LOCATION OF A TOP SECRET U.S. GOVERNMENT *CONCENTRATION CAMP* RIGHT HERE IN WASHINGTON STATE.

SPOOKY SHIT.

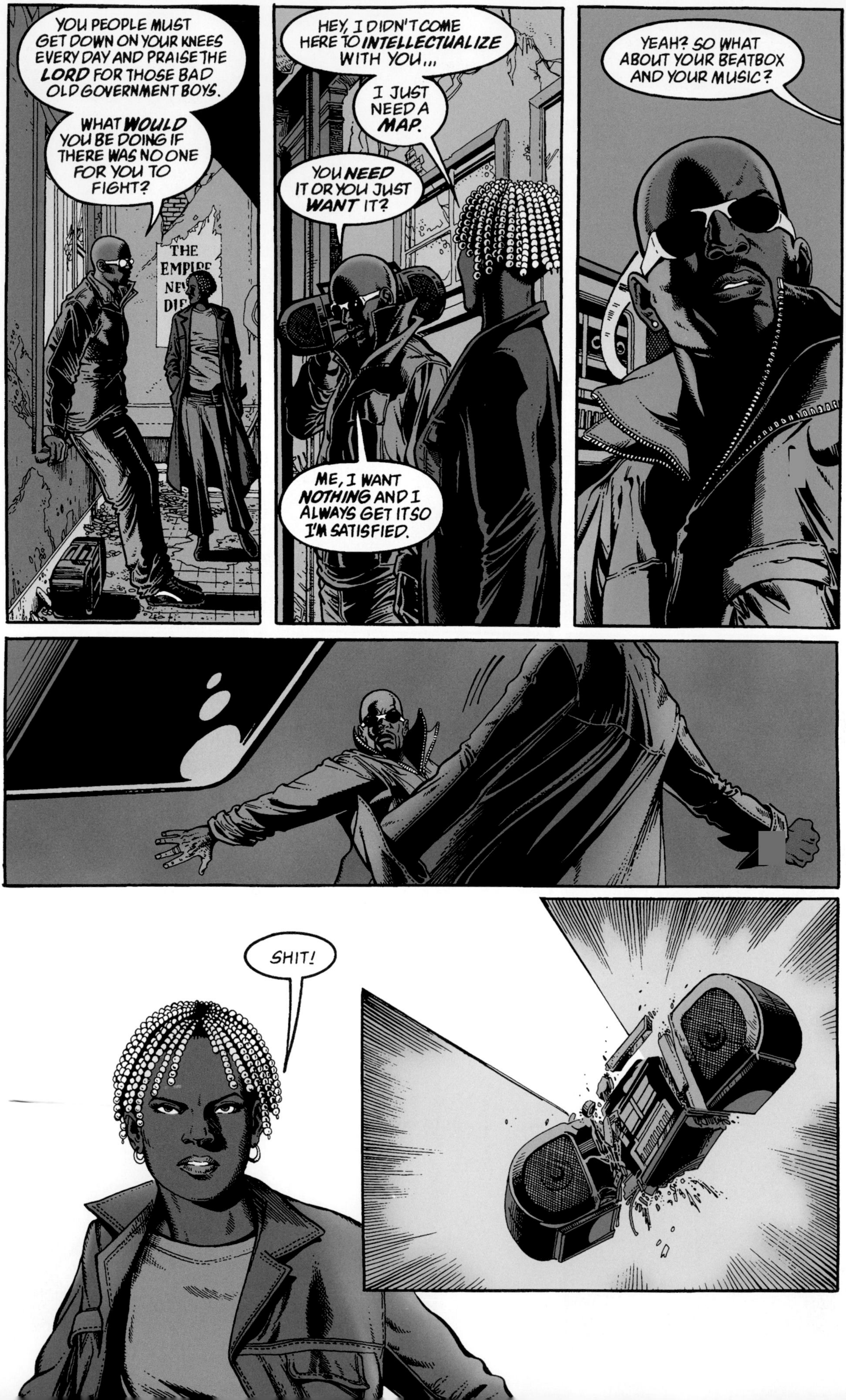
YOU PEOPLE MUST GET DOWN ON YOUR KNEES EVERY DAY AND PRAISE THE LORD FOR THOSE BAD OLD GOVERNMENT BOYS.
WHAT WOULD YOU BE DOING IF THERE WAS NO ONE FOR YOU TO FIGHT?
THE EMPIRE NEW DI
HEY, I DIDN'T COME HERE TO INTELLECTUALIZE WITH YOU...
I JUST NEED A MAP.
YOU NEED IT OR YOU JUST WANT IT?
ME, I WANT NOTHING AND I ALWAYS GET IT SO I'M SATISFIED.
YEAH? SO WHAT ABOUT YOUR BEATBOX AND YOUR MUSIC?
SHIT!

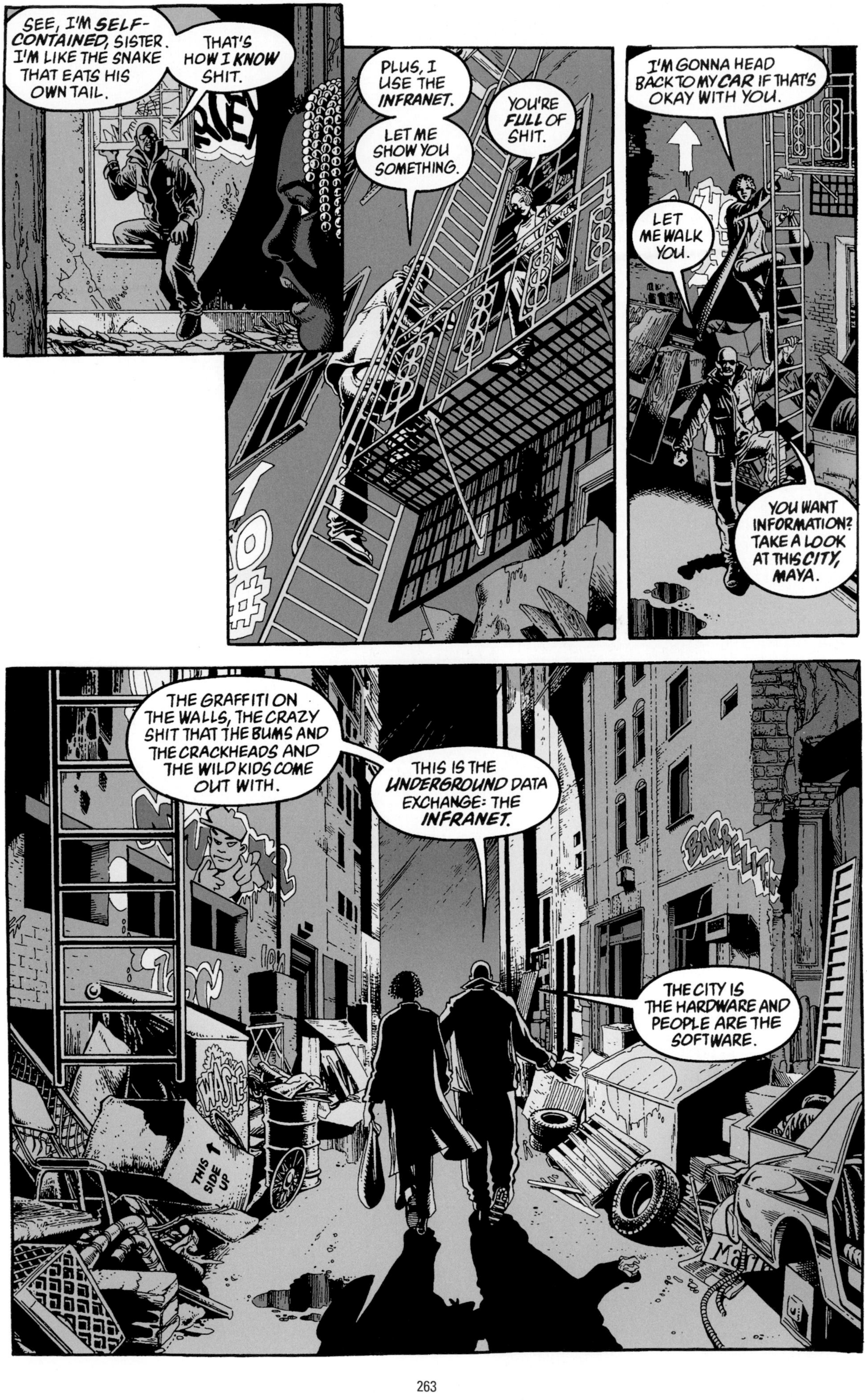

SEE, I'M **SELF-CONTAINED**, SISTER. I'M LIKE THE SNAKE THAT EATS HIS OWN TAIL.
THAT'S HOW I **KNOW** SHIT.
PLUS, I USE THE **INFRANET**.
LET ME SHOW YOU SOMETHING.
YOU'RE **FULL** OF SHIT.
I'M GONNA HEAD BACK TO MY **CAR** IF THAT'S OKAY WITH YOU.
LET ME WALK YOU.
YOU WANT **INFORMATION**? TAKE A LOOK AT THIS **CITY**, **MAYA**.
THE GRAFFITI ON THE WALLS, THE CRAZY SHIT THAT THE BUMS AND THE **CRACKHEADS** AND THE **WILD KIDS** COME OUT WITH.
THIS IS THE **UNDERGROUND** DATA EXCHANGE: THE **INFRANET**.
THE CITY IS THE HARDWARE AND PEOPLE ARE THE SOFTWARE.
THIS SIDE UP

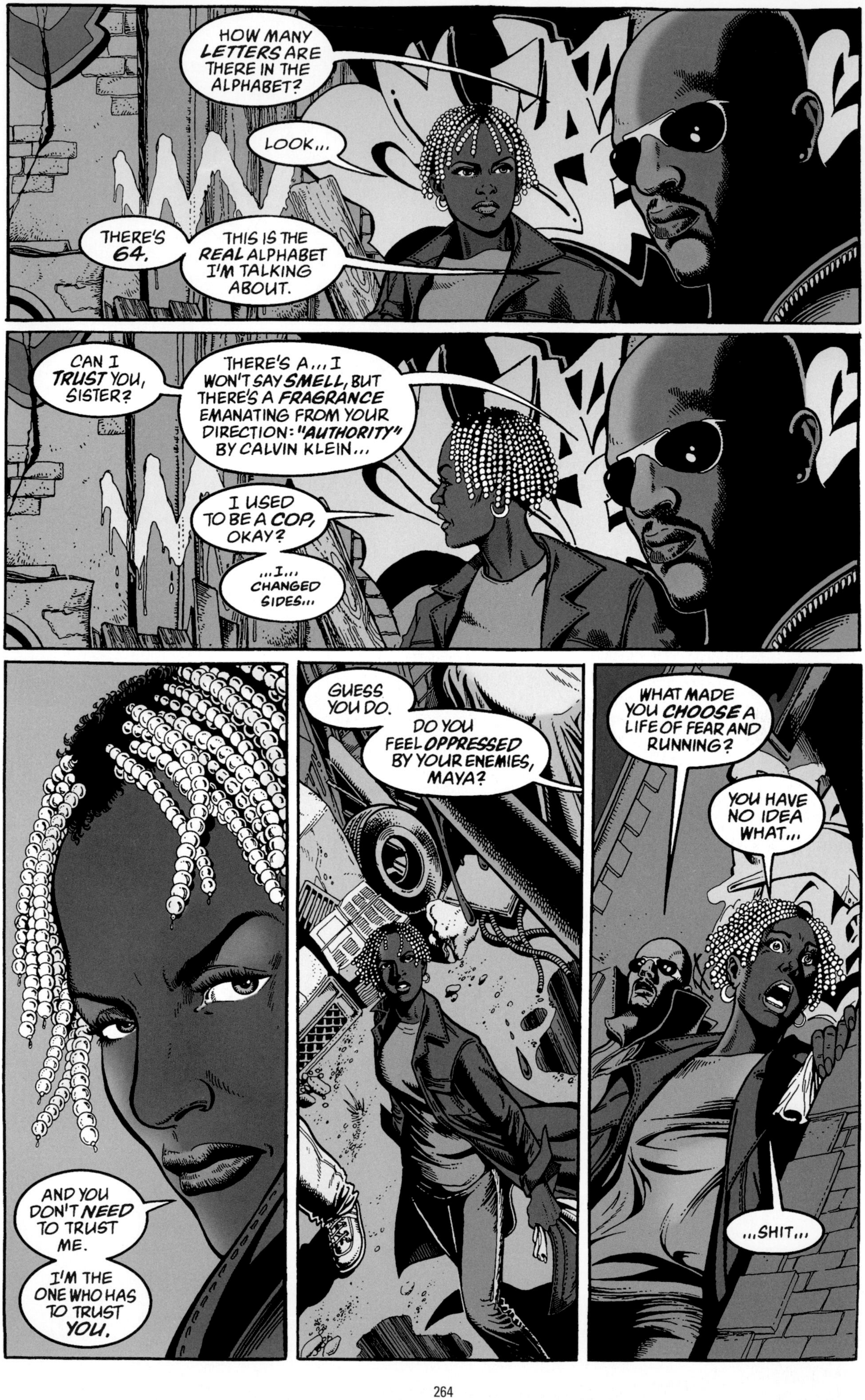
HOW MANY LETTERS ARE THERE IN THE ALPHABET?
LOOK...
THERE'S 64.
THIS IS THE REAL ALPHABET I'M TALKING ABOUT.
CAN I TRUST YOU, SISTER?
THERE'S A... I WON'T SAY SMELL, BUT THERE'S A FRAGRANCE EMANATING FROM YOUR DIRECTION: "AUTHORITY" BY CALVIN KLEIN...
I USED TO BE A COP, OKAY?
...I... CHANGED SIDES...
AND YOU DON'T NEED TO TRUST ME.
I'M THE ONE WHO HAS TO TRUST YOU.
GUESS YOU DO.
DO YOU FEEL OPPRESSED BY YOUR ENEMIES, MAYA?
WHAT MADE YOU CHOOSE A LIFE OF FEAR AND RUNNING?
YOU HAVE NO IDEA WHAT...
...SHIT...

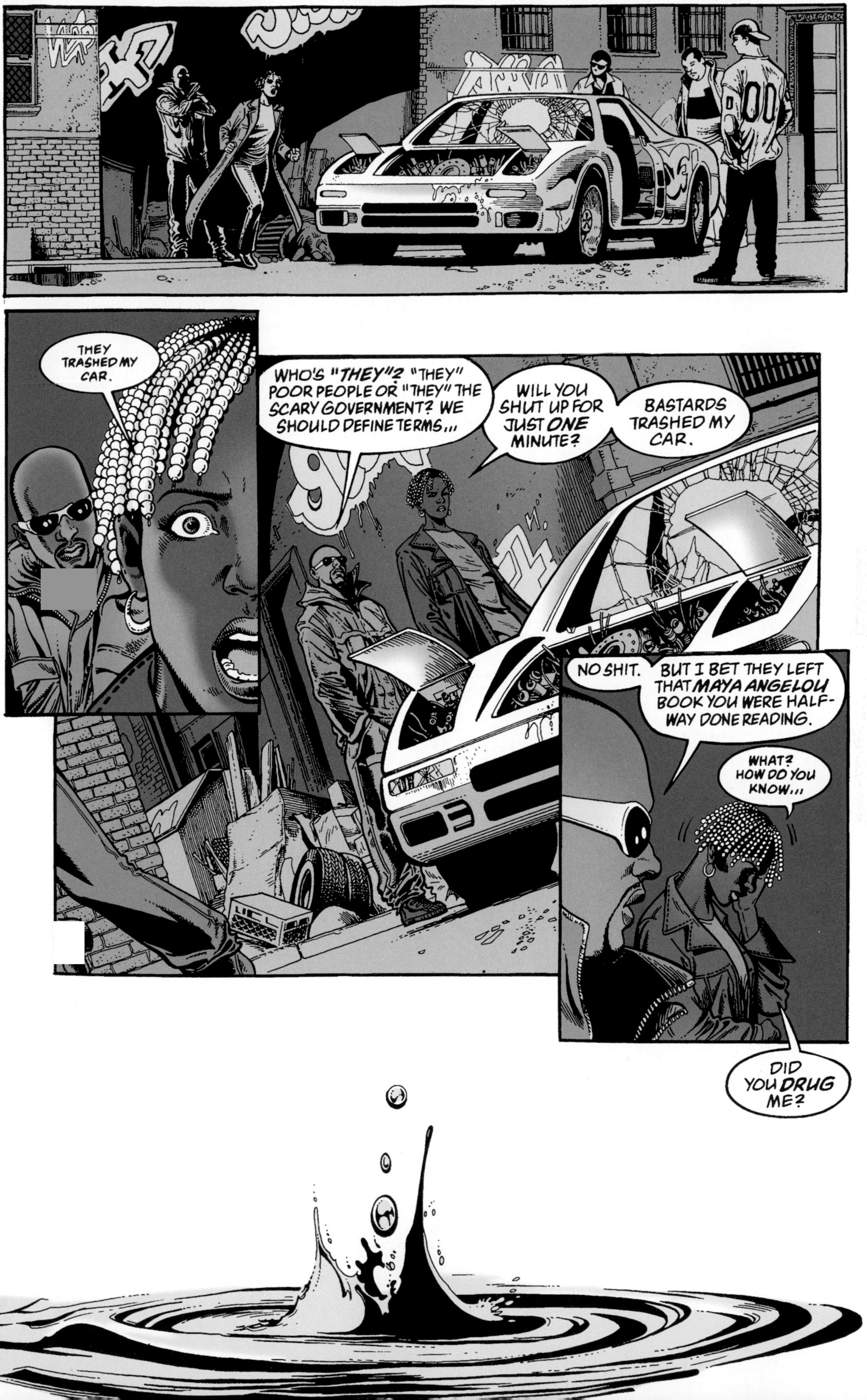
THEY TRASHED MY CAR.
WHO'S "THEY"? "THEY" POOR PEOPLE OR "THEY" THE SCARY GOVERNMENT? WE SHOULD DEFINE TERMS...
WILL YOU SHUT UP FOR JUST ONE MINUTE?
BASTARDS TRASHED MY CAR.
NO SHIT.
BUT I BET THEY LEFT THAT MAYA ANGELOU BOOK YOU WERE HALF-WAY DONE READING.
WHAT? HOW DO YOU KNOW...
DID YOU DRUG ME?

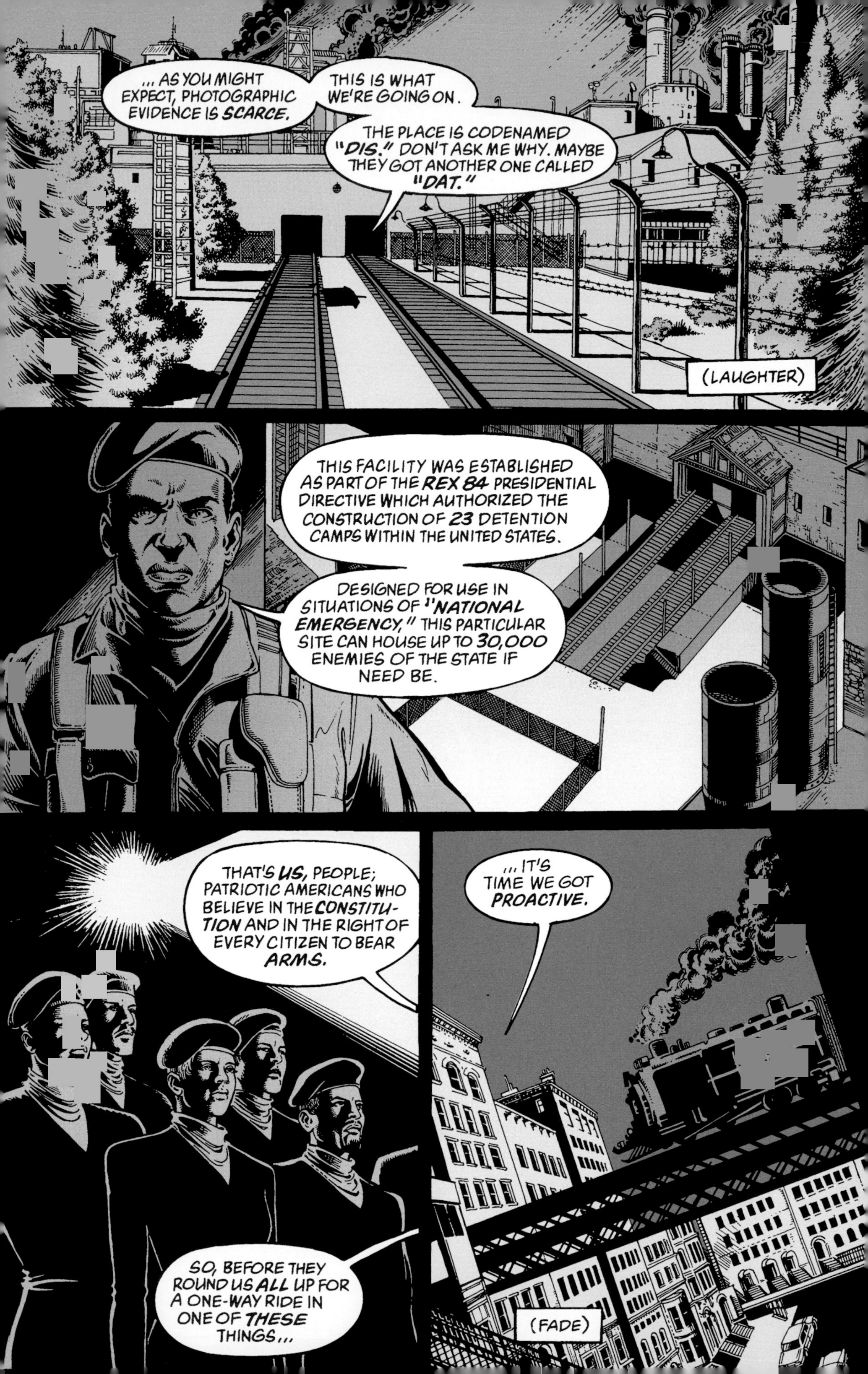

...AS YOU MIGHT EXPECT, PHOTOGRAPHIC EVIDENCE IS SCARCE.
THIS IS WHAT WE'RE GOING ON.
THE PLACE IS CODENAMED "DIS." DON'T ASK ME WHY. MAYBE THEY GOT ANOTHER ONE CALLED "DAT."
(LAUGHTER)
THIS FACILITY WAS ESTABLISHED AS PART OF THE REX 84 PRESIDENTIAL DIRECTIVE WHICH AUTHORIZED THE CONSTRUCTION OF 23 DETENTION CAMPS WITHIN THE UNITED STATES.
DESIGNED FOR USE IN SITUATIONS OF "NATIONAL EMERGENCY," THIS PARTICULAR SITE CAN HOUSE UP TO 30,000 ENEMIES OF THE STATE IF NEED BE.
THAT'S US, PEOPLE; PATRIOTIC AMERICANS WHO BELIEVE IN THE CONSTITUTION AND IN THE RIGHT OF EVERY CITIZEN TO BEAR ARMS.
SO, BEFORE THEY ROUND US ALL UP FOR A ONE-WAY RIDE IN ONE OF THESE THINGS...
...IT'S TIME WE GOT PROACTIVE.
(FADE)

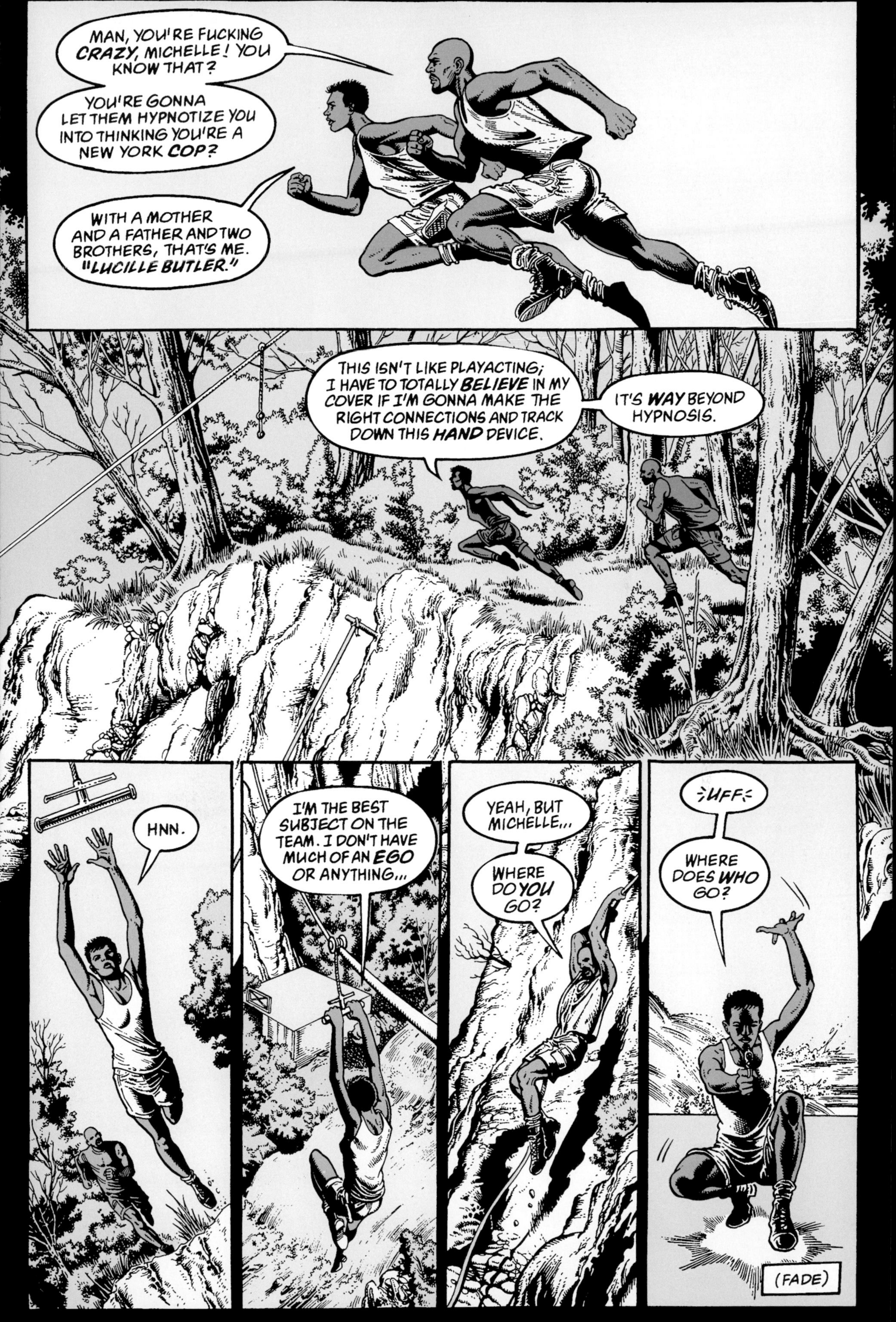
MAN, YOU'RE FUCKING CRAZY, MICHELLE! YOU KNOW THAT?
YOU'RE GONNA LET THEM HYPNOTIZE YOU INTO THINKING YOU'RE A NEW YORK COP?
WITH A MOTHER AND A FATHER AND TWO BROTHERS, THAT'S ME. "LUCILLE BUTLER."
THIS ISN'T LIKE PLAYACTING; I HAVE TO TOTALLY BELIEVE IN MY COVER IF I'M GONNA MAKE THE RIGHT CONNECTIONS AND TRACK DOWN THIS HAND DEVICE.
IT'S WAY BEYOND HYPNOSIS.
HNN.
I'M THE BEST SUBJECT ON THE TEAM. I DON'T HAVE MUCH OF AN EGO OR ANYTHING...
YEAH, BUT MICHELLE...
WHERE DO YOU GO?
UFF
WHERE DOES WHO GO?
(FADE)

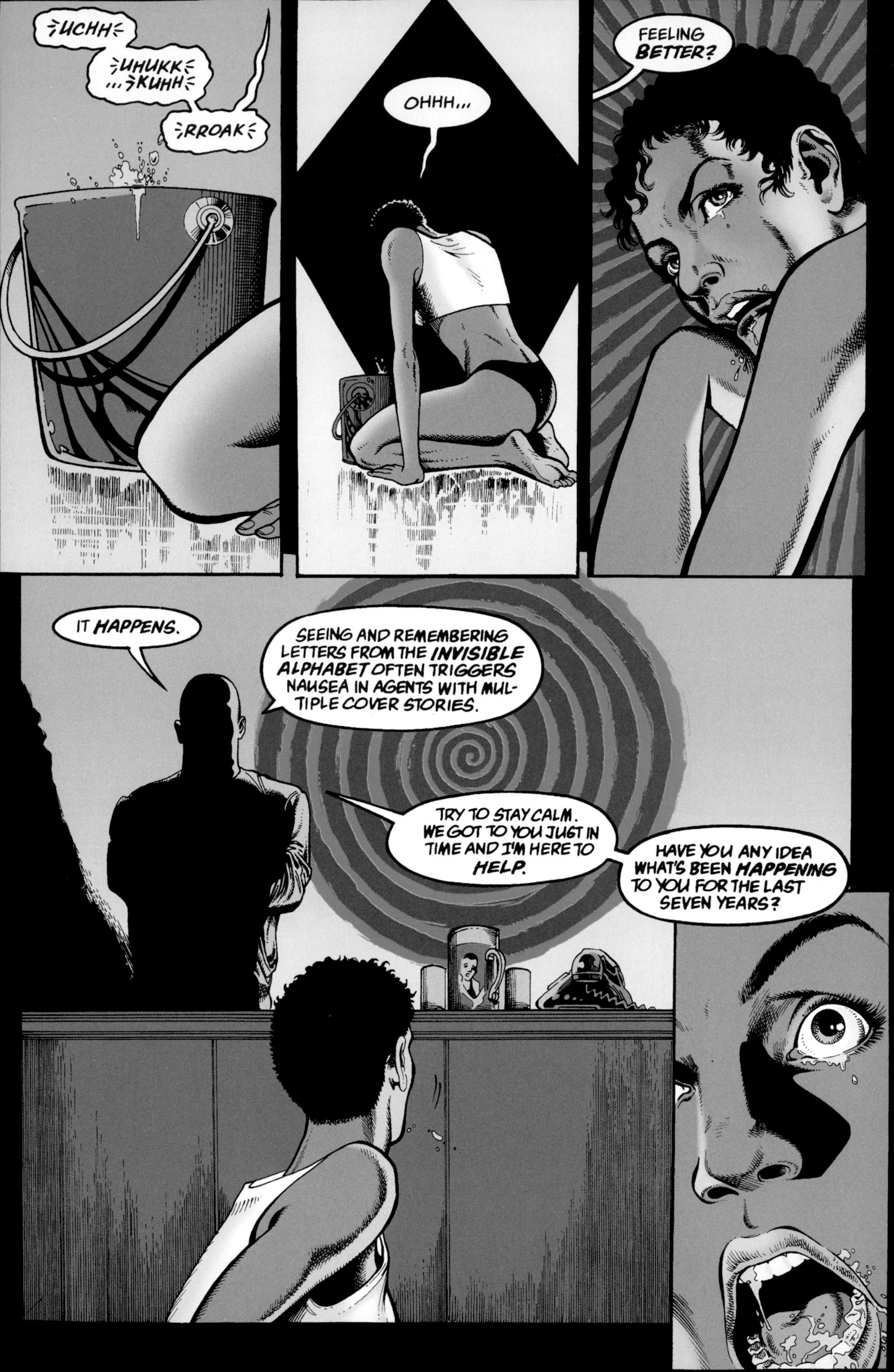
UCHH
UHUKK ...KUHH
RROAK
OHHH...
FEELING BETTER?
IT HAPPENS.
SEEING AND REMEMBERING LETTERS FROM THE INVISIBLE ALPHABET OFTEN TRIGGERS NAUSEA IN AGENTS WITH MULTIPLE COVER STORIES.
TRY TO STAY CALM. WE GOT TO YOU JUST IN TIME AND I'M HERE TO HELP.
HAVE YOU ANY IDEA WHAT'S BEEN HAPPENING TO YOU FOR THE LAST SEVEN YEARS?

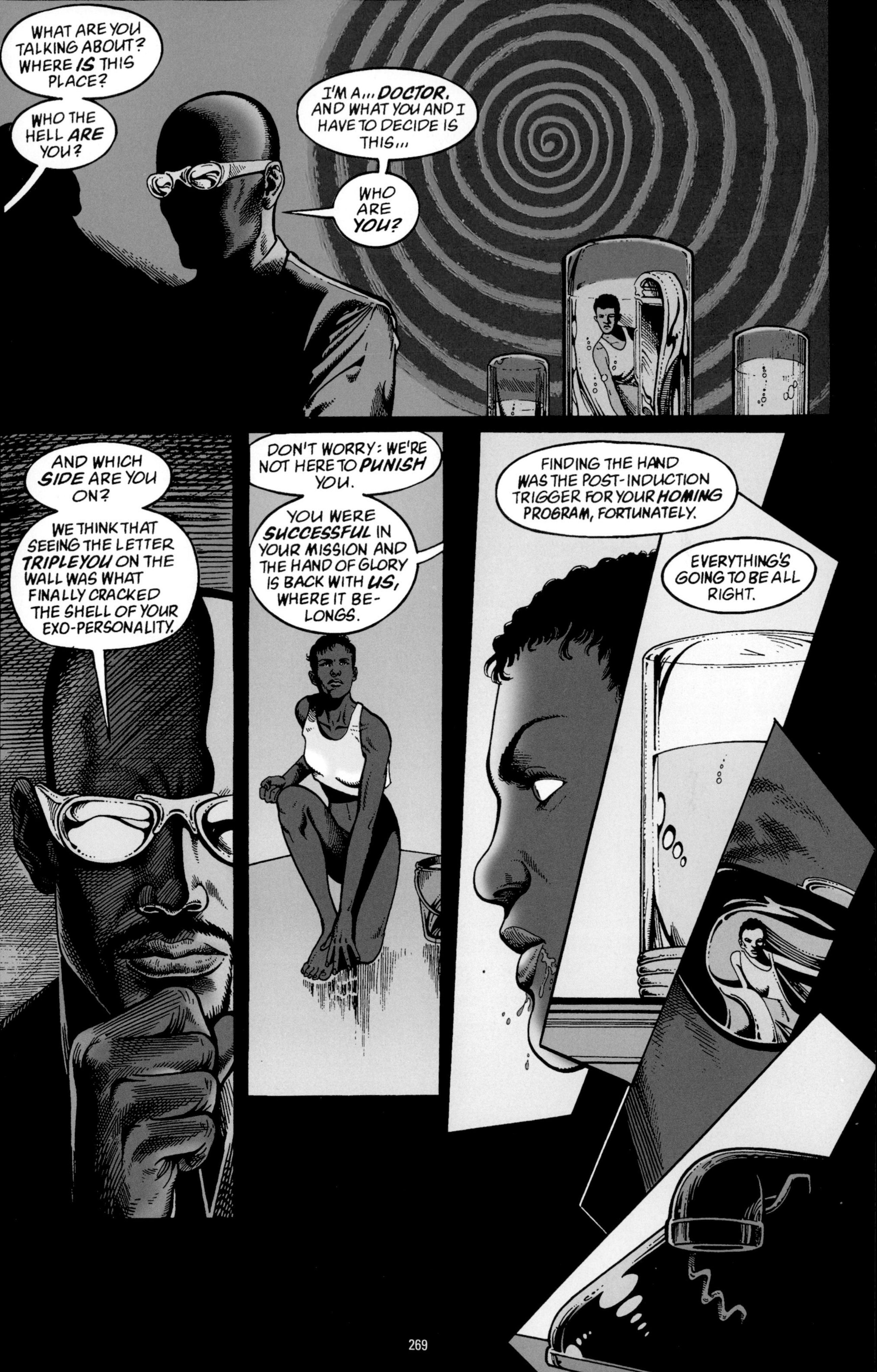
WHAT ARE YOU TALKING ABOUT? WHERE IS THIS PLACE?
WHO THE HELL ARE YOU?
I'M A... DOCTOR. AND WHAT YOU AND I HAVE TO DECIDE IS THIS...
WHO ARE YOU?
AND WHICH SIDE ARE YOU ON?
WE THINK THAT SEEING THE LETTER TRIPLEYOU ON THE WALL WAS WHAT FINALLY CRACKED THE SHELL OF YOUR EXO-PERSONALITY.
DON'T WORRY: WE'RE NOT HERE TO PUNISH YOU.
YOU WERE SUCCESSFUL IN YOUR MISSION AND THE HAND OF GLORY IS BACK WITH US, WHERE IT BE-LONGS.
FINDING THE HAND WAS THE POST-INDUCTION TRIGGER FOR YOUR HOMING PROGRAM, FORTUNATELY.
EVERYTHING'S GOING TO BE ALL RIGHT.

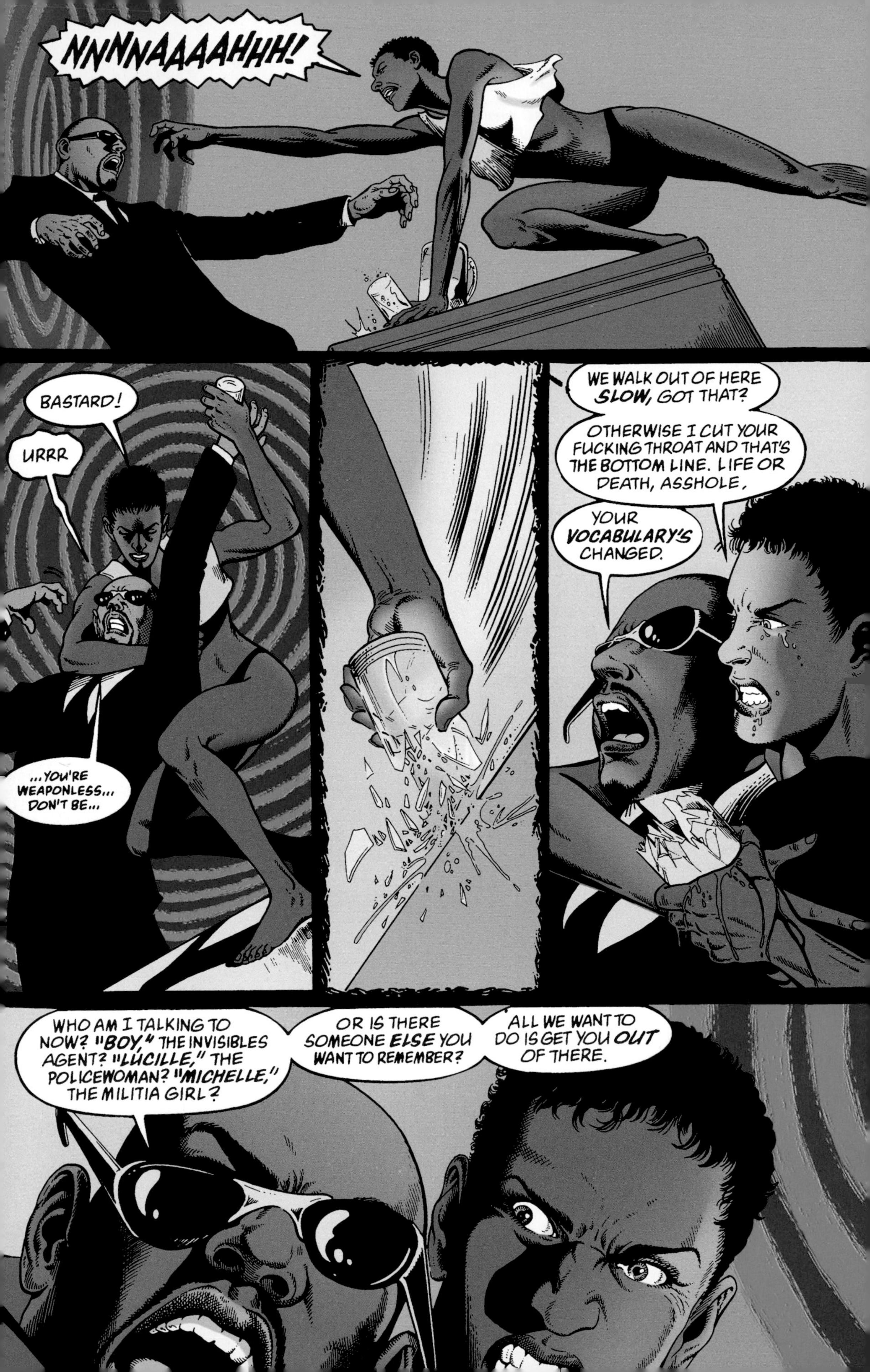
NNNNAAAAHHH!
BASTARD!
URRR
...YOU'RE WEAPONLESS... DON'T BE...
WE WALK OUT OF HERE SLOW, GOT THAT?
OTHERWISE I CUT YOUR FUCKING THROAT AND THAT'S THE BOTTOM LINE. LIFE OR DEATH, ASSHOLE.
YOUR VOCABULARY'S CHANGED.
WHO AM I TALKING TO NOW? "BOY," THE INVISIBLES AGENT? "LUCILLE," THE POLICEWOMAN? "MICHELLE," THE MILITIA GIRL?
OR IS THERE SOMEONE ELSE YOU WANT TO REMEMBER?
ALL WE WANT TO DO IS GET YOU OUT OF THERE.

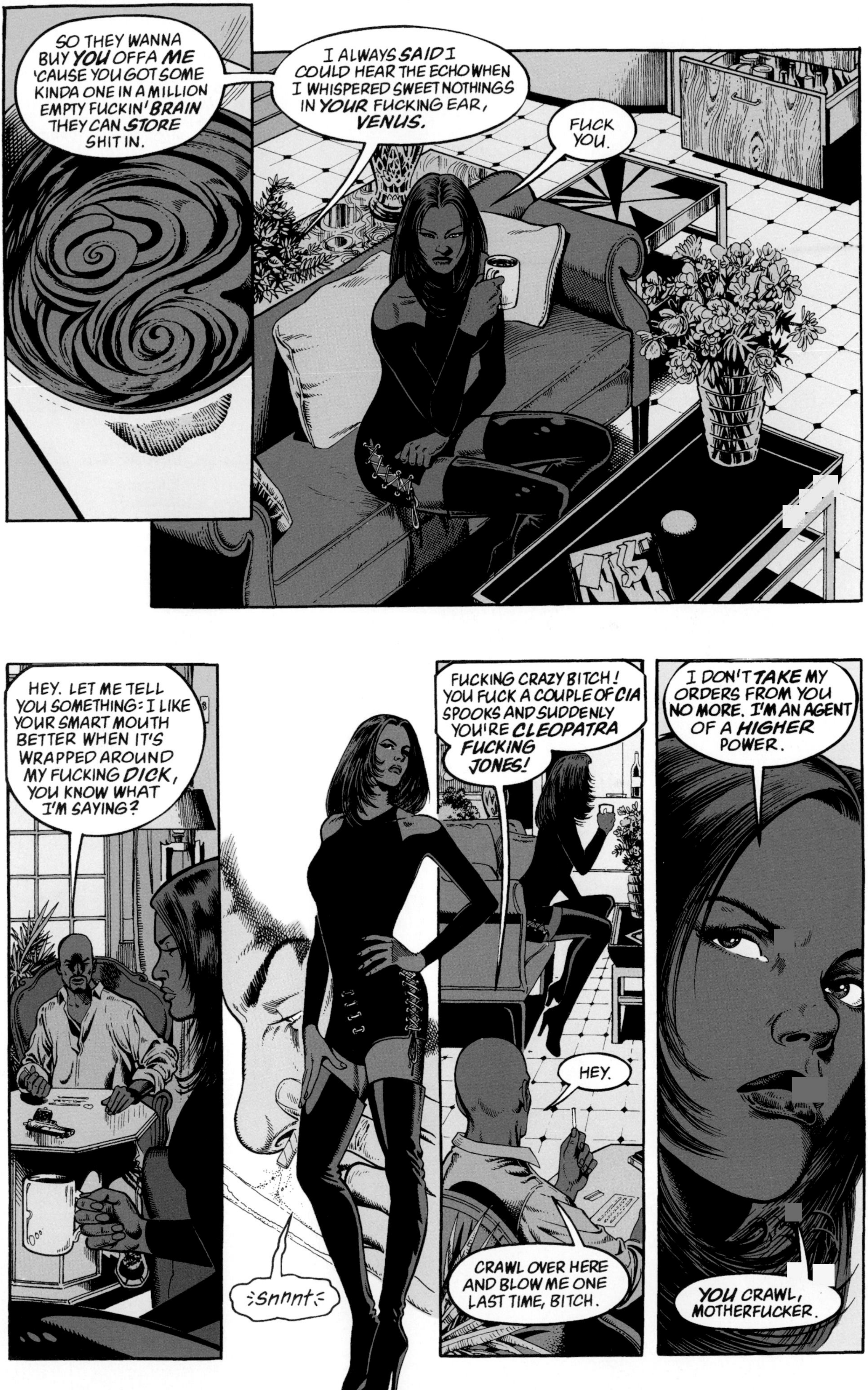
SO THEY WANNA BUY YOU OFFA ME 'CAUSE YOU GOT SOME KINDA ONE IN A MILLION EMPTY FUCKIN' BRAIN THEY CAN STORE SHIT IN.
I ALWAYS SAID I COULD HEAR THE ECHO WHEN I WHISPERED SWEET NOTHINGS IN YOUR FUCKING EAR, VENUS.
FUCK YOU.
HEY. LET ME TELL YOU SOMETHING: I LIKE YOUR SMART MOUTH BETTER WHEN IT'S WRAPPED AROUND MY FUCKING DICK, YOU KNOW WHAT I'M SAYING?
:snnnt:
FUCKING CRAZY BITCH! YOU FUCK A COUPLE OF CIA SPOOKS AND SUDDENLY YOU'RE CLEOPATRA FUCKING JONES!
HEY.
CRAWL OVER HERE AND BLOW ME ONE LAST TIME, BITCH.
I DON'T TAKE MY ORDERS FROM YOU NO MORE. I'M AN AGENT OF A HIGHER POWER.
YOU CRAWL, MOTHERFUCKER.

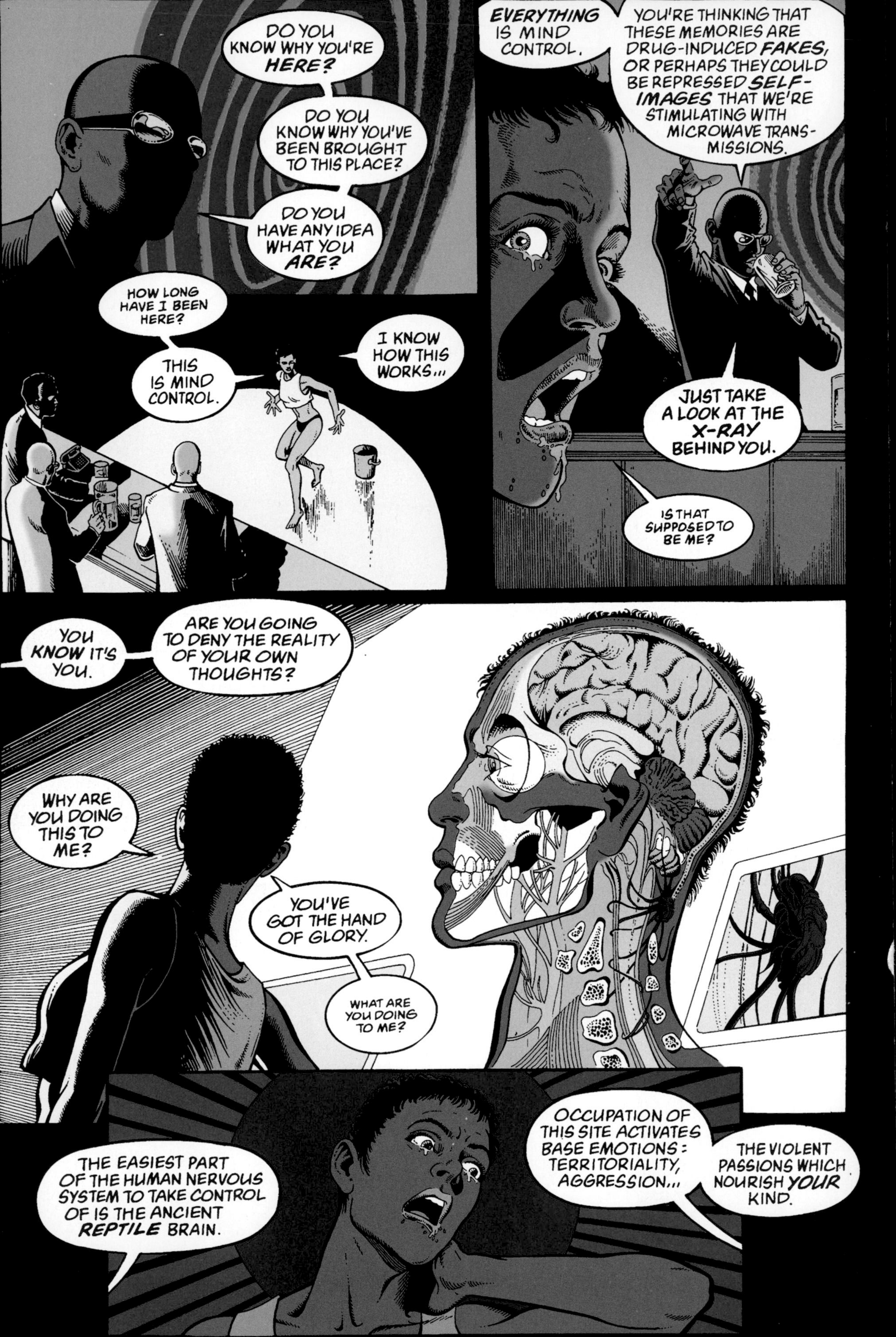
DO YOU KNOW WHY YOU'RE HERE?
DO YOU KNOW WHY YOU'VE BEEN BROUGHT TO THIS PLACE?
DO YOU HAVE ANY IDEA WHAT YOU ARE?
EVERYTHING IS MIND CONTROL.
YOU'RE THINKING THAT THESE MEMORIES ARE DRUG-INDUCED FAKES, OR PERHAPS THEY COULD BE REPRESSED SELF-IMAGES THAT WE'RE STIMULATING WITH MICROWAVE TRANS-MISSIONS.
HOW LONG HAVE I BEEN HERE?
THIS IS MIND CONTROL.
I KNOW HOW THIS WORKS...
JUST TAKE A LOOK AT THE X-RAY BEHIND YOU.
IS THAT SUPPOSED TO BE ME?
YOU KNOW IT'S YOU.
ARE YOU GOING TO DENY THE REALITY OF YOUR OWN THOUGHTS?
WHY ARE YOU DOING THIS TO ME?
YOU'VE GOT THE HAND OF GLORY.
WHAT ARE YOU DOING TO ME?
THE EASIEST PART OF THE HUMAN NERVOUS SYSTEM TO TAKE CONTROL OF IS THE ANCIENT REPTILE BRAIN.
OCCUPATION OF THIS SITE ACTIVATES BASE EMOTIONS: TERRITORIALITY, AGGRESSION...
THE VIOLENT PASSIONS WHICH NOURISH YOUR KIND.

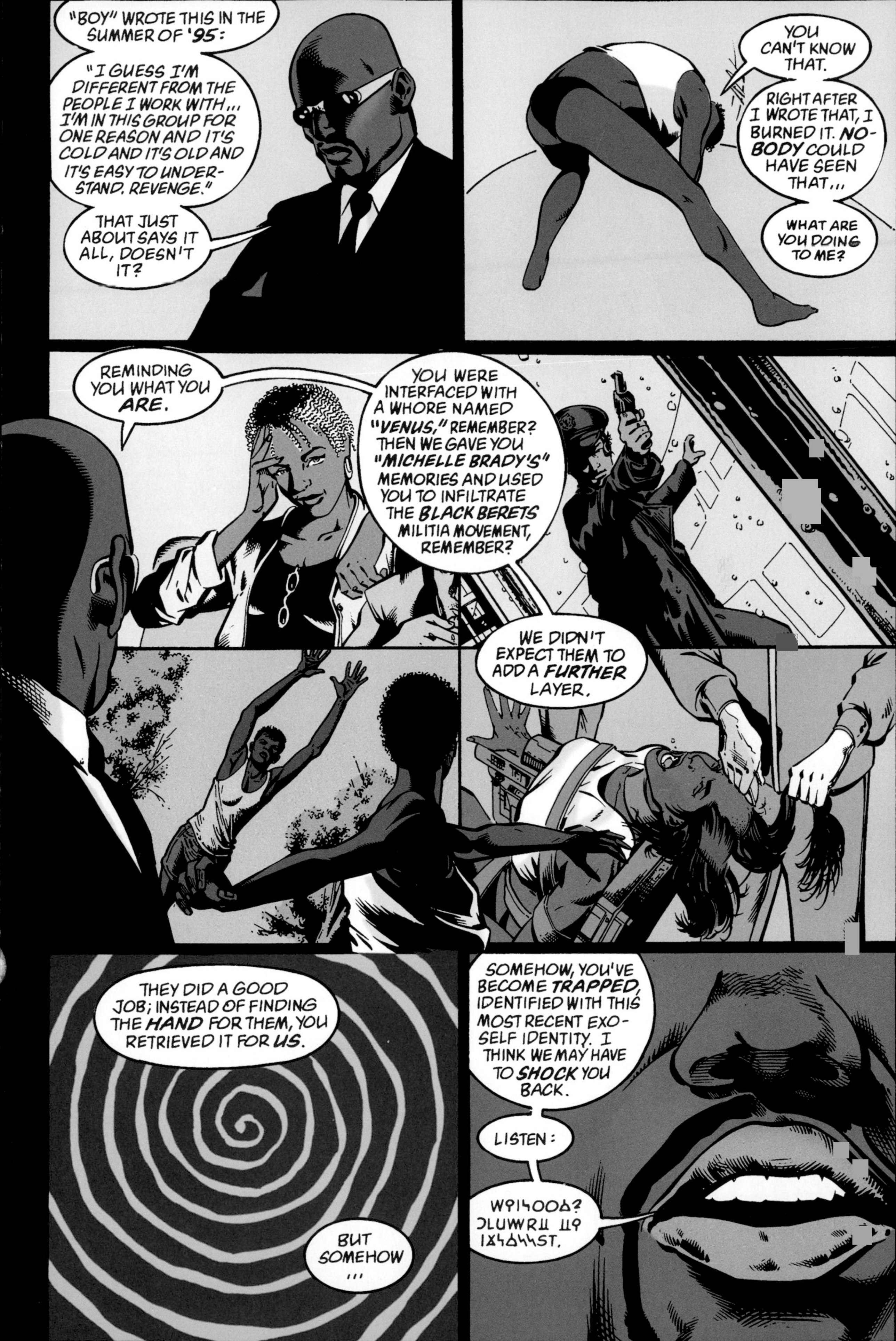

"BOY" WROTE THIS IN THE SUMMER OF '95:
"I GUESS I'M DIFFERENT FROM THE PEOPLE I WORK WITH... I'M IN THIS GROUP FOR ONE REASON AND IT'S COLD AND IT'S OLD AND IT'S EASY TO UNDERSTAND. REVENGE."
THAT JUST ABOUT SAYS IT ALL, DOESN'T IT?
YOU CAN'T KNOW THAT.
RIGHT AFTER I WROTE THAT, I BURNED IT. NOBODY COULD HAVE SEEN THAT...
WHAT ARE YOU DOING TO ME?
REMINDING YOU WHAT YOU ARE.
YOU WERE INTERFACED WITH A WHORE NAMED "VENUS," REMEMBER? THEN WE GAVE YOU "MICHELLE BRADY'S" MEMORIES AND USED YOU TO INFILTRATE THE BLACK BERETS MILITIA MOVEMENT, REMEMBER?
WE DIDN'T EXPECT THEM TO ADD A FURTHER LAYER.
THEY DID A GOOD JOB; INSTEAD OF FINDING THE HAND FOR THEM, YOU RETRIEVED IT FOR US.
BUT SOMEHOW...
SOMEHOW, YOU'VE BECOME TRAPPED, IDENTIFIED WITH THIS MOST RECENT EXO-SELF IDENTITY. I THINK WE MAY HAVE TO SHOCK YOU BACK.
LISTEN:

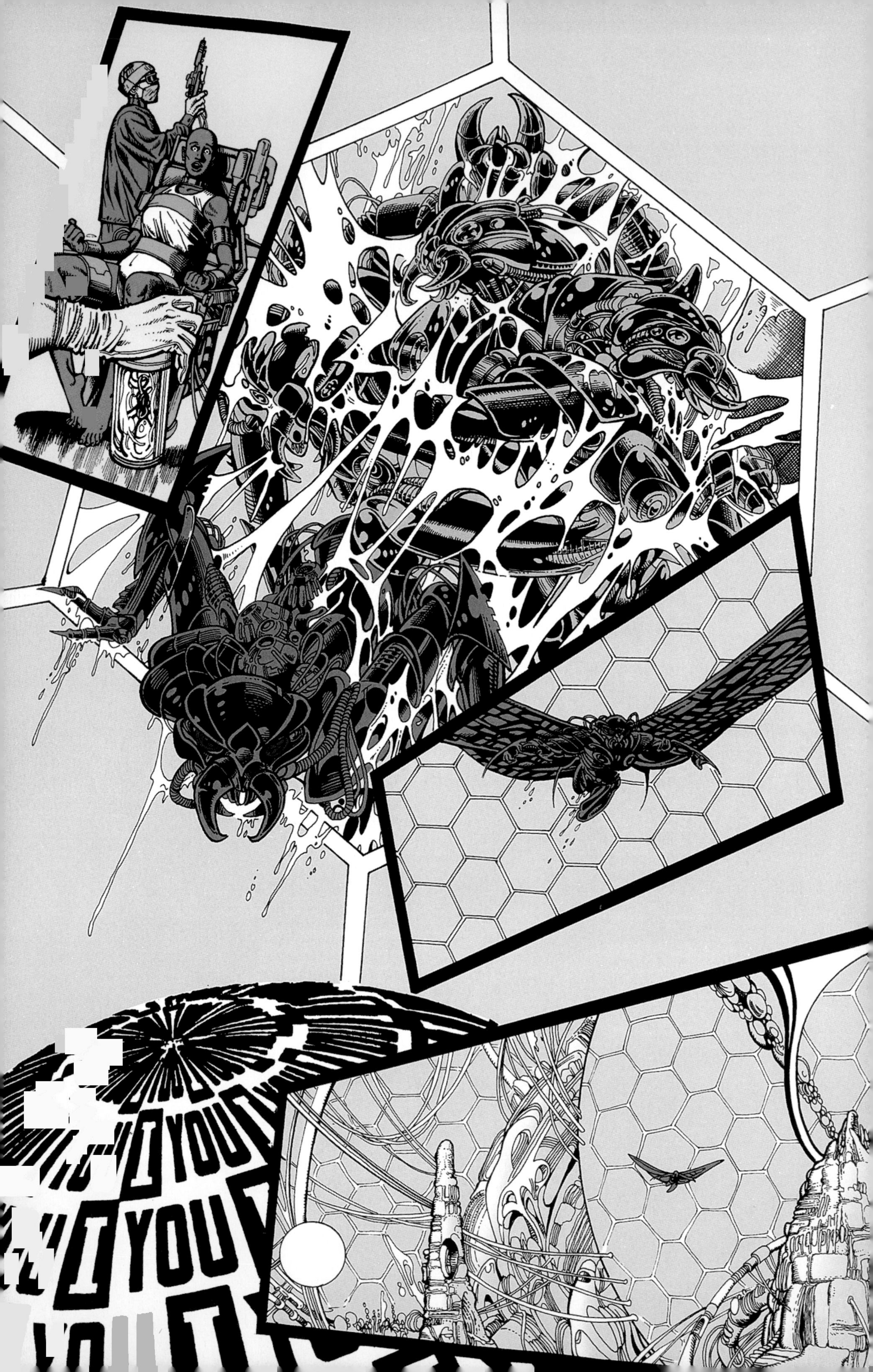
I YOU
I YOU

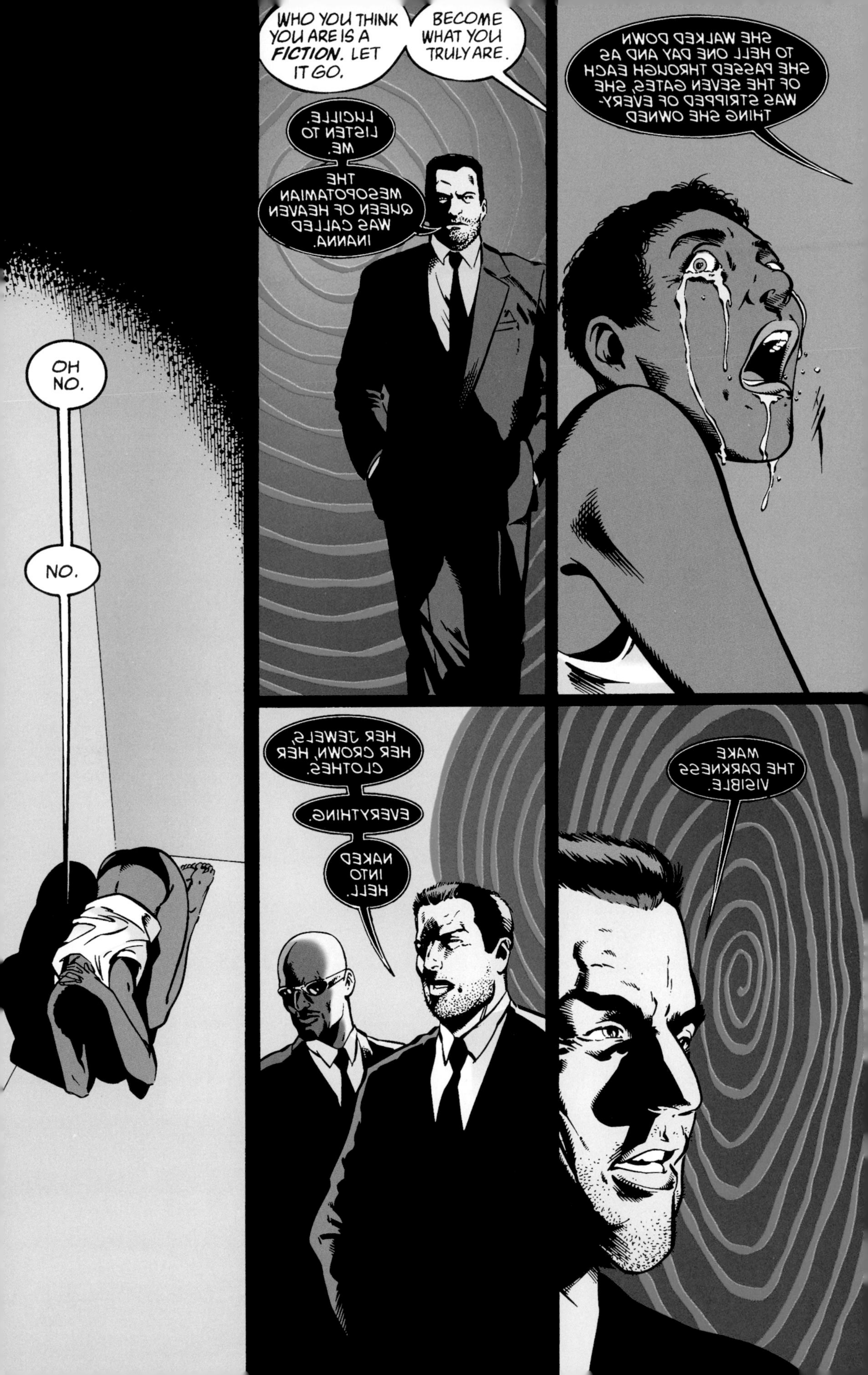
OH NO.
NO.
WHO YOU THINK YOU ARE IS A **FICTION.** LET IT GO.
BECOME WHAT YOU TRULY ARE.
LUCILLE. LISTEN TO ME.
THE MESOPOTAMIAN QUEEN OF HEAVEN WAS CALLED INANNA.
SHE WALKED DOWN TO HELL ONE DAY AND AS SHE PASSED THROUGH EACH OF THE SEVEN GATES, SHE WAS STRIPPED OF EVERY-THING SHE OWNED.
HER JEWELS, HER CROWN, HER CLOTHES.
EVERYTHING.
NAKED INTO HELL.
MAKE THE DARKNESS VISIBLE.

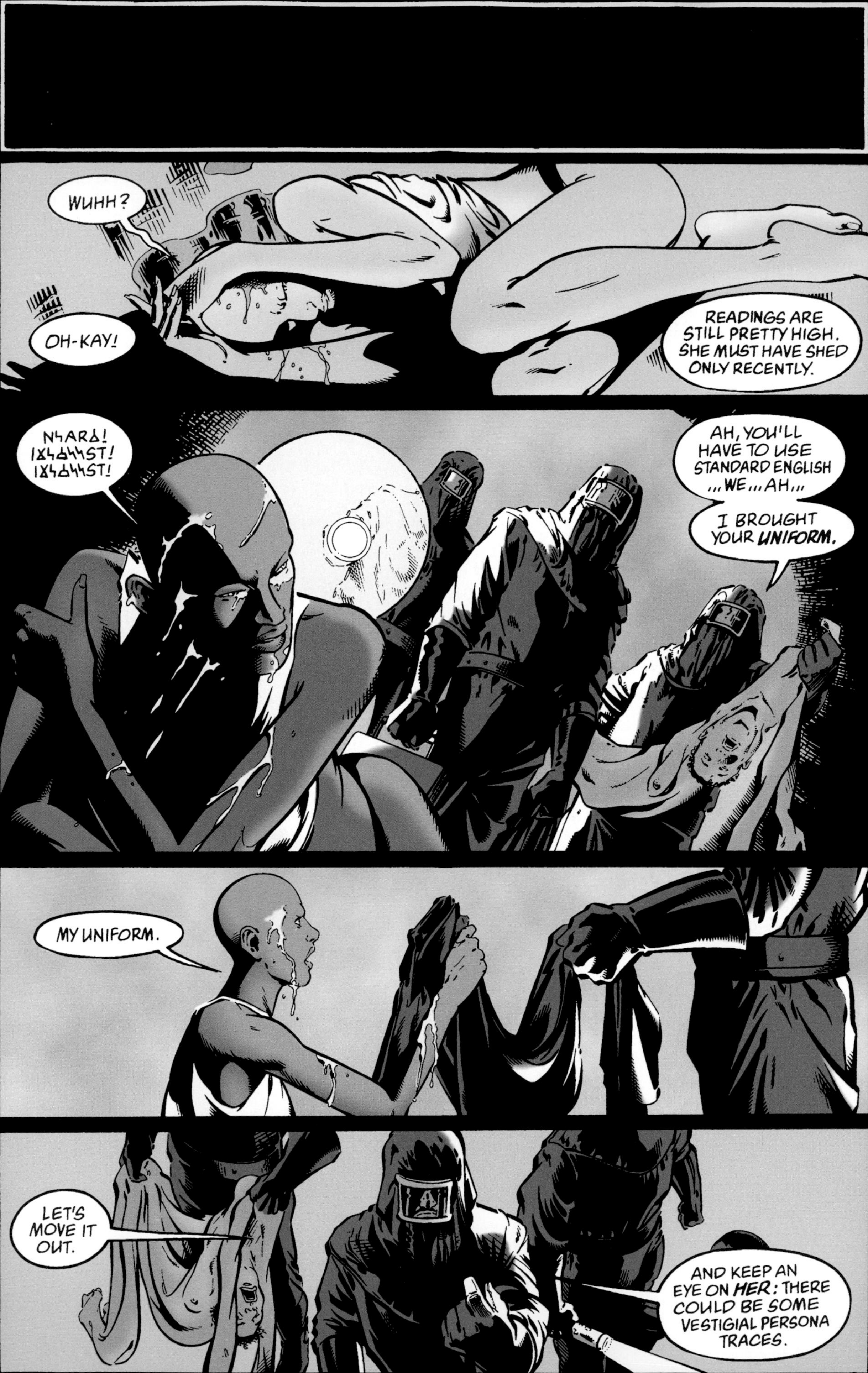
WUHH?
OH-KAY!
READINGS ARE STILL PRETTY HIGH. SHE MUST HAVE SHED ONLY RECENTLY.
AH, YOU'LL HAVE TO USE STANDARD ENGLISH ... WE ... AH ...
I BROUGHT YOUR UNIFORM.
MY UNIFORM.
LET'S MOVE IT OUT.
AND KEEP AN EYE ON HER: THERE COULD BE SOME VESTIGIAL PERSONA TRACES.

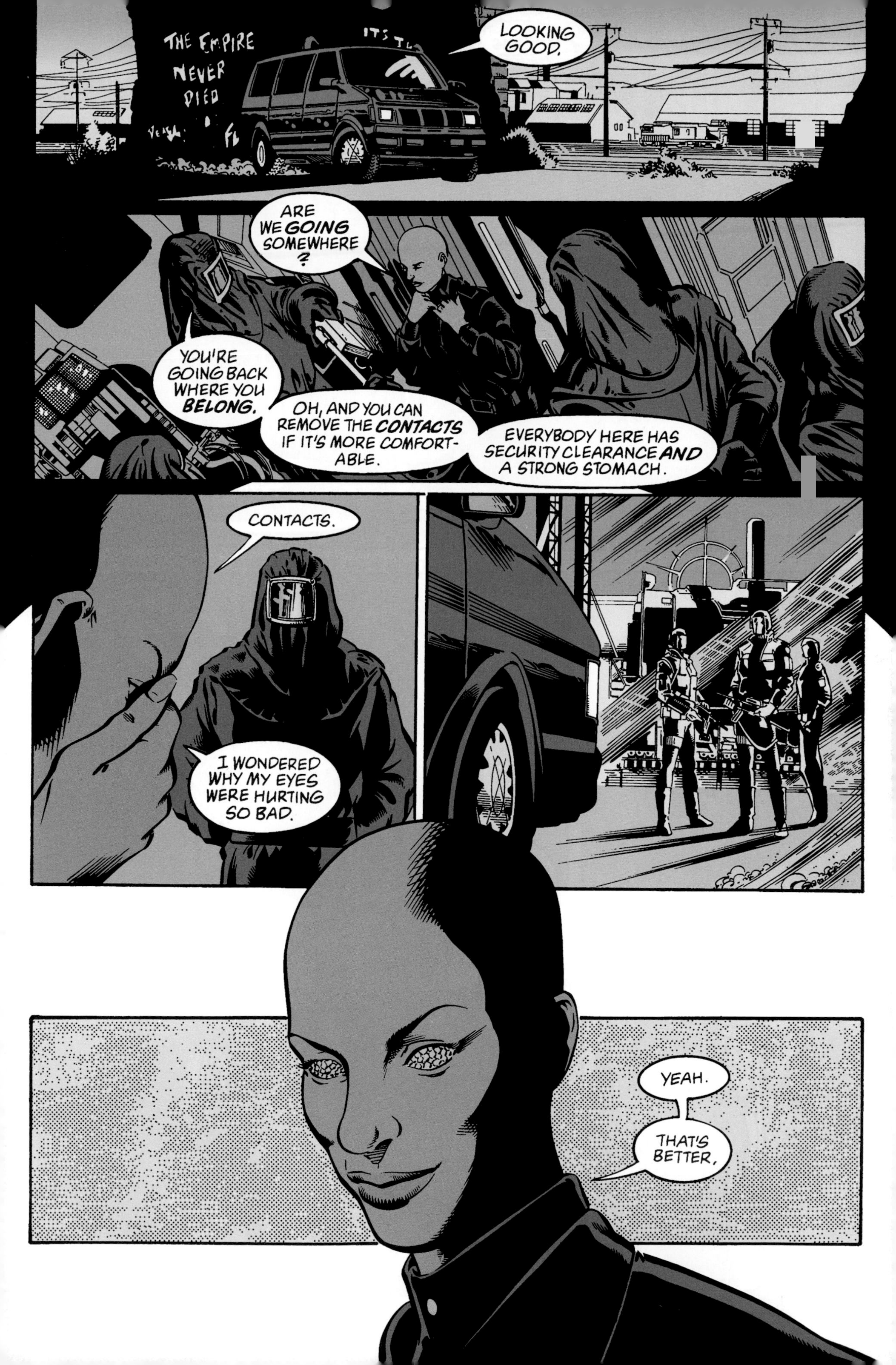
THE EMPIRE NEVER DIED
LOOKING GOOD.
ARE WE GOING SOMEWHERE?
YOU'RE GOING BACK WHERE YOU BELONG.
OH, AND YOU CAN REMOVE THE CONTACTS IF IT'S MORE COMFORT-ABLE.
EVERYBODY HERE HAS SECURITY CLEARANCE AND A STRONG STOMACH.
CONTACTS.
I WONDERED WHY MY EYES WERE HURTING SO BAD.
YEAH.
THAT'S BETTER.

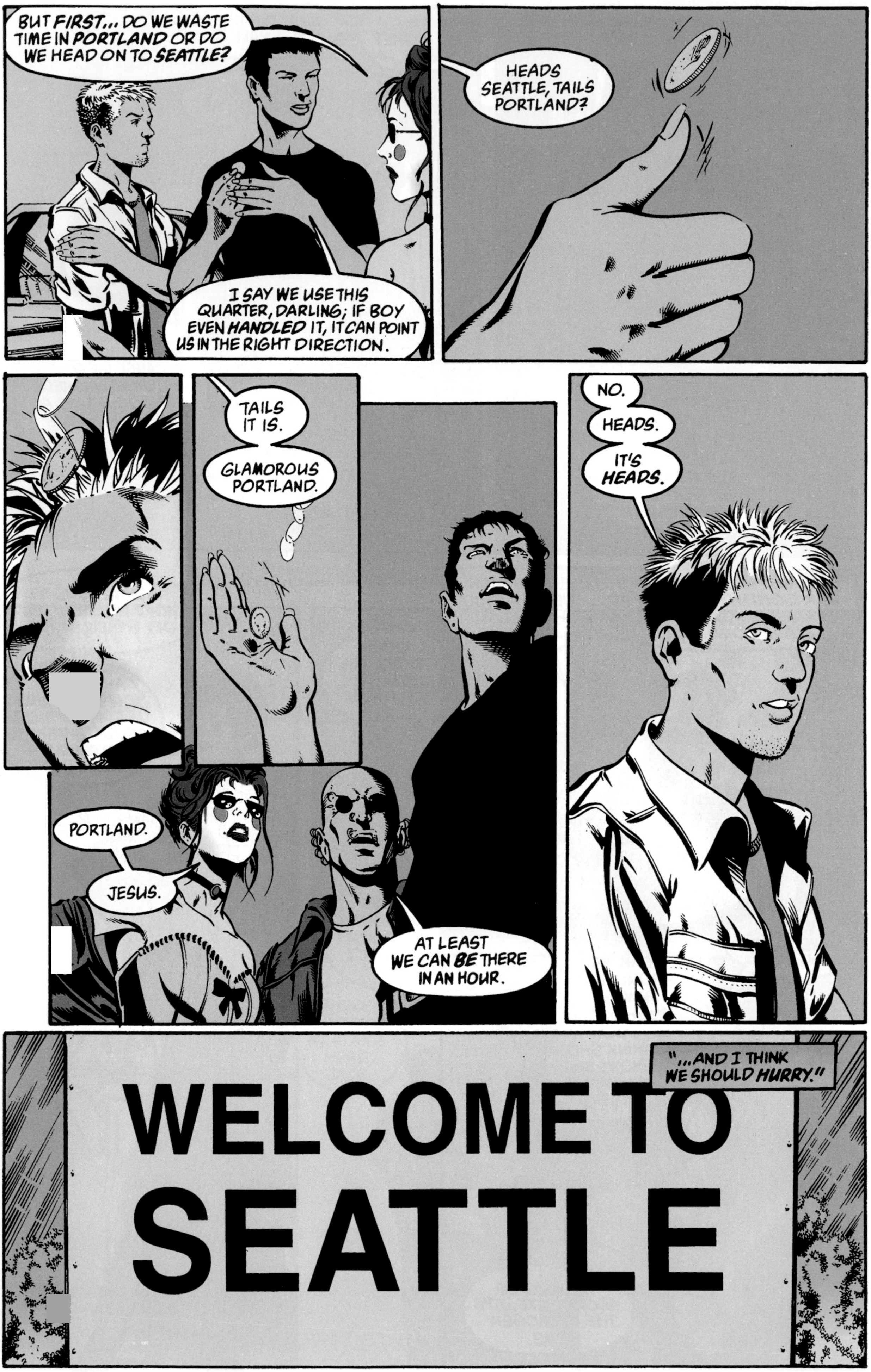
BUT FIRST... DO WE WASTE TIME IN PORTLAND OR DO WE HEAD ON TO SEATTLE?
I SAY WE USE THIS QUARTER, DARLING; IF BOY EVEN HANDLED IT, IT CAN POINT US IN THE RIGHT DIRECTION.
HEADS SEATTLE, TAILS PORTLAND?
TAILS IT IS.
GLAMOROUS PORTLAND.
PORTLAND.
JESUS.
AT LEAST WE CAN BE THERE IN AN HOUR.
NO.
HEADS.
IT'S HEADS.
"...AND I THINK WE SHOULD HURRY."
WELCOME TO SEATTLE

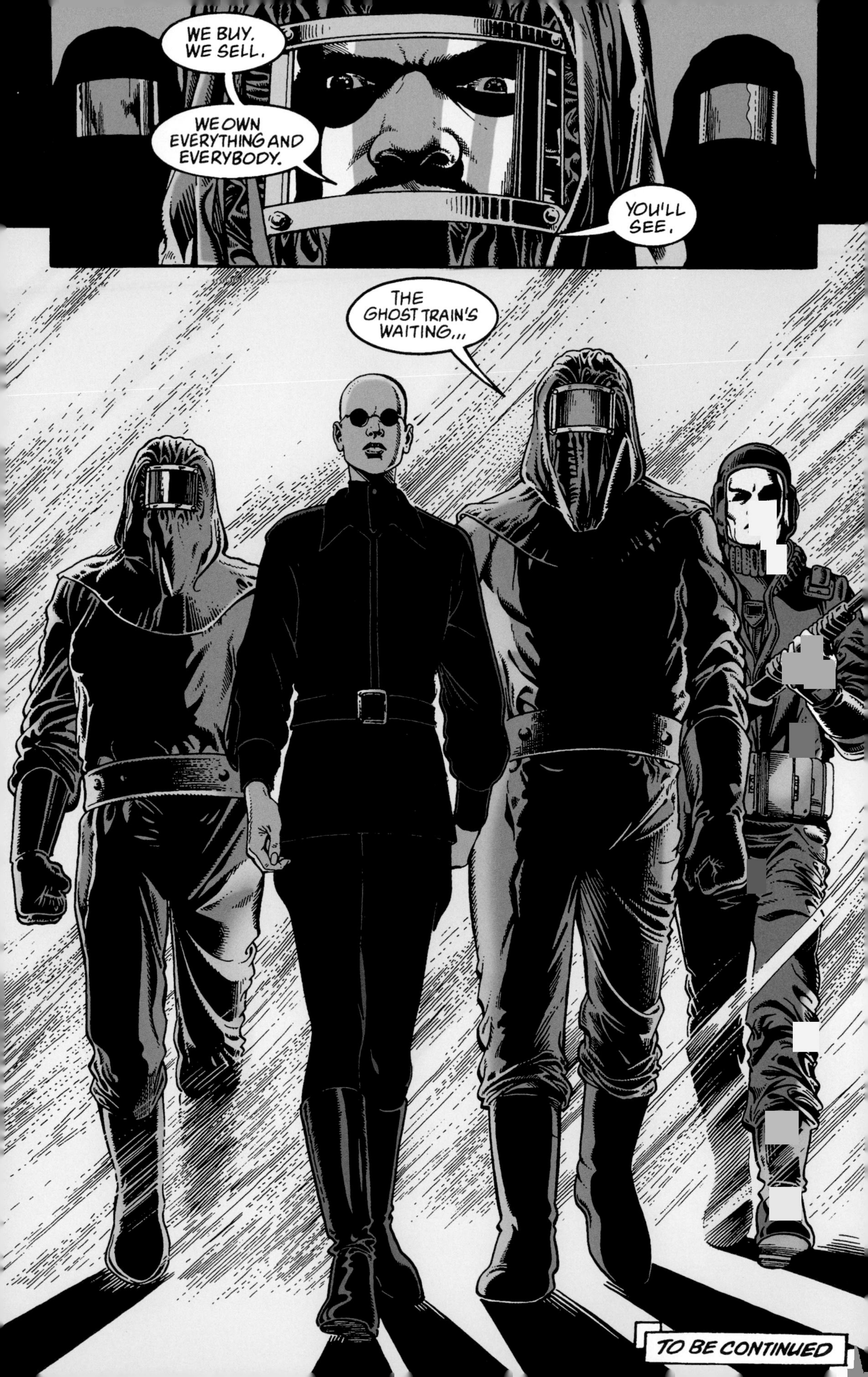
WE BUY. WE SELL.
WE OWN EVERYTHING AND EVERYBODY.
YOU'LL SEE.
THE GHOST TRAIN'S WAITING...
TO BE CONTINUED

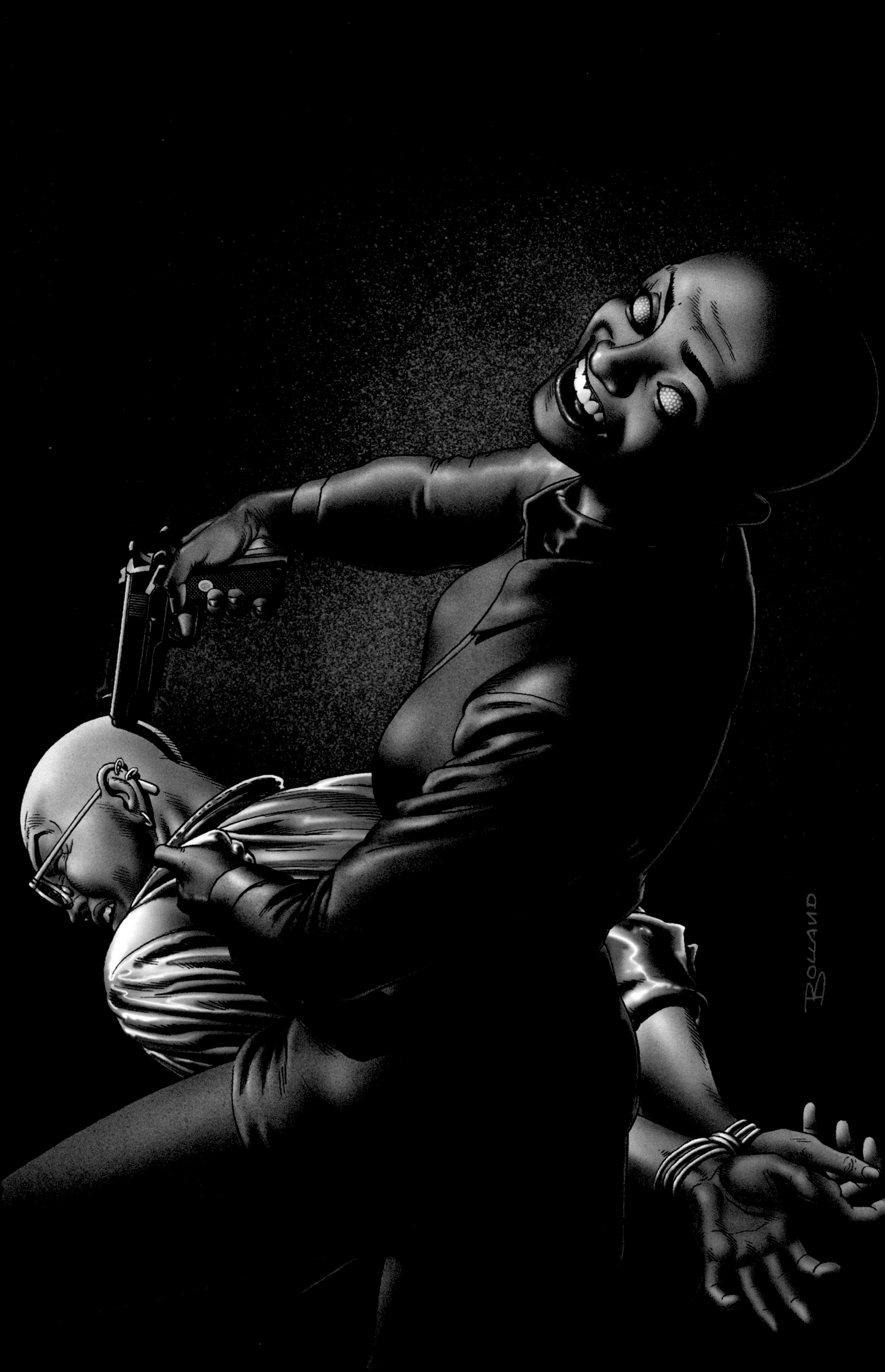
BOLLAND

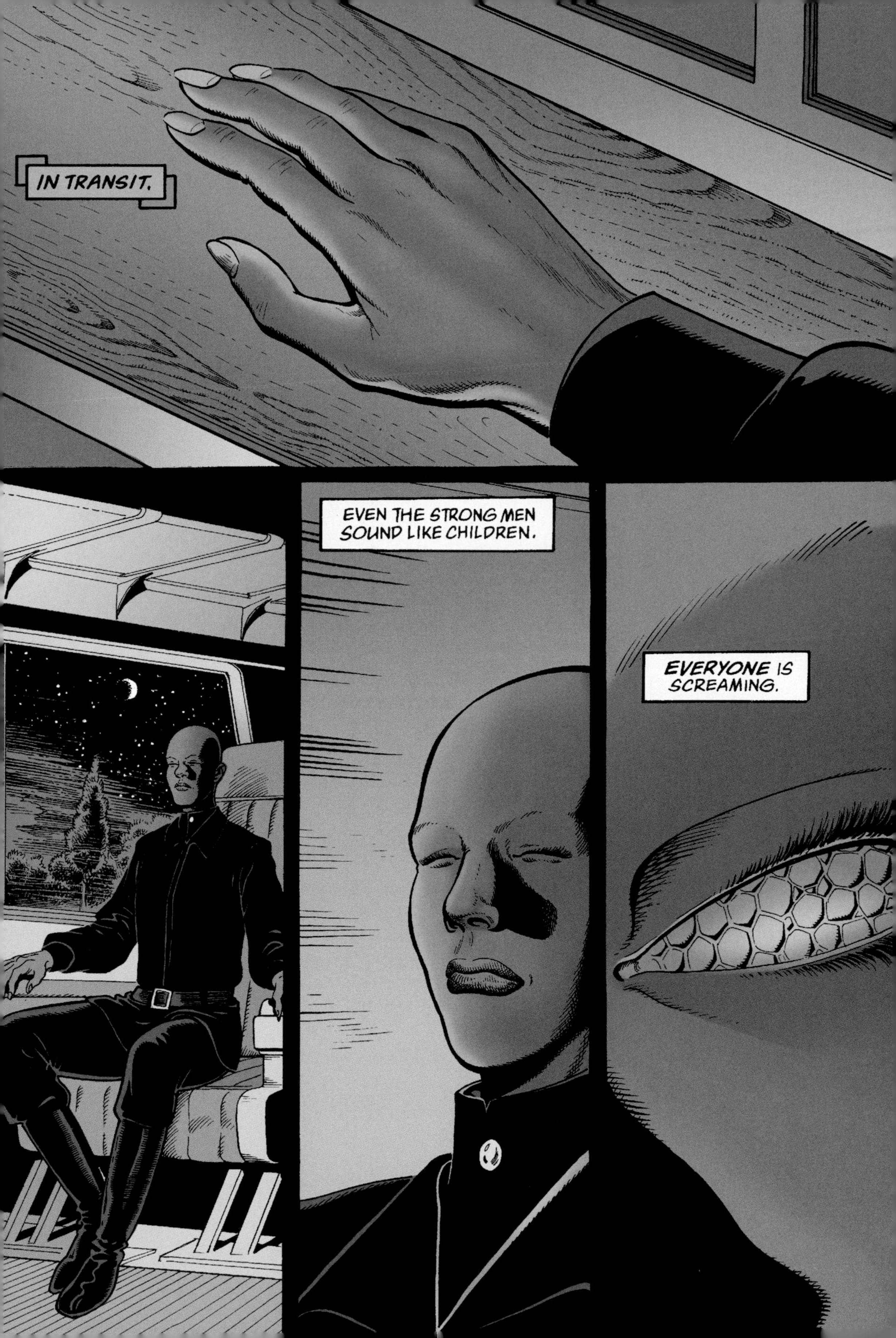
IN TRANSIT.
EVEN THE STRONG MEN SOUND LIKE CHILDREN.
EVERYONE IS SCREAMING.

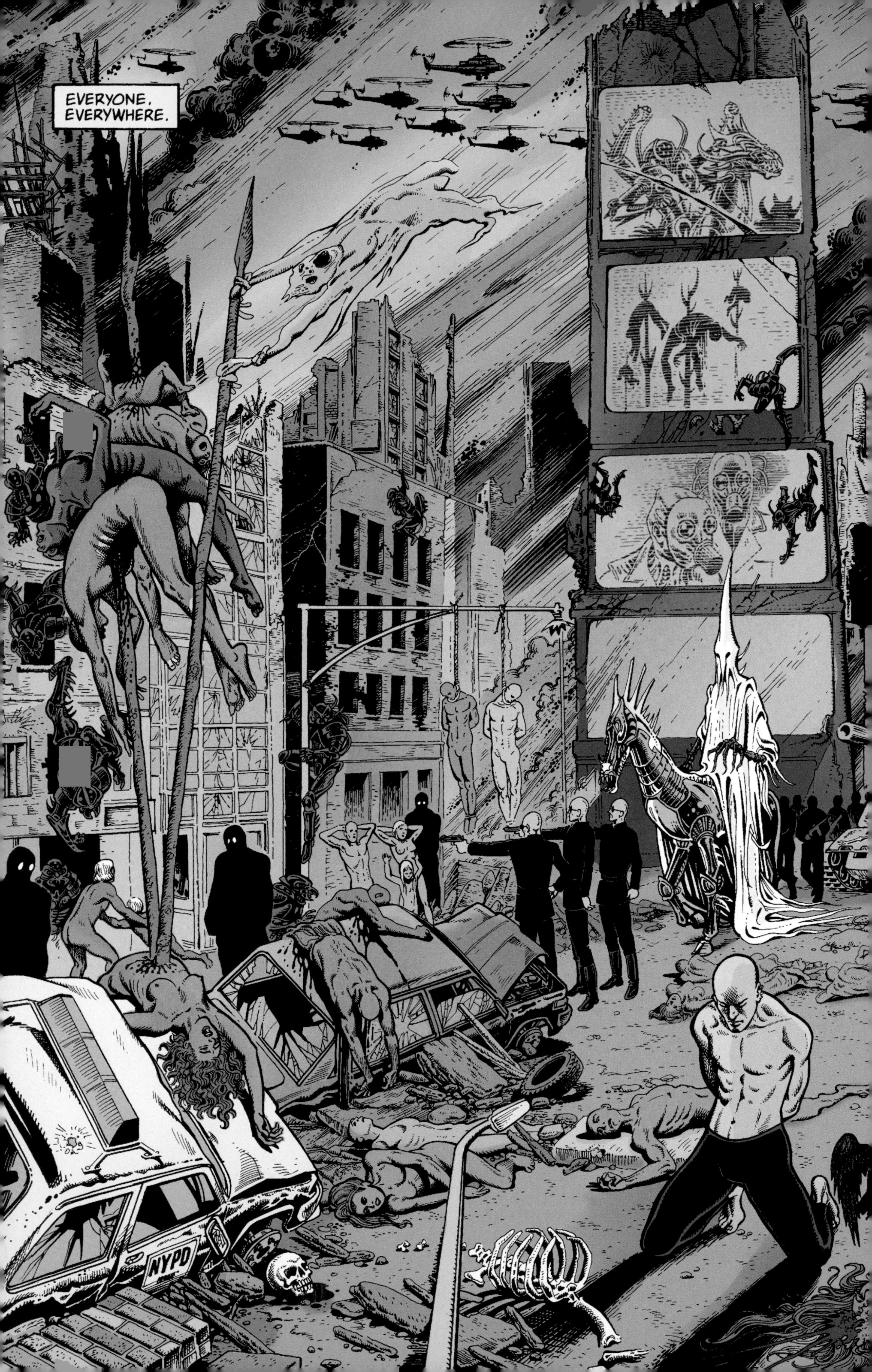
EVERYONE. EVERYWHERE.
NYPD

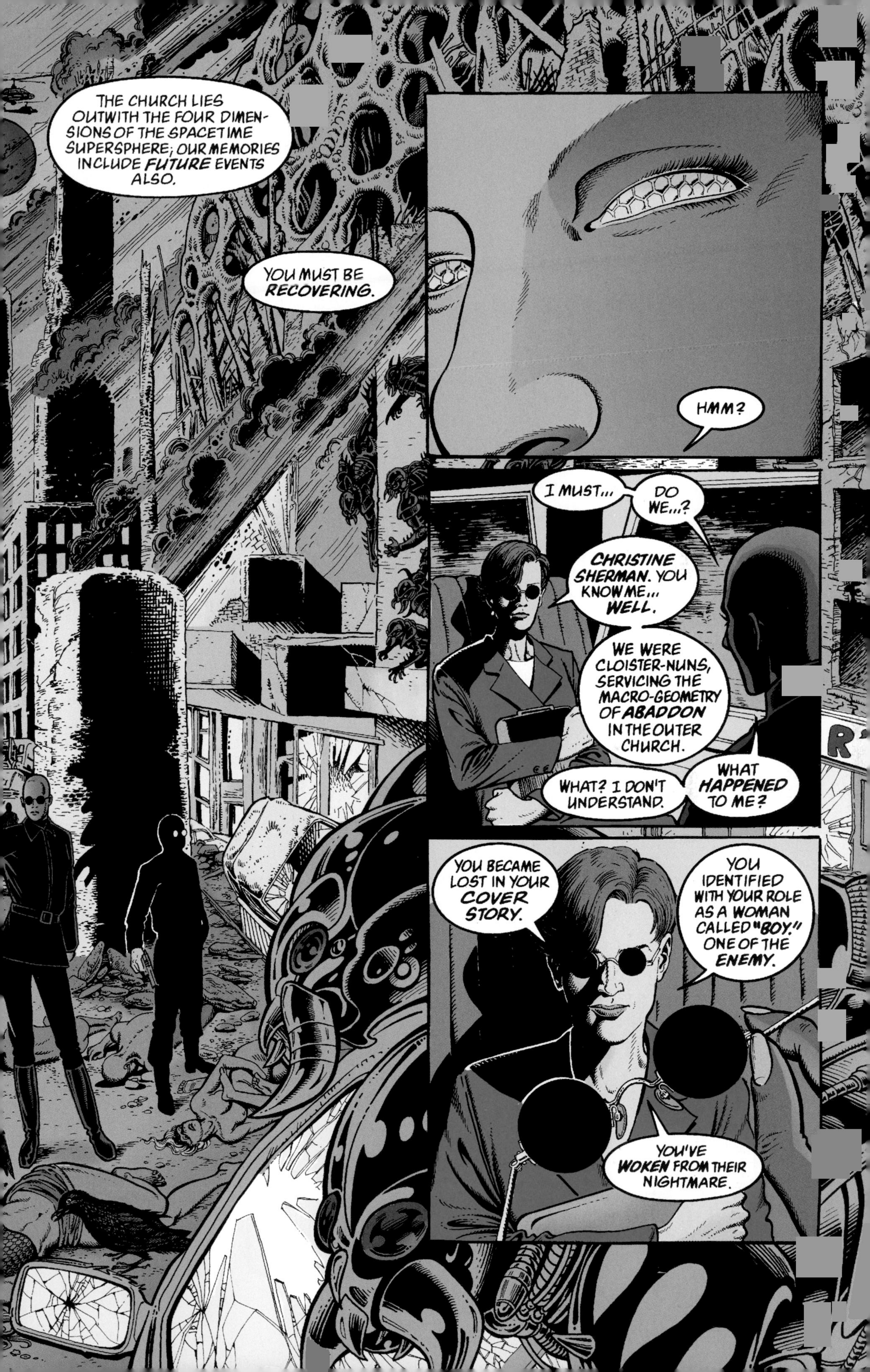

THE CHURCH LIES OUTWITH THE FOUR DIMENSIONS OF THE SPACETIME SUPERSPHERE; OUR MEMORIES INCLUDE FUTURE EVENTS ALSO.
YOU MUST BE RECOVERING.
HMM?
I MUST...
DO WE...?
CHRISTINE SHERMAN. YOU KNOW ME... WELL.
WE WERE CLOISTER-NUNS, SERVICING THE MACRO-GEOMETRY OF ABADDON IN THE OUTER CHURCH.
WHAT? I DON'T UNDERSTAND.
WHAT HAPPENED TO ME?
YOU BECAME LOST IN YOUR COVER STORY.
YOU IDENTIFIED WITH YOUR ROLE AS A WOMAN CALLED "BOY." ONE OF THE ENEMY.
YOU'VE WOKEN FROM THEIR NIGHTMARE.

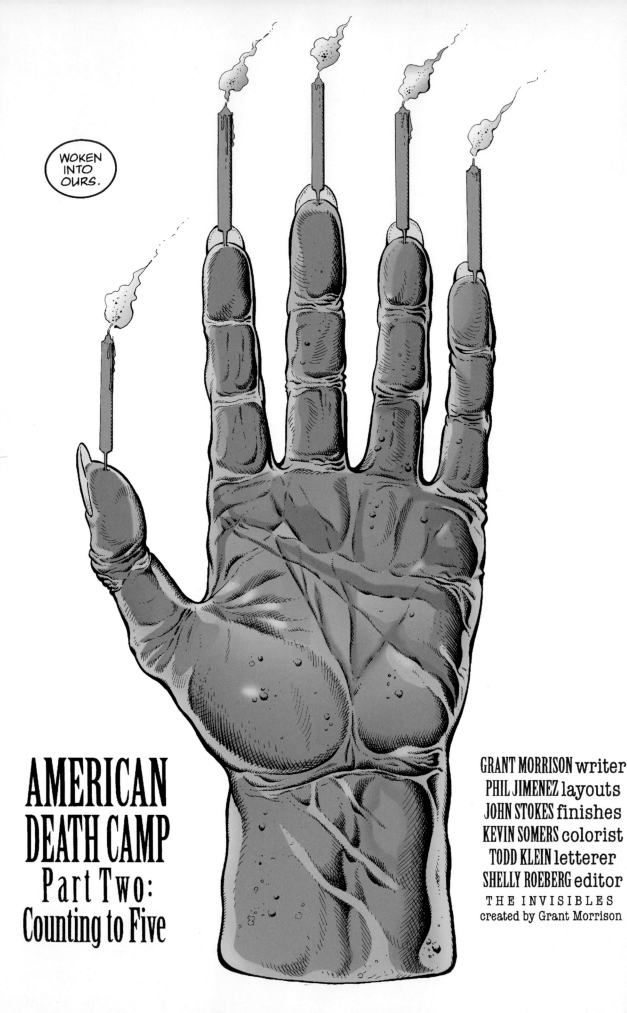

WOKEN INTO OURS.

AMERICAN
DEATH CAMP
Part Two:
Counting to Five

GRANT MORRISON writer
PHIL JIMENEZ layouts
JOHN STOKES finishes
KEVIN SOMERS colorist
TODD KLEIN letterer
SHELLY ROEBERG editor
THE INVISIBLES
created by Grant Morrison

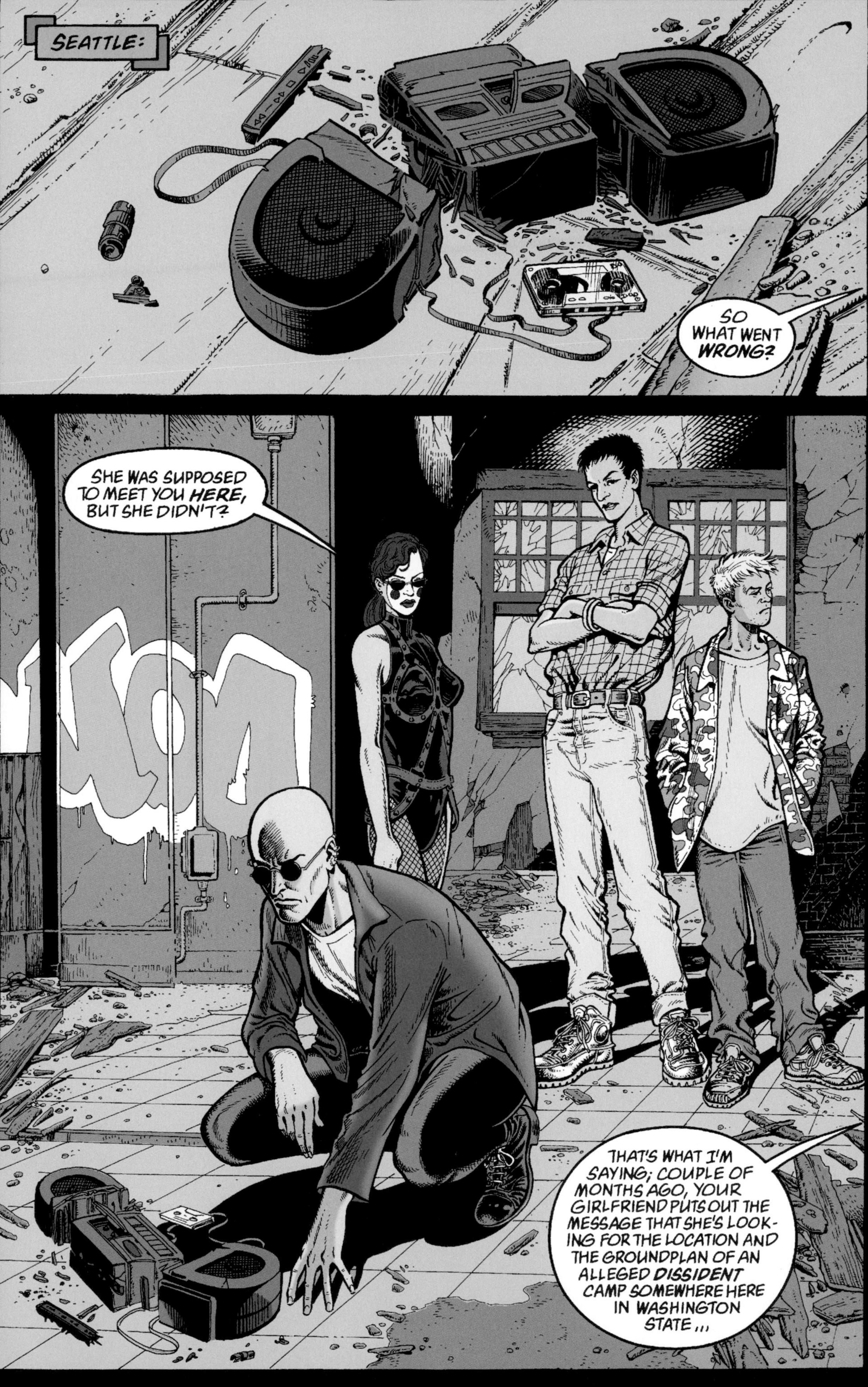
SEATTLE:
SO WHAT WENT WRONG?
SHE WAS SUPPOSED TO MEET YOU HERE, BUT SHE DIDN'T?
THAT'S WHAT I'M SAYING; COUPLE OF MONTHS AGO, YOUR GIRLFRIEND PUTS OUT THE MESSAGE THAT SHE'S LOOKING FOR THE LOCATION AND THE GROUNDPLAN OF AN ALLEGED DISSIDENT CAMP SOMEWHERE HERE IN WASHINGTON STATE...

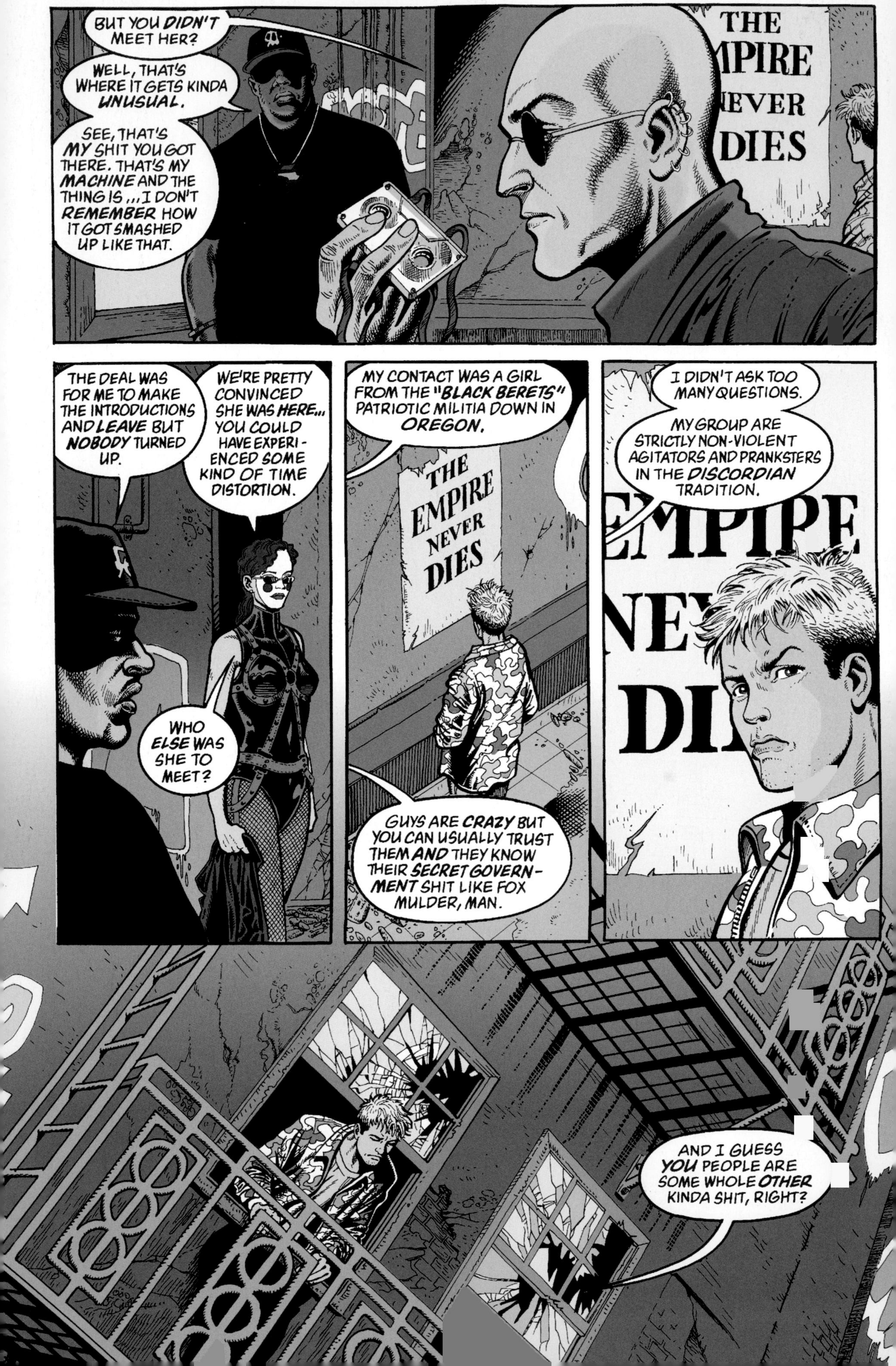
BUT YOU DIDN'T MEET HER?
WELL, THAT'S WHERE IT GETS KINDA UNUSUAL.
SEE, THAT'S MY SHIT YOU GOT THERE. THAT'S MY MACHINE AND THE THING IS ... I DON'T REMEMBER HOW IT GOT SMASHED UP LIKE THAT.
THE EMPIRE NEVER DIES
THE DEAL WAS FOR ME TO MAKE THE INTRODUCTIONS AND LEAVE BUT NOBODY TURNED UP.
WE'RE PRETTY CONVINCED SHE WAS HERE... YOU COULD HAVE EXPERI-ENCED SOME KIND OF TIME DISTORTION.
WHO ELSE WAS SHE TO MEET?
MY CONTACT WAS A GIRL FROM THE "BLACK BERETS" PATRIOTIC MILITIA DOWN IN OREGON.
THE EMPIRE NEVER DIES
GUYS ARE CRAZY BUT YOU CAN USUALLY TRUST THEM AND THEY KNOW THEIR SECRET GOVERN-MENT SHIT LIKE FOX MULDER, MAN.
I DIDN'T ASK TOO MANY QUESTIONS.
MY GROUP ARE STRICTLY NON-VIOLENT AGITATORS AND PRANKSTERS IN THE DISCORDIAN TRADITION.
AND I GUESS YOU PEOPLE ARE SOME WHOLE OTHER KINDA SHIT, RIGHT?

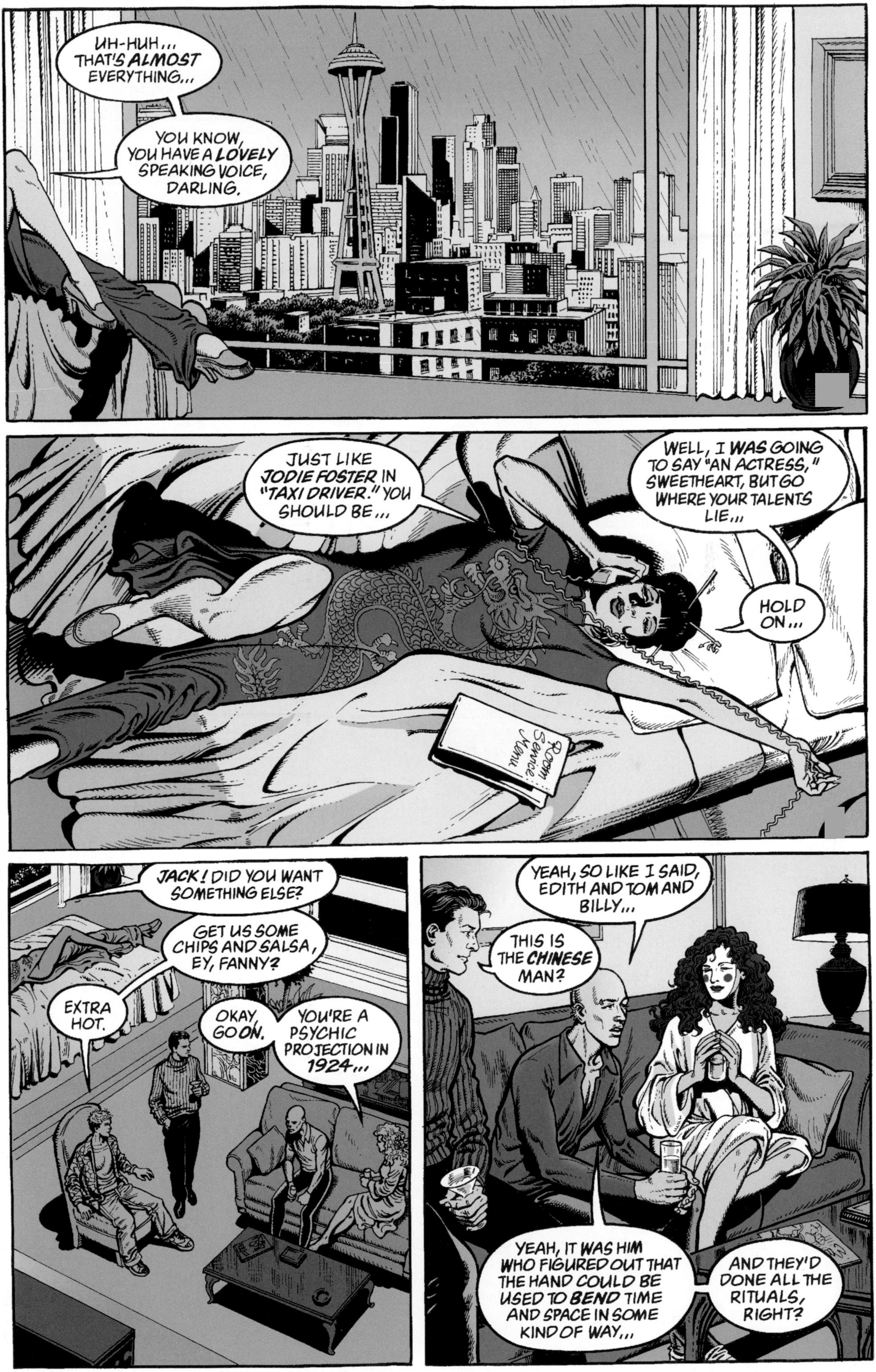

UH-HUH... THAT'S ALMOST EVERYTHING...
YOU KNOW, YOU HAVE A LOVELY SPEAKING VOICE, DARLING.
JUST LIKE JODIE FOSTER IN "TAXI DRIVER." YOU SHOULD BE...
WELL, I WAS GOING TO SAY "AN ACTRESS," SWEETHEART, BUT GO WHERE YOUR TALENTS LIE...
HOLD ON...
Room Service Menu
JACK! DID YOU WANT SOMETHING ELSE?
GET US SOME CHIPS AND SALSA, EY, FANNY?
EXTRA HOT.
OKAY, GO ON.
YOU'RE A PSYCHIC PROJECTION IN 1924...
YEAH, SO LIKE I SAID, EDITH AND TOM AND BILLY...
THIS IS THE CHINESE MAN?
YEAH, IT WAS HIM WHO FIGURED OUT THAT THE HAND COULD BE USED TO BEND TIME AND SPACE IN SOME KIND OF WAY...
AND THEY'D DONE ALL THE RITUALS, RIGHT?

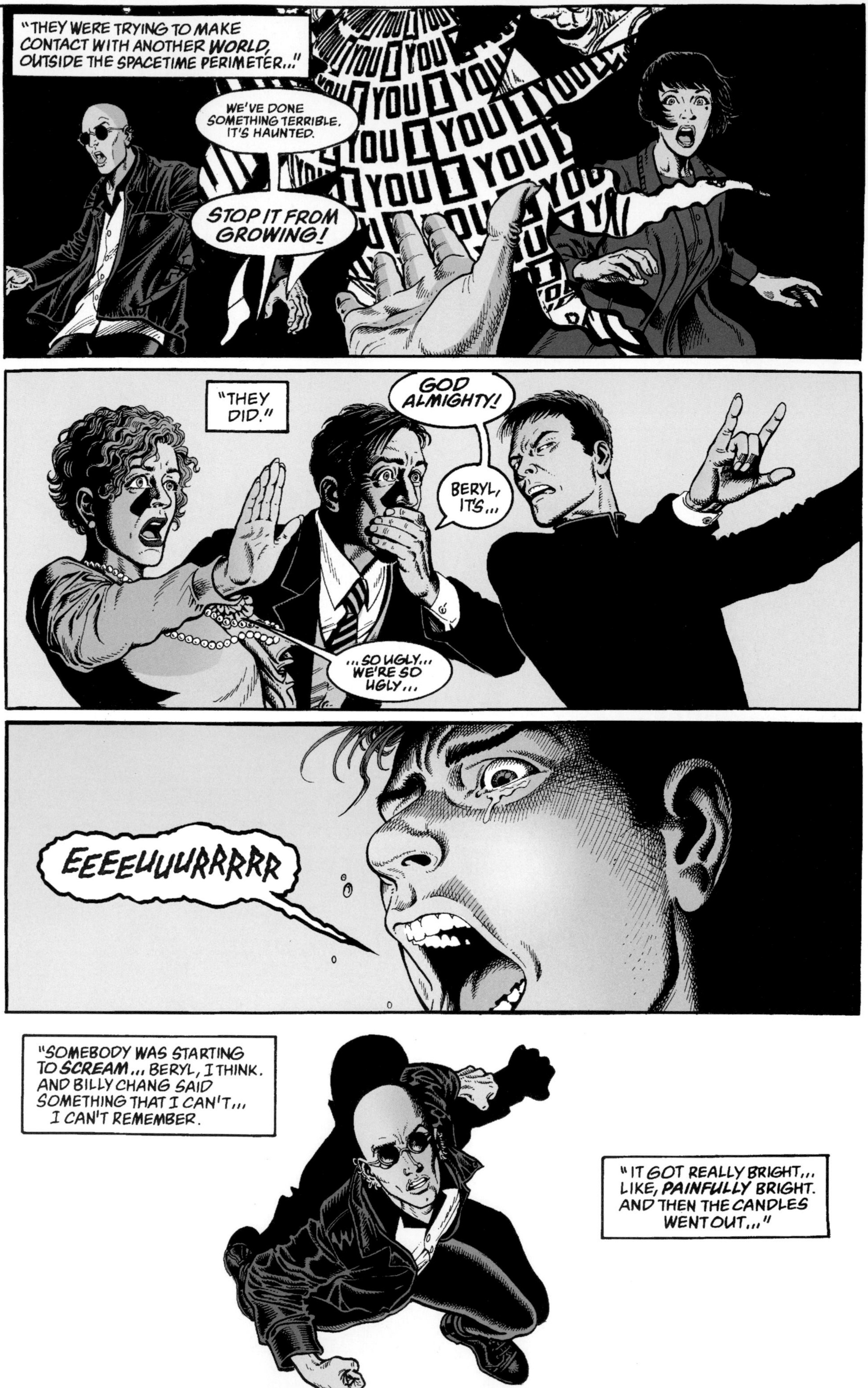
"THEY WERE TRYING TO MAKE CONTACT WITH ANOTHER WORLD, OUTSIDE THE SPACETIME PERIMETER..."
WE'VE DONE SOMETHING TERRIBLE. IT'S HAUNTED.
STOP IT FROM GROWING!
"THEY DID."
GOD ALMIGHTY!
BERYL, IT'S...
...SO UGLY... WE'RE SO UGLY...
EEEEUUURRRRR
"SOMEBODY WAS STARTING TO SCREAM... BERYL, I THINK. AND BILLY CHANG SAID SOMETHING THAT I CAN'T... I CAN'T REMEMBER.
"IT GOT REALLY BRIGHT... LIKE, PAINFULLY BRIGHT. AND THEN THE CANDLES WENT OUT..."

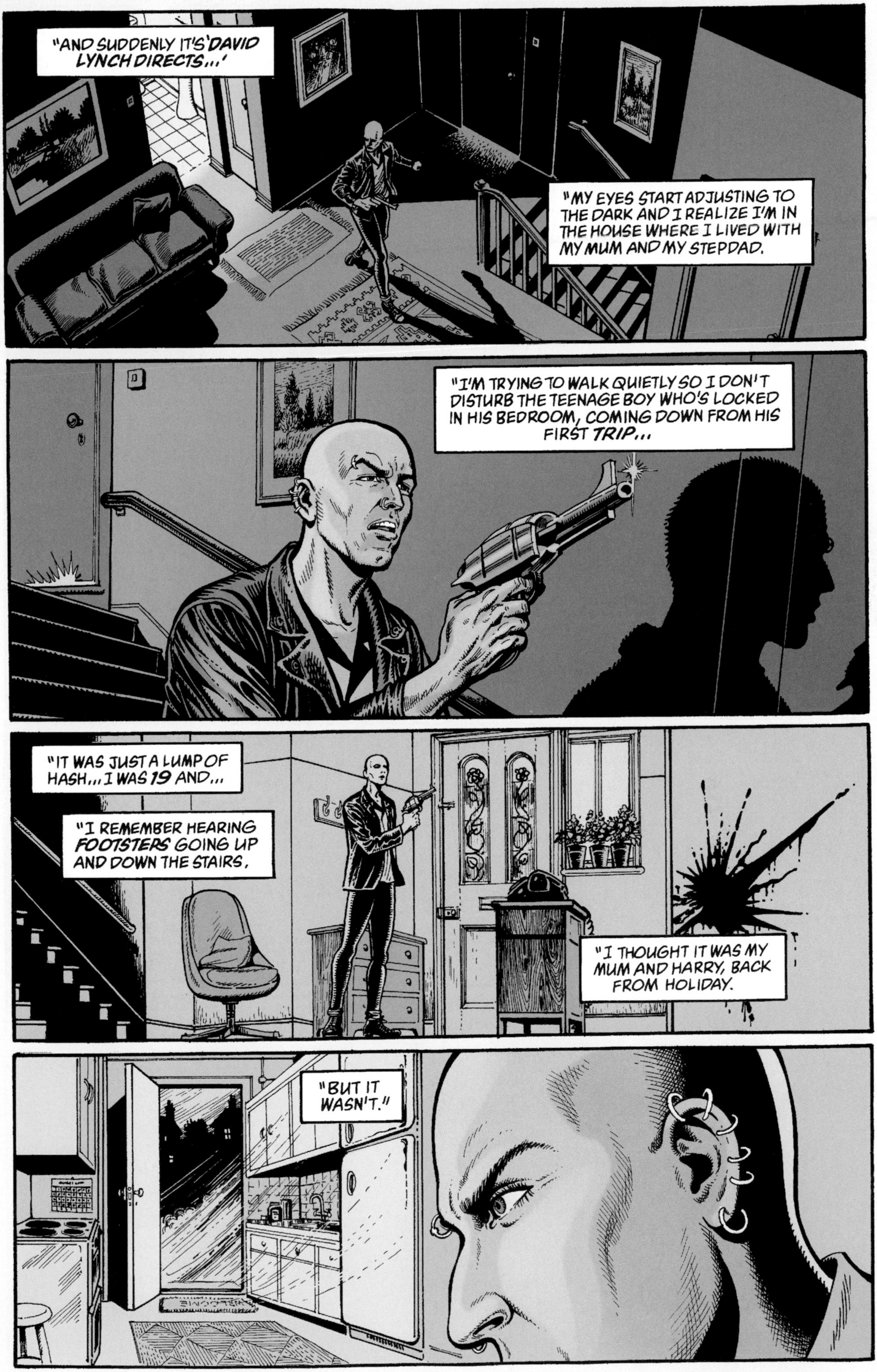
"AND SUDDENLY IT'S 'DAVID LYNCH DIRECTS...'
"MY EYES START ADJUSTING TO THE DARK AND I REALIZE I'M IN THE HOUSE WHERE I LIVED WITH MY MUM AND MY STEPDAD.
"I'M TRYING TO WALK QUIETLY SO I DON'T DISTURB THE TEENAGE BOY WHO'S LOCKED IN HIS BEDROOM, COMING DOWN FROM HIS FIRST TRIP...
"IT WAS JUST A LUMP OF HASH... I WAS 19 AND...
"I REMEMBER HEARING FOOTSTEPS GOING UP AND DOWN THE STAIRS.
"I THOUGHT IT WAS MY MUM AND HARRY, BACK FROM HOLIDAY.
"BUT IT WASN'T."

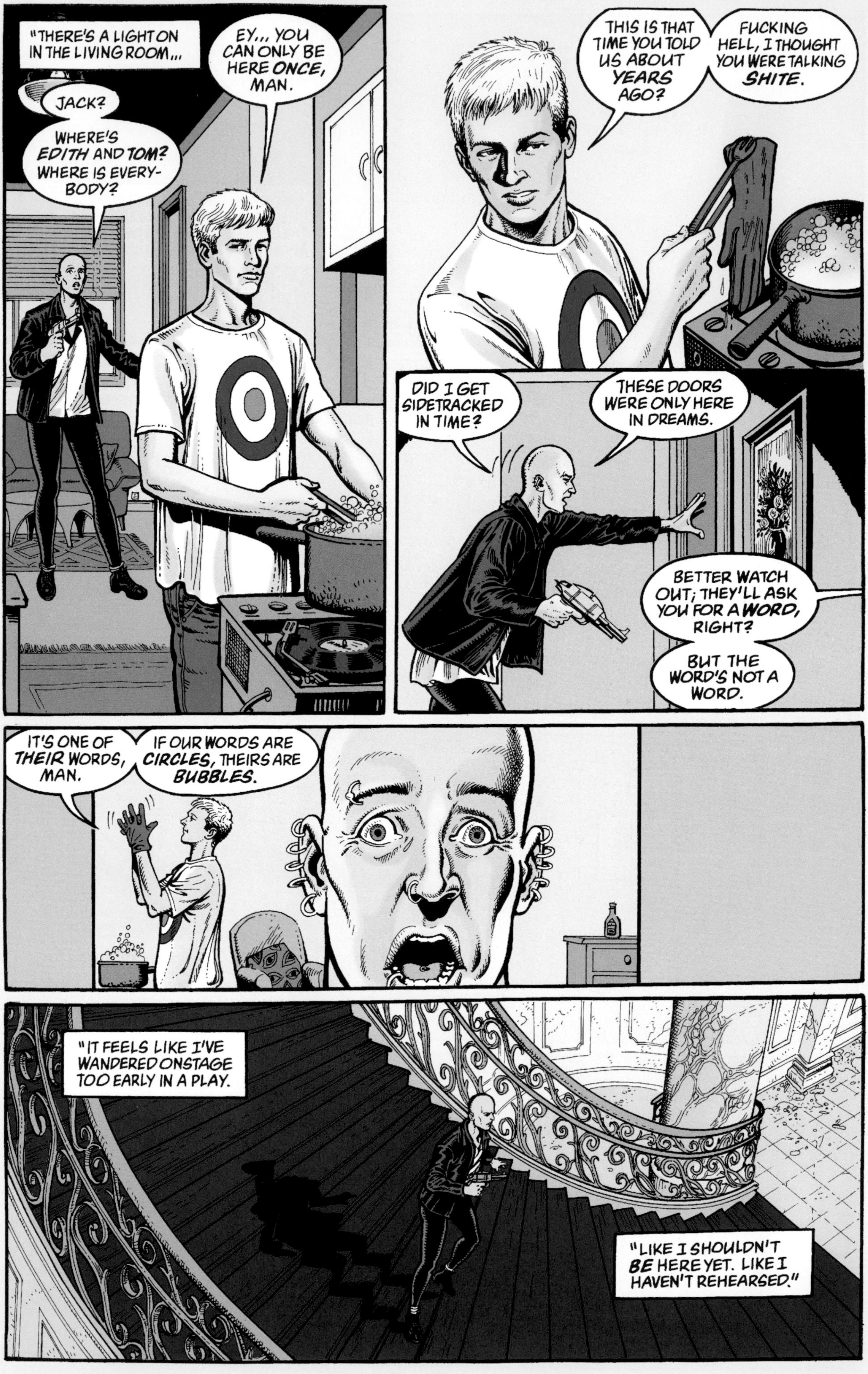
"THERE'S A LIGHT ON IN THE LIVING ROOM...
JACK?
WHERE'S EDITH AND TOM? WHERE IS EVERY-BODY?
EY... YOU CAN ONLY BE HERE ONCE, MAN.
THIS IS THAT TIME YOU TOLD US ABOUT YEARS AGO?
FUCKING HELL, I THOUGHT YOU WERE TALKING SHITE.
DID I GET SIDETRACKED IN TIME?
THESE DOORS WERE ONLY HERE IN DREAMS.
BETTER WATCH OUT; THEY'LL ASK YOU FOR A WORD, RIGHT?
BUT THE WORD'S NOT A WORD.
IT'S ONE OF THEIR WORDS, MAN.
IF OUR WORDS ARE CIRCLES, THEIRS ARE BUBBLES.
"IT FEELS LIKE I'VE WANDERED ONSTAGE TOO EARLY IN A PLAY.
"LIKE I SHOULDN'T BE HERE YET. LIKE I HAVEN'T REHEARSED."

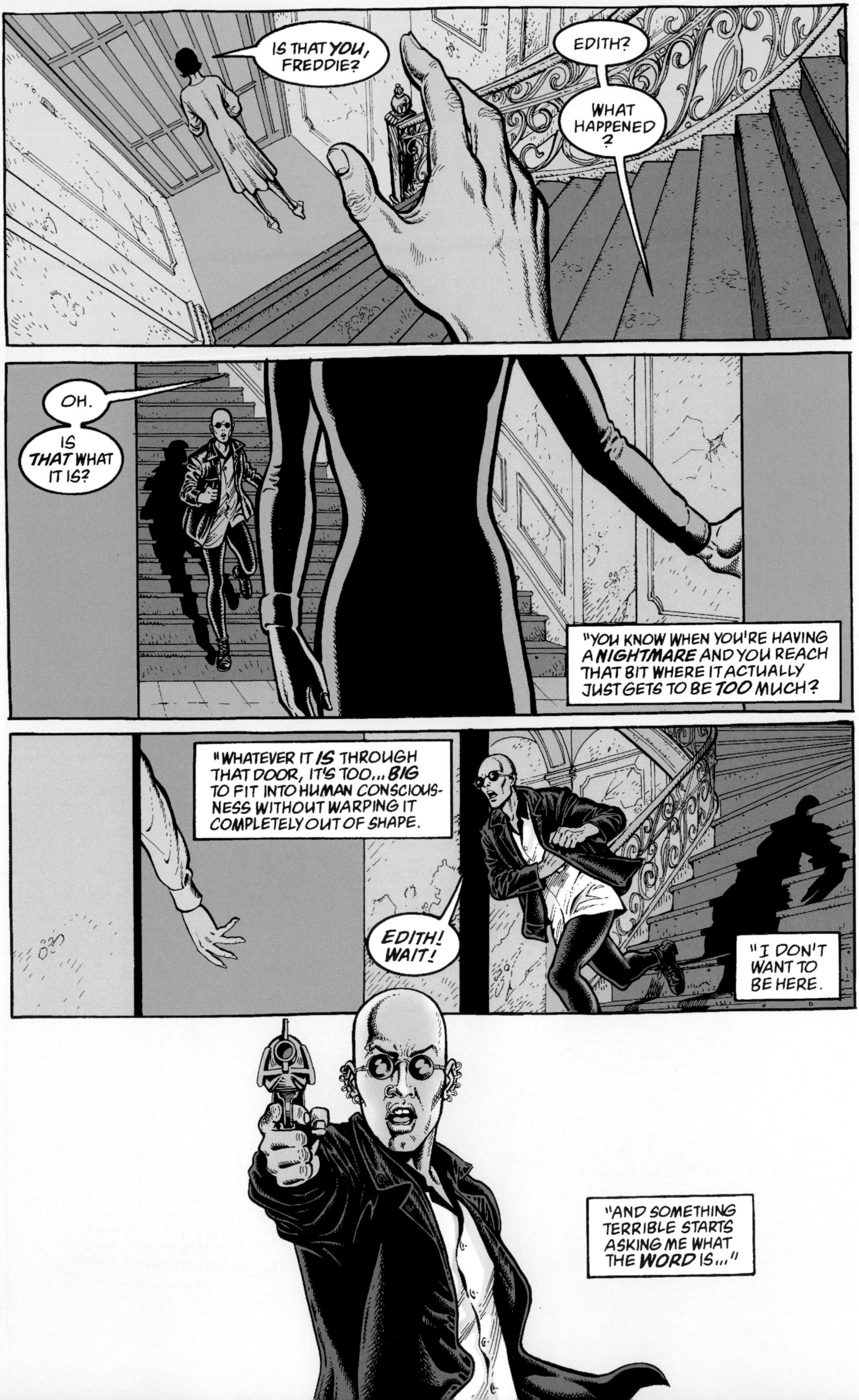
IS THAT YOU, FREDDIE?
EDITH?
WHAT HAPPENED?
OH.
IS THAT WHAT IT IS?
"YOU KNOW WHEN YOU'RE HAVING A NIGHTMARE AND YOU REACH THAT BIT WHERE IT ACTUALLY JUST GETS TO BE TOO MUCH?
"WHATEVER IT IS THROUGH THAT DOOR, IT'S TOO... BIG TO FIT INTO HUMAN CONSCIOUSNESS WITHOUT WARPING IT COMPLETELY OUT OF SHAPE.
EDITH! WAIT!
"I DON'T WANT TO BE HERE.
"AND SOMETHING TERRIBLE STARTS ASKING ME WHAT THE WORD IS..."

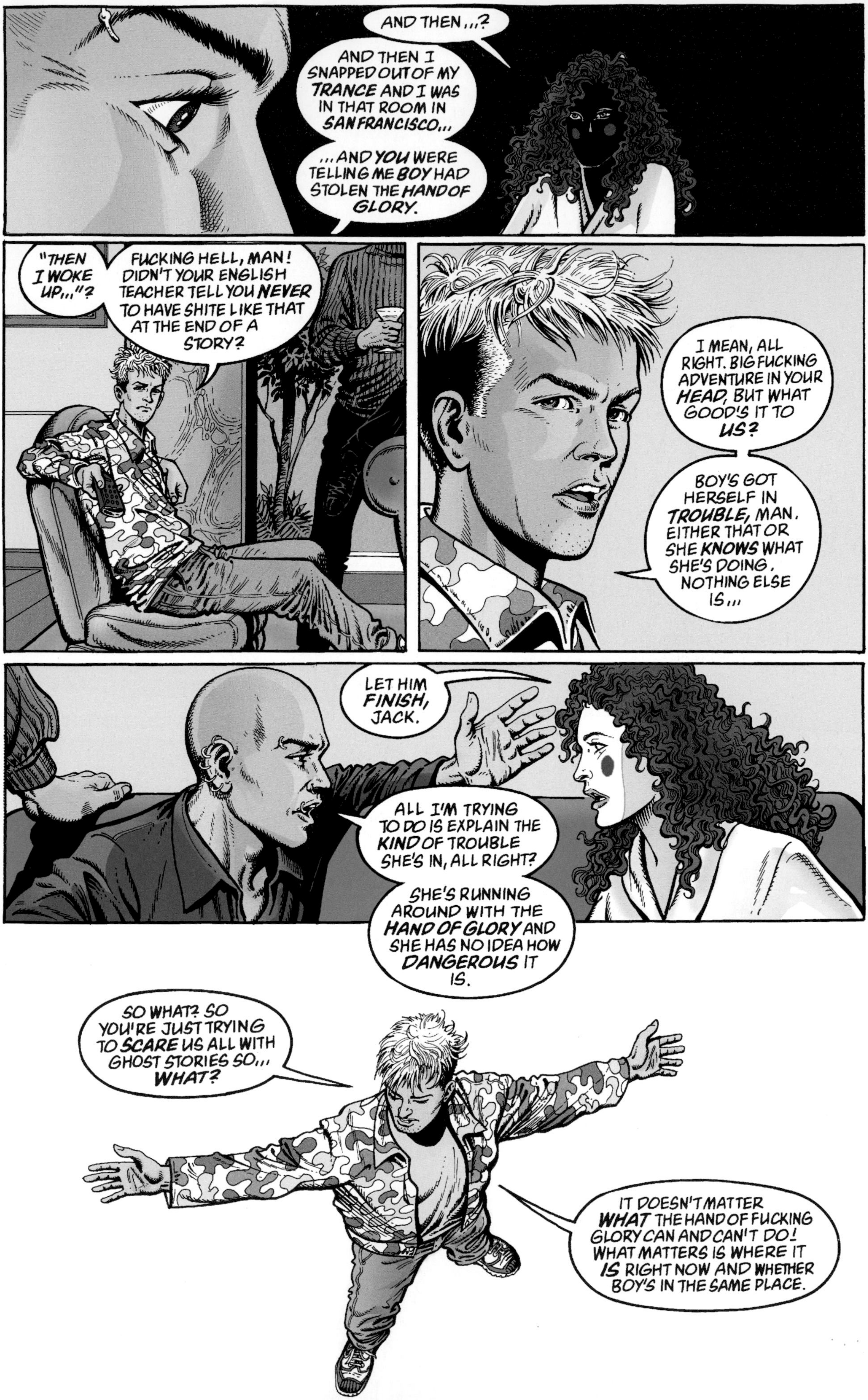
AND THEN ...?
AND THEN I SNAPPED OUT OF MY TRANCE AND I WAS IN THAT ROOM IN SAN FRANCISCO...
...AND YOU WERE TELLING ME BOY HAD STOLEN THE HAND OF GLORY.
"THEN I WOKE UP..."?
FUCKING HELL, MAN! DIDN'T YOUR ENGLISH TEACHER TELL YOU NEVER TO HAVE SHITE LIKE THAT AT THE END OF A STORY?
I MEAN, ALL RIGHT. BIG FUCKING ADVENTURE IN YOUR HEAD, BUT WHAT GOOD'S IT TO US?
BOY'S GOT HERSELF IN TROUBLE, MAN. EITHER THAT OR SHE KNOWS WHAT SHE'S DOING. NOTHING ELSE IS...
LET HIM FINISH, JACK.
ALL I'M TRYING TO DO IS EXPLAIN THE KIND OF TROUBLE SHE'S IN, ALL RIGHT?
SHE'S RUNNING AROUND WITH THE HAND OF GLORY AND SHE HAS NO IDEA HOW DANGEROUS IT IS.
SO WHAT? SO YOU'RE JUST TRYING TO SCARE US ALL WITH GHOST STORIES SO... WHAT?
IT DOESN'T MATTER WHAT THE HAND OF FUCKING GLORY CAN AND CAN'T DO! WHAT MATTERS IS WHERE IT IS RIGHT NOW AND WHETHER BOY'S IN THE SAME PLACE.

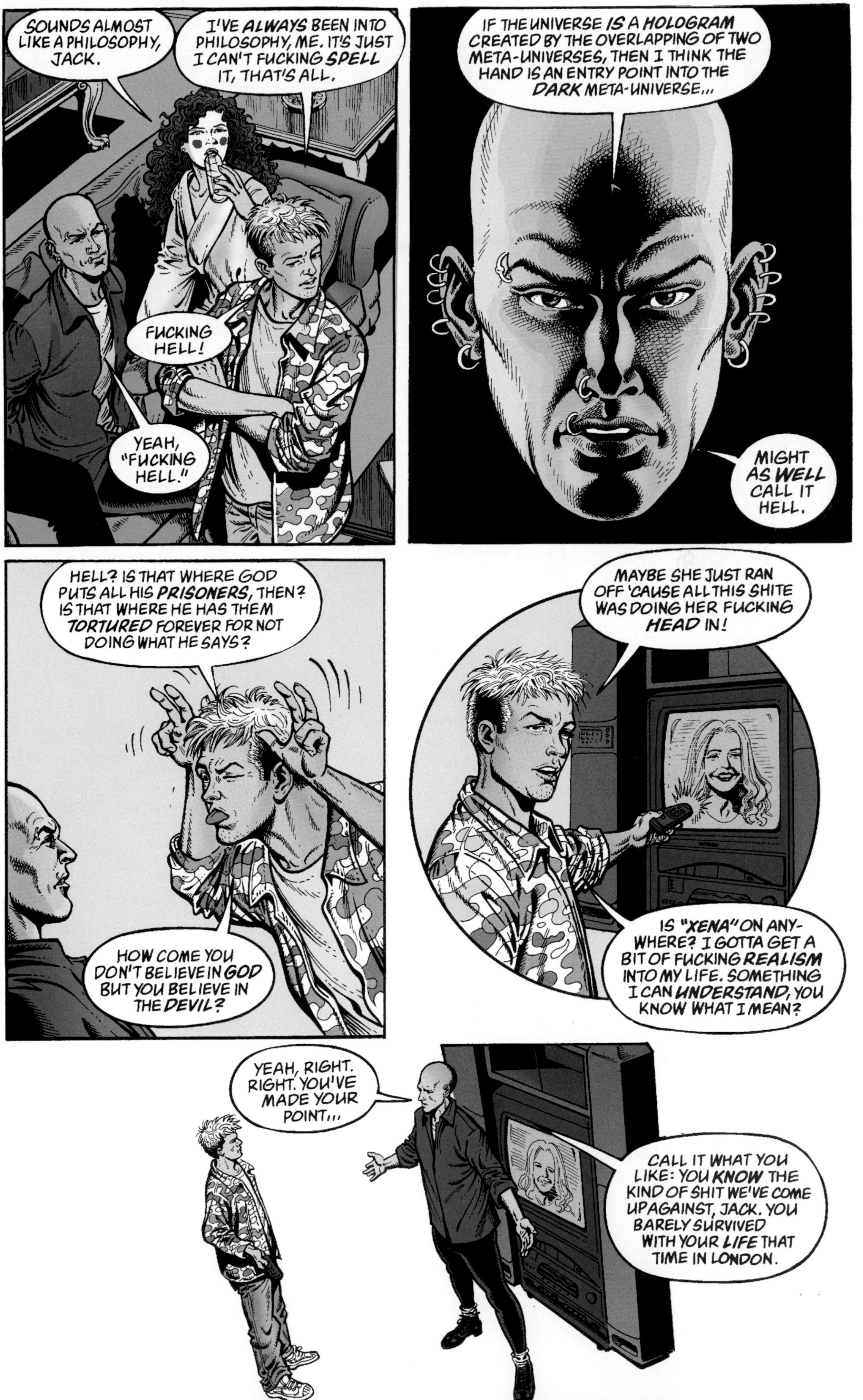
SOUNDS ALMOST LIKE A PHILOSOPHY, JACK.
I'VE ALWAYS BEEN INTO PHILOSOPHY, ME. IT'S JUST I CAN'T FUCKING SPELL IT, THAT'S ALL.
FUCKING HELL!
YEAH, "FUCKING HELL."
IF THE UNIVERSE IS A HOLOGRAM CREATED BY THE OVERLAPPING OF TWO META-UNIVERSES, THEN I THINK THE HAND IS AN ENTRY POINT INTO THE DARK META-UNIVERSE...
MIGHT AS WELL CALL IT HELL.
HELL? IS THAT WHERE GOD PUTS ALL HIS PRISONERS, THEN? IS THAT WHERE HE HAS THEM TORTURED FOREVER FOR NOT DOING WHAT HE SAYS?
HOW COME YOU DON'T BELIEVE IN GOD BUT YOU BELIEVE IN THE DEVIL?
MAYBE SHE JUST RAN OFF 'CAUSE ALL THIS SHITE WAS DOING HER FUCKING HEAD IN!
IS "XENA" ON ANY-WHERE? I GOTTA GET A BIT OF FUCKING REALISM INTO MY LIFE. SOMETHING I CAN UNDERSTAND, YOU KNOW WHAT I MEAN?
YEAH, RIGHT. RIGHT. YOU'VE MADE YOUR POINT...
CALL IT WHAT YOU LIKE: YOU KNOW THE KIND OF SHIT WE'VE COME UP AGAINST, JACK. YOU BARELY SURVIVED WITH YOUR LIFE THAT TIME IN LONDON.

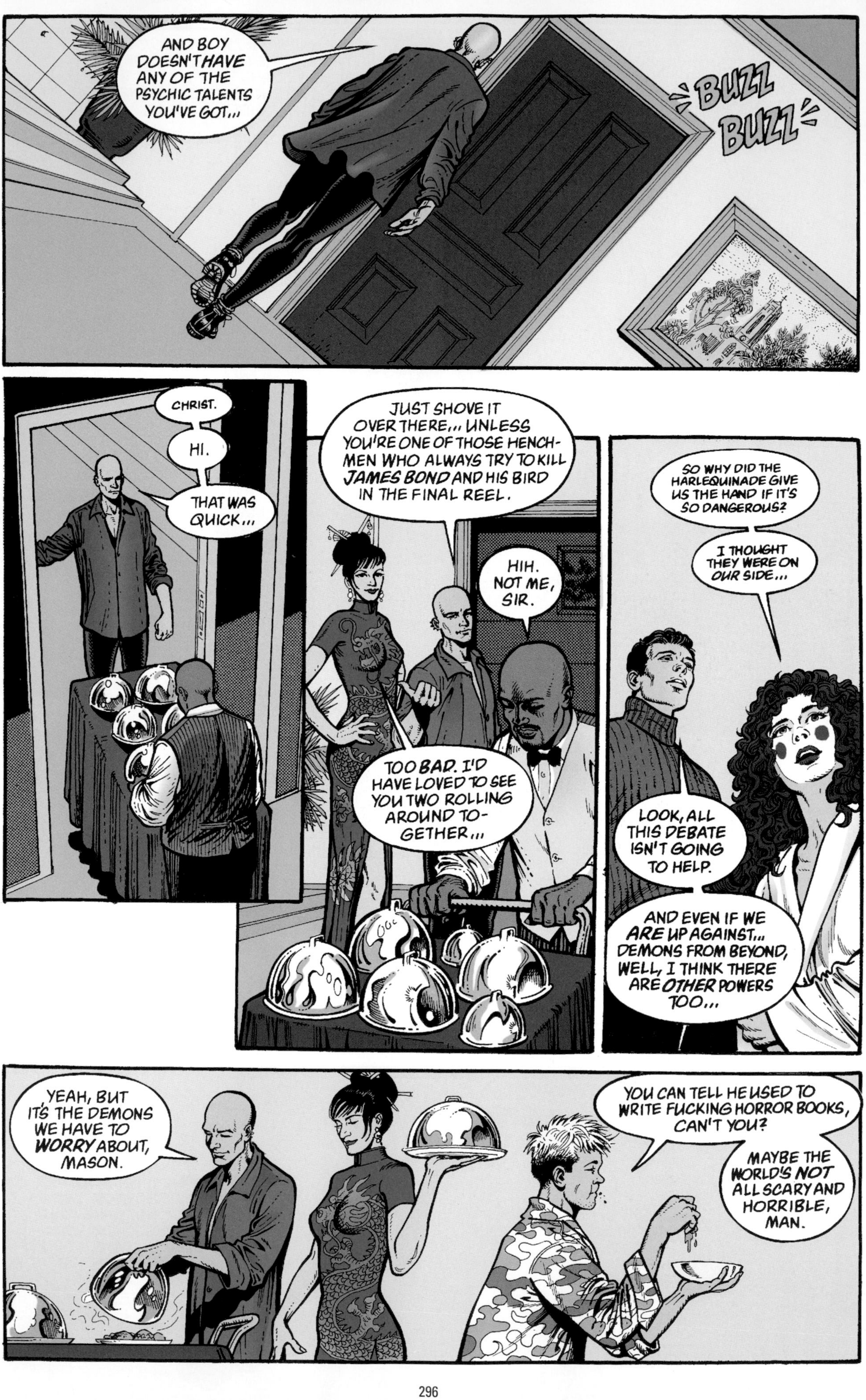
AND BOY DOESN'T HAVE ANY OF THE PSYCHIC TALENTS YOU'VE GOT...
BUZZ BUZZ
CHRIST.
HI.
THAT WAS QUICK...
JUST SHOVE IT OVER THERE... UNLESS YOU'RE ONE OF THOSE HENCHMEN WHO ALWAYS TRY TO KILL JAMES BOND AND HIS BIRD IN THE FINAL REEL.
HIH. NOT ME, SIR.
TOO BAD. I'D HAVE LOVED TO SEE YOU TWO ROLLING AROUND TOGETHER...
SO WHY DID THE HARLEQUINADE GIVE US THE HAND IF IT'S SO DANGEROUS?
I THOUGHT THEY WERE ON OUR SIDE...
LOOK, ALL THIS DEBATE ISN'T GOING TO HELP.
AND EVEN IF WE ARE UP AGAINST... DEMONS FROM BEYOND, WELL, I THINK THERE ARE OTHER POWERS TOO...
YEAH, BUT IT'S THE DEMONS WE HAVE TO WORRY ABOUT, MASON.
YOU CAN TELL HE USED TO WRITE FUCKING HORROR BOOKS, CAN'T YOU?
MAYBE THE WORLD'S NOT ALL SCARY AND HORRIBLE, MAN.

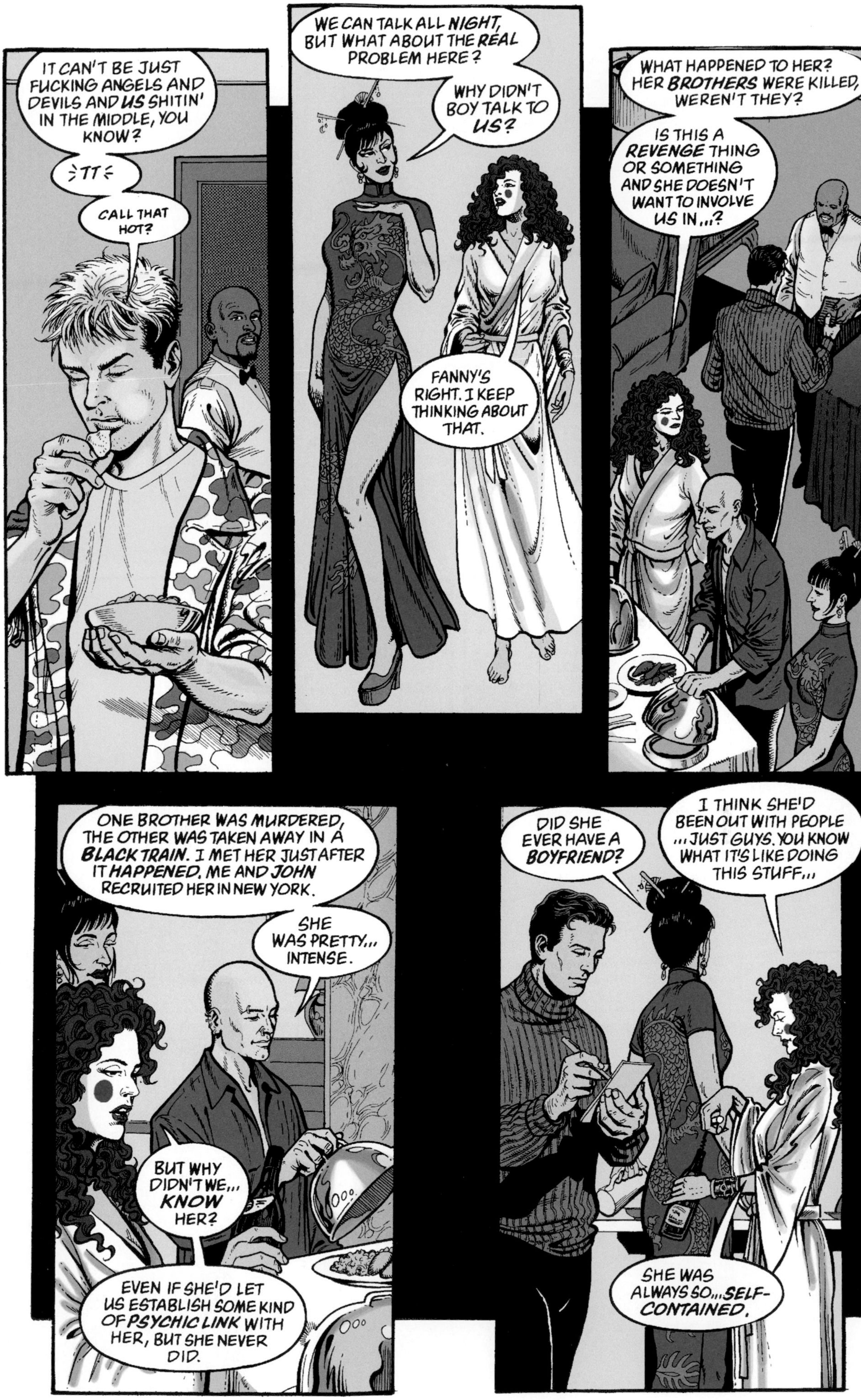
IT CAN'T BE JUST FUCKING ANGELS AND DEVILS AND US SHITIN' IN THE MIDDLE, YOU KNOW?
TT
CALL THAT HOT?
WE CAN TALK ALL NIGHT, BUT WHAT ABOUT THE REAL PROBLEM HERE?
WHY DIDN'T BOY TALK TO US?
FANNY'S RIGHT. I KEEP THINKING ABOUT THAT.
WHAT HAPPENED TO HER? HER BROTHERS WERE KILLED, WEREN'T THEY?
IS THIS A REVENGE THING OR SOMETHING AND SHE DOESN'T WANT TO INVOLVE US IN...?
ONE BROTHER WAS MURDERED, THE OTHER WAS TAKEN AWAY IN A BLACK TRAIN. I MET HER JUST AFTER IT HAPPENED, ME AND JOHN RECRUITED HER IN NEW YORK.
SHE WAS PRETTY... INTENSE.
BUT WHY DIDN'T WE... KNOW HER?
EVEN IF SHE'D LET US ESTABLISH SOME KIND OF PSYCHIC LINK WITH HER, BUT SHE NEVER DID.
DID SHE EVER HAVE A BOYFRIEND?
I THINK SHE'D BEEN OUT WITH PEOPLE ...JUST GUYS. YOU KNOW WHAT IT'S LIKE DOING THIS STUFF...
SHE WAS ALWAYS SO... SELF-CONTAINED.

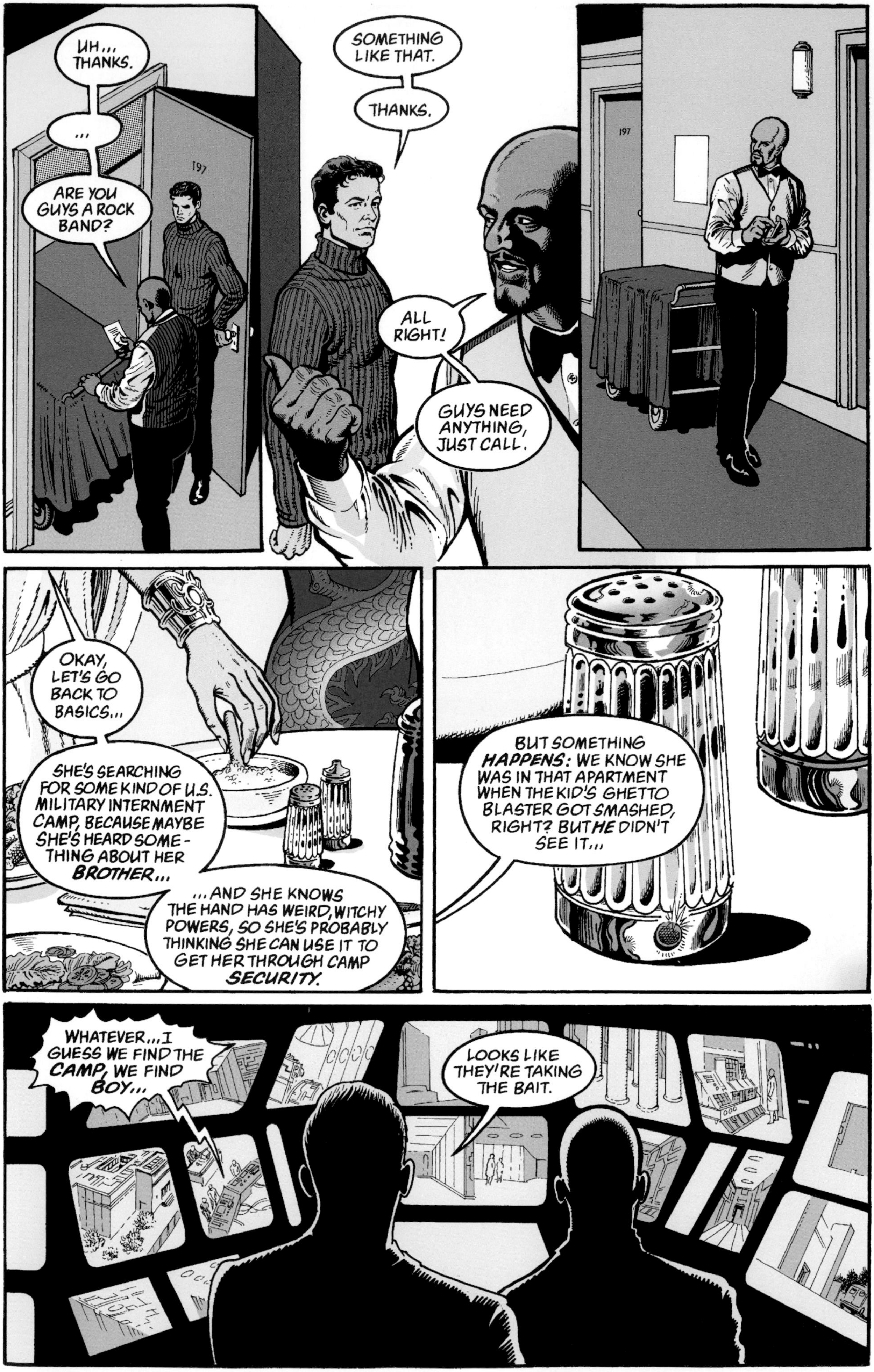
UH... THANKS.
...
ARE YOU GUYS A ROCK BAND?
SOMETHING LIKE THAT.
THANKS.
ALL RIGHT!
GUYS NEED ANYTHING, JUST CALL.
197
OKAY, LET'S GO BACK TO BASICS...
SHE'S SEARCHING FOR SOME KIND OF U.S. MILITARY INTERNMENT CAMP, BECAUSE MAYBE SHE'S HEARD SOME-THING ABOUT HER BROTHER...
...AND SHE KNOWS THE HAND HAS WEIRD, WITCHY POWERS, SO SHE'S PROBABLY THINKING SHE CAN USE IT TO GET HER THROUGH CAMP SECURITY.
BUT SOMETHING HAPPENS: WE KNOW SHE WAS IN THAT APARTMENT WHEN THE KID'S GHETTO BLASTER GOT SMASHED, RIGHT? BUT HE DIDN'T SEE IT...
WHATEVER... I GUESS WE FIND THE CAMP, WE FIND BOY...
LOOKS LIKE THEY'RE TAKING THE BAIT.

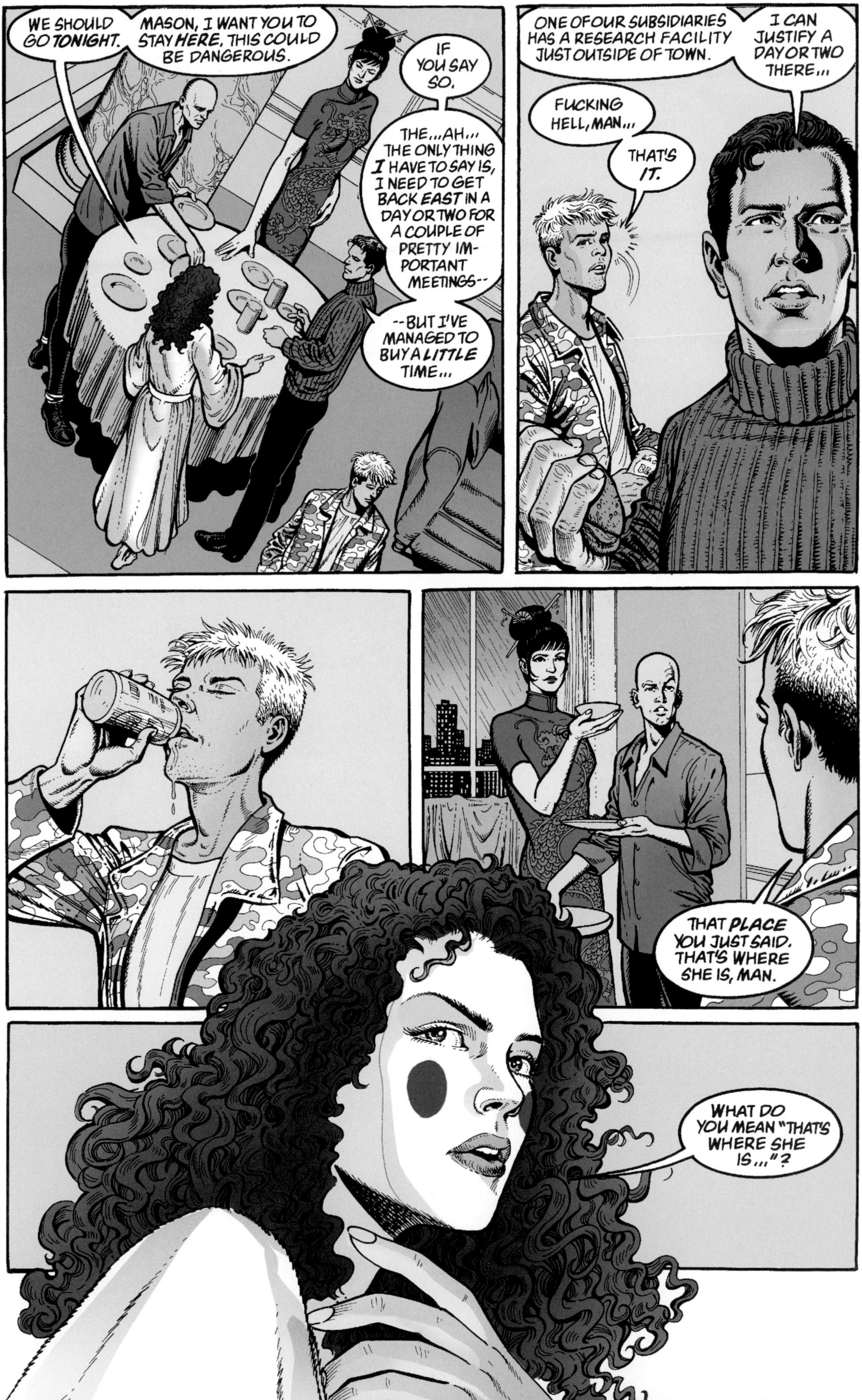

WE SHOULD GO TONIGHT.
MASON, I WANT YOU TO STAY HERE. THIS COULD BE DANGEROUS.
IF YOU SAY SO.
THE...AH... THE ONLY THING I HAVE TO SAY IS, I NEED TO GET BACK EAST IN A DAY OR TWO FOR A COUPLE OF PRETTY IMPORTANT MEETINGS--
--BUT I'VE MANAGED TO BUY A LITTLE TIME...
ONE OF OUR SUBSIDIARIES HAS A RESEARCH FACILITY JUST OUTSIDE OF TOWN.
I CAN JUSTIFY A DAY OR TWO THERE...
FUCKING HELL, MAN...
THAT'S IT.
THAT PLACE YOU JUST SAID. THAT'S WHERE SHE IS, MAN.
WHAT DO YOU MEAN "THAT'S WHERE SHE IS..."?

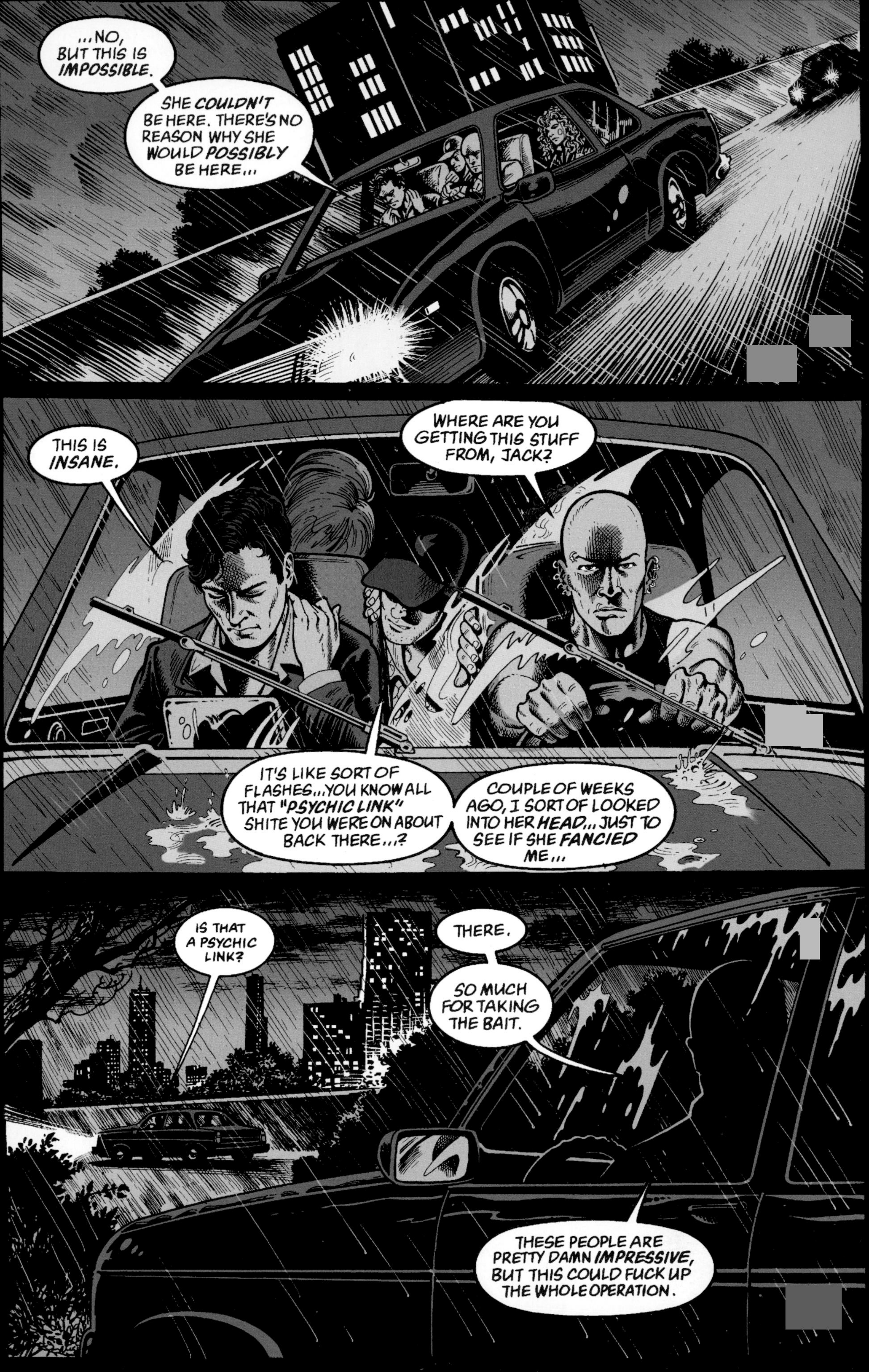
...NO, BUT THIS IS IMPOSSIBLE.
SHE COULDN'T BE HERE. THERE'S NO REASON WHY SHE WOULD POSSIBLY BE HERE...
THIS IS INSANE.
WHERE ARE YOU GETTING THIS STUFF FROM, JACK?
IT'S LIKE SORT OF FLASHES... YOU KNOW ALL THAT "PSYCHIC LINK" SHITE YOU WERE ON ABOUT BACK THERE...?
COUPLE OF WEEKS AGO, I SORT OF LOOKED INTO HER HEAD... JUST TO SEE IF SHE FANCIED ME...
IS THAT A PSYCHIC LINK?
THERE.
SO MUCH FOR TAKING THE BAIT.
THESE PEOPLE ARE PRETTY DAMN IMPRESSIVE, BUT THIS COULD FUCK UP THE WHOLE OPERATION.

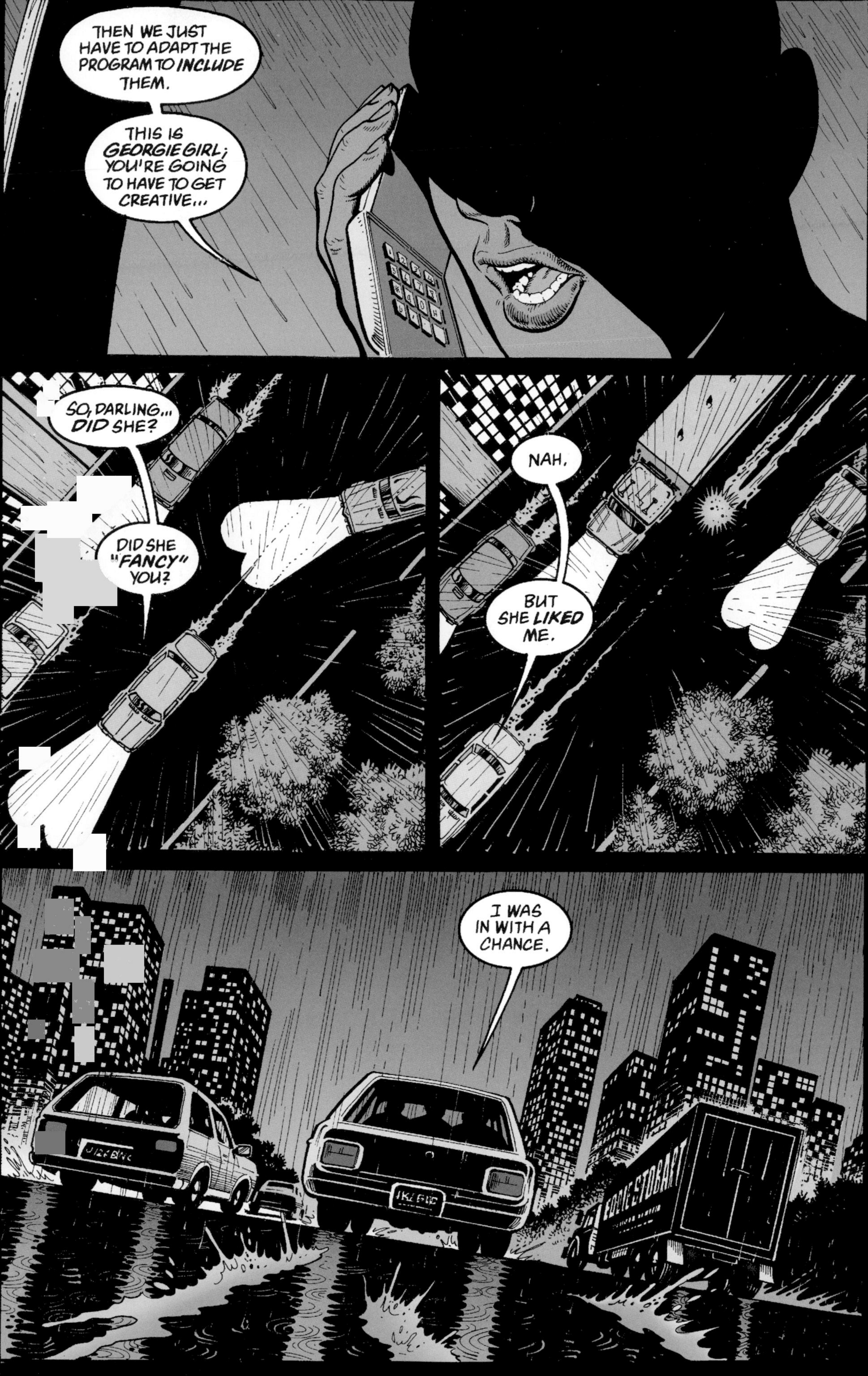
THEN WE JUST HAVE TO ADAPT THE PROGRAM TO INCLUDE THEM.
THIS IS GEORGIE GIRL; YOU'RE GOING TO HAVE TO GET CREATIVE...
SO, DARLING... DID SHE?
DID SHE "FANCY" YOU?
NAH.
BUT SHE LIKED ME.
I WAS IN WITH A CHANCE.
EDDIE STOBART

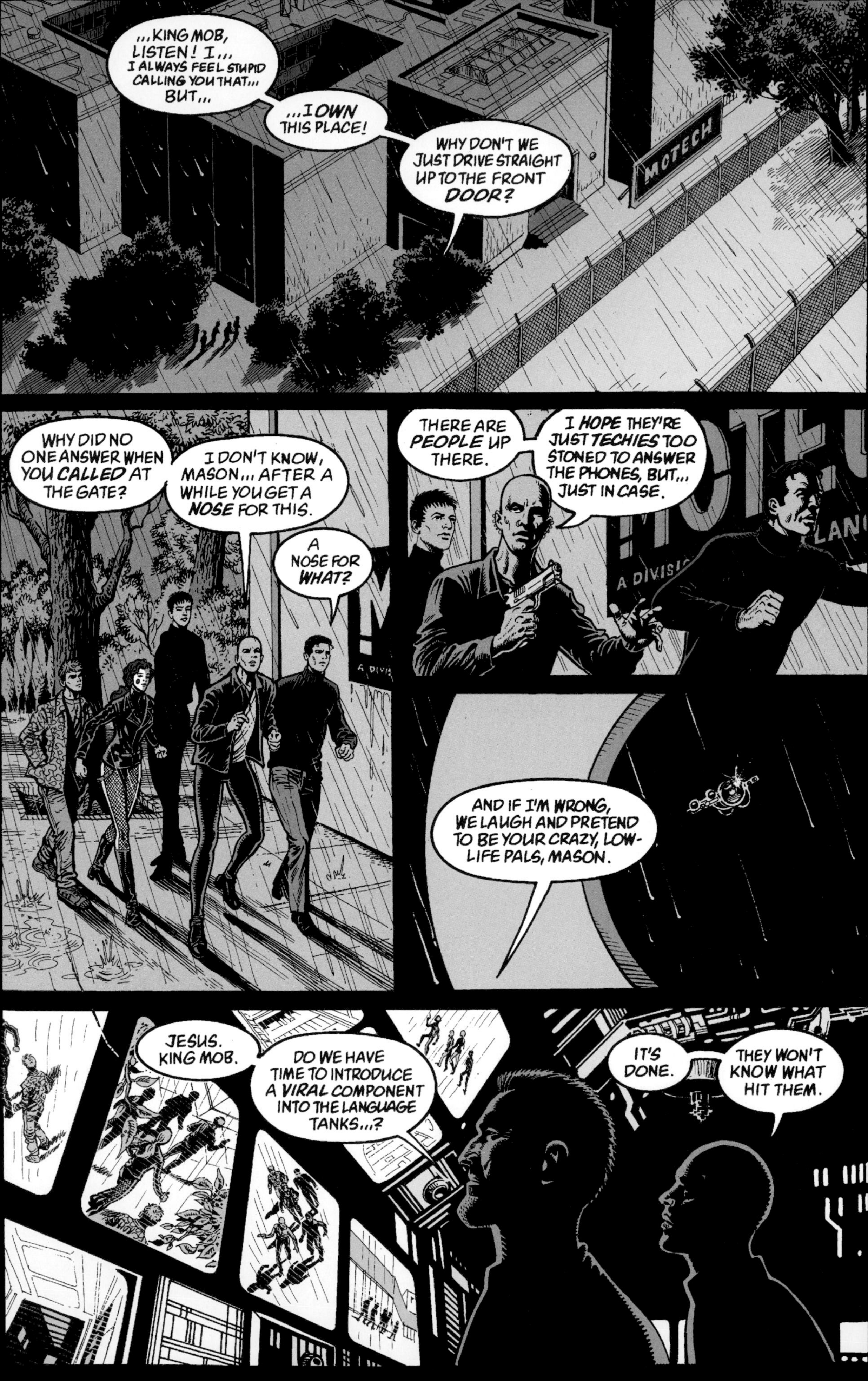
...KING MOB, LISTEN! I... I ALWAYS FEEL STUPID CALLING YOU THAT... BUT...
...I OWN THIS PLACE!
WHY DON'T WE JUST DRIVE STRAIGHT UP TO THE FRONT DOOR?
MOTECH
WHY DID NO ONE ANSWER WHEN YOU CALLED AT THE GATE?
I DON'T KNOW, MASON... AFTER A WHILE YOU GET A NOSE FOR THIS.
A NOSE FOR WHAT?
THERE ARE PEOPLE UP THERE.
I HOPE THEY'RE JUST TECHIES TOO STONED TO ANSWER THE PHONES, BUT... JUST IN CASE.
AND IF I'M WRONG, WE LAUGH AND PRETEND TO BE YOUR CRAZY, LOW-LIFE PALS, MASON.
JESUS. KING MOB.
DO WE HAVE TIME TO INTRODUCE A VIRAL COMPONENT INTO THE LANGUAGE TANKS...?
IT'S DONE.
THEY WON'T KNOW WHAT HIT THEM.

MISTRESS.

WELCOME TO *DIS*.

DIS?

HER RECALL'S DOWN, HER SPINAL INTERFACE IS STILL IN SHOCK.

OUR QUOTAS ARE STILL GOOD HERE, MISTRESS; EXTERMINATION AND CONVERSION PROGRAMS ARE ALL ON SCHEDULE *AND* WITHIN BUDGET...

WE'LL BE ALL SET TO BEGIN THE WAR AND SUMMON THE *KINGS* BY MID-"99...

I'LL TAKE OVER HERE.

MR. KADMON, SIR.

A NEW BATCH OF *MERCHANDISE* IS ALMOST READY FOR RETURN TOMORROW EVENING.

SHOULD BE A QUIET JOURNEY; THEY COME IN *REBELS*, THEY GO HOME WORKING FOR US.

SO THEY *FOUND* YOU?

DO I KNOW YOU?

OF COURSE. PERHAPS THIS WILL HELP RESTORE YOU TO UNITY.

DAVARIES WOOP·I·R OD DOIBXIS JAMCMAD.

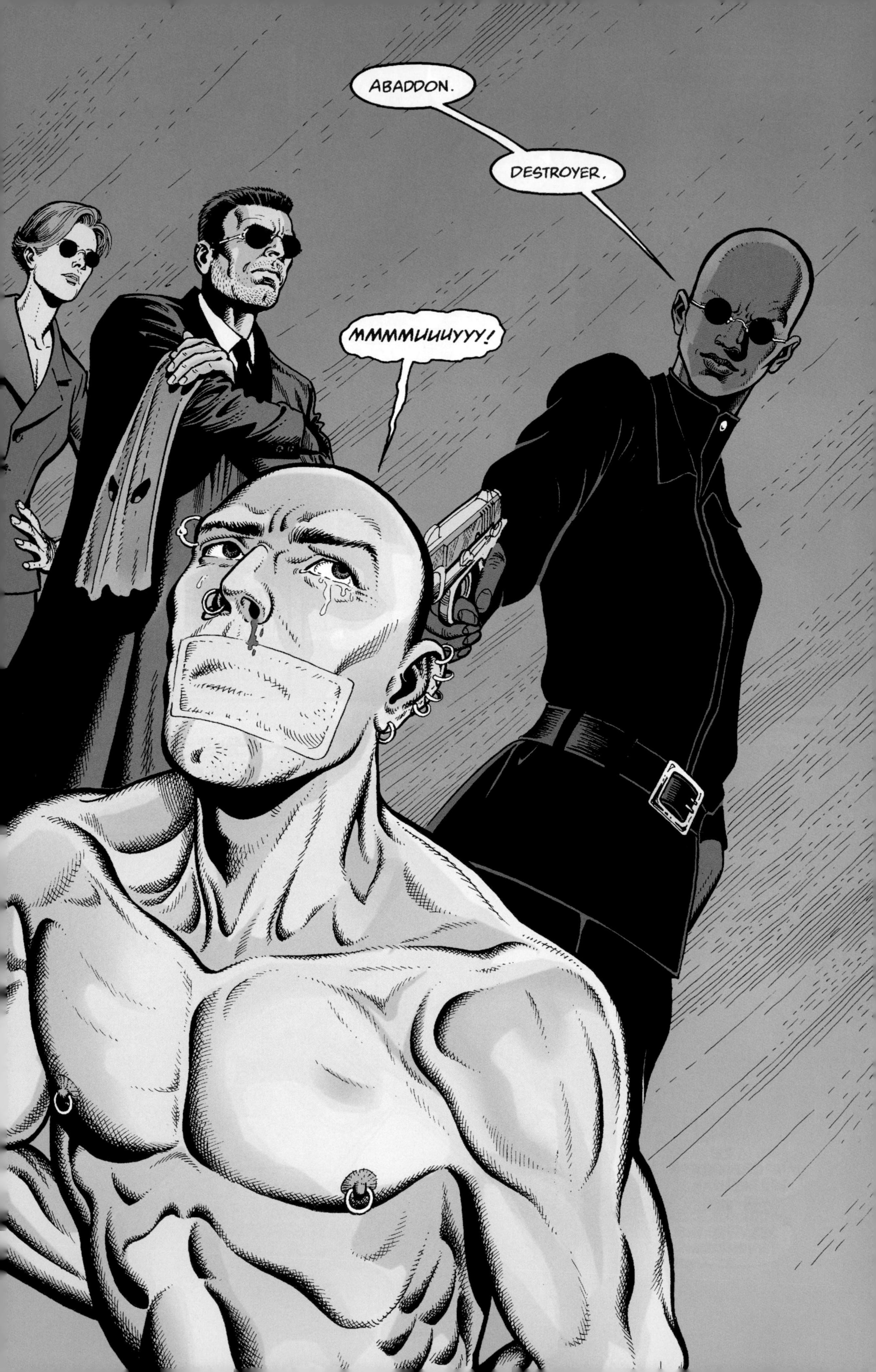
ABADDON.
DESTROYER.
MMMMUUUYYY!

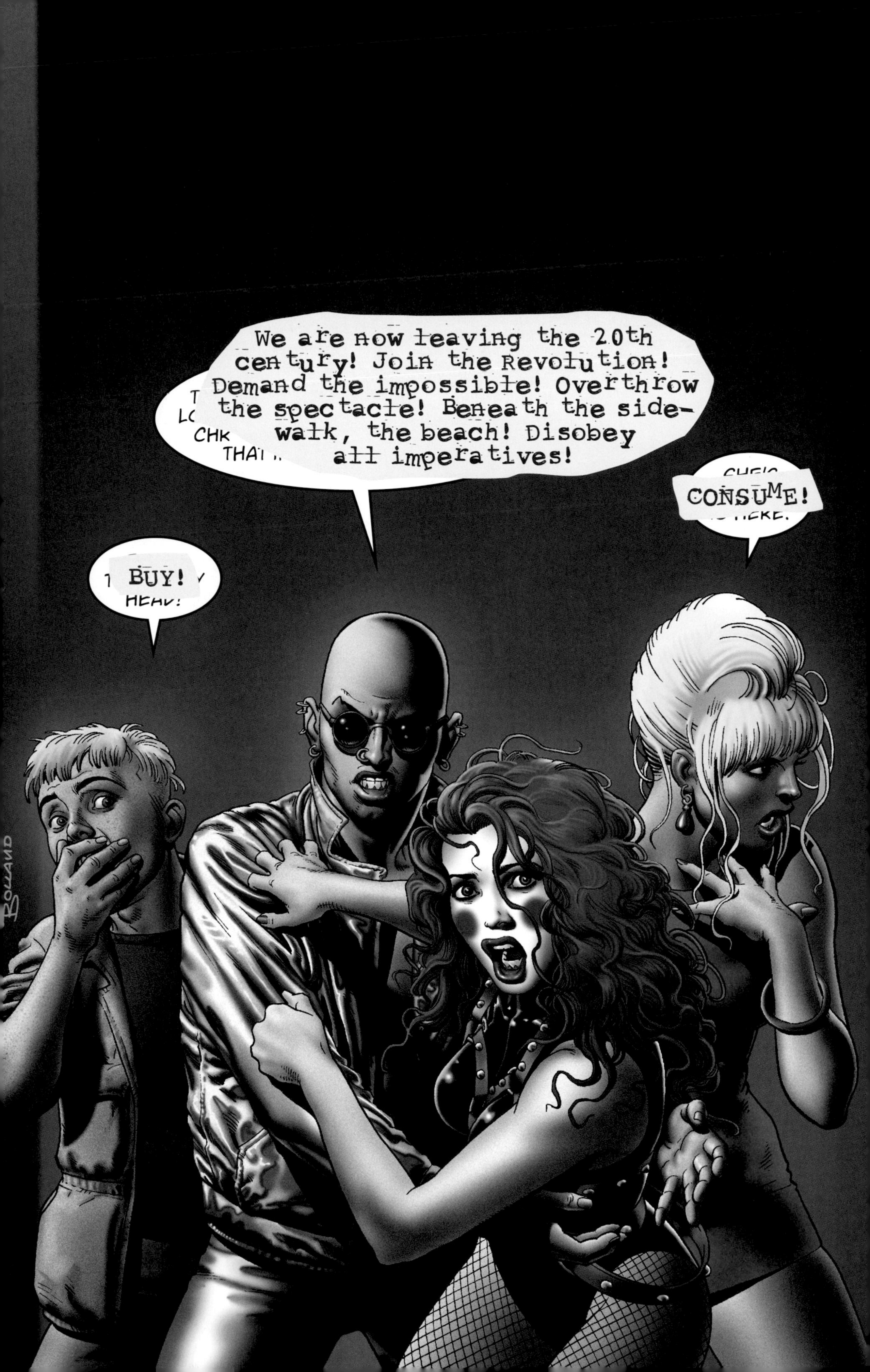
BUY!
We are now leaving the 20th century! Join the Revolution! Demand the impossible! Overthrow the spectacle! Beneath the side-walk, the beach! Disobey all imperatives!
CONSUME!
BOLLAND

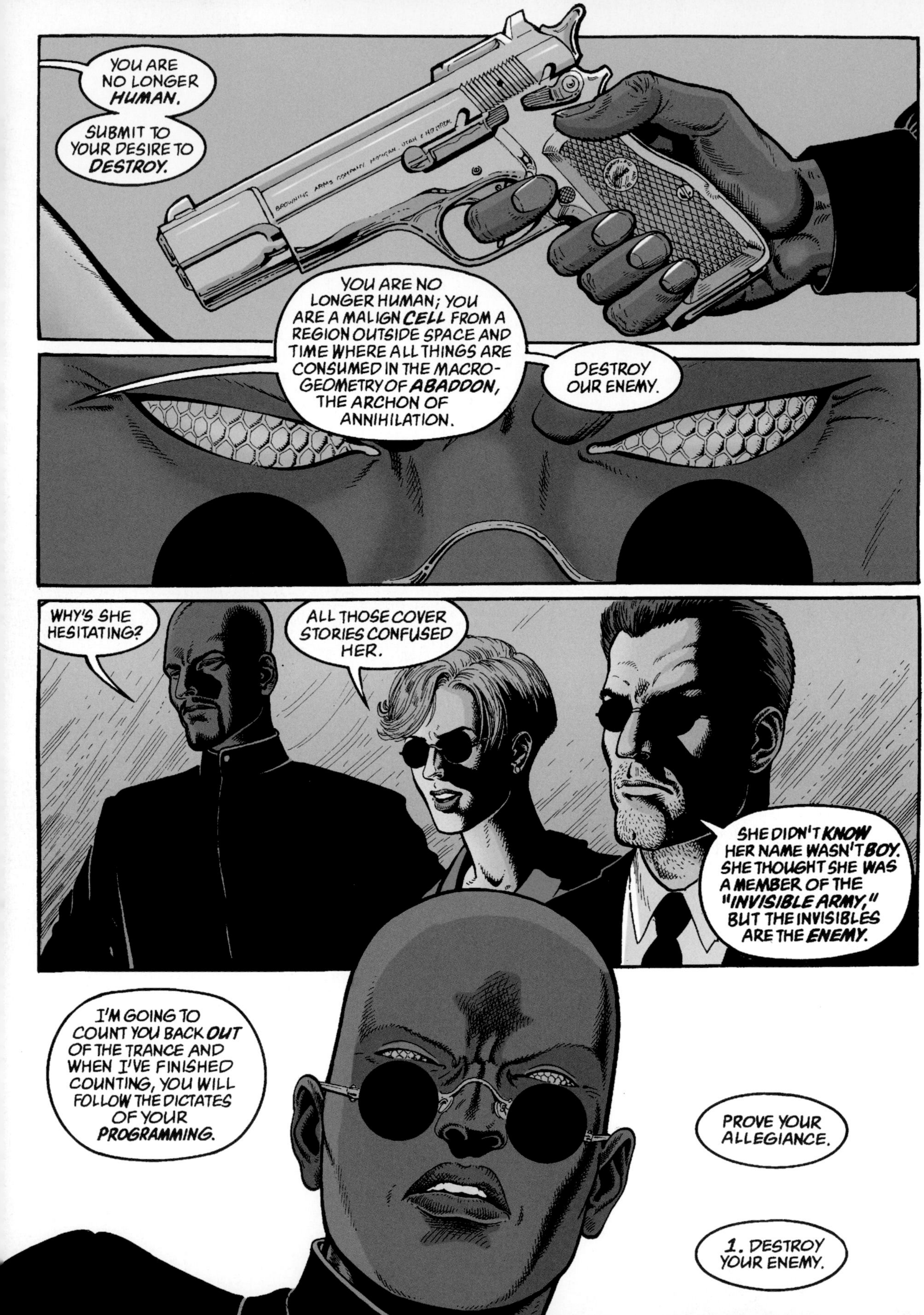
YOU ARE NO LONGER HUMAN.
SUBMIT TO YOUR DESIRE TO DESTROY.
YOU ARE NO LONGER HUMAN; YOU ARE A MALIGN CELL FROM A REGION OUTSIDE SPACE AND TIME WHERE ALL THINGS ARE CONSUMED IN THE MACRO-GEOMETRY OF ABADDON, THE ARCHON OF ANNIHILATION.
DESTROY OUR ENEMY.
WHY'S SHE HESITATING?
ALL THOSE COVER STORIES CONFUSED HER.
SHE DIDN'T KNOW HER NAME WASN'T BOY. SHE THOUGHT SHE WAS A MEMBER OF THE "INVISIBLE ARMY," BUT THE INVISIBLES ARE THE ENEMY.
I'M GOING TO COUNT YOU BACK OUT OF THE TRANCE AND WHEN I'VE FINISHED COUNTING, YOU WILL FOLLOW THE DICTATES OF YOUR PROGRAMMING.
PROVE YOUR ALLEGIANCE.
1. DESTROY YOUR ENEMY.

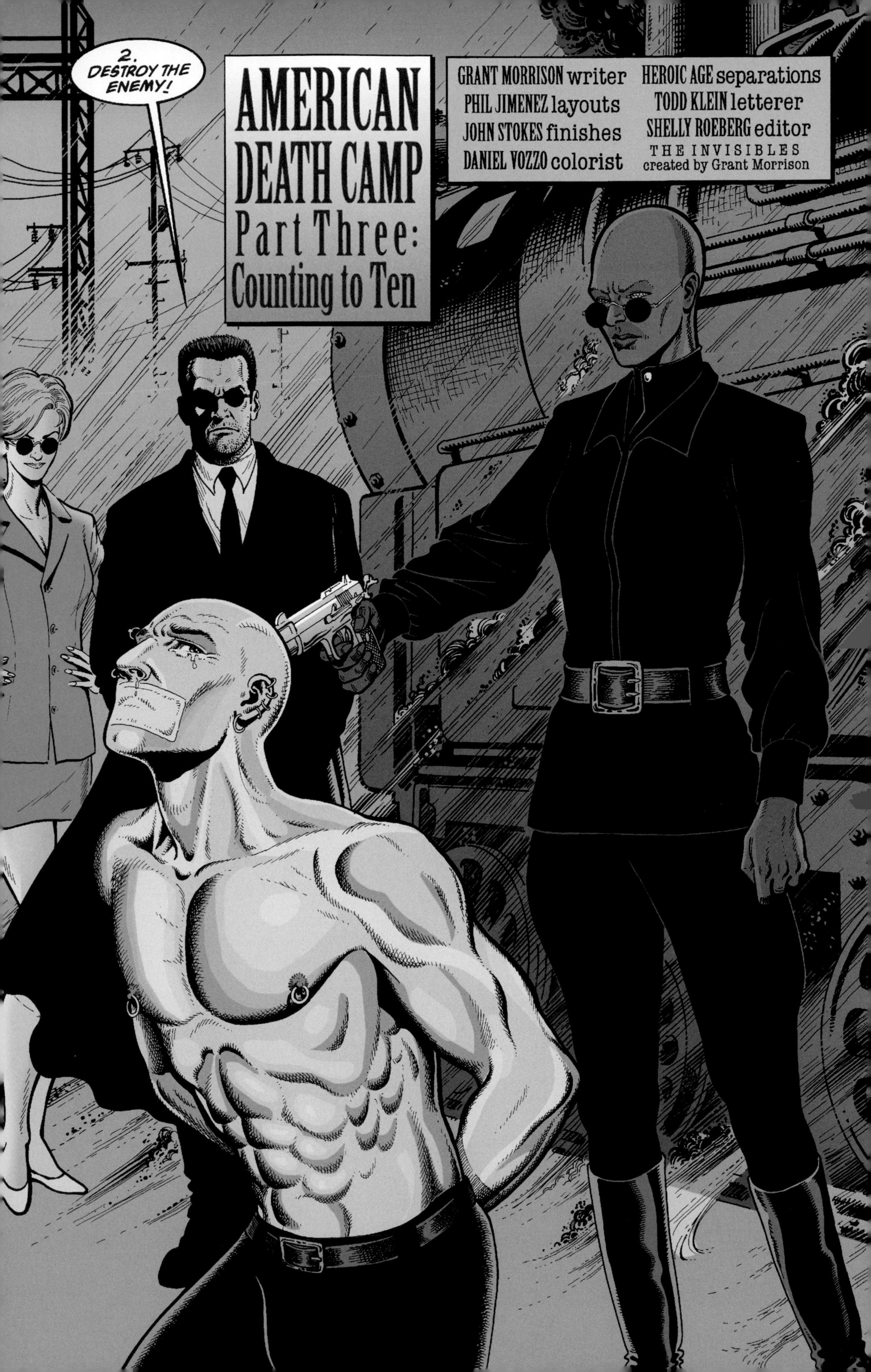
2. DESTROY THE ENEMY!
AMERICAN DEATH CAMP
Part Three: Counting to Ten
GRANT MORRISON writer
PHIL JIMENEZ layouts
JOHN STOKES finishes
DANIEL VOZZO colorist
HEROIC AGE separations
TODD KLEIN letterer
SHELLY ROEBERG editor
THE INVISIBLES
created by Grant Morrison

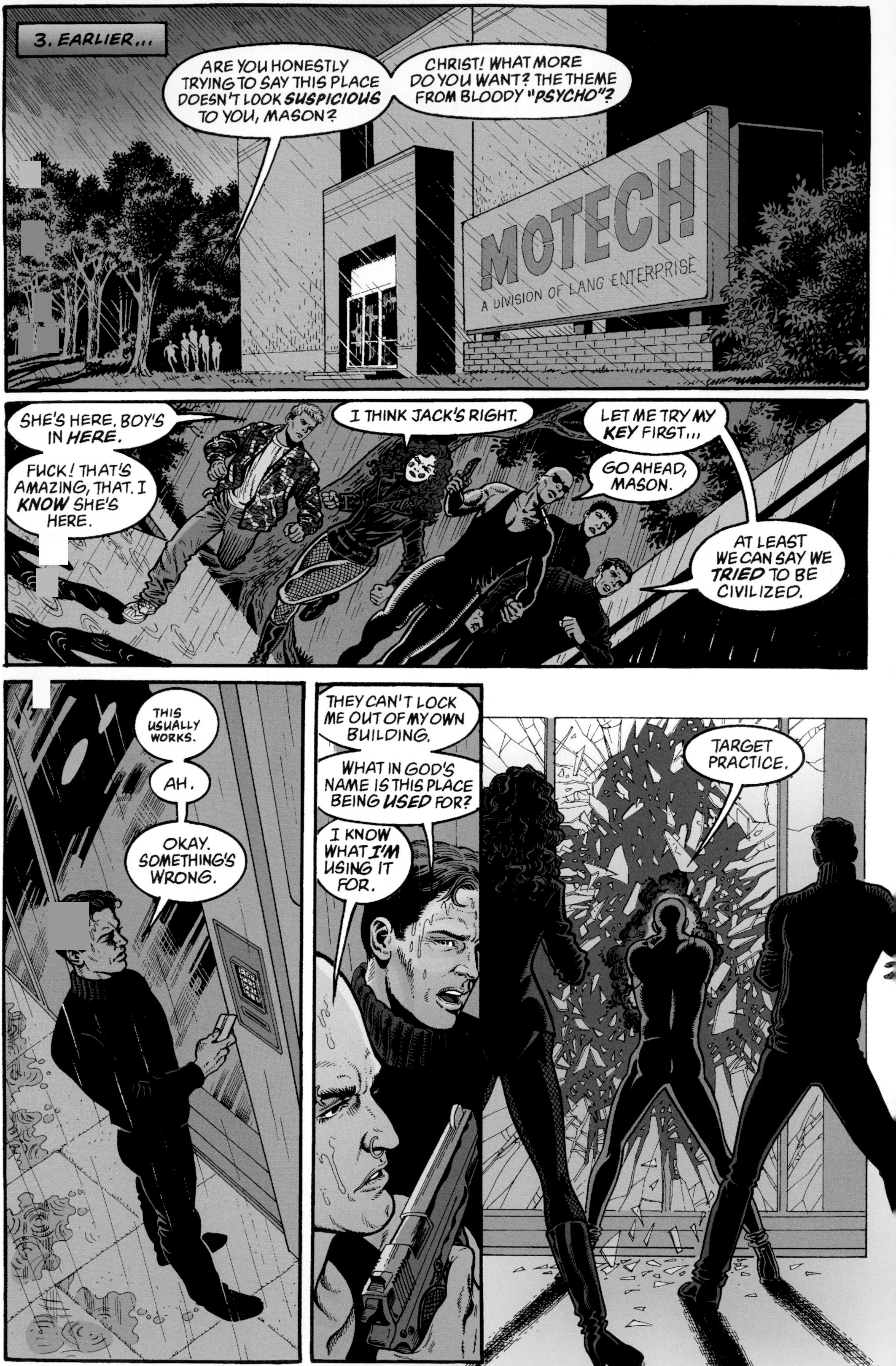
3. EARLIER...
ARE YOU HONESTLY TRYING TO SAY THIS PLACE DOESN'T LOOK SUSPICIOUS TO YOU, MASON?
CHRIST! WHAT MORE DO YOU WANT? THE THEME FROM BLOODY "PSYCHO"?
MOTECH
A DIVISION OF LANG ENTERPRISE
SHE'S HERE. BOY'S IN HERE.
FUCK! THAT'S AMAZING, THAT. I KNOW SHE'S HERE.
I THINK JACK'S RIGHT.
LET ME TRY MY KEY FIRST...
GO AHEAD, MASON.
AT LEAST WE CAN SAY WE TRIED TO BE CIVILIZED.
THIS USUALLY WORKS.
AH.
OKAY. SOMETHING'S WRONG.
THEY CAN'T LOCK ME OUT OF MY OWN BUILDING.
WHAT IN GOD'S NAME IS THIS PLACE BEING USED FOR?
I KNOW WHAT I'M USING IT FOR.
TARGET PRACTICE.

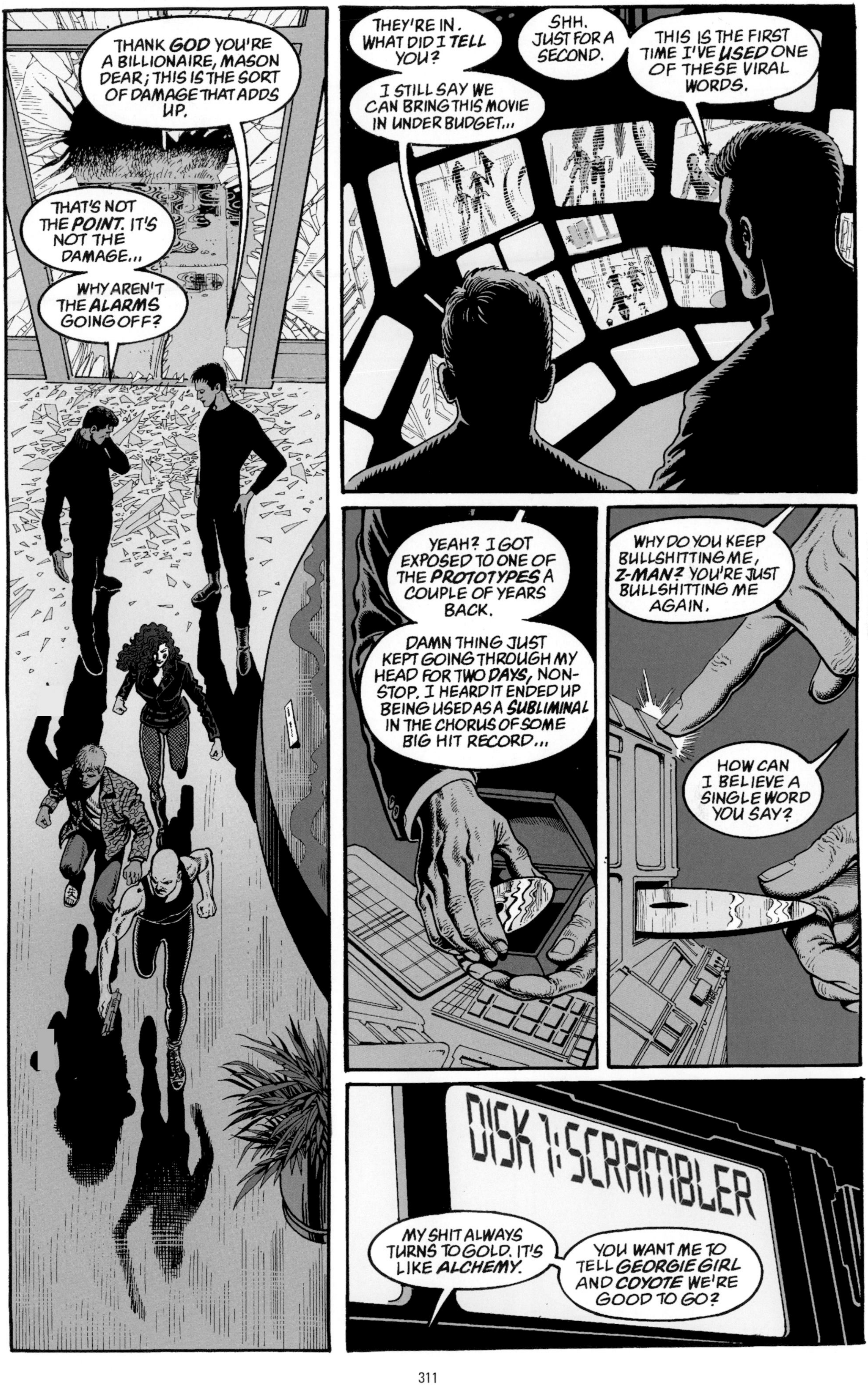
THANK GOD YOU'RE A BILLIONAIRE, MASON DEAR; THIS IS THE SORT OF DAMAGE THAT ADDS UP.
THAT'S NOT THE POINT. IT'S NOT THE DAMAGE...
WHY AREN'T THE ALARMS GOING OFF?
THEY'RE IN. WHAT DID I TELL YOU?
I STILL SAY WE CAN BRING THIS MOVIE IN UNDER BUDGET...
SHH. JUST FOR A SECOND.
THIS IS THE FIRST TIME I'VE USED ONE OF THESE VIRAL WORDS.
YEAH? I GOT EXPOSED TO ONE OF THE PROTOTYPES A COUPLE OF YEARS BACK.
DAMN THING JUST KEPT GOING THROUGH MY HEAD FOR TWO DAYS, NON-STOP. I HEARD IT ENDED UP BEING USED AS A SUBLIMINAL IN THE CHORUS OF SOME BIG HIT RECORD...
WHY DO YOU KEEP BULLSHITTING ME, Z-MAN? YOU'RE JUST BULLSHITTING ME AGAIN.
HOW CAN I BELIEVE A SINGLE WORD YOU SAY?
DISK 1: SCRAMBLER
MY SHIT ALWAYS TURNS TO GOLD. IT'S LIKE ALCHEMY.
YOU WANT ME TO TELL GEORGIE GIRL AND COYOTE WE'RE GOOD TO GO?

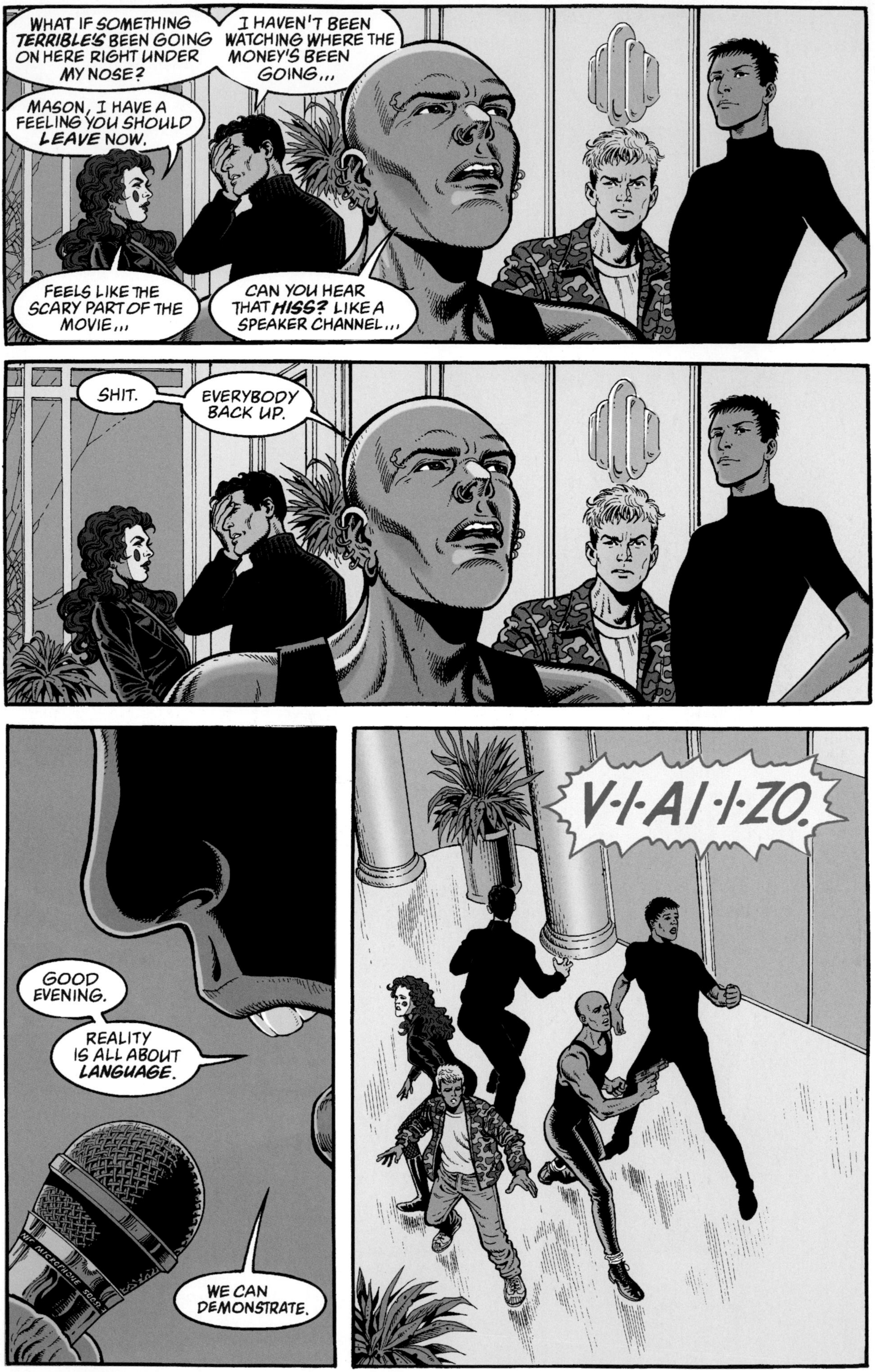
WHAT IF SOMETHING TERRIBLE'S BEEN GOING ON HERE RIGHT UNDER MY NOSE?
I HAVEN'T BEEN WATCHING WHERE THE MONEY'S BEEN GOING...
MASON, I HAVE A FEELING YOU SHOULD LEAVE NOW.
FEELS LIKE THE SCARY PART OF THE MOVIE...
CAN YOU HEAR THAT HISS? LIKE A SPEAKER CHANNEL...
SHIT.
EVERYBODY BACK UP.
GOOD EVENING.
REALITY IS ALL ABOUT LANGUAGE.
WE CAN DEMONSTRATE.
V-I-AI-I-ZO.

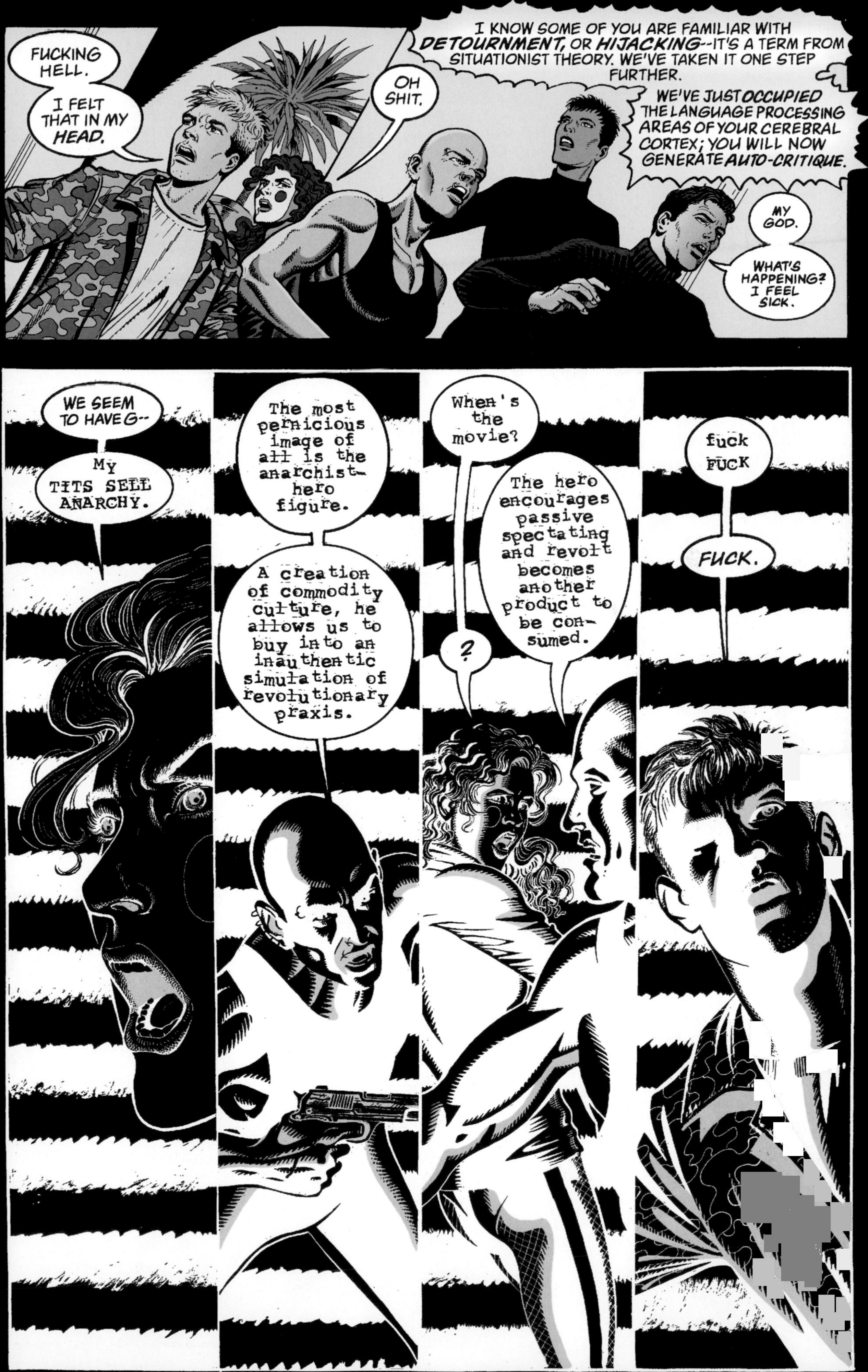

FUCKING HELL.
I FELT THAT IN MY HEAD.
OH SHIT.
I KNOW SOME OF YOU ARE FAMILIAR WITH DETOURNMENT, OR HIJACKING--IT'S A TERM FROM SITUATIONIST THEORY. WE'VE TAKEN IT ONE STEP FURTHER.
WE'VE JUST OCCUPIED THE LANGUAGE PROCESSING AREAS OF YOUR CEREBRAL CORTEX; YOU WILL NOW GENERATE AUTO-CRITIQUE.
MY GOD.
WHAT'S HAPPENING? I FEEL SICK.
WE SEEM TO HAVE G--
My TITS SELL ANARCHY.
The most pernicious image of all is the anarchist-hero figure.
A creation of commodity culture, he allows us to buy into an inauthentic simulation of revolutionary praxis.
When's the movie?
?
The hero encourages passive spectating and revolt becomes another product to be consumed.
fuck FUCK
FUCK.

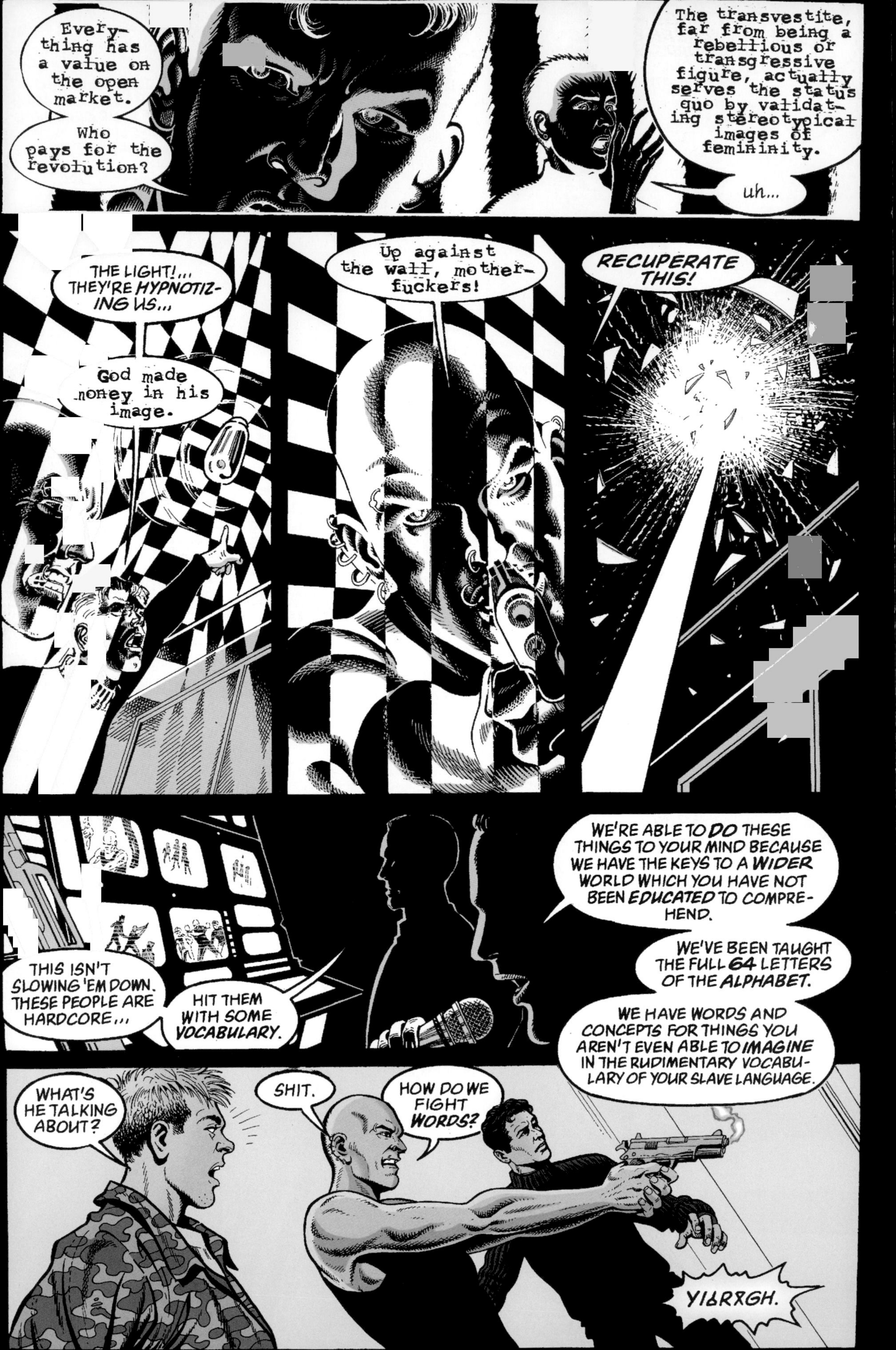
Every-thing has a value on the open market.
Who pays for the revolution?
The transvestite, far from being a rebellious or transgressive figure, actually serves the status quo by validating stereotypical images of femininity.
uh...
THE LIGHT!... THEY'RE HYPNOTIZING US...
God made money in his image.
Up against the wall, mother-fuckers!
RECUPERATE THIS!
THIS ISN'T SLOWING 'EM DOWN. THESE PEOPLE ARE HARDCORE...
HIT THEM WITH SOME VOCABULARY.
WE'RE ABLE TO DO THESE THINGS TO YOUR MIND BECAUSE WE HAVE THE KEYS TO A WIDER WORLD WHICH YOU HAVE NOT BEEN EDUCATED TO COMPREHEND.
WE'VE BEEN TAUGHT THE FULL 64 LETTERS OF THE ALPHABET.
WE HAVE WORDS AND CONCEPTS FOR THINGS YOU AREN'T EVEN ABLE TO IMAGINE IN THE RUDIMENTARY VOCABULARY OF YOUR SLAVE LANGUAGE.
WHAT'S HE TALKING ABOUT?
SHIT.
HOW DO WE FIGHT WORDS?

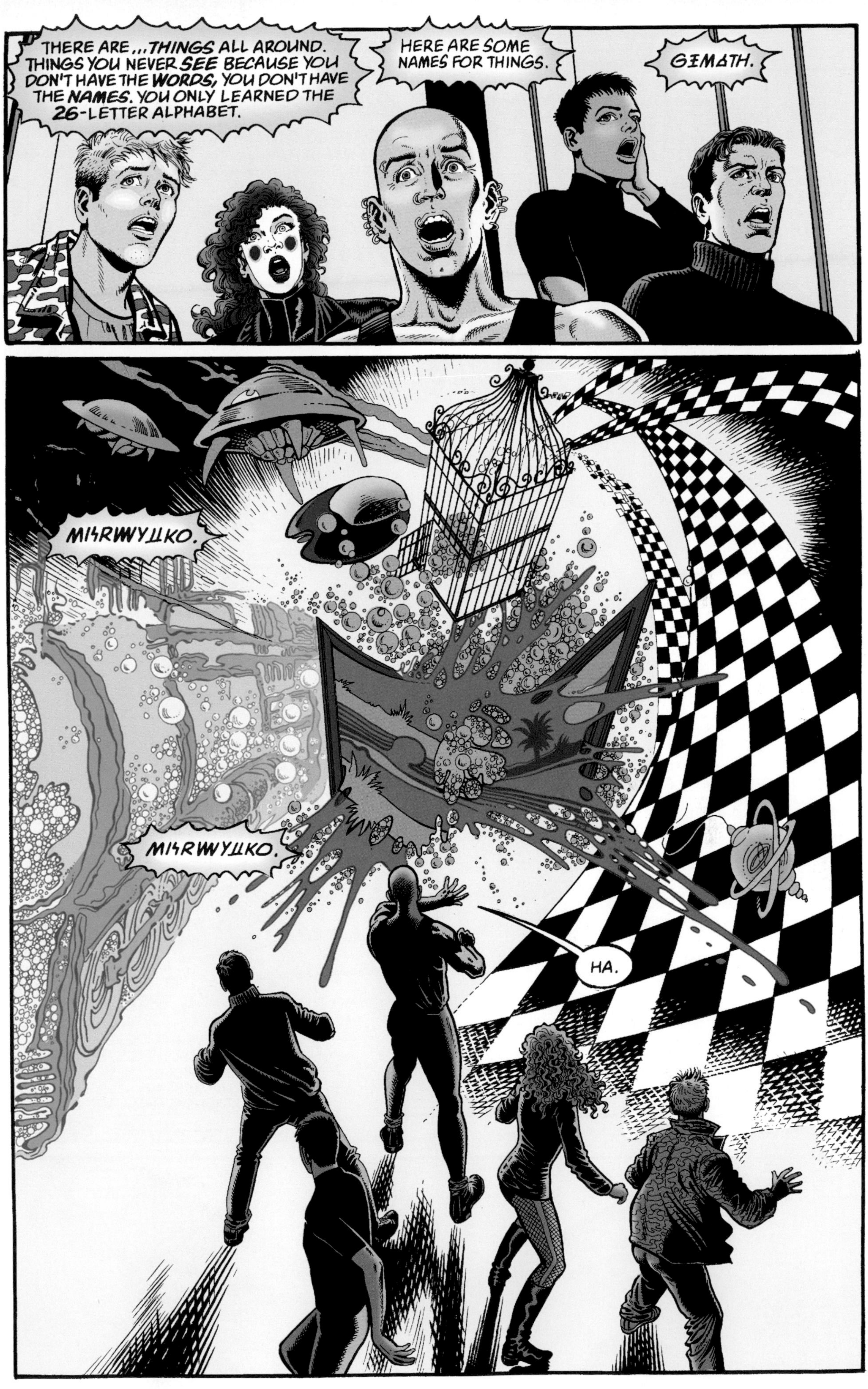
THERE ARE... THINGS ALL AROUND. THINGS YOU NEVER SEE BECAUSE YOU DON'T HAVE THE WORDS, YOU DON'T HAVE THE NAMES. YOU ONLY LEARNED THE 26-LETTER ALPHABET.
HERE ARE SOME NAMES FOR THINGS.
GIMATH.
MISRWYLLKO.
MISRWYLLKO.
HA.

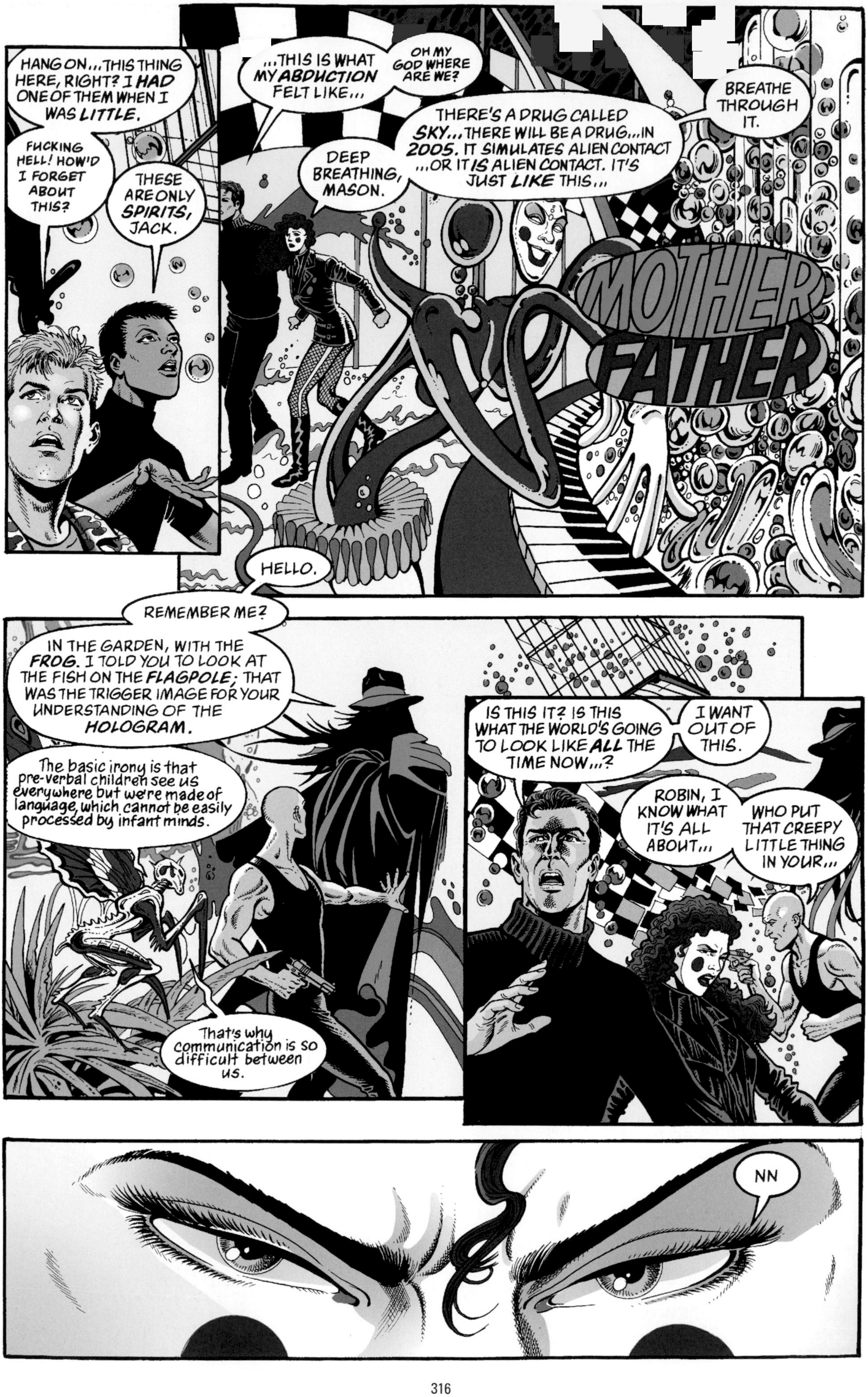
HANG ON... THIS THING HERE, RIGHT? I HAD ONE OF THEM WHEN I WAS LITTLE.
FUCKING HELL! HOW'D I FORGET ABOUT THIS?
THESE ARE ONLY SPIRITS, JACK.
...THIS IS WHAT MY ABDUCTION FELT LIKE...
OH MY GOD WHERE ARE WE?
DEEP BREATHING, MASON.
THERE'S A DRUG CALLED SKY... THERE WILL BE A DRUG... IN 2005. IT SIMULATES ALIEN CONTACT ...OR IT IS ALIEN CONTACT. IT'S JUST LIKE THIS...
BREATHE THROUGH IT.
MOTHER
FATHER
HELLO.
REMEMBER ME?
IN THE GARDEN, WITH THE FROG. I TOLD YOU TO LOOK AT THE FISH ON THE FLAGPOLE; THAT WAS THE TRIGGER IMAGE FOR YOUR UNDERSTANDING OF THE HOLOGRAM.
The basic irony is that pre-verbal children see us everywhere but we're made of language, which cannot be easily processed by infant minds.
That's why communication is so difficult between us.
IS THIS IT? IS THIS WHAT THE WORLD'S GOING TO LOOK LIKE ALL THE TIME NOW...?
I WANT OUT OF THIS.
ROBIN, I KNOW WHAT IT'S ALL ABOUT...
WHO PUT THAT CREEPY LITTLE THING IN YOUR...
NN

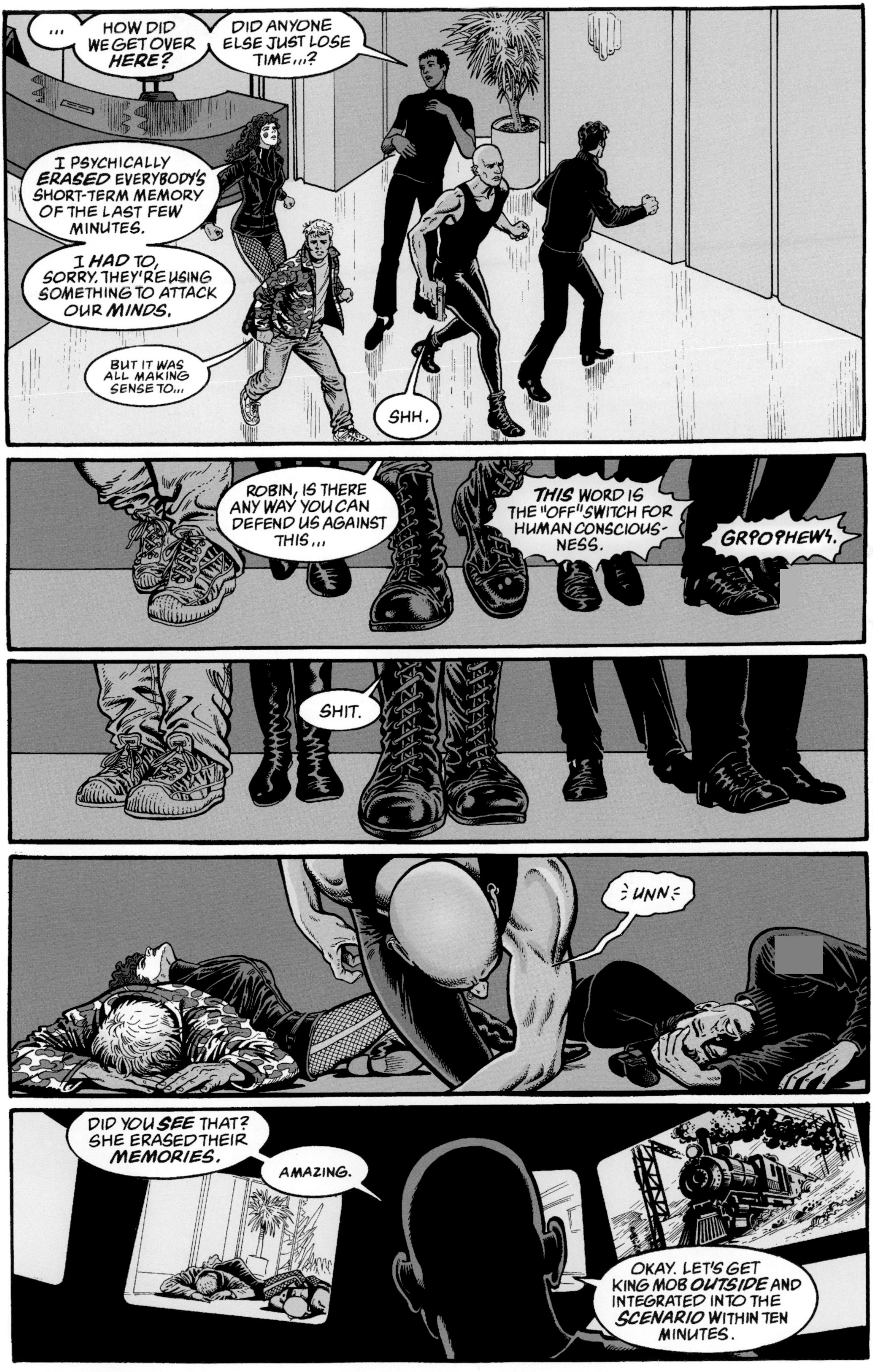
...
HOW DID WE GET OVER HERE?
DID ANYONE ELSE JUST LOSE TIME...?
I PSYCHICALLY ERASED EVERYBODY'S SHORT-TERM MEMORY OF THE LAST FEW MINUTES.
I HAD TO, SORRY. THEY'RE USING SOMETHING TO ATTACK OUR MINDS.
BUT IT WAS ALL MAKING SENSE TO...
SHH.
ROBIN, IS THERE ANY WAY YOU CAN DEFEND US AGAINST THIS...
THIS WORD IS THE "OFF" SWITCH FOR HUMAN CONSCIOUS-NESS.
GRPOPHEWY.
SHIT.
UNN
DID YOU SEE THAT? SHE ERASED THEIR MEMORIES.
AMAZING.
OKAY. LET'S GET KING MOB OUTSIDE AND INTEGRATED INTO THE SCENARIO WITHIN TEN MINUTES.

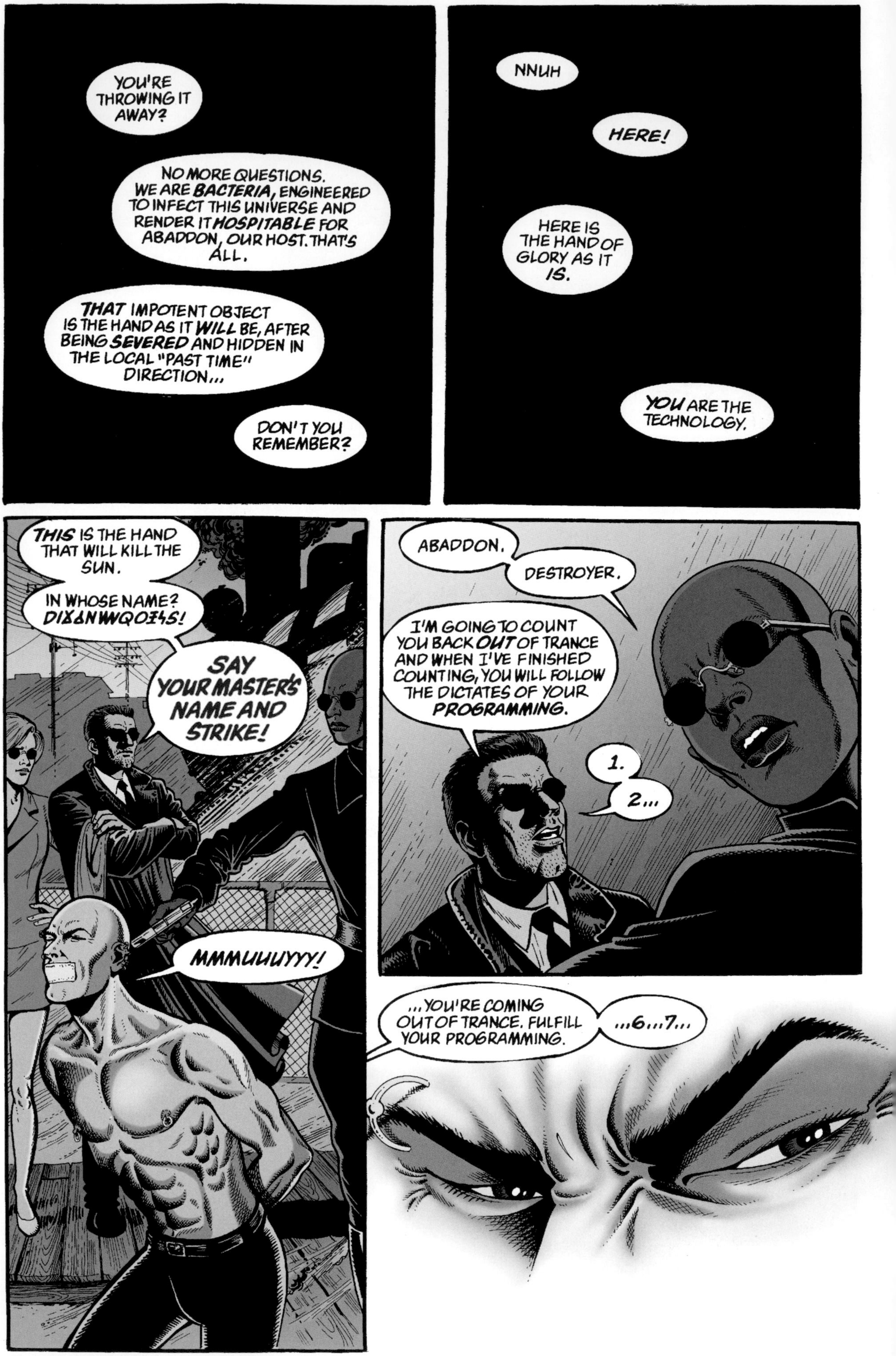
YOU'RE THROWING IT AWAY?
NO MORE QUESTIONS. WE ARE BACTERIA, ENGINEERED TO INFECT THIS UNIVERSE AND RENDER IT HOSPITABLE FOR ABADDON, OUR HOST. THAT'S ALL.
THAT IMPOTENT OBJECT IS THE HAND AS IT WILL BE, AFTER BEING SEVERED AND HIDDEN IN THE LOCAL "PAST TIME" DIRECTION...
DON'T YOU REMEMBER?
NNUH
HERE!
HERE IS THE HAND OF GLORY AS IT IS.
YOU ARE THE TECHNOLOGY.
THIS IS THE HAND THAT WILL KILL THE SUN.
IN WHOSE NAME?
SAY YOUR MASTER'S NAME AND STRIKE!
MMMUUUYYY!
ABADDON.
DESTROYER.
I'M GOING TO COUNT YOU BACK OUT OF TRANCE AND WHEN I'VE FINISHED COUNTING, YOU WILL FOLLOW THE DICTATES OF YOUR PROGRAMMING.
1.
2...
...YOU'RE COMING OUT OF TRANCE. FULFILL YOUR PROGRAMMING.
...6...7...

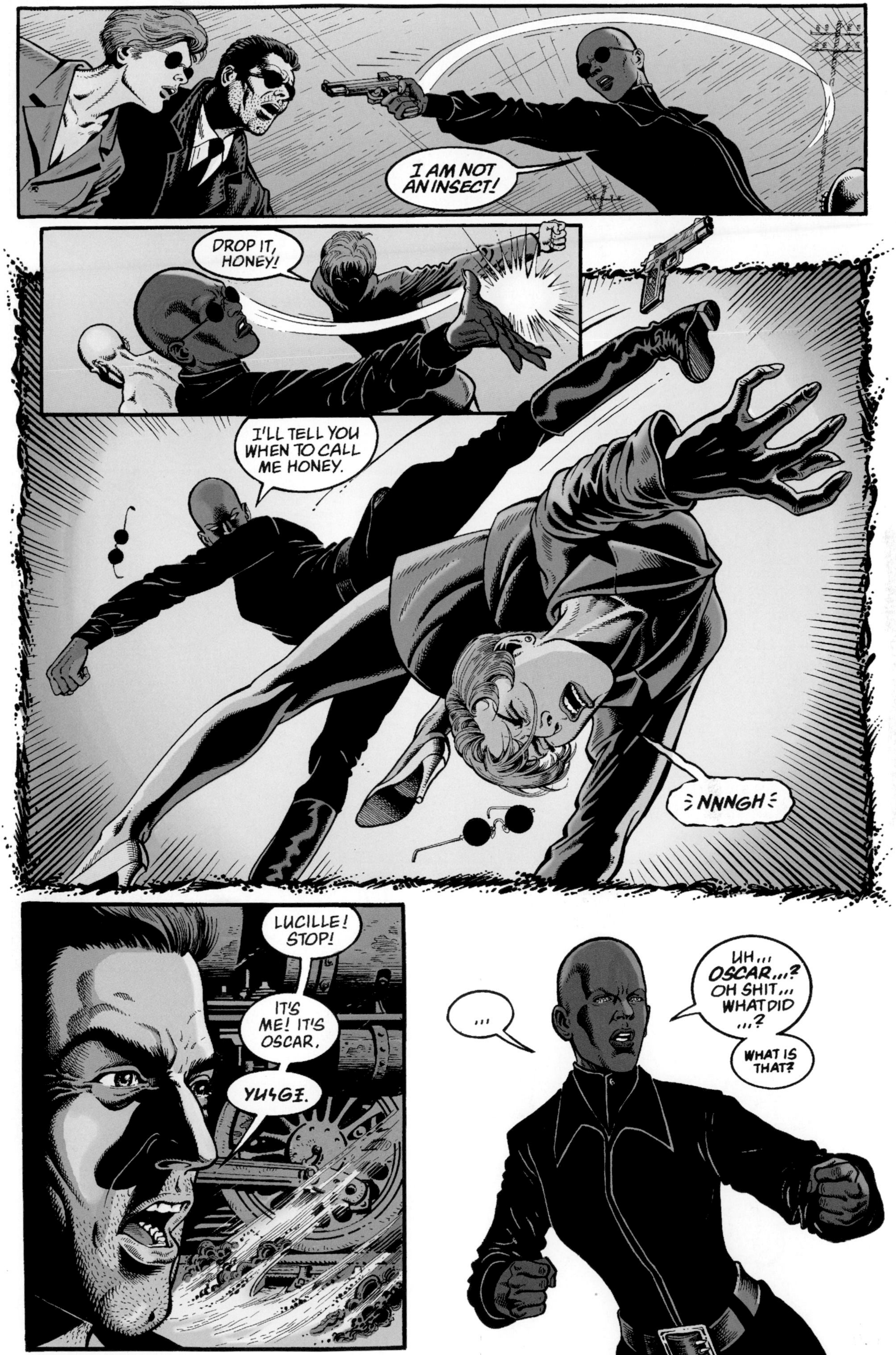
I AM NOT AN INSECT!
DROP IT, HONEY!
I'LL TELL YOU WHEN TO CALL ME HONEY.
NNNGH
LUCILLE! STOP!
IT'S ME! IT'S OSCAR.
YUSGI.
...
UH... OSCAR...? OH SHIT... WHAT DID ...?
WHAT IS THAT?

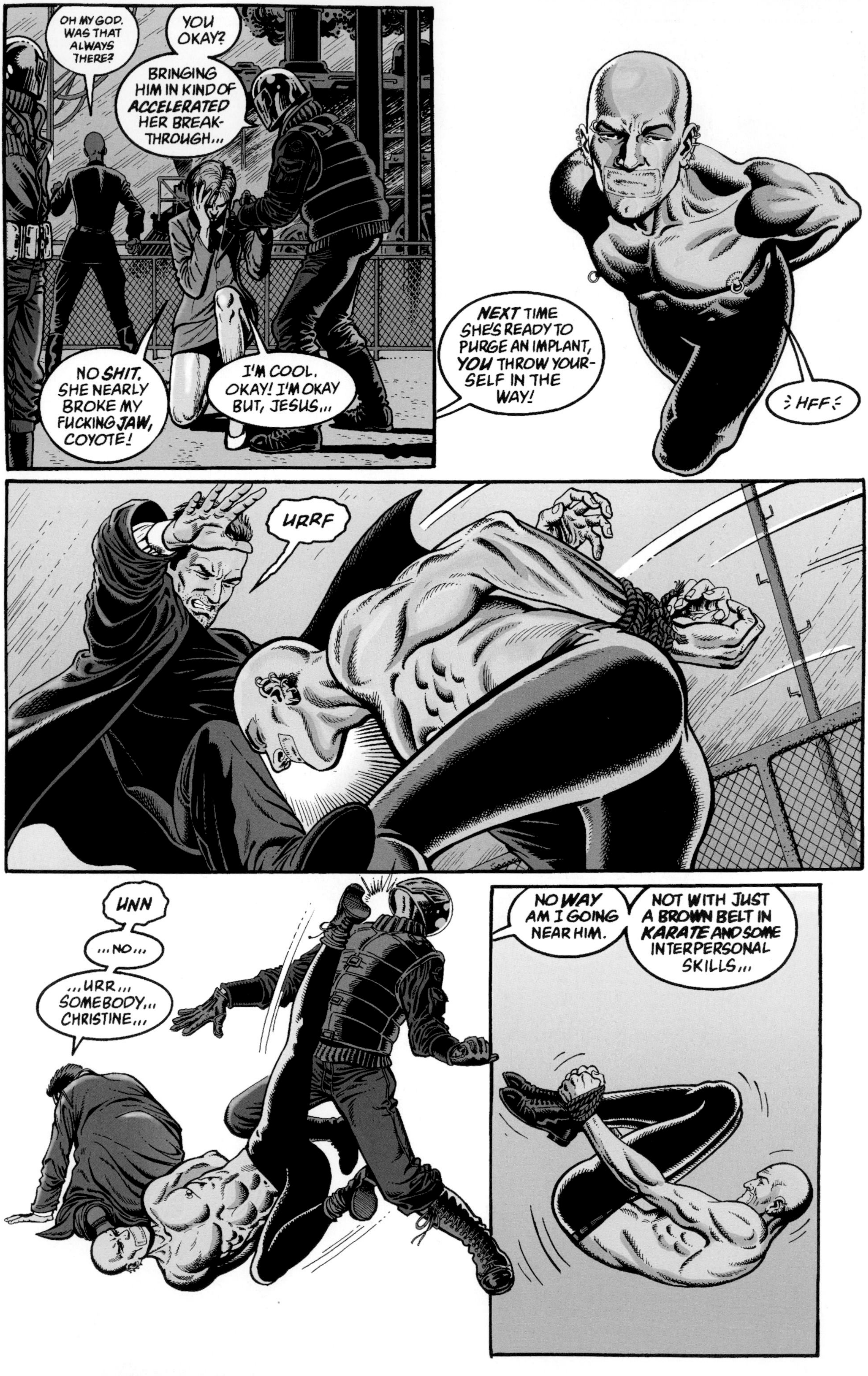
OH MY GOD. WAS THAT ALWAYS THERE?
YOU OKAY?
BRINGING HIM IN KIND OF ACCELERATED HER BREAK-THROUGH...
NO SHIT. SHE NEARLY BROKE MY FUCKING JAW, COYOTE!
I'M COOL. OKAY! I'M OKAY BUT, JESUS...
NEXT TIME SHE'S READY TO PURGE AN IMPLANT, YOU THROW YOUR-SELF IN THE WAY!
HFF
URRF
UNN
...NO...
...URR... SOMEBODY... CHRISTINE...
NO WAY AM I GOING NEAR HIM.
NOT WITH JUST A BROWN BELT IN KARATE AND SOME INTERPERSONAL SKILLS...

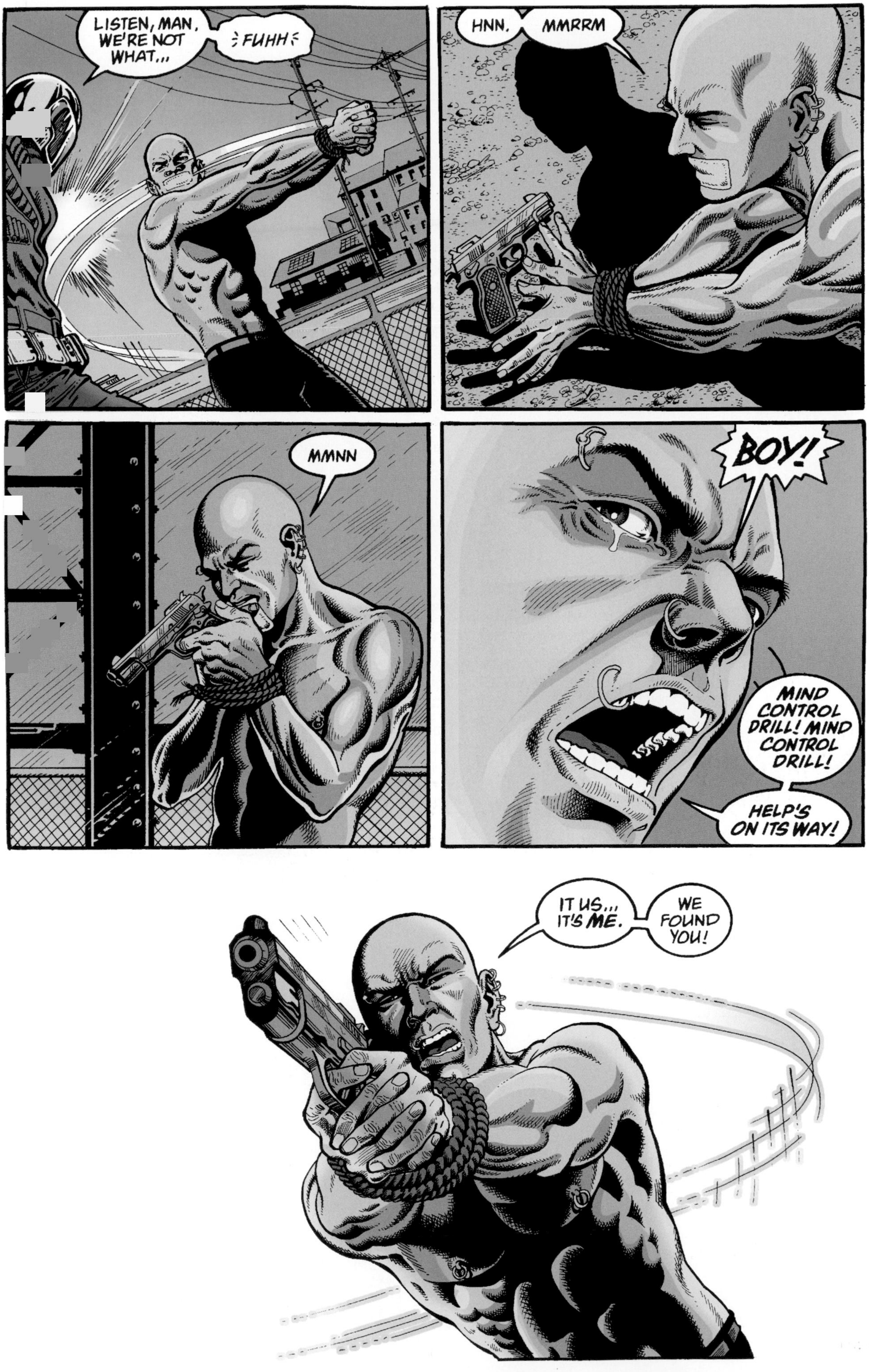
LISTEN, MAN, WE'RE NOT WHAT...
FUHH
HNN,
MMRRM
MMNN
BOY!
MIND CONTROL DRILL! MIND CONTROL DRILL!
HELP'S ON ITS WAY!
IT US... IT'S ME.
WE FOUND YOU!

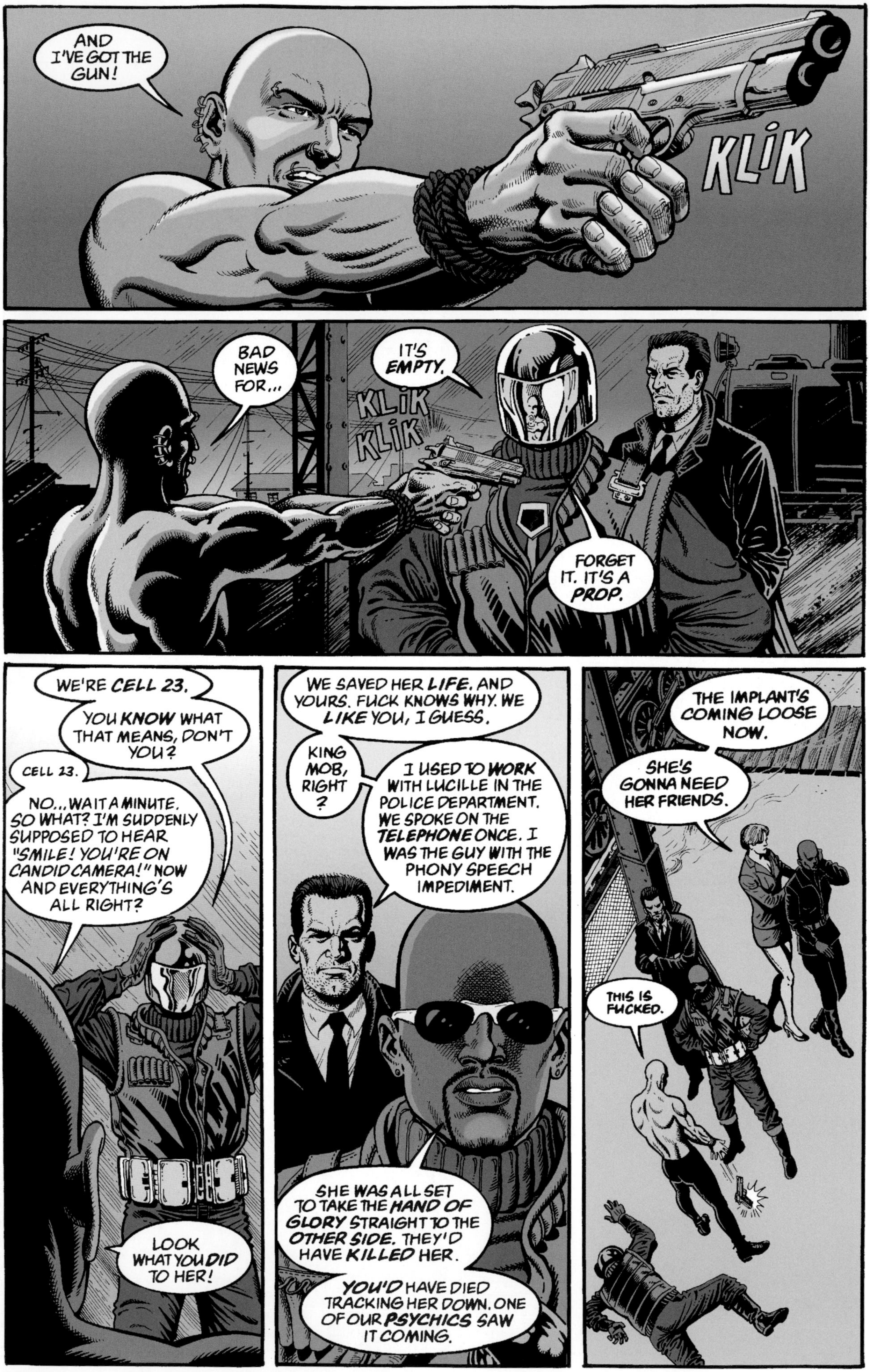
AND I'VE GOT THE GUN!
KLIK
BAD NEWS FOR...
IT'S EMPTY.
KLIK KLIK
FORGET IT. IT'S A PROP.
WE'RE CELL 23.
YOU KNOW WHAT THAT MEANS, DON'T YOU?
CELL 23.
NO...WAIT A MINUTE. SO WHAT? I'M SUDDENLY SUPPOSED TO HEAR "SMILE! YOU'RE ON CANDID CAMERA!" NOW AND EVERYTHING'S ALL RIGHT?
LOOK WHAT YOU DID TO HER!
WE SAVED HER LIFE. AND YOURS. FUCK KNOWS WHY. WE LIKE YOU, I GUESS.
KING MOB, RIGHT?
I USED TO WORK WITH LUCILLE IN THE POLICE DEPARTMENT. WE SPOKE ON THE TELEPHONE ONCE. I WAS THE GUY WITH THE PHONY SPEECH IMPEDIMENT.
SHE WAS ALL SET TO TAKE THE HAND OF GLORY STRAIGHT TO THE OTHER SIDE. THEY'D HAVE KILLED HER.
YOU'D HAVE DIED TRACKING HER DOWN. ONE OF OUR PSYCHICS SAW IT COMING.
THE IMPLANT'S COMING LOOSE NOW.
SHE'S GONNA NEED HER FRIENDS.
THIS IS FUCKED.

I DON'T CARE. I DON'T CARE *WHO* YOU ARE OR WHO YOU *THINK* YOU ARE...

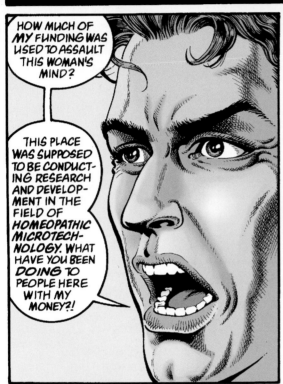

HOW MUCH OF *MY* FUNDING WAS USED TO ASSAULT THIS WOMAN'S MIND?

THIS PLACE WAS SUPPOSED TO BE CONDUCTING RESEARCH AND DEVELOPMENT IN THE FIELD OF *HOMEOPATHIC MICROTECHNOLOGY.* WHAT HAVE YOU BEEN *DOING* TO PEOPLE HERE WITH MY MONEY?!

MOTECH *STILL* LEADS THE FIELD, MR. LANG. WE MAKE IRREGULAR USE OF THE FACILITY FOR LARGE-SCALE SCENAR-IOS LIKE THIS ONE.

CELL 23 SPECIALIZES IN PSYCHODRAMATIC DEBUGGING OF SO-CALLED "INVISIBLES" OPERATIVES. THE SHORT STORY IS THAT WE'RE EXPERTS IN THE REMOVAL OF ENEMY EMOTIONAL *IMPLANTS.*

WHAT?

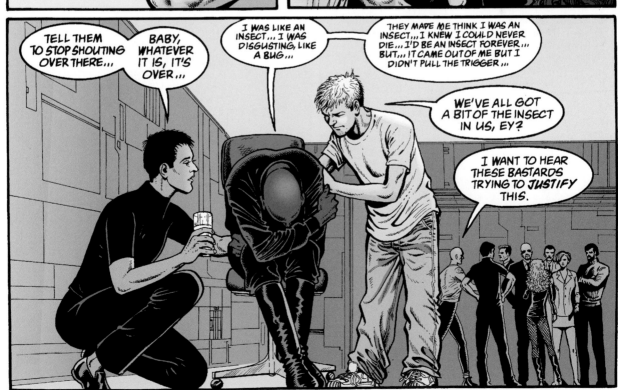

TELL THEM TO STOP SHOUTING OVER THERE...

BABY, WHATEVER IT IS, IT'S OVER...

I WAS LIKE AN INSECT... I WAS DISGUSTING, LIKE A BUG...

THEY MADE ME THINK I WAS AN INSECT... I KNEW I COULD NEVER DIE... I'D BE AN INSECT FOREVER... BUT... IT CAME OUT OF ME BUT I DIDN'T PULL THE TRIGGER...

WE'VE ALL GOT A BIT OF THE INSECT IN US, EY?

I WANT TO HEAR THESE BASTARDS TRYING TO *JUSTIFY* THIS.

SHUT UP OVER THERE, FOR GOD'S SAKE!

I SWEAR, IF A GIANT INSECT WALKED IN HERE RIGHT NOW, I'D FUCK IT TO *DEATH*.

I DON'T CARE *HOW* MANY LEGS IT'S GOT AS LONG AS IT'S BUYING THE DRINKS...

INSECTS! EVEN IF YOU *WERE* AN INSECT, WE'D STILL LOVE YOU, DARLING.

...OH JESUS, FANNY... I FEEL LIKE I'VE BEEN DEAD...

...I NEVER EVEN FOUND MY LITTLE MOUSE MARTY, I NEVER EVEN GOT TO BURY HIM ...HOW DID I KNOW IT...THE MOUSE AND MARTIN ARE THE SAME THING...

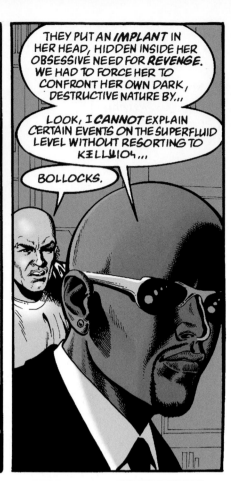

THEY PUT AN *IMPLANT* IN HER HEAD, HIDDEN INSIDE HER OBSESSIVE NEED FOR *REVENGE*. WE HAD TO FORCE HER TO CONFRONT HER OWN DARK, DESTRUCTIVE NATURE BY...

LOOK, I *CANNOT* EXPLAIN CERTAIN EVENTS ON THE SUPERFLUID LEVEL WITHOUT RESORTING TO K3LLЩ1O⊦...

BOLLOCKS.

LUCILLE, LISTEN. IT'S ME, OSCAR.

THEY PUT AN IMPLANT, A PSYCHIC BUG, IN YOUR HEAD BACK WHEN THEY TOOK *MARTIN* AND KILLED *EEZY D.* IT HAD TRIGGERED AND WAS READY TO KILL YOU.

REMEMBER.

OH NO... OH JESUS...OH... I CAN'T ...I ...

AAAUUUU!

AUUU NO!

IT'S JUST *THEIR WAY* OF BANISHING, JACK.

WHO IS THIS GUY?

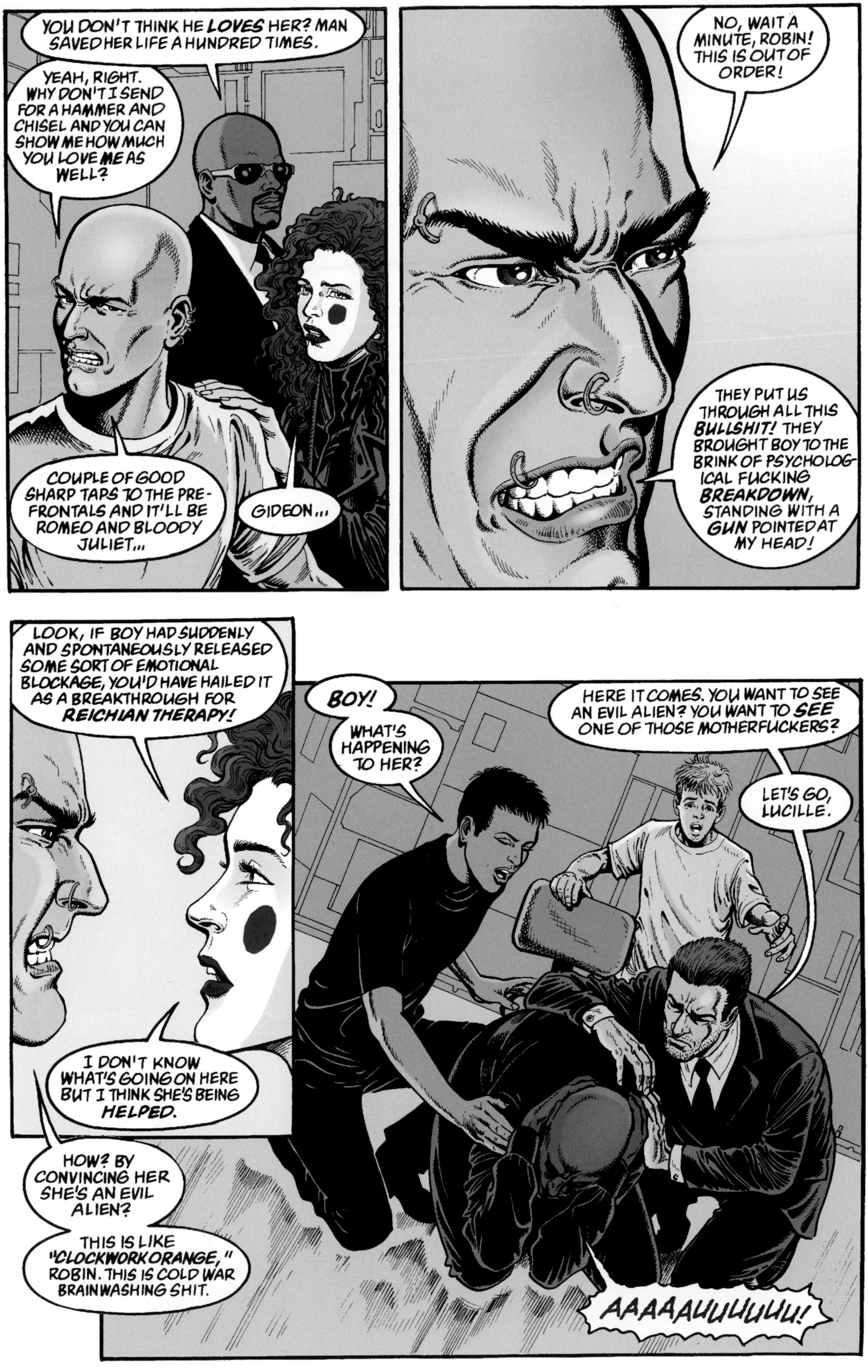
YOU DON'T THINK HE LOVES HER? MAN SAVED HER LIFE A HUNDRED TIMES.
YEAH, RIGHT. WHY DON'T I SEND FOR A HAMMER AND CHISEL AND YOU CAN SHOW ME HOW MUCH YOU LOVE ME AS WELL?
COUPLE OF GOOD SHARP TAPS TO THE PRE-FRONTALS AND IT'LL BE ROMEO AND BLOODY JULIET...
GIDEON...
NO, WAIT A MINUTE, ROBIN! THIS IS OUT OF ORDER!
THEY PUT US THROUGH ALL THIS BULLSHIT! THEY BROUGHT BOY TO THE BRINK OF PSYCHOLOG-ICAL FUCKING BREAKDOWN, STANDING WITH A GUN POINTED AT MY HEAD!
LOOK, IF BOY HAD SUDDENLY AND SPONTANEOUSLY RELEASED SOME SORT OF EMOTIONAL BLOCKAGE, YOU'D HAVE HAILED IT AS A BREAKTHROUGH FOR REICHIAN THERAPY!
I DON'T KNOW WHAT'S GOING ON HERE BUT I THINK SHE'S BEING HELPED.
HOW? BY CONVINCING HER SHE'S AN EVIL ALIEN?
THIS IS LIKE "CLOCKWORK ORANGE," ROBIN. THIS IS COLD WAR BRAINWASHING SHIT.
BOY!
WHAT'S HAPPENING TO HER?
HERE IT COMES. YOU WANT TO SEE AN EVIL ALIEN? YOU WANT TO SEE ONE OF THOSE MOTHERFUCKERS?
LET'S GO, LUCILLE.
AAAAAUUUUUU!

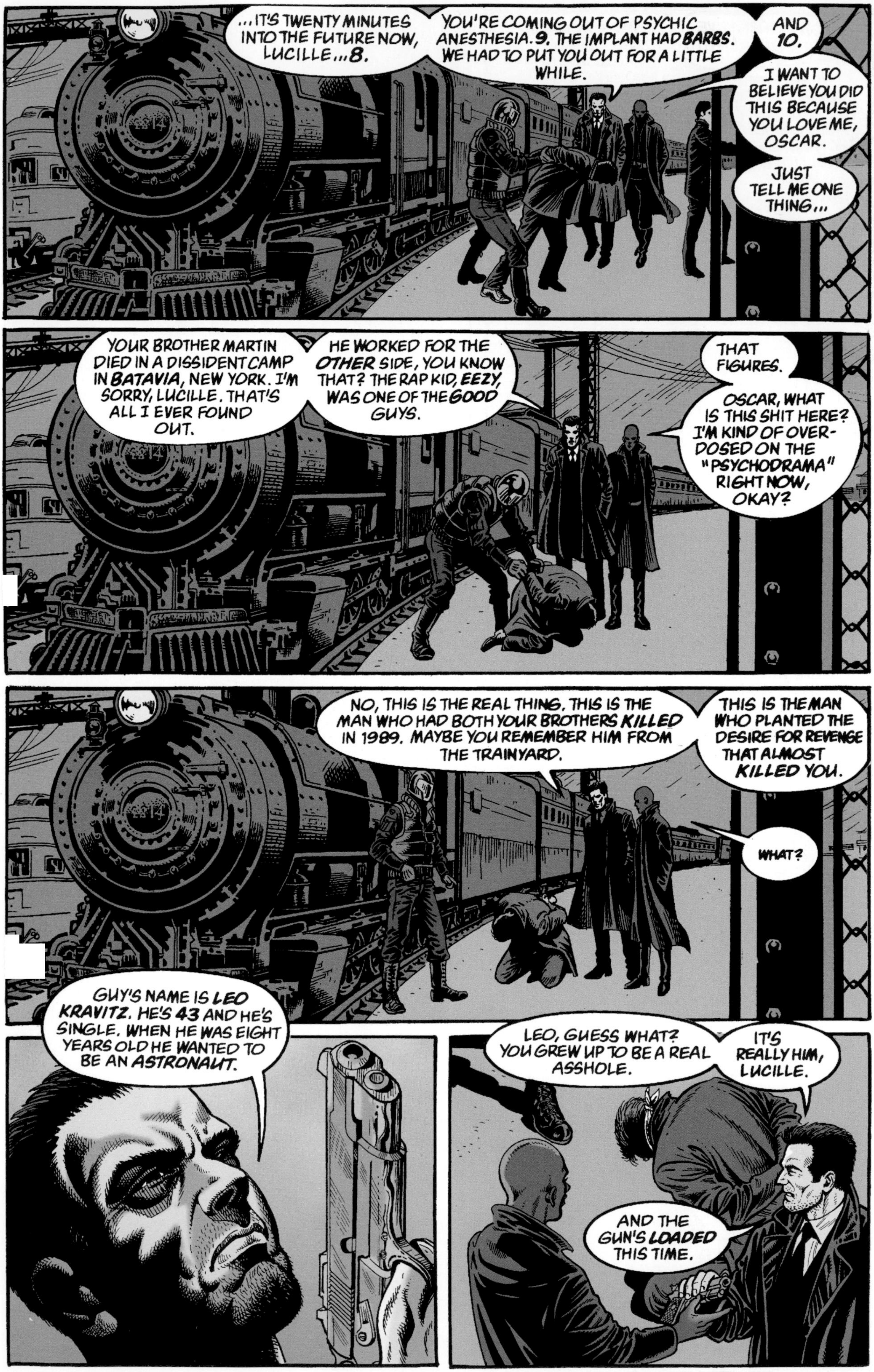

...IT'S TWENTY MINUTES INTO THE FUTURE NOW, LUCILLE...8.
YOU'RE COMING OUT OF PSYCHIC ANESTHESIA. 9. THE IMPLANT HAD BARBS. WE HAD TO PUT YOU OUT FOR A LITTLE WHILE.
AND 10.
I WANT TO BELIEVE YOU DID THIS BECAUSE YOU LOVE ME, OSCAR.
JUST TELL ME ONE THING...
YOUR BROTHER MARTIN DIED IN A DISSIDENT CAMP IN BATAVIA, NEW YORK. I'M SORRY, LUCILLE. THAT'S ALL I EVER FOUND OUT.
HE WORKED FOR THE OTHER SIDE, YOU KNOW THAT? THE RAP KID, EEZY, WAS ONE OF THE GOOD GUYS.
THAT FIGURES.
OSCAR, WHAT IS THIS SHIT HERE? I'M KIND OF OVER-DOSED ON THE "PSYCHODRAMA" RIGHT NOW, OKAY?
NO, THIS IS THE REAL THING. THIS IS THE MAN WHO HAD BOTH YOUR BROTHERS KILLED IN 1989. MAYBE YOU REMEMBER HIM FROM THE TRAINYARD.
THIS IS THE MAN WHO PLANTED THE DESIRE FOR REVENGE THAT ALMOST KILLED YOU.
WHAT?
GUY'S NAME IS LEO KRAVITZ. HE'S 43 AND HE'S SINGLE. WHEN HE WAS EIGHT YEARS OLD HE WANTED TO BE AN ASTRONAUT.
LEO, GUESS WHAT? YOU GREW UP TO BE A REAL ASSHOLE.
IT'S REALLY HIM, LUCILLE.
AND THE GUN'S LOADED THIS TIME.

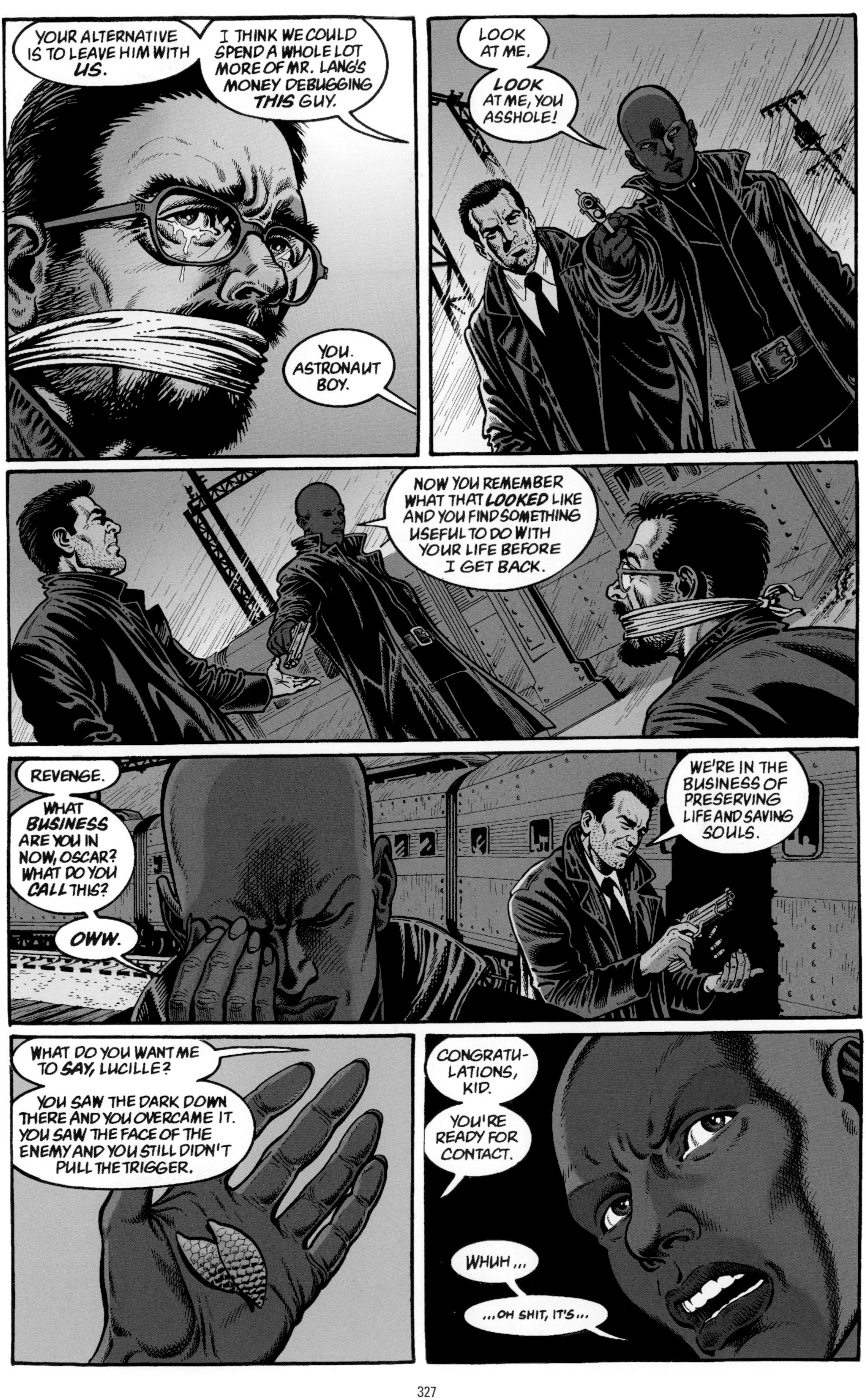
YOUR ALTERNATIVE IS TO LEAVE HIM WITH US.
I THINK WE COULD SPEND A WHOLE LOT MORE OF MR. LANG'S MONEY DEBUGGING THIS GUY.
YOU. ASTRONAUT BOY.
LOOK AT ME.
LOOK AT ME, YOU ASSHOLE!
NOW YOU REMEMBER WHAT THAT LOOKED LIKE AND YOU FIND SOMETHING USEFUL TO DO WITH YOUR LIFE BEFORE I GET BACK.
REVENGE.
WHAT BUSINESS ARE YOU IN NOW, OSCAR? WHAT DO YOU CALL THIS?
OWW.
WE'RE IN THE BUSINESS OF PRESERVING LIFE AND SAVING SOULS.
WHAT DO YOU WANT ME TO SAY, LUCILLE?
YOU SAW THE DARK DOWN THERE AND YOU OVERCAME IT. YOU SAW THE FACE OF THE ENEMY AND YOU STILL DIDN'T PULL THE TRIGGER.
CONGRATU-LATIONS, KID.
YOU'RE READY FOR CONTACT.
WHUH...
...OH SHIT, IT'S...

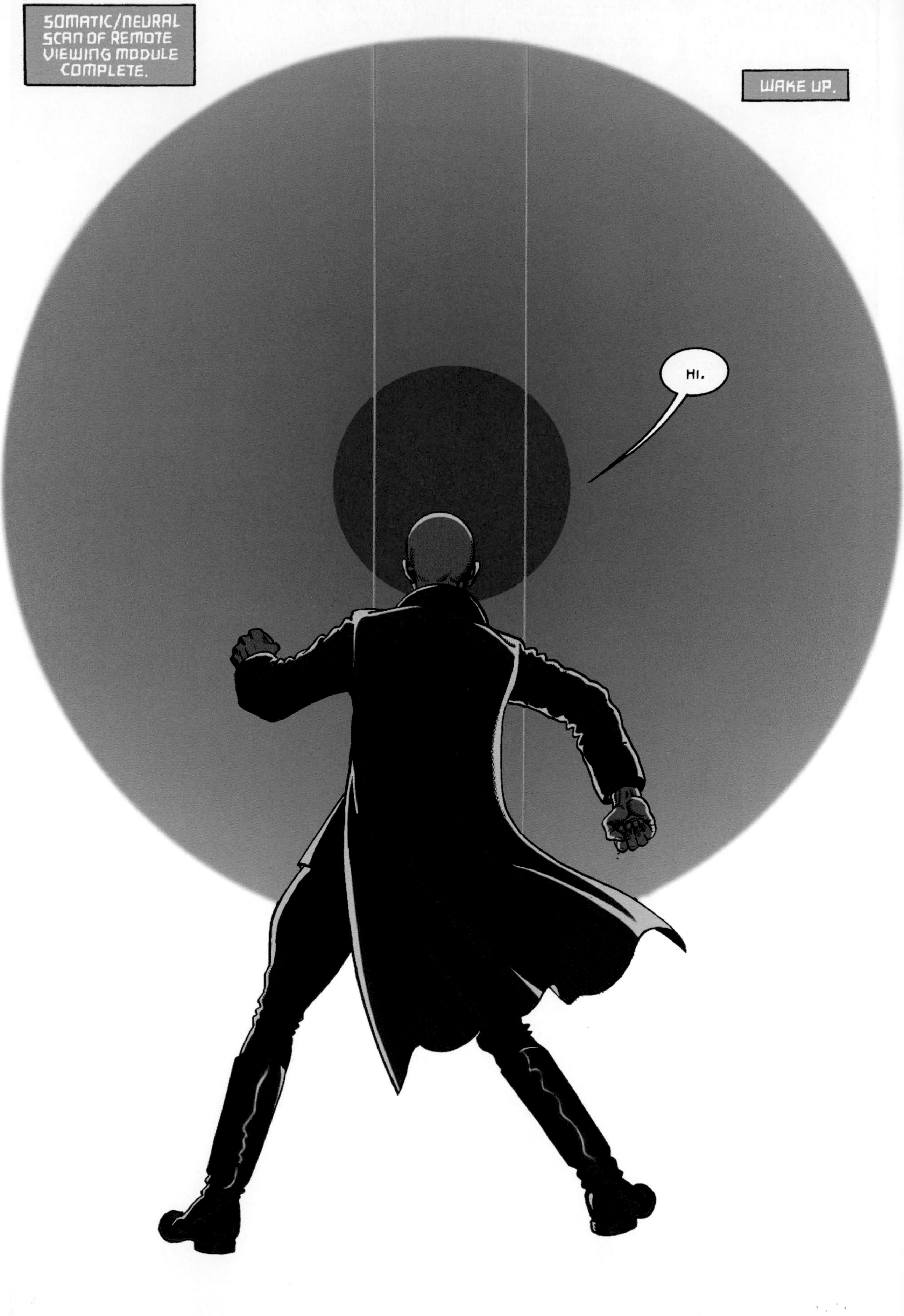
SOMATIC/NEURAL SCAN OF REMOTE VIEWING MODULE COMPLETE.
WAKE UP.
HI.

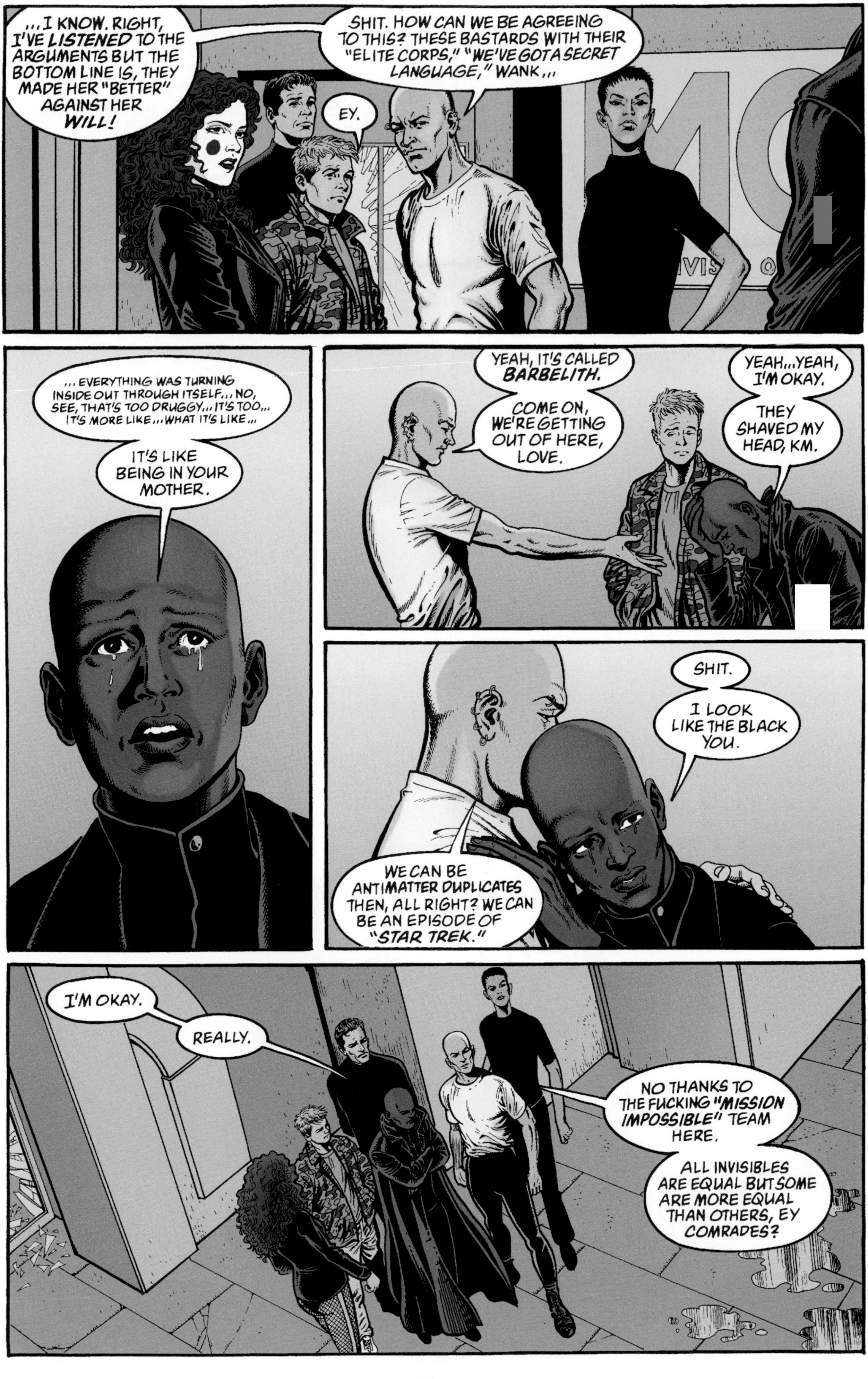
...I KNOW. RIGHT, I'VE LISTENED TO THE ARGUMENTS BUT THE BOTTOM LINE IS, THEY MADE HER "BETTER" AGAINST HER WILL!
SHIT. HOW CAN WE BE AGREEING TO THIS? THESE BASTARDS WITH THEIR "ELITE CORPS," "WE'VE GOT A SECRET LANGUAGE," WANK...
EY.
...EVERYTHING WAS TURNING INSIDE OUT THROUGH ITSELF... NO, SEE, THAT'S TOO DRUGGY... IT'S TOO... IT'S MORE LIKE... WHAT IT'S LIKE...
IT'S LIKE BEING IN YOUR MOTHER.
YEAH, IT'S CALLED BARBELITH.
COME ON, WE'RE GETTING OUT OF HERE, LOVE.
YEAH...YEAH, I'M OKAY.
THEY SHAVED MY HEAD, KM.
SHIT.
I LOOK LIKE THE BLACK YOU.
WE CAN BE ANTIMATTER DUPLICATES THEN, ALL RIGHT? WE CAN BE AN EPISODE OF "STAR TREK."
I'M OKAY.
REALLY.
NO THANKS TO THE FUCKING "MISSION IMPOSSIBLE" TEAM HERE.
ALL INVISIBLES ARE EQUAL BUT SOME ARE MORE EQUAL THAN OTHERS, EY COMRADES?

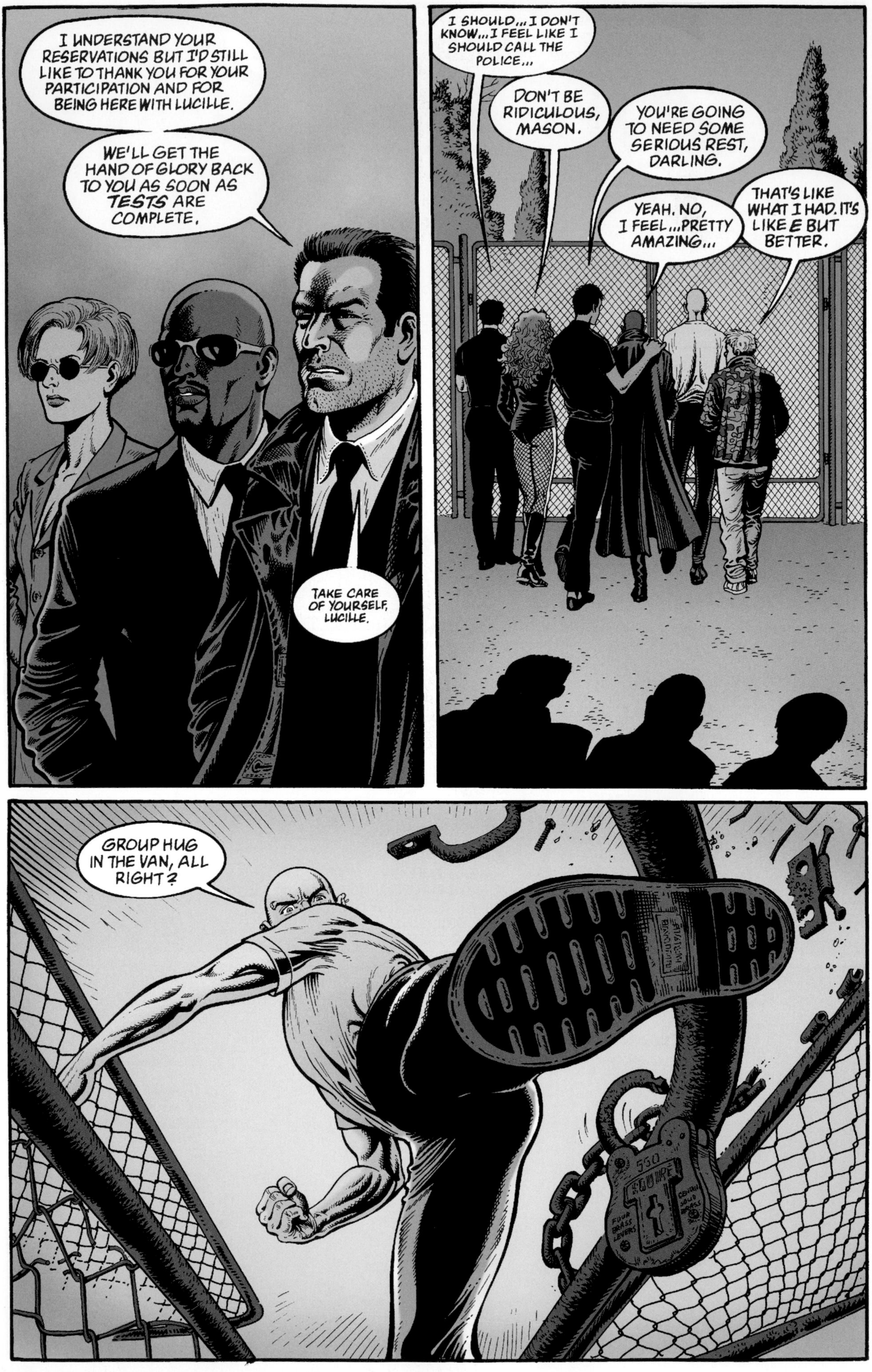
I UNDERSTAND YOUR RESERVATIONS BUT I'D STILL LIKE TO THANK YOU FOR YOUR PARTICIPATION AND FOR BEING HERE WITH LUCILLE.
WE'LL GET THE HAND OF GLORY BACK TO YOU AS SOON AS TESTS ARE COMPLETE.
TAKE CARE OF YOURSELF, LUCILLE.
I SHOULD... I DON'T KNOW... I FEEL LIKE I SHOULD CALL THE POLICE...
DON'T BE RIDICULOUS, MASON.
YOU'RE GOING TO NEED SOME SERIOUS REST, DARLING.
YEAH. NO, I FEEL... PRETTY AMAZING...
THAT'S LIKE WHAT I HAD. IT'S LIKE E BUT BETTER.
GROUP HUG IN THE VAN, ALL RIGHT?
550
SQUIRE
FOUR BRASS LEVERS

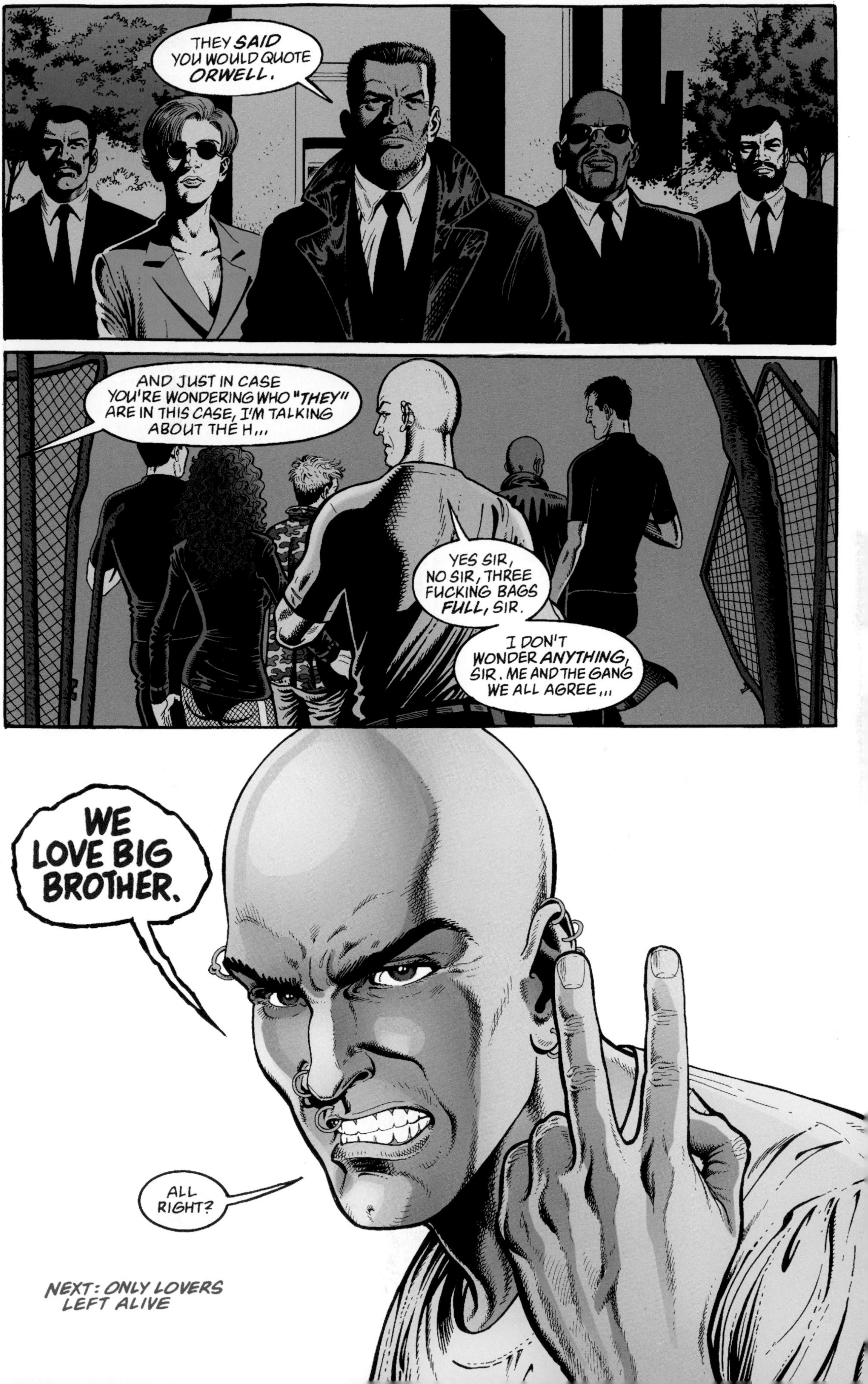
THEY SAID YOU WOULD QUOTE ORWELL.
AND JUST IN CASE YOU'RE WONDERING WHO "THEY" ARE IN THIS CASE, I'M TALKING ABOUT THE H...
YES SIR, NO SIR, THREE FUCKING BAGS FULL, SIR.
I DON'T WONDER ANYTHING, SIR. ME AND THE GANG WE ALL AGREE...
WE LOVE BIG BROTHER.
ALL RIGHT?
NEXT: ONLY LOVERS LEFT ALIVE

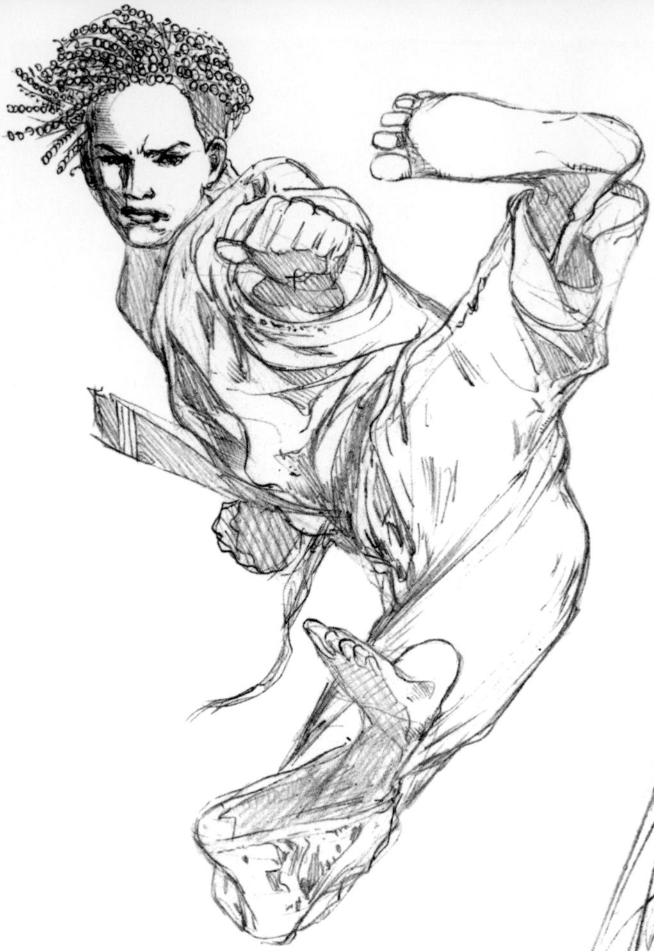

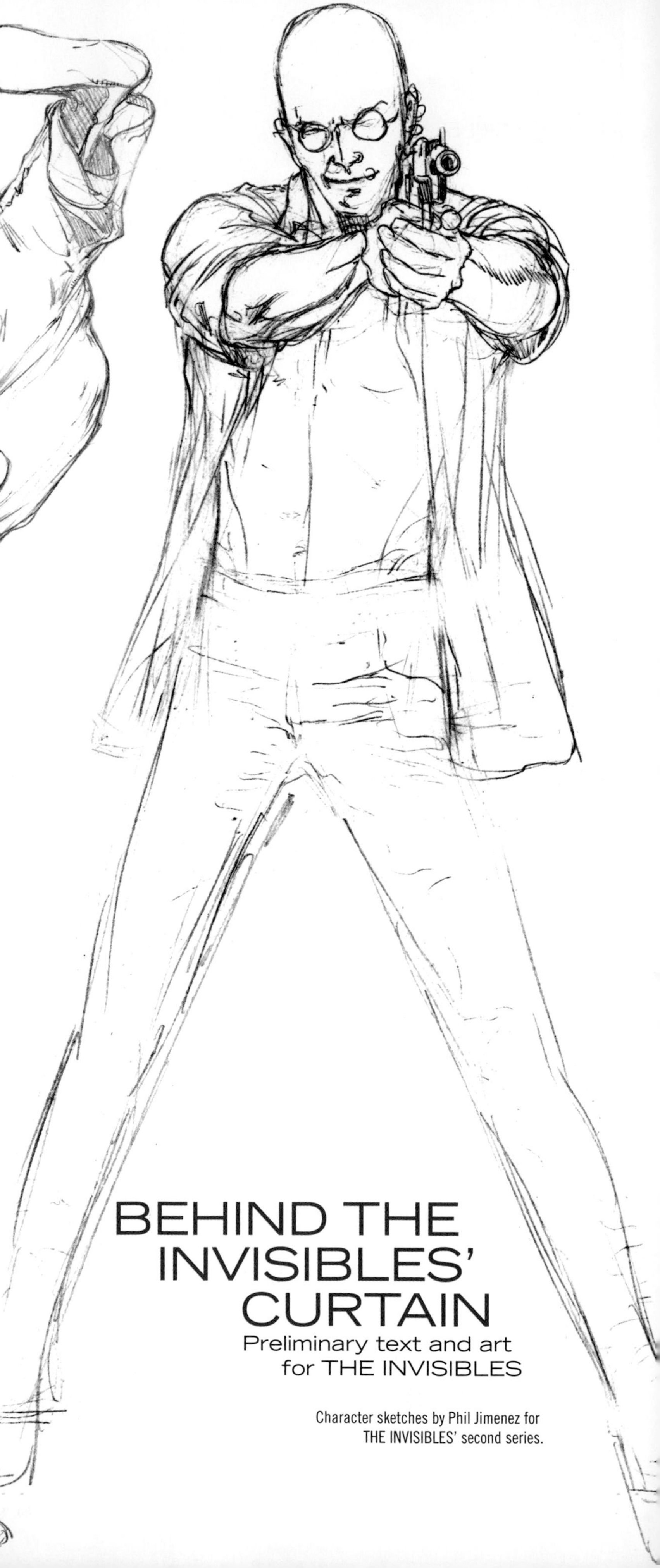

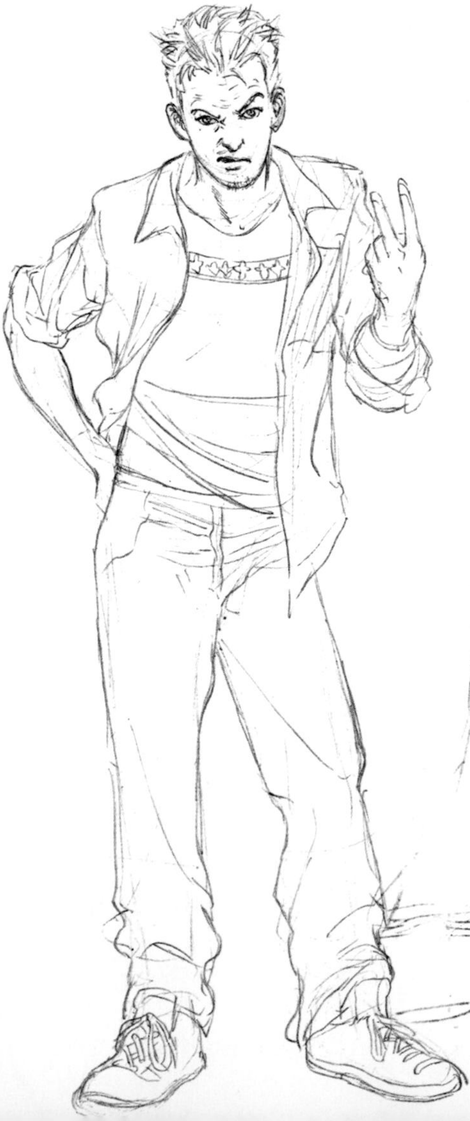

BEHIND THE INVISIBLES' CURTAIN

Preliminary text and art for THE INVISIBLES

Character sketches by Phil Jimenez for THE INVISIBLES' second series.

THE INVISIBLES VOLUME 2 Grant Morrison

I'll try to be brief here. We all know what's been happening in and with THE INVISIBLES and we all know about my desire to relaunch the book with Volume 2, so I'll proceed directly onto the reasoning behind what I'd like to do.

The first cold, hard fact is that the book isn't selling as well as it should be. There are various reasons for this, as far as I can see, including the fact that my grand idea of changing artists with every storyline is clearly not working. The major complaint in the letters I receive is that the art isn't good enough or is too inconsistent. Whether or not this is true, it's clear that the readers are not responding well to the rapid turnover of art teams and would probably prefer to see one good artist handle the book month in, month out. (Comics readers, including Vertigo fans, seem to be deeply conservative creatures at heart and I've become convinced that they want their comics to be as dependable as a McDonald's shitburger or a can of Pepsi. They also have very strong - and often wrongheaded, I feel - attitudes about what constitutes good and bad art and, in many cases, they feel THE INVISIBLES has let them down on that score.)

Also, the 'Arcadia' storyline, seen by many as 'difficult', came too early in the book's run and scared off a number of readers who would probably be a lot happier with the more straightforward stories which followed and which are currently running told in the title.

I'm sure the list could go on but rather than dwell on the mistakes, I'd like to look at ways to rectify them and that's where the Volume 2 plan comes in.

I've already explained in my letter columns that THE INVISIBLES has been conceived as a trilogy of books, designed to span the six years from first publication in 1994 to eventual completion (hollow laughter notwithstanding) in the year 2000. Volume 1 of the trilogy ends with

Notes on THE INVISIBLES' second series from Grant Morrison.

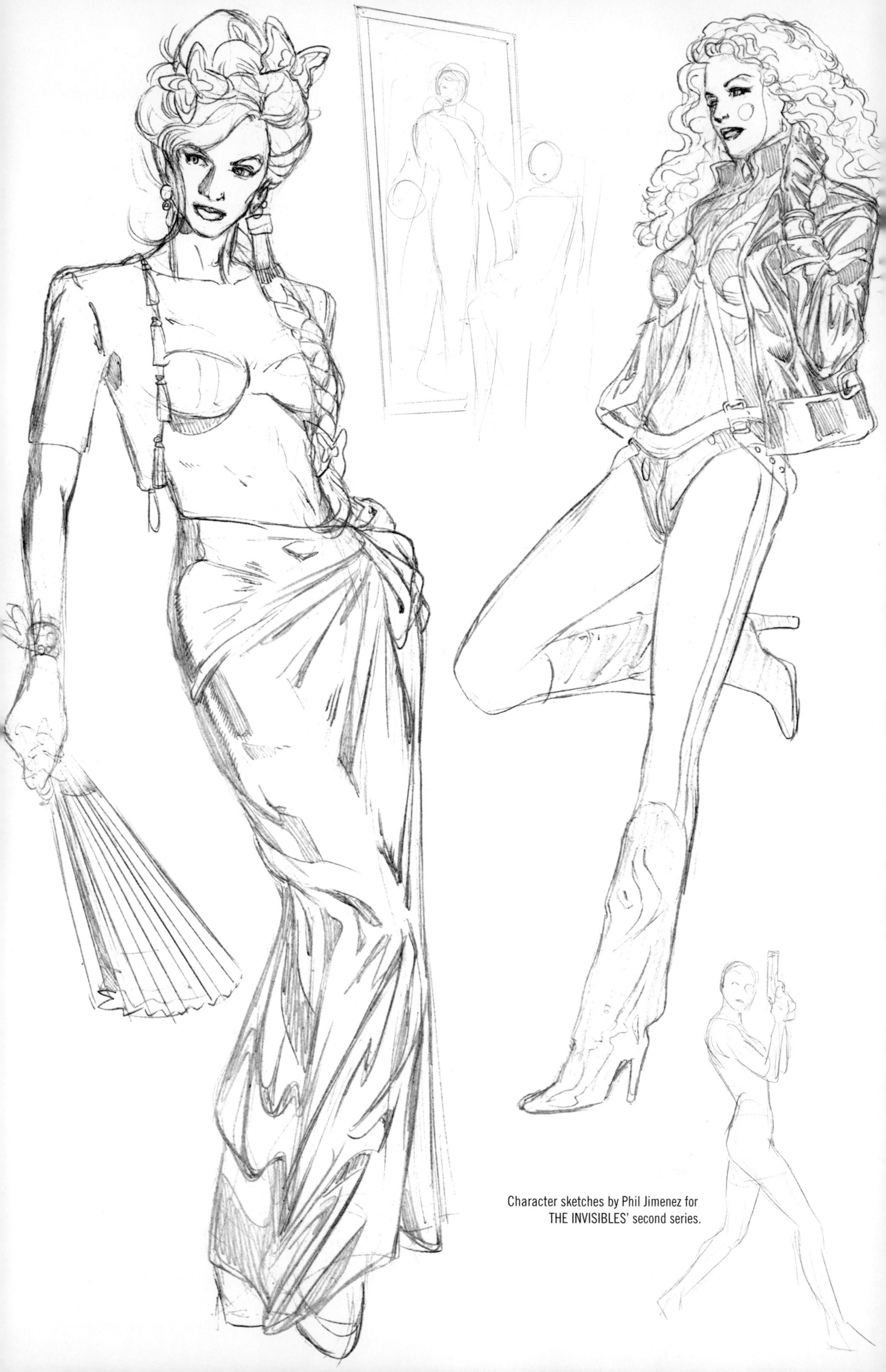

Character sketches by Phil Jimenez for THE INVISIBLES' second series.

issue 24. The readers who are already on board should have no problems with a relaunch, new readers won't know the difference and retailers will sell more books, which is surely the *raison d'etre* in these trying times. Following issue 2A of Volume 2, the book will relaunch once more with issue 1 of Volume 3. This is not an arbitrary marketing ploy but one built into the very structure of the story I'm hoping to complete.

So, it seems to me that starting again with a number one issue and having Phil and John on board as regular art team for a year at least would provide the kickstart THE INVISIBLES needs at this stage and *sell more copies* - again, the brutal reason behind what we do in the comics business in the first place.

The relaunch would also occur almost simultaneously with the first issue of my revamped JUSTICE LEAGUE, an event which will undoubtedly boost my profile once more and introduce me to a vast new 'Grant Morrison™' audience, many of whom may also be drawn to THE INVISIBLES, particularly when they see an art style on INVISIBLES which is much closer to the currently popular mainstream look. ('Closer' ? It's an exemplar!)

Creatively, the renumbering can be justified not only by the trilogy structure but by the fact that the focus of INVISIBLES will be shifting dramatically for Volume 2. The first volume was set almost entirely in the UK - a stumbling block for many US readers - and spent a great deal of time establishing the characters and the theoretical framework. Volume 2 moves the action to the USA and deals with mysteries and conspiracies which will be much more familiar to American readers, providing new explanations for the Roswell event, secret detention camps and underground military bases, black trains, unmarked helicopters, cattle mutilations and the various shadowy operations of the 'New World Order'. I can't pretend that it will be a completely new series - the characters are still the same and the whole storyline is still building up to the same series of revelations - but I do think that Volume 2 will have a very different flavor; it will be more accessible and will operate in conceptual territory much more familiar to US readers. It will be a book of American mysteries, quite